Coaching for Human Development and Performance in Sports

Rui Resende • A. Rui Gomes
Editors

Coaching for Human Development and Performance in Sports

Springer

Editors
Rui Resende
Life Quality Research Centre
University Institute of Maia
Maia, Portugal

A. Rui Gomes
School of Psychology
University of Minho
Braga, Portugal

ISBN 978-3-030-63911-2 ISBN 978-3-030-63912-9 (eBook)
https://doi.org/10.1007/978-3-030-63912-9

This Springer imprint is published by the registered company Springer Nature Switzerland AG.
The registered company address is: Gewerbestrasse 11, 6330 Cham, Switzerland

Foreword

It is an honor to write the Preface for *Coaching for Human Development and Performance in Sports*. Over the past three decades I have had the good fortune to work closely with many of the contributors to this book. Sports continue to hold a unique place in the hearts and minds of people across all nations. Increasing interest in and passion for sports has resulted in a greater focus on the central figure responsible for leading and training athletes—the sports coach. All indicators point to a robust expansion in the field of sports coaching, and those who study and support coaches.

In addition to the creation and expansion of national and international sport coaching frameworks, there is a dynamic and growing body of literature related to all aspects of coaching and coach education. Leading scientists and coach educators who have made significant contributions to this literature share their latest insights in this book. *Coaching for Human Development and Performance in Sports* is thoughtfully organized into three sections: Part I—Becoming a sports coach, Part II—Acting as a sports coach, and Part III—Challenges of sports coaching.

Part I is used to lay the foundation for quality coaching, coach education and its impact on coaching practice. The path to becoming a coach generally starts with playing the sport as an athlete. However, it is now widely acknowledged that athletic experience alone is insufficient qualification for becoming a quality coach. The journey to coaching mastery requires not only knowledge of the sport but also the ability to teach it, interpersonal skills critical for connecting with athletes, and self-awareness that comes through reflection and careful analysis of coaching practice. In addition to the expansion of formal coach education programs around the world, many sport organizations now provide digital learning platforms and customized learning support systems. I have noticed this is particularly evident in high-performance coaching contexts where coaching pressures often are high, yet coaching tenures frequently are short.

In Part II the focus shifts to the coaching process and how it is enacted across the full range of coaching contexts, including historically underrepresented contexts such as aging athletes and athletes with special needs. Although many coaching typologies exist, coaching contexts generally can be separated into developmental and high-performance sport. Yet, the growth of masters sport, the Paralympic movement, and nontraditional sports is challenging long held views on how to coach. There is no one type of athlete anymore—athletes come to sport across the lifespan, from widely different life histories and with a wide range of participation motives. For example, the addition of "uncoached" sports such as surfing, sport climbing, and skateboarding as demonstration sports for the 2020 Olympic Games in Tokyo will further stretch how we define quality coaching and the coaching process.

Finally, in Part III a wide array of issues facing coaches and the field of coaching are addressed, covering important topics such as athlete mental health, coaching life skills, use of technology, and coach well-being. Coaches today have unprecedented access to a virtually unlimited repository of coaching-related information. For example, while writing this preface I conducted a Google search using the term "sport coaching" and in less than one second received 633 million results. The sheer volume of information is overwhelming. Coaches need trusted sources to rely on for their coaching information. I believe there is a great opportunity for sport organizations, coach scientists, and coach developers to collaborate on creating online portals where coaches can quickly access information that has been vetted for credibility.

One area in particular that I see as a great challenge for coaches and those who support them is coach well-being. Although research generally shows that coaching as a profession is no more stressful than most other professions, there is a high turnover rate in many coaching contexts. Also, anecdotally I've noticed an increase in coach frustration and burnout. Whereas coaches once yielded complete authority with athletes, in many parts of the world the pendulum appears to have swung to the opposite end of the spectrum. The push for approaches such as "positive coaching," "holistic coaching," "autonomy-supportive coaching," and "transformational coaching" has inadvertently created conditions in some sport organizations where athletes now yield all the power. I do not believe either end of the spectrum is beneficial to coaching. Based on my experience with several high-profile sport organizations, the focus now is on creating an "optimal athlete experience," one in which athlete satisfaction is a key outcome. However, coaching often requires making athletes uncomfortable. Skill development requires high amounts of deliberate practice in competitive sport settings, something that is seldom perceived as enjoyable or comfortable. This is one of the great paradoxes of coaching that we collectively will have to resolve.

I have no doubt *Coaching for Human Development and Performance in Sports* will make an important contribution to the field. This text will serve as valuable reference point as we continue to unlock and share coaching and coach education discoveries. Regardless of your role—student, coach, coaching scientist, or coach educator—I believe *Coaching for Human Development and Performance in Sports* will become the type of book you return to often on your learning journey.

California State University, Fresno, CA, USA Wade Gilbert

Contents

Chapter 1
Coaching for Human Development and Performance in Sports: Introduction

Rui Resende and A. Rui Gomes

Abstract Sports can provide a huge contribution to human development and therefore be an important tool to society. Sports coaching is growing around the world spreading largely its field of action and intervention. The coaching professionalization is an important issue and this book attempts to contribute to our understanding of coaching and address this gap in the literature by organizing the chapters into three sections: (1) becoming a sports coach, (2) acting as a sport coach, and (3) challenges of sports coaching. The intention is to analyze how a coach develops as a professional; how a coach behaves in different contexts, and what are the challenges a coach is facing currently and in the future.

Introduction

Sport coaching is growing around the world leading to greater need to understand the profession of coaching. The role of the coach is wide-ranging especially when focusing on high performance. There is a solid foundation of our understanding about the education of coaches that provides useful resources and tools to help increase the quality of coaching for our athletes and for the broader population. However, several authors have highlighted that the theoretical foundations and principles of coaching are still contradictory and diverse (Bachkirova, 2017), despite the increasing number of publications in the last years (Griffo, Jensen, Anthony, Baghurst, & Kulinna, 2019; Trudel, Milestetd, & Culver, 2020).

This book attempts to contribute to our understanding of coaching and address this gap in the literature by organizing the chapters into three sections: (1) becoming a sports coach, (2) acting as a sport coach, and (3) challenges of sports coaching. The

R. Resende (✉)
Life Quality Research Centre, University Institute of Maia, Maia, Portugal
e-mail: rresende@ismai.pt

A. R. Gomes
School of Psychology, University of Minho, Braga, Portugal
e-mail: rgomes@psi.uminho.pt

R. Resende, A. R. Gomes (eds.), *Coaching for Human Development and Performance in Sports*, https://doi.org/10.1007/978-3-030-63912-9_1

intention is to analyze how a coach develops as a professional; how a coach behaves in different contexts, and what are the challenges a coach is facing currently and in the future. More specifically, chapters include on the section "becoming a sports coach" intend to set the stage for the coaching profession and their professional development. In the section on "acting as a sports coach", chapters focus on explaining how the coach can actuate, facing different contexts of sport participation and new fields of activity. In the third and final section, "challenges of sports coaching", chapters analyze new insights on sport coaching in different areas, including recommendations for future research in the area of sport coaching science.

Sport coaching is outlined in this book to help us better understand coaching as a profession within different contexts, the challenges to improve athletic performance and also how to increase coaching efficacy. The common theme between the three sections of the book is the sport coach. This book also attempts to answer how can the coach develops as a professional by taking into account the target audience who may have different motivations to be involved with sports. Emerging challenges to current coaches are also highlighted.

Part 1 is dedicated to clarifying what does it means to become a sports coach. Clarification of the key concepts about coaching is needed (Lyle, 2011), namely what is coaching, what is coaching education, what is philosophy of coaching, what is coaching efficacy, and what is the impact of coaching on athletes' performance and development. Specifically, Part 1 includes topics related to definitions and conceptualizations of coaching in the sport domain (chap. 1), how coaches learn to become coaches and what is the role of formal and informal sources of knowledge (chap. 2), how coaches set their philosophy of coaching and how they transmit their personal and professional values to athletes, teams and sports organizations in order to increase the efficacy of coaching (chap. 3), the relevance of transformational leadership behaviors on athletes development (chap. 4), and the global panorama of coaching profession around the world (chap. 5). Within this first part of the book, we intent to promote insights about the coach role in the society and how can coaching be conceptualized. Specifically, what different perspectives can emerge and represent sport coaching? What about the coach education: how can research puts in evidence its inadequacies and strengths, and point out some wisdom of how to best educate and train sports coaches? And how to increase leadership effectiveness of coaches: which tools can be used by coaches to develop athletes' skills and personal wellbeing? How is coaching activity organized and delivered by local and national institutions in order to guarantee credibility to the coaching profession?

Part 2 is dedicated to analyzing the factors that influence the activity of coaching across contexts and particularities of athletes and individuals that are orientated by coaches. Our main goal is to spread knowledge about the coach as a *multiple agent* of change and development from young to older individuals by demonstrating that they can act on distinct situations and populations (Nichol, Hall, Vickery, & Hayes, 2019). However, when we contrast the existing knowledge it is difficult to say what is specific and similar when assuming the coach activity across contexts and populations. In this way, Part 2 includes topics about what best describe the profession of coach (chap. 6), how to coach young athletes (chap. 7), how to coach high performance athletes (chap. 8), how to coach athletes in sport participation contexts (chap. 9), how to coach for adventures sports (chap. 10), how to coach aging individuals (chap. 11), and how to coach athletes with disabilities (chap. 12). This diversity of topics can stimulate the reflection about the differences on the coaching activity when dealing with individuals practicing sports for learning, participation, and professional purposes and about coaching athletes with disabilities or athletes on adventure sports. Within this second part of the book, we intent to promote insights about the broad spectrum areas of coaching activity. Specifically, what are the key concepts and skills to coach young athletes in order to promote learning and development over emphasizing winning? And what are the challenges and demands of coaching high performance athletes? What is the philosophy and practice of coaches of athletes whose focus on sport does not go through performance and winning, i.e., is there a coach for sport participating contexts? Also, the adventures sports need coaches and how can they contribute to promote challenging and safe experiences to the athletes? How to be successful in coaching aging athletes? What are the knowledge and skills to coach athletes with disabilities?

Part 3 is dedicated to analyzing the main challenges faced by coaches and by the coaching activity. This section was difficult to organize due the vast diversity of roles, functions, and actions that coaches can assume on their daily activity but we felt that topics related to promotion of athletes' mental health (chap. 13), teaching life skills to sports people (chap. 14), increasing the cohesion of teams (chap. 15), coaching girls and women (chap. 16), using the technology in order to increase the efficacy of coaching (chap. 17), dealing with stress and burnout of the coaching activity (chap. 18), and coach the coach in order to improve performance (chap. 19) they all represent important and useful topics in order to understand the complexities and challenges of being a coach. The final chapters of this section reflects about sports coaching and implications for future research in terms of coaches' leadership (chap. 20) and the trends of publication in sports coaching (chap. 21). Within this third part of the book, we intent to promote on the reader insights about actual challenges on sports coaching: what is the role of the coach in supporting athlete mental health and wellbeing? How can coaches increase life skills on youth athletes? How to develop the abilities of team members when they work collectively? What does it mean to coach girls and women on sports? The use of technology is really important to modern coaching? Can coaches be at risk for psychological problems due the tension they are submitted in their activities, particularly when leading professional athletes? And what about coaching the coach? What about the possibility of this "new" professional of coach of the coach? Is there a place for such a professional? And finally, how can research and practice in sports coaching grow and develop in the near future?

All in all, we believe this book will address important topics on coaching, giving to the reader a clear understanding of what is coaching, what is at stake when becoming a coach, and what challenges can arise when assuming this activity.

References

Bachkirova, T. (2017). Re-conceptualising coach education from the perspectives of pragmatism and constructivism. *Philosophy of Coaching: An International Journal, 2*(2), 29–50. https://doi.org/10.22316/poc/02.2.03

Griffo, J. M., Jensen, M., Anthony, C. C., Baghurst, T., & Kulinna, P. H. (2019). A decade of research literature in sport coaching (2005–2015). *International Journal of Sports Science & Coaching, 14*(2), 205–215. https://doi.org/10.1177/1747954118825058

Lyle, J. (2011). What is a coach and What is coaching. In I. Stafford (Ed.), *Coaching children in sport (pp. 5–16)*. Routledge.

Nichol, A. J., Hall, E. T., Vickery, W., & Hayes, P. R. (2019). Examining the relationships between coaching practice and athlete "outcomes": A systematic review and critical realist critique. *International Sport Coaching Journal, 6*(1), 13–29. https://doi.org/10.1123/iscj.2017-0105

Trudel, P., Milestetd, M., & Culver, D. M. (2020). What the empirical studies on sport coach education programs in higher education have to reveal: A review. *International Sport Coaching Journal, 7*(1), 61–73. https://doi.org/10.1123/iscj.2019-0037

Rui Resende is an Assistant Professor at University Institute of Maia – ISMAI, Portugal. He does research manly in Sports Pedagogy and Coach Education. He was a Volleyball athlete and coached teams at the high competition level in Portugal and also the junior national coach of the Portuguese national team. Presently is editor director of the Journal of Sport Pedagogy & Research and recently made his graduation as Coach Developer in the ICCE.

A. Rui Gomes is an Assistant Professor in the School of Psychology at the University of Minho, Portugal. He received his Ph. D. in Psychology from the University of Minho. He has research interests on human adaptation to stress, leadership and team performance, and training life skills and human performance. He leads the research group "Adaptation, Performance and Human Development", which was created in 2007 (www.ardh.pt). He leads the community and business intervention project "School of Life Skills" (www.e-cv.pt). As a sport psychologist, he consults athletes and their families, coaches, and sport managers.

Part I
Becoming a Sports Coach

Chapter 2
Coaching in the Sport Domain: Definitions and Conceptualisations

John Lyle

Abstract This chapter explores the definitions and meanings attached to sport coaching. It does not privilege any particular conceptualisation of sport coaching but reflects on how these should be interpreted. The chapter begins with an argument that sport coaching achieves its social significance from an association with particular forms of sport. This is followed by an acknowledgement that the term sport coaching acts as a 'referent' for an individual's identity, a role or occupation, an intervention process, or the social space occupied by the individuals, institutions, behaviours and practices that constitute the purposes, actions and understandings associated with sport coaching. Emphasis is placed on the process of intervention and the need for boundary markers for the coaching process. Following an overview of different discipline-led conceptualisations, the chapter explores the implications of these and presents a personal interpretation of how coaching may be conceptualised. This adopts a pragmatic approach to the coach's capacity to operationalise practice and embraces an optimistic view of the coach's resources. Stress is placed on the lack of integration of differing perspectives, but it is argued that a fuller account and understanding of sport coaching emerges from an aggregation of these diverse priorities in capturing and representing sport coaching.

Keywords Sport coaching · Conceptualisation · Intervention · Pragmatism · Coaching process

J. Lyle (✉)
Leeds Beckett University, Leeds, UK
e-mail: j.w.lyle@leedsbeckett.ac.uk

R. Resende, A. R. Gomes (eds.), *Coaching for Human Development and Performance in Sports*, https://doi.org/10.1007/978-3-030-63912-9_2

Coaching in the Sport Domain: Definitions and Conceptualisations

In this chapter, I explore definitions and conceptualisations attached to sport coaching. There are excellent treatments of the meanings attached to sport coaching in texts such as North (2017), Cassidy, Jones, and Potrac (2016) and Lyle and Cushion (2017), overviews such as Purdy (2018), and a recent account of the historical evolution of associated concepts in Lyle (2018a). This is not a review of literature. There would be limited value in merely rehearsing these very detailed and closely argued accounts, or to do justice to their nuanced arguments. It would impossible, and perhaps counter productive, to attempt merely to provide a synthesis of such work. As will be argued throughout the chapter, it would be inappropriate simply to create a composite or integrated account that satisfies all of the various perspectives on sport coaching and how it has been represented, interpreted and understood. Rather, the purpose of the chapter is to provide a critical reflection on sport coaching and, thereby, to invite the reader to appreciate how the term is used in the academic literature. The outcome should be a framework of critical thinking that will enable students of coaching science to approach the literature with a more insightful, questioning and less-accepting lens.

The basic question is 'what constitutes sport coaching and what meanings are attached to this term?' The term (although usually referred to as sports coaching, simply through historical convention) is in common usage, but it is inappropriate that the meanings implied, consciously or unconsciously, by what is such a widespread and varied practice in sport should be used indiscriminately or become taken-for-granted—or be without a considered foundation that renders practical issues, such as coach education, deployment, development strategies or professionalisation, less effective. The nature and substance of our conceptualisations impact on policy and practice. Language is important; it is through the use of language and how it is shared that meaning is socially constructed. In other words, this chapter is not yet another defence of a definition sport coaching but about creating a thinking tool with which to appraise critically any particular conceptualisation of the term.

We might start by asking why exploring definitions and conceptualisations is important. A privilege of academia is that it provides time and opportunity to think about what things are, and what they mean, and how these objects and ideas influence the understandings and actions of other groups—governmental agencies, policy makers, educationalists, practitioners and the public. In many respects, this is one of the most important roles that academia performs for society; that is, exploring and formalising meanings to understand what work they do and what implications they have. Others, particularly practitioners, whilst busy elsewhere, may not have time and the resources for this essential task. The problem that academics have, therefore, is that their scholastic endeavours are not obviously embraced by other groups in society. This is a problem of academic knowledge production, translation and use and is well recognised (Lyle, 2018b). Nevertheless, it would also do a disservice to the influence of academia to suggest that the ideas generated have not had some influence on coaching policy, coach education and development and indeed on practice, and there are numerous examples of this (North, 2017). Thus, articulating academic ideas remains important.

A further problem is that, as a relatively new area of academic enquiry, perhaps 40 years old at most, scholarly work in sport coaching is still at a relatively pre-paradigmatic stage. We have witnessed attempts by academics to understand sport coaching through behaviours, cognitions, context, and its social and relationship features. These different perspectives on sport coaching provide very valuable insights. However, as result of both disciplinary politics and problems in attempting to resolve apparently incompatible philosophical and methodological choices, there also appears to be conflict and contestation about what 'position' is best. It is inevitable then, that, as academic research matures, it seeks to explore what are in effect definitional and conceptual disagreements, by finding tools that provide additional (and I would argue, important) insights into the debate. It may seem an unnecessary task to conceptualise sport coaching when the practice is evident in our everyday lives. However, this generates a set of ideas that represent sport coaching; an explanation for what we see, experience and imagine. An effective conceptualisation will symbolise the practice of coaching, embracing its variety of purpose, intention and character. In turn, this allows us to address such questions as: what is and isn't coaching, what is its purpose, and what are its characteristic attributes? It is important to remember, however, that any conceptualisation will be contested; that is, it is open to challenge for the extent to which it is considered to represent sport coaching appropriately. The meanings implicit in such a set of ideas are a matter of interpretation, and this interpretation is dependent on more fundamental understandings that we hold about how best to explain social phenomena and human behaviour.

The Sport in Sport Coaching

Perhaps surprisingly, I begin, not with the term 'coaching', but with the word 'sport'. I would contend that many otherwise laudable attempts to define or circumscribe sport coaching focus on the 'coaching' element and pay insufficient attention to its siting in the sport context. There are many definitions of sport (Lagaert & Roose, 2016); a stricter, narrower definition characterises sport as an institutionalised (and culturally specific) form of physical activity, in which competition outcomes are determined by motor skills and there are clear rules of play. This is evident in traditional sports such as volleyball, athletics, kabaddi or hockey, but may also apply to adventure sports, and emerging 'sports' such as korfball, dodgeball, pickleball, and baton twirling (Liponski, 2003). There are also more general definitions that embrace almost all forms of physical activity and fitness (Council of Europe, 2002). However, sport also has many 'sport forms' in addition to competition performance itself, e.g. training/practice, rallying, casual play or amended games. Although, for many, it is not difficult to recognise sport from other forms of activity, there are 'grey areas' in relation to purpose and activity. Sport may be used for specific purposes, e.g. physical education in schools. There is also some confusion when truncated forms of sport, i.e. simply teaching basic skills in isolation from competition, is perceived to be a 'means to an end' in terms of subsequent leisure participation, or other societal or individual benefits.

It is reasonable to ask what this has to do with our definition and meaning of sport coaching. The basis of my argument is that there is a close relationship between meaning and context in terms of both discourse construction (how we use the term and what we relate it to) and practice (which activities we include and which we exclude). Not every manifestation of sport-related activity requires the same form of sport leadership; it is not sufficient to say that there is a basic or fundamental process of improving sport-related proficiency. Context and purpose become significant. Not all forms of sport, particularly recreational activity, will be coach-dependent. However, if we accept that sport coaching has a ubiquitous and impactful association with much of sport participation, albeit in domain-specific practices, it follows that the social significance of sport coaching is a reflection of the significance accorded to sport itself. Participation in sport is associated with health and well-being, with economic benefits, with a sense of identity from vicarious association with professional sport or national teams, with social advancement, with cultural exchange, with personal and esteem, with inculcating values in young people, and with the potential for personal development and self-fulfilment. Insofar as sport coaching contributes to the achievement of these benefits, it is a matter of some significance that we understand its contribution and place in the social world. Indeed, it is somewhat surprising that, given its social significance, sport coaching remains (in the UK) a largely voluntary activity and a 'hidden profession' (Lyle & Cushion, 2017). Part of understanding why this might be so is to explore and appreciate the meaning attached to sport coaching and how it is conceptualised.

Having established that sport coaches and sport coaching achieve their social significance from their association with sport, indeed, it might be argued that this is the defining attribute, it is hardly surprising that the variety of coaching roles and practices reflects the similarly diverse and distinctive provision of sport in all its richness. Without wishing to pre-empt my subsequent argument, this form of leadership will range from intermittent or short-term voluntary activity with young children, in resource-poor conditions, to resource-rich professional employment with Olympic performers. This may prompt you to ask whether we should attempt to establish any boundaries to what we mean by sport coaching. An acknowledgement of the environment in which coaches operate, and the range of predispositions and motivations of the sport participants, in addition to 'progress and refinement' in coaching practice, highlights the issue of whether any conceptualisation of sport coaching is time-and culture-bound. The answer is that any conceptualisation, whether popular or academic, will have antecedents and there will be a historicity attached to any social practice. We recognise that sport coaching has evolved over time and the traditional practices in, for example, soccer, rugby union and cricket in the UK, have evolved coaching roles, and associated meanings and mores, that reflect the social and sub-cultural conditions of the time, and become, to some extent and for some time, taken-for-granted. Similarly, developments in the organisation and administration of sport, along with policy and resource commitments, impact on coaching as a 'profession' (Lyle & Cushion, 2017; North, Piggott, Lara-Bercial, Abraham, & Muir, 2018). Nevertheless, I will argue that there is an underlying conceptualisation of coaching that helps us to make sense of what we currently experience as sport coaches. It has to be acknowledged that this is shaped by our own personal resources.

Preparing the Ground for a Definition

One of the traditional starting points is to offer a definition of sport coaching. Definitions are intended to bring clarity to how we think of the object in question; how to distinguish it from other objects and identify what meaning might be attached to it. Good practice suggests that the definition should identify the essence of the object but with sufficient elaboration to distinguish it from other similar objects. This is a demanding 'ask', for what are commonly relatively short, pithy statements. A basic familiarity with the academic literature in this field will establish that there are many, many definitions of sport coaching—or a recognition that the task is challenging (Horton, 2015). How can this be? One answer lies in the distinction between a narrow account of the essence of sport coaching—what it 'is'—and an elaboration that either adds a helpful contextual reference or defines what the writer thinks it 'should be' (Côté, Erickson, & Duffy, 2007). A simple definition of sport coaching would be 'a form of sport leadership', but this is circular and does not provide any clarity about what that 'form' might be. It is also about the role, rather than the process. Another simple statement such as, 'a process of improving sports performance', is process-orientated but immediately raises questions about what is meant by 'process', or 'performance', and implies that it is only to be considered coaching if 'improvement' is the aim.

To illustrate this further, I have selected a definition about which I am broadly supportive. A recent position statement (Lara-Bercial et al., 2017, p. 11) defines sport coaching as "a process of guided improvement and development in a single sport and at identifiable stages of development". The statement is process orientated but tells us nothing about what constitutes an 'acceptable' or characteristic process. To what does 'development' refer? We might understand the intention in the term 'guided', but does it have any boundaries? Why mention 'at identifiable stages of development'—what does this add? Overall, does this definition distinguish the process from other similar processes; does it help us to understand what it is not? There is a further elaboration of the definition in the above source, which stresses the "ongoing nurturing and education support of participants". This has clearly moved from 'what is' to 'what should be'. My simple message, through this illustration, is that it is very difficult to provide sufficient clarity to establish 'difference and specificity', and that how we conceive of a phenomenon, a social practice, is a reflection of a theoretical, conceptual or philosophical stance.

We need to move beyond mere definitions to capture, in much greater detail, the essence of sport coaching. This begins by acknowledging that the term sport coaching acts as a 'referent' for a number of social phenomena. In other words, in common usage, the use of the term may be associated with an individual's identity, a role or occupation, with an intervention process, or with the social space occupied by the individuals, institutions, behaviours and practices that constitute the purposes, actions and understandings associated with sport coaching. It is important, therefore, to be clear about the 'target' of any definitional attempt, while, at the same time, recognising that usages of the term will be interrelated and interdependent. It is understandable that the role of the sport coach, however defined, should become evident in a wide range of practice contexts. To reiterate, this chapter has been fashioned to recognise, and provide a reflection on, different approaches to the generation of a conceptualisation of sport coaching, but also to reinforce the principle that different conceptions may simply be partial versions of, or contributions to, a difficult-to-describe whole.

There is also an issue of cultural differences. The arguments set out in this chapter reflect academic writing and ideas in the English-speaking world—with an implicit understanding that these ideas represent powerful academic schools of thought. It would be incontrovertible that coaching practice will reflect cultural mores, norms, and expectations, although there is an interesting argument that the media-and major events-led globalisation of sport, and an accompanying mobility in coach deployment in high-performance sport, have created a universal, homogenous conception of coaching in that particular domain. However, my own experience has confirmed that there are cultural differences in the education and values attached to introducing young people to sport and that this is evident in coaching practice. It remains my contention, however, that there is a fundamental conception of sport coaching when operationalised; in other words, what we see in practice. Nevertheless, sport coaching is reflective of a developmental evolution over time and is subject to a number of layers of both cultural expectations and the political, social and economic ideas and policies attached to sport.

I will try not to fall into the trap of declaring that a simple definition is not possible but then attempting to provide one! As indicated above, the initial question is, 'what is it that you are attempting to define?' Sport coaching can be understood to refer to a role (provision of direction/assistance/support/leadership in a sport context), a social context (understood as a part of the sporting environment/resource within an institutional framework or set of relationships), a process (the collective activities and behaviours designed and delivered by the coach), and a set of interpersonal relationships (most commonly a relationship between coach and athlete(s)). These are stated without any elaboration about how each should be operationalised. Here, I declare a personal position. Each of these dimensions helps us to understand more fully what we mean by sport coaching, but, for me, the essence is the 'process of intervention' to prepare the athlete/team's performance capacity for participation in sport. Without this, the other dimensions have no meaning or context. If we assume for a moment that sport coaching is a form of leadership that involves guidance or direction intended to support sport participants, the term should include the process through which such guidance takes place. This might beg the question as to whether the many variants of sport coaching practice can be embraced by one descriptor. No matter how we conceive of the social world around us, it is evident that the term sport coaching is understood by specialists and non-specialists alike (although perhaps to a different depth of comprehension) as a descriptor of purposeful practice by individuals. However, there is also a 'system-wide' institutional network of organisations and institutions that aim to maintain and further develop coaching practice, either directly or indirectly. The 'system' and the individuals within it create a sense of how coaching is represented, and individual coaches operate within this framework—or challenge it!

It is important that I state my bias and how my background has influenced the way in which I present this chapter. I adhere to a pragmatic approach (which I elaborate later in the chapter); valuing knowledge that has an impact on practice. I also have an extensive background, both as performer and coach, in high-performance sport, in a team sport in which the coach plays a significant role in directing game performance. In addition, my academic interest is in how coaches cope with the multi-layered set of relationships and the environment within which they operate, rather than simply to better understand what those influences might be. This has undoubtedly influenced the emphasis I place on intervention, on competition preparation and on decision making. For example, and despite the entirely appropriate enjoinder to effective interpersonal behaviour, such behaviour, without reference to specific and purposeful intervention, is not the primary goal of the coaching 'contract'. It is a means to an end—accepting that such an 'end' may have myriad additional outcomes (social mobility, personal development, behaviour modification). I would contend, therefore, that it is important to appreciate the subtleties of context and meaning that are involved, and this is central to an appreciation of 'what we mean by sport coaching'. In circumstances in which there are purposes/objectives/goals that do not involve preparation for and participation in sport (implying competition forms of sport), the term coaching can only be applied as a generic descriptor of a delivery role and behaviour. Its meaning only becomes evident and 'attaches itself' to other complementary meanings and constructs when the purpose is identified. Thus, it is convenient, but unhelpful, if the sport leadership evident in youth clubs, social work, physical education, casual recreation, adventure holidays, and so on, is characterised as sport coaching. Generic descriptors such as medical practitioner, engineer, teacher, lawyer, salesperson or coach evoke an immediate sense of what this means (to the individual who interprets it)—but only in a most general sense.

Sport coaching occupies a social space—the myriad practices of individual coaches are accompanied by institutions and institutional processes that educate, facilitate, develop and support coaches. We often label this the 'coaching system'. Note, however, that these processes are not neutral; they serve to include and exclude, and in some case, regulate. We can rely on our own coaching practice as a lens through which to understand coaching, but North (2017) reminds us that the world of sport coaching is separate from our attempts in research to capture and represent it. I am often struck by the realisation that an individual's coaching practice does not change when being interpreted or conceptualised by competing academic schools of thought. Nevertheless, a conceptualisation of sport coaching and the setting of occupational boundaries can influence education and development (in addition to recruitment and deployment) and impact on the formulation of sport policy. In this way, our understanding of sport coaching and what it means to coach will impact on practice. The aggregation of these effects is one way to describe the 'profession' of coaching: the requirements and expectations placed on education, expertise, standards of practice, and accountable behaviour. Professional esteem is afforded to the coaching role by social recognition of its value and significance. Once again, the important point to highlight is that the reach, scope and remit of those within the profession and infrastructure of sport coaching is a reflection of how it is conceptualised by policy makers, who, in turn, are influenced to a greater or lesser extent by academic discourse.

This section of the chapter has attempted to reinforce the need for some 'boundary markers' (Lyle & Cushion, 2017) and some definitional clarity about how we should interpret the scope and essence of sport coaching. I also imply that this is a challenge; the use of the term sport coaching as an umbrella term for a family of coaching roles and domains (Lyle, 2011a) invites context-free generalisations that are less than helpful. However, it is also the case that most academic writing that deals with coaching or its practice does not feel the need to inform the reader about the scope of the coaching activity implied in the writing, nor of the characteristic practice of the practitioners (Lyle, 2018b). Without wishing to identify academic colleagues, I invite readers to examine a number of research papers in sport coaching and to test this hypothesis. Surprisingly, it also applies to academic 'position papers', particularly characteristic of academic writing that focuses on inter-personal relationships. These are implicitly held to be common to all forms of sport coaching. To some extent this is incontrovertible, but the coaching context evidences many and varied forms of interaction between athlete and coach.

Different Perspectives

To reach a conceptualisation of sport coaching we need to take a view on what is important about it, how it relates to the world around it, which questions are worth asking, and how we will frame the answers to these questions. Not surprisingly, there is no absolute consensus on this, and the different characterisations of coaching reflect our preferred perspectives on these philosophical and conceptual matters. There are some fundamental views on the nature of reality and how we understand the natural and social phenomena around us. This is termed our ontology, and is accompanied by our epistemology, which refers to the nature and scope of knowledge that supports what we know about the world (North, 2017). These more fundamental perspectives are the basis of more specific disciplinary or multi-disciplinary approaches.

These different disciplinary approaches (for example, psychology or sociology) not only have distinctive ways of understanding and explaining the world around us and have characteristic methods of investigating it, but also tend to address different issues. Psychology, for example, will focus on individuals' behaviour and cognitions; sociologists are focused on social structures, interrelationships and contextual factors. Each disciplinary approach has a tendency to validate its principles by pointing to the shortcomings of the alternatives. Nevertheless, the resultant conceptualisation is important; not only does it provide an understanding and interpretation of social phenomena, it has implications for education, development and effecting social change. We can think of it as providing a justification for our ideas—our conceptualisations.

Even a cursory familiarity with the academic literature on sport coaching will confirm that there are distinctive conceptualisations that arise from, or obtain their justification from, particular disciplinary perspectives—indeed, to some extent these have generated quite distinctive schools of thought. These have been described and appraised at length by North (2017) and I recommend this source for an excellent account of both the conceptualisations and their genesis. My purpose here is not to restate these competing conceptualisations but to examine a number of issues about which students of coaching science should be aware when relying on academic literature associated with a particular disciplinary approach: why are there different conceptualisations, are they really different, what function do they serve, and how do I, as a practitioner or student, interpret these representations of sport coaching? First, however, I provide a modest overview of these different conceptualisations; this is derived from North (2017), whose text will afford a much more comprehensive account.

North (2017) identifies the following perspectives: behaviourist, cognitive, strategic/functional, complexity, social, and normative. Each of these has a particular conceptualisation of coaching. The behaviourist perspective is said to conceive of coaching as a set of observable behaviours, within which it is possible to identify regularities that can be associated with effective practice. This is evident in the construction of analytical tools to capture and categorise behaviours (Cushion, Harvey, Muir, & Nelson, 2012). The cognitive perspective is rooted in psychology and emphasises the coach's cognitive organisation, storage and retrieval of knowledge. The focus is on the coach as a decision maker (Collins, Carson, & Collins, 2016; Harvey, Lyle, & Muir, 2015). A strategic/functional approach is less disciplinary based and may be termed a 'components approach'; there is an attempt to identify the key components or strategies adopted by coaches and how these are operationalised to best effect (Lara-Bercial & Mallett, 2016). The complexity perspective has been influential in conceiving of sport coaching as a site of interacting goals, actors and context, to the extent that it is described as messy, dynamic, emergent or ill-defined (Jones, Bowes, & Kingston, 2010). To some extent this has become a reference point for conceptions of sport coaching, and it rejects simplified explanations or representations of practice. The social perspective conceives of sport coaching as a social interaction between coach, athlete and other stakeholders, with a focus on interpersonal relationships (Jones & Corsby, 2015). There is an emphasis on social construction of knowledge and practice, and the power dynamics involved. Normative approaches tend to adduce eclectic arguments, rather than evidentiary bases, about how best to conceive of effective coaching practice, leading to prescriptions intended to influence coach education and development. North (2017) identifies Côté's 4Cs (Côté, Bruner, Erickson, Strachan, & Fraser-Thomas, 2010) and conceptions of the coach as 'orchestrator' (Jones, Bailey, & Thompson, 2013) or 'educator' (Jones, 2006) as examples.

One of the key questions to ask is what it is that academics disagree about. The firm conclusion is that they differ in their opinions as to what questions are worth asking and how sport coaching can best be understood from a particular perspective. The debate about what we mean by coaching is an example of a socially-derived construct and is most evident in the discourse about it. This manifests itself in academic writing, in public policy statements, in popular writing (press, media), and in dialogue between individuals. It is tempting to say that 'it is clear that everyone knows what coaching 'is' until they begin to explain it'. In reality, distinctive images and practices, exemplar roles and persons, and one's own experiences combine to 'paint a picture' that an individual holds to represent sport coaching—albeit a picture that benefits from reflection. Academics attempt to explain these representations and, to some extent, perhaps too much, to defend their stance in relation to others.

An example of a particular conceptualisation is Cassidy et al. (2016)) portrayal of sport coaching as a pedagogical and social enterprise. This is an exceedingly well-argued and well-written text. However, it evidences a number of the features of partial accounts described above. It is described as 'a leading perspective in the analysis of sport coaching' (p. 4); the authors feel it necessary to challenge other conceptions. They continue the caricaturing of coaching as a unidirectional technical exercise—a position that provides a 'stalking horse' for their academic agenda but is completely at odds with the experience and personal resources of coaches themselves. There is no doubt that sport coaching (as with all social endeavours) has an emotional, political, spiritual, and cultural context but the impression given is that practitioners and other academics have failed to identify this. The writers imply that the social factors are a 'higher order' perspective and to be valued above a 'what works' approach. In criticising the scientific functionalism (p. 176) said to characterise coaching, the authors perpetuate the partial perspective—of seeing 'what you want to see'. There is no doubt that (some) coaches implement a performance intervention programme based on performance sciences. However, any number of narratives from coaches (including those that conceive of coaching as a humanistic endeavour [Bennie & O'Connor, 2010]) will demonstrate that this is couched in a coach-athlete relationship and practice that acknowledges and attempts to accommodate to the emotional, developmental, social and cultural factors that the authors espouse.

There are reasonably straightforward answers to the questions posed earlier. Once we accept that different conceptualisations represent attempts to illustrate and understand sport coaching in a partial way that is based on a fallible process of capturing and representing the 'reality' of coaching (North, 2017), we realise that they are not inimical—simply addressing different questions and issues. The concepts, theories, narratives, metaphors and models do not provide a 'complete' account. Indeed, despite the editors' laudable intentions, the *Routledge Handbook of Sports Coaching*'s call for integration of the variety of disciplinary perspectives remains at the level of aggregation rather than integration (Potrac, Gilbert, & Denison, 2013). The different perspectives cannot be aggregated, being based on different foundations and with different purposes. We cannot fully represent sport coaching other than through our (largely disciplinary and therefore partial) lens. Therefore, it is inappropriate to say, 'coaching is . . .', but rather, 'from this perspective, sport coaching can be conceived of as . . .'.

The call for an inter-disciplinary approach has been answered by North (2017). Based on a critical realist evaluation of sport coaching, he moves someway towards a less disciplinary-bound approach, although integrating disciplinary perspectives into an embedded, relational and emergent (ERE) model of a sport coaching-specific ontology (see Chap. 6). The model is described as a tool to aid research and theorising; researchers are invited to look beyond observable practice to the underpinning causal layers that impact the coaches' 'resources, reasoning, reflecting and strategising' (pp. 175–176). Of particular interest is a set of concepts which he suggests can better describe and explain sport coaching. Individually these are not new concepts, but their value lies in the attempt to formulate a basis for integrated inter-disciplinary research. Sport coaching is said to be situated in time and space (particularly a collective historicity); to have a layered set of influences (socio-cultural, institutional, interpersonal and individual); to have a goal orientation; to be dependent on the resources available (at each level); to be the product of reasoning, reflecting and strategising; and to feature coaching actions that lead, imperfectly and over time, to outcomes.

There is also a political dimension to the way in which we conceive of sport coaching, and, as a consequence, how we scaffold policy and practice. For example, an extensive incorporation of sport leadership roles supports policies of inclusion (UK Coaching, 2017). The meaning attached to sport coaching also intimates what, at any given time, power brokers (those who determine strategy and resource allocation) choose to prioritise. This may also be related to what the wider society views as worthy of esteem. This is also linked, in what is currently a contentious debate, to notions of the professionalisation of sport coaching (Lyle & Cushion, 2017; North et al., 2018). There are obvious implications, in a practical sense, for research, provision of services and coach education structures. For an example of the importance of this reference point, and a case study of the interaction between national policy and the definition of sport and coaching, consider the case of the changing policy on sport (HM Government, 2015, Sport England, 2016) and coaching (UK Coaching, 2017) in the UK. There has been a deliberate attempt to obfuscate the meaning attached to sport coaching; first, by extending the terminology to refer to 'sport and physical activity', and, second, by emphasising the word 'coaching' in isolation. This satisfies the objectives of Government policy as it responds in policy terms to issues such as obesity, declining participation in sport, and an inactive population. However, it does little to circumscribe the boundaries of sport coaching and consequent implication for matters such as coach education and development and the professionalisation agenda. There will be a good deal of desirable and laudable leadership and delivery practice in the broader realm of physical activity (fitness classes, jogging, activity holidays, casual participation) and a good deal of children's physical activity resembles 'sport play'. It may even be the case that qualifications currently badged as 'coaching awards' are useful orientation and training mechanisms for leadership in these domains. Nevertheless, this is an example of a conceptualisation of sport coaching that has been devised for political purposes.

Where Are we? A Personal Interpretation

In immersing myself in the literature, I find myself asking two questions: first, does the author intend that there is a better, newer or deeper understanding of sport coaching or that the practice of coaching should be improved by this academic contribution? Second, has the author identified the coaching context(s) to which the findings/recommendations are intended to apply? I take the view that each and all perspectives contribute to our understanding of sport coaching. Setting aside for the moment the issue of what constitutes reality, as a coaching practitioner, my practice is not altered by the different conceptualisations described above—change comes as a result of coach education and development being influenced by different conceptions of coaching and by my own reflection and reasoning. Schools of thought emerge and evolve over time—was there no good practice before a particular approach took root? My practice could be simultaneously observed, investigated and explained through different lenses. Each would adopt mechanisms to capture an 'as best we can' representation and reproduction of my coaching practice, but to interrogate the results towards different priorities. It might be assumed that better understanding will lead to appropriate coach education and development, which, in turn, will improve practice. However, my experience is that much of the literature is dominated by the quest for understanding, with largely evidence-free prescriptions for education and development.

The coach is an active agent in determining practice. The extent and form of this is criticised, largely in terms of a perception that coaches do not reflect sufficiently on the assumptions and beliefs that they have about their practice and how they do or should behave. This is a fallacious argument. To what extent can we expect a 2-day trained first-aider to reflect critically on the treatments suggested by 'informed practice' in medicine? I suspect that this argument has merit; treatments (and resources) are determined by those with the knowledge and influence to incorporate them in practice. However, and as with beginner coaches, to what extent is it reasonable to expect these minimally trained practitioners to engage critically and with sufficient knowledge and insight in the genesis and appropriateness of such practices? The anticipated level of reflection is incompatible with the level of education and training, and their likely period of engagement as practitioners. I would not condone the unquestioning reproduction of taken-for-granted practices. Allowing that some coaches may well reflect critically, there remain questions about professional practice. Coaches may well be aware that they are accepting 'received wisdom' and that this is a consequence of power brokers who influence professional discourse, but see this as a practical alternative to 'testing out' alternative notions, given that their practice appears to be successful or effective.

Much of the literature has an unfortunate tendency to defend its ideas by attacking alternative approaches. Most disappointing is that many of the 'critical' writers take such an impoverished view of coaches. In aggregate (and with a little exaggeration) coaches are said not to reflect, simply to reproduce content and practice, to fail to take context into account, to neglect the interpersonal dimension, to rely only on a technical model, to take decisions without history or context and to adopt a unidirectional delivery style. There may well be coaches for whom some or much of this criticism would be valid (not, of course, those writers!), but the criticism stems from their partial account of practice. This is what North (2017) terms an 'epistemic fallacy'. Assuming a particular but partial view of what constitutes practice, researchers create a false 'standard' against which sport coaches are evaluated.

My own approach might best be described as pragmatic. The historical emergence of pragmatism through seminal figures, such as Piece, James, and Dewey, is readily available in the literature (cf. Bacon, 2012), and more recent treatments have documented its re-emergence in the late twentieth century (cf. Rescher, 2017). This brief description merely identifies those key principles that inform my approach to conceptualising sport coaching. There are a number of features of pragmatism that I believe help to understand and appreciate what is meant by sport coaching. First, the practical consequences of an idea or conception give it meaning. Second, experience and experimentation are the basis of understanding. Third, knowledge is fallible because the context, from which we derive our experience of it, is ever changing, and because we can only ever have a partial appreciation of it. Fourth, scepticism should arise from a confrontation with a particular problem, not from a more generalised state of 'doubt'. It is important to recognise that a conceptualisation is not an end in itself. It is an 'instrument' that helps us to understand our environment, or social world. This is abstracted from our direct experience, but this is 'tested' against the contribution of others, and against our own constant 'experimentation'. We have, therefore, a limited capacity to comprehend the complexity and scope of social phenomena. Our grasp of reality is fallible, but we deal with this by judging it against current and contextual standards of acceptance. This might be phrased as, 'how useful is my conceptualisation, not how 'true' is it'. Pragmatism also embraces the concept that developing and refining our conceptualisation is a social process.

Jenkins' (2017) stimulus paper criticises 'crude pragmatism' in understanding sport coaching, and an accompanying array of commentaries provide an excellent source of background reading and argument. The genesis of the argument is that a crude 'what works' approach by coaches should be replaced by a more reflective, values-infused approach—a philosophical pragmatism. However, this set of papers is marked by an unproblematic assumption of what is meant by sport coaching, almost no reference to coaching practice itself, and a focus, in general, on 'coaching philosophy' that might be better conceived of as coaching strategy. In addition, the assertion that such a 'crude' approach is superficial and not accompanied by deeper reflection, experimentation, or underpinning values is to misread both the evidence of individual coaches and the decision-making process. Pragmatists produce an 'early theorisation' that is workable and refined through practice. Our conceptualisations conform to the real, shared world but do so relatively, not absolutely: our knowledge and ideas exist in an ever-changing historical, cultural and social context. Emphasising this helps us to explain the development of ideas and practices but, I will argue, have less to do with the 'now' of practice; dealing with consequences makes us forward-looking. This will partly explain my emphasis on the practice of sport coaching—'what it is', rather than 'what it has become'. I will argue that sport coaching can be understood in terms of purpose and practice—values, context and resources provide an elaboration that distinguish it from similar social practices. I will argue that I leave 'crudeness' behind by emphasising not just 'what works', but 'what works in which situations' and how coaches can accommodate dealing with such a conundrum.

I am comfortable with all conceptualisations of sport coaching, while accepting that they have a disciplinary foundation and provide only a partial explanation for coaching practice. My questions centre (under my pragmatic umbrella) on how sport coaches cope with the operationalisation of practice. The centrepiece of this is a purposeful, planned intervention process towards identifiable goals. This may form part of a multi-year programme aimed at successful Olympic participation or a shorter-term series of episodic interventions. This explains my interest in coaches' expertise; their capacity for assimilating and accommodating to a multitude of, often competing, factors, which leads to a situation in which coaching can only be understood in the particularity of contextualised practice. In my view this places decision making, in its almost infinite variety, as a key element of coaching expertise. Of course, sport coaching is a social enterprise and comprises interpersonal relationships. It is entirely appropriate that academics should understand how coaching is shaped by this, but in placing performance intervention at the heart of sport coaching, I ask how this understanding impacts on the central purpose of coaching. I also believe that coaching practice can be better understood with reference to coaching domains (Lyle & Cushion, 2010). I do not entirely agree with Cassidy et al. (2016, p. 4) that these are 'artificial' demarcations (Lyle, 2011b), but they are certainly social constructions that are open to debate. Nevertheless, I find them a helpful analytical tool for expertise-led deployment and development. There are undoubtedly 'layers' of influence and a framework of socio-cultural and institutional causal forces that impact on the coaches' practice. There will always be an individual and relationship history to be taken into account. However, I find it helpful to distinguish between those matters that unpressured reflection will illuminate, but which may not be susceptible to immediate change, and the coaches' mechanisms for dealing with those factors that have an immediate impact but may also be 'held' tacitly.

One conceptualisation of coaching portrays it as a 'process' (Lyle, 1999), within a context of the management of sport performance (e.g., enhancement, maintenance, development). This dimension will be impacted by the other dimensions—professional context, social context (including ethical dimension), domain parameters, and athlete and coach resources. Thus, sport coaching is the management and delivery of an intervention (no matter how sophisticated, intensive or comprehensive) to assist/support/direct (leaving room for context-appropriate behaviour) an athlete/team to achieve specified sporting goals. This intervention is designed and planned to 'do the right thing, at the right time, in the right way ('right' can be substituted by 'appropriate'). It is a redundant exercise to debate whether there is a behavioural dimension, cognitive dimension, social dimension or inter-personal dimension. The answer is simple (even if said very clumsily)—'you cannot not do', 'you cannot not think', 'you cannot act outside context', and 'you cannot coach without athletes'. In other words, each and all of these dimensions are present at all times. This reinforces an integrated account of coaching but allows for a prioritising of focus and interest. It also points to the poverty of academic contributions that seek to focus on one dimension without reference to the others (particularly the nexus of goals, domain and intervention).

Key Points

The professionalisation of sport coaching as a valued occupation is a current and recurring theme in sport coaching literature (Cassidy et al., 2016; Lyle & Cushion, 2017; North, 2017). It may seem obvious, but perhaps worthy of greater attention, that the professionalisation process and agenda are dependent upon the scope and meaning attached to the term. It is important that we are able to distinguish sport coaching from other, perhaps similar, pursuits. However, the boundaries of sport coaching in policy and professionalisation must be such that its practice—entry, education, qualifications, values, expertise, quality control and regulation—is of sufficient weight as to be commensurate with professional status. It seems to me that professionalisation in a tradition sense is a worthwhile ambition and distant policy initiative but that more tightly defined and managed sport coaching in terms of employment, deployment and licensing is more likely to lead to a higher level of professionalism. It is for that reason that the meaning attached to sport coaching, its association with sporting practice, matters of inclusion and exclusion, its domain properties, and, crucially, a need to recognise and acknowledge the strengths and limitations of seeing sport coaching through disciplinary eyes, are matters that may appear consigned to abstract conceptual debate but have surprisingly practical consequences.

Conclusion

I have an optimistic view of coaches and coaching. They reason and reflect; they strategise both deliberatively and in pressured situations. They are aware of their own resources/capabilities and those of others. They assimilate history and context, but at times, in everyday practice, they may focus with a narrower perspective on the immediacy of intervention. They operate within a framework of interdependent goals, ambitions and motivations—institutional and personal—which they understand and work towards, recognising that it is not a linear pathway (no-one ever said it was!) and that goals may be contested by other coaches and athletes. However conceptualised, sport coaching involves higher-order expertise. There is a very broad range of definitions and conceptualisations with which to embrace this expertise; yes, influenced by disciplinary positions or conceptual preferences, but perhaps also redolent of our continued use of sport coaching as a unitary construct for what is a loosely-bound aggregation of roles and purposes.

References

Bacon, M. (2012). *Pragmatism: An introduction*. Cambridge, England: Polity Press.

Bennie, A., & O'Connor, D. (2010). Coaching philosophies: Perceptions from professional cricket, rugby league and rugby union players and coaches in Australia. *International Journal of Sports Science & Coaching, 5*(2), 309–320.

Cassidy, T., Jones, R. L., & Potrac, P. (2016). *Understanding sports coaching: The pedagogical, social and cultural foundations of coaching practice* (3rd ed.). London: Routledge.

Collins, L., Carson, H. J., & Collins, D. (2016). Metacognition and professional judgement and decision making: Importance, application and evaluation. *International Sports Coaching Journal, 3*(3), 355–361.

Côté, J., Bruner, M., Erickson, K., Strachan, L., & Fraser-Thomas, J. (2010). Athlete development and coaching. In J. Lyle & C. Cushion (Eds.), *Sports coaching: Professionalisation and practice* (pp. 63–84). Edinburgh: Churchill Livingstone, Elsevier.

Côté, J., Erickson, K., & Duffy, P. (2007). Developing the expert performance coach. In D. Farrow, J. Baker, & C. MacMahon (Eds.), *Developing sport expertise* (pp. 96–112). London: Routledge.

Council of Europe (2002). *European sport charter* (Revised). Available in http://rm.coe.int/16804c9dbb.

Cushion, C. J., Harvey, S., Muir, B., & Nelson, L. (2012). Developing the coach analysis and intervention system (CAIS): Establishing validity and reliability of a computerised systematic observation instrument. *Journal of Sports Sciences, 30*(2), 201–216.

Harvey, S., Lyle, J., & Muir, B. (2015). Naturalistic decision making in high performance team sport coaching. *International Sport Coaching Journal, 2*(2), 152–168.

HM Government. (2015). *Sporting future: A new strategy for an active nation*. London: Cabinet Office, HM Government.

Horton, P. (2015). The role of the coach. In C. Nash (Ed.), *Practical sports coaching* (pp. 3–15). London: Routledge.

Jenkins, S. P. R. (2017). Beyond 'crude pragmatism' in sports coaching: Insights from C. S. Pierce, William James and John Dewey. *International Journal of Sports Science & Coaching, 12*(1), 8–19.

Jones, R. L. (2006). *The sports coach as educator: Re-conceptualising sports coaching*. London: Routledge.

Jones, R. L., Bailey, J., & Thompson, A. (2013). Ambiguity, noticing and orchestration: Further thoughts on managing the complex coaching context. In P. Potrac, W. Gilbert, & J. Denison (Eds.), *The Routledge handbook of sports coaching* (pp. 271–283). London: Routledge.

Jones, R. L., Bowes, I., & Kingston, K. (2010). Complex practice in coaching: Studying the chaotic nature of coach-athlete interactions. In J. Lyle & C. Cushion (Eds.), *Sports coaching: Professionalisation and practice* (pp. 15–25). Edinburgh: Churchill Livingstone, Elsevier.

Jones, R. L., & Corsby, C. (2015). A case for coach Garfinkel: Decision making and what we already know. *Quest, 67*, 439–449.

Lagaert, S., & Roose, H. (2016). Exploring the adequacy and validity of 'sport' definitions: Reflections on a contested and open concept. *International Review for the Sociology of Sport, 51*(4), 485–498.
Lara-Bercial, S., & Mallett, C. J. (2016). The practices and development of pathways of professional and Olympic serial winning coaches. *International Sport Coaching Journal, 3*(3), 221–239.
Lara-Bercial, S., North, J., Hämäläinen, K., Oltmanns, K., Minkhorst, J., & Petrovic, L. (2017). *European sport coaching framework*. Champaign, Il: Human Kinetics.
Liponski, W. (2003). *World sports encyclopedia*. St Paul, MN: MBI.
Lyle, J. (1999). The coaching process: An overview. In N. Cross & J. Lyle (Eds.), *The coaching process: Principles and practice for sport* (pp. 3–24). Oxford: Butterworth Heinemann.
Lyle, J. (2011a). What is a coach and what is coaching? In I. Stafford (Ed.), *Coaching children in sport* (pp. 5–16). London: Routledge.
Lyle, J. (2011b). Sport development, sports coaching and domain specificity. In B. Houlihan & M. Green (Eds.), *The Routledge handbook of sports development* (pp. 487–500). London: Routledge.
Lyle, J. (2018a). Reflecting on the development of a conceptual framework for sport coaching. *International Sport Coaching Journal, 5*(1), 90–98.
Lyle, J. (2018b). The transferability of sport coaching research: A critical commentary. *Quest, 70* (4), 419–437.
Lyle, J., & Cushion, C. (2010). Narrowing the field: Some key questions about sports coaching. In J. Lyle & C. Cushion (Eds.), *Sports coaching: Professionalisation and practice* (pp. 243–252). Edinburgh: Churchill Livingstone.
Lyle, J., & Cushion, C. (2017). *Sport coaching concepts: A framework for coaching practice*. Edinburgh: Churchill Livingstone, Elsevier.
North, J. (2017). *Sport coaching research and practice: Ontology, interdisciplinarity and critical realism*. London: Routledge.
North, J., Piggott, D., Lara-Bercial, S., Abraham, A., & Muir, B. (2018). The professionalization of sport coaching. In R. Thelwell & M. Dicks (Eds.), *Professional advances in sports coaching: Research and practice*. London: Routledge.
Potrac, P., Gilbert, W., & Denison, J. (2013). Introduction. In P. Potrac, W. Gilbert, & J. Denison (Eds.), *Routledge handbook of sports coaching* (pp. 1–2). London: Routledge.
Purdy, L. (2018). *Sports coaching: The basics*. London: Routledge.
Rescher, N. (2017). *Pragmatism: The restoration of its scientific roots*. London: Routledge.
Sport England. (2016). *Coaching in an active nation*. London: Sport England.
UK Coaching. (2017). *Our strategy 2017–2021*. Leeds: UK Coaching.

John Lyle is a Professor in the Carnegie School of Sport, Leeds Beckett University. He established the first Masters degree in coaching studies in the UK, and is the author of a number of influential textbooks. His academic experience is complemented by a considerable personal experience as a coach, involvement in sport coaching policy in the UK, and engagement in the delivery of high performance coach development. He has coached and played volleyball at international level and was also a professional soccer player.

Chapter 3
Coaching Educational Programs: (Re)Conceptualising how Coaches Learn

Charles L. T. Corsby, Gethin L. Thomas, and Manuel Santos

Abstract Research developments within sports coaching have stressed coaches as highly influential actors in shaping, creating and developing athletes' experiences. It is therefore unsurprising to see that coach education and development has been subject to considerable investigation (e.g., Chesterfield, G., Jones, R. L., & Potrac, P., Sport Educ Soc 15:299–314; 2010; Nelson, L., & Cushion, C., Sports Psychol 20:174–183; 2006; Piggott, Phys Educ Sport Pedagogy 20:283–298; 2013; Townsend, R. C., & Cushion, C., Sport Educ Soc 22:528–546; 2015). This chapter presents a brief insight to this associated literature, specifically concerning the conduct, experiences, and development of coach education. The discussion considers the location of sports coaching research, coach education and higher education provision. In doing so, a case study is presented that illustrates the educational and methodological possibilities for coaches to consider within their professional development. Specific attention will be paid to the future implications for coaches and their associated development in the form of 'action research' as a methodology; of which, the approach is presented as holding the possibility of both 'deconstructing' and 'reconstructing' coaching practice. The argument here draws upon (Cassidy, Jones, and Potrac's, *Cultural and pedagogical foundations of coaching practice*. Routledge, London, 2016) recommendations of 'practical theorists' and, by way of example, the chapter concludes by offering the experiences of a Doctoral student engaging in action research as a live case study.

Keywords Coach education · Coach development · Practical theorist · Doctorate in sports coaching

C. L. T. Corsby (✉) · G. L. Thomas · M. Santos
Cardiff Metropolitan University, Cardiff, Wales, UK
e-mail: ccorsby@cardiffmet.ac.uk; glthomas@cardiffmet.ac.uk; mdsantos@cardiffmet.ac.uk

R. Resende, A. R. Gomes (eds.), *Coaching for Human Development and Performance in Sports*, https://doi.org/10.1007/978-3-030-63912-9_3

Coaching Educational Programs: (re)Conceptualising how Coaches Learn

In recent years, considerable attention has been paid to the examination of coach education (e.g., Adams, Cropley, & Mullens, 2016; Allison, 2016; Chesterfield, Jones, & Potrac, 2010). This chapter presents a brief insight into this literature, specifically concerning the conduct, experiences, and development of coach education. The principal purpose is to further locate sports coaching as a discipline of study and, in doing so, critically review coach education and development. Specific attention will be paid to the developmental principles and methodological possibilities of postgraduate education for coaches in the form of a case study. In terms of the chapter's structure, the opening section provides a brief overview and insight into the conceptual and empirical developments within coach education literature. Following this, the chapter attempts to locate the discipline of sports coaching before presenting a case study of an existing doctoral programme that stands as a complementary 'pathway' to coach accreditation. The recommendations discussed are underpinned by Cassidy, Jones, and Potrac (2016) assertion of coaches as 'practical theorists' and the associated value of 'action research' as a methodology. The chapter concludes by offering the experiences of a student engaging in the doctoral programme as a live case study.

Coach Education: Conceptual and Empirical Developments

Research developments within sports coaching have highlighted coaches as highly influential actors in shaping, creating and developing athletes' experiences. It is therefore unsurprising to see coach education and development has been subject to considerable investigation (e.g., Chesterfield et al., 2010; Nelson & Cushion, 2006; Piggott, 2012, 2013; Townsend & Cushion, 2015). According to Nelson, Cushion, and Potrac (2006), the learning experiences of coaches can be categorised as being formal, non-formal, and informal. Formal learning has been defined as taking place in an "institutionalised, chronologically graded and hierarchically structured education system" (Coombs & Ahmed, 1974, p. 8). Coach education programmes resemble these formal situations, occurring only in short blocks at a time with significant months or years in between teaching sessions (Knowles, Gilbourne, Borrie, & Nevill, 2001). To date, the academic attention towards coach education has concerned preparing coaches through these educational structures (e.g., Chesterfield et al., 2010).

Building upon this line of inquiry, Piggott (2013) described three fundamental assertions drawn from this (growing) body of literature: (1) coach education has been synonymously used with formal education; (2) coach education is a sub-category of coach learning and; (3) coach learning is a sub-category of coach development. Despite consensus that the education of coaches is a critical component, Cushion and colleagues have previously criticised the effectiveness of formal learning on these courses as ranging from genuine 'education' to 'indoctrination' (Cushion et al., 2010). The accusation, according to Nelson et al. (2006), is that National Governing Bodies (NGB's) hold some flawed assumptions about coaches and coaching which position the courses towards 'indoctrination' (Piggott, 2012).

From this perspective, despite limited critical analysis, coach education courses have typically operated from competency-based assessment. Yet, there remains no evidence to directly link coach education certification (accreditation) to coaching competency, suggesting the competencies achieved by coaches cannot be attributed to the courses on offer. Thus, despite recognising an exposure to sports science (e.g., physiology, biomechanics) and sports specific content, coaches have tended to value their informal 'in-the-field' experiences (Adams et al., 2016). Similarly, Townsend and Cushion's (2015) interrogation of elite cricket's haphazard culture illustrated a tension between the highly individualised legitimised knowledge and the prescribed body of knowledge provided in cricket coach education. Drawing upon Bourdieu's work, the scholars identified a gap in our understanding of the power-ridden, socially political, and constructed reality of coach education (Townsend & Cushion, 2015). Such a finding resonates with Chesterfield et al. (2010) description of the 'studentship' (Graber, 1991) and 'impression management' (Goffman, 1959) that coaches engage in to satisfy course expectations. In doing so, the content has thus been accused of largely ignoring the pedagogical and socio-cultural aspects relating to the coach's role (Cassidy, Jones, & Potrac, 2009). Such attainment of qualifications has been further problematised by Blackett, Evans, and Piggott (2015) study of sporting directors' perception of coaches' dispositions, coaching knowledge and ability to maintain respect. Here, recruitment of 'fast-tracked' head coaches often occurred earlier in the coaches' playing careers, resulting in some candidates generating more cultural and symbolic capital, and consequently, positioned more favourable for the positions. The nepotism illustrated in this paper further adds to the concerns of reproducing taken-for-granted bodies of knowledge, valorising playing styles as 'coaching', and the pitfalls of mere accreditation.

However, in spite of such criticisms levelled at coach education, Jones and Allison's (2014) examination of candidates' experiences on an elite professional preparation programme identified that periodic course gatherings provided participants with a 'community of security'. The findings proposed that the value of the course was not in developing competencies, but rather, to provide coaches refuge from their everyday workplace anxieties. Such a finding echoed previous work calling for more peer-based learning opportunities to better support coaches; for example, problem-based learning (Jones & Turner, 2006); Communities of practice (Culver & Trudel, 2008); and Theory-to-practice (Jones, Morgan, & Harris, 2012). In doing so, many professional development programmes have responded to accusations of 'decontextualized' and 'divorced' knowledge by including 'in-situ' mentoring programmes across their accreditation (e.g., The Football Association).

Taking lead from nursing, education, and business, Jones, Harris, and Miles (2009) reviewed the literature concerning the formalised role of mentoring. A subsequent body of research has emerged placing an emphasis on the role and value of the coach educator, particularly relating to 'mentoring' as an opportunity to challenge, legitimise, and recreate coaching practices. Indeed, Adams et al. (2016) recommended that, alongside reflective practice, mentoring can better combine the informal with the formal learning (i.e., seminar course delivery) on such courses. The proposed justification underpinning mentoring has been to enhance the skills, knowledge, and understanding of employees at all levels through a "formalised process whereby a more knowledgeable and experienced person actuates a supportive role" (Roberts, 2000, p. 162). Yet, despite the ostensible merits, Jones et al. (2009) identified several potential pitfalls and unfounded claims to mentoring. Such criticisms included: (1) an impartial picture of what 'tends' to happen and what potentially 'could' happen; (2) overly simplistic accounts of the mentor-mentee relationship that ignores the relationality of pedagogic interactions (e.g., Cushion, Griffiths, & Armour, 2017); and finally (3) an anaemic analysis of the power dynamics, legitimation and conflict the participants must negotiate to 'buy-in'.

In an attempt to address such pitfalls, Potrac (2016) investigated the subjective experiences of mentors working within The FA Grassroots Club Mentor Programme. The findings from the project highlighted the tensions and challenges mentors faced and further alluded to the contested nature of club football settings. Similar to previous research (e.g., Piggott, 2013; Potrac & Jones, 2009; Thompson, Potrac, & Jones, 2015), the mentors were subject to a rite of passage that required they 'prove' their knowledge and skills. In doing so, the mentors described the need to understand the 'person' they were working with, which often lead to persistent difficulties in 'shifting' the coaching beliefs and practices. As such, Potrac's (2016) recommendations for coach education included a more (critical) consideration of coaches, coach educators, mentors and significant others' network of interrelationships.

Building upon this line of inquiry, Cushion et al. (2017) explored the myriad of power relations and interactions of coach educators working in clubs and with academy managers. The argument here asserted that coaching practice is situationally tied to both the emergent and historically bound practices of coaches and thus, the social structures that educators are subject to must be examined (see Hodkinson, Biesta, & James, 2007). The subsequent findings from the study placed coach educators as structured by, and structuring of, the context they worked within. Indeed, the coach educators' practice and learning required negotiation and legitimation within each 'field of struggle', resulting in a controlled and maintained body of knowledge (Cushion et al., 2017). Coach educators thus remained central to influencing and reshaping the protected language, rhetoric and ideology of coach education.

The value of such work has illuminated the dispositions and assumptions underpinning coach education and the experiences of coach educators. However, despite appropriate criticism, to tarnish all coach education as 'divorced from reality' would be an injustice to the courses, with coaches often citing particular elements as useful (e.g., Jones & Allison, 2014). For, as Piggott (2012) identified, some smaller NGBs have been cited as generating more meaningful interaction between coaches through task orientations that have been deemed more useful by attendees. For example,

McCullick, Belcher, and Schempp (2005) investigated the perceptions of 30 participants (25 course candidates and five coach educators) from a Ladies Professional Golf Association (LPGA) coach education course. Here, the findings illustrated that coaches recognised and enjoyed the presence of 'knowledgeable' others as useful and important for their development. Similarly, Leduc, Culver, and Werthner (2012) examined coach learning on a formal coach education programme that was grounded in a constructivist approach to learning. Drawing upon Jarvis (2006, 2007, 2009) and Moon's (2001) theoretical frameworks, the authors reaffirmed the difficulties coach education faces in moving the beliefs and practices of coaches. On one hand, some coaches were able to engage with the material, resulting in cognitive, emotive and practical changes. While, on the other hand, some participants cited confidence, time and an unease to change as explanations for limited engagement. The concerns raised here resonate with the work of Partington and Cushion (2012), who observed an 'epistemological gap' between coaches' knowledge, action and explanations.

The literature highlighted and considered thus far has shed light on the contemporary issues raised within coach education literature (and some wider). By way of answering some of the prominent issues within coach education, Allison, Abraham, and Cale (2016) presented The Football Association's (FA) commitment to supporting the coach developer, educator and consequently coaches: better coaches; better players. Here, Allison's (2016) introduction provides a refreshing recognition of, not just traditional 'functional' and 'applied' research that dominates courses, as reported by Adams et al. (2016), but knowledge that grapples with the 'complexity' of coaching; innovative learning and assessment that values theory and practice. Valuing the former to inform the latter, the development of better synergies between NGBs and Higher Education (HE), therefore, provides the platform for developing coaches as 'practical theorists' (Cassidy et al., 2016). That is, demanding that coaches deliberately think about their values, beliefs, dispositions, objectives and intentions as a precursor to action (Flyvberg, 2001).

However, the implication of this argument for coach education is twofold. Firstly, the initial idea raises concerns about the depth and scope of sports coaching research more generally, and to what coaches on education courses are currently exposed (e.g., Adams et al., 2016). Questions akin to: What is defined as relevant sports coaching 'knowledge'? Where do coaches go for 'new' knowledge? And, 'what' do coaches find? Fundamental to this assertion, then, is sports coaching research must aim to generate clear, considerate and critical ideas that resonate with the coaches' experiences. Indeed, placing the emphasis on 'insightful' research, Jones (2019) recognised the importance of 'quality' research that both informs and enhances the work of sports coaches, and thus, avoiding "valuable knowledge being left on the table" (p. 157). Consequently, rather than solely taking issue with the 'levelness' of coach education, the second interrelated implication of this argument relates to debating the purpose and integration of such (often contested) coaching knowledge. That is, paying attention to the relationship between coaches, HE courses, coach education and industry expectations. Here, in keeping with Jones (2019), we take issue with the creep of 'accreditation' in HE courses, by calling for coach education and development to embrace the spirit of 'practical theorists'; an argument centred on working with the coach and their way of 'being'. Therefore, rather than viewed as parallel, embedded or even alternative, the essence of educating coaches lies in developing a 'quality of mind' that holds the potential to combat the 'academic vs. practitioner' debate; an argument more recently reproduced by Ewing (2019). In turn, better preparing coaches to manage their everyday complexities, make informed (and critical) judgments on the knowledge they are exposed to, and mapping a pathway grounded in the experiences for coaches to genuinely develop.

In terms of the remainder of this Chapter, while it is hoped the content stimulates professional practitioners, researchers and coaches to carefully examine their role in educating coaches, the purpose stretches beyond critical 'discussion'. The subsequent sections focus on locating and presenting a doctoral programme that encapsulates the role of combining theory and practice to develop sports coaches as 'practical theorists'. Attempting to address the concerns above, the course is presented as an example of illuminating how coaching research can be coupled with increasing use and exploitation in practice. Here, the Doctorate in Sports Coaching (DSC) was designed as a high-level, leading-edge knowledge and skills training for coaches 'in-the-field' and 'on-the-ground'. The content outlined below stands as a 'live' example that combines the academic study of coaching (i.e., research informed practice), pedagogy (i.e., consideration of learning and teaching) and the 'practice' of coaches (i.e., 'on-the-field' activity). Viewing these structures as interconnected, rather than separate entities, the chapter presents 'action research' as a design that holds the potential to complement both the 'deconstruction' and 'reconstruction' of coaching; of challenging the taken-for-granted and evolving the processes and practices of coaches' work.

Locating Sports Coaching: Research and Education

Despite coach education aiming to be developmental, such courses are often criticised for being detached from the reality of coaching practice and of failing to develop new and progressive knowledge for practitioners (Jones & Turner, 2006). Coaches' learning, in these situations, are restricted by having to engage with existing knowledge and limited opportunities to interact in critical thought and subsequent depth of learning. Notwithstanding the acknowledgment by many researchers and practitioners that coaching is a complex process (Cassidy et al., 2016), the notion that at the heart of coaching lies mechanical reduction and sequential 'models' continues to exist (e.g. Lyle & Cushion, 2016; Robinson, 2014). This persistence to strive for linear functionality has been evident throughout coach education programmes where coaching 'toolkits' and 'effective' practice models are prevalent (Piggott, 2012). Thus, prior to presenting the practical case study, it is our intention to outline our ontological (i.e., assumptions concerning nature of reality) and epistemological (i.e., assumptions concerning the nature of knowledge) position for sport coaching. The purpose here is underpinned by Jones'

(2019) consideration for quality research that can inform coaching practice, and the subsequent education of coaches.

In line with Jones, Edwards, and Viotto Filho (2016) we locate coaching within the interpretivist and critical paradigms, guided by a relativist and a subjective, interactive epistemology. Viewed from this perspective coaching knowledge cannot be taught a priori (Flyvberg, Landman, & Schram, 2012) and develops principally through in-depth familiarity with context, and shared understandings of practice. In these settings, the coaching self is not an independent and self-contained individual but is located firmly within social and cultural arrangements (e.g. Jones et al., 2016; Santos, Jones, & Mesquita, 2013). This allows for the pursuit of an interpretive and critical agenda whilst not denying the existence of an agreed target goal. As highlighted by Jones et al. (2016) this perspective aims to move beyond critiques of modelling and rationality as related to coaching and to present a practical epistemological reality.

As alluded to previously, positioning coaching in such a way provides a direction for educating and developing coaches as 'practical theorists' whereby cutting-edge content is made relevant, accessible, and can be immediately integrated into practice (Cassidy et al., 2016). This is an approach focused on the transformative acts of coaches; creating clear ideas for coaches to think with as opposed to being firm directives (Jones, 2019). As an example, we present the 'Doctorate in Sports Coaching' as a way of fostering the notion of 'practical theorist' to educate coaches. The point made here is not to be considered as a recommendation that all coaches must achieve level eight qualifications to practice, but rather, that coach education (and development) structures should harness the sentiment of working with the coach and their way of 'being'; informed and underpinned by high-quality 'coaching' research.

Practical Implications: Doctorate in Sports Coaching (DSC)

The development of the DSC in 2016 arose from a demand for high-level, leading-edge knowledge and skills training, coupled with increasing the use and exploitation of coaching research in practice. In line with the first UKCGE Report on 'Professional Doctorates' (Hoddell, Street, & Wildblood, 2002), the DSC qualification can be defined as;

A programme of advanced study and research which, whilst satisfying the University criteria for the award of a doctorate, is designed to meet the specific needs of a professional group external to the University, and which develops the capability of individuals to work within a professional context (ibid, p. 62).

Consequently, the DSC intends to improve the relevance of postgraduate degrees to the profession of sports coaching. In doing so, the programme aims to develop 'practical theorists' with an appreciation of the symbiotic and synergetic relationship between theory and practice. Echoing the words of Macdonald et al. (2002, p. 149) it seeks to take theory "off the table and into the field" providing a deeper critical understanding of coaching and a more realistic learning programme for coaches that reflects the complexity of practice (Jones, Potrac, Cushion, & Ronglan, 2011). The distinct emphasis lies in nurturing further the direct link between intellectual knowledge and moment-to-moment personal and social action (Reason & Torbert, 2001). Participants are required to become 'practical theorists' through rejecting the traditional distinction between academic and practitioner knowledge (Cassidy et al., 2016). Hence, coaches develop themselves through possessing considerable knowledge of theory or theories and cultivating the courage to experiment with these ideas within their own coaching practice. In line with the recommendations of the Quality Assurance Agency for Higher Education, the purpose is to develop individuals' "professional practice and to support them in producing a contribution to (professional) knowledge" (QAA, 2008, p. 25). It offers a unique opportunity for professional and career enhancement in sports coaching through critical analysis and innovative practice.

In terms of design, the overall structure of the DSC programme consists of three elements: taught modules, a professional development report, and research project. The DSC starts with completion of a taught component comprising of four compulsory modules designed to (1) generate critical thought and creativity akin to transformative learning, and (2) to encourage such insights' application to practice. Running alongside the taught component students complete a 'professional development report' where participants' engage in critique and interpretation of 'evidence informed' professional practice to inform continuing development. Following the completion of both these elements, students conduct a research project where they are strongly encouraged to carry out a piece of action research for their study of coaching practice.

An example of the 'theory to practice' aim of the DSC and the consequent development of 'practical theorists' is illustrated within 'The Pedagogical Foundations of Coaching' teaching module. Similar to the use of educational theorist by other coaching scholars (e.g. Jones, Thomas, Nunes, & Viotto Filho, 2018; Nelson, Groom, & Potrac, 2016), the work of Lev Vygotsky is explored and applied to better understand and inform coaching practice. The module consists of ten three-hour seminars conducted fortnightly over a period of two academic terms of 10 weeks. The number of participants each year varies from three to six students dependent on the amount of individuals enrolled on the programme. During the first seminar, the initial focus is on the aims, learning outcomes, assessment procedures and teaching method. In the second part, a Vygotskian concept is introduced to students, and they are set a task of considering this idea in relation to their coaching practice and to produce a reflective written log by the next seminar. A structured whole class and small group discussion on the implementation into practice of the concept given in the first session forms the first half of the second seminar. During the second half of the seminar, students are presented with the next Vygotskian concept and the process continues as in the previous class. The remainder of the seminars in the module follow this fortnightly pattern covering Vygotskian concepts, discussions groups, and student presentations, with a final session to formally evaluate the unit.

The Vygotskian concepts given to students on the module include an introduction to cultural historical theory, mediation, psychological tools, conceptual formation, higher mental functions, zone of proximal development, more capable other and perezhivane. Students engage, for example, with Vygotsky's dialectical ideas on concept formation (Vygotsky, 1987) in their coaching practice, which he considered to result from an interaction between everyday (spontaneous) concepts and formal scientific ones. Vygotsky proposed this dialectical view of reality to overcome a traditional Cartesian dualism vision (Liu & Matthews, 2005). He focused on combining opposing views into a continuous whole to enhance the development of new knowledge and understanding. For students on the DSC this means acknowledging that understanding results from experience of direct interaction with the environment (e.g. informal learning); alongside knowing mediated by given scientific concepts (Jones et al., 2018). In this way, scientific concepts mediate individual thoughts, providing structure to everyday thinking and problem solving (Vygotsky, 1987). Hence, knowledge given (i.e. scientific concepts) is gradually embedded in everyday coaching practice and vice versa (Jones et al., 2018).

Through challenging the taken-for-granted practices of coaches, then, the DSC holds the promise to enhance the processes and practices of coaching enabling sports coaching education to take a step forward as a whole. As research has recently established, the main knowledge source of both novice and experienced coaches are interactive experiences within practical coaching contexts (Chesterfield et al., 2010). In this regard, the DSC adopts (but not exclusively) an early conceptualisation of 'action research' as a research design for coaches to combine theory and practice (Carr, 2006). Here, it is proposed that 'action research' holds the potential to complement both the 'deconstruction' and 'reconstruction' of coaching research to support the development of careful, critical and considerate practitioners. In doing so, such an argument moves beyond Alison's (Allison, 2016) appreciation of research in coach education by attempting to address theory–practice inconsistencies among practitioners.

Action Research

In recent years, there has been a significant growth in the use of action research as a form of inquiry into social and educational issues (Coghlan & Brannick, 2014). The introduction of the phrase 'action research' is commonly attributed to Kurt Lewin (1890–1947) to describe a way of investigating allowing "the significantly established laws of social life to be tried and tested in practice" (Carr, 2006, p. 423). Lewin is also recognised as the creator of the action research method, which includes a spiral of steps, each composed of "a circle of planning, action and fact finding about the result of the action" (Lewin, 1946, p. 205). In its initial guise, the growth of action research was stifled by the positivistic culture within the social sciences that was prevalent in the United States during the mid-twentieth century (Carr, 2006). By the 1950s the inability of action research to conform to positivistic methodological requirements led to its decline as form of investigation (Sanford, 1970).

The re-emergence of action research as a form of inquiry took place in the context of educational and curriculum investigation in the United Kingdom (UK) during the 1970s (for example, Stenhouse, 1975). Action research in the UK differed from the American version through its adoption of an interpretive stance and its rejection of a positivistic research methodology, shifting attention to the perspectives of social actors (Kemmis, 1988). Through adopting education practice as its focus, action research became an approach whereby "practitioners could test the 'educational theories' implicit in their own practice by treating them as experimental hypotheses to be systematically assessed in specific educational contexts" (Carr, 2006, p. 424). This was a step taken to where a pedagogic professional could and should be researching his or her own practice as opposed to the more traditional research-development-diffusion model (Carr & Kemmis, 1986).

In the development of our own coach education courses, to ensure critical reflection of social theories in practice, we have drawn on an initial conceptualisation of action research (Carr, 2006). This is an interpretive position whereby students have to make sense of and share their pedagogical experiences (Jones et al., 2012). By encouraging participants to engage with both new knowledge and what they already tacitly know, the main aim is to advance knowledge (Carr, 2006). Students are encouraged to question their own assumptions while also placing importance on critical reflective engagement with new theoretical knowledge in practice. Such an approach upholds several important fundamental characteristics associated with action research. The aim is to generate understanding and knowledge through cycles of action and critical reflection (Coghlan & Brannick, 2014). By engagement with recurring iterative and cyclical processes of planning, action and evaluation the students focus on relevant issues in order to produce knowledge that is actionable (Coghlan, 2019). As such, primacy is given to the relational, with individuals involved working collaboratively in seminars and towards creating knowledge in action throughout the cyclical processes (Bradbury, 2015). Within the classroom and on the practice field inter-subjectivity is crucial whereby people continuously interact socially, culturally, and historically within relationships. Acknowledging the interconnection and history of these social structures allows participants to identify and challenge existing patterns while critically considering potential emergent and developmental solutions within their own context (Bradbury, 2015). Knowledge is constructed through transformative action by building on the past, interacting in the present with the aim of shaping the future (Coghlan, 2019). The practical knowing that emerges from relationships within complex emergent systems allows for students to contribute for the self and others. Hence, within action research social action has a practical and emancipatory focus (Bradbury, 2015). Within the next section a case study of an existing doctoral programme, underpinned by this action research methodology, will be presented; as an example of a complementary pathway to coach accreditation.

A Doctorate in Sports Coaching Case Study

At the age of 31, coaching volleyball has been a defining part of who I am. For 14 years I have been coaching volleyball, from beginners to adults, both male and female squads. Thus, undertaking a degree in sports science (that contained a specialisation in coaching volleyball), and a master's degree focused on pedagogical practice was a logical step to further my education and 'coaching' knowledge. Of course, embodying principles of 'life-long learner' and 'continual professional development', I found some anxiety concerning 'how' and 'where' to go following MSc study. In addition, I often shared the frustration of coaches that felt the disconnect between academics and coaches, theory and practice, while my frustration to improve my coaching practice was not satisfied by professional development opportunities (such as NGB-led coaching qualifications). I felt 'beyond' the professional development I received (level three qualification), and yet, I also found myself criticising those coaches, or 'theorists', that preferred to 'sit at the desk' rather than join me on the court. I was at a crossroad; I had the skills to learn but not the accessibility or support to engage with 'new' material. I was searching for new knowledge that resonated with my practice and beliefs about 'what' coaching is.

Looking back, my experiences reflected an episode described by Cassidy et al. (2016) in which a coach demonstrates dissatisfaction with the language employed by a 'theorist' whose terminology did not reflect my everyday struggles. This 'policy guru', despite an espoused educator, did not share my vocabulary. After many years struggling for 'new' knowledge, I decided to undertake the Doctorate in Sports Coaching. While my contribution in this chapter is a first-person account, the purpose is to bring-to-life the connection (and gap) between theory and practice. Specific attention will be paid to the impact that action research had (and still has) in shaping my coaching practices.

As alluded to above, merging the (perceived) gap between theory and practice remains a crucial challenge for educators of coaches; one that mainstream research, higher education institutes and coach education courses are still debating. The major appeal of undertaking the doctoral degree, then, related to the innovative, cyclical nature of the modules. Here, the cycles attempted to interweave theory and practice by introducing one (or several) theoretical concept(s) in a progressive manner that allowed for experimentation in my coaching practice. Unlike a typical research-based doctoral degree, the bouts of theory and practice are followed by insightful discussions based on the application of theory in our coaching contexts. These cycles of applying theory into practice allowed for a deconstruction and deeper understanding of practice, followed by a critical reflection (and reconstruction) on the process that further informs practice. Such a process is based upon Lewin's proposed cyclical structure of action research (Kemmis & McTaggart, 2005). In turn, the structure provided an opportunity to tie theory and practice in a way that moves "theory from the table to the field" (MacDonald et al., 2002, p. 149). For instance, as part of the Vygotsky-inspired module, I was challenged to experiment with Vygotsky's ideas on concept formation, which ignited a cultural-historical analysis of my coaching context. Here, the focus was on comprehending how my pedagogical practices (and consequently, athletes' learning) were influenced by volleyball in the UK lacking any cultural and historical roots. Further examples of theoretically inspired action research projects have also been disseminated and published (Pritchard, 2019; Santos, 2019; Santos & Morgan, 2019).

Here, claims that coaching is an inherently complex endeavour are addressed by using an action research design to make sense of practice, and therefore, living the complexity and messiness of the coaching field through a theoretical perspective. Yet, the cyclical nature of this process allowed my coaching practice to be underpinned by a theoretical lens, examining the laws of social life in a real-world context (Carr, 2006). Rather than treating theory and practice as two separate entities, the living of theory in practice takes lead from Apple's (1999) call for 'connected theory', practice, and issues. Thus, such entanglement between theory and practice combines a curiosity for theoretical underpinning, while encouraging considerate practical experimentation; that is, living the theory to provide opportunities to critically appreciate real-life context. Indeed, following this line of inquiry and development, I more recently wrestled with notions of creativity (inspired by jazz musicians), which have been translated in publication (See Santos & Morgan, 2019). This study, underpinned by pedagogical principles, positioned creativity as a shared collaborative process. The findings illustrated how players developed a curiosity for experimentation, enhanced appreciation of the game and, consequently, impacted upon their communication and solutions (Santos & Morgan, 2019).

While 'mainstream' coach education programmes have been accused of ignoring the emergent power differences and 'legitimised' knowledge (e.g., Cushion et al., 2017), the course clearly defines coaching as 'contextually-bound' activity, shaped by social and cultural rules, and underpinned by the assumptions and values of those involved. Thus, rather than protecting a body of knowledge that has been accused of being 'divorced' from reality, the purpose has been to challenge some of these values (and assumptions), bringing to the forefront what may previously have been implicit (Flyvberg, 2001). As alluded to in the previous examples, this reflective endeavour is based upon a premise to better analysing practice through embodying the idea of the practical theorist; of continually (and critically) engaging within new knowledge, while respecting existing structures and practices. Returning to the roots of what Hemmestad, Jones, and Standal (2010) described as the 'practical wisdom', my coach development experience is based upon the 'backwards-and-forwards' between theory and practice. It is a position I believe can be embraced by practitioners and educators to necessarily and appropriately propel coaches' practice forward; of which, can be facilitated by the action research design adopted in the DSC.

Key Points

The principal purpose of this chapter has been to further locate sports coaching as a discipline of study and, in doing so, critically review coach education and development. In questioning the conduct, experiences, and development of coaches, the main issue raised is that of the need to develop coach education courses that reflects the complex socio-political landscape of coaching. Central to this argument is the academic study of coaching, and the associated branch of knowledge, must be viewed as part of, rather than separate to, the (practical) activities (i.e., Academic Vs. Practitioner). Indeed, we have argued that by transforming the representation of coaching (i.e., how coaching is portrayed), we can start to (re)conceptualise what we strive for coaches to learn and manage within their respective contexts. Consequently, taking lead from Flyvberg (2001), Cassidy et al.'s (2016) recommendations of coaches as 'practical theorists', we believe, holds the potential to develop coaches that deliberately think about values, beliefs, dispositions, objectives and intentions as a precursor to action. To further bring these key points to life we offer the experiences of a Doctoral student engaging in 'action research' as a case study:

Conclusion

The field of sports coaching has come to recognise the multi-faceted relationships and interactions between coach, athlete and context (e.g., Cassidy et al., 2016). It is therefore unsurprising to see that coach education and development has been subject to considerable investigation (e.g., Chesterfield et al., 2010; Nelson & Cushion, 2006; Piggott, 2012, 2013; Townsend & Cushion, 2015). Despite recognising the relevance of an exposure to sports science (e.g., physiology, biomechanics) and sports specific content, fundamental to the critique offered, is the value that coaches place on their informal 'in-the-field' experiences (Adams et al., 2016). Consequently, recent literature (e.g., Blackett et al., 2015; Cushion et al., 2017) has gone some way to illustrate that coaching and coach education are socially and politically driven, which cannot be viewed as linear processes. This chapter has sought to present a brief insight into this associated literature, specifically concerning the conduct, experiences, and development of coach education. More generally, the discussion considered the location of sports coaching research, coach education and higher education provision.

While the principal aim of this chapter was to further locate sports coaching as a discipline of study, we argue that by transforming the representation of coaching (i.e., how coaching is portrayed and conceptualised), we can start to (re)-conceptualise the education of coaches; of what we strive for coaches to learn and manage within their respective contexts. Indeed, taking lead from Flyvberg (2001), we suggest coach development must encourage coaches to deliberately think about their values, beliefs, dispositions, objectives and intentions as a precursor to action.

Using examples from a Doctorate in Sports Coaching (DSC), the discussion moves beyond criticisms of coaches as technical experts to consider coach development in the form of 'action research'. Grounded in theory, it is proposed the methodology's general character provides scope for both 'deconstructing' and 'reconstructing' coaching practice. This chapter, then, builds upon, and echoes, Cassidy et al. (2016) recommendations of developing coaches as 'practical theorists'.

References

Adams, D., Cropley, B., & Mullens, R. (2016). Developing specialised youth soccer coaching qualifications: An exploratory study of course content and delivery mechanisms. *International Sport Coaching Journal, 3*, 31–45. https://doi.org/10.1123/iscj.2014-0148

Allison, W. (2016). The FA's coach education and development programme: Research informing practice. In W. Allison, A. Abraham, & A. Cale (Eds.), *Advances in coach education and development: From research to practice* (pp. 1–15). London: Routledge.

Allison, W., Abraham, A., & Cale, A. (2016). *Advances in coach education and development: From research to practice*. London: Routledge.

Apple, M. (1999). *Ideology and curriculum*. New York: Routledge.

Blackett, D., Evans, A., & Piggott, D. (2015). Why the best way of learning to coach the game is playing the game; conceptualizing 'fast-tracked' high-performance coaching pathways. *Sport, Education and Society, 22*(6), 744–758. https://doi.org/10.1080/13573322.2015.10754994

Bradbury, H. (2015). Introduction: How to situate and define action research. In H. Bradbury (Ed.), *The SAGE handbook of action research* (3rd ed., pp. 1–9). London: Sage.

Carr, W. (2006). Philosophy, methodology and action research. *Journal of Philosophy of Education, 40*(4), 421–435.

Carr, W., & Kemmis, S. (1986). *Becoming critical: Education, knowledge and action research*. Lewes: Falmer.

Cassidy, T., Jones, R. L., & Potrac, P. (2009). Understanding sports coaching: The social. In *Cultural and pedagogical foundations of coaching practice* (2nd ed.). London: Routledge.

Cassidy, T., Jones, R. L., & Potrac, P. (2016). Understanding sports coaching: The social. In *Cultural and pedagogical foundations of coaching practice* (3rd ed.). London: Routledge.

Chesterfield, G., Jones, R. L., & Potrac, P. (2010). 'Studentship' and 'impression management': Coaches' experiences of an advanced soccer coach education award. *Sport, Education and Society, 15*, 299–314.

Coghlan, D. (2019). *Doing action research in your own organization* (5th ed.). London: Sage.

Coghlan, D., & Brannick, T. (2014). *Doing action research in your own organization* (4th ed.). London: Sage.

Coombs, P., & Ahmed, M. (1974). *Attacking rural poverty: How non-formal education can help*. Baltimore: John Hopkins University Press.

Culver, D., & Trudel, P. (2008). Clarifying the concept of communities of practice in sport. *International Journal of Sports Science & Coaching, 3*(1), 1–10.

Cushion, C., Griffiths, M., & Armour, K. (2017). Professional coach educators in-situ: A social analysis of practice. *Sport, Education and Society, 24*(5), 533–546. https://doi.org/10.1080/13573322.2017.1411795

Cushion, C., Nelson, L., Armour, K., Lyle, J., Jones, R., Sandford, R., & O'Callaghan, C. (2010). *Coach learning and development: A review of literature* (Leeds, sports coach UK). Retrieved from: http://www.sportscoachuk.org/index.php? PageID_5&sc_23&uid_1321

Ewing, T. K. (2019). Rethinking head coach credentials: Playing experience, tertiary qualifications and coaching apprenticeships. *International Sport Coaching Journal*. https://doi.org/10.1123/iscj.2018-0092

Flyvberg, B. (2001). *Making social science matter: Why social inquiry fails and how it can succeed again*. Cambridge: Cambridge University Press.
Flyvberg, B., Landman, T., & Schram, S. (2012). Introduction: New directions in social science. In B. Flyvberg, T. Landman, & S. Schram (Eds.), *Real social science: Applied phronesis* (pp. 1–14). Cambridge: University Press.
Goffman, E. (1959). *The presentation of self in everyday life*. Reading: Penguin Books.
Graber, K. (1991). Studentship in pre-service teacher education: A qualitative study of undergraduate students in physical education. *Research Quarterly for Exercise and Sport, 62*(1), 41–51.
Hemmestad, L. B., Jones, R. L., & Standal, Ø. F. (2010). Phronetic social science: A means of better researching and analysing coaching? *Sport, Education and Society, 15*(4), 447–459.
Hoddell, S., Street, D., & Wildblood, H. (2002). *Doctorates – Converging or diverging patterns of provision. Quality Assurance in Education, 10*(2), 61–70.
Hodkinson, P., Biesta, G., & James, D. (2007). Understanding learning cultures. *Educational Review, 59*(4), 415–427.
Jarvis, P. (2006). *Towards a comprehensive theory of human learning*. London: Routledge.
Jarvis, P. (2007). *Globalisation, lifelong learning and the learning society: Sociological perspectives*. London: Routledge.
Jarvis, P. (2009). *Learning to be a person in society*. London: Routledge.
Jones, R. (2019). Sports coaching research: A brief look around and forward. In C. Corsby & C. N. Edwards (Eds.), *Exploring research in sports coaching and pedagogy: Context and contingency* (pp. 153–158). Newcastle upon Tyne, UK: Cambridge Scholars Publishing.
Jones, R. L., & Allison, W. (2014). Candidates' experiences of elite coach education: A longitudinal study ('tracking the journey'). *European Journal of Human Movement, 33*, 110–122.
Jones, R. L., Edwards, C., & Viotto Filho, I. A. T. (2016). Activity theory, complexity and sports coaching: An epistemology for a discipline. *Sport, Education and Society, 21*(2), 200–216.
Jones, R. L., Harris, R., & Miles, A. (2009). Mentoring in sports coaching: A review of the literature. *Physical Education and Sport Pedagogy, 14*(3), 267–284.
Jones, R. L., Morgan, K., & Harris, K. (2012). Developing coaching pedagogy: Seeking a better integration of theory and practice. *Sport, Education and Society, 17*(3), 313–329.
Jones, R. L., Potrac, P., Cushion, C., & Ronglan, L. T. (2011). *The sociology of sports coaching*. London: Routledge.
Jones, R. L., Thomas, G. L., Nunes, R. L., & Viotto Filho, T. (2018). The importance of history, language, change and challenge: What Vygotsky can teach sports coaches. *Motriz; Journal of Physical Education, 24*(2). https://doi.org/10.1590/s1980-6574201800020008
Jones, R. L., & Turner, P. (2006). Teaching coaches to coach holistically: Can problem-based learning (PBL) help? *Physical Education and Sport Pedagogy, 11*(2), 181–202.
Kemmis, S. (1988). Action research. In J. P. Keeves (Ed.), *Educational research, methodology and measurement: An international handbook* (pp. 173–179). Oxford: Pergamon Press.
Kemmis, S., & McTaggart, R. (2005). Participatory action research: Communicative action and the public sphere. In N. K. Denzin & Y. S. Lincoln (Eds.), *Handbook of qualitatative research* (3rd ed., pp. 559–603). London: Sage.
Knowles, Z., Gilbourne, D., Borrie, A., & Nevill, A. (2001). Developing the reflective sports coach: A study exploring the process of reflective practice within a higher education programme. *Reflective Practice, 2*, 185–207.
Leduc, M., Culver, D., & Werthner, P. (2012). Following a coach education programme: Coaches' perceptions and reported actions. *Sports Coaching Review, 1*(2), 135–150.
Lewin, K. (1946). Action research and minority problems. *Journal of Social Issues, 2*(4), 33–46.
Liu, C. H., & Matthews, R. (2005). Vygotsky's philosophy: Constructivism and its criticisms examined. *International Education Journal, 6*(3), 386–399.
Lyle, J., & Cushion, C. (2016). *Sport coaching concepts* (2nd ed.). Oxon: Routledge.
MacDonald, S., Kirk, D., Metzler, M., Nilges, L. M., Schempp, P., & Wright, J. (2002). It's all very well in theory: Theoretical perspectives and their applications in contemporary pedagogical research. *Quest, 54*, 133–156.

McCullick, B., Belcher, D., & Schempp, P. (2005). What works in coaching and sport instructor programs? The participants' view. *Physical Education and Sport Pedagogy, 10*(2), 121–137.
Moon, J. (2001). *Short courses & modules: Improving the impact of learning, training & professional development*. London: Kogan Page Limited.
Nelson, L., & Cushion, C. (2006). Reflection in coach education: The case of the national governing body coaching certificate. *The Sports Psychologist, 20*, 174–183.
Nelson, L., Cushion, C., & Potrac, P. (2006). Formal, nonformal and informal coach learning: A holistic conceptualisation. *International Journal of Sports Science & Coaching, 1*(3), 247–259.
Nelson, L., Groom, R., & Potrac, P. (2016). *Learning in sports coaching*. London: Routledge.
Partington, M., & Cushion, C. (2012). Performance during performance: Using Goffman to understand the behaviours of elite youth football coaches during games. *Sports Coaching Review, 1*(2), 93–105.
Piggott, D. (2012). Coaches' experiences of formal coach education: A critical sociological investigation. *Sport, Education and Society, 17*(4), 535–554.
Piggott, D. (2013). The open society and coach education: A philosophical agenda for policy reform and future sociological research. *Physical Education & Sport Pedagogy, 20*(3), 283–298.
Potrac, P. (2016). Delivering the FA grassroots club mentor programme. In W. Allison, A. Abraham, & A. Cale (Eds.), *Advances in coach education and development: From research to practice* (pp. 77–86). London: Routledge.
Potrac, P., & Jones, R. L. (2009). Micropolitical workings in semi-professional football. *Sociology of Sport Journal, 26*, 557–577.
Pritchard, R. (2019). Marrying theory to practice: Using Vygsotky to underpin game sense pedagogy. In C. L. Corsby & C. N. Edwards (Eds.), *Exploring research in sports coaching and pedagogy: Context and contingency* (pp. 101–110). Newcastle-Upon-Tyne: Cambridge Scholars Publishing.
QAA. (2008). *Framework for higher education in England, Wales and Northern Ireland*. London, UK: QAA.
Reason, P., & Torbert, W. (2001). The action turn: Towards transformational social science. *Concepts and Transformation, 6*(1), 1–37.
Roberts, A. (2000). Mentoring revised: A phenomenological reading of the literature. *Mentoring and tutoring: Partnership in learning, 8*(2), 145–169.
Robinson, P. E. (2014). *Foundations of sports coaching* (2nd ed.). Oxon: Routledge.
Sanford, N. (1970). Whatever happened to action research? *Journal of Social Issues, 26*(4), 3–23.
Santos, M. (2019). Collaborative creativity: From jazz to coaching. In C. L. Corsby & C. N. Edwards (Eds.), *Exploring research in sports coaching and pedagogy: Context and contingency* (pp. 93–100). Newcastle-Upon-Tyne: Cambridge Scholars Publishing.
Santos, S., Jones, R. L., & Mesquita, I. (2013). Do coaches orchestrate? The working practices of elite Portuguese coaches. *Research Quarterly for Exercise and Sport, 84*(2), 263–272.
Santos, M., & Morgan, K. (2019). Developing creative team games players: From jazz to sport coaching. *International Journal of Sports Science and Coaching, 14*(2), 117–125.
Stenhouse, L. (1975). *An introduction to curriculum research and development*. London: Heinemann.
Thompson, A., Potrac, P., & Jones, R. L. (2015). 'I found out the hard way': Micropolitical workings in professional football. *Sport, Education and Society, 20*(8), 976–994.
Townsend, R. C., & Cushion, C. (2015). Elite cricket coach education: A Bourdieusian analysis. *Sport, Education and Society, 22*(4), 528–546. https://doi.org/10.1080/13573322.2015.1040753
Vygotsky, L. (1987). Thinking and speech (N. Minick, trans.). In *The collected works of L. S. Vygotsky. Problems of general psychology* (Vol. 1, pp. 39–285). New York: Plenum Press.

Charlie Corsby is a lecturer in Sport Coaching at the Cardiff School of Sport and Health Sciences, Cardiff Metropolitan University. Charlie obtained a Ph.D. (Sports Coaching) in 2017 and his research interests relate to the everyday affairs of coaches to gain influence and control of others. To date, Charlie's work has drawn upon the work of Harold Garfinkel and ethnomethodology to explore coaches' everyday interactions and observations.

Gethin Thomas is a Senior Lecturer in Sport Coaching and Programme Director for the MSc in Sport Coaching and Pedagogy at Cardiff School of Sport and Health Sciences, Cardiff Metropolitan University. His research interest focuses on the pedagogy of sport coaching in relation to exploring, understanding and locating the educational function of coaches, thus viewing them as more capable others and learning as a social practice. Gethin obtained his Ph.D. at the University of Exeter working in partnership with the Economic and Social Research Council and Rugby Football Union.

Manuel Santos is an Associate Tutor at the Cardiff School of Sport and Health Sciences, Cardiff Metropolitan University. Alongside his teaching and coaching responsibilities, Manuel is in his final year studying for a Doctorate in Sport Coaching at Cardiff Metropolitan University. His research interests are on creativity in sport, currently focused on the development of creative coaching practice.

Chapter 4
Coaching Efficacy: The Leadership Efficacy Model

A. Rui Gomes

Abstract This chapter introduces the leadership efficacy model applied to sports coaching. It is proposed in the model that leadership efficacy depends on the congruence between the conceptual cycle of leadership and the practical cycle of leadership and also by considering the leadership styles assumed by coaches and the moderating influence of the antecedent factors of leadership. This chapter discusses how these three elements of the model (leadership cycles, leadership styles, and the antecedent factors of leadership) apply to sports coaches and concur to explain their efficacy in leading athletes and teams. The model includes four hypotheses (congruence of leadership cycles, optimal leadership profile, favourability of conditions for leadership, and optimized congruence hypothesis of leadership) that will be presented according empirical finding about leadership and sports coaching. The final part of the chapter presents some practical implications of the model to the work of coaches.

Keywords Coach efficacy · Sport leadership · Leadership efficacy model · Coaches philosophy

Coaching Efficacy: The Leadership Efficacy Model

The leadership efficacy model, which was first named the Triphasic Model of Leadership Efficacy (Gomes, 2014a), proposes that leadership efficacy depends on the congruence between the conceptual cycle of leadership and the practical cycle of leadership and also considers the moderating influence of the antecedent factors of leadership. The model was triphasic due to the linear relation established among leadership philosophy, leadership practice, and leadership criteria. This *new* leadership efficacy model reinforces the cycles of leadership as a central element of

A. R. Gomes (✉)
School of Psychology, University of Minho, Braga, Portugal
e-mail: rgomes@psi.uminho.pt

R. Resende, A. R. Gomes (eds.), *Coaching for Human Development and Performance in Sports*, https://doi.org/10.1007/978-3-030-63912-9_4

leadership efficacy (triphasic relation) and recognizes the antecedents of leadership as moderators of leadership efficacy. However, the model introduces the styles of leadership (Gomes & Resende, 2014) and the concept of the "optimal profile of leadership" to explain the linear relations established among leadership philosophy, leadership practice, and leadership criteria.

The leadership efficacy model intends to explain coach efficacy by considering three main factors: leadership cycles, leadership styles, and the antecedent factors of leadership. The integration of these three factors helps us to understand the efficacy achieved by coaches, both at a subjective level (e.g., athletes' satisfaction with leadership) and at an objective level (e.g., athlete and team performance). Figure 4.1 presents the leadership efficacy model.

Leadership Efficacy Model

Leadership Cycles and the Triphasic Relation

Leadership cycles refer to the dynamic relations established between what coaches believe about their leadership (conceptual cycle) and what coaches effectively do when leading athletes and teams (practical cycles). The juxtaposition of both cycles increases leadership efficacy, particularly when these relations respect the athletes' preferences for leadership behaviours and when the cycles are based on the optimal profile of leadership (as will be explained later).

Cycles are developed according to the linear relations among three factors: the philosophy of leadership, leadership practice/leadership in practice, and leadership criteria, named as triphasic relation (Gomes, 2014a). The philosophy of leadership refers to values, beliefs, assumptions, attitudes, principles, and priorities assumed by coaches and that influence both the practice and criteria of leadership. Leadership practice refers to specific behaviours assumed by coaches to fulfil their coaching philosophy. Leadership criteria include personal and professional indicators that help coaches monitor whether they are meeting the tenets of their philosophy and the practice of coaching.

In the leadership efficacy model, linear relations are assumed among the philosophy of leadership, leadership practice, and leadership criteria, meaning that efficient coaching starts by defining a leadership idea or goal (the philosophy of leadership) that is then translated into a specific plan of action (leadership practice) and ends in the formulation of subjective or objective indicators of the accomplishment of the ideas and behaviours (leadership criteria). For example, the coach may believe that "only hard work leads to success" (philosophy); this idea may influence the coach to use goal setting programmes to establishes the specific levels of effort and commitment of athletes during training sessions (practice); by the end of each week, the coach delivers to athletes the "athletic progress graph" through which they can monitor the performance achieved during training sessions in the areas of goal setting (leadership criteria). The coach will eventually begin by defining this

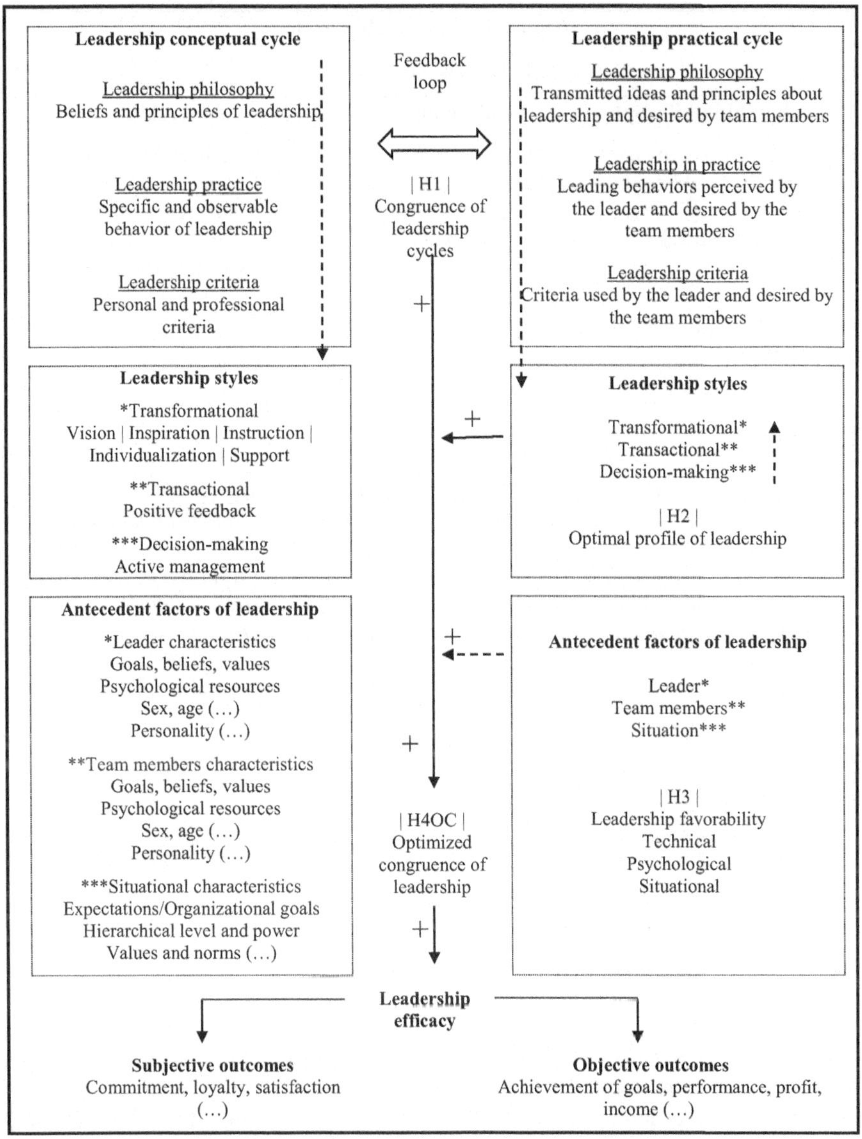

Fig. 4.1 Leadership Efficacy Model

leadership plan by thinking alone or by listening to all technical staff (and even the athletes) to establish the final plan (this is the conceptual cycle of leadership). Then, the coach presents the plan to the athletes, starting by inspiring the athletes to commit to the idea of "only hard work leads to success" (philosophy); next, the coaches explain and implement the plan during training sessions (leadership in practice); and finally, the coaches deliver the "athletic progress graph" to athletes (effectiveness

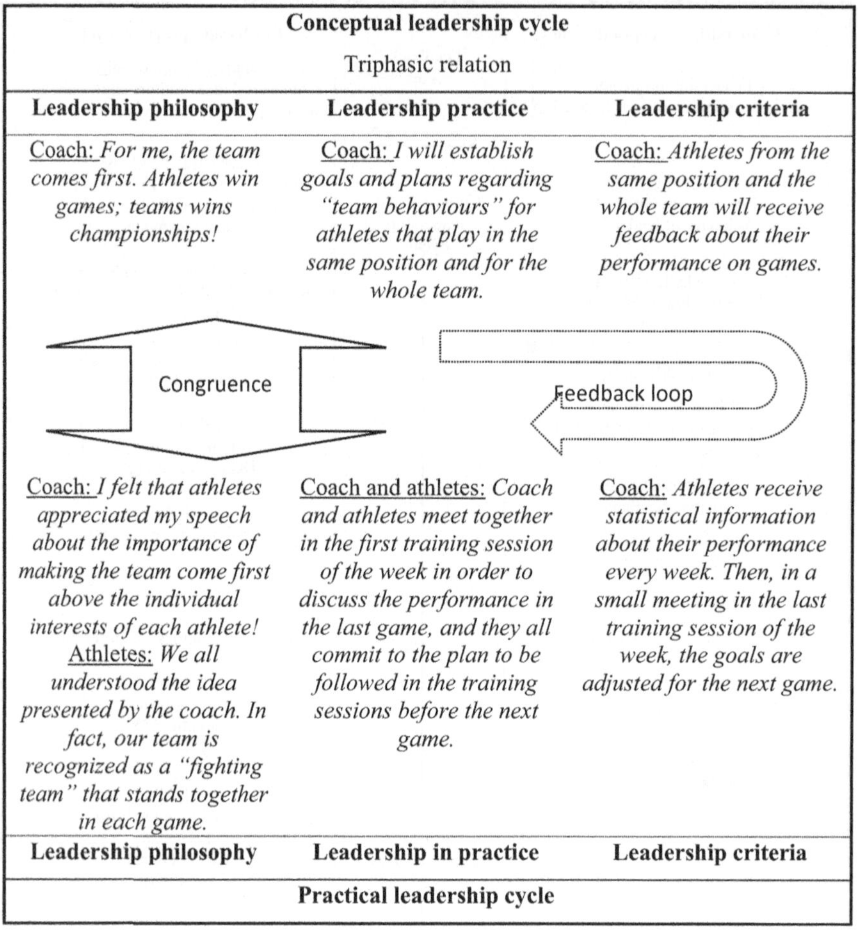

Fig. 4.2 Example of a leadership cycle

criteria). This process is the practical cycle of leadership. Of course, both cycles are not independent or static. To the contrary, when the practical cycle begins, it is possible that the coach understands the need to make adjustments to the leadership plan to better achieve the intended coaching idea. This exchange between cycles is guaranteed by the feedback loop.

In sum, leadership cycles represent the "brain" of coach activity by including the "why" of being a coach (set of ideas that turns a certain person into a coach), the "how" of being a coach (set of specific behaviours that turns a certain person into a coach), and "how much" change is produced by the coach (set of indicators that convert the ideas and behaviours of a person into a coach). Figure 4.2 presents an example of the congruence established between the conceptual and practical cycles of leadership.

Leadership Styles

Leadership styles are the second component of the leadership efficacy model. Leadership styles refer to specific behaviours used by coaches to achieve a specific goal when leading athletes, teams, and organizations (and at a broader level, it can include communities and society). To establish a style of leadership, it is necessary to achieve four conditions:

(a) Theoretical observation: styles of leadership correspond to specific behaviours that can be observed (and identified) when the coach is leading athletes and teams.
(b) Theoretical variance: styles of leadership include different behaviours that share the same goal of leadership, and because of that, they can be organized together.
(c) Theoretical independence: each style of leadership should be perceived similarly by the coach and the athletes and should be perceived distinctly from other sets of coaches' behaviours.
(d) Theoretical impact: styles of leadership achieve "usefulness" when it is possible to establish relations, positive or negative, with subjective or objective measures of leadership efficacy.

The leadership efficacy model includes three areas of leadership styles, transformational, transactional, and decision making, which are all capable of influencing the efficacy of coaching, particularly transformational styles.

Transformational Leadership This style can be defined as the leaders' tendency to produce major changes in the attitudes, beliefs, and values of followers to a point where the goals of an organization and the vision of the leader are internalized, and followers achieve performances beyond expectations (Bass, 1985). The leadership efficacy model integrates five transformational factors of leadership:

(a) Vision: coaches' ability to present an enthusiastic and optimistic vision of athletes' futures.
(b) Inspiration: coaches' positive expectations and behaviours are directed towards promoting the success and continuous efforts of athletes.
(c) Instruction: coaches' actions are focused on positively teaching technical sports skills.
(d) Individualization: coaches' tendency to consider the needs and personal and sport expectations of athletes.
(e) Support: coaches' personal concern regarding athletes' well-being and interest in building positive relationships based on confidence.

Transactional Leadership This style can be defined as leaders' tendency to respond to team members' behaviours and performance using positive or negative feedback; this tendency is built on an exchange system between what leaders want and what team members give (Avolio & Bass, 2004). The leadership efficacy model integrates two transactional factors of leadership:

(f) Positive feedback: coaches' reinforcement and recognition of the good performance and effort of athletes.
(g) Negative feedback: coaches' punishments intended to manage athletes' inadequate performance.

Decision-Making Leadership This style can be defined as coaches' tendency to be active or passive in sharing leadership power and decision making with team members in regard to deciding important aspects of team functioning (Gomes & Resende, 2014). The leadership efficacy model integrates two decision-making factors of leadership:

(h) Active management: coaches' power management behaviours regarding whether they make decisions in a more decentralized process (involving team members) or in a more centralized process (assuming all the decision-making power).
(i) Passive management: coaches' avoidance or delay in taking responsibility for decision making when it is necessary to solve important problems.

The optimal leadership profile (Bass & Avolio, 1994; Gomes, 2014b) assumes that higher frequencies of transformational behaviours followed by the use of positive feedback and active management (particularly the decentralized form), and lower use of negative feedback and passive management will stimulate higher leadership efficacy (see Fig. 4.3). It should be said that other leadership factors could be considered in order to formulate the optimal leadership profile, as long as they are theoretically and empirically supported.

In sum, leadership styles represent the "heart" of coach activity by including the specific behaviours used by coaches to accomplish their leadership plans that are first defined at the conceptual level and then at a practical level (i.e., leadership cycles).

Antecedent Factors of Leadership

Antecedent factors of leadership represent the third domain of the leadership efficacy model, influencing leadership efficacy by moderating the effects produced by the leadership cycles and styles of leadership. That is, antecedent factors do not directly influence leadership, but they act as facilitators of leadership, enhancing the positive influence of coaches on athletes and team performance, or inhibitors of leadership, decreasing the positive influence of coaches on athletes and team performance. There are three types of antecedent factors.

Leader Characteristics Factors that identify the coaches and that are likely to influence, positively or negatively, their actions. These characteristics include personal factors (e.g., gender, age, or socio-educational level), stable mental factors (e.g., personality, life goals, personal beliefs and values), and dynamic mental factors (e.g., tolerance for adversity, coping with problems). It is important that

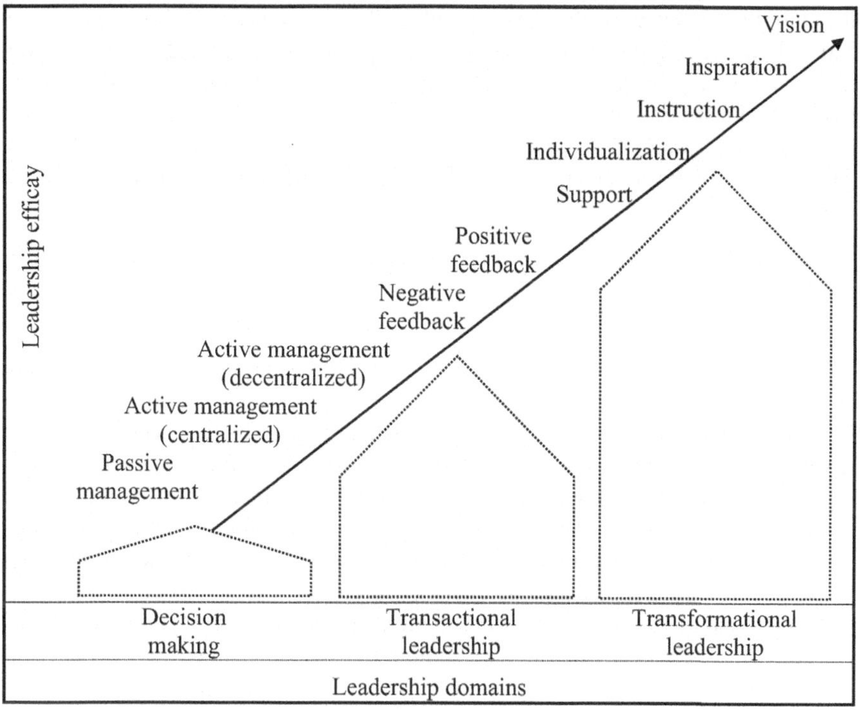

Fig. 4.3 Leadership styles and leadership efficacy

coaches have self-knowledge about their personal functioning because these factors may influence the success of coaching. In this sense, coaches should analyse the need to adjust their actions according to their characteristics as a person.

Team Member Characteristics Factors that identify the members of the team (i.e., athletes) and that are likely to positively or negatively influence the action of the coach. These characteristics include personal factors (e.g., gender, age, or socio-educational level), stable mental factors (e.g., personality, life goals, personal beliefs and values), and dynamic mental factors (e.g., tolerance for adversity, coping with problems). It is important that the coach understand the personal functioning of team members because these factors may influence the success of coaching. In this sense, coaches should analyse the need to adjust their actions according to the characteristics of the team members.

Situational Characteristics Factors that identify the context of coaches' activity, including the type of responsibility that they assume in the organization (e.g., hierarchical level, autonomy, responsibility, and power), the type of organization in which they are working (e.g., local or national club), and the external environment that identifies their work (e.g., level of professionalization, regional, national, or international competitions). These three situational levels may represent facilitating or inhibiting factors of coaches' actions. For example, the sports demands faced by the club, the expectations and goals established for the coach's activity, the organizational culture, the power assumed by the coach, the material and financial conditions given to the coach, among others, represent aspects that may affect the coaches work. Obviously, improvements in the situational conditions correspond to greater possibilities of coaches' success. In this sense, coaches should analyse the need to adjust their actions to maximize the resources and opportunities that exist in the sports context.

Antecedent factors related to the coach, team members, and situation can be combined to indicate the favourability of conditions for leadership, which can occur at three levels:

(a) Technical favourability: orientation of the leader to the tasks (value given to the mission and goals of the team) and task maturity of team members (competence and knowledge of team members about what needs to be performed).
(b) Psychological favourability: orientation of the leader to the relationships (interest in the personal and human aspects of the team members, namely, their needs, expectations, and values) and psychological maturity of team members (feelings of self-confidence and motivation of team members to accept responsibility for designated roles and tasks).
(c) Situational favourability: identifies the material conditions (e.g., resources, budgets), the human condition (e.g., number of team members, experience and maturity of team members), and the environmental conditions (e.g., players on the same market, deadlines) provided to the leader.

These concepts of technical, psychological, and situational favourability (Fiedler, 1993; Hersey & Blanchard, 1996; Likert, 1967) came together in the leadership efficacy model as moderator variables of leadership efficacy, meaning that they can facilitate the action of the coach (e.g., when team members are mature and the situation benefits the task and relationship orientation of the leader), or they can debilitate the action of the coach (e.g., when the situation undermines the coach's actions and team members are not mature, making the task and relationship orientation of the leader almost irrelevant). Figure 4.4 presents the three dimensions of the favourability of conditions for leadership.

In summary, antecedent factors of leadership represent the "arms and legs" of coaching activity (i.e., stamina) by increasing or decreasing the potential of the leadership plan (i.e., leadership cycles) and the way it is presented to athletes and teams (i.e., leadership styles).

Leadership Cycles and Leadership Styles

Leadership cycle congruency can increase leadership efficacy. Congruence occurs when coaches assume linear relations among leadership philosophy, leadership practice, and leadership criteria, both at the conceptual and practical levels, and

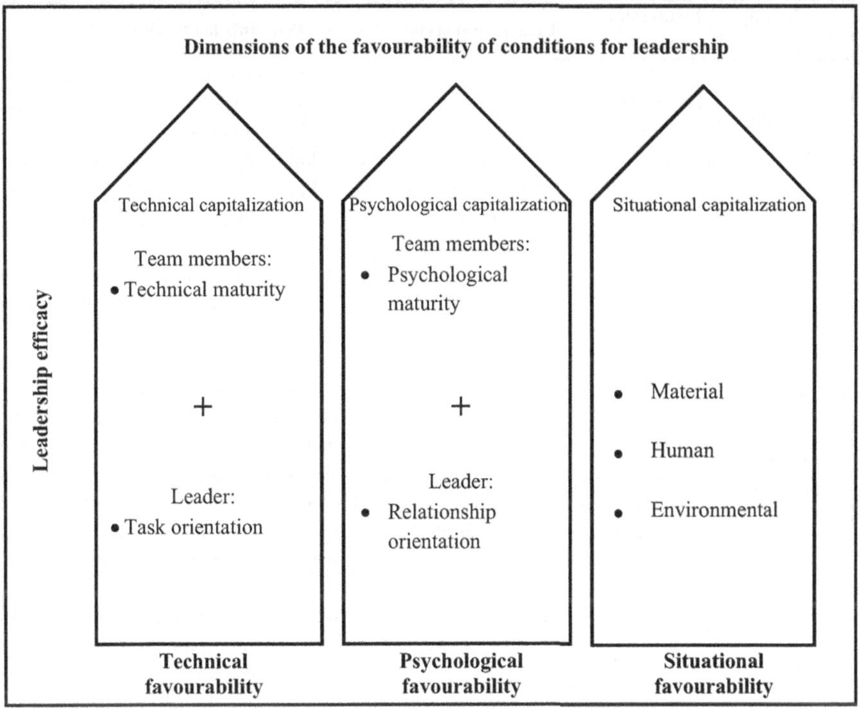

Fig. 4.4 Antecedent factors of leadership and leadership efficacy

when this congruence is based on team member preferences about leadership. However, *simply* assuming good matches between leadership cycles and *simply* assuming linear relations among the philosophy, practice, and criteria of leadership that respect team member preferences does not automatically guarantee leadership efficacy. If such a guarantee was possible, it would be enough to educate coaches in establishing these relations to augment their chances of achieving sport success. On the other hand, some ideas and goals assumed by leaders can indeed produce bad results for team members, meaning that leadership is not always related to positive changes in individuals, teams, communities, and even societies (see Bass, 1998, for the concept of *pseudo-transformational* leaders). Therefore, the *quality* of leadership cycles should be considered when evaluating the impact produced by leaders. In the leadership efficacy model, the quality of leadership cycles is evaluated by the leadership styles used by the leaders, meaning that they can influence the effects produced by leaders on team members. This influence occurs in multiple forms because we should consider, at least, nine styles of leadership that can be combined in different ways and in cumulative forms, producing distinct profiles of leadership. The result is that there is no single right way to lead, but there are multiple possibilities that can be adopted by leaders. However, we should mention that this consideration does not mean that *anything goes* when leading others. In fact, some

Leadership cycle	Leadership tasks	Leadership styles	Why this leadership style?
Leadership philosophy	1 Establishing the mission	Vision	o Allows the leaders to get a collective sense of team members regarding the established mission.
Leadership practice	2 Joining the team	Active management (decentralized)	o Allows the leader to achieve the collective involvement of team members regarding the established mission.
		Active management (centralized)	o Allows the leader to attain the collective mobilization of team members towards achieving the established mission.
	3 Defining the plan of action	Instruction	o Allows the leader to stimulate the will of team members to progress when performing the tasks related to the established mission.
		Individualization	o Allows the leader to stimulate the sense of personal value of team members regarding the established mission.
		Support	o Allows the leader to stimulate personal trust with team members that can facilitate the accomplishment of the established mission.
	4 Applying the plan of action	Inspiration	o Allows the leader to obtain the maximum effort of team members towards achieving the established mission.
Leadership criteria	5 Defining the outcomes	Positive feedback	o Allows the leader to attain the prolonged efforts of team members towards achieving the established mission.
		(Negative feedback)	o Allows the leader to achieve corrections of the negative actions of team members regarding the established mission.

Fig. 4.5 Application of leadership styles throughout the leadership cycle

leadership styles seem to produce better results in leadership efficacy, as we will explain later.

Figure 4.5 presents a proposal for how to apply the leadership styles through the leadership cycle to maximize the quality and effects produced by leadership philosophy, leadership practice, and leadership criteria. This integration is performed according to a proposal of five tasks that leaders must complete when leading individuals and teams. The figure includes one leadership style for establishing the leadership philosophy (e.g., vision), five leadership styles for establishing the leadership practice (e.g., active management, instruction, individualization, support, and inspiration), and two leadership styles for establishing the leadership criteria (positive feedback and negative feedback). This last leadership style is in parenthesis because coaches may have alternative behaviours to change the undesirable behaviours of athletes without provoking negative reactions by them, such as disagreement in a positive way or even positive corrective instruction. As stated, coaches may assume different leadership styles in each area of the leadership cycle or even distinct combinations of leadership styles throughout the leadership cycle. The proposed combination of leadership styles in Fig. 4.5 may be more *logical* by considering how the cycles and styles of leadership match the tasks performed by coaches when leading athletes and teams.

It Is all about Ideas

Leadership cycles should occur linearly from leadership philosophy to leadership practice and then to leadership criteria, both at the conceptual and practical levels. This process implies that leaders should start their work by defining a philosophy of leadership based on a mission that team members are enthusiastic about. For that, leaders should reflect on their values, beliefs, and goals and about the needs, expectations, and goals of all the individuals involved in the situation (i.e., team members, managers, clients, social and legal regulators, among others). By considering these three factors (the goals of leader, the goals of the team members, and the requirements of the situation), the leader can define a philosophy of leadership that can augment the chances of bringing together all the individuals involved in the *leadership scenario*. This implies that coaches should be careful in defining their leadership philosophy to augment the success of their actions when working with teams and athletes.

According to Hardman and Jones (2013), the definition of coaching philosophy involves four philosophical concepts: ontology (what does it mean to be a coach), axiology (the values assumed by the coach), ethics (the moral or immoral judgements of the coach), and phenomenology (thoughts about the experience of being a coach). To establish a leadership philosophy, coaches should define the meaning of being a coach, which reflects the values assumed by the coach and the ethics of sports activity; this definition can, ultimately, influence the final experience of being a coach. The establishment of the philosophy assumed by coaches should reflect these four aspects, as proposed below.

(a) Meaning of being a coach (ontology). The philosophy should be determined by the common *purpose* of contributing to stimulating athletes' potentialities that can impact human development in a broad sense (i.e., not only the development of physical or motor skills). This common purpose should be reflected in a particular mission that encourages the best efforts and commitment of all those involved in the leadership situation.

(b) Values of being a coach (axiology). The philosophy should correspond to a mission based on a positive vision of the future that is *simple* (but not simplistic) and *specific* for team members (i.e., all team members understand what the mission is all about). This positive vision can transcend the immediate and individual interests of each team member, stimulating them to believe that with hard work and maximum effort, they can transcend their levels of achievement and improve their abilities.
(c) Moral options of being a coach (ethics). The philosophy should articulate a mission that is based on the *ethical values* and *social norms* of the context in which coaches and athletes are situated. Athletes should understand the ethical values of sports and how these values relate to the purpose of improving their potentialities and achieving high performance in competitions.
(d) Personal experience of being a coach (phenomenology). The philosophy should reflect the *personal vocation* and *enthusiasm* of the coach as the leader of the team towards the established mission. The coach should be optimistic and confident about the possibility of achieving a better scenario for all the individuals involved in the situation.

These four aspects characterize the formulation of the leadership philosophy, which is the first step of the leadership cycle of the leadership efficacy model. As stated, both the conceptual and practical cycles are linear, meaning that they follow a logical relation across the philosophy, practice, and criteria of leadership. However, is it possible to have nonlinear relations across these three factors, meaning that practice and criteria can determine the philosophy of leadership?

Perhaps this question is much more *a hypothetical* possibility than a *real* possibility in the daily work of coaches, but it should be admitted that the process is not exactly the same. In fact, when the process starts by developing a leadership philosophy, coaches may be thinking in a more logical and sustained way by considering the ontology, axiology, ethics, and phenomenology of their activity as coaches. This is the *ideal* process through which to establish a leadership philosophy and ideal profile of coaching. This approach is the *ideological* process of coaching.

However, it should be admitted that leadership philosophy may be determined by following distinct processes of formulation. For example, coaches can define their goals and principles based on their leadership practice, *altering* the order of the leadership cycle: leadership practice TO leadership philosophy. In this case, we may have coaches who base their ideas about coaching on their past experience and the fact that they have worked over the years. As stated by Gomes (2014a), this approach sustains on the idea of "practice makes the leader", meaning that coaches may rely on "trial and error" strategies to establish their activity as coaches (i.e., their philosophy of leadership). This approach is the *experimental* process of coaching.

The other possible profile occurs when coaches define their goals and principles based on their leadership criteria, *altering* the order of the leadership cycle: leadership criteria TO leadership philosophy. In this case, we may have coaches that formulate their ideas about coaching on what produces or augments the chances of achieving success as coaches. When the leadership criteria determine the leadership philosophy, coaches may see their activity as "good" or "bad" if it leads to success or failure in training and competition situations. Again, as stated by Gomes (2014a), this approach sustains on the idea of "if it works don't fix it", meaning that leading well or leading poorly is evaluated according to the result achieved in each moment by coaches and athletes. This approach is the *results-oriented* process of coaching.

In sum, the leadership cycle is a key concept for the leadership efficacy model, establishing a relation among philosophy, practice, and criteria of leadership. These linear relations should start with defining the leadership philosophy based on a *good* idea that team members enthusiastically support. It is correct to assume that other combinations can occur in the leadership cycle, producing other ways to establish a leadership philosophy. In this sense, it seems that the leadership efficacy model *is all about ideas*; however, this is not the case. For this proposal, maximum efficacy depends on linear relations from leadership philosophy to leadership practice and then to leadership criteria that include the meaning of being a coach (ontology), the values of being a coach (axiology), the moral options of being a coach (ethics), and the personal experience of being a coach (phenomenology). This approach is the best strategy for producing *good* coaching ideas.

Leadership Efficacy Model Hypotheses

The three factors of the leadership efficacy model result in four hypotheses that test the entire model (see Fig. 4.6).

H1. Congruence of Leadership Cycles | Triphasic Relation
The efficacy of leadership increases when the leader establishes a linear relationship between how he or she intends to use the leadership position (conceptual cycle) and the effective way in which the leadership position is used when leading athletes and teams (practical cycle). The congruence between cycles of leadership should occur by considering the perspectives of both coaches and athletes.

H2. Optimal Leadership Profile
Leadership efficacy increases when the leader sustains the congruence between leadership cycles by using higher levels of transformational leadership, higher levels of positive feedback and lower levels of negative feedback from transactional leadership, and higher levels of active (decentralized) management of decision making and lower levels of passive management.

In this sense, the optimal profile of leadership is characterized by the following leadership styles: (a) decision making based on higher use of active decentralized management of leadership than centralized management of leadership, (b) transactional leadership based on higher use of positive feedback and lower use of negative feedback, and, especially, (c) the use of higher levels of transformational leadership. An optimal leadership profile is expected to augment leadership efficacy when compared with the suboptimal profile of leadership, which is based on

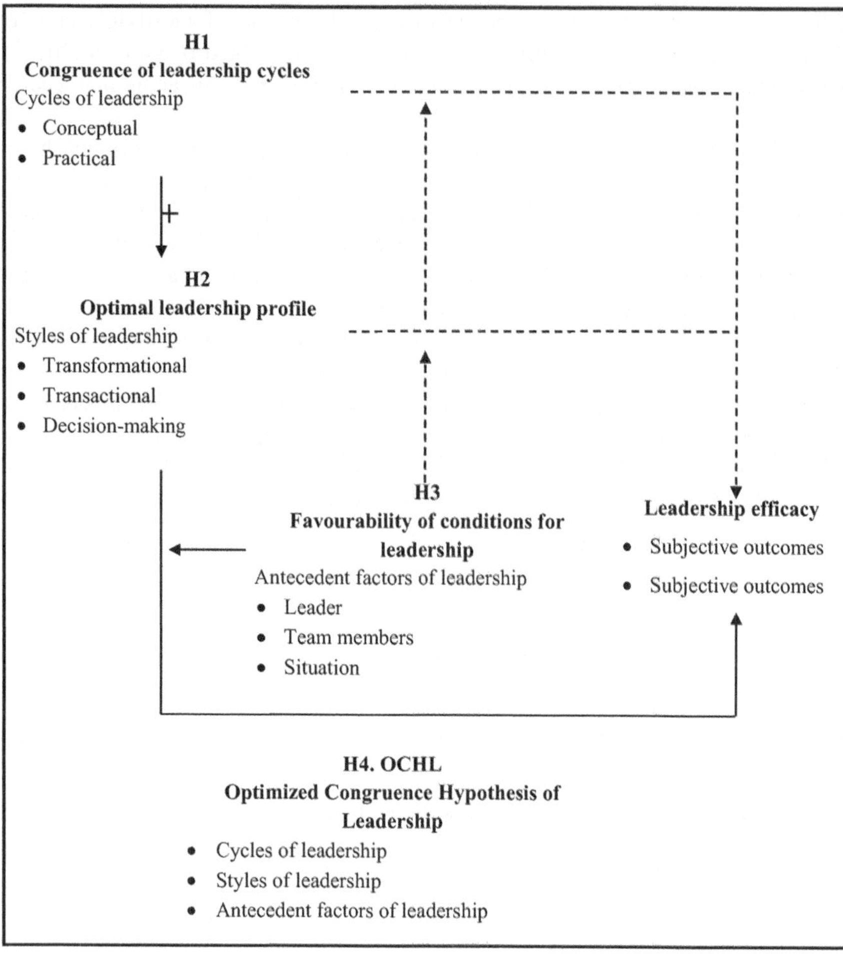

Fig. 4.6 Leadership Efficacy Model Hypotheses. *Note.* Discontinuous arrows separately test the H1, H2, and H3 hypotheses; continuous arrows test the H4. OCHL hypothesis

less use of transformational leadership, more use of negative feedback and less use of positive feedback, and the higher use of passive management and centralized active management. When both profiles are compared, the optimal profile of leadership has a better chance of increasing coaches' efficacy, both at the subjective level (i.e., team cohesion, athletes' satisfaction) and the objective level (goal achievement, performance). Therefore, leadership styles may maximize (i.e., facilitators) or minimize (i.e., inhibitors) the leader's cycles of leadership, moderating leadership efficacy.

H3. Favourability of Conditions for Leadership
The efficacy of leadership increases when the leader has antecedent factors that operate as facilitators of his/her actions or when the leader has antecedent factors that operate as inhibitors of his/her actions but adopts strategies to minimize the

antecedent factors. These factors are related to the personality of the leader, the characteristics of the team members, and the specific conditions provided by the organization in which the leader is working. Therefore, these factors may maximize (i.e., facilitators) or minimize (i.e., inhibitors) the leader's cycles of leadership, moderating leadership efficacy.

H4. OCHL | Optimized Congruence Hypothesis of Leadership
The efficacy of leadership increases when the leader establishes a congruence between the conceptual and practical cycles of leadership (congruence of leadership cycles), uses leadership styles based on the optimal profile of leadership when determining the leadership plan, and considers the antecedent factors of leadership.

Empirical Findings

Research about Leadership Cycles and Triphasic Relation

The leadership efficacy model attributes a central role to the linear relations established among leadership philosophy, leadership practice, and leadership criteria to explain leadership efficacy. Philosophy, practice, and criteria deserve equal attention and importance as "central elements" explaining the activity and success of coaches. That is, coaches may have "good", "stimulating", "visionary" ideas for athletes and teams, but the ideas do not extend beyond "utilitarian intentions" if coaches fail to incorporate them into effective plans of actions in their work with athletes and teams. Additionally, coaches may translate the ideas into well-designed plans for training and action in their work with athletes and teams, but again, they do not extend beyond "utilitarian intentions and actions" if the coaches do not establish the effectiveness indicators of the ideas and actions to be adopted by all the team members. Therefore, establishing interesting ideas for coaching athletes is central to the efficacy of coaches, but it is a very narrow perspective for analysing the work of coaches. The "big picture" of coaching activity should also include how coaches translate the ideas into specific plans of action and how coaches monitor the accomplishment of the ideas and plans of action.

When we analyse the literature, it is obvious that the philosophy of coaching is the key factor of research and a main concept of coaching education programmes. As referred to by Jenkins (2010), coaching philosophy is central to comprehending coaches' leadership styles and actions, representing a major aspect of coach education publications and training (Cassidy, Jones, & Potrac, 2009). The consequence of this overvaluation of the philosophy of coaching is that we have a much greater understanding of the ideas and principles that coaches value in their work than we have about how they implement and monitor the ideas and principles. For example, Lyle (1999) studied the coaching philosophies of 43 senior coaches and identified 24 values (e.g., "respect for others" and "partnership") that characterize a coach's philosophy.

Another problem with knowledge about the philosophy of coaching is that several studies rely on single cases (which limit the results generalization), and most of them lack detailed information about methodology or data analysis techniques (Gould, Pierce, Cowburn, & Driska, 2017). Nevertheless, the findings of these studies are worthy of recognition. Callary, Werthner, and Trudel (2013) studied the underlying values that influenced the actions of a female hockey coach and concluded that five core values guided her actions (equity, connectedness, holistic development, respect, and effort). Vallée and Bloom (2016), providing their own example of Chantal Vallée as a basketball coach, identified principles of coaching that contributed to winning five consecutive championships (enacting a vision, athlete empowerment, teaching life skills, and lifelong learning and personal reflection). In a similar study performed with Russ Rose, a coach who won four successive NCAA national championships with a university volleyball team, concluded that "coaching for accountability" and "self-responsibility" were central aspects that characterized the philosophy of this coach (Yukelson & Rose, 2014). Interestingly, Gavazzi (2015) found similar coaching values guiding the philosophy of Urban Meyer, a highly successful Ohio State University football coach. Specifically, this coach referred to values and actions related to setting clear expectations and guidelines for his players that emphasize team accountability and player responsibility. In a more methodologically rigorous case study (employing member checking, a critical *friend*, and audit trail procedures), Hodge, Henry, and Smith (2014) analysed the philosophy of Graham Henry and Wayne Smith, head and assistant coaches, respectively, of the New Zealand All Blacks, the most successful rugby team of all time. As already demonstrated in other studies, these coaches valued leadership based on shared responsibility, autonomy, and supportive coaching. However, these important values changed when coaches faced major problems with athletes as, for example, unsuccessful periods of competition or even athletes engaged in undisciplined behaviours such as binge drinking. These aspects confirm the feedback loop of the leadership efficacy model, meaning that coaches can indeed change their course of action when they feel there are mismatches between their intended ideas, actions, and criteria (conceptual cycle) and the application of their leadership plan for the specific coaching context (practical cycle).

Although these studies are of interest, they have two major shortcomings. First, these studies offer a limited perspective of coaching activity by not analysing the *impact* of philosophy on coaches' actions and effectiveness criteria. Second, as already indicated, most of these studies are based on single cases, lacking detailed information about methodology or data analysis techniques. As confirmed by Jenkins (2010), the link between coaching philosophy and coaching actions needs to be more deeply explained. In an attempt to better explain these relations, Gould et al. (2017) examined the coaching philosophy of J. Robinson, one of the most respected and successful NCAA wrestling coaches in the United States, and found clear relations between the coach's philosophy and the way he proposed the development of mental skills in Robison Intensive Wrestling Camps. However, this study previously defined the analysis of the relations between a coaching philosophy and coaches' actions specifically directed to the development of psychological skills in athletes as a goal. This approach can facilitate the establishment of connections between the philosophy and practices of coaches and limit the analysis of other areas of coaching impact produced by coaches. When these relations are not predetermined, coaches may experience more difficulties in establishing logical connections between philosophy and behaviours. In fact, there are indications that the relations established among leadership philosophy, leadership practice, and leadership criteria are far from simple and far from "spontaneous occurrences". This assumption was demonstrated by McCallister, Blinde, and Weiss (2000) in a study with youth baseball and softball coaches, finding that coaches were capable of identifying a wide range of values and skills that are important to teach their athletes, but they had difficulty explaining how these values were then translated into their work with athletes. The fact that these coaches had little formal training in coaching could be a reason for this failure, but as we will see below, it is a very limited explanation.

Although research is already scarce in clarifying the relations between the philosophy and practices of coaches, the scenario may be more challenging if we add a third element of coach activity, the leadership criteria, that is, the personal and professional indicators that coaches use to analyse the impact produced by their philosophy and practices on athletes and teams. Without criteria, it is difficult to understand the profound impact of coaches on the wellbeing and performance of athletes, and without criteria, it is almost impossible to understand stability and change in the course of the actions of coaches. In fact, it is because of leadership criteria that coaches decide to maintain and reinforce their philosophy and behaviours (meaning they are producing the expected impact on athletes and teams), and it is also possible that it is because of leadership criteria that coaches decide to change their ideas and course of actions (meaning they are not producing the expected impact on athletes and teams). This result was evident in the previous study by Hodge et al. (2014), demonstrating that some *critical incidents* occurred in the team (i.e., deviations from what the coaches were expecting) that changed the leadership approach adopted by the coaches. It is very difficult to understand these changes in the course of action if we do not evaluate the previous expectations of coaches' impacts (i.e., leadership criteria) and what happens when coaches confront reality.

In an attempt to capture the *big picture* of the philosophy, practice, and criteria of coaches, Gomes, Araújo, Resende, and Ramalho (2018) interviewed ten elite coaches from different sports. All of these coaches possessed the maximum certification to lead their teams, and they were very successful in terms of sports results, which was very different from the coaches studied by McCallister et al. (2000). Gomes et al. (2018) found congruence between coaches in some areas of their work with athletes, namely, the value of athlete motivation, the value of building positive relationships with athletes, the value of cohesion, and the need for formal and informal rules that regulate the team's functioning. For all these areas, coaches established *full property matches* among the philosophy, practice, and criteria of leadership. However, these linear relationships occurred for only 21% of the established matches, meaning that for the majority of the data provided by the coaches, it was not possible to establish matches among philosophy, practice, and criteria. Therefore, this study aligns with the findings of McCallister et al. (2000), making the role of the formal training of coaches less evident in their ability to successfully complete the leadership cycles (relation among philosophy, practice, and criteria), which may be quite amazing if we think about the demands and sophistication of formal programmes of coach education.

In summary, it is evident that there is a long way to go to understand the philosophy of coaching and the impact produced on the coaches' behaviours and effectiveness criteria. However, the pursuit of this understanding is a rewarding journey, allowing us to understand how coaches build their convictions about coaching and how these values impact the development of athletes and teams.

Research about Leadership Styles

The leadership efficacy model incorporates leadership styles to give the leadership cycles a *meaning of action*. The linear relations established among leadership philosophy, leadership practice, and leadership criteria, which occurred both at the conceptual and practical levels of coaches' functioning (congruence hypothesis), are central to explaining leadership efficacy. However, the way these relationships occurred is worth noting. In practical terms, this process signifies that a coach can achieve congruence between conceptual and practical cycles of leadership by adopting different styles of leadership, thus producing distinct effects on athletes and teams and on leadership efficacy.

In the leadership efficacy model, coaches may achieve congruence between cycles of leadership by selecting leadership behaviours from three leadership domains (transformational, transactional, and decision making), and it is proposed that the "optimal profile of leadership" may have a major impact on coaches' leadership. This profile is constituted by active decentralized leadership management (from decision-making leadership), positive feedback (from transactional leadership), and by vision, inspiration, instruction, individualization, and support (from transformational leadership). This set of behaviours offers better possibilities of achieving leadership efficacy when compared with a "suboptimal profile of leadership" based on less use of transformational leadership, more use of negative feedback than positive feedback, and the tendency to manage power by adopting centralized active management or, even worse, by adopting passive management.

The study of leadership styles is a main topic in the literature, producing very robust findings about leaders' actions related to better results for team members and organizations. It should be noted that the research findings are more substantial for demonstrating the impact of leadership styles on subjective measures of leaders' efficacy (as is the case for team members' satisfaction and work commitment) than for demonstrating an unequivocal impact on objective measures (as is the case for teams and organizations' performance) (for a review, see Kaiser, Hogan, & Craig, 2008; Lowe, Kroeck, & Sivasubramaniam, 1996). Nevertheless, the results reveal that certain profiles of leadership are better than others in explaining the impact produced by leaders on individuals, groups and teams, organizations, communities, and societies.

One of the major distinctions relates to the differential impacts produced by transactional leadership and transformational leadership. For the first case, leadership is based on an exchange between something that the leaders want team members to do to achieve a certain goal or task and something that team members want to have in return for their efforts in doing what the leaders want. In transformational leadership, the relationships between the leader and team members surpass the instrumental exchange system of transactional leadership by exhibiting a true commitment by the leader and team members regarding a vision and a mission that involve all of them and that stimulate the maximum levels of effort that can indeed produce performance beyond expectations (see Bass, 1985; Wang, In-Sue, Courtright, & Colbert, 2011).

This increase in the positive impact of transformational leadership over transactional leadership on distinct aspects of followers' psychological experiences at work and on performance was called the *augmentation effect* of transformational leadership (Bass, 1985). Research over the years has been very consistent in demonstrating better results for transformational leadership than for transactional leadership (Bycio, Hackett, & Allen, 1995; Hater & Bass, 1988; Judge & Piccolo, 2004; Molero, Cuadrado, & Morales, 2007; Waldman, Bass, & Yammarino, 1990). Birasnav (2014), in a study with managers from service firms, found that transformational leadership has strong and positive effects on the knowledge management process and organizational performance after controlling for the effects of transactional leadership. Additionally, Zwingmann et al. (2014) analysed the health promoting effects of transformational leadership, contingent reward, and laissez-faire leadership across 16 countries and found that a strong transformational leadership climate was associated with better perceived health in eight countries and that the augmentation effect was significant in six countries.

The augmentation effect was also confirmed in sports contexts. Rowold (2006), in a study of martial arts, found that transformational leadership added unique variance beyond that of transactional leadership for predicting leader effectiveness. Gomes and Resende (2014), in a study with futsal and soccer athletes, also confirmed the augmentation effect, with transformational leadership adding unique variance over decision-making leadership and transactional leadership for variables related to satisfaction with leadership and coach-athlete compatibility.

The augmentation effect is the demonstration of higher effects of transformational leadership over transactional leadership. However, the leadership efficacy model also proposes decision making as an area of coaches' leadership. The model includes passive management to describe the tendency of the leader to avoid decisions and responsibilities when that is important to followers and teams and active management to describe the opposite tendency of leaders who assume their responsibilities whenever necessary. Active management can occur in a more centralized form, when leaders make decisions with little or no consultation with team members, or in a more decentralized form, when leaders make decisions only after some consultation with team members. In essence, passive management under the leadership efficacy model is similar to *laisse-faire management* from transformational leadership theory (Bass, 1985; Bass & Riggio, 2006), but active management under the leadership efficacy model does not correspond to *active management* under the Bass model. For the leadership efficacy model, the focus is on how leaders manage the power of decision making with team members (centralizing or decentralizing the decisions), while for transformational leadership theory, the focus is on how leaders act when deviations from rules and standards occur, by preventing these deviations from occurring (being more active) or by resolving the deviations when they occur (being more passive). For Bass (1985), decision-making leadership is included in other dimensions of transformational and transactional leadership, meaning that a leader can be transactional or transformational by using more negotiated or imposed strategies of power management. This approach is obviously possible, but it probably does not reflect *equivalent* forms of leadership, giving decision making theoretical autonomy and independence from the transactional and transformational leadership. This conception is supported by major approaches to leadership that treat decision making as a *singular* form of leadership; for instance, situational leadership theory proposes that the levels of authority and of empowerment by the leader should consider the levels of team members' competence and commitment (Blanchard, 2007; Sosik & Jung, 2018). Additionally, path-goal theory proposes that leaders should select the most appropriate behaviours (i.e., directive, supportive, participative, or achievement oriented) according to the personal characteristics of followers and environmental characteristics in order to increase followers' motivation to perform and reach high levels of productivity (House & Mitchell, 1997). Contributions from these models point out distinct leadership options that can modify the final profile of leaders' ways of acting and including them as inherent parts of transactional and transformational styles limits the comprehension of how they exert power over athletes and teams. For example, a leader assuming the profile of centralized active management, positive feedback, and all five transformational behaviours may be different from a leader assuming the profile of decentralized active management, positive feedback, and all five transformational behaviours. If decision making is excluded from the analysis, these distinct patterns are also disregarded by the analysis.

In summary, the leadership efficacy model includes three areas of leadership and nine styles of leadership, covering very distinct domains of leadership. By including decision making in addition to transactional and transformational leadership, the model offers researchers the possibility to test a more comprehensive profile of leadership styles when explaining leadership efficacy (optimal profile of leadership).

Research about the Antecedent Factors of Leadership

The leadership efficacy model incorporates antecedent factors of leadership because some factors *outside* the specific dynamics established between leaders and team members can influence leadership efficacy. These factors are the leader as a person, the team members as persons, and the situation in which the leadership occurs. All of these factors assume the role of facilitators or inhibitors of leadership by enhancing or decreasing the positive influence of coaches on athletes and team functioning.

Starting with the leader characteristics, there is a long tradition in leadership research of analysing whether some traits, such as intelligence, self-confidence, determination, integrity, and sociability, are related to leadership effectiveness (Sosik & Jung, 2018). Some of these traits are more referenced in the research, as is the case of the big five personality model (i.e., emotional stability, openness, conscientiousness, extraversion, and agreeableness; McCrae & Costa Jr, 1992). The results from this model indicate that leaders who are positive, adaptive, interpersonally engaging and aware, and developmental in nature are the most effective leaders (DeRue, Nahrgang, Wellman, & Humphrey, 2011; Judge, Bono, Ilies, & Gerhardt, 2002; Sosik & Jung, 2018).

The team members' characteristics and situational characteristics also represent important factors in the comprehension of leadership, reinforcing the need for congruence between the leader's style of action and the characteristics of the subordinates and the work setting (see House, 1971). For example, path-goal theory emphasizes the personal characteristics of followers (e.g., perceived ability and locus of control) and environmental characteristics (e.g., task structure, authority system, or work group characteristics) as key factors in achieving organizational goals (House & Mitchell, 1997). Additionally, the contingency theory proposed by Fred Fiedler aggregates leadership into task- and relationship-oriented leadership, which should be applied according to three critical situational factors: (i) the quality of the leader-follower relations, (ii) the leader's position of power (i.e., authority to reward or punish followers based on his or her position in the organization), and (iii) the task structure (i.e., whether the task is clearly defined and easily understood or ambiguous and complex) (Sosik & Jung, 2018).

The conjunction of the characteristics of the leaders, athletes, and situations are recognized in some important models of sports leadership, such as the multidimensional model of leadership (Chelladurai, 2007), the mediational model of leadership (Smith & Smoll, 1996), and the working model of coaching effectiveness (Horn, 2008). The results are very substantial, revealing that several variables may indeed be important to explaining leadership efficacy in sports contexts. For example, coaches' personalities (Laborde, Guillén, Watson, & Allen, 2017) and resilience (Weinberg, Butt, & Culp, 2011) and coaches' coping strategies for dealing with stressors (Norris, Didymus, & Kaiseler, 2017; Olusoga, Butt, Maynard, & Hays, 2010) seem to be important variables in explaining how coaches assume their roles and tasks. In the case of athletes, variables related to their sex, age, or sport experience (e.g., Beam, Serwatka, & Wilson, 2004; Riemer & Toon, 2001;

Sherman, Fuller, & Speed, 2000), amotivation and sport anxiety (Charbonneau, Barling, & Kelloway, 2001; Horn, Bloom, Berglund, & Packard, 2011; Stenling, Ivarsson, Hassmén, & Lindwall, 2017), and even narcissism (Arthur, Woodman, Ong, Hardy, & Ntoumanis, 2011) seem to be related to the way coaches' leadership is perceived by athletes. Additionally, situational factors, such as the type of sport practised by athletes (Riemer & Chelladurai, 1995) and the sports results achieved by the team (Gomes, Lopes, & Mata, 2011) also impact the way athletes perceive their coaches.

In summary, the antecedent factors of the leadership efficacy model may help us understand leadership efficacy; they act as moderators of the influence exerted by coaches on athletes and teams. By including antecedent factors in the study of sports coaching, we may have a better perspective of why some specific coaches leading some specific athletes in a particular situation achieve success, while other specific coaches working with some specific athletes in a given situation do not achieve success.

Practical Implications

The leadership efficacy model includes some practical implications for the coaches' work, which are mainly derived from three components of the model: leadership cycles, leadership styles, and the antecedent factors of leadership.

Implications for the Leadership Cycles and Triphasic Relation

The main idea of leadership cycles is that when coaches establish linear relations between what they want to do (conceptual cycle) and what they effectively do when leading athletes and teams (practical cycle), both from the perspective of coaches and athletes, they maximize their efficacy with regard to their athletes and teams (congruence hypothesis). This congruence includes the relations established among leadership philosophy, leadership practice/leadership in practice, and leadership criteria (Gomes, 2014a).

Some aspects can increase the chances of the congruence hypothesis applying in leadership cycles.

(a) Leadership plans should be designed by starting from the philosophy of leadership, and only then should leadership practices (specific behaviours that will be adopted to fulfil the coaching philosophy) and the leadership criteria (specific indicators used to monitor the accomplishment of the philosophy and practice of leadership) be established.
(b) The philosophy of leadership does not need to be complex or extremely elaborate to be successful; on the contrary, it should be positive (i.e., pointing out a

stimulating and challenging mission for the team), specific (i.e., pointing out a concrete and comprehensive mission for the team), based on personal vocation (i.e., reflecting the personal enthusiasm of the coach for the mission), and ethically acceptable (i.e., pointing out a mission that is based on the personal and social standards of sports).

(c) The practice of leadership should include specific actions that can concretize the philosophy of leadership. A good plan of action should include specific strategies to unite the team regarding the mission, the specific plan of action, which can concretize the philosophy of leadership, and how to apply the plan of action in daily work with athletes.

(d) The leadership criteria should be based on observable and quantifiable indicators that can monitor the achievement of the leadership philosophy and the progress of leadership practices.

(e) Coaches may not monitor all of their ideas and actions used in daily work with athletes, but they should, at least, monitor the central ideas that they intend to implement in their teams over the sport season.

(f) Coaches should be careful when applying their leadership plans to their teams (conceptual cycle of leadership); they should listen to athletes about the leadership plan and then observe their reactions in training and competition (practical cycle of leadership). This feedback loop between the conceptual and practical cycles of leadership can improve the impact produced by coaches on athletes and teams, leading to an increase in leadership efficacy.

(g) Using linear cycles of leadership will prevent *erratic* leadership plans that are adopted without first establishing a philosophy of leadership. For example, coaches who believe that their activity is mostly a question of experience may define their leadership plans based on what worked in the past without reflecting on the leadership principles that should guide their actions; additionally, coaches who believe that their activity is a question of achieving the desired sports results may define their leadership plans based on what gives athletes better chances of achieving a higher performance without reflecting on the leadership principles that should guide their actions.

Implications for the Leadership Styles

The main idea of leadership styles is that some leadership behaviours may increase the *quality* of the leadership cycles, augmenting the efficacy of leadership with regard to athletes and teams; thus, some practical implications should be presented.

(a) Coaches can increase the impact of their leadership (i.e., congruence among leadership philosophy, leadership practice, and leadership criteria) by using the optimal profile of leadership (mainly based on transformational leadership, followed by positive feedback and decentralized active management).

(b) Coaches should avoid the suboptimal profile of leadership related to passive management, centralized active management (especially if the alternative behaviour of decentralized active management can be used), and negative feedback to prevent decreases in the impact of leadership efficacy on athletes and team functioning.

(c) Leadership styles should be selected based on the goals of the coaches, the needs of the athletes, and the requirements of the situation. For example, behaviours related to vision and inspiration may be important to motivate change and the commitment of athletes to the team mission; behaviours related to individualization and support may be important to understand the athletes' personal expectations and needs; behaviours related to instruction and positive feedback may be important when athletes are performing under pressure; and behaviours related to active management may be important when coaches have to determine important aspects of training and competition.

Implications for the Antecedent Factors of Leadership

The antecedent factors of leadership can maximize or debilitate the efficacy of coaching, meaning that coaches should consider some implications of these factors on the leadership plans.

(a) Coaches can increase the impact of their leadership by adjusting their leadership based on their own personal characteristics, the characteristics of the athletes, and the requirements of the situation. Although antecedent factors do not represent central aspects of coaches' activities, they can exert substantial impact on leadership efficacy.
(b) Coaches can increase technical favourability in their teams by establishing cycles of leadership based on behaviours related to vision (to define the mission and goals of the team), inspiration (to stimulate the maximum effort of athletes), instruction (to promote the desire for the progression and improvement of athletes) and positive feedback (to stimulate continuous efforts by and feelings of pride in athletes).
(c) Coaches can increase psychological favourability in their teams by establishing cycles of leadership based on behaviours related to individualization (to increase feelings of personal contribution by athletes towards the team mission), support (to promote positive relationships of trust with athletes), and decentralized active management (to stimulate feelings of responsibility and the desire for autonomy in athletes).
(d) Coaches can increase situational favourability in their teams by establishing cycles of leadership based on behaviours related to vision and instruction (to convince decision makers—such as club managers—to create better conditions for coaches' activities), and they should adapt leadership behaviours according the athletes' maturity (to capitalize on the skills and experience of athletes).

Leadership cycle	Leadership tasks	Purposes of leadership	Leadership styles	Leadership impact
Leadership philosophy	1 Establishing the mission	Coaching is about achieving a challenging and positive mission	Vision	Collective sense of the mission
Leadership practice	2 Joining the team	Coaching is about involving everybody in a challenging and positive mission	Active management (decentralized)	Collective involvement
			Active management (centralized)	Collective mobilization
	3 Defining the plan of action	Coaching is about challenging athletes to continuously improve	Instruction	Desire of progression
		Coaching is about getting the best of everybody	Individualization	Personal value
		Coaching is about building strong and positive relationships	Support	Trust relationships
	4 Applying the plan of action	Coaching is about motivating the best of everybody	Inspiration	Maximum effort
Leadership criteria	5 Defining the outcomes	Coaching is about recognizing efforts and achievements	Positive feedback	Prolonged effort
		Coaching is about preventing and dealing with errors and failures	(Negative feedback)	Change negative actions

Fig. 4.7 The leadership activity of coaches

Key Points

The activity of coaches (as that of other leaders) is complex and very dynamic. Such activity is complex because coaches must address a significant number of factors that can impact their final efficacy when leading athletes and teams. For example, for the leadership efficacy model, these factors can be aggregated into three areas (leadership cycles, leadership styles, and leadership antecedent factors). Such activity is dynamic because coaches' actions occur in contexts that change constantly, meaning that in very narrow periods of time, the coach can be considered a successful professional (the established goals are fulfilled), but if the situation changes dramatically, the coach could turn into an unsuccessful professional (the established goals are not fulfilled). This context can be understood as the "hungry sports machine", requiring not only maximum effort and dedication from coaches and athletes but also requiring maximum performance and sports success.

Considering the multitude of sports expectations regarding the coach's activities, many of them not completely controllable by the coaches, it is important to reflect on how coaches can organize their ideas, goals, and actions. Figure 4.7 summarizes an organization of cycles and styles of leadership according to the main tasks involved in the coach's activity. Some aspects should be reinforced.

(a) The three phases of the leadership cycle (leadership philosophy, leadership practice, and leadership criteria) indicate five tasks for coaches (establishing the mission, uniting the team, defining the plan of action, applying the plan of action, and defining the outcomes).
(b) Establishing the mission seems more related to the philosophy of leadership because coaches have to think about the purpose of their work with athletes and teams.
(c) Uniting the team seems more related to leadership practices because coaches have to think about how to involve athletes in accomplishing the mission. This goal can be reached by using decentralized active management (stimulating the collective involvement of athletes) or by centralized active management (stimulating the collective mobilization of athletes). In fact, open processes of decision making have the potential to promote cohesion due the sense of the personal *authorship* of the athletes in the establishment of the mission; by contrast, closed processes of decision making put more responsibility on the ability of coaches to convince (and hence mobilize) athletes towards accomplishing the mission.
(d) Defining the plan of action seems more related to leadership practices because coaches have to challenge athletes to continuously improve, stimulate the best efforts of each one, and then build strong and positive relationships. These three aspects may increase the possibilities of success in achieving the established mission. A *good* plan of action may depend on the ability of coaches to provide positive instruction, individualization, and support to athletes to stimulate their maximum efforts in concretizing the team mission.
(e) Applying the plan of action seems more related to leadership practices because coaches have to motivate athletes to give their best in training and competitions. By using the behaviour of inspiration, coaches may promote attitudes that maximize the efforts of athletes.
(f) Defining the outcomes seems more related to the leadership criteria because coaches have to determine the indicators that will be used to monitor the accomplishment of the mission. Despite the indicators that are formulated, coaches may increase the success of their plans if they assume a positive approach regarding the effort exhibited by athletes. In fact, by using positive feedback, coaches may stimulate continuous efforts by athletes, which is essential for achieving the outcomes and thus the established mission. During this process of achieving the outcomes, error and failure will occur. One of the possible reactions is to use negative feedback; however, it is not the only or the most interesting behaviour to use; coaches may respond with disagreement (when it is important to change actions related to the achievement of the outcomes) or even corrective instruction (when it is important to change the *way* actions are performed by the athletes in order to achieve the outcomes).
(g) The leadership cycles and tasks are enhanced by using the most appropriate leadership styles; they should be selected based on the impact that coaches want

to produce on athletes and teams. Of course, there are other leadership styles that can be applied, and they can be combined to produce multiple effects on athletes and teams. However, once again, these styles should not be used indiscriminately or without forethought. These styles should serve a certain cycle of leadership (leadership philosophy, leadership practice, and leadership criteria).

Conclusion

In this chapter, we present the leadership efficacy model, which explains one of the most fascinating topics of leadership: the effects produced by the action of leaders on individuals, groups and teams, communities, and even societies. It is evident that coaches exert influence on athletes at different levels (psychological, physically, technical, tactical, among others); however, what specific factors contribute to explaining this influence and how it occurs is still a topic of debate in the literature.

One century of academic studies on leadership have produced several theoretical explanations and united many researchers, who have all given their best to explain what leadership is all about and how it can be developed in leaders and interested individuals. It is correct that scientists have not reached agreement on these issues. However, it is a worthwhile effort because leading others with the purpose of stimulating their maximum efforts regarding a positive and common mission represents one of the most extraordinary forms of influence between human beings.

References

Arthur, C. A., Woodman, T., Ong, C. W., Hardy, L., & Ntoumanis, N. (2011). The role of athlete narcissism in moderating the relationship between coaches' transformational leader behaviors and athlete motivation. *Journal of Sport & Exercise Psychology, 33*(1), 3–19.

Avolio, B. J., & Bass, B. M. (2004). *Multifactor leadership questionnaire. Manual and sampler set* (3rd ed.). Redwood City: Mind Garden.

Bass, B. M. (1985). *Leadership and performance beyond expectations*. New York: Free Press.

Bass, B. M. (1998). *Transformational leadership: Industrial, military, and educational impact*. Mahwah, NJ: Erlbaum.

Bass, B. M., & Avolio, B. J. (1994). *Improving organizational effectiveness through transformational leadership*. Newbury Park, CA: Sage.

Bass, B. M., & Riggio, R. E. (2006). *Transformational leadership* (2nd ed.). Mahwah, NJ: Lawrence Erlbaum Associates.

Beam, J. W., Serwatka, T. S., & Wilson, W. J. (2004). Preferred leadership of NCAA division I and II intercollegiate student-athletes. *Journal of Sport Behavior, 27*, 3–17.

Birasnav, M. (2014). Knowledge management and organizational performance in the service industry: The role of transformational leadership beyond the effects of transactional leadership. *Journal of Business Research, 67*(8), 1622–1629. https://doi.org/10.1016/j.jbusres.2013.09.006

Blanchard, K. (2007). *Leading at a higher lever: Blanchard on leadership and creating high performance organizations*. Upper Saddle River, NJ: Pearson-Prentice Hall.

Bycio, P., Hackett, R. D., & Allen, J. S. (1995). Further assessments of Bass's (1985) conceptualization of transactional and transformational leadership. *Journal of Applied Psychology, 80*(4), 468–478.

Callary, B., Werthner, P., & Trudel, P. (2013). Exploring coaching actions based on developed values: A case study of a female hockey coach. *International Journal of Lifelong Education, 32* (2), 209–229. https://doi.org/10.1080/02601370.2012.733974

Cassidy, T., Jones, R., & Potrac, P. (2009). *Understanding sports coaching: The social, cultural and pedagogical foundations of coaching practice* (2nd ed.). London: Routledge.

Charbonneau, D., Barling, J., & Kelloway, E. K. (2001). Transformational leadership and sports performance: The mediating role of intrinsic motivation. *Journal of Applied Social Psychology, 31*(7), 1521–1534. https://doi.org/10.1111/j.1559-1816.2001.tb02686.x

Chelladurai, P. (2007). Leadership in sports. In G. Tenenbaum & R. C. Eklund (Eds.), *Handbook of sport psychology* (3rd ed., pp. 113–135). Hoboken, New Jersey: John Wiley & Sons.

DeRue, D. S., Nahrgang, J. D., Wellman, N., & Humphrey, S. E. (2011). Trait and behavioral theories of leadership: An integration and meta-analytic test of their relative validity. *Personnel Psychology, 64*(1), 7–52.

Fiedler, F. E. (1993). The leadership situation and the black box in contingency theories. In M. M. Chemers & R. Ayman (Eds.), *Leadership theory and research: Perspectives and directions.* New York: Academic Press.

Gavazzi, S. M. (2015). Turning boys into men: The incentive based system in urban Meyer's plan to win. *International Sport Coaching Journal, 2*, 298–304. https://doi.org/10.1123/iscj.2015-0064

Gomes, A. R. (2014a). Leadership and positive human functioning: A triphasic proposal. In A. R. Gomes, R. Resende, & A. Albuquerque (Eds.), *Positive human functioning from a multidimensional perspective: Promoting high performance* (Vol. 3, pp. 157–169). New York: Nova Science.

Gomes, A. R. (2014b). Transformational leadership: Theory, research, and application to sports. In C. Mohiyeddini (Ed.), *Contemporary topics and trends in the psychology of sports* (pp. 53–114). New York: Nova Science Publishers.

Gomes, A. R., Araújo, V., Resende, R., & Ramalho, V. (2018). Leadership of elite coaches: The relationship among philosophy, practice, and effectiveness criteria. *International Journal of Sports Science & Coaching, 13*(6), 1120–1133. https://doi.org/10.1177/1747954118796362

Gomes, A. R., Lopes, H., & Mata, R. T. (2011). Leadership, cohesion and satisfaction: Differences between swimming and handball Portuguese teams. *Revista Mexicana de Psicologia, 28*(1), 31–42.

Gomes, A. R., & Resende, R. (2014). Assessing leadership styles of coaches and testing the augmentation effect in sport. In C. Mohiyeddini (Ed.), *Contemporary topics and trends in the psychology of sports* (pp. 115–137). New York: Nova Science Publishers.

Gould, D., Pierce, S., Cowburn, I., & Driska, A. (2017). How coaching philosophy drives coaching action: A case study of renowned wrestling coach J Robinson. *International Sport Coaching Journal, 4*(1), 13–37.

Hardman, A., & Jones, C. (2013). Philosophy for coaches. In R. L. Jones & K. Kingston (Eds.), *An introduction to sports coaching: Connecting theory to practice* (2nd ed., pp. 99–111). New York: Routledge.

Hater, J. J., & Bass, B. M. (1988). Superiors` evaluations and subordinates perceptions of transformational and transactional leadership. *Journal of Applied Psychology, 73*(4), 695–702.

Hersey, P., & Blanchard, K. (1996). *Management of organizational behaviour: Utilizing human resources* (7th ed.). Englewood Cliffs, New Jersey: Prentice-Hall.

Hodge, K., Henry, G., & Smith, W. (2014). A case study of excellence in elite sport: Motivational climate in a world champion team. *The Sport Psychologist, 28*, 60–74. https://doi.org/10.1123/tsp.2013-0037

Horn, T. S. (2008). Coaching effectiveness in the sport domain. In T. S. Horn (Ed.), *Advances in sport psychology* (3rd. ed., pp. 239–267). Champaign, IL: Human Kinetics.

Horn, T. S., Bloom, P., Berglund, K. M., & Packard, S. (2011). Relationship between collegiate athletes' psychological characteristics and their preferences for different types of coaching behavior. *The Sport Psychologist, 25*, 190–211.

House, R. J. (1971). A path-goal theory of leader effectiveness. *Administrative Science Quarterly, 16*(3), 321–328.

House, R. J., & Mitchell, T. (1997). Path-goal theory of leadership. In R. P. Vecchio (Ed.), *Leadership: Understanding the dynamics of power and influence in organizations* (pp. 259–273). Notre Dame, Indiana: University of Notre Dame Press.

Jenkins, S. (2010). Coaching philosophy. In J. Lyle & C. Cushion (Eds.), *Sports coaching: Professionalisation and practice* (pp. 233–242). London: Churchill Livingstone Elsevier.

Judge, T. A., Bono, J. E., Ilies, R., & Gerhardt, M. W. (2002). Personality and leadership: A qualitative and quantitative review. *Journal of Applied Psychology, 87*(4), 765–780.

Judge, T. A., & Piccolo, R. F. (2004). Transformational and transactional leadership: A meta-analytic test of their relative validity. *Journal of Applied Psychology, 89*(5), 755–768.

Kaiser, R. B., Hogan, R., & Craig, S. B. (2008). Leadership and the fate of organizations. *American Psychologist, 63*(2), 96–110.

Laborde, S., Guillén, F., Watson, M., & Allen, M. S. (2017). The light quartet: Positive personality traits and approaches to coping in sport coaches. *Psychology of Sport & Exercise, 32*, 67–73. https://doi.org/10.1016/j.psychsport.2017.06.005

Likert, R. (1967). *The human organizations: Its management and value*. New York: McGraw-Hill.

Lowe, K. B., Kroeck, K. G., & Sivasubramaniam, N. (1996). Effectiveness correlates of transformational and transactional leadership: A meta-analytic review of the MLQ literature. *Leadership Quarterly, 7*(3), 385–425.

Lyle, J. (1999). Coaching philosophy and coaching behaviour. In N. Cross & J. Lyle (Eds.), *The coaching process* (pp. 25–46). Oxford: Butterworth-Heinemann.

McCallister, S. G., Blinde, E. M., & Weiss, W. M. (2000). Teaching values and implementing philosophies: Dilemmas of the youth sport coach. *The Physical Educator, 57*, 34–45.

McCrae, R. R., & Costa, P. T., Jr. (1992). Discriminant validity of the NEO-PIR facet scales. *Educational and Psychological Measurement, 52*, 229–237. https://doi.org/10.1177/001316449205200128

Molero, I., Cuadrado, M. N., & Morales, J. F. (2007). Relations and effects of transformational leadership: A comparative analysis with traditional leadership styles. *The Spanish Journal of Psychology, 10*, 358–368.

Norris, L. A., Didymus, F. F., & Kaiseler, M. (2017). Stressors, coping, and Well-being among sports coaches: A systematic review. *Psychology of Sport and Exercise, 33*, 93–112.

Olusoga, P., Butt, J., Maynard, I., & Hays, K. (2010). Stress and coping: A study of world class coaches. *Journal of Applied Sport Psychology, 22*, 274–293.

Riemer, H. A., & Chelladurai, P. (1995). Leadership and satisfaction in athletics. *Journal of Sport & Exercice Psychology, 17*, 276–293.

Riemer, H. A., & Toon, K. (2001). Leadership and satisfaction in tennis: Examination of congruence, gender and ability. *Research Quarterly for Exercise and Sport, 72*, 243–256.

Rowold, J. (2006). Transformational and transactional leadership in martial arts. *Journal of Applied Sport Psychology, 18*(4), 312–325.

Sherman, C. A., Fuller, R., & Speed, H. D. (2000). Gender comparisons of preferred coaching behaviors in Australian sports. *Journal of Sport Behavior, 23*, 389–402.

Smith, R. E., & Smoll, F. L. (1996). The coach as a focus of research and interventions in youth sports. In F. L. Smoll & R. E. Smith (Eds.), *Children and youth in sport. A biopsychosocial perspective* (pp. 125–141). Brown & Benchmark: Madison, WI.

Sosik, J. J., & Jung, D. (2018). *Full range leadership development* (2nd ed.). New York, NY: Routledge.

Stenling, A., Ivarsson, A., Hassmén, P., & Lindwall, M. (2017). Longitudinal associations between athletes' controlled motivation, illbeing, and perceptions of controlling coach behaviors: A

Bayesian latent growth curve approach. *Psychology of Sport & Exercise, 30*, 205–214. https://doi.org/10.1016/j.psychsport.2017.03.002

Vallée, C. N., & Bloom, G. A. (2016). Four keys to building a championship culture. *International Sport Coaching Journal, 3*, 170–177. https://doi.org/10.1123/iscj.2016-0010

Waldman, D. A., Bass, B. M., & Yammarino, F. J. (1990). Adding to contingent-reward behavior-the augmenting effect of charismatic leadership. *Group & Organization Studies, 15*(4), 381–394.

Wang, G., In-Sue, O., Courtright, S. H., & Colbert, A. E. (2011). Transformational leadership and performance across criteria and levels: A meta-analytic review of 25 years of research. *Group & Organization Management, 36*(2), 223–270. https://doi.org/10.1177/1059601111401017

Weinberg, R. S., Butt, J., & Culp, B. (2011). Coaches' views of mental toughness and how it is built. *International Journal of Sport and Exercise Psychology, 9*(2), 156–172.

Yukelson, D., & Rose, R. (2014). The psychology of ongoing excellence: An NCAA coach's perspective on winning consecutive multiple national championships. *Journal of Sport Psychology in Action, 5*(1), 44–58. https://doi.org/10.1080/21520704.2013.866604

Zwingmann, I., Wegge, J., Rudolf, M., Richter, P., Wolf, S., & Schmidt, M. (2014). Is transformational leadership healthy for employees? A multilevel analysis in 16 nations. *Zeitschrift für Personalforschung, 28*(1–2), 24–51. https://doi.org/10.1688/ZfP-2014-01

Rui Gomes is an Assistant Professor in the School of Psychology at the University of Minho, Portugal. He received his Ph.D. in Psychology from the University of Minho. He has research interests on human adaptation to stress, leadership and team performance, and training life skills and human performance. He leads the research group "Adaptation, Performance and Human Development", which was created in 2007 (www.ardh.pt). He leads the community and business intervention project "School of Life Skills" (www.e-cv.pt). As a sport psychologist, he consults athletes and their families, coaches, and sport managers.

Chapter 5
Coaching Impact: The Transformational Coach in Sports

Jennifer Turnnidge and Jean Côté

Abstract There is growing recognition that effective coaching is not only about developing better athletes, but also about developing better people. To achieve this important goal, behavioural frameworks are needed to help coaches foster high-quality interpersonal relationships through their interactions with athletes. This chapter focuses on the principles of Transformational Coaching and how these principles can be practically implemented into real world sport settings. Recent research suggests that Transformational Coaching can be conceptualized using 11 distinct coaching behaviours. This chapter will (a) provide an overview of these 11 behaviours, (b) elaborate on how Transformational Coaching behaviours can foster positive developmental experiences, and (c) offer practical strategies for incorporating Transformational Coaching into everyday coach-athlete interactions.

Keywords Coaching effectiveness · Transformational coaching · Development

Coaching Impact: The Transformational Coach in Sports

The purpose of this chapter is to illustrate how Transformational Coaching can provide a viable avenue for understanding and facilitating effective coach-athlete relationships, and ultimately, for fostering athlete development in sport. The chapter begins with an overview of a framework that outlines the elements of coaching effectiveness necessary for athlete development in sport, and positions Transformational Coaching within this framework. The remainder of the chapter focuses specifically on the behaviours that coaches can use to integrate the principles of Transformational Coaching into their everyday coach-athlete interactions. Lastly, this chapter outlines practical applications related to how Transformational Coaching can influence positive experiences in sport.

J. Turnnidge (✉) · J. Côté
Queen's University, Kingston, ON, Canada
e-mail: 5jm14@queensu.ca; jc46@queensu.ca

R. Resende, A. R. Gomes (eds.), *Coaching for Human Development and Performance in Sports*, https://doi.org/10.1007/978-3-030-63912-9_5

Coaching Effectiveness

It is well documented that effective coaching plays a vital role in facilitating athlete development (Cushion & Lyle, 2010). Previous research consistently demonstrates that coaches' interactions with their athletes can influence the quality of youth's sport experiences (e.g., Erickson, Côté, Hollenstein, & Deakin, 2011; Vella, Oades, & Crowe, 2013). Côté and Gilbert (2009) proposed that coaching effectiveness is comprised of three key elements: (a) coaches' knowledge, (b) the outcomes that result from the consistent application of that knowledge, and (c) the specific context in which coaching occurs. Within this definition, coaches' knowledge represents the integration of professional (i.e., sport-specific/instruction), interpersonal (i.e., relational), and intrapersonal (i.e., capacity for introspection and reflection) knowledge that is manifested in coaches' behaviours. Athletes' developmental outcomes are conceptualized by the 4 C's (competence, confidence, connection, and character; Côté, Bruner, Erickson, Strachan, & Fraser-Thomas, 2010) and developmental coaching contexts refers to a typology of generic coaching settings that are determined by the age and competitive level of the athletes.

One of the underlying aims of the coaching literature has been to gain a deeper understanding of how effective coaches express their knowledge through their behaviours. Accordingly, over the last 40 years, researchers have shed light on various aspects of coaching behaviours, including (a) what behaviours are exhibited by effective coaches, (b) how effective behaviours are shaped by coach, athlete, and situational variables, and (c) how specific coaching behaviours can facilitate athletes' development in sport (Vierimaa, Turnnidge, Evans, & Côté, 2016). Indeed, there is a wealth of evidence on effective coaches' behaviours in practice and competition and across a wide range of sports (e.g., Claxton, 1988; Cushion & Jones, 2001; DeMarco, Mancini, & Wuest, 1996; Lacy & Darst, 1989; Lacy & Goldston, 1990; Potrac, Jones, & Cushion, 2007; Trudel, Côté, & Bernard, 1996) that can be discussed according to Côté and Gilbert's (2009) three types of coaches' knowledge/behaviours.

Professional Knowledge/Behaviours

Traditionally, coaching research has focused on understanding coaches' teaching of sport-specific skills. In reviewing the literature, Erickson and Gilbert (2013) proposed that (a) instructional, (b) support and encouragement, and (c) management behaviours represent the core behaviours of the coaching process for athletes' development of sport specific skills. Indeed, previous research highlights that instruction-based behaviours are integral to coaching effectiveness (e.g., Curtis, Smith, & Smoll, 1979; Ford, Yates, & Williams, 2010; Segrave & Ciancio, 1990). In addition to instruction, coaches spend a significant proportion of their time providing support and encouragement when interacting with athletes in training and competition (e.g., corrective feedback, praise; Smith, Zane, & Smoll, 1983). Although such behaviours can be linked with positive athlete outcomes, researchers have expressed caution regarding the overuse or ingenuine use of support or encouragment behaviours (e.g, Claxton, 1988; Potrac, Jones, & Armour, 2002). Erickson and Gilbert (2013) also drew attention to coaches' use of management behaviours to organize the sport environment (e.g., setting up drills, telling athletes where to go). Generally, studies suggest that effective coaches use such management behaviours less than instruction or support/encouragement behaviours (e.g., Erickson et al., 2011; Lacy & Goldston, 1990). Overall, research examining coaches' use of professional knowledge/behaviours provides valuable insight into how these behaviours can contribute to the quality of athletes experiences. Indeed, previous studies illustrate how the content, temporal patterning (e.g., timing, stage of practice), and recipient (e.g., individual, small group, team) of professional knowledge/behaviours can all play important roles in facilitating athletes' skill acquisition (e.g., Cushion, Harvey, Muir, & Nelson, 2012; Erickson et al., 2011).

Interpersonal Knowledge/Behaviours

Although behaviours such as instruction, support/encouragement, and management are integral components of the coaching process, it is important to acknowledge that there may be other aspects of coaching effectiveness that are not fully captured by coaches' professional knowledge/behaviours. Consistent with this contention, there is growing recognition that more research is needed on coaches' interpersonal knowledge/behaviours. In an effort to address this need, coaching researchers have employed frameworks such as self-determination theory (Deci & Ryan, 2002) and achievement goal theory (Nicholls, 1989) to understand coaches' interpersonal behaviours (e.g., Erickson & Côté, 2016; Smith, Quested, Appleton, & Duda, 2016; Webster et al., 2013). Although such research lends valuable insight into how motivational theories can influence athlete development, it may be worthwhile for researchers to investigate how other interpersonal-based approaches, such as leadership frameworks, may be used to enhance our understanding of coaches' interpersonal knowledge/behaviours.

Full-Range Leadership Model One theory that may hold significant potential for investigating such knowledge/behaviours is the Full- Range Leadership Model (Bass & Riggio, 2006). According to this framework, leadership behaviours can be understood along two axes: One axis ranging from passive to active and the other axis ranging from least effective to most effective. The original framework encompasses laissez-faire, transactional, and transformational (TFL) behaviours. Neutral and toxic leadership were added to the full-range leadership model when it was adapted to the sport context (Turnnidge & Côté, 2016). Please see Fig. 5.1 for a schematic representation of the model in the sport context.

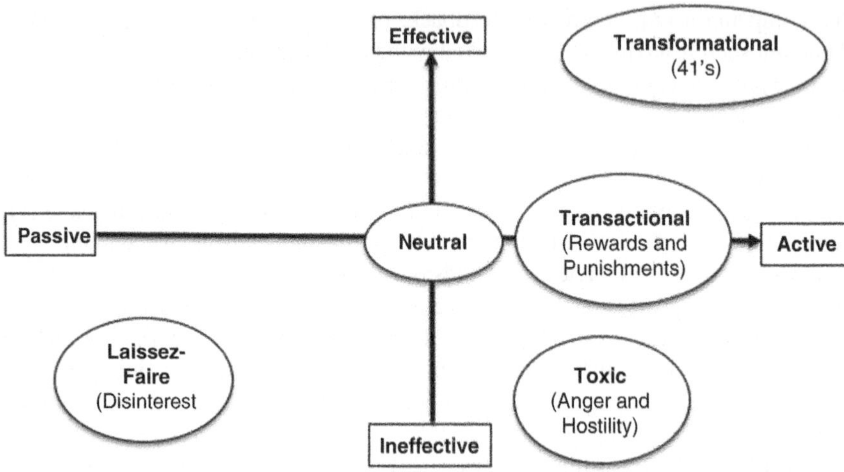

Fig. 5.1 Schematic representation of the full-range leadership model adapted for the sport context (Bass & Riggio, 2006; Turnnidge & Côté, 2017)

Toxic and Laissez-Faire Leadership Toxic leadership refers to a form of leadership that is both active and ineffective. Although toxic was not included in the original model, this form of leadership was added when applying the Full-Range Leadership Model in the sport context. Drawing upon research from organizational and military settings on abusive supervision and toxic leadership (e.g., Aryee, Chen, Sun, & Debrah, 2007; Pelletier, 2010), toxic leadership involves behaviours such as expressing anger and hostility towards athletes (e.g., threats, intimidation) and modelling anti-social behaviours (e.g., aggression).

Whereas toxic leadership represents an active form of leadership, laissez-faire reflects an ineffective and passive form of leadership. Often referred to as *non-leadership*, laissez-faire behaviours involve ignoring one's responsibilities, avoiding decision-making, and displaying indifference towards one's followers (Bass & Riggio, 2006). Previous research suggests that toxic and laissez-faire behaviours are associated with negative outcomes, including role conflict and ambiguity, lower levels of well-being, and reduced effectiveness (e.g., Barling & Frone, 2017; Haslam, Reicher, & Platow, 2010; Skogstad, Einarsen, Torsheim, Aasland, & Hetland, 2007). It is thus possible, that coaches who employ such behaviours may similarly contribute to negative developmental outcomes for athletes.

Neutral Moving along the continuum, neutral coaching involves behaviours that do not have a discernable leadership tone. For example, coaches may use simple instruction/organizational behaviours (e.g., "Go over here"), vague feedback (e.g., "Go, go, go") or passive praise (e.g., "Good job" without a clear target or rationale). Previous research has raised concerns regarding such nonspecific coaching behaviours because they offer limited information or meaning to athletes and may lessen the potential influence of coaches' more relevant and constructive behaviours

(Cushion & Jones, 2001). Nonetheless, there is a paucity of research examining these behaviours and thus more studies are needed to examine the potential influence of neutral behaviours on athlete development.

Transactional Leadership Transactional leadership represents a more active form of leadership which involves behaviours that are contingent on the adequacy of followers' abilities to execute specific standards or tasks. This may include assigning or discussing the positive and/or negative consequences for certain types of behaviours or monitoring followers to detect error or failures to meet specific standards. Previous research indicates that transactional behaviours can be reasonably effective in promoting positive follower outcomes (Judge & Piccolo, 2004), but are insufficient for optimal follower development. This finding relates to the *augmentation hypothesis*, which suggests that transactional behaviours represent the necessary foundation for effective leadership and that TFL behaviours can build upon this foundation to promote higher levels of positive development. As such, TFL behaviours may be particularly well-suited for facilitating positive development in the sport context.

Transformational Leadership TFL involves empowering, inspiring, and challenging one's followers to facilitate individual, team, and organizational outcomes (Bass, 1997). This type of leadership is comprised of four dimensions, collectively referred to as the 4 I's: Idealized influence, inspirational motivation, intellectual stimulation, and individualized consideration. First, *idealized influence* refers to leaders who foster trust and respect and serve as role models for their followers. Second, *inspirational motivation* relates to leaders who motivate and challenge their followers by displaying enthusiasm, articulating a compelling vision, and providing meaning to their followers' tasks. Third, leaders engage in *intellectual stimulation* by facilitating their followers' efforts to be creative and innovative and by encouraging their followers to offer novel ideas. Lastly, *individualized consideration* refers to leaders who display genuine care and concern for their followers' development and achievement.

The Full-Range Leadership Model has been successfully applied in several contexts including business, health care, military, physical education, and sport (e.g., Barling, Weber, & Kelloway, 1996; Charbonneau, Barling, & Kelloway, 2001; Morton, Keith, & Beauchamp, 2010). Although previous studies indicate that coaches' leadership behaviours may have important implications for athlete outcomes, including athlete satisfaction, effort, performance, and group cohesion (e.g., Arthur, Woodman, Ong, Hardy, & Ntoumanis, 2011; Callow, Smith, Hardy, Arthur, & Hardy, 2009; Charbonneau et al., 2001; Rowold, 2006; Vella et al., 2013), the processes through which TFL behaviours shape athlete development has been investigated extensively in the last few years.

TFL in Sport In an effort to further understand how leadership behaviours are manifested in the sport context, Turnnidge and Côté (2019) developed an observational instrument to examine coaches' real-time leadership behaviours in sport. Drawing upon literature reviews, qualitative interviews, and video observation, the

Table 5.1 Coaching behaviours of the coach leadership assessment system

Higher-order dimension	Lower-order dimension
Idealized influence	1 – Discussing/modelling pro-social values or behaviours 2 – Showing vulnerability/humility
Inspirational motivation	3 – Discussing goals/expectations 4 – Expressing confidence in athlete(s)' capabilities 5 – Implementing a collective vision 6 – Providing meaningful and challenging tasks and roles
Intellectual stimulation	7 – Eliciting athlete input 8 – Sharing decision making/leadership responsibilities 9 – Emphasizing the learning process
Individualized consideration	10 – Showing interest in athletes' needs 11 – Recognizing individual roles/contributions
Transactional	12 – Discussing rewards/penalties 13 – Searching for/responding to errors
Neutral	14 – Neutral
Laissez-faire	15 – Showing disinterest
Toxic	16 – Expressing anger/hostility 17 – Discussing and modelling anti-social values or behaviours
N/A	X – Uncodable

Coach Leadership Assessment System (CLAS) was developed. The CLAS is comprised of 17 behavioural categories across five higher order dimensions: transformational (11 codes), transactional (2 codes), neutral (1 code), laissez-faire (1 code), and toxic (2 codes) coaching, as well as an uncodable category (please see Table 5.1 for a summary). The coding system also analyzes coaches' leadership behaviours in relation to their content (e.g., instruction/feedback, organization, and general communication), recipient (e.g., team, individual athlete), and context (e.g., warm-up, scrimmage).

The CLAS can help researchers and practitioners to operationalize the theoretical constructs of the Full-Range Leadership Model, with an emphasis on TFL, within the context of coach-athlete interactions in sport. Further, this tool outlines a range of leadership behaviours that are rooted in the coaching literature and practices of youth sport coaches, that can be used as a guide for practically implementing leadership behaviours in real-world sport settings. As such, the following sections will focus on describing each of the evidence-based 11 Transformational Coaching behaviours by providing examples of how coaches can apply these behaviours when interacting with athletes. Please see Table 5.2 for a summary of the 11 Transformational Coaching behaviours.

Table 5.2 Transformational Coaching behaviours

Higher Order Dimension	Leadership Tone	Description	Strategies
Idealized influence	1–Discussing/ modelling pro-social values or behaviours	Discussion or modelling of behaviours that are intended to benefit others and that are often prompted by empathy, morality, or a sense of social responsibility, rather than a desire for personal gain (e.g., helping others).	– Translating values into actions (e.g., showing respect by speaking to coaches, athletes, officials, etc. in a calm and effective tone) – Practicing what you preach (e.g., participating in warm up or community events).
	2–Showing vul-nerability/ humility	Behaviours through which coaches recognize gaps in their knowledge or under-standing. Could involve ask-ing for help or apologizing for mistakes.	– Acknowledging gaps in knowledge (e.g.," I don't know the answer right now."). – Recognizing and apolo-gizing for mistakes (e.g., "sorry, I didn't explain that drill very well.").
Inspirational motivation	3–Discussing goals/ expectations	Behaviours through which the coach expresses expecta-tions for a particular training session, a particular drill, or as a part of a larger picture, such as an upcoming game or goals for the season. Can also include discussions of goal (s), goal setting, etc.	– Highlighting the objec-tives of a specific drill, including both what the athletes are expected to do and how they should do it.
	4–Expressing confidence in athlete(s)' capabilities	Behaviours through which the coach conveys an opti-mistic or enthusiastic attitude regarding what the athlete (s) can achieve.	– Providing encouragement (e.g., "I know you've got this.").
	5–Implementing a collective vision	Behaviours through which the coach encourages team spirit/collaborative attitude among team members.	– Sharing symbols (e.g., team mottos, equipment) and stories (e.g., stories of past successes).
	6–Providing meaningful and challenging tasks and roles	Behaviours through which the coach highlights the value/meaning of certain activities/drills or provides reasoning behind decisions.	– Offering rationales and explanations (e.g., "It's really important that you keep your head down because it helps you to conserve energy.").
Intellectual stimulation	7–Eliciting ath-lete input	Behaviours that convey a view of the athlete(s) as con-tributing members of the sit-uation and which encourage athlete(s) to solve problems and to look for alternative	– Asking questions (e.g., "how can we improve our endurance?"). – Reframing assumptions (""'what can we learn from a

(continued)

Table 5.2 (continued)

Higher Order Dimension	Leadership Tone	Description	Strategies
		solutions, have open discussions, or contribute new and alternative ideas.	drill when things do not go as expected?").
	8–Sharing decision making/ leadership responsibilities	Behaviours through which the coach provides opportunities for the athlete(s) to make decisions, show initiative, leadership (e.g., demonstrating skills, leading a warm-up, etc).	– Providing choices – Offering opportunities to lead or mentor teammates
	9–Emphasizing the learning process	Behaviours through which coaches encourage athlete(s) to value effort, learning from mistakes, and/or engage in challenging tasks.	– Encouraging effort rather than outcome (e.g., "Don't worry about that shot, keep going!").
Individualized consideration	10–Showing interest in athletes' feelings/ needs/ concerns	Behaviours through which a coach recognizes and/or adapts to an athlete's individual needs or considers their unique abilities.	– Discussing athletes' lives in and out of sport (e.g., "how did that test go yesterday?"). – Adapting activities (e.g., "I know your shoulder has been a bit sore, so I think we'll only do two sets today.").
	11–Recognizing athlete achievements/ Contributions	Behaviours through which coaches show appreciation for athlete(s) efforts.	– Thanking athletes for their contributions and accomplishments in and out of sport (e.g., cheering on their teammates, participating in community events). – Providing supportive and enthusiastic feedback (e.g., "excellent job on that turn, Jake!").

Transformational Coaching in Sport

Idealized Influence First, idealized influence involves the behaviours of (a) *discussing and modelling pro-social values* and (b) *showing vulnerability and humility* with one's athletes. Coaches can apply the principle of idealized influence by making an active effort to demonstrate their personal values in their everyday settings. For instance, a coach who values respect could translate this value into action by modelling appropriate behaviours (e.g., shaking hands, helping others, beginning/ending practice on time), discussing the importance of such behaviours (e.g., having conversations about behaving respectfully with coaches, athletes, parents, or officials), or providing feedback on athletes' use of these behaviours. Coaches can also demonstrate idealized influence by modelling behaviours that they want their athletes to exhibit. Some examples of this may include coaches who participate in warm-up or conditioning drills with their athletes to emphasize the importance of these activities or coaches who lead community initiatives to reinforce the organization's philosophy of contributing to the community both in and out of sport.

Another way coaches can engage with idealized influence is by *showing vulnerability or humility* with their athletes. This may include being accountable or apologizing for one's mistakes (e.g. "Sorry everyone, I don't think I explained that drill very well."), acknowledging gaps in one's knowledge or capabilities (e.g., "That's a great question, I don't know the answer right now, but maybe we can look it up and find out together."), or sharing personal experiences with their athletes. For instance, if an athlete is experiencing a plateau in their performance, a coach may share stories of how they've experienced plateaus themselves (e.g., as an athlete, coach, or student). By showing vulnerability and humility, coaches can help to facilitate more open and honest communication between themselves, which may ultimately lead to perceptions of trust and respect.

Linking Idealized Influence Behaviours to the Research By discussing and modelling their personally held values, coaches who use idealized influence behaviours may be perceived as important role models. In doing so, coaches can increase the likelihood that their athletes will identify with these prosocial values and behaviours, and ultimately encourage athletes to adopt these values themselves. Idealized influence behaviours may also contribute to athlete development by fostering relationships based on mutual trust. Previous studies suggest that leaders who act as role models by consistently doing what is right, rather than what is personally beneficial, can facilitate the development of trust (e.g., Jung & Avolio, 2000; Kelloway, Turner, Barling, & Loughlin, 2012). With regards to showing vulnerability and humility, limited research has examined this behaviour in relation to coach-athlete relationships. However, evidence from the organizational psychology literature suggests that apologizing can positively influence followers' perceptions of their leaders (Tucker, Turner, Barling, Reid, & Elving, 2006).

Inspirational Motivation The second dimension of transformational coaching is inspirational motivation. Inspirational motivation can be applied by coaches who create a shared understanding of what their athletes would like to achieve, how they will achieve it, and why these achievements are important (e.g., how it can facilitate the athletes' development in or out of sport or how it may connect to the team's goals for the season). Coaches can develop this shared understanding by *discussing goals and expectations with their athletes*. It is important to note that there are many ways to tailor these discussions, such as changing: (a) who leads the discussion (e.g., coach-led vs. athlete-led), (b) whom is involved in the discussion (e.g., the whole team vs. an individual athlete), or (c) the content of the discussion (e.g., sport-related, such as technique vs. non-sport-related, such as balancing school and sport).

Coaches can also apply the principle of inspirational motivation by *expressing confidence in their athletes' capabilities* to achieve their goals. These capabilities can relate to sport-specific outcomes, such as mastering a specific technique or tactical strategy and to personal development outcomes, such as teamwork or communication. Coaches can actively demonstrate their belief in their athletes by talking optimistically or enthusiastically about their athletes' capabilities (e.g., "You've got this, Amy!" or by providing challenging tasks (e.g., "Ryan, I think you can handle this higher intensity, so we're going to go for it today."). By expressing confidence, coaches can convey a sense of trust in their athletes' abilities, which may positively influence their perceptions of competence and confidence.

Another aspect of inspirational motivation involves using behaviours that help athletes connect themselves and their activities to the bigger picture. For example, coaches can *implement a collective vision* for the team by (a) developing a team vision or sharing team symbols or stories (e.g., creating a team motto, wearing team uniforms, participating in a team cheer), (b) discussing team norms and roles (e.g., discussing team protocols for competitions), and (c) encouraging connections to the team (e.g., providing opportunities for peer bonding). Coaches can also foster connections to the bigger picture by *providing meaningful and challenging tasks and roles*. For instance, coaches can highlight the value of certain activities or drills (e.g. "This drill is important because..."), provide rationales for decision making (e.g., "We decided to move you to defense because..."), and illustrate the connections between specific activities and roles and the team's collective vision (e.g., "This conditioning drill will help us to maintain our speed in the finals next week.").

Linking Inspirational Motivation to the Research The behaviours related to inspirational motivation resonate with several lines of research both in and out of sport. For example, the behaviour of discussing goals and expectations is consistent with the work of Camiré, Trudel, and Forneris (2009), who found that athletes' perceptions of the quality of their coach-athlete communications were enhanced when the athletes knew what was expected of them. Similarly, the behaviour of expressing confidence is supported by the work of Fraser-Thomas and Côté (2009) which revealed that coaches who demonstrated unfaltering belief in their athletes' capabilities enhanced their athletes' confidence and motivation. Fraser-Thomas and Côté (2009) further posited that coaches' beliefs in their athletes can be demonstrated through their enthusiasm and encouragement. Since coaches are perceived as credible sources of an athlete's abilities, they can influence an athlete's perceptions of their potential (e.g., Feltz & Lirgg, 2001).

Finally, by implementing a collective vision and offering meaningful and challenging tasks and roles, coaches can encourage their athletes to discover meaning and value in the activities and roles themselves (Avolio, Zhu, Koh, & Bhatia, 2004). Previous research in organizational settings indicates that leaders who set a collective vision for their team enable followers to find a *higher purpose* or *meaning* in their tasks (e.g., Arnold, Turner, Barling, Kelloway, & McKee, 2007; Sparks & Schenk, 2001). By helping athletes understand the bigger picture, coaches increase the likelihood that their athletes' motivations for engaging in activities is internally driven (Shamir, House, & Arthur, 1993; Sheldon, Turban, Brown, Barrick, & Judge, 2003). As such, coaches can create an environment that fosters athletes' motivation and interest.

Intellectual Stimulation

Third, coaches can implement intellectual stimulation by actively involving athletes in the coaching process. For instance, coaches can *elicit athlete input* (e.g., "What could we do differently to improve this drill?"). To elicit athlete input, coaches can provide opportunities for their athletes to critically reflect on sport- and non-sport issues by encouraging them to (a) solve problems and consider alternative solutions and (b) contribute new ideas and perspectives. Coaches can also apply the principle of intellectual stimulation by *sharing decision-making and leadership responsibilities*. Examples of this behaviour can include offering choices (e.g. "Would you rather scrimmage at the beginning or end of practice?") or providing opportunities to lead others (e.g., leading warm-up, mentoring teammates). Coaches can also enact the principle of intellectual stimulation by *emphasizing the learning process*. More specifically, coaches can provide instructions and feedback that focus on the process, rather than the outcome (e.g., "Great effort, Jason!). Using the behaviours of intellectual stimulation can help athletes re-frame their perceived challenges as learning opportunities (e.g., "I know this is a frustrating loss, but what can we take away from this?") and can set the stage for more creative and engaging sessions.

Linking Intellectual Stimulation to the Research The behaviours associated with intellectual stimulation share marked commonalities with certain elements of autonomy-supportive coaching. Indeed, autonomy-supportive coaching similarly involves offering athletes choices, providing initiative-building opportunities, and acknowledging athletes' perspectives (Mageau & Vallerand, 2003). An extensive body of literature demonstrates that adopting this interpersonal style is linked with a myriad of positive outcomes, including higher levels of sportspersonship and psychological well-being, as well as lower levels of athlete burnout (e.g., Mageau & Vallerand, 2003; Mallett, 2005). As such, these findings lend support to the contention that intellectual stimulation behaviours have important implications for the outcomes that youth derive from their sport participation.

The behaviours associated with intellectual stimulation also resonate with mastery-oriented behaviours (Smith, Cumming, & Smoll, 2008). Intellectual stimulation creates an environment in which followers are willing to learn, to adopt new approaches, and to think for themselves (e.g., Bass & Riggio, 2006). Intellectual stimulation also involves encouraging followers to view mistakes as a fundamental part of the learning process (Bass & Riggio, 2006). Similarly, mastery-oriented coaching behaviours encourage athletes to select challenging tasks and to view mistakes as valuable sources of feedback (Smith et al., 2008). This emphasis on athletes' active engagement in the learning process can facilitate competence and confidence (e.g., Sarrazin, Vallerand, Guillet, Pelletier, & Cury, 2002).

Overall, the behaviours associated with intellectual stimulation can positively contribute to athlete development. For example, in an organizational context, Sivanathan, Arnold, Turner, and Barling (2004) suggested that by pushing followers to think for themselves and to take initiative, leaders can convey a sense of trust in their followers' abilities, which can positively influence their perceptions of competence and confidence. Coaches who employ intellectual stimulation behaviours in the sport context may similarly facilitate these positive developmental outcomes of their athletes.

Individualized Consideration

Finally, the principle of individualized consideration may be enacted in practice by coaches who make a genuine effort to *show interest* in their athletes' lives, both in and out of sport. Examples of this behaviour include listening to athletes' concerns, incorporating their feedback, or discussing their hobbies. For instance, a coach may discuss an athlete's upcoming musical recital or may adjust their practice activities to accommodate an athlete's heavy exam schedule. Overall, this principle encourages coaches to view youth not just as athletes, but as young people whose lives are affected by their experiences with family, school, other extra-curricular activities, and the community.

Another aspect of individualized consideration is *recognizing athlete achievements and contributions*. Coaches can manifest this behaviour in several ways such as by (a) providing opportunities for athletes to demonstrate their skills, (b) offering feedback on their achievements both in and out of sport (e.g., "Great passing technique, Alex!" or "I heard you had a really interesting project at the school science fair!"), and (c) drawing attention to their contributions and roles (e.g., "Thanks for helping clean up after practice, it means a lot." or "I know it can be hard to be on the sidelines, but you did an amazing job supporting your teammates today."). These behaviours should be targeted towards not only performance-related achievements, but towards achievements related to personal development as well. For instance, coaches can recognize athletes who display leadership skills or exhibit pro-social behaviours in their interactions with their teammates, opponents, and officials. It may be particularly beneficial for coaches to consider the importance of pro-social behaviours and personal achievements since these elements are often overlooked within competitive sport environments. Lastly, coaches should try to choose the appropriate moment, as well as the appropriate method, for providing individualized recognition. Coaches can learn to select these moments and methods by observing their athletes to better understand how personal and situational factors shape athletes' responses to coach behaviours.

Linking Individualized Consideration to the Research At its core, the behaviours associated with individualized consideration align with the adoption of a person-centred approach to coaching. These behaviours resonate with Douglas and Carless' proposition (Douglas & Carless, 2008) that a *person-centred*, rather than *athlete-centred*, approach should be adopted in order to recognize the fact that sport is just one of the many contexts of a young person's life. A person-centred approach also supports Miller and Kerr's (2002) suggestion that coaches should consider how their behaviours will contribute to youth's development in the future, even if they no longer participate in sport. Additionally, individualized consideration behaviours parallel the work of Stuntz and Spearance (2010), which suggests that coaches' communication with their athletes about outside-sport topics may lead to more adaptive athlete outcomes. For instance, Stuntz and Spearance's findings revealed that athletes' whose coaches knew more about their lives outside sport reported higher levels of sport enjoyment and commitment. Together, these studies indicate that adopting individualized consideration behaviours may help coaches to foster positive sport experiences since it signals to youth that they are cared for and valued.

Transformational Coaching: Practical Implications

Overall, the concepts discussed in this chapter have important implications for researchers and practitioners wishing to enhance the quality of coaches' leadership behaviours in youth sport, and ultimately facilitate athletes' positive development. Indeed, these concepts can be incorporated into everyday coaching practices, and into the design, evaluation, and dissemination of initiatives to improve coaches' leadership behaviours.

Although there are numerous ways in which coaches may improve their coaching knowledge/behaviours, such as first-hand experience and peer mentoring, formal Coach Development Programs (CDPs) represent an important cornerstone of coaches' professional development (Lefebvre, Evans, Turnnidge, Gainforth, & Côté, 2016). According to Evans, McGuckin, Gainforth, Bruner, and Côté (2015), CDPs refer to "learning activities applied systematically through education, social interaction, and/or personal reflection with the goal of changing coach behaviours" (Evans et al., 2015, p. 871). Recent systematic reviews of the CDP literature revealed that the uptake and relevance of CDPs may be enhanced by placing a greater emphasis on (a) coaches' interpersonal knowledge/behaviours (Lefebvre et al., 2016), (b) integrating behaviour change theories into the design and implementation of CDPs (Allan, Vierimaa, Gainforth, & Côté, 2017), and (c) systematic evaluation of interpersonal CDPs (Evans et al., 2015). A worthwhile direction of researchers and practitioners may thus be to explore how these findings can be integrated into the design, implementation, and evaluate on of an effective and sustainable CDP. Such programs would contribute to our understanding of how education programs may lead to changes in coaches' leadership behaviours and athletes' outcomes.

In an effort to address this call for intervention research, Turnnidge and Côté (2017) developed the Transformational Coaching Workshop (TCW). Drawing upon previous transformational leadership interventions (e.g., Barling et al., 1996; Beauchamp, Barling, & Morton, 2011; Vella et al., 2013), the TCW is a facilitator led, interactive workshop designed to educate coaches on the full-range leadership model and enhance coaches' capability, opportunity, and motivation to practically implement transformational coaching behaviours into their everyday coach-athlete interactions. Findings from a pilot test of the TCW with eight youth soccer coaches provide some preliminary support for the effectiveness of the workshop (Lawrason, Turnnidge, Martin, & Côté, 2018). Indeed, coaches spent more time displaying idealized influence, inspirational motivation, intellectual stimulation, and instruction/feedback behaviours following the workshop. Coaches also spent less time displaying neutral and organizational/management behaviours after the workshop. These findings highlight the potential for educational interventions to positively influence coaches' use of transformational coaching behaviours. Nonetheless, it is important to acknowledge the preliminary nature of these findings and thus further research is needed to assess the effectiveness of the TCW with larger samples of coaches, as well as the influence of the TCW on athletes' developmental outcomes.

Key Points

The exploration of sport coaching through a transformational coaching lens offers exciting opportunities for both research and practice. Drawing upon the coaching and leadership literature, it is evident coaches' interpersonal knowledge/behaviours play an integral role in shaping the quality of athletes' sport experiences. As such, it is crucial for coaches to gain a deeper understanding of how to apply evidence-informed interpersonal knowledge/behaviours in their coaching practice. The 4 I's of transformational coaching, and the associated 11 behaviours, provides a salient framework for operationalizing the "how" of sport coaching. It is hoped that coaches will reflect on how these behavioural principles align with their own coaching practice and encourage them to develop strategies for integrating these behaviours into their everyday coach-athlete interactions.

Conclusion

Overall, the aim of this chapter was to examine coaches' leadership behaviours in sport and the processes by which coaches' leadership behaviours influence athlete development. This chapter offers insight into how research on coach leadership can be translated into real-world, youth sport settings. By enhancing coaches' use of effective leadership behaviours, researchers and practitioners may be able to positively contribute to young athletes' performance, continued participation, and personal development through sport.

References

Allan, V., Vierimaa, M., Gainforth, H. L., & Côté, J. (2017). The use of behaviour change theories and techniques in research-informed coach development programmes: A systematic review. International Review of Sport and Exercise Psychology. Advanced online publication. doi: https://doi.org/10.1080/1750984X.2017.1286514.

Arnold, K. A., Turner, N., Barling, J., Kelloway, E. K., & McKee, M. C. (2007). Transformational leadership and psychological Well-being: The mediating role of meaningful work. *Journal of Occupational Health Psychology, 12*(3), 193.

Arthur, C. A., Woodman, T., Ong, C. W., Hardy, L., & Ntoumanis, N. (2011). The role of athlete narcissism in moderating the relationship between coaches' transformational leader behaviors and athlete motivation. *Journal of Sport and Exercise Psychology, 33*(1), 3–19.

Aryee, S., Chen, Z. X., Sun, L. Y., & Debrah, Y. A. (2007). Antecedents and outcomes of abusive supervision: Test of a trickle-down model. *Journal of Applied Psychology, 92*, 191–201.

Avolio, B. J., Zhu, W., Koh, W., & Bhatia, P. (2004). Transformational leadership and organizational commitment: Mediating role of psychological empowerment and moderating role of structural distance. *Journal of Organizational Behavior: The International Journal of Industrial, Occupational and Organizational Psychology and Behavior, 25*(8), 951–968.

Barling, J., & Frone, M. R. (2017). If only my leader would just do something! Passive leadership undermines employee wellbeing through role stressors and psychological resource depletion. *Stress and Health, 33*(3), 211–222. https://doi.org/10.1002/smi.2697

Barling, J., Weber, T., & Kelloway, E. K. (1996). Effects of transformational leadership training on attitudinal and financial outcomes: A field experiment. *Journal of Applied Psychology, 81*, 827–832. https://doi.org/10.1037/0021-9010.81.6.827

Bass, B. M. (1997). Does the transactional–transformational leadership paradigm transcend organizational and national boundaries? *American Psychologist, 52*(2), 130–139.

Bass, B. M., & Riggio, R. E. (2006). *Transformational leadership* (2nd ed.). New York, NY: Psychology Press.

Beauchamp, M. R., Barling, J., & Morton, K. L. (2011). Transformational teaching and adolescent self-determined motivation, self-efficacy, and intentions to engage in leisure time physical activity: A randomized controlled pilot trial. *Applied Psychology: Health and Well-Being, 3*, 127–150. https://doi.org/10.1111/j.1758-0854.2011.01048.x

Callow, N., Smith, M. J., Hardy, L., Arthur, C. A., & Hardy, J. (2009). Measurement of transformational leadership and its relationship with team cohesion and performance level. *Journal of Applied Sport Psychology, 21*(4), 395–412. https://doi.org/10.1080/10413200903204754

Camiré, M., Trudel, P., & Forneris, T. (2009). High school athletes' perspectives on support, communication, negotiation and life skill development. *Qualitative Research in Sport and Exercise, 1*(1), 72–88.

Charbonneau, D., Barling, J., & Kelloway, E. K. (2001). Transformational leadership and sports performance: The mediating role of intrinsic motivation. *Journal of Applied Social Psychology, 31*, 1521–1534. https://doi.org/10.1111/j.1559-1816.2001.tb02686.x

Claxton, D. B. (1988). A systematic observation of more and less successful high school tennis coaches. *Journal of Teaching in Physical Education, 7*(4), 302–310.

Côté, J., Bruner, M. W., Erickson, K., Strachan, L., & Fraser-Thomas, J. (2010). Athlete development and coaching. In J. Lyle & C. Cushion (Eds.), *Sport coaching: Professionalism and practice* (pp. 63–78). Oxford: Elsevier.

Côté, J., & Gilbert, W. (2009). An integrative definition of coaching effectiveness and expertise. *International Journal of Sports Science & Coaching, 4*(3), 307–323. https://doi.org/10.1260/174795409789623892

Curtis, B., Smith, R. E., & Smoll, F. L. (1979). Scrutinizing the skipper: A study of leadership behaviors in the dugout. *Journal of Applied Psychology, 64*(4), 391–400. https://doi.org/10.1037/0021-9010.64.4.391

Cushion, C., Harvey, S., Muir, B., & Nelson, L. (2012). Developing the coach analysis and intervention system (CAIS): Establishing validity and reliability of a computerised systematic observation instrument. *Journal of Sports Sciences, 30*(2), 201–216.
Cushion, C. J., & Jones, R. L. (2001). A systematic observation of professional top-level youth soccer coaches. *Journal of Sport Behaviour, 24*, 354–376.
Cushion, C., & Lyle, J. (2010). Conceptual development in sports coaching. In J. Lyle & C. Cushion (Eds.), *Sports coaching: Professionalisation and practice* (pp. 1–14). Edinburgh: Churchill Livingstone.
Deci, E. L., & Ryan, R. M. (2002). *Handbook of self-determination research.* Rochester, NY: University Rochester Press.
DeMarco, G., Mancini, V., & Wuest, D. (1996). Reflections on change: A qualitative and quantitative analysis of a baseball coach's behavior. *Journal of Sport Behavior, 20*(2), 135–163.
Douglas, K., & Carless, D. (2008). Using stories in coach education. *International Journal of Sports Science & Coaching, 3*(1), 33–49.
Erickson, K., & Côté, J. (2016). A season-long examination of the intervention tone of coach-athlete interactions and athlete development in youth sport. *Psychology of Sport and Exercise, 22*, 264–272. https://doi.org/10.1016/j.psychsport.2015.08.006
Erickson, K., Côté, J., Hollenstein, T., & Deakin, J. (2011). Examining coach-athlete interactions using state space grids: An observational analysis in competitive youth sport. *Psychology of Sport and Exercise, 12*, 645–654. https://doi.org/10.1016/j.psychsport.2011.06.006
Erickson, K., & Gilbert, W. (2013). Coach–athlete interactions in youth sport. In J. Côté & R. Lidor (Eds.), *Conditions of children's talent development in sport* (pp. 129–156). Morgantown, WV: Fitness Information Technology.
Evans, M. B., McGuckin, M., Gainforth, H. L., Bruner, M. W., & Côté, J. (2015). Coach development programmes to improve interpersonal coach behaviours: A systematic review using the re-aim framework. *British Journal of Sports Medicine, 49*(13), 871–877. https://doi.org/10.1136/bjsports-2015-094634
Feltz, D. L., & Lirgg, C. D. (2001). Self-efficacy beliefs of athletes, teams, and coaches. In R. N. Singer, H. A. Hausenblas, & C. Janelle (Eds.), *Handbook of sport psychology* (2nd ed., pp. 340–361). New York: John Wiley & Sons.
Ford, P. R., Yates, I., & Williams, A. M. (2010). An analysis of practice activities and instructional behaviours used by youth soccer coaches during practice: Exploring the link between science and application. *Journal of Sports Sciences, 28*(5), 483–495.
Fraser-Thomas, J., & Côté, J. (2009). Understanding adolescents' positive and negative developmental experiences in sport. *The Sport Psychologist, 23*(1), 3–23.
Haslam, S. A., Reicher, S. D., & Platow, M. J. (2010). *The new psychology of leadership: Identity, influence and power.* New York, NY: Psychology Press.
Judge, T. A., & Piccolo, R. F. (2004). Transformational and transactional leadership: A meta-analytic test of their relative validity. *Journal of Applied Psychology, 89*(5), 755.
Jung, D. I., & Avolio, B. J. (2000). Opening the black box: An experimental investigation of the mediating effects of trust and value congruence on transformational and transactional leadership. *Journal of Organizational Behavior, 21*(8), 949–964.
Kelloway, E. K., Turner, N., Barling, J., & Loughlin, C. (2012). Transformational leadership and employee psychological Well-being: The mediating role of employee trust in leadership. *Work & Stress, 26*(1), 39–55.
Lacy, A. C., & Darst, P. W. (1989). The Arizona State University observation instrument (ASUOI). In P. W. Darst, D. B. Zakrajsek, & V. H. Mancini (Eds.), *Analysing physical education and sport instruction* (pp. 369–377). Champaign, IL: Human Kinetics.
Lacy, A. C., & Goldston, P. D. (1990). Behavior analysis of male and female coaches in high school girls' basketball. *Journal of Sport Behavior, 13*(1), 29.
Lawrason, S., Turnnidge, J., Martin, L., & Côté, J. (2018). Assessing the effectiveness of a transformational coaching workshop for changing youth sport coaches' behaviours. *The Sport Psychologist, 50*(1).

Lefebvre, J. S., Evans, M. B., Turnnidge, J., Gainforth, H. L., & Côté, J. (2016). Describing and classifying coach development programmes: A synthesis of empirical research and applied practice. *International Journal of Sports Science & Coaching, 11*, 887–899. https://doi.org/10.1177/1747954116676116

Mageau, G. A., & Vallerand, R. J. (2003). The coach–athlete relationship: A motivational model. *Journal of Sports Science, 21*(11), 883–904.

Mallett, C. (2005). Self-determination theory: A case study of evidence-based coaching. *Sport Psychologist, 19*, 417–429.

Miller, P. S., & Kerr, G. A. (2002). Conceptualizing excellence: Past, present, and future. *Journal of Applied Sport Psychology, 14*(3), 140–153.

Morton, K. L., Keith, S. E., & Beauchamp, M. R. (2010). Transformational teaching and physical activity: A new paradigm for adolescent health promotion? *Journal of Health Psychology, 15*, 248–257.

Nicholls, J. G. (1989). *The competitive ethos and democratic education*. Cambridge, MA: Harvard University Press.

Pelletier, K. L. (2010). Leader toxicity: An empirical investigation of toxic behavior and rhetoric. *Leadership, 6*(4), 373–389.

Potrac, P., Jones, R., & Armour, K. (2002). "It's all about getting respect": The coaching behaviors of an expert English soccer coach. *Sport, Education and Society, 7*(2), 183–202.

Potrac, P., Jones, R., & Cushion, C. (2007). Understanding power and the coach's role in professional English soccer: A preliminary investigation of coach behaviour. *Soccer & Society, 8*(1), 33–49.

Rowold, J. (2006). Transformational and transactional leadership in martial arts. *Journal of Applied Sport Psychology, 18*, 312–325. https://doi.org/10.1080/10413200600944082

Sarrazin, P., Vallerand, R., Guillet, E., Pelletier, L., & Cury, F. (2002). Motivation and dropout in female handballers: A 21-month prospective study. *European Journal of Social Psychology, 32*, 395–418. https://doi.org/10.1002/ejsp.98

Segrave, J. O., & Ciancio, C. A. (1990). An observational study of a successful pop warner football coach. *Journal of Teaching in Physical Education, 9*(4), 294–306.

Shamir, B., House, R. J., & Arthur, M. B. (1993). The motivational effects of charismatic leadership: A self-concept based theory. *Organization Science, 4*(4), 577–594.

Sheldon, K. M., Turban, D. B., Brown, K. G., Barrick, M. R., & Judge, T. A. (2003). Applying self-determination theory to organizational research. *Research in Personnel and Human Resources Management, 22*, 357–393. https://doi.org/10.1016/S0742-7301(03)22008-9

Sivanathan, N., Arnold, K. A., Turner, N., & Barling, J. (2004). Leading well: Transformational leadership and Well-being. In *Positive psychology in practice* (pp. 241–255).

Skogstad, A., Einarsen, S., Torsheim, T., Aasland, M. S., & Hetland, H. (2007). The destructiveness of laissez faire leadership behavior. *Journal of Occupational Health Psychology, 12*(1), 80–92. https://doi.org/10.1037/1076-8998.12.1.80

Smith, R. E., Cumming, S. P., & Smoll, F. L. (2008). Development and validation of the motivational climate scale for youth sport. *Journal of Applied Sport Psychology, 20*, 116–136. https://doi.org/10.1080/10413200701790558

Smith, N., Quested, E., Appleton, P. R., & Duda, J. L. (2016). A review of observational instruments to assess the motivational environment in sport and physical education settings. *International Review of Sport and Exercise Psychology, 9*, 134–159. https://doi.org/10.1080/1750984X.2015.1132334

Smith, R. E., Zane, N. W., & Smoll, F. L. (1983). Behavioral assessment in youth sports: Coaching behaviors and children's attitudes. *Medicine and Science in Sports and Exercise, 15*(3), 208–214.

Sparks, J. R., & Schenk, J. A. (2001). Explaining the effects of transformational leadership: An investigation of the effects of higher-order motives in multilevel marketing organizations. *Journal of Organizational Behavior: The International Journal of Industrial, Occupational and Organizational Psychology and Behavior, 22*(8), 849–869.
Stuntz, C. P., & Spearance, A. L. (2010). Cross-domain relationships in two sport populations: Measurement validation including prediction of motivation-related variables. *Psychology of Sport and Exercise, 11*, 267–274. https://doi.org/10.1016/j.psychsport.2010.02.007
Trudel, P., Côté, J., & Bernard, D. (1996). Systematic observation of youth ice hockey coaches during games. *Journal of Sport Behavior, 19*(1), 50.
Tucker, S., Turner, N., Barling, J., Reid, E. M., & Elving, C. (2006). Apologies and transformational leadership. *Journal of Business Ethics, 63*(2), 195–207. https://doi.org/10.1007/s10551-005-3571-0
Turnnidge, J., & Côté, J. (2016). Observing coaches' leadership behaviours in sport: The development of the coach leadership assessment system (CLAS). *Journal of Sport and Exercise Psychology, 38*, S265.
Turnnidge, J., & Côté, J. (2017). Transformational coaching workshop: Applying a person-centered approach to coach development programs. *International Sport Coaching Journal, 4*, 314–325.
Turnnidge, J., & Côté, J. (2019). Observing coaches' leadership behaviours. The development of the coach leadership assessment system (CLAS). *Measurement in Physical Education and Exercise Science*, 1–13. https://doi.org/10.1080/1091367X.2019.1602835
Vella, S., Oades, L., & Crowe, T. (2013). The relationship between coach leadership, the coach–athlete relationship, team success, and the positive developmental experiences of adolescent soccer players. *Physical Education and Sport Pedagogy, 18*, 549–561. https://doi.org/10.1080/17408989.2012.726976
Vierimaa, M., Turnnidge, J., Evans, B., & Côté, J. (2016). Tools and techniques used in the observation of coach behaviour. In P. Davis (Ed.), *Psychology of effective coaching* (pp. 111–132). New York, NY: Nova Science.
Webster, C. A., Wellborn, B., Hunt, K., Lafleche, M., Cribbs, J., & Lineberger, B. (2013). MPOWER: An observation system for assessing coach autonomy support in high school varsity boys' soccer practices. *International Journal of Sports Science and Coaching, 8*, 741–754. https://doi.org/10.1260/1747-9541.8.4.741

Jennifer Turnnidge is a Post-Doctoral Fellow in the School of Kinesiology and Health Studies at Queen's University. Using both quantitative and qualitative methods, she is interested in exploring how coach-athlete and peer relationships can promote positive development in sport. Specifically, her work focuses on developing, implementing, and evaluating evidence-informed resources to promote high quality interpersonal relationships in sport.

Jean Côté is a professor in the School of Kinesiology and Health Studies at Queen's University in Kingston (Canada). His research interests are in the areas of children in sport, coaching, positive youth development, and sport expertise.

Chapter 6
Coaching Around the World: On Becoming a Profession

Sergio Lara-Bercial, John Bales, and Julian North

Dedication: In memory of the late Prof Pat Duffy who initiated and led many of the developments described in this chapter.

Abstract This chapter explores the notion of the professionalization of coaching and coaches based on the current work and previous experiences of the International Council for Coaching Excellence (ICCE). It provides a historical review of the evolution of the notion of coaching as a profession through key texts published by ICCE as well as existing research and policy documents. The themes identified are then traced through a brief examination of examples from four different countries (Canada, Portugal, Croatia and South Africa) with coaching systems at different stages of maturity. Implications for practitioners, and for the future of coaching as a profession are drawn, and recommendations for the future are proposed.

Keywords Coaching profession · Coach education · Coach development · Coaching systems · Coach recognition · Coaching practice

Coaching Around the World: On Becoming a Profession

Everyday millions of people around the world engage in sport. A small minority do so as professional competitive athletes, whilst for most, sport is a leisure activity linked to enjoyment, self-improvement and physical and mental wellbeing.

S. Lara-Bercial (✉)
Leeds Beckett University and International Council for Coaching Excellence, Leeds, UK
e-mail: s.lara-bercial@leedsbeckett.ac.uk

J. Bales
International Council for Coaching Excellence, Leeds, UK

J. North
Leeds Beckett University, Leeds, UK
e-mail: J.North@leedsbeckett.ac.uk

R. Resende, A. R. Gomes (eds.), *Coaching for Human Development and Performance in Sports*, https://doi.org/10.1007/978-3-030-63912-9_6

Regardless of the purpose of the activity, the common link amongst many sport participants is the presence of a coach who guides their efforts on a day to day basis. Millions of coaches across the globe therefore support participants and athletes reach their personal goals and fulfil their aspirations. In doing so, coaches play a very significant role in society and are increasingly recognised as being an important vocational/occupational group supporting the social fabric (Council of the European Union and the Representatives of Governments of Member States, 2017b).

Coaching matters, not least because they constitute one of the most significant 'workforces' in terms of scale. In Europe, for instance, conservative estimates propose that there are over nine million coaches operating across the 27 Member States (Lara-Bercial et al., 2016a, b). To put this into perspective, across the European Union there are approximately six million teachers, 1.6 million doctors and 1.6 million police officers (Eurostat, 2019). A significant workforce indeed. Yet, the educational background of these nine million coaches, the requirements to carry out their coaching practice, and their working status and remuneration, to mention but a few important factors, vary significantly from country to country and from sport to sport.

Despite the above, it is only over the last twenty or thirty years that governments and international and national sport federations, associations and governing bodies of sport have started to realise the significance of the work coaches do and the implications of the ways in which they are recruited, educated, developed, deployed and employed. It is within this time period that the debate around the professionalisation of coaching and coaches has become a mainstream topic at government and federation level, and that many countries have started to explore the policy and legislative requirements to ensure coaches meet minimum standards of education and practice, as well as facilitating and promoting appropriate recognition and rewards for this professional role.

This chapter will offer an overview of the history and evolution of the question of professionalisation from the perspective of the International Council for Coaching Excellence (ICCE), exploring the key challenges surrounding this very complex topic, and including a selection of case studies covering four different countries (i.e., Canada, South Africa, Croatia and Portugal) which, in facing similar challenges, have arrived at different solutions through varied pathways.

A Brief History of Coaching

A detailed account of the history of sport coaching is beyond the scope of this chapter. However, a brief reflection about the origins and evolution of coaching is important to better understand how we got to where we are in terms of the key challenges that relate to its professionalisation.

Sport coaching is not new. Even if the term coaching does not arise until the 1800s,[1] sport historians argue that forms of coaching have existed throughout human history (Parlebas, 2012). In ancient civilisations these were particularly relevant in the military and in the education of the children of noble and royal families. In addition, "coaches" were also important in training those who took part in popular contests, from the Olympians of Greece, to the gladiators of Rome and the Caber Tossers of the Highlands in Scotland. With the advent of the modern Olympic Games in Athens in 1896 and the birth of mass popular sports such as Football, Rugby, Tennis or Cricket in the late 1800s and their rapid expansion throughout the British Empire, coaching became an important component of the sporting experience. The main driver for the emergence of the figure of the coach was a desire to support performance in competition, which went from gentlemanly educational past-times to life and death like affairs (Mason, 2011). The search for competitive advantages for athletes and teams to maximise the chances of success, was therefore an important influence on the emergence of the coach.

Fast forward 100 years. Competitiveness remained an important driver aided by the professionalisation and monetisation of certain mass sports (i.e., soccer, basketball, tennis, golf, etc) and the opportunity that sport offered to demonstrate global supremacy and feed national pride during the cold-war years (Holt, 1990). These two main mechanisms led to the role of the coach being increasingly valued and acknowledged as central to performance during the twentieth century. As a result, the education and, in some cases, the employment of coaches began to feature as key elements of the global sport system (Green & Houlihan, 2005).

Notwithstanding the above, the coaching landscape on the ground tended to look very different depending on what side of the "iron-curtain" a country was.[2] In western nations, coach education was typically housed within the boundaries of the various national federations or governing bodies of sport and professional coaches were employed by clubs and, in the case of Olympic sports, by the relevant federation. By contrast, in countries in the Eastern block and in most of Asia, coach education was the prerogative of higher education institutions and, therefore, the coaching workforce was solely comprised of university graduates. In the latter, coaches were mainly employed by the state and deployed across national schools of sport, universities and state funded professional teams. Despite these significant

[1]Although different versions exist, most historians agree that the word "coach" originates from the Hungarian "Kocsi". Koscis were a type of horse-drawn carriages built in the town of Kocs in Hungary in the late 1400s that became the gold standard for this type of vehicle around Europe leading to the word being used henceforth to refer to all carriages in many languages (i.e., Kutsche in German, Coche in Spanish and Coach in English). It was only hundreds of years later in the 1800s that the word started to be used by lectures and tutors at Oxford University to refer to the act of taking students on a journey to where they were at the beginning of the studies to where they wanted to be on completion. This terminology was later adopted in the sport context too and hence sport instructors becoming known as coaches in English-speaking countries.

[2]For the purpose of simplification, the West-East divide is used. The authors fully appreciate that this is a much more nuanced and grained picture.

disparities between East and West, there were also similarities: namely, sport and thus coaching, had primarily a very clear performance orientation and a pyramidal structure wherein talent identification and development were the top priority. Sport for all and mass participation had not entered the picture yet. This type of structure and system meant that in most countries, coaching was also a minority occupation given the scarcity of professional opportunities and the lack of a substantial community sport scene.

This all started to change through the 1980s, the 1990s and exploded with the turning of the twenty-first century. Whilst professional sport continued to grow both in following and revenue generating power, more and more, children and adults alike, started to demand opportunities to play sport for all, and not only for the elite athletes or the affluent. A big part of this shift in the West was down to the interest of governments to engage citizens in physical activity to palliate the effects of changing lifestyles: notably sedentarism. With this growing demand, especially in youth sport, federations began to provide education (or in some cases just expanded their exiting offer) for this new audience of mostly volunteer coaches who were needed to service this mass provision.

In the East, the move toward sport for all was delayed for some time and in some cases is still developing. For most countries, nothing changed much until long after the fall of the Berlin wall and the break-up of both the USSR and the Republic of Yugoslavia. Whereas in western nations, the sport system was much more open and flexible and mass participation provision had been increasingly prioritised since the 80s, the sport system in all Eastern countries was completely geared towards high performance sport. The main goal was to identify the most talented young athletes as early as possible to put them through a comprehensive and often scientifically guided process of accelerated development in the hope of Olympic glory (Gilbert, 1979). National sport schools and training centres, and state funded professional sport were the norm. This system all but collapsed in the wake of the massive changes that altered the very core of these countries in the early 1990s. Toomas Tõnise, Secretary General of the Estonian Olympic Committee, explained the evolution of the Estonian coach education system in a keynote at the Inaugural Conference on Sport of the Estonian EU Presidency in 2017.

> When we became an independent nation again, we found ourselves with a very small amount of coaches, and they were all the remnants of the USSR performance-driven university-based system. But a few years into our new path, we now had a vast number of people that wanted to participate in sport and no-one to coach them. We had a big problem and had to develop a coach education and deployment system totally from scratch (Tõnise, 2017).

In addition, a significant phenomenon that has impacted on coaching particularly since the 2000s is the so-called "professionalisation of youth sport" (Farrey, 2008). In certain countries and sports, an arms race has emerged comprising two main elements. On the one hand, federations and clubs have invested heavily in human and capital resource to unearth and nurture talented children as early as possible. It is no longer unusual to, for instance, see children as young as 6 recruited by soccer academies to name one sport. On the other hand, parents have progressively started to spend significantly more time and money to expose children to a variety of sports at an earlier age. In some cases this is driven by a desire to raise physically active children and in others by a pre-established plan to maximise their children's chances to become a professional athlete or a combination of both (Ginsburg, Durant, & Baltzel, 2006). For coaches, these factors have translated into more profitable employment opportunities. These can be through freelance work or through full or part-time employment within clubs and federations, especially in key sports (i.e., soccer, tennis, basketball, golf, swimming, etc).

In sum, the sporting landscape has evolved dramatically from the days of ancient Greece and Rome. Whether in high performance sport, youth performance development, or at the mass participation level, coaching and coaches have become a ubiquitous, important and sought-after commodity. The emergence of the figure of the coach as an important contributor to society has brought with it a series of challenges and opportunities that have the potential to significantly transform the way coaches are educated, developed, deployed and employed. These issues can be considered under the common thread of what has been referred to as the 'professionalisation of coaching'. The rest of the chapter will explore this issue and provide examples of how four different countries have attempted to tackled it.

Conceptual Implications: Professionalisation and the International Council for Coaching Excellence

The professionalisation of coaching has become an important discussion point in research and policy circles. This section of the chapter will provide an abbreviated account of the way the International Council for Coaching Excellence (ICCE) has strived to bring the issue of professionalisation to the fore of the debate at the highest levels of policy-making, and review the key issues identified in the scientific literature as well as in key policy documents in order to map the current landscape.

The ICCE was founded in 1997 with the mission to "Lead and support the development of coaching globally" (ICCE, 2017). As a not-for-profit international cooperative, the ICCE Strategy contains four key pillars: (1) Develop the organisation; (2) Supporting coaching development systems; (3) Giving coaching a strong voice; and (4) Building coaching as a profession. ICCE currently represents over 50 countries and works in partnership with key sporting bodies such as the International Olympic Committee, the World Anti-Doping Agency, The Association of Summer and Winter Olympic International Federations and the European Commission.

As one of the cornerstones of its strategy, the professionalisation of coaching has been a top priority and key driver since the ICCE's inception. In this respect, two main avenues have been explored, namely coach education and development, and coaching policy and regulation. The two are inextricably interwoven and thus will be treated jointly in the following paragraphs.

As mentioned, through the 1980s and 90s, the global coaching landscape started to change, and the coaching community began to consider key emerging phenomena which required attention. Amongst these, for instance:

- The increased world-wide demand for coaching,
- The number of coaches gaining full or part time paid positions,
- The need to promote and yet manage the increased mobility of the coaching workforce,
- The increased accountability and expectations placed on coaches, and
- The disparity between coach education and development systems across the world.

It is probably fair to say that, thanks to the opportunity afforded by the existence of the European Union, which brings together 27 Member States, Europe is the world region where ICCE has worked most intensely and where most joined-up thinking has taken place. The increasing interest and support for the role of the coach in society shown by the European Commission has to a great extent facilitated the pursuit of key areas of work by ICCE and its members and partners. This analysis will therefore start in Europe and expand outwards thereafter.

The main emphasis in Europe over the last 20 years has been around the harmonisation and homogenisation of coaching qualifications to both raise their quality and facilitate coaches' mobility between countries. The first major step on the journey towards the standardisation of coaching qualifications was through the efforts of the European Network of Sport Education (formerly ENSSE).[3] The Coaching Committee of ENSE (which included the European Coaching Council, ICCE's European arm) initiated work in relation to the creation of a common reference point for the development and validation of coaching qualifications. The result of this process was the development of the 5-level structure for coach training in 1999.

The European 5-Level Structure for Coach Education

The 5-level structure intended to: (a) provide a scheme for the analysis of the coach education systems in each of the EU countries; (b) foster the harmonisation and homogenisation of the various education systems; and (c) facilitate the free movement of coaches within the EU. The 5-level structure contained clearly defined levels of coaching practice and education for levels 3, 4 and 5. The framework did not define the nature of levels 1 and 2, recognising they were subject to great variability within and between countries, and between national governing bodies and international federations. In addition, the structure incorporated minimum guidelines in

[3]For a full account of this process please go to https://www.coachlearn.eu/project-reports.html

relation to the education of coaches at each level and stated the required domains of competence and fields of knowledge (Table 6.1).

This framework was promptly adopted across the EU, most notably in Belgium, Denmark, France, Germany, Ireland, Italy, Netherlands, Portugal, Spain and Sweden. In addition, some international federations such as the European Handball Federation and the Federation Equestre Internationale used the structure to design their coach education systems. However, the 5-level framework had some drawbacks. For instance, it led to a stronger focus on the national systems, yet it lacked the unifying and translational power across the EU that was hoped for.

Despite the positive welcome and adoption rate, in the 5 years the 5-level structure was in operation, it became evident that there were elements of the structure that had not been implemented or gained full acceptance within the EU's coaching community. It also struggled to resolve the relationship between vocationally and university-based coach education. Perhaps more importantly, the framework had not fully addressed the coaching capacities needed at each coaching level, nor recognised that coaching expertise is developed not only via formal education, but also through non-formal and informal development opportunities. More specifically, that coaching expertise is derived from many years of on-the-job experience and cannot simply be attained through the completion of a degree course. In addition, the trend towards competence-based learning suggested that the input-based (i.e., number of study hours) 5-level structure needed to be updated. Moreover, in the wider, global context, the ICCE had also indicated the need for a more effective framework to guide the recognition of coaching qualifications between different countries (ICCE, 2000). As a result, in 2004, the 5-level framework was reviewed as part of the broader Aligning a European Higher Education Structure in Sport Science project (AEHESIS) which ran between 2004 and 2007. This review led to the publication of the European Framework for the Recognition of Coaching Competences and Qualifications (EFRCCQ; ENSE, 2007).

The European Framework for the Recognition of Coaching Competences and Qualifications

The EFRCCQ started by defining coaching as:

'The guided improvement, led by a coach, of sports participants and teams in a single sport and at identifiable stages of the athlete/sportsperson pathway.' (p. 5).

It then went on to propose that:

- Coach education should be competence-based and that coaches should be trained to do the job and to fulfil specific coaching roles (i.e., apprentice coach, coach, senior coach and master coach). Therefore, qualifications should be linked to occupational roles rather than levels.
- The format of coach education programmes should include a range of learning modes and be able to recognise prior learning.

Table 6.1 The European 5-Level Structure for Coach Education (ENSE, 1999)

	LEVEL III	LEVEL IV	LEVEL V
Keywords			
Execution	X	X	X
Co-ordination	(X)[a]	X	X
Teaching		X	X
Research		(x)	X
Management		(x)	X
Supervision			X
Strategic Planning			X
Tasks	To coach one or several sportsmen and to co-ordinate a team of several assistant coaches (level I and II). At this level, the coach is mainly concerned with the execution of basic activities.	To coach is responsible for all aspects of the sports practice, of the sport activity organisation. At this level, the coach has reached a higher .level in training. The management and research fields are not a priority at this level.	The coach is now responsible for all aspects of the sports practice, as an "ideas man", promoter and organiser, whilst drawing on multidisciplinary scientific training, both general and specific. At this level, the coach is competent to intervene to all the areas of performance training structure.
Activities			
Training sportsmen	Plans, implements and assesses training	Idem	Devises, plans, executes and assesses the training process
Competition	Assists the sportsmen during competition	Advises the sportsmen during competition	Idem
Talent detection	Participates in identifying talents	Idem	Develops strategy to detect talent
Coaches' training		Supervises coaches internship	Analyses the demands of coaches' training, devises programmes, produces subject Matter
Safety	Takes the necessary steps to ensure the athletes' safety	Idem	Idem
Research	Keeps abreast of progress in knowledge	Idem	Formulates the needs in research and implements research action
Co-ordination of Staff			Co-ordinates a team of contributors

(continued)

Table 6.1 (continued)

	LEVEL III	LEVEL IV	LEVEL V
Promotion sports activity		Organises, manages and promotes the sport activity	Devises, organises and manages the promotion of sport activity
Admission Conditions	Practical experience in the specific sport Level I and II certificates (if they are included in the national training system)	Level III certificate	Secondary education diploma/certificate, which gives access to higher education. Practical experience in the specific sport. (Level III or IV certificate can be taken into account)
Minimum Duration	300 hours 2 years practical coaching experience (validated by the competent authorities)	600 hours idem	2400 hours (4 years of university studies): – 1200 hours of basic education in sport sciences – 1200 hours of specific education in the chosen sport idem

[a]Brackets denote where a competence may be desirable but not compulsory at each level.

- Coaching expertise is built up through a combination of practical experience, knowledge and life-long experiences, formal training programmes and self-reflection.
- Coaches should be supported on a journey of Long-Term Coach Development.
- Coach education should take into account the context and domain in which the coach will work (i.e., participation vs performance) and provide related content and experiences.
- Coach education levels should be underpinned by systems of quality assurance and linked to the emerging National and European Qualifications Frameworks (i.e., recommended between levels 3 and 7 of EQF; European Commission, 2008).
- There is a large number of institutions and sectors involved in coach education and greater cooperation is needed to support recognition and portability of coaching qualifications within and between educational institutes, federations and countries.
- The introduction of a coach licensing system was recommended. As part of the process of moving coaching towards the status of a regulated profession it was recommended that all coaches should hold a sport-specific coaching licence.

Figure 6.1 summarises the key features of the EFRCCQ structure and their relationship to EQF and NQFs.

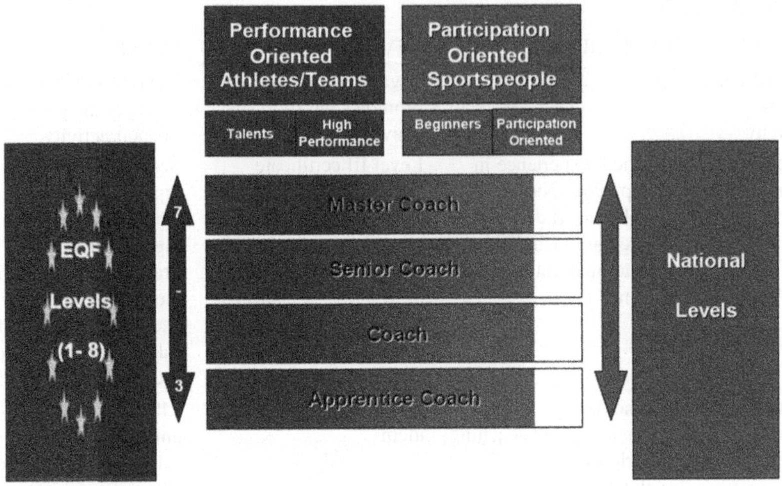

Fig. 6.1 Main features of the EFRCCQ (ECC, 2007)

The EFRCCQ was formally adopted on September 22nd 2007 through the signing of the Rio Major Convention for the Recognition of Coaching Competence and Qualifications whereby all ECC members committed to using the framework as their reference point for the period 2008–2011. The EFRCCQ led to an overhaul of coach education and development in countries such as the UK, Ireland, Portugal and Germany. However, uncertainty over broader developments in educational frameworks in the EU (i.e., the emerging European Qualifications Framework for Lifelong Learning) meant that the new framework encountered a certain level of resistance in others. In addition, the incremental expansion of the EU in 2004 and 2007 to 27 countries introduced novel complexities to the education of coaches. In many of the expansion countries, coach education had been strongly embedded within the higher education sector, and this was not addressed in the context of the EFRCCQ review. The clarification and progressive implementation of the broader developments in Europe's system for the recognition of qualifications in the years following the publication of the EFRCCQ allowed nations and sports to further understand the new landscape and start making the required changes to their systems.

Notwithstanding the above, the Rio Major Convention stipulated that the EFRCCQ would be the main reference point between 2007 and 2011 at which time, a new review should take place to assess its validity and impact and continue to evolve it. Against this backdrop, at a global level, the ICCE had also identified the need to develop a universal framework for the recognition of coaching competences and qualifications to drive the advance of coaching world-wide. It was thus agreed with ECC that the resulting International Sport Coaching Framework (ISCF; ICCE, ASOIF, & LBU, 2013) would also serve as the planned review of the EFRCCQ to continue to guide the development of coaching the EU for the period 2011–2016.

The International Sport Coaching Framework (ISCF)

In 2011, the ICCE brought together a multi-agency working group in conjunction with the Association of Summer Olympic International Federations (ASOIF) and Leeds Beckett University to develop the ISCF using the EFRCCQ as a starting point. The ISCF was conceived as an *'an internationally recognised reference point for the development of coaches globally'* (ICCE, ASOIF, & LBU, 2013, p. 10). The decision to partner with ASOIF recognised the significant role International Federations play in the education and development of coaches, especially in countries with non-existent or emerging coaching systems. The Framework built on the principles introduced by the EFRCCQ, adding further guidance and detail, including considering broader coaching systems features such as recruitment, employment and deployment, as well education systems.

The ISCF defined coaching as *'a process of guided improvement and development in a single sport and at identifiable stages of development'* (p. 14). The addition of "development" to the definition provided by the EFRCCQ signalled the recognition that coaching entails a long-term process of development which goes beyond episodic sessional improvements. The ISCF also further developed the segmentation of sport participation and performance into six coaching 'domains': e.g., Coaches of Children; Coaches of Adolescent Participants; Coaches of Adult Participants; Coaches of Emerging Athletes; Coaches of Performance Athletes; and Coaches of Elite Athletes). Moreover, the Framework evolved the four coaching roles proposed in the EFRCCQ to coaching assistant, coach, senior/advanced coach and master/head coach.

Importantly, the ISCF defined six primary functions which coaches have to fulfil independent of role, context or domain, proposed a set of underlying competences for each of the primary functions, and described the knowledge basis which underpin the competences of the coach. Figure 6.2 provides a summary of these new concepts.

In addition, the ISCF placed greater emphasis on the different ways in which coaches learn (i.e., mediated and unmediated learning opportunities) and thus on the creation of flexible and individualised learning pathways and on the importance and varied role played by coach developers and educators beyond that of knowledge transfer in formal settings. It also set clear guidelines with regards to the alignment of achievement standards (i.e., qualifications) with coaching roles and provided a broad mechanism for the recognition of coaching qualifications and prior learning amongst countries and between different sectors of education.

In sum, the ISCF provided a clear reference point for the creation of coach education and development systems. Since its publication, the Framework has helped governments and institutions realise the importance of coaching and coach education and create new and ambitious plans for its development. For example, it has gained support from organisations such as the International Olympic Committee, the European Commission and the World Anti-Doping Agency. Countries as diverse as the USA, South Africa, Poland, Italy, Japan, Saudi Arabia and the Philippines have used it to guide their efforts in coach education and development.

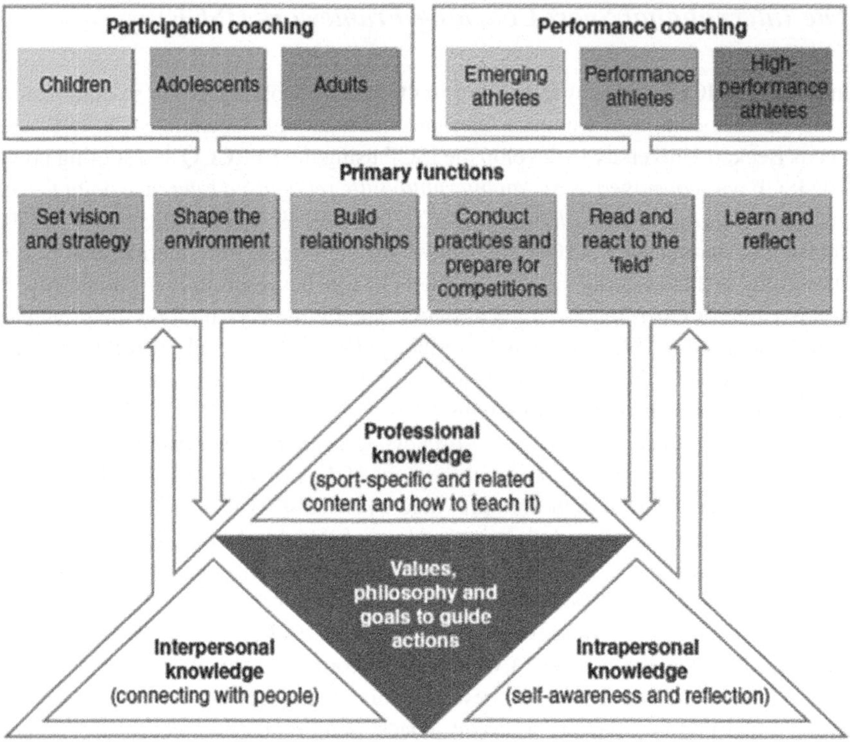

Fig. 6.2 Functional coaching competence and coaching knowledge (reproduced from ISCF v1.2, ICCE, ASOIF, & LBU, 2013)

Despite these advances, a number of challenges to the professionalisation of coaching still remain globally as identified by ICCE President Mr. John Bales in the opening address of the Global Coach Conference 2015 in Vierumaki, Finland (Bales, 2015). These include:

- The identification of coaching as a profession where volunteer and paid coaches can coexist and are trained and recognised in a professional manner. This is progressing apace in some sports and countries, yet still lacks traction and credibility in certain areas.
- The low degree of representation of coaches at the decision-making level in key sporting organisations and institutions. There is thus a significant need to strengthen "the voice of the coach" (Duffy et al., 2013).
- The recognition of prior learning and the compatibility of coaching qualifications between different sectors of the education pathway (i.e. between further and higher education institutions; and between national and international federations and further and higher education).
- The development of occupational standards and minimum standards for the deployment of coaches.

- The creation of enhanced quality assurance in coach education and development, including the potential role of ICCE as an endorsing body, and
- The creation of a platform of higher education institutions involved in coach education.

Moreover, Lara-Bercial et al. (2016a) identified further limitations of the ISCF especially within the EU context:

- Lack of guidance regarding adequate assessment and quality assurance of coaching qualifications.
- Limited guidance in relation to certification, licensing, mutual recognition and recognised prior learning.
- Use of a very functional, reductionist view of competence.
- Low emphasis and guidance on the need for practicum periods.
- Lack of tools to facilitate adoption and implementation.

As a result of this analysis and building on an Erasmus+ grant from the European Commission, the ICCE and ECC embarked in a review of the ISCF from a European Perspective through Project CoachLearn. The outcomes of this project led to the publication of the European Sport Coaching Framework (ESCF, Lara-Bercial et al., 2016a, b).

The European Sport Coaching Framework

The ESCF aimed to tackle some of the issues raised in the analysis of the ISCF and its current use, as well as contextualising it more to the European landscape and structures. In doing so it added the following features:

- Identification of the five drivers of "The Coaching System" as Coaching Practice, Coaching Expertise, Coach Development, Coach Certification and Recognition and Athlete-Centred Vision (see Fig. 6.3 below)
- Emphasis on the nature of coaching as a *'blended occupational area'* (p. 13) wherein volunteer and part and full-time remunerated coaches co-exist and where their proportions vary according to social, cultural and economic factors between countries and sports.
- Further refining of the six primary functions of the coach outlined in the ISCF and the associated task-related competencies.
- Promotion of a broader, expertise-based view of competence wherein the cognitive resources that coaches require to perform the primary functions (i.e., knowledge, representation, retrieval, interpretation, decision-making, anticipation, etc) and how previous experiences shape them, are brought to the fore alongside the more traditional manifestations of "what coaches do". Expertise is thus seen as having 'cognitive, behavioural and social dimensions' (Lara-Bercial et al., 2016a, b, p. 33) with implications for coach education and development (see following bullet point).

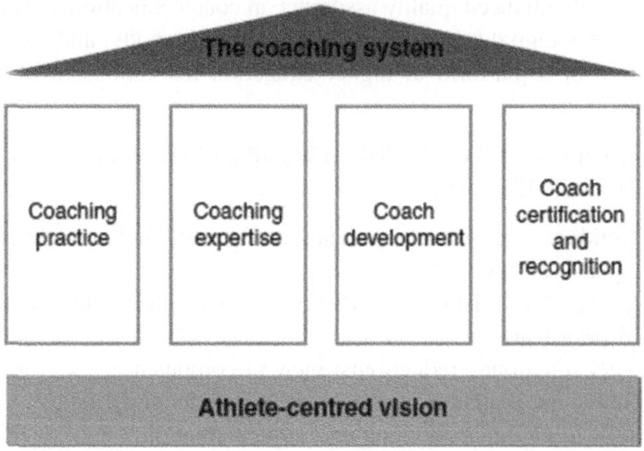

Fig. 6.3 The five drivers of coaching systems (reproduced from ESCF; Lara-Bercial et al., 2016a, b)

- Making a strong case for coaching qualifications to have a practical focus and to allocate enough time and resources to experiential learning modes. This also calls for the elevation and re-consideration of the role and importance of coach developers and how they are selected, recruited and developed.
- Connecting the notion of expertise and degree of responsibility with the previously defined coaching roles, and linking them to national and European qualification frameworks.
- Support for effective coach licensing and tracking systems where appropriate as development, planning and quality assurance tools for the further refinement and building of the coaching system.

All the above have implications for the way coach education, development and employment is construed, planned for and implemented. For this reason, a significant contribution of the ESCF and Project CoachLearn was the development of a comprehensive set of tools[4] to support the application of the above principles:

- Tool 1: Coaching system mapping tool.
- Tool 2: European education landscape factsheet and FAQ.
- Tool 3: Participant development model builder.
- Tool 4: Coaching qualification curriculum builder.
- Tool 5: Qualification mapping and conversion tool.
- Tool 6: Step-by-step guide to the recognition of prior learning and work-based experience.

Seen in total, there has been a considerable evolution of coaching system ideas and tools (to support professional development) over the last 20 years supported by

[4]All tools are downloadable for free from https://www.coachlearn.eu/tools.html

the work of the ICCE. This is especially so in Europe, where the importance of coaching has now been recognised at the highest levels of policy such as in the European Commission's Workplan for Sport 2017–2020 (Council of the European Union and the Representatives of Governments of Member States, 2017a) and the Council Conclusions of the Estonian Presidency in 2017 (Council of the European Union and the Representatives of Governments of Member States, 2017b). Notwithstanding these advances, progress towards professionalisation are still problematic. The ESCF identified varying traditions and expectations about what coaching is, what coaches do and how they should be recognised and rewarded based on three key areas (ESCF, p. 49):

> ***1. The social status of the coach.*** *In some countries and sports, coaches, not just in performance sport but in any domain, are highly esteemed as professionals, similar to teachers and doctors. In other countries and sports, coaching is less valued.*
>
> ***2. The employment status of coaches.*** *The proportion of volunteer, part-time paid and full-time paid coaches varies considerably between countries and sports. As previously mentioned, coaching has therefore been classed as a blended occupational area.*
>
> ***3. The qualification status of coaches.*** *It is estimated that only around four million of the nine million coaches in the European Union meet qualification standards. Again, there is great variability between countries and sports. In some cases, coaches are expected, either by law or by social tradition, to hold minimum qualifications to be able to coach; in others, such expectations do not exist.*

The discussion around the potential for sport coaching to become a profession has, however, not only taken place at policy level. Increasingly, academic literature has considered the pros and cons of professionalisation coming to a variety of conclusions and views. The next section will briefly summarise the major current positions based on North, Piggott, Lara-Bercial, Abraham, and Muir's (2019) recent work.

Professionalisation in the Academic Literature

One of the ways in which academics have tried to make sense of professionalisation is through a 'traits approach'. This approach, rooted in traditional professions such as medicine and law, simply tries to identify the distinct traits that warrant defining an occupational area as a profession. Notably, this method has been used by key authors in recent years (e.g. Duffy et al., 2011; Lyle & Cushion, 2017; Taylor & Garratt, 2008, 2010). Reviewing these literature, North and colleagues identified the following traits of professions:

- Existence of an independent, self-regulating organisation.
- Exclusive membership with clear entry criteria.
- Distinct and shared culture, values, ethics and identity.
- Expertise and effective practice.
- Dedicated and advanced education.
- Distinct underpinning knowledge base.

- Career structures and pathways with associated progression and remuneration.
- Workforce tracking and management via professional registers or licensing systems.
- Recognition of the profession by public office and the law.

When the potential for coaching to become a profession has been measured by the traits approach it has not fared well. Given its blended nature and relatively low maturity as an occupation, in most countries and sports, coaching tends to score poorly against many of the above identified criteria. For these reasons, some authors have openly criticised this approach and suggested it offers an inappropriate vision for coaching change (Cassidy, Jones, & Potrac, 2016; Lyle & Cushion, 2017; Taylor & Garratt, 2013).

For example, Lyle and Cushion (2017) contend that coaching has a very weak profile against the traits and that it has made very small progress towards meeting some of these criteria in the last 40 years (i.e., limited educational practice, low/no barriers for entry, non-existence of self-organising and self-regulating coaching organisations, lack of remuneration and poor levels of recognition at public and policy levels). They conclude that given this alleged low level of development over the last few decades, professionalisation should not be pursued by coaching and instead offered the notion of "professionalism" as an alternative. We will discuss this idea in later sections.

Another critical view of sport coaching as a profession has focused on what North et al. referred to as the 'maligned managerialism' perspective (p. 8; Cassidy et al., 2016; Taylor & Garratt, 2010). These authors propose that attempts to unify and standardise coach education systems are too functionalist, bureaucratic and controlling and that coaching, and coach development cannot be reduced to the codification of professional knowledge and the description and pursuit of a rigid set of competencies. They argue that coaching practice is much more nuanced and socially embedded and therefore based on craft knowledge which is not recognised by current education systems. According to these authors, this type of managerialist approach engenders resentment and frustration amongst coaches and thus should also be avoided in favour of more grounded systems (Cassidy et al., 2016).

In addition, North and colleagues claim that certain authors have argued that progress towards professionalisation is hampered by the apparent lack of separation between different types of coaching occupations (Lyle & Cushion, 2017; Malcolm, Pinheiro, & Pimenta, 2014). These commentators propose that the lack of clear boundaries between different roles (i.e., coaches, instructors and leaders) or between coaching domains and contexts (i.e., participation, performance development, high performance) has held back progression towards professionalisation. As a result, Lyle and Cushion (2017) make a case for a much tighter definition of coaching which encompasses only those working in environments where the optimisation of performance of both individuals and teams is the priority (i.e., performance development or high performance coaching).

In sum, this group of authors advocate for a move away from previous conceptions of professionalisation as system change and instead propose a focus on individual responsibility and service based on the notion of "professionalism". In a nutshell, the idea of professionalism revolves around the key principle that coaches should 'act as professionals' and that this is characterised by a series of attitudes, behaviours, knowledge and skills gained over lengthy periods of formal, non-formal and informal learning grounded in a shared occupation identity and vocation bound by a social contract. The responsibility for professional conduct lies here directly with the individual rather than with any formal structure or body.

Against this background of a relatively damning assessment of the potential for coaching to become a profession, North et al. have offered a counterargument which provides a more optimistic position. First, they contend that the traits approach has been, perhaps erroneously, used as an 'all or nothing analytical tool' (p. 23) which given the sociocultural constraints around coaching, will frequently find it wanting when compared to the traditional professions. They then argue against the polarisation of the debate around the notions of "professionalisation" and individual "professionalism" as two incompatible and mutually exclusive options, rather than parallel components of the same system. Depending on the sociocultural determinants of the system, the level of professionalisation and professionalism within a sport or country will vary. Some countries may be high or low in both or high in one and low in the other. The traits approach, North et al. argue, has therefore much more significant value as a guiding developmental tool rather than as an all or nothing evaluation gauge.

Used in this way, the traits approach provides a much more favourable assessment of the evolution of sport coaching as a profession in recent decades. North and colleagues provide evidence that in many cases coaching has moved forwards in areas such as the creation of an evidence-based body of knowledge, participant-centred systems of education and delivery, a greater emphasis on in situ learning and formative as well as normative assessment, and a general growth trend in the number of available paid positions. For example, anecdotal reports indicate that the percentage of full time employed coaches in the youth academy system in England has gone from 10% to 50% since the advent of the Elite Performance Player Plan in 2011 (Canham, 2019; Premier League, 2011).

The perception of the authors of this chapter, perhaps unsurprisingly given the overlap of writers between the two, is relatively similar to that of North and colleagues. In our work for ICCE, we have continuously been exposed to the efforts of countries, and national and international federations, to professionalise coaching. From the USA and Brazil, to South Africa, Singapore, Saudi Arabia and Australia, and of course all across Europe, stakeholders over the last 20 years have attempted in different ways to professionalise coaching.

It is important to note that our perception of the motivations behind this work is that they are rooted primarily in a desire to improve and guarantee a minimum level of quality and safety within coaching practice for the sake of the millions of participants, especially children, who take part in sport every day around the world.

Regardless of what motivates an organisation or country to take steps towards professionalisation, North et al. contend that given the blended nature of coaching, and the lack of self-organisation on the part of coaches, state-led interventions are required to make significant improvements to coaching. Again, our experience within the ICCE work in this respect is very similar. Over the last 20 years we have seen first-hand dozens of countries and federations lead efforts to professionalise coaching. Each attempt has been different, and each attempt has had successes, setbacks and multiple iterations over the course of its existence. Our conclusion is that, despite the overall common issues framing the problem of professionalisation, how this plays out in the real world depends highly on the history, traditions, and socioeconomical and legislative constraints present in a particular context. When it comes to professionalisation, there is not and never will be a one size fits all solution.

To the contrary, each attempt to professionalise coaching will have to be preceded by a clear agreement on the motivations and extent to which coaching will be professionalised, a careful analysis of the general and idiosyncratic components of the existing system and how they aid or hinder the process, and a significant amount of lobbying and buy-in by stakeholders prior to and all long the process. To illustrate this point and to round up the chapter, what follows are four brief case studies representing four significantly different country-specific attempts to professionalise coaching in Canada, Portugal, South Africa and Croatia.[5] Each case study will succinctly explore four key elements: (a) Motivations for professionalisation; (b) Process undertaken; (c) Current status, key features and rationale; and (d) Impact.

Portugal: The National Plan for Coach Education (2013)

Motivations for professionalisation despite a long-standing tradition of coaching and coach education, coaching was only partially regulated by law in Portugal from 2012. Prior to that, each federation decided if and to what level coaching was regulated and what were the pre-requirements for a person to carry out functions as a coach. This made for a very heterogeneous system where high quality coach education in some sports co-existed with lower standards in others. The Portuguese government, realising the scale of the coaching workforce and taking into account developments within the European Union (i.e., the advent of the European Qualifications Framework and the rise in importance of coaching at European Commission level) decided to overhaul the profession of coaching. The main motivations behind this decision were to more strongly recognise and reward the role of coaches in Portuguese society, to bring coaching at a par with other professions, and to develop homogenous coach education of the highest quality which integrates all educational sectors (i.e., federations, vocational education and higher education). All these goals

[5]The authors would like to thank Mr. Mario Moreira from the Portuguese Institute for Youth and Sport, Mrs. Desire Vardhan from the South African Sport Confederation and Olympic Committee and Miss Adela Čujko and Martina Jeričevič from the Central State Office for Sport in Croatia for their time and their willingness to share their knowledge regarding the evolution of the professionalization of coaching in their respective countries.

fit into the overall goal of providing the highest possible quality of sport experiences for participants and athletes across Portugal.

The process the approval of the Law for the Access to the Activities of the Profession of Sport Coaching (Assembleia da República, 2012; Law 40/2012 of 28th August) was the result of a long and, ambitious process which started with the approval of the Foundational Law for Physical Activity and Sport in 2007 (Assembleia da República, 2007; Law 5/2007 of 16th January). In getting to this point, the role of the Portuguese Coaches Confederation (now "Treinadores Portugal") and the influence of the European Coaching Council to lobby for these changes at ministerial level was very important. A series of consultations with all stakeholders took place to ensure buy-in. This was not an easy task and there was initial resistance, especially from some national federations who did not want to disrupt the status quo. The determination to bring about change at governmental level was key to a successful outcome. The approval of the 2012 law paved the way for the development of the National Plan for Coach Education (Instituto do Desporto de Portugal, 2013) which has since regulated coaching qualifications in Portugal. Recently, an updated Law for the Access to the Activities of the Profession of Sport Coaching has been passed (Assembleia da República, 2019; Law 106/2019 of sixth September) which includes modifications based on the application of the law since 2012.

Key features and current status the 2007 law provided the basic regulation for the practice of coaching and laid the foundation for the development of the law of 2012 and its updated version of 2019. The key features of the law and national plan include

- Coaching recognised as a full profession.
- Clear rules in relation to who can practice the profession of coaching and what are the requirements for deployment.
- Application of regulation to all sport disciplines and levels of practice (i.e., remunerated and non-remunerated and grassroots and performance sport).
- Standardisation of coaching qualifications across all disciplines.
- A move to competence-based education.
- Creation of the Coaching Licence required to be able to coach at any level.
- Monitoring and tracking of coaches via licence database.

Impact despite early resistance, the new system has now been embedded across the country and there are signs that it has had a positive effect. These include a marked upward trend in the number of qualified and licensed coaches since 2013, a broader range of providers of coach education across different sectors (i.e., federations, vocational and higher education), and an increase in sport participation throughout all sports. It is significant too that the amendments to the 2012 law approved in 2019 have been guided by feedback from stakeholders (i.e. education providers, employers and coaches themselves) and are in the main aimed at facilitating access to and progression through the profession, rather than creating additional hurdles or deterrents.

Croatia: The National Plan for Sport 2019–2026

Motivations for (re)professionalisation thanks to its past as a former communist Yugoslav republic heavily influenced by USSR policies, coaching in Croatia has always been regulated as a profession. Access to the profession was, in the main, only given via the completion of a three-year bachelor's degree in sport coaching and it was aimed at the training of Olympic and professional athletes and teams. Since Croatia became an independent country in the 1990s, the sport system has been slowly transitioning from a focus on performance only to a sport-for-all approach. This move has also been motivated by Croatia featuring consistently near the bottom of the EU table for levels of physical activity in the population (Eurobarometer, 2019). The difficulties that Croatia is facing given its history and existing legislation around coaching is that there are not enough coaches qualified to degree level to cater for the interest from a wider participant base. In addition, the current law and economic landscape makes it very difficult and expensive for clubs to employ coaches full time and the government does not offer clubs, nor coaches any incentives to formalise their involvement in coaching. The Croatian government has realised this and has sought to redress the balance of the professionalisation of coaching in its recently approved National Sports Programme 2019–2026 (Central State Office for Sport Croatia, 2019).

The process sport in Croatia has been regulated by a series of Sports Acts. The 2006 Sports Act was in place up until it was superseded by the 2016 Sports Act, which also founded the Central State Office for Sport which has since governed on all matters pertaining to sport since the 2016 law was enacted. The 2016 act perpetuated the requirements of needing a three-year degree to be able to work as a coach and also added a small number of additional routes to be granted access to the occupation. Since coming into being, the suitability of the 2016 sport act was put into question and in the summer of 2019, the National Sport Plan 2019–2026 was approved.

Key Features and Current Status The 2019–2016 Plan proposes to:

- Amend the legal framework related to the pre-requisites to gain employment as a coach. This directive is aimed at removing barriers to becoming and working as a coach and is thus "softening" existing regulation; and to
- Align the educational offer in relation to sport jobs with the needs of the sector, and thus design new tailored programmes to build a suitable workforce.

Impact given its recent adoption, no impact of the National Sport Plan has been measured to date (at the time of writing this chapter in October 2019). However, below is a summary of the expectations as they relate to coaching:

- Increased number of qualified coaches.
- Increased number of part—and full-time employed coaches.
- Decreased number of coaches practising without the relevant qualifications.

- Existence of a greater number of purpose-built coaching qualifications informed by the need of the sector.
- Higher number of authorised coach education providers.

South Africa: The South African Coaching Framework

The motivations following a poor performance in the Beijing 2008 games, the South African Sport Confederation and Olympic Committee (SASCOC) decide to undertake a review of high performance sport. A central part of this review was an audit of coach education provision by sport federations. The survey unearthed a number of issues: heterogenous provision, low levels of professionalism and commitment to coaching within federations, no long-term planning and overreliance on international federation qualifications. These results led to all South African sport stakeholders to agree on the need for a coordinated coaching system, the South African Coaching Framework (SACF) by 2011 (SASCOC, 2011). The vision presented in the Framework is to create an effective, inclusive, cohesive and ethical coaching system that promotes transformation and excellence in an active and winning nation. The main goals of the SACF were to:

- Have more appropriately skilled, qualified and experienced coaches working with our athletes at all stages of their development.
- Ensure all sports coaches have a sports coaching licence that is issued to sports coaching through a SAQA (South African Qualifications Authority) recognized professional body, thus establishing coaching as a profession in South Africa.
- To develop coaches of high performance athletes with a view of improving the performances at the Olympic, Paralympic and world level participation.

The process the creation of the Framework occurred through a process of widespread consultation with national federations, provincial sports councils, SASCOC, government departments, universities, and qualification authorities. Multiple consultations were held over a two-year period to develop and refine the Framework, and to establish the readiness of federations to implement it. To support development and implementation, a number of bodies were created. These include the South African Coaches Commission, the Implementation Group, and the Coaching Standards Group. Central to the process was the constant engagement with international experts from academia and from ICCE. The SACF was launched in November 2011.

Key features and current status in line with the then emerging ISCF, the SACF was built on the premise of providing the right coach for the right participant at the right time and thus advocates for differentiated education for coaches working in different domains of the sport sector. Equally, the Framework adopted a 'long term coach development' approach by recognising that coaches develop over time and that coach education and development opportunities should aim to provide coaches with the competences to fulfil five different coaching roles (i.e., apprentice coach, coaching assistant, coach, senior coach and master coach). Finally, the SACF also recognised the important role that coach developers play and therefore promoted a 'long term coach developer development' model to create a suitable workforce. Perhaps more importantly, the Framework aimed to establish a legislative framework for coaching by 2016. One of the key provisions in this legislation would be the recognition of SASCOC as the Professional Body for Sports Coaching which would award the newly created 'coach licence'. The creation of this new professional body was approved by SAQA in 2016. In 2018, the amendment of the Sport and Recreation Act ratified that anyone wishing to practise as a sport coach, train or guide athletes or participants preparing for any sport shall be a licensed member of the professional body for sports coaching in line with relevant regulations governing sports coaching in the Republic. This amendment provided a much-needed boost towards the professionalisation of sports coaching advocated for in the SACF. More recently, the General Council proposed that the newly created professional body should become independent and be placed outside of SASCOC to guarantee its impartiality. This transition to an independent body took place in June 2019.

Impact although it has been a long and arduous process, the advent of the SACF put in place a number of important structures that appear to have made an impact on the South African coaching system. A very significant marker of progress is the continued growing number of National Federations (61 to date) that have signed up to the Framework and have, to different degrees, aligned their coaching systems to the guidance provided within. Perhaps the greatest achievement has been the creation of the legislative framework and the independent professional body which aims to accelerate the alignment of federations to the SACF and the desire for coaches to belong to this body.

Since the professional body became an independent body in June 2019, hundreds of coaches and coach developers have achieved professional status. This figure is expected to rise significantly in the coming years as more and more coaches seek to have their qualifications and experience recognised. It is important to note that the existence of a growing workforce of professional coach developers points at the impact of the SACF going beyond the professionalisation of coaches, but also of the support structures around them. This was a foundational principle of the SACF which used a systems-based approach as opposed to a qualification-based change process.

In relation to performance impact, since the cataclysmic results of Beijing 2008 where a single silver medal was the full tally of the South African team results have improved. At the London Olympiad 6 medals were brought back to South Africa while in Rio the haul reached 10. Of course, the reasons for this increase are multifaceted, but it is plausible to think that the advent of the SACF and its ramified effects may have contributed to it. The extent of this contribution warrants further investigation.

Canada: The Evolving Professionalization of Coaching

The motivations Coaching in Canada has a very strong tradition of volunteerism, which has made the evolution towards a coaching profession a challenging path that is still incomplete. The roots of attempts to professionalize coaching in Canada date back to the 1980s, when a group of national coaches, dissatisfied with their lack of influence in their federations and feeling that administrators were compromising their technical decisions, created the Canadian Association of National Coaches. It soon became evident that similar issues were at play with coaches at other levels of the sport system (e.g. provincial and club head coaches), and that the goal they were searching for was a coaching profession where coaches would be recognized for their expertise and remunerated accordingly.

The organization thus evolved into the Canadian Professional Coaches Association, with the vision that it would become an independent, self-regulated professional association that serves to "protect the public" by providing a workforce that adheres to high ethical and education standards and disciplines any members who might contravene the code of ethics. A set of professional membership criteria was put in place that included a university degree and experience based qualifications, a code of conduct, and a disciplinary policy and process was established.

Thus, contrary to the situation in Croatia, South Africa, and to an extent, Portugal, the motivation for professionalization was very much at the individual rather than government level. Despite very strong concerns about ethical conduct in sport (i.e., two critical incidents were the Ben Johnson doping scandal in 1988 and a very high profile sexual abuse case involving professional hockey players in 1995), the government was not prepared to regulate coaching. This was complicated by the fact that in Canada professions are a provincial responsibility, but no province was willing to move towards regulating coaching.

Professional associations in other fields (law, medicine, etc) are monopolies, where only members of the professional association are legally entitled to practice. In Canadian coaching, where the majority of coaches are volunteers, this created the fear that this volunteer workforce would be lost or alienated, and that professionalising coaching would result in much higher costs to participate in sport—a fear that is born out in sports that have a tradition of paying their coaches (e.g. swimming, figure skating, equine, etc).

The process In the absence of provincial legislation to regulate coaching, the Canadian Professional Coaches Association, which was re-branded as Coaches of Canada, protected the title "Chartered Professional Coach" (ChPC), and established professional-level qualifications and regulations for coaches to be able to use this title. This effectively serves to differentiate coaches with the higher educational standards and commitment to ethical standards. However, it is not a legal requirement to hold these qualifications or be a member of a professional body, and therefore, enforcement of professional including ethical standards has proven exceptionally difficult to implement and maintain—i.e., when a coach breaks the code of conduct, the relevant sport association does not have jurisdiction over the coach if he or she is not a member, and since membership is not mandatory the coach can often avoid being disciplined.

Key features and current status Although an independent professional association no longer exists—Coaches of Canada was folded into the CAC (the Coaching Association of Canada, a government funded organization with the mandate to lead the coach education system in Canada) in 2014—coaches are encouraged to earn the ChPC designation, that "tells employers, athletes, and parents that you have the knowledge, experience, and ethical standards to coach in a professional manner in a National Coaching Certification Program stream or context." (CAC website).

The ChPC is therefore the professional designation for sport coaches in Canada. It states that a professional coach (CAC website):

- Is trained to deliver expert and safe coaching, which benefits everyone,
- Has learned the shared body of coaching knowledge,
- Follows ethical standards, and
- Is accountable to stakeholder expectations (sports organization and community).
  Figure 6.4 describes the expectations of a professional coach and the various pathways to achieve the ChPC designation (note that pathways 1, 2 and 4 require a university degree and pathway 3 an NCCP—tailored advanced coaching diploma).

Impact Although the attempt to develop a regulated profession with an independent professional association has not been successful, the efforts have resulted in a number of significant developments:

- **Development of professional standards for coaches:** clear expectations for the education and experience requirements, and acceptable ethical conduct of professional level coaches have been established. These expectations are being actively promoted by the Coaching Association of Canada.
- **Protected title:** the use of ChPC as a quality symbol to designate a professional standard of practice.
- **Linkage to higher education:** according to Marcotte (1998), the development of the largely volunteer-based National Coaching Certification Program resulted in a decline in university standards for coaches. The push for professionalization has re-kindled the importance of higher education for professional level coaches.
- **Appreciation of the need to license coaches:** in the absence of government legislation to regulate coaching, sport organizations are establishing licensing processes that provides mechanisms to promote continuous professional development of coaches as well as to remove unethical ones.
- **A foundation for future professionalization:** The sport environment in Canada has changed dramatically since the initial efforts to professionalize coaching were undertaken, with many more paid coaches at all levels and in a much wider range of sports. In addition, the concept of a blended profession as put forward by ICCE has encouraged a new viewpoint into how volunteer and paid coaches can support and complement each other. Although there are no immediate plans to revitalize a professional body in Canada, the experience of past efforts combined with the changing coaching landscape means it should not be ruled out in the near future.

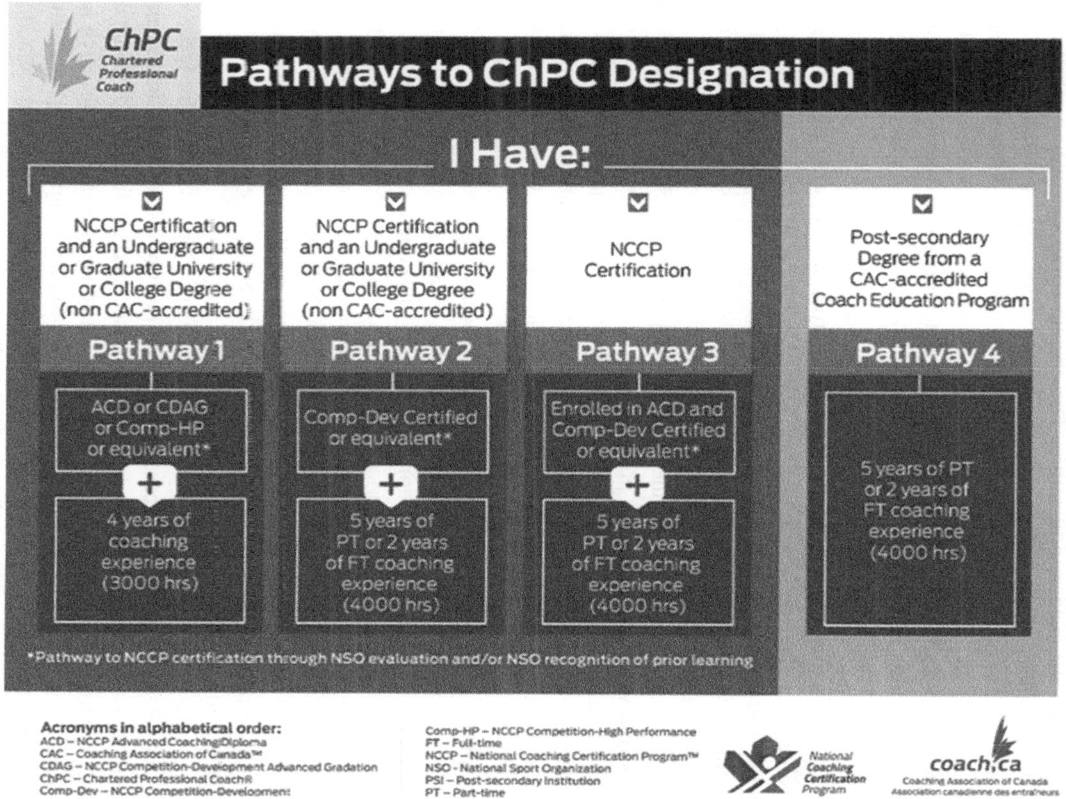

Fig. 6.4 Pathway to Chartered Professional Coach Designation (Coaching Association of Canada, 2019; reproduced with permission from Coach Canada)

Key Points

This chapter has offered a brief history of attempts to facilitate the development of coaching, including coaching as a profession, through the work of the ICCE and ECC. It has also briefly analysed the current debate around the professionalisation of coaching within the academic literature. The chapter concluded with a set of four short case studies examining the evolution and current status of the professionalisation of coaching in four different countries across three continents. After this full circle journey from history to policy analysis, to academia and back to the applications of all the above on the ground, the authors would like to share some closing conclusions and parting thoughts that we hope will be of use primarily to coaches but also other key stakeholders:

- In our view, and as the case studies prove, the professionalisation of coaching is possible given the right conditions.
- Having said the above, what these conditions are and what professionalisation may mean, will depend strongly on the historical traditions linked to coaching in a particular context, and on the socioeconomical circumstances.
- Moreover, the experience of the authors supporting coaching organisations around the world suggests that professionalisation "is not for everyone" and it is not a quick process. Systems must be ready for professionalisation—the way must be paved, political will must exist and adequate resources must be made available. Only then professionalisation efforts should occur. Coaches, however, can play an active role in this preparation work.
- If the process of professionalising coaching is placed on a continuum from coach-led to government-led, the existing examples of success appear to point at governments' desire for professionalisation and subsequent interventions as the key success factor. In our experience, a sector of the coaching workforce may resist this attempts to professionalise the occupation because of the financial, fiscal and administrative implications for coaches. Yet, our work also shows how in the long term, the system tends to re-balance itself as the new structures become embedded and become part of the fabric of the overall sport structure of the country or federation.
- In line with the above, professionalisation is a very political issue. For it to be effective, it seems that in most cases, legislation must be passed and comprehensive frameworks and systems to deal with the associated implications developed. Gaining political support early is paramount. In some successful cases such as Portugal, coaches associations have been shown to play a significant part in this process and thus coaches may wish to consider joining their relevant association.
- The case studies also suggest that professionalising coaching takes time and thus coaches, policy makers and system builders should be mindful of early signs of resistance from stakeholders or setbacks of the process.

Conclusion

This chapter has shown how the professionalisation debate is more alive than ever before. The growing status of sport and coaching in twenty-first century society has catapulted the issue of the regulation of coaching to the forefront of many international and national organisations' priorities. The chapter shows that whether or not coaches, federations or governments have a desire for regulation and professionalisation, the evolution of the sport system, and the ever higher demands and expectations placed on coaches, have created a trend towards regulation and system improvement. At the very least, organisations and stakeholders have started considering how these issues could play out in their specific environments.

The chapter has shown some examples of how these processes have developed in different countries. There are many more examples globally and ICCE is currently working on a variety of projects like the Erasmus+ co-funded CoachForce21 and PEAK projects to further investigate this phenomenon. Over the next few years, ICCE will develop a position statement on this issue and a set of tools to support countries and federations explore their context and propose tailored solutions to this dilemma.

References

Assembleia da República. (2007). *Foundational Law for Physical Activity and Sport #5/2007 (16th January). Diário da República, 1.ª série — N.° 11* (pp. 356–363). Assembleia da República: Lisboa.

Assembleia da República. (2012). *Sport Coaching Law #40/2012 (28th August). Diário da República, 1.ª série — N.° 166* (pp. 4753–4758). Assembleia da República: Lisboa.

Assembleia da República. (2019). *Sport Coaching Law #106/2019 (9th June). Diário da República, 1.ª série — N.° 171* (pp. 51–68). Assembleia da República: Lisboa.

Bales, J. (2015). *The challenges for coaching.* Vierumaki, Finland: Opening address of ICCE's Global Coach Conference.

Canham, M. (2019). *Personal communication at Premier League Coach Development event.* Nottingham, UK. Premier League.

Cassidy, T., Jones, R. L., & Potrac, P. (2016). *Understanding sports coaching: The pedagogical, social and cultural foundations of coaching practice* (3th ed.). London: Routledge.

Central State Office for Sport Croatia. (2019). *National Sport Programme 2019–2026.* Zagreb: Central State Office for Sport.

Coaching Association of Canada. (2019). *Pathway to chartered professional coach designation.* Retrieved from https://www.coach.ca/apply-now-or-renew-p158441#ELIGIBILITYCRITERIA.

Council of the European Union and the Representatives of Governments of Member States. (2017a). *European Union Work Plan for Sport 2017–2020.* Brussels: Council of the European Union.

Council of the European Union and Representatives of Government States. (2017b). *Conclusion of the Estonian presidency on the role of the coach in 21st century society.* Brussel: Council of the European Union.

Duffy, P., Hartley, H., Bales, J., Crespo, M., Dick, F., Vardhan, D., … Curado, J. (2011). Sport coaching as a 'profession': Challenges and future directions. *International Journal of Coaching Science, 5*(2), 93–123.

Duffy, P., North, J., Curado, J., & Petrovic, L. (2013). *Coach Net: The further development of a coordinated network for Sport Coaching in Europe*. A report for the European Union. Leeds: Leeds Metropolitan University and the International Council for Coaching Excellence. Duffy et al., 2011–Coaching as a blended profession.

ECC & ENSE. (2007). *Review of the EU 5-level structure for the recognition of coaching qualifications*. Cologne: European Coaching Council & European Network of Sport Education.

ENSE. (1999). *Report on sports occupations in the European Union: European structures for the 5-levels of coach training* (2nd ed.). Cologne: European Network of Sport Education.

European Commission. (2008). *The European Qualifications Framework for Lifelong Learning*. Luxembourg: Publications Office of the European Union.

Eurostat. (2019). *Data on the number of teachers, doctors and police and armed forces in the EU*. Retrieved from https://ec.europa.eu/eurostat/home?

Farrey, T. (2008). *Game on: The all-american race to make champions of our children*. New York: ESPN.

Gilbert, D. (1979). *The miracle machine*. New York: Putnam.

Ginsburg, R. D., Durant, S., & Baltzel, A. (2006). *Whose game is it anyway?* Chicago: Mariner Books.

Green, M., & Houlihan, B. (2005). *Elite sport development: Policy learning and political priorities*. Abingdon: Routledge.

Holt, R. (1990). *Sport and the British: A modern history*. Oxford: Oxford University Press.

ICCE. (2000). *The Magglingen declaration*. Magglingen: ICCE.

ICCE. (2017). *ICCE: Celebrating 20 years of global coaching development*. Leeds: International Council for Coaching Excellence.

ICCE, ASOIF, & LBU. (2013). *The international sport coaching framework v1.2*. Champaign, IL: Human Kinetics.

Instituto do Desporto de Portugal. (2013). *Programa nacional de formação de treinadores*. Lisboa: Instituto do Desporto de Portugal.

Lara-Bercial, S., North, J., Petrovic, L., Oltmanns, K., Minkhorst, J., & Hämäläinen, K. (2016a). *Report on qualification frameworks and employment and mobility tools in the European Union: Implications for sport coaching and the european sport coaching framework*. Coach Learn: Leeds.

Lara-Bercial, S., North, J., Petrovic, L., Oltmanns, K., Minkhorst, J., & Hämäläinen, K. (2016b). *European Sport Coaching Framework*. Champaign, IL: Human Kinetics.

Lyle, J., & Cushion, C. (2017). *Sports coaching concepts: A framework for coaches' practice*. London: Routledge.

Malcolm, D., Pinheiro, C., & Pimenta, N. (2014). Could and should sport coaching become a profession? Some sociological reflections. *International Sport Coaching Journal, 1*(1), 42–45.

Marcotte, G. (1998). La professionnalisation des entraineurs et entraineures en sport. *Avante, 4*(3), 148–153.

Mason, T. (2011). *Sport in Britain: A social history*. Cambridge: Cambridge University Press.

North, J., Piggott, D., Lara-Bercial, S., Abraham, A., & Muir, B. (2019). The professionalization of sport coaching. In R. Thelwell & M. Dicks (Eds.), *Professional advances in sports coaching: Research and practice* (pp. 3–21). London: Routledge.

Parlebas, P. (2012). *Diccionario de praxiologia motriz*. Madrid: Paidotribo.

Premier League. (2011). *The elite player performance plan*. London: Premier League.

SASCOC. (2011). *The South African coaching framework*. Johannesburg: SASCOC.

Taylor, W. G., & Garratt, D. (2008). *The professionalisation of sports coaching in the UK: Issues and conceptualisation*. Leeds: Sports Coach UK.

Taylor, W. G., & Garratt, D. (2010). The professionalisation of sports coaching: Relations of power, resistance and compliance. *Sport, Education and Society, 15*(1), 121–139. https://doi.org/10.1080/13573320903461103

Taylor, W. G., & Garratt, D. (2013). Coaching and professionalisation. In P. Potrac, W. Gilbert, & J. Denison (Eds.), *Routledge handbook of sports coaching* (pp. 27–39). London: Routledge.
Tõnise, T. (2017). The evolution of sport coaching in Estonia. In *Oral communication, Sport Conference of the Estonian Presidency of the European Union*. Tallin: Estonia.

Sergio Lara-Bercial is a Reader in Sport Coaching in the Carnegie School of Sport of Leeds Beckett University and the Manager for Strategy & Development for the International Council for Coaching Excellence. Sergio has extensive international experience in the development and evaluation of coach education systems and has consulted for organisations around the globe. Sergio is also a youth performance coach who has led basketball teams to 17 national and international titles.

John Bales is the President of the International Council for Coaching Excellence, former CEO of the Coaching Association of Canada and former Olympic coach. Under John's leadership, ICCE has developed widely adopted reference documents such as the International Sport Coaching Framework, the International Coach Developer Framework and the International Coaching Degree Standards. John regularly consults with multiples stakeholders across the globe to support the development of coaching as profession.

Julian North is a Reader in Sport Coaching in the Carnegie School of Sport of Leeds Beckett University and the Director of its Research Centre for Sport Coaching. He has been a social and sport researcher for nearly 30 years in a variety of policy, practice and academic roles in the UK and Australia. Julian has authored numerous articles, books, book chapters, and reports in sport, coaching and beyond. He is the current acting Chair of the Research Committee of the International Council for Coaching Excellence.

Part II
Acting as a Sports Coach

Chapter 7
Coaching Profession: Acting as a Coach

Paul Potrac, Brian Gearity, Adam Nichol, Callum Morgan, and Edward Hall

Abstract Through the adoption of a dramaturgical perspective, this chapter positions coaching as being somewhat akin to a theatrical social performance. From this standpoint, coaching work entails much more than the routine application of pre-packaged knowledge and methods. It also requires coaches to carefully consider (and reflect upon) their interactions with others, inclusive of how they manage and display various emotions within the coaching environment ((Cassidy, T., Jones, R., & Potrac, P., *Understanding sports coaching: The social, cultural and pedagogical foundations of coaching practice*. Routledge, London, 2016); (Nelson, L., Potrac, P., Gilbourne, D., Allanson, A., Gale, L., & Marshall, P., *Sociology of Sport Journal 19*:19-40, 2014)). In terms of its structure, the chapter begins by introducing the notion of dramaturgy. This background material is followed by an overview of the classic dramaturgical writings of Erving Goffman and Arlie Russell Hochschild. Here, we highlight some essential features of their respective theorising that can stimulate critical reflection upon the dramaturgical aspects of coaching ((Cassidy, T., Jones, R., & Potrac, P., *Understanding sports coaching: The social, cultural and pedagogical foundations of coaching practice*. Routledge, London, 2016)). After the theoretical backdrop is presented, the focus then shifts to reviewing the (limited) available literature addressing how coaches engage in various acts of impression and emotion management to achieve their goals. In concluding the chapter, the main

P. Potrac (✉)
Department of Sport, Exercise and Rehabilitation, Northumbria University, Newcastle, UK

School of Public Health, Physiotherapy and Sport Science, University College Dublin, Dublin, Ireland
e-mail: paul.potrac@northumbria.ac.uk

B. Gearity
School of Professional Psychology, University of Denver, Denver, CO, USA
e-mail: Brian.Gearity@du.edu

A. Nichol · C. Morgan · E. Hall
Department of Sport, Exercise and Rehabilitation, Northumbria University, Newcastle, UK
e-mail: adam.nichol@northumbria.ac.uk; callum.morgan@northumbria.ac.uk; edward.hall@northumbria.ac.uk

R. Resende, A. R. Gomes (eds.), *Coaching for Human Development and Performance in Sports*, https://doi.org/10.1007/978-3-030-63912-9_7

arguments are summarised and a number of ‘key points’ that coaches (and coach educators) may wish to critically reflect upon are presented.

Keywords Dramaturgy · Impression management · Emotion management

Coaching Profession: Acting as a Coach

> A great deal of the work of organisations - decision making, the transmission of information, the close co-ordination of physical tasks - is done face-to-face, requires being done in this way, and is vulnerable to face-to-face effects. Differently put…as agents of social organisations of any scale, from states to households, can be persuaded, cajoled, flattered, intimidated, or otherwise influenced by effects only achievable in face-to-face dealings (Goffman, 1983, p. 3).

> What perhaps matters most then, is not exactly what the coach does, but how others perceive the impression given by the coach (Cassidy, Jones, & Potrac, 2016, p. 99).

In recent years, scholars have progressively questioned the sanitised and unproblematic representations of coaching that have traditionally dominated the coaching literature and much coach education provision (e.g., Cassidy et al., 2016; Jones & Wallace, 2005; Potrac, Jones, Gilbourne, & Nelson, 2013; Potrac, Mallett, Greenough, & Nelson, 2017). By addressing some of the ways in which coaching is characterised by ideological diversity, poor co-ordination, and the potential for conflict between social actors (e.g., coaches, athletes, administrators, and parents, among others), this work highlights the limitations of viewing coaching as a linear activity that ought to be practiced only in relation to bio-scientific, technical and tactical knowledges (Cassidy et al., 2016; Jones & Wallace, 2005). Indeed, coaching has, instead, been increasingly positioned as a complex, social endeavour; one where coaches are engaged in a fluid and dynamic process of obtaining, maintaining, and advancing the trust, confidence and support of various situational stakeholders (Cassidy et al., 2016; Gale, Ives, Nelson, & Potrac, 2019; Jones, 2019; Potrac et al., 2017). From this standpoint, coaches’ interactions and relationships with contextual stakeholders are seen to not only influence the space, resources and time afforded to them to implement their coaching philosophy, but also the working climate in which they seek to achieve their coaching goals (Cassidy et al., 2016; Thompson, Potrac, & Jones, 2015). Rather than being straightforwardly generated, secured and advanced, the support coaches receive and the influence they have is arguably grounded in their dynamic relationships with others. That is, they are dependent on how athletes, support staff, administrators, parents and sponsors experience, interpret, and evaluate the coach’s choices and actions; all of which can change over time and from situation to situation (Cassidy et al., 2016; Jones, Potrac, Cushion, & Ronglan, 2011; Potrac, Jones, & Nelson, 2014).

Through the adoption of a dramaturgical perspective, this chapter positions coaching as being akin to a theatrical social performance; coaches perform individually and/or collectively in front of a scrutinising audience, who evaluate their actions in relation to the qualities and attributes that a coach claims and is expected to possess (Cassidy et al., 2016). Importantly, this audience evaluation shapes the nature of future interactions and engagements, the influence a coach has on others, and the ongoing treatment of the coach, as well as the ways a coach feels about his or her self in the role (Edgley, 2013; Jones et al., 2011; Jones, Armour, & Potrac, 2004; Potrac et al., 2017). From this standpoint then, coaching work entails much more than the routine application of pre-packaged knowledge and methods. It also requires coaches to carefully consider (and reflect upon) their interactions with others, inclusive of how they manage and display various emotions within the coaching environment (Cassidy et al., 2016; Nelson et al., 2014).

In terms of its structure, this chapter begins by briefly introducing the notion of dramaturgy. This background material is followed by an overview of the classic dramaturgical writings of Erving Goffman and Arlie Russell Hochschild. We do not provide an exhaustive overview of these works or their associated critiques. Instead, we highlight some essential features of their respective theorising that can stimulate critical reflection upon the dramaturgical aspects of coaching (Cassidy et al., 2016). After the theoretical backdrop is provided, the focus shifts to reviewing the limited available literature addressing how coaches engage in various acts of impression and emotion management to achieve their goals. Finally, the chapter concludes by summarising the key arguments presented in this chapter.

What Is Dramaturgy?

Originally a theatrical term, dramaturgy refers to the ways in which actors (and other theatrical professionals) stage and adapt performances and texts to best communicate a work's meanings to an audience (Schulman, 2017). Rather than focusing on imaginary characters and fictional texts, those adopting a dramaturgical perspective in sociology are primarily concerned with examining nonfiction performances (Schulman, 2017). That is, how "people stage performances in real life" (Schulman, 2017, p. 5). Here, specific attention is given to social actors' appearances (i.e., dress and other features that identify the actor's role, status or condition), manner (i.e., the actor's attitude towards a role and how they are playing the role- being haughty, meek or aggressive among others), the use of props (objects that are used to support a desired image in the eyes of others), and the staging of activity (the physical layout and other background items) (Scott, 2015).

According to Schulman (2017), dramaturgical inquiry has much to offer to our understanding of social life, both theoretically and practically. For example, he eloquently argued that this perspective can allow us to: (a) understand 'how 'and 'why' we might judge others based on their appearances and performances; (b) become more aware of how our sense of self may arise and stand out in our engagements with others; (c) be a more thoughtful people watcher, and; (d) appreciate the many social influences on how we and others act and responsively treat each other. Importantly, for us at least, Schulman (2017) also suggested two further benefits to the dramaturgical study of everyday life. The first is concerned with how dramaturgical frameworks can help us critically consider how people (such as coaches) use various impression management tactics as they attempt to exercise influence and power on and through others (e.g., athletes, support staff, administrators, parents) in everyday social and organisational life. Indeed, he believes dramaturgical inquiry allows us to document and consider the various ways in which people attempt to influence the thoughts, feelings and actions of others and, relatedly, the consequences of these efforts. He also suggested that our individual skill set stands to benefit from being able to incorporate dramaturgical knowledge into everyday lives. In the context of sport coaching, these arguments resonate strongly with us, especially in terms providing a meaningful vocabulary for helping coaches to understand and develop the 'soft' (i.e., being able to make people feel valued, being seen to be trustworthy) and 'hard' (e.g., dealing with pressure or resistance from others) interpersonal skills that are increasingly recognised as an important feature of coaches' efforts to successfully influence the thoughts, feelings and actions of others (Potrac, 2019).

Theoretical Framework: The Dramaturgical Theorising of Erving Goffman and Arlie Russell Hochschild

The theoretical framework deployed in this chapter is principally informed by the respective works of Erving Goffman (1959, 1969a, b) and Arlie Russell Hochschild (Hochschild, 1983, 1997, 2000, Hochschild & Machung, 2003). Goffman is widely lauded as the leading exponent of dramaturgical theorising in sociology. In particular, his text addressing the *Presentation of the Self in Everyday Life* (Goffman, 1959) is recognised as making a ground-breaking contribution to our understanding of how, in the quest to fulfil societal and organisational expectations, individuals frequently "play roles, negotiate situations, and to a larger extent are forced to be actors" (Marsh, Keating, Eyre, Campbell, & McKenzie, 1996, p. 73; Jones et al., 2011). In this book, Goffman's nuanced analysis of everyday social life provided rich empirical and conceptual insights into how individuals and groups seek to present themselves to others, the tactics they utilise in an attempt to manage the impressions they give off, and, relatedly, protect or advance the version of the self that is exhibited to others (Cassidy et al., 2016; Jones et al., 2011). At the heart of Goffman's dramaturgical writings is the view that individuals are not completely free to choose the version of the self that they wish to have others accept (Jones et al., 2011). Rather, they obliged to "define themselves in congruence with the statuses, roles, and relationships that they are accorded by the social order" (Branaman, 2000; p. 48). Importantly, however, he argued that our thoughts, actions and feelings are not entirely determined by society. We are not the passive recipients of socialisation. We are, instead, able to manipulate social encounters and situations strategically, especially in terms of the impression that others form of us. Here, Goffman eloquently noted:

> an individual does not. . .merely go about his [sic] business. He goes about constrained to sustain a viable image of himself in the eyes of others. Some local circumstances always reflect upon him, and since these experiences will reflect upon him, and since these circumstances will vary unexpectedly and constantly, footwork or rather self-work, will be continuously necessary (Goffman, 1971, p. 185).

For Goffman (1959) then, face-to-face interaction plays a pivotal role in our efforts to influence how others think about and experience our actions, intentions, and, indeed, competency.

Schulman (2017) draws our attention to six key principles that underpin Goffman's dramaturgical theorising. These are:

- People are performers who use impression management to convey a persona or sense of who they are to others.
- People work in teams and collectively express the characteristics of social situations.
- People perform in different social spaces referred to as regions of performance.
- People prioritise giving credible performances.
- People avoid communicating 'out of character' and taking any actions that could contradict the requirements of a performance and spoil it.
- When people produce 'spoiled' (e.g., failure to demonstrate the characteristics and attributes associated with a social role or position) performances or someone spoils their performances, they try to repair any damage by engaging in curative steps.

For Goffman (1959), performance incorporates "all the activity of an individual that occurs during a period marked by his [sic] continuous presence before a set of observers and which has some influence on the observers" (p. 32). In essence, Goffman (1959) argued that our performances matter. They are pivotal in our attempts to navigate the social landscape and achieve our desired goals, as they influence how we connect, bond and generally get along (or not) with others (Jones et al., 2004). Our performances come with no guarantees in terms of their outcomes or influence on others, however. Here, Goffman (1959) distinguished between calculated impressions and secondary impressions. While the former refers to an impression of the self that an individual purposefully seeks to convey to others, the latter is concerned with the impression that the individual leaves in the mind of these others (Schulman, 2017). This may or may not include the calculated impression that an individual sought to create (Leary, 1995; Schulman, 2017).

Related to the notion of performance is Goffman's concept of 'front'. This refers to "that part of an individual's performance which regularly functions in a general and fixed fashion to define the social situation for those who observe performance" (Goffman, 1959, p. 22). For Goffman (1959), the front is comprised of the appearance, manner, props and setting that were introduced in the previous subsection on dramaturgy. In constructing and managing a particular front, an individual may be required to consistently exhibit and instantaneously demonstrate the attributes that he or she claims for the front during interaction with others in order maintain it (Cassidy et al., 2016). In illustrating the front in action, Goffman (1959, p. 30) gave the example of a baseball umpire:

> [i]f a baseball umpire is to give the impression that he [sic] is sure of his judgement, he must forgo the moment of thought which might make him sure of his judgement. He must give an instantaneous decision so that the audience will be sure of his judgement.

Goffman's dramaturgical framework also addresses the regions in which our social performances occur. He labelled these the front and back regions (or stages). The front region is the label give to the place where our performances occur. In coaching, for example, this could be the training ground or the meeting room, among other settings. In the front region, the actors seek to present an idealised image of themselves to an audience whilst simultaneously seeking to conceal aspects that might discredit the impression they are seeking to give off. The back region, in contrast, refers to the place or places where they can step out of character and, to some degree, relax or drop the front that is presented in the front region. It is also the setting where actors can plan, rehearse, and reflect upon their performances. Importantly, the audience is normally not allowed access to the back region.

Goffman (1959) recognised that performances are not just conducted by individuals; They are also staged by groups or teams. For Goffman (1959, p. 85), a performance team refers to "any set of individuals who co-operate in staging a single routine" that seeks to create a desired and unified team impression (Scott, 2015). This concept has considerable utility for sports coaching, especially as many coaches are required to create and sustain performances with, and for, collaborators (e.g., head coach, assistant coaches, and support staff), as well as for their audience (e.g., athletes, parents, and administrators) (Schulman, 2017). According to Goffman (1959), actors engaged in team performances strive to avoid incidents, which are "unexpected events that disrupt the version of reality fostered by the participants and make the performance grind to an embarrassing halt" (Scott, 2015, p. 88). These can include unmeant gestures (i.e., an actor gives off a contradictory impression), inopportune intrusions (i.e., when an audience member catches a performer out of character in the back region), faux pas (i.e., when a performer unthinkingly endangers the image that the group wishes to project) and causing a scene (i.e., a performer explicitly challenges the consensus projected by the team) (Scott, 2015).

To prevent these incidents from happening (as much as is possible), Goffman (1959) conceptualised three defensive attributes and strategies that individuals and groups could draw upon. These are dramaturgical loyalty, dramaturgical discipline, and dramaturgical circumspection. Dramaturgical loyalty refers to the moral obligation that a performer has to not betray the shared secrets of the team (e.g., the planning of their show, the backstage realities, and their off-stage identities) (Scott, 2015). Dramaturgical discipline, meanwhile, concerns "an actor's careful management of their personal front so as to appear nonchalant, while concealing the extensive work that they are doing to create this very impression" (Scott, 2015,

p. 88). Dramaturgical discipline, then, entails an actor remembering and positively executing their role in the group's performance, managing their own verbal and non-verbal communication, carefully monitoring the team's performance as a whole, and having the presence of mind to prevent any incidents from occurring (Scott, 2015). Finally, dramaturgical circumspection refers to the "exercise of prudence, care, and honesty" in the staging of a team performance (Goffman, 1959, p. 212). This includes putting measures in place to avoid or minimise any anticipated incidents and preparing for likely contingencies (Scott, 2015). Dramaturgical circumspection can be exercised in a variety of ways. This can, for example, include a head coach limiting the number of assistant coaches and support staff and selecting only those whom he or she trusts. This could be done to "minimise the risk of any [team] member acting improperly, embarrassingly or treacherously" (Scott, 2015, p. 89). Another action may be the use of straightforward and well-rehearsed scripts that minimise the possibility of a performer "fluffing their lines and blowing the team's cover" (Scott, 2015, p. 213). For example, an assistant coach contradicting or appearing confused when relaying agreed messages, which were prepared in the back region with the head coach, to athletes in a team meeting.

Influenced by the dramaturgical writings of Goffman, Hochschild's (1983, 1997, 2000; Hochschild & Machung, 2003) theorising charts the interplay between impression management, social interaction and emotion (Potrac & Marshall, 2011). Indeed, in her now classic text, *The Managed Heart*, Hochschild illuminated the relationship in the workplace between the emotions that an individual may feel and those that are acted out for the benefit of others, inclusive of the consequences of such performances. At the heart of her work are the concepts of emotion management and emotional labour, surface acting and deep acting, and feeling rules and display rules. For Hochschild (2000, p. 7), emotion management is concerned with how a social actor seeks to manage their emotions and "create publicly observable facial and bodily display" for the consumption of others. She argued that, as a consequence of our socialisation experiences, we learn what emotions are appropriate or inappropriate in particular social settings and situations. The failure to demonstrate to others the emotions that are expected in a particular circumstance can negatively impact upon their evaluation of us and, importantly, the ways in which they responsively treat us (Potrac & Marshall, 2011). Relatedly, emotional labour refers to the emotion work that a social actor is expected to engage in within the workplace. Indeed, Hochschild (1983, p. 7) defined emotional labour as that which:

> . . .requires one to induce or suppress feeling in order to sustain the outward countenance that produces the proper state of mind in others [such as] the sense of being cared for in a convivial safe place. This kind of labour calls for communication of mind and feeling, and it sometimes draws on a source of self that we honour as deep and integral to our individuality. . .Emotional labour is sold for a wage and, therefore, has exchange value.

Arguably, emotional labour takes on greater significance and impact in today's service-oriented society than at any other point in history. For example, in the USA, we can think of a collegiate coach 'smiling' and 'reassuring' prospective athletes (and their parents) that the coach and university will take good care of them. Here, the coach suppresses a more authentic interaction and emotions related to their knowledge of impending harms (e.g., physical injury or pressures to prioritise sport over schooling) to reap the benefit of getting the athlete to attend their university. Similarly, female coaches breaking barriers in male dominant sports may exchange their emotional labour for some other benefits. These might include an increased salary, acceptance into traditionally exclusionary settings, or a promotion in title or rank.

Hochschild's work (1983, 2000) also highlighted how emotion management and emotional labour are framed by socially constructed (and reconstructed) feeling and display rules. Here, display rules refer to when and how particular overt expressions of emotion should occur. For example, a coach may expect to put on a 'happy' and 'enthusiastic face' in order to sustain a social encounter (e.g., a pre-season meeting with the parents of players) as the display rules he or she learnt through their socialisation experiences suggest that they ought to demonstrate positivity in this situation to others (Cassidy et al., 2016; Turner & Stets, 2005). On the other hand, feeling rules address the specific emotions that an individual (e.g., a coach) should experience in a particular situation (e.g., joy following significantly improved athlete performance) and also their duration (i.e., momentarily or more longer lasting). Here, Hochschild (2000, p. 180) noted:

> . . .acts of emotion management are not only simply private acts; they are used in exchanges under the guidance of feeling rules. Feeling rules are standards used in emotion conversations to determine what is rightly owed in the currency of feeling. Through them, we tell what is 'due' in each relation, each role. We pay tribute to each other in the currency of managing the act. In interaction, we pay, overpay, underpay, play with paying, acknowledge our due, pretend to pay, or acknowledge what is emotionally due to another person.

Taking inspiration from Goffman's theorising, Hochschild (1983, 2000) suggested that we engage in a certain amount of acting when hiding and displaying our emotions to others. Indeed, she argued that a social actor can engage in surface acting and deep acting. Surface acting refers to a social actor's desire to deceive others in terms of the emotions that they are feeling without trying to deceive him or herself about their true feelings (Cassidy et al., 2016). For example, a coach may wish to be seen to engage with a parent in a calm and diplomatic manner whilst really feeling intensely angry at that parent's behaviour or comments. Surface acting is, then, concerned with how an individual manages their body language and paraverbal communication (i.e., pitch, pace) to convince others of the emotion that they are experiencing, which can include the 'put on' smile, the 'fake laugh', "the posed shrug, [and] the controlled sigh" (Hochschild, 2000, p. 35). Deep acting focuses on the "conscious mental action" that an individual may use to believe in the emotion that he or she wishes to express to others (Hochschild, 2000, p. 36). In drawing upon the work of the renowned theatre director and method actor, Constantin Stanislavski, she examined how an individual's public display of emotion can sometimes be a "natural result of working on the feeling; the actor does not try to seem happy or sad but rather expresses spontaneously a real feeling that is self-induced" (Hochschild, 2000, p. 35). When engaging in deep acting, social actors can utilise two principal strategies or resources. The first involves training memories or imaginations to believe the emotions being experienced. For example, a coach may transfer memories of emotions from a past situation to a current one. Equally, a coach may use exhortations, which refer to the efforts he or she might make to feel particular emotions (e.g., "I psyched myself up for the budget meeting with the administrators" or "I mustered up some gratitude for the players' efforts even though I was deeply disappointed with the outcome of today's game") (Cassidy et al., 2016; Hochschild, 2000; Potrac & Marshall, 2011).

While Hochschild's research predominantly addressed how individuals variously manage (e.g., hide, show, manipulate) emotions in their relations with others, other scholars (e.g., Lois, 2003; Lumsden & Black, 2017; Rafaeli & Sutton, 1991) have sought to extend upon her ground-breaking theorising by also examining how the management of emotions is also a group project. Indeed, Charmaz, Harris, and Irvine (2019, p. 135) suggested that "managing one's own emotions is frequently a means to shape what an audience feels". For example, a coach may carefully use tone and facial expressions to convey concern and urgency, yet optimism, in a half-time team talk to athletes who are behind in an important match. In this situation, a coach could, arguably, be engaging in three forms of emotion management simultaneously: a) surface acting, by pretending to be more calm or confident than he or she is; b) deep acting, by changing his or her own thoughts in an attempt to create a real feeling of calm rather than a façade; and c) interpersonal emotion management, by trying to judiciously calibrate the athletes' thoughts and emotions (Charmaz et al., 2019). Importantly, Charmaz et al. (2019) also highlighted how interpersonal emotion management can be undertaken in an adversarial, as well as a collaborative fashion. Indeed, two or more people might not agree (implicitly or explicitly) on the desired emotion and the means of generating them (Charmaz et al., 2019). In some circumstances, people may knowingly resist efforts to shape their own or others' emotions. For example, an athlete who is disappointed at not being selected for a starting position on a team may want to dwell on their anger and disappointment, engage in disruptive behaviour, and may not react positively to the coach's consoling words and advice (Charmaz et al., 2019).

The Coach as Social Performer: Some Dramaturgical Insights from the Literature

While Goffman and Hochschild never conducted their research in a sports coaching context, a small group of scholars have drawn upon (and continue to utilise) their theoretical insights to examine the impression (and emotion) management strategies of coaches (Cassidy et al., 2016; Jones et al., 2011; Potrac, 2019). Such work has investigated what coaches do, when, how, why, and to what cost and/or benefit. For example, scholars have begun to address the emotional demands and challenges that coaches face in their everyday practice. Here, for example, Nelson et al. (2014) used

Hochschild's concepts to examine the emotion management and emotional labour of a semi-professional football coach. In this study, the coach described how he tried to manage the outward expression of his emotions according to the display rules that he considered to be dominant (or normal) in his sporting subculture. Specifically, he articulated how he had to suppress the emotions he felt in his interactions with players and supporters and, instead, engage in surface acting. For example, in his work with the players he noted:

> Last night I didn't feel too good, going to a training session…So you're thinking, "I don't fancy this tonight". However, I can't show that to the players…I have to put an act on (Nelson et al., 2014, p. 475).

Similarly, in terms of engaging with the club's supporters, the coach in the study explained that, although he disliked having to interact with certain supporters in the clubhouse after matches, he knew his employer expected him to attend these gatherings and present himself as a 'polite', 'engaging' and 'upbeat' coach, who was genuinely interested in their thoughts and views. In his own words:

> It's just a nightmare. You get frustrated and you also get angry. You want to turn around to them and say, "What have you done? What level have you played at? What qualifications have you got? But you know you can't (Nelson et al., 2014, p. 477).

These extracts clearly illustrate Hochschild's (1983) concept of emotional labour in action; the coach recognised that a particular display and management of emotion in his coaching role was expected by his employers.

The long-term engagement in emotional labour was not easy for the coach in this study. Indeed, he articulated how he ultimately felt the need to take a break from his coaching work, as he became fatigued by the perceived need to engage in inauthentic behaviours and emotional displays. He also revealed how a reduction in his emotional stamina led to a situation where his credibility and sincerity were questioned by others in the club environment. In his own words:

> I think, especially with adults, you gradually get found out, and there is only so much you can do before the players start realising (Nelson et al., 2014, p. 478).

It is also important to recognise that engaging in emotional labour is not always a negative activity for coaches. Potrac and Marshall (2011), for example, considered how emotion work (both intra and interpersonally) can also provide coaches with a sense of challenge, satisfaction and excitement. In illustrating this point, a track and field coach noted:

> Overall, I feel that the emotional labour I invest in my coaching offers many positives. I coach through choice, because I enjoy it. While coaching does come with an emotional cost, it is also hugely rewarding. By engaging in emotional labour, I am able to support athletes more effectively, to help them achieve their goals and competitive ambitions. The reward is seeing this happen, in watching those you work with enjoy their training, growing in confidence and ability. For many of the athletes I work with, they desperately want to succeed. This brings with it a high emotional cost to me as a coach, in managing their emotions and expectations. However, it also brings with it a huge feeling of satisfaction in a job well done when they do achieve (Potrac & Marshall, 2011, p. 66).

Goffman's (1959) notions of dramaturgical circumspection and dramaturgical discipline have been used to examine how individual coaches' seek to construct, maintain, and advance the image of themselves that they give off to the scrutinising audiences in their respective coaching environments (e.g., athletes, other coaches, support staff, and administrators). In relation to dramaturgical discipline, Jones et al.'s (2004) study of coaching practice in elite sport highlighted that, while coaches are often intellectually and emotionally committed to their working role, they conscientiously seek to avoid "unmeant gestures when performing it" (Goffman, 1959, p. 217). For example, one coach noted:

> You've got to think on your feet. Whereas if you start bawling or saying, "Where is so and so?" [using a panicky voice], you're not being professional. You can make a joke out of it and throw your notes down, "Come on let's piss off to the pub". You make light of it, but you try to show that you're not bothered; you're in control and know what you are doing. You've got to adapt, think on your feet and have things in your mind, first reserve, second reserve type of thing, which isn't easy, but it has to be done.

As the beginning of this chapter alluded to, the scenes, roles, actions and emotions presented thus far show a reality of coaching far from sanitised or unproblematic. For us, it is important that coaches understand that these social norms and interaction rules were built up over time, vary across contexts, and that a coach's engagement with them can lead to an array of positive or negative effects. Indeed, the value of the dramaturgical perspective lies in its potential to help coaches see that the social world is not simply 'natural' or 'just the way things are'. Instead, it can enable them to critically develop their knowledge of, and practical engagement with, the socio-political terrains in which their work as coaches is embedded (Potrac, 2019).

In reflecting the comments above, another coach highlighted how his understanding of subcultural expectations led him to attach great store to his social competencies and interactions with others. For example, in order to successfully navigate his coaching workplace, the coach emphasised the need to appear knowledgeable when interacting with athletes in training sessions and team meetings. In his own words:

> Football players will test you. I find that when you go to a new club…they will test you to see if you know. They usually pump you with questions. They'll say they've never done that before, and if I can't say why I want it done that way, if I can't give a good reason, then I've got trouble. You can't afford to lose the players. If they have no respect for your coaching ability, then you've had it, you've lost respect and the coaching sessions become difficult. So, you've got to know your subject; it is the most important thing. You can get away with being a bit quiet or a bit noisy, but if you don't know your subject then you have real problems (Potrac, Jones, & Armour, 2002, p. 192).

The fear of being stigmatised by players and assistant coaches was also the subject of Jones' (2006) autoethnography, which examined the relationship between his own dysfluency and the front that he attempted to project to others. Following a problematic experience of giving a pre-game team talk he documented the following:

> Maybe nobody noticed, maybe it wasn't that bad of a stumble? Of course it was, what an idiot I must have looked. Why me? And, why just then? I could come clean about it, maybe

> the players would respect that?...Thoughts about 'coming out' continue to pervade my mind. It's the struggle between who I am and who I want to be. Politically, maybe I should forsake attempts to cover up, yet the fear of social ridicule and rejection is too strong. Sensitivity is not easily found in football dressing rooms (Jones, 2006, p. 1016).

With regard to dramaturgical circumspection, the literature has highlighted the importance that coaches in elite sport attach to the meticulous planning and preparation that they undertook in the back region. On one level, this planning focused on the techniques, strategies and tactics to be learned or practiced. One coach, for example, noted:

> I have to show how tiny movements give clues to the man in possession. You see, a difference of only 3 inches can be significant, as it's that much closer or further away from the defender, and I have to make sure the players know how much difference that really makes to the execution of a move. I also have to know exactly how I'm going to present that [to the players] (Jones et al., 2004, p. 569).

The work of Potrac and Jones (2009) has provided some initial insights into how coaches' planning can extend beyond techniques and tactics to include their interactions with particular individuals. Specifically, this study illustrated how the participant coach gave considerable attention to how he managed conflict with a senior player, who was resistant to the coach's programme and methods. In this respect, the coach was concerned that the player's derogatory comments might lead to the coach's employers questioning his credibility as the team's head coach. In his own words:

> I knew David was pretty close to the Chairman, so I had to be pretty careful in terms of how I dealt with him...I started setting things up in training so that he'd fail. He just didn't have the technical ability or the speed to play in the position he wanted, so I decided to exploit that. We'd set up some patterns of play and the players would be working hard and every time he'd be in the wrong place, make a bad pass, or have a crap touch. After a couple of sessions, I began to hear complaints from the players about him. His status within the group changed and he became more and more isolated (Potrac & Jones, 2009, p. 569).

The coach also described how he formed a performance team with several senior players, whom he trusted and had personally recruited to the club, to further limit with the potential incidents that David might cause. Here, he noted:

> I [also] spoke [privately] to the [senior] boys about what was happening. I suggested that maybe the players should get together and tell David that they weren't happy with his attitude and performance, which might be more meaningful than if I did it. So, they started letting David know they weren't happy with him and soon the other players began to join in. In the end, I think that played a large part in why David left the club...It also looked better for me because I wasn't seen [by the Chairman] as the person who was throwing out an established player (Potrac & Jones, 2009, p. 570).

In this example, it is clear that the coach sought to control the problematic situation with David. He did this in multiple ways. Firstly, he maintained a desired 'front' in the eyes of the chairman by not aggressively challenging David's behaviour or being seen to treat David unfairly; happenings that would have constituted incidents that the coach believed would have spoiled his identity in the club setting. Secondly, he designed practices that resulted in David's identity being spoiled, instead. This primarily occurred through the other players' negative reactions to David's technical and physical limitations being exposed on the training ground. Finally, he recruited allies (the senior players), who he worked with in the back region to orchestrate further negative reactions towards David from the players in the front region.

The limited available coaching literature (e.g., Jones et al., 2004; Potrac & Jones, 2009) has also highlighted how coaches' engagement in dramaturgical circumspection includes being seen to visibly care about athlete learning and well-being. Specifically, this literature has indicated that, in order to create an idealised image of themselves in the eyes of athletes, they provide additional coaching sessions and feedback, produce and share learning resources, and take an interest in the athletes' lives outside of sport. In this respect, one former elite coach noted:

> You're actually showing them you care, and whilst you show them that you think about them and the other side of life, you stand to gain a great deal in terms of your working relationship with them (Jones et al., 2004, p. 158).

Here, the coach's discussion highlighted how this was not just caring for caring's sake, but was, instead, tied to two important benefits. These included: (a) the perceived athletic performance gains that caring practice contributed to; (b) athletes' support for, confidence in, and compliance towards the coaches' agenda and 'personality', and relatedly; (c) a coach's efforts to develop, maintain and advance a positive reputation in an industry characterised by insecure employment and a surplus of (coaching) labour (Potrac et al., 2013). Arguably, caring practice is, for some coaches, firmly embedded within the everyday socio-political realities of their working relationships with others.

While coaches can take various actions to build, maintain and advance their respective 'fronts', there are occasions when things do not go according to the script or plan. One strategy that coaches have described they use to handle such disruptions is self-deprecating humour (Jones et al., 2004). Specifically, coaches have suggested that such humour can be used proactively to build a working consensus with others or as a reactive strategy to dampen the implications of potentially discrediting events (e.g., Jones et al., 2004; Jones et al., 2011; Ronglan & Aggerholm, 2014). With regard to the latter, it has been suggested that such humour can limit the 'fall-out' from performance disruptions by lessening the expectation of leader infallibility (Cassidy et al., 2016); it can be used as a tool to lessen or prevent the spoiling of a coaching identity. Humour then has the potential to locate incidents within the normative range of behaviour. Finally, it was also suggested that humour can help a coach display his or her 'human side', which can foster the development of productive working relationships with others. In a coach's own words:

> I use self-irony; reveal weaknesses and show 'human traits', in a way. The players chuckle when I ask for help to handle technical gadgets that the players know everything about. It's important to be able to laugh at oneself and to be relaxed regarding one's own limitations. Self-importance really doesn't work in Norwegian culture (Ronglan & Aggerholm, 2014 p. 41).

Practical Implications

Rather than provide prescriptions regarding what coaches should and should not do, we instead invite coaches to reflect on the questions below using the theoretical concepts and literature utilised in this chapter.

Within a sporting context of your choice, consider the following questions:

- What do you consider to be the expectations of coaches' behaviours and interactions in your chosen setting? How do people respond when they consider a coach to have met, exceeded, or not fulfil these expectations? What consequences might this have for a coach's on-going relationships with others (e.g., athletes, other coaches, administrators, among others)? How do these expectations develop in society and how did you learn them?
- Who are the situational stakeholders that you will need to achieve the confidence of, and support from, as a coach? In seeking to develop and maintain a credible coaching front, what interactional strategies will you use? What will you do or not do and what does this say about your character? In situations where you are trying to affect others and control the outcome of an interaction, what ethical principles or values are involved?
- What display rules and feeling rules are dominant in your sport setting? How do others react if these norms are contravened? What emotions will you show or hide in your chosen setting? To whom and to what extent? When? How? Why?
- How will you present yourself to others in this setting? What will you consider and do in terms of your appearance and manner, use of props (i.e., coaching equipment and learning resources for athletes) and staging of the physical setting (e.g., how a team meeting room is organised or laid out)?
- How will your reading of this chapter influence your planning activities individually and/or with your co-coaches? What will you do differently? Why? What will you avoid doing? Why?

Key Points

We encourage coaches (and other readers) to consider the following key points:

(a) To recognise the importance of everyday interaction in coaching. It is through your interactions that you generate connections with others, gain their support, and determine the influence that you are able to exert. The failure to connect with others or live up to their expectations can significantly impact the support you receive, the influence you have, and the atmosphere in which you strive to achieve your coaching goals.

(b) We believe that dramaturgical theorising provides important ideas that coaches can think and act with. For example, coaches can benefit from giving careful consideration to the 'front' or 'image' of themselves that they wish to create in the eyes of significant others (e.g., athletes, parents, administrators, support staff, among others). This includes reflecting on our manner (inclusive of the emotions we show) and appearance, our use of coaching props and the staging of the coaching environment, as well as the micro-dynamics of our individual and team performances as coaches. Such critical knowledge is not normally included in coach education provision but is essential to our efforts to 'professionalise' coaching.

(c) As a field, we need to develop a more detailed and nuanced body of knowledge addressing the ways in which coaches are both tacticians and targets of influence. Indeed, there is much more to learn in terms of how coaches seek to influence others towards desired outcomes, as well as how coaches are, themselves, the subject of others' attempts to influence and navigate the sometimes problematic aspects of joint action (Grills & Prus, 2019; Potrac, 2019).

Conclusion

In this chapter, we have sought to consider some of the dramaturgical features of coaching work. Whilst we are unable to explore 'all' of their dimensions, we hope that the integration of some of Goffman's (1959) and Hochschild's (1983, 2000) theorising with pertinent coaching literature, will contribute to increasing the readers' understanding of, and engagement with, the interactive and emotionally laden challenges that are an inherent feature of coaching. For us, coaching is "an obligation driven social activity" (Jones et al., 2011, p. 26) that requires coaches (individually and collectively) to consciously plan for and critically reflect upon how they present themselves and their ideas, choices, actions and emotions to others (Cassidy et al., 2016). Developing and maintaining an idealised image in the eyes of a scrutinising audience is not an easy task; it is an embodied and dynamic challenge that requires us to consider how we feel and make others feel" with our achievements inextricably linked to the quality of our social engagements and practices (Cassidy et al., 2016, p. 99). We certainly believe that such issues warrant consideration in coach certification and development programmes (Potrac, Nichol, & Hall, 2020).

References

Branaman, A. (2000). Goffman's social theory. In C. Lemert & A. Branaman (Eds.), *The Goffman reader* (pp. xlv–lxxxii). Oxford: Blackwell Publishers.

Cassidy, T., Jones, R., & Potrac, P. (2016). *Understanding sports coaching: The social, cultural and pedagogical foundations of coaching practice* (3rd ed.). London: Routledge.

Charmaz, K., Harris, S., & Irvine, L. (2019). *The social self and everyday life: Understanding the world through symbolic interactionism*. Hoboken, NJ: Wiley Blackwell.

Edgley, C. (2013). Introduction. In C. Edgley (Ed.), *The drama of social life: A dramaturgical handbook* (pp. 1–12). Burlington, VT: Ashgate Publishing Limited.

Gale, L., Ives, B., Nelson, L., & Potrac, P. (2019). Trust and distrust in community sports work: Tales from the 'shop floor'. *Sociology of Sport Journal, 36*(3), 244–253.

Goffman, E. (1959). *The presentation of self in everyday life*. London: Penguin.

Goffman, E. (1969a). *Strategic interaction*. Philadelphia: University of Pennsylvania Press.
Goffman, E. (1969b). *Where the action is*. London: Penguin.
Goffman, E. (1971). *Relations in public: Microstudies of the public order*. New York, NY: Basic Books.
Goffman, E. (1983). The interaction order. *American Sociological Review, 48*, 1–17.
Grills, S., & Prus, R. (2019). *Management motifs: An interactionist approach for the study of organisational interchange*. Switzerland: Springer.
Hochschild, A. (1983, 2000). The managed heart. Commercialisation of human feeling. Berkeley, CA: University of California Press.
Hochschild, A. (1997). *The time bind: When work becomes home and home becomes work*. New York, NY: Metropolitan Holt.
Hochschild, A. R. (2000). *The managed heart: Commercialisation of human feeling*. Berkeley, CA: University of California Press.
Hochschild, A., & Machung, A. (2003). *The second shift: Working parents and the revolution at home*. London: Penguin.
Jones, R. (2006). Dilemmas, maintaining 'face' and paranoia: An average coaching life. *Qualitative Inquiry, 12*(5), 1012–1021.
Jones, R. (2019). *Studies in sports coaching*. Newcastle Upon Tyne: Cambridge Scholars Publishing.
Jones, R., Armour, K., & Potrac, P. (2004). *Sports coaching cultures: From practice to theory*. London: Routledge.
Jones, R., Potrac, P., Cushion, C., & Ronglan, L. T. (Eds.). (2011). *The sociology of sports coaching*. London: Routledge.
Jones, R., & Wallace, M. (2005). Another bad day at the training ground: Coping with ambiguity in the coaching context. *Sport, Education and Society, 10*(1), 119–134.
Leary, M. (1995). *Self-presentation: Impression management and interpersonal behaviour*. Oxford: Oxford University Press.
Lois, J. (2003). *Heroic efforts: The emotional culture of search and rescue volunteers*. New York, NY: New York University Press.
Lumsden, K., & Black, A. (2017). Austerity policing, emotional labour and the boundaries of police work: An ethnography of a police force control room in England. *The British Journal of Criminology, 58*(3), 606–623.
Marsh, I., Keating, M., Eyre, A., Campbell, R., & McKenzie, J. (1996). *Making sense of society: An introduction to sociology*. London: Longman.
Nelson, L., Potrac, P., Gilbourne, D., Allanson, A., Gale, L., & Marshall, P. (2014). Thinking, feeling, acting: The case of a semi-professional soccer coach. *Sociology of Sport Journal, 19*(1), 19–40.
Potrac, P. (2019). Exploring politics and political astuteness in coaching: Some critical reflections. In C. Corsby & C. Edwards (Eds.), *Exploring research in sports coaching and pedagogy: Context and contingency* (pp. 13–21). Newcastle Upon Tyne: Cambridge Scholars Publishing.
Potrac, P., & Jones, R. (2009). Micro-political workings in semi-professional football coaching. *Sociology of Sport Journal, 26*, 557–577.
Potrac, P., Jones, R., & Armour, K. (2002). "It's all about getting respect": The coaching behaviours of a top-level English football coach. *Sport, Education and Society, 7*(2), 183–202.
Potrac, P., Jones, R., Gilbourne, D., & Nelson, L. (2013). Handshakes, BBQs, and bullets: A tale of self-interest and regret in football coaching. *Sports Coaching Review, 1*(2), 79–92.
Potrac, P., Jones, R., & Nelson, L. (2014). Interpretivism. In L. Nelson, R. Groom, & P. Potrac (Eds.), *Research methods in sports coaching* (pp. 31–41). London: Routledge.
Potrac, P., Mallett, C., Greenough, K., & Nelson, L. (2017). Passion and paranoia: An embodied tale of emotion, identity, and pathos in sports coaching. *Sports Coaching Review, 6*(2), 142–161.
Potrac, P., & Marshall, P. (2011). Arlie Russell Hochschild: The managed heart, feeling rules, and emotional labour: Coaching as an emotional Endeavour. In R. Jones, P. Potrac, C. Cushion, & L. T. Ronglan (Eds.), *The sociology of sports coaching* (pp. 54–66). London: Routledge.

Potrac, P., Nichol, A., & Hall, E. (2020). Critically understanding and engaging with the (micro) political dimensions of coaches' work in an advanced undergraduate coaching course. In B. Callary & B. Gearity (Eds.), *Coach education and development: Instructional strategies* (pp. 45–57). London: Routledge.
Rafaeli, A., & Sutton, R. (1991). Emotional contrast strategies as means of social influence. Lessons from criminal interrogators and bill collectors. *Academy of Management Journal, 34*(4), 749–775.
Ronglan, L. T., & Aggerholm, K. (2014). 'Humour helps': Elite sports coaching as a balancing act. *Sports Coaching Review, 3*(1), 33–45.
Schulman, D. (2017). *The presentation of self in contemporary social life*. Los Angeles, CA: Sage.
Scott, S. (2015). *Negotiating identity: Symbolic interactionist approaches to social identity*. Cambridge: Polity Press.
Thompson, A., Potrac, P., & Jones, R. (2015). 'I found out the hard way': Micro-political workings in professional football. *Sport, Education, & Society, 20*(8), 976–994.
Turner, J., & Stets, J. (2005). *The sociology of emotions*. Cambridge: Cambridge University Press.

Paul Potrac, PhD, is a Professor of Sport Coaching in the Department of Sport, Exercise and Rehabilitation at Northumbria University, a full Visiting Professor in the School of Public Health, Physiotherapy and Sport Science at University College Dublin, and a Visiting Professor in the Cariff School of Sport and Health Sciences at Cardiff Metropolitan University. His research focuses on the dramaturgical, political, and emotional dimensions of coaching and coach education. He has co-authored several books on coaching, including Sport Coaching Cultures, Understanding Sports Coaching, Learning in Sport Coaching, and the Sociology of Sport Coaching. He is also an Associate Editor for the Sports Coaching Review Journal.

Brian Gearity, PhD, is the Founding Director and Assistant Professor of the Master of Arts in Sport Coaching and several online graduate certificate programs at the University of Denver. He is Editor-in-Chief for National Strength and Conditioning Association's practitioner journal *NSCA Coach*, and is on the editorial board for *Sport Coaching Review; Qualitative Research in Sport, Exercise, and Health; Strength & Conditioning Journal;* and *Journal of Aging and Physical Activity*. Along with Dr. Bettina Callary, he is co-editor of the book, "*Coach education and development in sport: Instructional Strategies.*"

Adam Nichol is a PhD Researcher and Associate Lecturer in the Department of Sport, Exercise and Rehabilitation at Northumbria University, Newcastle upon Tyne. His research is centred on understanding *how*, *when*, *why*, and *under which circumstances* the (inter)actions of coaches' influence (or do not influence) others.

Callum Morgan is a PhD student in the Department of Sport, Exercise, and Rehabilitation at Northumbria University. Callum's PhD focuses on the dramaturgical, relational, and emotional features of everyday working life for coach educators. Specifically, his thesis seeks to generate new ethnographic insights into how coach educators prepare for, enact, and reflect upon the individual and collective performances that comprise their work, as well as the emotions they experience, conceal, and show to others.

Edward Hall is a Senior Lecturer in Sports Coaching at Northumbria University, UK. His research focuses on the relational, (micro) political and emotional complexities of sports coaching. Edward's work principally explores how networks of social relations influence the thoughts, feelings and (inter)actions of sport professionals, and how sense is made of experiences, relationships and the self.

Chapter 8
Coaching Youth Athletes

Gordon A. Bloom, Lea-Cathrin Dohme, and William R. Falcão

Abstract Sport settings have long been viewed as environments that can foster youth athletes' positive psychological development. Consequently, sport coaches are increasingly called upon to create environments that nurture this development. The purpose of this chapter is to provide insight into some of the most influential conceptual and empirical research findings that help guide coaching practices in building learning environments that are structured to meet the needs and desires of youth athletes. This will be accomplished by reviewing four popular and empirically tested coaching frameworks: Mastery Approach to Coaching, Positive Youth Development in Sport, Life Skills Development Model, and Humanistic Coaching. Insights gained from these frameworks informed our recommendations for creating ideal youth sport environments: promote learning and development over winning, create a supportive environment, intentionally plan and promote the development of positive developmental outcomes (PDO), facilitate opportunities to practice PDO, promote and facilitate the transfer of PDO, and consider athletes' individual differences and wider social environment. Given the worldwide movement towards appropriate developmental opportunities for children and youth, this chapter offers helpful recommendations for coaches and other important stakeholders involved in children's development.

Keywords Positive Development · Life Skills · Humanistic Coaching

---

G. A. Bloom (✉)
McGill University, Montreal, Canada
e-mail: gordon.bloom@mcgill.ca

L.-C. Dohme
Cardiff Metropolitan University, Cardiff, Wales, UK
e-mail: LDohme@cardiffmet.ac.uk

W. R. Falcão
HEC Montreal, Montreal, Canada

R. Resende, A. R. Gomes (eds.), *Coaching for Human Development and Performance in Sports*, https://doi.org/10.1007/978-3-030-63912-9_8

Coaching Youth Athletes

Over the past 50 years, researchers have found that coaching behaviours influenced children's self-perceptions, adherence levels to sport, and psychosocial development (Smith & Smoll, 2002; Smith, Smoll, & Curtis, 1979). As a result, guiding frameworks emerged describing the processes, pathways, and outcomes associated with the engagement in sport throughout childhood and adolescence (e.g., Côté, 1999; Gould & Carson, 2008a). Most notably, experts outlined that youth athletes' positive development is not an automated outcome of sport participation; instead it is triggered through appropriate training patterns and social influences (Côté, Baker, & Abernethy, 2007; Côté & Vierimaa, 2014).

Coaches are increasingly called upon to create environments that foster positive developmental outcomes in youth athletes. This bears great responsibility, as coaches are dealing with athletes at a time during which they are easily influenced by authoritative adults and are subject to the challenges of adolescence (Holt, 2016). Research has significantly increased our understanding of these needs, as well as the environmental conditions that foster them. This enhances the ability of sport organizations, coach educators, and coaches to explicitly plan for the creation of high quality, positive, and youth athlete-centred environments. The purpose of this chapter is to provide insight into some of the most influential conceptual and empirical research findings that help guide coaching practices in building learning environments that are structured to meet the needs and desires of youth athletes.

Conceptual and Empirical Findings

This section will cover some of the theoretical frameworks and empirical findings regarding youth sport coaching. Although there are multiple theories describing youth sport coach behaviours and the positive outcomes that can accrue from youth sport participation, this chapter will focus on four frameworks: Mastery Approach to Coaching, Positive Youth Development in Sport, Life Skills Development Model, and Humanistic Coaching. These theories of youth sport coaching help us understand the historical background and current knowledge in coaching youth athletes. Readers interested in other frameworks and theories for coaching youth athletes can also refer to the Developmental Model of Sport Participation (Côté, Lidor, & Hackfort, 2009), Transformational Leadership (Turnnidge & Côté, 2018), and Autonomy-Supportive coaching (Carpentier & Mageau, 2016). This information can be accessed through resources such as Potrac, Gilbert, and Denison's (2013) Handbook of Sport Coaching, or Green and Smith's (2016) Handbook of Youth Sport.

Mastery Approach to Coaching

The Mastery Approach to Coaching (MAC) is an education program that aims to promote athlete motivation, team cohesion, and coach-athlete interactions by creating an atmosphere that encourages skill development and limits athletes' fear of failure (Smith, Smoll, & Cumming, 2007). The MAC originated from the work of Ronald Smith, Frank Smoll and their colleagues whose work has established a firm foundation for the knowledge and ideal behaviours of youth sport coaches. Among their conclusions, Smith and Smoll (2002) found coach behaviours impacted the psychosocial and affective responses of youth sport participants, and participation did not automatically result in beneficial effects. The results of their research led to the creation of intervention and training programs geared to ensure positive outcomes of youth sport participation. Their program of research began in the 1970s when they investigated coaches' behaviours and their effects on youth athletes (Smith et al., 1979; Smith, Smoll, & Hunt, 1977; Smoll, Smith, Curtis, & Hunt, 1978). Together, this research created an empirical foundation for the development of psychologically based youth sport coach intervention programs.

Theoretical Underpinnings Smith, Smoll and colleagues' work was guided by the Mediational Model of Leadership (MML: Smoll & Smith, 1989), a theoretical model suggesting the effects of coaching behaviours on athletes' experiences are mediated by the meaning they attach to behaviours. These perceptions, in turn, influence children's affective reactions to their sporting experiences and ultimately, the psychological impact of their sport involvement. In essence, athlete's recall and understanding of their coach's behaviours, combined with the significance they attribute to these behaviours, mediate the effects of coaching behaviours on the youth sport experience.

The MML recognises that coaches' behaviours, as well as athletes' perception of and reaction to coaches' behaviours are influenced by situational factors, as well as coaches' and athletes' individual characteristics. The situational factors are described as the nature of the sport, level of competition (i.e., recreational versus competitive), practice sessions versus games, previous success/failure, present status in competitions and training, and interpersonal relationships within the team. Players' individual characteristics include the athlete's age, gender, perceptions of coaching norms, preferred coaching behaviours, sport-specific achievement motives, competitive anxiety, general self-esteem, and athletic self-esteem. Finally, coach characteristics include the coach's goals, behavioural intentions, instrumentalities (i.e., perceived probability that a certain outcome will occur as a result of a behaviour), perceived norms associated with the role of the coach, inferred player motives, self-monitoring, and the coach's gender. Overall, the MML offers a comprehensive model that allowed Smith and Smoll to determine how observable coaching behaviours, athletes' perception and recall of these behaviours, and athletes' attitudes related to each other.

In order to measure coaches' behaviours described in the MML, Smith et al. (1977) developed the Coaching Behavior Assessment System (CBAS). The CBAS allows individuals to observe and code coaches' behaviours during practices and games. It consists of 12 categories, which are divided into reactive and spontaneous behaviours. Reactive behaviours are defined as immediate responses to preceding athlete or team behaviours (e.g., reinforcement, instructions, punishment). Spontaneous behaviours are defined as responses that are initiated by the coach without preceding stimulation (e.g., general technical instructions, general communication). Research based on the CBAS has established relationships between coach behaviours and athlete variables specified in the conceptual model.

Empirical Findings Research applying the MML and CBAS found that coaches frequently responded to situations with specific patterns of behaviours, which in turn impacted youth athletes' levels of adherence, self-perception, anxiety, and liking of the coach and sport (e.g., Cumming, Smoll, Smith, & Grossbard, 2007; Smith, Shoda, Cumming, & Smoll, 2009; Smoll, Smith, Barnett, & Everett, 1993; Smoll, Smith, & Curtis, 1978). The first field study using the CBAS involved the observation of 51 male Little League Baseball coaches during 202 games in the United States (Smoll, Smith, Curtis, & Hunt, 1978). The results were cross-referenced with data collected from 542 players through interviews and questionnaires designed to assess athletes' recall and perceptions of their coaches' behaviours, general self-esteem, and overall enjoyment of the sport. Findings suggested that athletes responded most favourably to coaches who showed high levels of supportive and instructional behaviours. In addition, these behaviours influenced athletes' liking of the coach more than the team's win-loss records. Finally, findings indicated that coaches had limited awareness of their behaviours. In sum, the findings indicated that coaches' behaviours significantly effected youth athletes' motivation and sport experience, yet coaches needed training that would increase their awareness of adaptive and maladaptive coaching behaviours. Consequently, Smith, Smoll, and colleagues developed and evaluated a coach training program aimed at modifying coaches' behaviours to promote athlete well-being.

Coach Training Program This line of intervention research began with the design, implementation, and evaluation of the Coach Effectiveness Training (CET) program (Smith et al., 1979). The CET was an empirically derived coach intervention program that aimed to instil five distinct coaching principles (Smith & Smoll, 2002; Smoll & Smith, 2002). First, it taught coaches to create climates that focused on youth athletes' enjoyment and ability to master skills as opposed to beating others. A fundamental component of this principle was learning that personal success or failure was not measured on a win-loss ratio, but on coaches' ability to motivate athletes to give maximum effort. Second, coaches were taught to utilize a positive approach to coaching by using reinforcement, appropriate instructions, and encouragement. In addition, punitive behaviours such as scolds or penalties were strongly discouraged. Third, coaches were taught to establish an environment in which it was the norm to help and support one another to increase team cohesion and athletes' personal commitment. Fourth, coaches were encouraged to include athletes in decision-making processes regarding the team. Finally, coaches were taught to engage in self-monitoring to increase awareness of their own coaching behaviours. Consequently, several studies were conducted to evaluate the effectiveness of the CET program (e.g., Smith et al., 1979; Smith, Zane, Smoll, & Coppel, 1983). For example, Smith et al. (1979) delivered the CET program to 18 Little League Baseball coaches and assigned 13 other coaches to an experimental control group. To assess the effects of the CET on coaches and their players, all coaches were scored on the CBAS and 325 male players were individually interviewed. Findings pointed towards the effectiveness of the program as youth athletes of trained coaches showed a significant increase in sporting enjoyment, commitment, and self-esteem, decreased levels of anxiety, and more favourable evaluation of their coach and teammates despite win-loss ratios.

While the CET program proved successful, Smith, Smoll, and colleagues upgraded the program in response to the emergence of the achievement goal theory (Nicholls, 1984) and the extensive research that it triggered. According to achievement goal theory, two types of goals guide athletes' behaviours, namely task and ego goals. Athletes that are task orientated aim to continually learn and master activities, frequently judge themselves in a self-referenced manner, and focus on investing maximum effort to become better. In comparison, athletes that are ego orientated aim to beat and outperform others. Commonly, task orientation is perceived as more adaptive towards athletes' positive physical and psychosocial development compared to ego orientations (Nicholls, 1984). Smith et al. (2007) incorporated these principles into their CET program and termed this upgraded program the Mastery Approach to Coaching (MAC).

The aim of the MAC had many similarities to the CET, such as to increase youth athletes' intrinsic motivation and promote positive coach-athlete interactions that foster personal development as opposed to winning. However, the MAC simplified the five principles of the CET into two themes, namely emphasizing positive reinforcement and measuring success based on maximum effort. In addition, the MAC explicitly described what a mastery climate looked like, how it was developed, and modelled desirable and undesirable responses to specific situations (e.g., athlete mistakes). Finally, the duration of the workshop was reduced from 2 hours to 75 minutes and supported by a 28-page workbook, as well as self-monitoring forms that related to the behavioural guidelines that were being reinforced.

Smith, Smoll and colleagues conducted a series of research studies to examine the effectiveness of the MAC training program (e.g., Smith et al., 2007; Smith, Smoll, & Cumming, 2009; Sousa, Smith, & Cruz, 2008). For example, Smith et al. (2007) recruited 37 American community-based basketball coaches and 216 of their athletes. The MAC was delivered to 20 coaches. Athletes were tested on the Sport Anxiety Scale-2 (Smith, Smoll, Cumming, & Grossbard, 2006) and Motivational Climate Scale for Youth Sports (Smith, Cumming, & Smoll, 2008) before and after the coaches had been exposed to the MAC. Similar to the evaluation of the CET program, the findings of the study revealed that athletes of trained coaches showed higher enjoyment and self-esteem, and lowered cognitive and somatic anxiety than athletes of untrained coaches (Smith et al., 2007). In addition, Cumming et al. (2007) examined the effects of motivational climates and win-loss percentages on athletes' evaluations of their coaches and enjoyment of their team experience. Results indicated that athletes' sport enjoyment and perceptions of the coach were more strongly related to coaching behaviours than to the team's or athlete's win-loss records.

Parents' Impact on Youth Sport Coaching More recently, Smith, Smoll, and colleagues shifted the focus of their research from investigating the influence of coaches to looking at how parents impacted youth athletes (e.g., O'Rourke, Smith, Smoll, & Cumming, 2014; Schwebel, Smith, & Smoll, 2016; Smoll & Smith, 2012). In particular, Smith, Smoll, and colleagues' earlier work found that, similar to coach-initiated climates, parent-initiated climates could also be task or ego orientated. Parents who encouraged a task orientated motivational climate commonly viewed success through self-improvement, task mastery, and the exhibition of maximum effort, whereas parents who encouraged an ego orientated motivational climate projected a definition of success that was based on social comparison and the importance of winning (Schwebel et al., 2016). In one of their first studies, O'Rourke et al. (2014) compared the effects of coaches and parents' behaviours on athletes' self-esteem, performance anxiety, as well as intrinsic and extrinsic motivation. Quantitative data was collected from 238 youth swimmers who were part of an Olympic development program and possessed highly involved parents. Findings indicated significant correlations between both coaches and parents' behaviours and athletes' psychological outcomes. In particular, mastery climates showed positive correlations with athletes' self-esteem and autonomy, and negative correlations with performance anxiety. In turn, ego oriented climates correlated negatively with athletes' self-esteem and autonomy, and positively with performance anxiety. Finally, O'Rourke et al. found that parent-related correlations were consistently higher than coaches, despite both having some impact on youth athletes' psychological outcomes. Accordingly, parents may impact athletes' self-esteem, anxiety, and autonomous regulation significantly more than coaches. This led O'Rourke et al. to call for more research examining the impact of parents' goal-directness on youth athletes' psychosocial outcomes.

In an effort to address this call, Schwebel et al. (2016) created and tested the validity of the Perceived Parent Success Standards Scale (PPSSS), a 12-item scale that was designed to assess the effects of parent-initiated motivational climates on youth athletes. The PPSSS consists of ego ("I beat other people") and mastery ("I master something I could not do before") subscales. Each item begins with: "When I play sports, it is most important to my parents that...". The measure has strong factorial and construct validity and thus provides a precise assessment of the relationship between youth athletes and perceived parental success criteria. Schwebel et al. (2016) used the PPSSS and the Motivational Climate Scale for Youth Sports (MCSYS; Smith et al., 2007) to compare the influence of coach- and parent-initiated motivational climates on 543 athletes in a recreational sport program, an environment commonly characterised by less involved parents. Findings supported those of O'Rourke et al. (2014), suggesting that parental success criteria impacted athletes' psychosocial outcomes more than coach-initiated motivational climates. Specifically, parents' success standards were found to influence athletes' self-esteem and intrinsic and extrinsic motivation more than coaches' success standards. The exception was athletes' performance anxiety which was found to be influenced more by coach-initiated mastery climates than parental standards. Also, parental ego standards were found to dampen the relationships between coach mastery climate and athletes' level of anxiety and ego goal orientation. This latter finding suggested that parental success standards could influence athletes' response to coach created motivational climates. Given this evidence, Schwebel et al. (2016) suggested that motivational climate interventions may also be beneficial for parents. As such, coaches should aim to work in close collaboration with parents to negotiate and standardize the values and goal-orientations that are being instilled in the athletes.

In sum, Smith, Smoll, and colleagues have changed our way of looking at coach-athlete and parent-athlete relations by highlighting their impact on athletes' sport experiences. Moreover, they postulated that the key to a positive athletic experience was how well coaches and parents related to their athletes and which achievement standards they reinforced. Finally, they recommended that coaches and parents should be trained to provide mastery orientated environments for young athletes. Therefore, their results urge coaches to work alongside parents to enable the reinforcement of standardized values and goal orientations.

Positive Youth Development in Sport

Positive Youth Development (PYD) is an approach based on the positive psychology movement that aims to counteract the deficit-reduction approach that historically dominated the developmental sciences (Holt, 2016). Instead of focusing on "fixing" individuals' deficiencies, positive psychology sets out to promote individuals' strengths (Holt, 2016). PYD offers a framework that adopts this strength-based approach, which regards youth as "resources to be developed" rather than "problems to be managed" (Roth & Brooks-Gunn, 2003, p. 94). More specifically, the PYD approach focuses on the development of youths' strengths, talents, and interests, as well as positive values to sustain long-term prevention of unhealthy and risky behaviours, such as substance abuse or academic failure (Damon, 2004). Schulman and Davies (2007) defined PYD as "the acquisition of all the knowledge, skills, competencies, and experiences required to successfully transition from adolescence to adulthood" (p. 4). PYD has been identified as particularly reliable in sustaining positive behaviours and improving individual's lives as it recognizes that human development is influenced by personal (e.g., resilience and interests) and environmental characteristics (e.g., schools and neighbourhoods), which are dynamic and ever changing (Damon, 2004). This section will begin with a historic overview of this paradigm, before offering insight into recent research findings.

Theoretical Underpinnings The PYD in sport framework originated from Lerner, Fisher, and Weinberg's (2000) seminal work in developmental psychology. Lerner et al. described five desirable developmental outcomes (known as the "five Cs of PYD") that ensued from a successful PYD approach: competence, confidence, connection, caring/compassion, and character. The framework recognises that development takes place within a system in which public policies impact behaviours at a community level. Consequently, Lerner et al. (2000) suggested that policies and community programs need to be developed in a way that explicitly reinforces the five Cs. Lerner and colleagues have conducted a longitudinal investigation since 2002 to validate the development of the five Cs through youth programs (Lerner, 2009; Lerner et al., 2014).[1] To date, data has been collected from approximately 7000 adolescents and their parents using comprehensive questionnaires that assessed parents' demographic information (e.g., marital status, ethnicity, religion, socioeconomic status), their children's habits (e.g., hours of sleep per night, afterschool activities), as well as children's measures of the five Cs, problem behaviours, and developmental regulations (Lerner et al., 2005). Results offered the first empirical evidence that well-developed community programs fostered the five Cs and identified positive relationships between PYD and children's self-regulation, as well as school and community engagement. Finally, the presence of PYD was found to significantly decrease the likelihood of depression, as well as deviant and risk behaviours in adolescents.

Sport programs have long been understood as ideal platforms for young individuals to develop physically, psychologically, emotionally, socially, and intellectually (Fraser-Thomas, Côté, & Deakin, 2005). Inspired by Lerner and colleagues' work, Côté, Bruner, Erickson, Strachan, and Fraser-Thomas (2010) adapted the PYD framework to the sport domain. In their investigations, Côté et al. found that participants perceived caring/compassion as part of character due to the close relationship between these constructs in sport. Consequently, Côté et al. proposed a reduction from five to four ideal outcomes of youth sport participation, namely competence, confidence, connection, and character; also known as the four Cs of PYD in sport. Within this theoretical framework, competence was defined as individuals' abilities in a specific sport; confidence as the degree of certainty an individual possesses about his/her ability to succeed in general; connection as the positive interpersonal relationships that originate from the need to belong and feel cared for; and character as individuals' moral development and sportspersonship. Together, the four Cs have become widely accepted in the youth sport developmental literature. For instance, Holt et al. (2017) conducted a qualitative meta-study of PYD in sport research that offered support for the development of the four Cs through youth sport programs. Among their findings, the most common outcomes of youth sport participation included improved competence, fundamental movement

[1]Every year, Lerner and colleagues write a "wave report" that summarizes the findings of their research. See (https://4-h.org/wp-content/uploads/2016/02/4-H-Study-of-Positive-Youth-Development-Wave-9-Report.pdf) for an example of their work.

skills, motivation, self-awareness, teamwork, communications skills, leadership skills, autonomy, and respect for others (Holt et al., 2017). All of these outcomes relate to the four Cs, highlighting the impact the PYD in sport framework has had on youth sport coaching research and practice. Still, it is important to note that mere sport participation does not guarantee the development of positive developmental outcomes (PDO; Danish, Forneris, Hodge, & Heke, 2004). Instead, it is the responsibility of coaches, teachers, and parents to appropriately facilitate positive youth development in the context of youth sport.

Empirical Findings Empirical research investigating the development of the four Cs through sport provides support and recommendations to improve the promotion of PYD outcomes in sport contexts (e.g., Côté, Turnnidge, & Evans, 2014; Fraser-Thomas et al., 2005; Fraser-Thomas & Côté, 2009; Holt, Sehn, Spence, Newton, & Ball, 2012; Holt, Tamminen, Tink, & Black, 2009). For example, Holt et al.'s (2012) case study examined school staff members and students' perceptions of the factors that either facilitated or impeded PYD during school-based recreational activities, including physical education, intramural sports, and school sport teams. Data was collected through individual interviews with eight teachers and 59 children from grades 5–9 of a Canadian inner-city elementary school that explicitly aimed to elicit PYD outcomes in their students. According to Holt et al., physical education and team sports fostered students' empathy and social connection. Specifically, teachers and coaches facilitated PYD outcomes when they established clear boundaries during lessons, emphasized the value of respect, and provided students with input and choices over activities. Fewer PDO were achieved when teachers did not explicitly promote PYD during intramural activities. This led to a lack of student boundaries and consequences, which in turn led to negative student interactions, such as damaging equipment, not listening to the referee, swearing at the referee and at each other, and occasional aggressive physical behaviour. These findings highlight the important role teachers and coaches play in facilitating PYD. Petitpas, Cornelius, and Van Raalte (2008) reinforced this statement stating: "youth development programs are only as effective as the adults that deliver them" (p. 62).

Over the past 10 years, research has focused on the coaching behaviours that foster PYD (e.g., Camiré, Forneris, Trudel, & Bernard, 2011; Falcão, Bloom, & Gilbert, 2012; Petitpas et al., 2008). For instance, Camiré et al. (2011) examined the strategies that exceptional coaches implemented to facilitate PYD through sport. Data was collected from high school coaches of adolescents between the ages of 13 and 19. In total, coaches used five general strategies to facilitate PYD including: (a) the development of well-thought out coaching philosophies that prioritized the physical, psychological, and social development of athletes; (b) the development of meaningful relationships with youth athletes through training and additional team bonding actives; (c) the intentional planning of developmental strategies for coaching practice; (d) the creation of opportunity for athletes to practice PDO; and (e) the explicit teaching of the transfer of PDO to other life domains such as school and other community programs. While these coaches offered helpful strategies for the creation of PYD, they also found its facilitation was challenging. Common challenges were the level of time and creativity necessary to offer PYD, not having enough human resources (e.g., assistant coaches or volunteers) to put PYD into practice, and tensions between parents and coaches due to contradictive developmental values.

An increase in coach training program interventions to promote PYD outcomes emerged to help coaches improve their knowledge and application of PYD (e.g., Falcão et al., 2012; Harwood, 2008). For example, Falcão et al. (2012) created and delivered a two-hour coach education workshop designed to promote PDO in youth athletes. Six youth sport coaches from both recreational and competitive leagues from two sport associations in a lower-income area of an urban Canadian city participated in this study. Results suggested the workshops enhanced coaches' knowledge and understanding of their athletes. In addition, coaches felt more competent to create and implement activities that promoted athlete cohesion and communication, as well as competence, confidence, connection, and character/caring. Together, these findings demonstrated the value of designing coach training initiatives that offered learning opportunities to foster PDO for youth sport participants.

In sum, the PYD movement in sport has reinforced that youth sport programs can foster positive psychosocial outcomes, such as the four Cs (Côté et al., 2010). Nevertheless, it is important to remember that the mere exposure to sport does not produce PYD, instead the sport environment must be explicitly designed to foster specific goals and pedagogical strategies that promote PYD. Similar to Smith, Smoll, and colleagues' work, researchers studying PYD in youth sport also found the importance of training influential adults, such as parents, coaches, and teachers, to enhance the sport environments for young athletes.

Life Skills Development Model

The Life Skills Development Model (LSDM) is a theoretical framework that explains how sport participation can lead to the development of life skills such as goal setting, time and stress management, emotional regulation, moral development, teamwork, and confidence (Gould, Carson, Fifer, Lauer, & Benham, 2009). Within this framework, life skills are defined as "internal personal assets, characteristics, and skills . . . that can be facilitated or developed in sport and are transferred for use in non-sport settings" (Gould & Carson, 2008b, p. 287). As such, life skills outcomes differ from PYD outcomes in that PYD outcomes only qualify as life skills if they are successfully transferred to settings beyond the sport context. The concept of PYD is thus broader than that of life skills, whereby all life skills focus on PYD, yet not all PYD efforts develop life skills (Gould & Carson, 2008a). Life skills are commonly developed when a coach, parent, or program leader intentionally emphasizes the importance of transferring learned psychological skills to other life situations. Overall, the LSDM serves as a guiding framework for research and youth sport programs aiming to foster the development of life skills (Gould & Carson, 2008a, 2008b; Pierce, Gould, & Camiré, 2017).

Theoretical Background The LSDM was developed by Gould and Carson (2008a) after conducting a review of the life skills development through sport literature and has since been used by various researchers to examine and enhance the process of life skills development and transfer in youth sport (e.g., Camiré, Trudel, & Forneris, 2012; Trottier & Robitaille, 2014). The model consists of five components describing factors that influence the development of life skills through youth sport participation, including (a) athletes' make-up, (b) coaches' strategies to teaching life skills, (c) processes by which life skills development occurs and impacts behaviours, (d) possible outcomes of sport participation, and (e) the transferability of life skills to non-sport settings (Gould & Carson, 2008a). The first component outlines that coaches need to account for athletes' individual characteristics (i.e., internal assets such as personality traits and external assets such as parents and peers) and previous experiences of youth sport participation when aiming to effectively teach life skills. Similar to the MAC and PYD, the second component highlights that coaches influence athletes' life skills development through their attitudes, as well as direct and indirect coaching behaviours. Direct coaching behaviours include the reinforcement of clear and consistent rules, high quality instructions, the provision of leadership and decision making opportunities, individualised attention to athletes, fairness, and effective team building. Indirect coaching behaviours are characterised by the demands of the sport, program success, modeling, social reinforcement, and positive social norms. The third component of the LSDM describes other processes that influence youth athletes' life skills development including the wider social environment and athletes' utility of life skills strategies. The fourth component offers an overview of potential positive and negative physical, intellectual, and psychosocial outcomes of sport participation, including fitness and health benefits or injury, increased school engagement or drop out, and stress management or burnout. The final component outlines the factors influencing the transferability of life skills from sport to non-sport settings, including athletes' belief that life skills are valued in other settings, a comprehension of life skills transfer, the confidence to apply life skills to other domains, and others' support and reinforcement. Specific to the latter component, Pierce et al. (2017) suggested that coaches developed athletes' ability to transfer life skills by regularly discussing this process, raising awareness of transfer opportunities, and by offering athletes chances to practice life skills within and outside coaching practices (e.g., through decision making, team bonding, and leadership opportunities). Taken together, the LSDM outlines the pivotal role coaches play in the development and transfer of athletes' life skills.

Empirical Findings Studies using the LSDM have focused on identifying the life skills youth learned through sport participation, and which strategies coaches used to foster life skills transfer among their athletes (Bean, Kendellen, & Forneris, 2016; Camiré et al., 2012; Pierce, Kendellen, Camiré, & Gould, 2018; Whitley, Wright, & Gould, 2016). For example, Bean et al. (2016) examined the life skills that promoted positive development and empowered female youth from low-income Canadian families. The program was largely based on Hellison's (2011) Teaching Personal and Social Responsibility model, where coaches encouraged youth participants to engage in personal responsibility, effort, self-coaching, leadership, and life skills transfer. In particular, coaches in this program encouraged participants to put forth their best effort and take responsibility for their actions, facilitated opportunities for participants to practice their learned life skills, and explained how and why transferring life skills to other domains was important. After implementing the program, Bean et al. interviewed eight youth female participants who reported learning both intrapersonal skills (i.e., emotional regulation, focus, and goal setting) and interpersonal skills (i.e., respect, responsibility, and social skills), as well as transferring these skills to non-sport settings such as their academic, social, and family life. Furthermore, the authors provided examples of strategies that coaches used to facilitate the development and transfer of life skills. This included the teaching of breathing and relaxation techniques, helping participants set goals, and playing cooperative games that emphasized teamwork and communication.

In another study that was conceptualized with the LSDM, Camiré et al. (2012) interviewed nine high school coaches and 16 of their athletes to examine the philosophies and strategies coaches used to foster the transfer of life skills to other domains. Findings revealed that coaches learned about their athletes' background, followed coaching philosophies that emphasized personal development, and used strategies that taught life skills. For example, coaches modelled and discussed core values such as respect and fair play, used teachable moments showing how lessons learned in sport were applicable to other domains, and organized volunteer work to teach athletes leadership and community involvement (Camiré et al., 2012).

Taken together, the LSDM has been researched and implemented in various settings, providing a foundation that describes how coaches can teach life skills to youth sport participants and foster their ability to transfer these skills to other life domains. Similar to the PYD and MAC approaches, LSDM highlights the significance of teaching supporting adults such as coaches, parents, and teachers how to best develop and encourage the transfer of life skills in youth sport participants.

Humanistic Coaching

Humanistic coaching is a philosophy that focuses on promoting athletes' personal growth and development by empowering athletes and fostering collaborative interpersonal relationships between coaches and athletes (Lombardo, 1987; Lyle, 2002). It focuses on including athletes as active agents of their sporting experience by encouraging them to make decisions and problem-solve, which fosters the achievement of personal, athletic, cognitive, and emotional competencies. While humanistic coaching shares similarities with the aforementioned approaches (e.g., emphasis on personal growth and development), it is unique in building collaborative coach-athlete relationships that emphasize athletes' freedom and autonomy. Humanistic coaching entails a change of coaches' attitudes, from making decisions to sharing responsibility, from information-giver to a facilitator of learning, from setting rules and standards to agreeing on them (Lombardo, 1987). Coaches using humanistic coaching strategies commonly individualize training and teach athletes to make positive decisions in and away from the sport setting.

Theoretical Underpinnings Humanistic psychology is an approach proposing individuals are inherently motivated to grow and improve, while also taking control of their lives (Maslow, 1954; Rogers, 1969). The humanistic psychology approach believes that individuals are driven towards achieving a sense of fulfillment, growth, and personal achievement, referred to as self-actualization (Coulter, Megan, Mallett, & Carey, 2016; Maslow, 1954). This perspective emphasizes the importance of making choices and continuously growing to achieve personal satisfaction and fulfilment (Rogers, 1969; Rowley & Lester, 2016). Humanistic psychology follows five principles (Maslow, 1954; Rogers, 1969; Shaffer, 1978). First, it emphasizes the personal and subjective interpretation of one's experience. Second, it takes a holistic stance to interpreting individuals and rejects a dualist or reductionist view of humans. Third, it describes freedom and autonomy as central concepts to human behaviour. More specifically, it views individuals as inherently motivated to achieve self-actualization, which in turn requires freedom to experience and choose. Fourth, humanistic psychology is anti-reductionist by not attempting to analyze experience as a combination of individual components, but viewing it instead as a unique and personal phenomenon. Finally, it does not attempt to define human nature, instead it views it as a unique and dynamic process during which individuals continuously learn and develop. Taken together, humanistic psychology has an optimistic view of humanity that emphasizes individuality and holistic interpretation while also highlighting individuals' autonomy to make decisions and take control of their lives. These humanistic principles have been applied to other fields of science, such as education and coaching.

Humanistic coaching emerged in response to the limitations of coach-centered methods which are characterized by a lack of personal empathy and one-way communication whereby information is only transmitted from the coach to the athlete (Lombardo, 1987; Nelson, Cushion, Potrac, & Groom, 2014). This traditional coaching style is described as autocratic, authoritative, and performance-oriented (Lyle, 2002). In comparison, humanistic coaching advocates athletes' autonomy and freedom, collaborative coach-athlete relationships, and is oriented towards growth and development (Lyle, 2002). Six coaching behaviours are used to describe humanistic coaching (Lombardo, 1987; Lyle, 2002; Nelson et al., 2014). First, coaches must be responsive to change to accept the continuous evolution of sport coaching. Second, developing freedom and autonomy for athletes encourages them to pursue self-actualization (i.e., personal achievement, fulfilment, growth, and development). To this end, the authenticity of freedom is more important than the amount of freedom itself. Third, coaches must set clear goals that focus on personal growth and development. This allows athletes to understand what is expected of them and how they can progress in the sport setting. Fourth, coaches must gradually relinquish control until athletes attain the autonomy and freedom that will allow for the aforementioned self-actualization. This transition must be gradual so that participants can adjust to new challenging circumstances that can enhance athletes' potential to problem-solve. Fifth, providing problem-solving opportunities to challenge athletes to learn in a self-directed and independent way where athletes learn by doing and trying. It is the coaches' responsibility to provide athletes with optimal levels of challenge to foster opportunities to improve performance and self-awareness. Finally, coaches must adjust and adapt their behaviours and leadership style to the needs, characteristics, and abilities of individual athletes.

Empirical Findings Research examining humanistic coaching has mostly focused on professional and Olympic contexts showing that coaches using this appraoch fostered holistic development by taking an athlete-centered stance, building positive collaborative relationships, and providing problem-solving opportunities for athletes (Bennie & O'Connor, 2010; Jones, Armour, & Potrac, 2003; Lara-Bercial & Mallett, 2016). For example, Bennie and O'Connor (2010) interviewed six coaches and 25 of their athletes from professional sport leagues and found that coaches who followed humanistic principles believed success on the field was a consequence of developing the individual as an athlete and a person by allowing their players to achieve a balance between sport and life. More specifically, coaches encouraged athletes to seek personal intersts beyond sports, such as pursing academic interests in their time away from training. Coaches also developed a greater awareness of their players' personal needs by talking to them about non sport issues in their lives (Bennie & O'Connor, 2010).

To date, only a few studies have empirically examined humanistic coaching in youth sport settings (Falcão, Bloom, & Bennie, 2017; Falcão, Bloom, Caron, & Gilbert, 2019; Solana-Sánchez, Lara-Bercial, & Solana-Sánchez, 2016). For example, Falcão et al. (2017) developed, delivered, and evaluated a humanistic coaching workshop for coaches of high school athletes. During the workshop researchers presented the humanistic coaching principles and facilitated interactive activities in which coaches developed humanistic coaching behaviours and strategies. The results of this study found that coaches applied the humanistic principles by giving problem-solving opportunities and challenging athletes with thought-provoking questions, building collaborative coach-athlete relationships by engaging in athletes lives beyond sport (e.g., asking about athletes' experiences in school and with their family), as well as seeking athletes' input about practices and allowing them to make decisions about the team (Falcão et al., 2017). As a result of using these behaviours, coaches noticed a number of developmental outcomes in their athletes, such as increased autonomy, communication skills, motivation, and willingness to help teammates (Falcão et al., 2017). These findings were supported by two subsequent studies examining the experiences of youth high school athletes of coaches who had participated in a humanistic coaching workshop (Falcão, Bloom, Caron, & Gilbert, 2019; Falcão, Bloom, & Sabiston, 2020). Among their findings, high school athletes felt empowered to make decisions, enjoyed their sport experience, built stronger relationships with their coaches, and reported engaging in less antisocial behaviours compared to athletes of coaches who had not participated in the workshop. In addition, Solana-Sánchez et al. (2016) investigated the philosophical, methodological, and pedagogical tenets of the Sevilla Football Club Youth Academy that were used to develop the personal and athletic skills of their athletes. Among their findings, the program emphasized developing athletes' ability to make decisions and solve problems. To that end, coaches used games for understanding (cf. Bunker & Thorpe, 1982) that promoted decision making and in-depth knowledge of the sport (Solana-Sánchez et al., 2016). Consequently, the authors concluded that the Sevilla Football Club emphasized athletes' active engagement in their practice and provided a holistic approach to coaching soccer. Both of these studied provided examples of the application of humanistic behaviours with youth athletes. Similar to the previous approaches, humanistic coaching emphasizes athletes' personal growth and development, yet it is unique in the extent to which it highlights the role of coaches in providing athletes freedom to choose and experience by acting as facilitators of athletes' learning process.

Practical Implications

The previous section provided insight into the theoretical underpinnings and empirical findings of four coaching frameworks. Together, these frameworks contribute to the growing body of research that aims to understand and foster youth athletes' positive development through sport participation. These models offer useful recommendations for coaching practice and coach education. As a result, this section begins by synthesizing and presenting six practical coaching strategies that facilitate the development of positive outcomes in youth sport participants, as well as their transfer to other life domains. Following this section, recommendations are provided outlining how these coaching strategies can be taught through coach education programs.

Implications for Coaching

Based on the conceptual and empirical findings presented in this chapter, six coaching strategies are recommended to foster PDO in youth sport participants. Each coaching strategy is explained below, and practical examples are offered.

Promote Learning and Personal Development over Winning Coaching behaviours significantly impact the psychosocial and affective responses of youth sport participants (Holt, 2016; Smith & Smoll, 2002). To cultivate PDO among youth athletes, it is fundamental that coaches prioritize athletes' personal development and learning over winning (Bean et al., 2016; Camiré et al., 2012; Smith et al., 2007). To do so, coaches should (a) promote and praise effort, task mastery, enjoyment, and persistence, (b) limit athletes' fear of failure by promoting challenges and failure as opportunities for growth, (c) consciously avoid the creation of an ego orientated coaching climate, (d) avoid punishment or punitive behaviours particularly after mistakes or failure, and (e) communicate a belief in athletes' ability to improve (Camiré et al., 2011; Cumming et al., 2007). To identify if coaches promote these values and behaviours, they can ask themselves questions such as "why do I coach?", "what are my objectives for coaching?", "what do I get out of coaching?", and "why did I get into coaching?" (Gould, Medbery, & Collins, 2003). The answers to these questions offer insight into coaches' beliefs, values, and behaviours.

Create a Supportive Environment Positive relationships between athletes, their coaches, and teammates have consistently been reported to foster valuable developmental outcomes in youth athletes, including commitment, intrinsic motivation, and effort (Fraser-Thomas et al., 2005; Gould & Carson, 2008b). To foster positive coach-athlete relationships coaches can (a) empower athletes through decision making and problem solving opportunities, (b) offer positive reinforcement, (c) focus on athletes' strengths, talents, and interests, (d) have realistic expectations of athletes, (e) refrain from judgemental comments, (f) model positive behaviours such as respect, sportsmanship, empathy, patience, and warmth, (g) show interest in athletes' lives beyond the sport context, and (h) acknowledge athletes' perspectives and values (Côté et al., 2010; Falcão et al., 2017; Pierce et al., 2018). Specific to the latter two behaviours, coaches should make a conscious effort to connect with their athletes regarding issues outside of sport. To also foster positive relationships between athletes, coaches are encouraged to create environments conducive of mutual support and social interaction. This can be achieved through the provision of team building activities (Cumming et al., 2007; Falcão et al., 2012).

Intentionally Plan and Promote the Development of PDO While the emphasis of learning and personal development and the creation of supportive environments build a strong foundation for the development of PDO, their development is still not guaranteed (Camiré et al., 2011; Smith & Smoll, 2002). Instead, coaches have to explicitly plan and systematically integrate their development into their everyday coaching practice (Bean et al., 2016). To enhance this process, several behaviours are recommended. First, coaches should engage in self-monitoring and reflection processes (Smoll & Smith, 2002). These have the potential to increase coaches' awareness of their own coaching behaviours, as well as situations that offer ideal opportunities for teaching PDO (Smoll & Smith, 2002). Second, coaches should regularly plan for and reflect upon the development of PDO (Falcão et al., 2012). Particularly in the early stages, the conscious facilitation of athletes' positive development can be challenging and time consuming. Over time coaches will be able to make the behaviour an integral part of their practice. Third, coaches should dedicate time to discuss positive development in practice to develop athletes' understanding of this topic. Fourth, coaches can bring in older athletes who can share their experience of developing and using PDO throughout their sporting careers to foster athletes' understanding of the value and importance of well-developed PDO.

Finally, coaches can teach athletes key words or catchy slogans that trigger their use of PDO within the sport context. For instance, the All Blacks Rugby team uses the slogan "Better People Make Better All Blacks" (Hodge, Henry, & Smith, 2014).

Facilitate Opportunities to Practice PDO Talking about PDO is the first step towards explicitly teaching them. The next step is to offer athletes opportunities to practice and refine their PDO (Holt, 2016). This process helps athletes internalise and apply learned skills into practice (Pierce et al., 2018). For instance, when considering the PDO focus in the sport of golf, coaches can teach their athletes to employ a specific performance routine before taking a shot, while explaining the importance of focus on shot accuracy. In addition, coaches can provide athletes with leadership, decision making, and problem-solving opportunities. For example, during rugby practice, coaches could nominate two captains who are responsible for a group of players. Each captain needs to clearly communicate playing strategies to his/her team and solve problems throughout the session. Before the session comes to a close, coaches should gather athletes together to reflect on the captains' performance in a supportive manner (Bean et al., 2016). To foster this process further, coaches can engage athletes in individual conversations or team briefs that are guided by open-ended questions or encourage athletes to keep a reflective journal (Camiré et al., 2011; Fraser-Thomas et al., 2005). For example, after teaching athletes focus through a structured performance routine, coaches can ask questions such as "How did you find using the performance routine to help you focus?" or "What else could you do to help you focus before your shot?" Finally, coaches should aim to facilitate challenging, yet achievable training sessions that allow athletes to master new tasks and skills. Despite the aspect of challenge, goals should be process orientated to foster a mastery climate and, if possible, established in collaboration with athletes to provide an empowering and autonomy supportive environment (Falcão et al., 2012; Smith & Smoll, 2002).

Promote and Facilitate the Transfer of PDO Similar to the development of PDO within the sport context, it is important to explicitly discuss and practice the transfer of skills into other life domains. Thus, coaches should identify situations outside the sport context in which PDO can be applied (Danish, Taylor, & Fazio, 2003; Gould & Carson, 2008a). Akin to the development of PDO, coaches can facilitate this process through (a) discussions that emphasise the link between sport and other life domains, (b) examples from coaches or older athletes of the successful transfer of PDO from sport to other life domains, (c) open-ended, reflective questioning (e.g., Why is the transfer of PDO important? Can you give me an example of a skill you successfully transferred to another life domain?), and (d) enhancement of athletes' confidence to transfer PDO by offering praise for transfer attempts, viewing transfer failure as valuable learning opportunities, and setting goals for future skill transfer (Gould & Carson, 2008b; Pierce et al., 2017).

After developing a sound understanding of the notion of transfer, it is important to provide athletes with concrete opportunities for transfer (Bean et al., 2016). To facilitate this process coaches can encourage or facilitate athletes' engagement in community services, team fundraisers, or volunteer opportunities. These offer athletes the opportunity to experience various amounts of community involvement, teamwork, organisation, respect, and leadership (Camiré et al., 2011; Petitpas et al., 2008). Finally, coaches should inquire about athletes' experiences of PDO transfer to help athletes reflect upon, evaluate, and monitor the extent to which they successfully apply skills to other contexts (Pierce et al., 2018).

Consider Athletes' Individual Differences and wider Social Environment When aiming to foster PDO, it is important to consider athletes' individual internal and external assets (Gould & Carson, 2008b). Specifically, athletes have different personal and physical attributes, as well as different family and coaching backgrounds, all of which influence their personal make-up and receptiveness to developmental goals. Coaches are encouraged to invest time interacting with their athletes to learn about their background and personal interests. Additionally, parents and teachers can also influence youth athletes' developmental process (Côté, 1999; O'Rourke et al., 2014; Schwebel et al., 2016). Consequently, coaches should strive to form collaborations with these agents to enhance the likelihood of PDO to be transferred to other life domains (Pierce et al., 2018). To do so, coaches are encouraged to openly share and discuss their coaching strategies and intended PDO with parents and teachers (Camiré et al., 2011). Regular progress meetings and collaborative reflections with parents and teachers can increase the likelihood of all agents reinforcing the same values and offering appropriate practice opportunities.

In sum, this section provided an overview of six coaching strategies recommended to foster PDO in youth sport participants. It is envisaged that these strategies will enhance coaches' abilities to fulfil their responsibility of teaching youth athletes sport and life skills, offering them the opportunity to develop into fulfilled and contributing community members. Together, this outlines the need for youth sport coaches to be well-trained (Lauer & Dieffenbach, 2013). Consequently, the following section outlines how the recommended coaching strategies can be taught through coach education.

Implications for Coach Education

Despite the fact that coaches need to be well-trained, the reality is that most youth sport coaches do not receive formal coach education that prepares them to create youth sport environments conducive of PDO (Coatsworth & Conroy, 2007; Lauer & Dieffenbach, 2013). Considering that the mere participation in youth sport programs does not guarantee the development of PDO, more initiatives, such as Smith et al.'s (2007) MAC program are needed to appropriately educate youth sport coaches (Camiré et al., 2011). After reviewing the youth sport coaching literature, several recommendations for coach education programs can be made. First, coach education programs should teach how and why to create mastery orientated coaching climates when working with youth athletes. Specifically, programs should emphasise the importance of prioritizing athletes' learning, personal development, enjoyment, and maximum effort over winning. Second, programs should encourage the development of athlete-centred, supportive, and safe environments in which mistakes and failure are viewed as valuable learning opportunities. Consequently, coaches should be taught to utilize positive behaviours such as reinforcement, praise, and encouragement. Third, programs should offer sessions that provide examples of youth sport program curriculums that have successfully embedded the development of PDO as an integral part of their practice. This should be followed by an opportunity for coaches to develop, present, discuss, and gain feedback on their own curriculum. Fourth, live coaching sessions or DVD-based scenes in which coach developers or successful coaches model the explicit facilitation of PDO should be offered. After reflecting upon the sessions, coaches should develop session plans themselves or in small groups that also provide ample opportunities for youth sport participants to develop and practice PDO. To enhance their learning, coaches should enact these sessions, be observed by coach developers and fellow program attendees, and receive constructive feedback on their performance. Fifth, to foster creativity, programs should help coaches identify situations within and outside the sport context in which youth athletes can develop, apply, and practice their PDO. Examples from domains such as school, family, and community programs should be provided. Finally, coaches should be encouraged to work alongside other adults who impact youth athletes' development to enable the repeated reinforcement of standardized values and goal orientations. To increase coaches' motivation to engage in this process, programs should teach coaches strategies that foster positive relationships with key social agents. This could include sessions on effective communication and leadership styles and providing templates for activities such as collaborative reflections and process meetings.

Key Points

The chapter outlined conceptual, empirical, and practical aspects that have the potential to further promote the professionalization of youth sport coaches. Frameworks such as the Mastery Approach to Coaching, Positive Youth Development in Sport, Life Skills Development Model, and Humanistic Coaching provide valuable guidance structured to inform practices that promote sport environments that meet the needs and desires of youth athletes. To enhance coaches' capability to provide such environments, we believe that coach education programmes should strive to bridge the gap between theory and practice more effectively by teaching coaches the knowledge and practical skills needed to provide positive youth sport environments structured to intentionally and systematically develop PDO.

Conclusions

The chapter explained how youth sport coaches could foster athletes' positive psychological development. Coaches are expected to teach both sport and life skills that are intended to help millions of children around the world flourish athletically and personally to become well-rounded and contributing citizens. After reviewing four popular and empirically tested coaching frameworks, including the Mastery Approach to Coaching, Positive Youth Development in Sport, the Life Skills Development Model, and Humanistic Coaching, six strategies were recommended to support the development of PDO in youth sport participants: (a) promoting learning and personal development over winning, (b) creating supportive environments, (c) intentionally planning and promoting the development of PDO, (d) facilitating opportunities to practice PDO, (e) promoting and facilitating the transfer of PDO, and (f) considering athletes' individual differences and wider social environment. While a gap between best-practice recommendations, everyday coaching practice, and the education of youth sport coaches still exists, it is encouraging to see that sport organisations all around the world are making efforts to promote and enhance the provision of positive youth sport environments, by providing increasing opportunities for the education and recognition of adequately trained and supported youth sport coaches. In sum, a worldwide movement towards appropriate developmental opportunities for children and youth is noticed. We hope that this chapter will positively contribute to this movement and offer helpful recommendations for coaches and other important stakeholders involved in children's development.

References

Bean, C., Kendellen, K., & Forneris, T. (2016). Moving beyond the gym: Exploring life skill transfer within a female physical activity-based life skills program. *Journal of Applied Sport Psychology, 28*, 274–290. https://doi.org/10.1080/10413200.2015.1124155

Bennie, A., & O'Connor, D. (2010). Coaching philosophies: Perceptions from professional cricket, rugby league and rugby union players and coaches in Australia. *International Journal of Sports Science & Coaching, 5*, 309–320. https://doi.org/10.1260/1747-9541.5.2.309

Bunker, D., & Thorpe, R. (1982). A model for the teaching of games in secondary schools. *Bulletin of Physical Education, 18*, 5–8.

Camiré, M., Forneris, T., Trudel, P., & Bernard, D. (2011). Strategies for helping coaches facilitate positive youth development through sport. *Journal of Sport Psychology in Action, 2*, 92–99. https://doi.org/10.1080/21520704.2011.584246

Camiré, M., Trudel, P., & Forneris, T. (2012). Coaching and transferring life skills: Philosophies and strategies used by model high school coaches. *The Sport Psychologist, 26*, 243–260. https://doi.org/10.1123/tsp.26.2.243

Carpentier, J., & Mageau, G. A. (2016). Predicting sport experience during training: The role of change-oriented feedback in athletes' motivation, self-confidence and needs satisfaction fluctuations. *Journal of Sport and Exercise Psychology, 38*, 45–58. https://doi.org/10.1123/jsep.2015-0210

Coatsworth, J. D., & Conroy, D. E. (2007). Youth sport as a component of organized afterschool programs. *New Directions for Youth Development, 115*, 57–74. https://doi.org/10.1002/yd.223

Côté, J. (1999). The influence of the family in the development of talent in sport. *The Sport Psychologist, 13*, 395–417. https://doi.org/10.1123/tsp.13.4.395

Côté, J., Baker, J., & Abernethy, B. (2007). Practice and play in the development of sport expertise. In G. Tenenbaum & R. C. Eklund (Eds.), *Handbook of sport psychology* (3rd ed., pp. 184–202). New York, NY: Wiley.

Côté, J., Bruner, M., Erickson, K., Strachan, L., & Fraser-Thomas, J. (2010). Athlete development and coaching. In J. Lyle & C. Cushion (Eds.), *Sport coaching: Professionalism and practice* (pp. 63–84). Oxford, UK: Elsevier.

Côté, J., Lidor, R., & Hackfort, D. (2009). ISSP position stand: To sample or to specialize? Seven postulates about youth sport activities that lead to continued participation and elite performance. *International Journal of Sport & Exercise Psychology, 9*, 7–17. https://doi.org/10.1080/1612197X.2009.9671889

Côté, J., Turnnidge, J., & Evans, M. B. (2014). The dynamic process of development through sport. *Kinesiologia Slovenica, 20*, 14–26.

Côté, J., & Vierimaa, M. (2014). The developmental model of sport participation: 15 years after its first conceptualization. *Science & Sports, 29*, 63–69. https://doi.org/10.1016/j.scispo.2014.08.133

Coulter, T., Megan, G., Mallett, C., & Carey, A. (2016). Abraham Maslow: Hierarchy of coach and athlete needs. In L. Nelson, R. Groom, & P. Potrac (Eds.), *Learning in sports coaching: Theory and application* (pp. 63–74). New York, NY: Routledge.

Cumming, S. P., Smoll, F. L., Smith, R. E., & Grossbard, J. R. (2007). Is winning everything? The relative contributions of motivational climate and won-lost percentage in youth sports. *Journal of Applied Sport Psychology, 19*, 322–336. https://doi.org/10.1080/10413200701342640

Damon, W. (2004). What is positive youth development? *Annals of the American Academy of Political and Social Science, 591*, 13–24. https://doi.org/10.1177/0002716203260092

Danish, S., Forneris, T., Hodge, K., & Heke, I. (2004). Enhancing youth development through sport. *World Leisure, 46*, 38–49. https://doi.org/10.1080/04419057.2004.9674365

Danish, S. J., Taylor, T. E., & Fazio, R. J. (2003). Enhancing adolescent development through sports and leisure. In G. R. Adams & M. Berzonsky (Eds.), *Blackwell handbook of adolescence* (pp. 92–108). Malden, MA: Blackwell.

Falcão, W. R., Bloom, G. A., & Bennie, A. (2017). Coaches' experiences learning and applying the content of a humanistic coaching workshop in youth sport settings. *International Sport Coaching Journal, 4*, 279–290. https://doi.org/10.1123/iscj.2017-0027

Falcão, W. R., Bloom, G. A., & Gilbert, W. D. (2012). Coaches' perceptions of a coach training program designed to promote youth developmental outcomes. *Journal of Applied Sport Psychology, 24*, 429–444. https://doi.org/10.1080/10413200.2012.692452

Falcão, W. R., Bloom, G. A., Caron, J. G., & Gilbert, W. D. (2019). Youth sport student-athletes' perceptions of humanistic coaching. *International Journal of Sport Psychology, 50*, 523–547. https://doi.org/10.7352/IJSP.2019.50.523

Falcão, W. R., Bloom, G. A., & Sabiston, C. M. (2020). The influence of humanistic coaching on youth development through sport. *International Journal of Sports Science & Coaching, 15*, 610–620. https://doi.org/10.1177/1747954120933975

Fraser-Thomas, J., & Côté, J. (2009). Understanding adolescents' positive and negative developmental experiences in sport. *The Sport Psychologist, 23*, 3–23. https://doi.org/10.1123/tsp.23.1.3

Fraser-Thomas, J., Côté, J., & Deakin, J. (2005). Youth sport programs: An avenue to foster positive youth development. *Physical Education and Sport Pedagogy, 10*, 19–40. https://doi.org/10.1080/1740898042000334890

Gould, D., & Carson, S. (2008a). Life skills development through sport: Current status and future directions. *International Review of Sport and Exercise Psychology, 1*, 58–78. https://doi.org/10.1080/17509840701834573

Gould, D., & Carson, S. (2008b). Personal development through sport. In H. Hebestreit & O. Bar-Or (Eds.), *The young athlete* (pp. 287–301). Oxford, UK: Blackwell.

Gould, D., Carson, S., Fifer, A., Lauer, L., & Benham, R. (2009). Stakeholders' perceptions of social-emotional and life skill development issues characterizing contemporary high school sports. *Journal of Coaching Education, 2*, 20–44. https://doi.org/10.1123/jce.2.1.20

Gould, D., Medbery, R., & Collins, K. (2003). Coaching philosophy-developing winners in football and life. In D. Gould (Ed.), *Coaching academy playbook* (pp. 3–9). Morristown, NJ: The National Football Foundation and College Hall of Fame.

Green, K., & Smith, A. (2016). *Routledge handbook of youth sport*. New York, NY: Routledge.

Harwood, C. (2008). Developmental consulting in a professional football academy: The 5Cs coaching efficacy program. *The Sport Psychologist, 22*, 109–133. https://doi.org/10.1123/tsp.22.1.109

Hellison, D. R. (2011). *Teaching personal and social responsibility through physical activity*. Champaign, IL: Human Kinetics.

Hodge, K., Henry, G., & Smith, W. (2014). A case study of excellence in elite sport: Motivational climate in a world champion team. *The Sport Psychologist, 28*, 60–74. https://doi.org/10.1123/tsp.2013-0037

Holt, N. L. (2016). *Positive youth development through sport* (2nd ed.). London, UK: Routledge.

Holt, N. L., Neely, K. C., Slater, L. G., Camiré, M., Côté, J., Fraser-Thomas, J., . . . Tamminen, K. A. (2017). A grounded theory of positive youth development through sport based on results from a qualitative meta-study. *International Review of Sport and Exercise Psychology, 10*, 1–49. https://doi.org/10.1080/1750984X.2016.1180704

Holt, N. L., Sehn, Z. L., Spence, J. C., Newton, A. S., & Ball, G. D. C. (2012). Physical education and sport programs at an inner city school: Exploring possibilities for positive youth development. *Physical Education and Sport Pedagogy, 17*, 97–113. https://doi.org/10.1080/17408989.2010.548062

Holt, N. L., Tamminen, K. A., Tink, L. N., & Black, D. E. (2009). An interpretive analysis of life skills associated with sport participation. *Qualitative Research in Sport and Exercise, 1*, 160–175. https://doi.org/10.1080/19398440902909017

Jones, R. L., Armour, K. M., & Potrac, P. (2003). Constructing expert knowledge: A case study of a top-level professional soccer coach. *Sport, Education and Society, 8*, 213–229. https://doi.org/10.1080/13573320309254

Lara-Bercial, S., & Mallett, C. J. (2016). The practices and developmental pathways of professional and Olympic serial winning coaches. *International Sport Coaching Journal, 3*, 221–239. https://doi.org/10.1123/iscj.2016-0083

Lauer, L., & Dieffenbach, K. (2013). Psychosocial training interventions to prepare youth sport coaches. In P. Potrac, W. Gilbert, & J. Denison (Eds.), *Routledge handbook of sports coaching* (pp. 451–462). New York, NY: Routledge.

Lerner, R. M. (2009). The positive youth development perspective: Theoretical and empirical bases of a strength-based approach to adolescent development. In C. R. Snyder & S. J. Lopez (Eds.), *Oxford handbook of positive psychology* (2nd ed., pp. 149–163). Oxford, UK: Oxford University Press.

Lerner, R. M., Fisher, C. B., & Weinberg, R. A. (2000). Toward a science for and of the people: Promoting civil society through the application of developmental science. *Child Development, 71*, 11–20. https://doi.org/10.1111/1467-8624.00113

Lerner, R. M., Lerner, J. V., Almerigi, J., Theokas, C., Phelps, E., Gestsdottir, S., . . . & von Eye, A. (2005). Positive youth development, participation in community youth development programs, and community contributions of fifth grade adolescents: Findings from the first wave of the 4-H study of positive youth development. *Journal of Early Adolescence, 25*, 17–71. https://doi.org/10.1177/0272431604272461

Lerner, R. M., Wang, J., Chase, P. A., Gutierrez, A. S., Harris, E. M., Rubin, R. O., & Yalin, C. (2014). Using relational developmental systems theory to link program goals, activities, and outcomes: The sample case of the 4-H study of positive youth development. *New Directions for Student Leadership, 144*, 17–30. https://doi.org/10.1002/yd.20110

Lombardo, B. J. (1987). *The humanistic coach: From theory to practice*. Springfield, IL: Charles Thomas.

Lyle, J. (2002). *Sports coaching concepts: A framework for coaches' behaviour*. London, UK: Routledge.

Maslow, A. H. (1954). *Motivation and personality*. New York, NY: Harper.

Nelson, L., Cushion, C. J., Potrac, P., & Groom, R. (2014). Carl Rogers, learning and educational practice: Critical considerations and applications in sports coaching. *Sport, Education and Society, 19*, 513–531. https://doi.org/10.1080/13573322.2012.689256

Nicholls, J. G. (1984). Achievement motivation: Conceptions of ability, subjective experience, task choice, and performance. *Psychological Review, 91*, 328–346. https://doi.org/10.1037/0033-295X.91.3.328

O'Rourke, D. J., Smith, R. E., Smoll, F. L., & Cumming, S. P. (2014). Relations of parent- and coach-initiated motivational climates to young athletes' self-esteem, performance anxiety, and autonomous motivation: Who is more influential? *Journal of Applied Sport Psychology, 26*, 395–408. https://doi.org/10.1080/10413200.2014.907838

Petitpas, A. J., Cornelius, A., & Van Raalte, J. (2008). Youth development through sport: It's all about relationships. In N. L. Holt (Ed.), *Positive youth development through sport* (pp. 61–70). Abington, UK: Routledge.

Pierce, S., Gould, D., & Camiré, M. (2017). Definition and model of life skills transfer. *International Review of Sport and Exercise Psychology, 10*, 186–211. https://doi.org/10.1080/1750984X.2016.1199727

Pierce, S., Kendellen, K., Camiré, M., & Gould, D. (2018). Strategies for coaching for life skills transfer. *Journal of Sport Psychology in Action, 9*, 11–20. https://doi.org/10.1080/21520704.2016.1263982

Potrac, P., Gilbert, W., & Denison, J. (2013). *Routledge handbook of sports coaching*. New York, NY: Routledge.

Rogers, C. R. (1969). *Freedom to learn*. Columbus, OH: Merrill.

Roth, J. L., & Brooks-Gunn, J. (2003). What exactly is a youth development program? Answers from research and practice. *Applied Developmental Science, 7*, 94–111. https://doi.org/10.1207/S1532480XADS0702_6

Rowley, C., & Lester, C. (2016). Carl Rogers: Person-centred learning in coaching. In L. Nelson, R. Groom, & P. Potrac (Eds.), *Learning in sports coaching: Theory and application* (pp. 75–85). New York, NY: Routledge.

Schulman, S., & Davies, T. (2007). Evidence of the impact of the 'youth development model' on outcomes for young people – A literature review. *London, UK: The National Youth Agency: Information and Research.*

Schwebel, F. J., Smith, R. E., & Smoll, F. L. (2016). Measurement of perceived parental success standards in sort and relations with athletes' self-esteem, performance anxiety, and achievement goal orientation: Comparing parental and coach influences. *Child Development Research, Article ID 7056075*, 1–13. https://doi.org/10.1155/2016/7056075

Shaffer, J. B. P. (1978). *Humanistic psychology*. Englewood Cliffs, NJ: Prentice Hall.

Smith, R. E., Cumming, S. P., & Smoll, F. L. (2008). Development and validation of the motivational climate scale for youth sports. *Journal of Applied Sport Psychology, 20*, 116–136. https://doi.org/10.1080/10413200701790558

Smith, R. E., Shoda, Y., Cumming, S. P., & Smoll, F. L. (2009). Behavioral signatures at the ballpark: Intraindividual consistency of adults' situation-behavior patterns and their interpersonal consequences. *Journal of Research in Personality, 43*, 187–195. https://doi.org/10.1016/j.jrp.2008.12.006

Smith, R. E., & Smoll, F. L. (2002). *Way to go, coach!: A scientifically-proven approach to youth sports coaching effectiveness*. Portola Valley, CA: Warde Publishers.

Smith, R. E., Smoll, F. L., & Cumming, S. P. (2007). Effects of a motivational climate intervention for coaches on young athletes' sport performance anxiety. *Journal of Sport & Exercise Psychology, 29*, 39–59. https://doi.org/10.1123/jsep.29.1.39

Smith, R. E., Smoll, F. L., & Cumming, S. P. (2009). Motivational climate and changes in young athletes' achievement goal orientations. *Motivation and Emotion, 33*, 173–183. https://doi.org/10.1007/s11031-009-9126-4

Smith, R. E., Smoll, F. L., Cumming, S. P., & Grossbard, J. R. (2006). Measurement of multidimensional sport performance anxiety in children and adults: The sport anxiety Scale-2. *Journal of Sport & Exercise Psychology, 28*, 479–501. https://doi.org/10.1123/jsep.28.4.479

Smith, R. E., Smoll, F. L., & Curtis, B. (1979). Coach effectiveness training: A cognitive-behavioral approach to enhancing relationship skills in youth sport coaches. *Journal of Sport Psychology, 1*, 59–75. https://doi.org/10.1123/jsp.1.1.59

Smith, R. E., Smoll, F. L., & Hunt, E. (1977). A system for the behavioural assessment of athletic coaches. *Research Quaterley, 48*, 401–407. https://doi.org/10.1080/10671315.1977.10615438

Smith, R. E., Zane, N. W. S., Smoll, F. L., & Coppel, D. B. (1983). Behavioral assessment in youth sports: Coaching behaviors and children's attitudes. *Medicine & Science in Sports & Exercise, 15*, 208–214.

Smoll, F. L., & Smith, R. E. (1989). Leadership behaviors in sport: A conceptual model and research paradigm. *Journal of Applied Social Psychology, 19*, 1522–1551. https://doi.org/10.1111/j.1559-1816.1989.tb01462.x

Smoll, F. L., & Smith, R. E. (2002). *Children and youth in sport* (2nd ed.). Dubuque, IA: Kendall/Hunt.

Smoll, F. L., & Smith, R. E. (2012). *Parenting young athletes: Developing champions in sport and life*. Lanham, MD: Rowman & Littlefield.

Smoll, F. L., Smith, R. E., Barnett, N. P., & Everett, J. J. (1993). Enhancement of children's self-esteem through social support training for youth sport coaches. *Journal of Applied Psychology, 78*, 602–610. https://doi.org/10.1037/0021-9010.78.4.602

Smoll, F. L., Smith, R. E., & Curtis, B. (1978). Behavioral guidelines for youth sport coaches. *Journal of Physical Education and Recreation, 49*, 46–47.

Smoll, F. L., Smith, R. E., Curtis, B., & Hunt, E. (1978). Toward a mediational model of coach-player relationships. *Research Quarterly, 49*, 528–541. https://doi.org/10.1080/10671315.1978.10615567

Solana-Sánchez, A., Lara-Bercial, S., & Solana-Sánchez, D. (2016). Athlete and coach development in the Sevilla Club de Fútbol youth academy: A values-based proposition. *International Sport Coaching Journal, 3*, 46–53. https://doi.org/10.1123/iscj.2015-0085

Sousa, C., Smith, R. E., & Cruz, J. (2008). An individualized behavioral goal-setting program for coaches. *Journal of Clinical Sport Psychology, 2*, 258–277. https://doi.org/10.1123/jcsp.2.3.258

Trottier, C., & Robitaille, S. (2014). Fostering life skills development in high school and community sport: A comparative analysis of the coach's role. *The Sport Psychologist, 28*, 10–21. https://doi.org/10.1123/tsp.2012-0094

Turnnidge, J., & Côté, J. (2018). Applying transformational leadership theory to coaching research in youth sport: A systematic literature review. *International Journal of Sport and Exercise Psychology, 16*, 327–342. https://doi.org/10.1080/1612197X.2016.1189948

Whitley, M. A., Wright, E. M., & Gould, D. (2016). Coaches' perspectives on teaching life skills to underserved south African children and youth. *International Journal of Sports Science & Coaching, 11*, 312–326. https://doi.org/10.1177/1747954116643464

Gordon Bloom is a Professor in the Department of Kinesiology and Physical Education at McGill University in Montreal, Canada. His research examines coaching effectiveness related to the knowledge, leadership skills, and behaviours employed by both elite and youth sport coaches that create positive environments for excellence and participation in sports.

Lea-Cathrin Dohme is a Lecturer in Sport & Exercise Psychology in the Cardiff School of Sport & Health Sciences at Cardiff Metropolitan University, United Kingdom. Prior to this appointment, she completed a postdoctoral fellowship at McGill University in Montreal, Canada. Her research focuses on understanding and improving the development of youth athletes. This includes examining the knowledge and strategies employed by coaches and parents that foster or inhibit this development. To improve athletes' positive development, Dr. Dohme engages in the development and delivery of international coach education initiatives.

William Falcão is a Postdoctoral Fellow in Sports Management at HEC Montreal in Canada. His research interests include sport coaching, coach education, sport programming, and athlete development through sport. In particular, his doctoral work completed at McGill University entailed the development, implementation, and assessment of a coach training protocol that fostered the personal development, health, and well-being of young athletes.

Chapter 9
Coaching High Performance Athletes

Justine Allen and Bob Muir

Abstract This chapter provides a review of the recent research examining coaching high performance athletes. We first explore who are the athletes and coaches and what are the contexts that comprise this coaching domain. Recognising the diversity within this domain and diversity of approaches researchers have adopted our review attempts to span disciplinary boundaries and develop themes that represent commonalities in the process and practices of coaching high performance athletes. The research findings are discussed under five themes: vision, philosophy, quality relationships, high performing culture and coaching strategies. We offer our views on these findings and areas for further development through research. The chapter then turns to the implications for coaches and researchers. Here we offer an integrated framework that may provide some structure through which to navigate the complex and dynamic process and practices of coaching high performance athletes and connect disciplinary-based theory and concepts to understand the realities of coaching in this domain.

Keywords Coaching domain · Vision · Philosophy · Quality relationships · Coaching strategies

Research interest in coaching is increasing (Griffo, Jensen, Anthony, Baghurst, & Kulinna, 2019) and particularly in the context of coaching high performance athletes. This focus on high performance is perhaps driven by the notion that 'the best coaches work with the best athletes' and therefore, examining coaching in high performance sport will provide insights about coaching that are applicable to others. However, it is important to note that "successful coaches adjust their approach to the

J. Allen (✉)
Faculty of Health Sciences and Sport, University of Stirling, Stirling, UK
e-mail: justine.allen@stir.ac.uk

B. Muir
Carnegie School of Sport, Leeds Beckett University, Leeds, UK
e-mail: B.Muir@leedsbeckett.ac.uk

R. Resende, A. R. Gomes (eds.), *Coaching for Human Development and Performance in Sports*, https://doi.org/10.1007/978-3-030-63912-9_9

athletes, settings and circumstances, because they know the most effective coaching is context specific" (United States Olympic Committee [USOC], 2017, p. 27). Reflective of such consideration, researchers have proposed the use of coaching domains to conceptualise the more or less coherent aggregation of practices and behaviours resulting from the demands and needs of the coaching context and participants (Lyle & Cushion, 2017; North, 2009). This chapter focuses on the coaching domain of high performance athletes and the processes and practices of coaching in this domain. Beyond the scope of this chapter was exploration of the coach as performer and coach as learner (for a review see Rynne, Mallett, & Rabjohns, 2017).

We begin the chapter by exploring the *conceptualisation of high performance athletes, contexts, and coaches*. Next, we *examine the research that seeks to provide insight into coaching high performance athletes*. It is important to note two features of this research: (1) there is a relative lack of empirical research in this coaching domain upon which to base this review; (2) coaching research has been largely informed and guided by the application of concepts and theories from specific disciplines such as psychology, sociology, and pedagogy. Dependent on the disciplinary lens adopted, coaching is portrayed as ordered, regulated, controllable, planned, purposeful and structured *or* dynamic, complex, uncertain, innovative, flexible, improvised, uncontrollable and imbued with unattainable goals (Lyle & Cushion, 2017; Muir, 2018; North, 2017). Although, the resulting behavioural, cognitive and social approaches provide valuable insight into parts of coaching they seldom provide more comprehensive accounts that consider the layered ecology of coaching (Muir, 2018; North, 2017). Leading some researchers to argue for a move beyond disciplines to develop a "more inclusive, 'and/or' rather than 'either/or' conception of coaching practice, reflecting the more interdisciplinary nature of problems that coaches navigate in their day-to-day reality" (Muir, 2018, p. 69). Through our review we have attempted to explore across disciplinary boundaries organising the research findings under key emerging themes. We then consider the *implications for coaches* and to do so adopt *a conceptual framework for coaching* which offers a structure to make sense of the 'reality' of coaching high performance athletes and locate the findings of research more broadly. Finally, we offer several *key points for researchers*.

Review of Literature

High Performance Athletes, Contexts, and Coaches

In order to advance our understanding of coaching high performance athletes, it is important to first consider what constitutes high performance sport and who are high performance athletes. The International Sport Coaching Framework 1.2 (International Council for Coaching Excellence [ICCE], Association of Summer Olympic International Federations [ASOIF], & Leeds Metropolitan University [LMU], 2013), similar frameworks (e.g., USOC Coaching Framework, 2017; European Coaching Framework (Lara-Bercial et al., 2017) and researchers (e.g. Lyle & Cushion, 2017; North, 2009) distinguish between forms of sport engagement (e.g., participation, development, performance). Participation sport emphasises involvement and enjoyment, while performance sport accentuates competition and achievement (ICCE et al., 2013). Within performance sport athletes are further categorised as emerging, performance, and high performance. High performance athletes are a small group of "world-class athletes competing in world championships and major events and high level leagues" (ICCE & ASOIF, 2012, p. 16) with a long term commitment to excellence. The USOC Coaching Framework (2017) describes this sport engagement as comprising "highly competitive sport experiences limited to a select few who are highly committed to achieving the highest possible level of expertise" (p. 12). Therefore, high performance athletes are those engaged in contexts where emphasis is on preparation for and performance in competitive sport for achievement of performances that are, comparatively speaking, of the highest level.

An exploration of the research on coaching high performance athletes indicates that researchers have examined a range of sporting contexts such as Collegiate sport (e.g., Callary, Werthner, & Trudel, 2013; Vallée & Bloom, 2016; Yukelson & Rose, 2014); Olympic/Paralympic sport (e.g., Dixon, Lee, & Ghaye, 2012; Lara-Bercial & Mallett, 2016; Mallett & Lara-Bercial, 2016; Ritchie & Allen, 2015; Ritchie, Allen, & Kirkland, 2018); Professional sport (e.g., Bennie & O'Connor, 2010; Cruickshank, Collins, & Minten, 2013; Gomes, Araújo, Resende, & Ramalho, 2018); and Masters sport (e.g., Medic, Young, Starkes, & Weir, 2012). Many or even most athletes in these contexts would certainly be characterised as highly competitive and committed to preparation for, and achievement of, high level performances. However, Collegiate and Masters sport athletes' level of performance might be considered relative to their particular context rather than of the highest level of expertise for their sport. Furthermore, a relative newcomer to researchers' attention is Adventure Sports (e.g., Cooper & Allen, 2018, 2020; Simon, Collins, & Collins, 2017). The competitive versions of these sports such as Winter Olympic sports are comparable to contexts in previous high performance sport research (e.g., Din, Paskevich, Gabriele, & Werthner, 2015; Lyons, Rynne, & Mallett, 2012; Simon et al., 2017). However, those athletes performing to the highest level of expertise in non-competitive Adventure Sport settings such as mountaineering or kayaking might challenge the notions of 'who are high performance athletes' and 'what are high performance sport contexts'. The diversity of contexts and definitions of 'elite' athletes indicate a far from homogenous group (Swann, Moran, & Piggott, 2015) and yet they are frequently considered under the umbrella of high performance sport. When seeking to derive insight from our review of literature about this coaching domain it is important to consider this diversity and the situated nature of coaching.

Turning our attention to coaches working in this domain, it is important to consider that working with high performance athletes does not guarantee the coach engages in quality coaching or indeed could be considered an expert coach. Coaches may, in fact, be considered 'experts by association'. Coaches are often employed based on their athletic success (Gilbert, Côté, & Mallett, 2006; Trudel & Gilbert,

2006) and appointed without adequate training (Mallett, Rossi, Rynne, & Tinning, 2016). Similar practices are likely in the recruitment and appointment of coaches into high performance contexts (Mallett & Lara-Bercial, 2016) and perhaps exacerbated by the practice of 'fast-tracking' former elite performers into high performance coaching roles. Such practices have been questioned with particular concerns including coaches' limited actual coaching practice (Blackett, Evans, & Piggott, 2018; Rynne, 2014), lack of reflection and self-awareness resulting in uncritical adoption of coaching practices (Blackett, Evans, & Piggott, 2017; Watts & Cushion, 2017), and the limited evidence of a relationship between coaching success and coaches own playing experience (Ewing, 2019; Schempp, McCullick, Grant, Foo, & Wieser, 2010). Equally, however some coaches fast-tracked into these contexts and roles, along with other coaches in this domain, are indeed high performing coaches, demonstrating quality coaching. The point here is that expertise and quality coaching is not guaranteed by virtue of who a coach works with or the context they work in.

Despite diversity in the contexts, athletes, and coaches deemed to be high performance, a commonality of this coaching domain is the emphasis on preparation for and performance at the highest level compared with others in the sport. The coach plays a central role in this coach-athlete-performance relationship (Abraham, Collins, & Martindale, 2006; Lyle & Cushion, 2017; Mallett & Lara-Bercial, 2016). Although not exclusively, coaches' are frequently responsible for guiding athletes' preparation and performances in the international sporting arena and they are held accountable for producing winning outcomes (Kristiansen & Roberts, 2010; Mallett & Côté, 2006; Mallett & Lara-Bercial, 2016). Coaches' tasks go beyond direct interventions with athletes to include indirect task related activity (e.g., programming, management of staff, research), administrative tasks (e.g., budgets, reports), and public relations activities (e.g., media, liaising with stakeholders, sharing with coaches) (Lyle & Cushion, 2017; Rynne & Mallett, 2012). Applying criteria that assist in establishing boundaries between coaching domains, performance coaching has been characterised as involving a planned, progressive, and individualised process, with intensive commitment to preparation and formalised competition, long and short term objectives including specific competition objectives, and extensive interpersonal contact between coach and performer (Lyle, 2002; Lyle & Cushion, 2017). The coaching process will, however, differ in focus, scale, and intensity in other coaching domains such as participation coaching for children, adolescents or adults and performance coaching for emerging or performance athletes (Lyle, 2002; Lyle & Cushion, 2017). Furthermore, operationalisation of the coaching process in the high performance domain is set amidst a context which has been characterised for its dynamic, complex, unpredictable and even chaotic nature (Purdy & Jones, 2011).

With such diversity in this domain, it is no wonder that several researchers have suggested that 'structured improvisation', seeking to bring order to chaos (Bowes & Jones, 2006; Cushion, 2007; Cushion, Armour, & Jones, 2003), is useful when considering coaching high performance athletes (Mallett, 2010). It is also perhaps unsurprising that coaches in this domain have been characterised as detailed planners, who are organised and deliberate and yet adaptable and fluid in their practice and usually engage in highly complex decision making (Mallett, 2010). Furthermore, to effectively operationalise coaching, coaches are likely to require a range of in-depth knowledge resources and the capability to integrate this knowledge within their practice (Abraham, Muir, & Morgan, 2010; Côté & Gilbert, 2009; Lyle, 2002; Lyle & Cushion, 2017; North, 2017). In summary, despite representation as a single coaching domain (coaching high performance athletes), there is substantial diversity among athletes, contexts, and coaches all of which should be taken into account when considering the research that follows. In the next section we review the research on coaching high performance athletes seeking to provide some structure through which to understand coaching of, for, and with high performance athletes.

Foundations and Practices of Coaching High Performance Athletes

Researchers continue to work to better understand coaching high performance athletes and, although not mutually exclusive, continue to examine coaching in Olympic and international sport (e.g., Consterdine, Newton, & Piggin, 2013; Hansen & Andersen, 2014; Lara-Bercial & Mallett, 2016; Purdy & Jones, 2011; Ritchie & Allen, 2015) and high performance clubs, teams, and individuals (e.g., Abrahamsen & Pensgaard, 2012; Bennie & O'Connor, 2010; Cruickshank et al., 2013; Junggren, Elbæk, & Stambulova, 2018; Mills & Denison, 2013). Coaching in professional sport falls under these two contexts. Furthermore, some participant samples are not defined by a specific context and instead include a mix of national level and international athletes (e.g., Keegan, Harwood, Spray, & Lavallee, 2014; Santos, Jones, & Mesquita, 2013).

Participants in the research reviewed for this chapter were most often coaches and, to a lesser extent, athletes. Relatively few studies included both coaches and athletes (for exceptions see Din et al., 2015; Junggren et al., 2018; Lara-Bercial & Mallett, 2016) and even fewer included other stakeholders such as performance director, specialist coaches, support staff (for exceptions see Cruickshank et al., 2013; Fletcher & Streeter, 2016). With regards to research design, most research was cross-sectional with only a few studies adopting longitudinal (e.g., Abrahamsen & Pensgaard, 2012; Hall, Gray, & Sproule, 2016), ethnographic or case study approaches (e.g., Junggren et al., 2018; Lyons et al., 2012; Purdy & Jones, 2011). The most common method employed was semi-structured interviews. This almost always involved a single interview with each participant (for exceptions see Barker-Ruchti, Rynne, Lee, & Barker, 2014; Mills & Denison, 2013). Quantitative questionnaires, generally with athletes, have also been employed (e.g., Abrahamsen & Pensgaard, 2012; Gillet, Vallerand, Amoura, & Baldes, 2010). Only a few studies employed other methods such as observations (e.g., Hall et al., 2016; Purdy & Jones, 2011) or adopted multiple methods (e.g., Consterdine et al., 2013; Lyons et al., 2012; Muir, 2018; van Puyenbroeck, Stouten, & Vande Broek, 2017).

Access for researchers to the high performance coaching domain can be challenging and may provide an explanation for the prominence of interviews as the favoured method of research. Interviews provide a useful glimpse into this coaching domain, particularly if researchers are interested in coaches' and athletes' perceptions of coaching processes and practices. Insights from this self-report method, however, may be limited by the accuracy of participants' memory and recall as well as more deliberate impression management and self-presentation strategies. In addition, coherence between coaches' verbal recollections of what they do and their actual behaviour in practice has been questioned (Muir, 2018; Partington & Cushion, 2013). Although there is some research to suggest that this is not evident for all coaches (e.g., Cooper & Allen, 2020; Grecic, MacNamara, & Collins, 2013). The over reliance on a single method for evidence collection has been problematised and researchers reminded that interviews are just one method for gathering rich information (Culver, Gilbert, & Sparkes, 2012; Sparkes & Smith, 2009). Greater use of longitudinal or ethnographic designs and employing multiple methods will be useful to further our understanding of the situated and layered nature of coaching high performance athletes (North, 2017).

As discussed earlier in the chapter, there is marked diversity across contexts, athletes, and coaches within the high performance coaching domain. In addition, considering the characteristics of the research described above and its inherent limitations, next we cautiously present an overview of the research findings. Although our review suggests some commonalities, these are presented at a more general level and as such risk appearing to devalue the detail, subtleties and diversity integral to this coaching domain. That is not our intention. Instead, we have organised the discussion into five themes as a means to make sense of the diverse recent research examining coaching high performance athletes. These themes are: Vision; Philosophy; Quality Relationships; High Performing Culture; and Coaching Strategies.

Vision: A Sense of Purpose and Direction

From our review of the research, it was evident that a clear sense of purpose and direction expressed through a detailed vision of what is necessary to win was the foundation of coaches' work with high performance athletes. The capacity to see into the future provided a platform from which coaches were able to simplify the complexity of their sports, undertake thorough action planning, constantly review and monitor progress to adjust where necessary. Not only did this vision provide direction and a sense of purpose it also assisted coaches to navigate the uneven terrain of the journey associated with the pursuit of successful performance in sport at the highest level (Lara-Bercial & Mallett, 2016; Mallett & Lara-Bercial, 2016). Mallett and Lara-Bercial's research with serial winning Professional and Olympic coaches found that coaches all expressed a clear vision that included an assessment of key performance elements that would underpin future successful performance, innovation to 'future proof' performances, and consideration of the many parts of the process, seeing how they would fit together and simplifying the inherent complexity to prioritise those key to success. Coaches in other research also emphasised the importance of clear goals (e.g., Dixon et al., 2012; Fletcher & Streeter, 2016; Gomes et al., 2018; Hodge, Henry, & Smith, 2014; Mills & Denison, 2013). For example, the endurance coaches of international athletes in Mills and Denison's study appeared very much in control of the targets and goals for athletes' training. Somewhat in contrast, Hodge et al. found that the coaches of the New Zealand All Blacks international rugby team expected players to set their own goals and challenges, believing this was more beneficial for players' motivation than those imposed externally. Indeed, this formed a central part of the coaches' strategy to nurture the holistic development of the players beyond rugby captured in their phrase 'Better People make Better All Blacks'. In their case study of a British high performance swimming club, Fletcher and Streeter found the vision, initially driven by the coach, was a shared club vision that focused on individual and collective improvement. Overtime the vision had evolved going beyond swimming performance, to place greater emphasis on the swimmers' wider lives.

Another consistent finding from the review was the coaches' plan for how to enact their vision. From the research it was clear coaches had a long-term plan and an idea of how the plan would unfold over a period of time, bringing necessary elements together in the process. The plan was not a static entity but rather a clear and detailed set of expectations affording on-going review and adjustment where needed to maintain momentum and progression towards the achievement of specified goals (Din et al., 2015; Fletcher & Streeter, 2016; Mallett & Lara-Bercial, 2016; Nash, Sproule, & Horton, 2011; Ritchie & Allen, 2015). For example, Din et al.'s study of coaches and athletes who together had won medals at Winter Olympic Games found that the coaches communicated a vision and accompanying detailed, meticulous and responsive plan that focused on "teaching athletes what they needed to do to perform on demand against the world's best rather than pitching the idea of winning Olympic gold medals to their athletes" (p. 596). The plan was individualised and whilst it provided a path to competitive success, it also included many adaptations and changes. Ritchie and Allen's (2015) examination of Olympic track and field coaches' perceptions of their role and practices during major events found that the coaches' detailed preparation and planning prior to the event was critical for optimal performance on the day of competition. Supporting these findings, Purdy and Jones (2011) study of a group of international rowers, found that the rowers were unhappy with the coaches' inability to clearly convey their vision. As a result, the rowers began to doubt the competency of the coaches and the resulting friction negatively affected the training environment and the rowers' attention to training tasks.

In summary, this research indicated that coaches expressed a vision for future performance, key ingredients for success, and deemed the vision critical for coaching high performance athletes. This vision, therefore, appears to be a cognitive representation of what is possible and importantly *how* it is possible. Furthermore, the vision these coaches described appeared to be more encompassing than just the individual athlete or team performance, extending to include all key stakeholders, their roles and contributions. Similar concepts have been proposed regarding athletes' potential such as coaches' mental models for athlete performance (e.g., Côté, Salmela, Trudel, Baria, & Russell, 1995) and improving a team's performance through developing a shared mental model (e.g., Richards, Collins, & Mascarenhas, 2012). There appears to be links with expertise and the integration of professional, interpersonal and intrapersonal knowledge (Abraham et al., 2006; Côté & Gilbert, 2009; Lyle & Cushion, 2017) as well as Mason's (2002) concept of noticing, a foundational element of orchestration (Jones, Bailey, & Thompson, 2013; Jones & Wallace, 2005). Coaches can only intervene, halt proceedings or change course to get things 'back on track', if they notice the need to act in the first place. Noticing relies on coaches consciously attending to moments of importance or disruption. However, people are 'sensitised' or 'primed' to notice certain things. In this sense, coaches' vision and their mental model of their sport, provides the framework against which expectations are monitored. Ritchie and Allen's study (2015) and Santos et al.'s (2013) examination of national and international coaches in Portugal are two examples where orchestration and noticing were central concepts in the research. Although providing somewhat contrasting perspectives on coaching, these studies provide some insight into this aspect of coaching high performance athletes. Future research might consider how the vision can be conceptualised, what distinguishes a useful from less useful vision, how it is and could be developed, and under what circumstances it might be adapted, adjusted, or even abandoned.

Philosophy: Developing the Person

Coaches' reasoning, reflecting, strategising, actions and behaviours are underpinned by their personal resources[1] (Muir, 2018; North, 2017). Among the various concepts that can be drawn upon to explore coaches' resources, one in particular has received more attention than most within the research on coaches working with high performance athletes—that of philosophy (Bennie & O'Connor, 2010; Carless & Douglas, 2011; Dixon et al., 2012; Gomes et al., 2018; Junggren et al., 2018; Lara-Bercial & Mallett, 2016; Mallett & Lara-Bercial, 2016). Through our review of the research for this chapter we noticed commonalities in the way coaches' philosophies were reported. The central features reflected humanistic ideals for coaching (Lombardo,

[1]In the work by North (2017) and Muir (2018) resources are conceptualised as a family term that covers a wide range of causal powers, potentials and liabilities that coaches' draw on to reason, reflect, strategise and carry out actions. In this regard, resources encompass a broad variety of concepts already established in coaching and broader learning literature including among others: abilities, attitudes, behaviours, beliefs, biases, capabilities, characteristics, competencies, dispositions, emotion, frames of mind, habits of mind, knowledge, memory, motives, personal perspectives/theories, personality, philosophy, points of view, skills, understandings, values, volition and will.

1987), specifically, a focus on personal development; care and consideration for athletes; and respect and honesty.

With regards to a focus on personal development, Bennie and O'Connor's (2010) study with coaches and athletes from three professional sports teams in Australia found that coaches sought to develop players both 'on and off the field of play' and not solely focused on sporting performance outcomes. Hodge et al. (2014) found the philosophy of coaches in their study emphasised supporting players to become more self-reliant and resilient. Almost inseparable from a personal development focus, studies showed that coaches' reported care and consideration for the athletes they worked with. For example, Carless and Douglas (2011) explored the philosophy of a professional golf coach finding her philosophy was based on care for the person and focused on 'listening first' to determine what they needed. Professional cricketers in Smith, Young, Figgins, and Arthur's (2017) study reported that their coaches considered the individual through "first, an individual approach to the players' training and development; and second, a more general approach to dealing with the players in an individual way." (p. 8). Coaches and athletes in Lara-Bercial and Mallett's (2016) study also reported that the coaches were genuine and caring in their support of athletes both professionally and personally. They also found that coaches espoused and enacted high moral standards including honesty, loyalty and respect for athletes. Furthermore, even when hard decisions had to be made these coaches indicated that they considered the impact on athletes and, from the athletes' perspective, knowing that coaches focused on their 'best interests' supported them through challenging times. Gomes et al. (2018) found that professional Portuguese coaches reported valuing respect between coaches and athletes and showing respect was a means to build relationships with athletes.

In summary, the research reviewed described coaches' well-developed philosophy as an important foundation for their work with high performance athletes. It described how coaches' values and beliefs, an integral part of their philosophy, guided their reasoning, strategising, actions and behaviours. However, it is important to acknowledge concerns about the way that philosophy has been used within the research as a 'catch all' metaphorical dumping ground that assumes a shared understanding of its properties and application (Cushion & Partington, 2014; Lyle & Cushion, 2017). Concerns have also been raised about the accuracy of coaches' self-reports (i.e., via interviews) and the congruence between coaches' espoused theories for practice and their theories in use (Gomes et al., 2018; Harvey, Cushion, Cope, & Muir, 2013; Muir, 2018). Some studies examined coaches' *and* athletes' perceptions (Mallett & Lara-Bercial, 2016) *and* employed observations (Junggren et al., 2018) to explore, more thoroughly the relationship between intentions and actions. As has been argued elsewhere, more research is needed and researchers should look to employ a conceptual framework, common vocabulary, and multiple perspectives to interrogate coaching philosophies (Lyle & Cushion, 2017).

Quality Relationships: Relationships, Collaboration, and Managing Stakeholders

Researchers recognise that coaching is an interpersonal process that involves at the very least a coach and an athlete (Lyle & Cushion, 2017; North, 2017). It is perhaps not surprising then that increasingly the relationship between the coach and athlete (s) is viewed as a critical feature of coaching (Jowett, 2017; Jowett & Shanmugam, 2016; Lyle & Cushion, 2017; North, 2017), including coaching high performance athletes (Gould & Maynard, 2009; Mallett & Lara-Bercial, 2016; Ritchie & Allen, 2015). Our review of the research in this domain suggested that: (1) coaches and athletes believe the formation of trusting, stable and enduring working relationships built on mutual respect and support provides a foundation from which performance success was achieved; (2) some coaches and athletes reported the importance of developing collaborative ways of working and; (3) coaches reported that they recognised and deliberately fostered relationships with and amongst the support team and other key stakeholders (Bennie & O'Connor, 2010; Din et al., 2015; Dixon et al., 2012; Fletcher & Streeter, 2016; Gomes et al., 2018; Hodge et al., 2014; Junggren et al., 2018; Lara-Bercial & Mallett, 2016; Mallett & Lara-Bercial, 2016; Ritchie & Allen, 2015; Smith et al., 2017).

Largely without exception, researchers examining coaching high performance athletes identified the salience, even foundational nature, of coach-athlete relationships. For example, Lara-Bercial and Mallett (2016) found that coaches and athletes believed that quality coach-athlete relationships were fundamental to athletes' success, in part, because this contributed to a psychosocial environment that allowed athletes to "concentrate on the task at hand and to train and perform to the best of their ability" (p. 235). Coaches and athletes in Din et al.'s (2015) study indicated that open and honest communication, even when this involved difficult conversations, was a critical foundation for the relationship. Similarly, cricketers in Smith et al.'s (2017) study reported that coaches were honest in their communication which lead players to respect the coach.

In several studies researchers found explicit collaboration between coaches and athletes (Din et al., 2015; Fletcher & Streeter, 2016; Hodge et al., 2014; Junggren et al., 2018; Lara-Bercial & Mallett, 2016). Rather than coaches leading and athletes following, coaches were working *with* high performance athletes, actively engaging them in the process. An example of this collaboration was the Dual Management approach Hodge et al. found, where a group of players and coaches would regularly meet, sharing decision making and leadership. Similarly, Fletcher and Streeter and Junggren et al. also found shared leadership and responsibility were part of the ethos of the high performance swimming clubs in their studies. Junggren et al. found that this collaboration went even further. The coach and athlete were considered an inseparable unit from which "their relationship, interaction, and knowledge-sharing produce 'emergent effects' related to the development and performance of both athletes and coaches… [Suggesting that] the coach and the athlete need one another to develop, grow and succeed" (p. 1117). In contrast, Purdy and Jones (2011) found that the rowers in their study expressed dissatisfaction with the coaches' use of negative tone and inability to explain the relevance of the training. Rather than coaches working to deliberately foster the rowers' ownership, instead the rowers 'took' ownership of their development and relied less on the coaches. Furthermore, Mills and Denison (2013) suggested that although the endurance coaches in their study were "well meaning, clever, thoughtful, reflective and ultimately considerate coaches" (p. 143), these coaches also believed that their control over the detail and structure of athletes' training was critical for athletes to succeed.

High performance contexts invariably include a range of personnel forming the support team such as assistant and specialist coaches, sport scientists, manager, medical staff and performance director as well as other key stakeholders including media, agents, and athletes' families. Another key finding from our review was that managing the team that supports the athletes was considered by coaches and athletes as crucial to ensuring conditions were favourable for athletes to thrive (Din et al., 2015; Fletcher & Streeter, 2016; Gomes et al., 2018; Hodge et al., 2014; Lara-Bercial & Mallett, 2016; Ritchie & Allen, 2015; Waters, Phillips, Panchuk, & Dawson, 2019). Features that coaches and athletes in this research considered important for effective management included: (1) building and managing relationships with each member and stakeholder; (2) establishing roles and systems; (3) encouraging support personnel to take responsibility for their contribution to the vision; (4) clear, open communication and cooperation among personnel; (5) encouraging debate and discussion; (6) monitoring and reconciling differing opinions; (7) coaches 'managing up', recognising the political landscape and influencing superiors; (8) adapting to circumstances and the needs of wider contexts; and (9) in some cases, head coaches taking a more strategic approach, adopting a management rather than hands-on-coaching role. For example, Din et al. found that coaches' directive leadership behaviour provided clear and concise communication with athletes, sport scientists, and staff with the intention of ensuring everyone knew their distinct role and was accountable for their contribution to preparation. They also found that coaches were decisive 'conductors', managing and leading the group of athletes, sport scientists and support staff to become a unified team and 'bring the best out of everyone'. This meant making final, often tough, decisions when necessary and keeping specialists on task and aligned to the vision and plan. In one of the few studies that has included the sport scientists' perspective, Waters, et al. found that quality relationships between athletics sprint coaches and biomechanists were critical to their work. Participants reported that where these relationships were considered dysfunctional, a key feature was a lack role clarity. In addition, Hodge et al. found that the coaches also focused on how players connected with people around them, such as teammates, family, and fans. They believed that good connections and performances came from behaving respectfully, being self-aware and self-reliant.

In summary, the research supports the view that coaching in the high performance domain is highly relational (Mallett & Lara-Bercial, 2016) and coaches and athletes consider building and maintaining quality relationships as fundamental for their success. In addition, the relational nature of coaching extends beyond the coach-athlete relationship to include collaborations with and among athletes and management of support teams and stakeholders. Much of the research reviewed in this chapter describes relationships and their characteristics in broad terms and as such the conceptual understanding of relationships in this coaching domain is largely under developed. An exception is researchers' examinations of power, where, drawing from different theorists, they have identified the complex, social, relational, oppressive and productive nature of power in coaching (e.g., Mills & Denison, 2013; Purdy & Jones, 2011).

In addition to the conceptualisations of power, the work of Jowett and colleagues (see Jowett, 2017; Jowett & Shanmugam, 2016) including examinations of conflict (e.g., Wachsmuth, Jowett, & Harwood, 2018a) provides researchers with another conceptualisation of the coach-athlete relationship. It is important to note, however, that while many of the participant samples in research utilising Jowett's model, to date, have included performance, and to a lesser extent high performance, athletes (e.g., Felton & Jowett, 2013, 2015; Hampson & Jowett, 2014), very few have explicitly focused on this group (e.g., Jowett & Cockerill, 2003). Therefore, conclusions from this research for this domain should be considered with some caution. Other concepts that may also prove useful to further our understanding of quality relationships in this coaching domain include benevolence (Martela & Ryan, 2016) (e.g., Lara-Bercial & Mallett, 2016) and relatedness within self-determination theory (Ryan & Deci, 2000). The recent application of the concept of care to sport coaching (Cronin & Armour, 2019), in particular, within Collegiate sport (see Fisher, Larsen, Bejar, & Shigeno, 2019 for a review) and recently in high performance sport (Dohsten, Barker-Ruchti, & Lindgren, 2020) provides another framework from which to examine relationships in this domain. Researchers should look to employ clear conceptual frameworks enabling connections to be made across research findings and advance our understanding the nature of quality relationships in this domain.

High Performing Culture: High Expectations, Accountability, and Drive for Improvement

A consistent finding in the research examining coaching high performance athletes was the facilitation of a 'culture of high performance or excellence' which was viewed as a central driver for athletes' performance and crucial to sustained athletic success (Cruickshank & Collins, 2012; Cruickshank et al., 2013; Din et al., 2015; Fletcher & Arnold, 2011; Fletcher & Streeter, 2016; Hodge et al., 2014; Lara-Bercial & Mallett, 2016). This research suggests that coaches were viewed as the cultural leaders who sought to develop and sustain the *high performing* culture, however, other key stakeholders such as Performance Directors may also be important cultural leaders. Based on their study of a professional English Rugby Football Club, Cruickshank et al. (2013) suggested the culture was deliberately engineered but was achieved subtly rather than being imposed by 'cultural leaders'. This involved "the careful facilitation of stakeholders' actions and beliefs... [that focused on] the consistent uptake of performance-optimising behaviour" (p. 287). The research reviewed also suggested that leadership was shared among coaches and athletes, however, this is not always the case (e.g., Barker-Ruchti et al., 2014; Mills & Denison, 2013).

Three common features of the high performing culture were identified: (1) clear expectations; (2) personal accountability and; (2) a drive for continual improvement. Researchers described coaches who conveyed expectations for how athletes' should approach and engage in training and competition as well as how they should behave away from these environments (Cruickshank et al., 2013; Din et al., 2015; Gomes et al., 2018; Hodge et al., 2014; Lyons et al., 2012; Nash et al., 2011). For example, Smith et al. (2017) found that cricketers reported their coaches conveyed performance expectations that included continued improvement, effort in training and exemplary behaviour in non-performance areas. In addition, Lyons et al.'s (2012) ethnographic study of an Olympic Ski Cross coach's work with three athletes found that athletes acknowledged expectations from external stakeholders, however, as these expectations aligned with the athletes' goals and the athletes' considered their own goals were more significant, they were able to some extent, dismiss external expectations. Purdy and Jones (2011) found that rowers also had expectations for how their coaches should work with them. They found that a lack of congruence between the athletes' expectations for the coaches and the coaches' actions was a source of frustration and tension that impacted on their training.

Our review also found that coaches sought to develop athletes' personal responsibility and accountability (Fletcher & Streeter, 2016; Hodge et al., 2014; Lyons et al., 2012; Nash et al., 2011) as well as challenging athletes whose actions were not consistent with expectations (Din et al., 2015; Gomes et al., 2018). An important feature appeared to be accountability that was individualised for the athletes' needs (Hodge et al., 2014; Junggren et al., 2018; Lara-Bercial & Mallett, 2016) and supported through close monitoring of athletes' performances which allowed athletes to track their progress (Lara-Bercial & Mallett, 2016). Furthermore, Junggren et al. found that similar to other high performance athletes, swimmers had individual development plans, however, these swimmers were also encouraged to take responsibility for their training and apply what 'felt right to them'. This was supported by collaboration with the coaches who sought to assist swimmers to "filter and combine different pieces of knowledge that fit into the swimmer's individual perspective" (p. 1114).

Another consistent finding was coaches' and athletes' reports that a drive for continual improvement in performance was a central feature of the culture (Cruickshank et al., 2013; Din et al., 2015; Dixon et al., 2012; Fletcher & Streeter, 2016; Gomes et al., 2018; Hodge et al., 2014; Junggren et al., 2018; Lara-Bercial & Mallett, 2016; Mallett & Coulter, 2016). Hodge et al. found that coaches focused on improving players' strengths and encouraging an attitude to training of trying to be the best they could be. The coaches in Junggren et al.'s study encouraged swimmers to 'test even minor details' of their training and performance. Din et al described a "devotion to analysis and an unending search for the details that would make the difference between a good performance and a podium performance" (p. 599). Furthermore, the successful Olympic coach in Mallett and Coulter's case study described striving for improvement as a coach, seeing his own development as a means to assist the improvement of the athletes he coached. Lara-Bercial and Mallett found that although the coaches in their study possessed self-belief in their coaching attributed to their previous achievements and work ethic, they also had a 'healthy' self-doubt in their ability to be successful again which led them to continue to pursue avenues to be successful in the future. Junggren et al. found that the coaches viewed knowledge-sharing as a central value of the swimming club's culture where swimmers' and coaches' both had the 'right to contribute' and open-mindedness and learning from everybody were valued and evident in practice. This even went as far as embracing disagreements and differences of opinion as a positive contribution to development. However, although there may have been disagreements with the detail there was agreement with the underlying purpose—the process of continuing to improve.

In summary, in the research reviewed, coaches and athletes reported that a high performing culture was crucial to sustained performance improvement and success and provided some indication of more general characteristics of this culture, specifically clear expectations, accountability, and drive for continual improvement. There was frequent use of terms which have become commonplace in popular science and everyday sport (e.g., culture, high expectations, cultural leader, being the best they can be, leaving no stone unturned). Consequently, the results from such studies and their subsequent interpretations should not be taken as unproblematic prescriptions for 'effective' coaching practice (Potrac, Jones, & Cushion, 2007). For example, researchers might consider the potential impact continual striving has on coaches' (and athletes) well-being. Furthermore, much has already been written about the need to critically consider prevailing ideologies, power dynamics, subcultures, traditions, hidden curriculums and micro-politics in sport coaching cultures (cf. Jones, Potrac, Cushion, & Ronglan, 2011).

The concept of culture is a useful example. If defined at all, a broad view of culture was provided where culture is an understanding, that is shared by everyone in the organisation or group, in relation to the behaviours and ways of working required for consistent competitive results (Hodge et al., 2014; Junggren et al., 2018; Lara-Bercial & Mallett, 2016). In contrast, Fletcher and Streeter (2016) were one of the few to conceptualise culture, drawing on notions of organisational culture from Jones, Gittins, and Hardy's (2009) high performance environment model. Within this model culture relates to the extent to which organisations balance a focus on competing agendas: achievement, well-being, innovation, and internal processes. Junggren et al. (2018) adopted a different approach to culture, using Schein's (2010) conceptualisation of organisational culture and its three layers: cultural artefacts, espoused beliefs and values, and basic assumptions, to examine coaching practices in a Danish swimming club. Both approaches may provide useful starting points from which to clarify and interrogate the concept of culture. To develop further our understanding of culture within this domain, there is a need for future research to more critically engage with the concept, to more clearly define its meaning and explore how it shapes coaches', athletes' and other key stakeholders' resources, reasoning, reflecting, strategies, actions and behaviours (Muir, 2018).

Coaching Strategies: An Optimally Challenging and yet Supportive Learning-Focused Environment

When reviewing the research for this chapter, it became clear that the strategies coaches employ with the aim of maximising athletes' preparation and performance are diverse and numerous. Some examples include: forms of practice (playing versus training forms) (Hall et al., 2016); use of planned disruptions (Kegelaers, Wylleman, & Oudejans, 2020); optimising team functioning (Collins & Durand-Bush, 2016); conflict management (Wachsmuth, Jowett, & Harwood, 2018b); use of humour (Ronglan & Aggerholm, 2014); facilitating athletes' autonomous decision making (Richards et al., 2012), reflection on action (Hansen & Andersen, 2014) and self-regulation (Collins & Durand-Bush, 2014); video-based feedback (Magill, Nelson, Jones, & Potrac, 2017); and in-competition roles (Mouchet & Duffy, 2020; Ritchie & Allen, 2015). Due to space limitations in this chapter, we have focused on one sub-category of coaching strategies that has received significant attention from researchers—the psychosocial environment of training and competition and the actions of coaches that shape it.

Researchers examining the coach-created psychosocial environment (i.e., motivational climate) in high performance sport found: (1) continued demonstration that the coach plays a central role in shaping the psycho-social environment (Hodge et al., 2014; Keegan, Harwood, et al., 2014; Keegan, Spray, Harwood, & Lavallee, 2014; Lara-Bercial & Mallett, 2016; Lyons et al., 2012); (2) features of the climate that were task-involving[2] and autonomy supportive[3] were more prominent than features that were ego-involving and controlling (Abrahamsen & Kristiansen, 2015; Abrahamsen & Pensgaard, 2012; De Backer, Boen, De Cuyper, Høigaard, & Vande Broek, 2015–study 2; Hodge et al., 2014; Keegan, Harwood, et al., 2014; Kristiansen, Ivarsson, Solstad, & Roberts, 2019; Lara-Bercial & Mallett, 2016; Lyons et al., 2012; Nash et al., 2011; van Puyenbroeck et al., 2017); 3) perceptions of an ego-involving climate were frequently moderate (Abrahamsen & Kristiansen, 2015; Kristiansen et al., 2019; van Puyenbroeck et al., 2017); 4) task-involving or autonomy supportive climates were preferred by athletes and associated with

[2]Achievement goal theory (Ames, 1992; Nicholls, 1984) distinguishes between task-involving (i.e., emphasis on individual's self-referenced ability, learning and effort) and ego-involving (i.e., emphasis on normative ability and outperforming others) climates.

[3]Self-determination theory (Ryan & Deci, 2000) distinguishes between autonomy supportive behaviours (i.e., acknowledge athletes' agency and perspectives and facilitates athletes' active engagement in their development) and controlling behaviours (i.e., coaches seek to control participants through physical or psychological means).

'desirable' outcomes such as self-determined motivation and actual performance (Gillet et al., 2010; Keegan, Harwood, et al., 2014; Lyons et al., 2012), stronger team identification and task and social cohesion (De Backer et al., 2015—study 2), lower perceptions of the coach as a stressor (Kristiansen et al., 2019), athletes' proactive behaviour (taking charge, voicing opinions, upward influence) (van Puyenbroeck et al., 2017); and athletes' learning and adaptation, personal growth, well-being, and enjoyment (Lyons et al., 2012); (5) strategies and actions which shaped the climate's task-involving and autonomy supportive nature included: facilitating individualised learning; challenging athletes to solve problems; employing 'healthy' competition focused on stretching individual's performance capability; closely monitoring athletes to allow individuals to track their progress; coaches were demanding of effort and attention to tasks and yet supportive recognising individuals' needs and circumstances; coaches' behaviours had a degree of stability and dependability which supported athletes; and the training environment felt relaxed and yet focused on the task at hand (Din et al., 2015; Fletcher & Streeter, 2016; Hodge et al., 2014; Lara-Bercial & Mallett, 2016; Nash et al., 2011).

Several studies also identified the dynamic nature of the psychosocial environment. More specifically, that ego-involving features maybe more prominent at different times or to different athletes (Abrahamsen & Kristiansen, 2015; Abrahamsen & Pensgaard, 2012; Keegan, Harwood, et al., 2014; Kristiansen et al., 2019) and that coaches' strategies varied depending on the athletes and circumstances (Dixon et al., 2012; Lara-Bercial & Mallett, 2016; Lyons et al., 2012). For example, Abrahamsen and Pensgaard found that athletes' perceptions of the climate changed over the season becoming less task-involved and more ego-involved later in the season. Somewhat in contrast, Keegan, Harwood et al. found that athletes' reported that prior to competition, coaches promoted a mastery focus and could be positive and pressure avoiding. In addition, Abrahamsen and Kristiansen found that even within a highly task-involving climate athletes may still experience stress at certain times due to greater salience of ego-involving aspects of the climate such as pre-season where athletes are focused on team selection. Similarly, Kristiansen et al. suggested that athletes' status in the team may result in them experiencing the climate differently. Specifically, injured or marginal players (i.e., those fighting for or less secure in their place on the team) appeared more sensitive to the ego-involving cues within the environment. With regards to autonomy support and control, Lyons et al. noted that the coach 'shifted along the continuum' between autonomy supportive and controlling coaching behaviours. Furthermore, whilst coaches in Lara-Bercial and Mallett's study reported they preferred a more collaborative (task-involving and autonomy supportive) way of working with athletes, they also recognised that they moved to more directive practices when appropriate to the context, situation, individuals and time-constraints.

Although not based on conceptualisations of task/ego-involvement (Ames, 1992; Nicholls, 1984) or autonomy support/control (Ryan & Deci, 2000), other research examining coaches' interpersonal strategies also suggested that coaches employ a range of strategies dependent on the athlete and context. For example, Consterdine et al. (2013) found that the Olympic athletics coach in their study paid deliberate attention to his language, pitch and intonation, body language, which he tailored to each athlete with the intention of general positive communication and encouraging athletes to take personal responsibility for their actions. Furthermore, the researchers reported that the coach also challenged athletes and was both calculating and caring in how he worked with athletes in order to move athletes closer to the desired outcomes. Similarly, in their examination of Norwegian cross-country skiing coaches' actions to stimulate athletes' reflection, Hansen and Andersen (2014) found that coaches tended to individualise their actions and use democratic interaction behaviours to stimulate athletes to consider key features of their training. However, the researchers also found that this shifted from providing the solutions when athletes were struggling to challenging athletes' reflection further when the athletes were performing well. Somewhat in contrast to these findings, several studies (e.g., Din et al., 2015; Mills & Denison, 2013; Purdy & Jones, 2011) have found that coaches employed more controlling ways of working with athletes. For example, the coaches in Mills and Denison's study felt they should be in control of training plans and that they knew more than the athletes. Mills and Dension problematised these practices, questioning how this prepares athletes to make decisions in the chaos of competition. Furthermore, Cruickshank and Collins (2015) examined the 'dark side' of leaders' behaviours in their study with professional coaches and Olympic sport programme directors. They found that all participants reported using Machiavellian behaviours (i.e., cunning, manipulative, deceitful) to shape relationships and further the team's interest and performance. However, the researchers noted that the behaviours were employed deliberately to lead to specific outcomes and often involved shaping the conditions so that use of undesirable behaviours was viewed by others as less undesirable or even acceptable.

In summary these studies suggest a psychosocial environment that emphasises task-involvement and support for athletes' autonomy providing an optimal balance between challenge and support. That is, training that challenges athletes and yet remains supportive with a certain amount of stability to enable athletes to thrive. Although not exclusively, conceptualisations of the psychosocial environment have been based on achievement goal theory (AGT) (Ames, 1992; Nicholls, 1984) or self-determination theory (SDT) (Ryan & Deci, 2000). In comparison to research in other domains (e.g., children or adolescents), much less is known about the coaching strategies and resulting motivational climate in this coaching domain, therefore, further research is needed (Harwood, Keegan, Smith, & Raine, 2015; Keegan, Spray, et al., 2014; Occhino, Mallett, Rynne, & Carlisle, 2014). In addition, transformational leadership behaviours (Bass, 1985) were recently examined in studies with professional cricketers (Smith et al., 2017) and football managers (Mills & Boardley, 2016). From a conceptual and theoretical perspective, it is important to note that transformational leadership (and the contrasting transactional leadership) is not a theory and researchers may find it useful to consider the extent to which the interpersonal strategies might be incorporated within or extend existing theories such as AGT and SDT. Furthermore, each of these conceptualisations tends to pit one set of interpersonal strategies against another (e.g., task-involving versus ego-involving), leading to suggestions that one represents 'good' coaching and the other 'poor' coaching. This polarisation of strategies does not recognise the dynamic nature of coaching or, as some of the research in this chapter demonstrates, that coaches appear to knowingly employ a range of interpersonal strategies to meet the needs of athletes varying in accordance with circumstances.

Implications for Coaching

At the beginning of the chapter we mentioned that we did not want to lose sight of the diversity among athletes, contexts, and coaches, nor did we want to trivialise or ignore the complex, behavioural, cognitive and social nature of coaching. And yet, through our review of the research we were able to identify a number of common themes about the process and practices of coaching high performance athletes. Rather than suggest that all coaching in high performance sport should confirm to these themes, instead we offer an integrative perspective on coaching high performance athletes. This conceptual framework acknowledges the relative (it depends) nature of coaching whilst also providing structure to make sense of the 'reality' of coaching high performance athletes and locate the findings of research more broadly.

The conceptual framework (see Fig. 9.1) draws on earlier work of Abraham, Muir and colleagues[4] who suggested that '*high performing*' coaches are constantly seeking to maximize their effectiveness through challenging *personal* 'theories of practice' (i.e. ideas) through reference to *formal* 'theories of practice' (i.e. understanding). As has been described earlier, the desire to continually improve through an openness to on-going learning, and willingness to critically reflect overtime enables the '*high performing*' coach to: (a) present a personal, reasoned explanation for their strategies and goals; (b) explain and provide reasons for actions taken to meet their goals; and (c) evaluate the personal and collective effectiveness of their strategies (Thompson, 2000).

The central premise underpinning the framework is that '*high performing*' coaches' reasoning, reflecting, strategising, actions and behaviours (i.e. their practice) are based on their existing beliefs, values, knowledge and perspectives (i.e. self) about the needs and wants of their athletes (the 'who'), the demands of their sport (the 'what') and of skill acquisition and learning (the 'how') within their embedded context (i.e., the context, culture and politics within which they operate). Thus, Abraham, Muir and colleagues suggested '*high performing*' coaching practice rests on the coach's ability to draw on knowledge from several overlapping domains to develop optimal learning environments for athletes. It involves a continuous process of decision-making about when and how to intervene in order to maintain momentum and progression towards the achievement of specified goals.

[4]cf. Abraham et al. (2010), Abraham & Collins (2011), Muir, Morgan, Abraham, and Morley, (2011), Muir, Till, Abraham, and Morgan (2015).

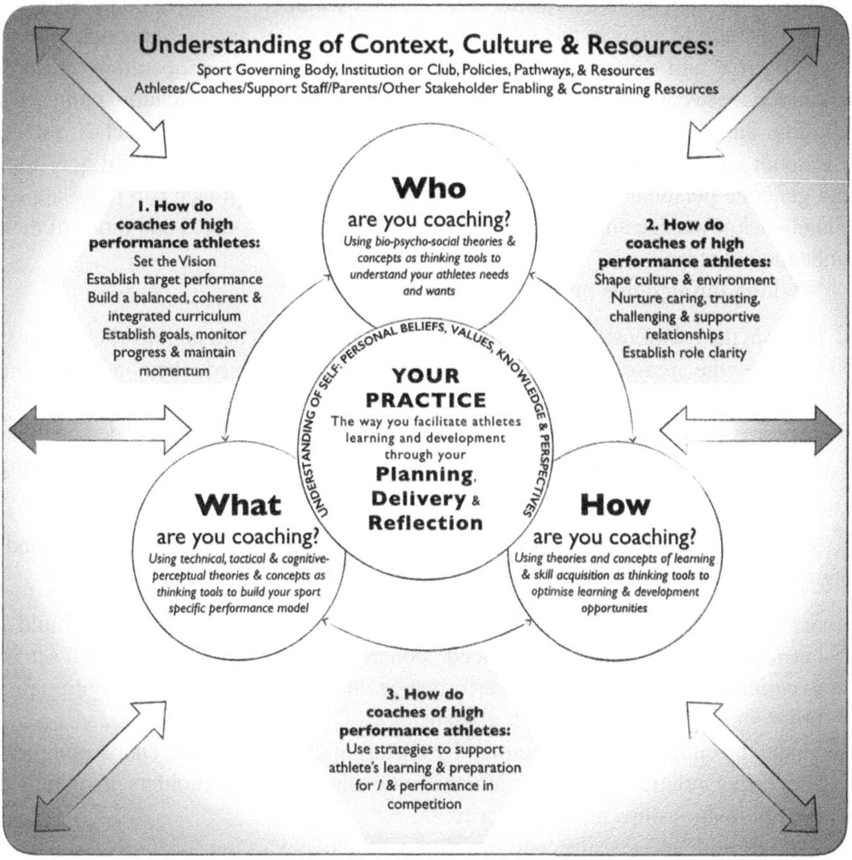

Fig. 9.1 A conceptual framework to explore coaches' resources, reasoning, strategies actions and behaviours (adapted from Muir, 2018)

Muir (2018) used the framework as a 'thinking tool' to explore the resources, reasoning, actions and behaviours of forty coaches that work with Olympic and national age group athletes across ten sports over an 8-year period.[5] The study illustrated 'how' coach learning and development can be more meaningfully embedded in coaches' everyday practice contexts. By starting with coaches lived experiences, learning situations were developed to stimulate reflection on existing practices and provoke coaches to consider their underpinning reasoning and resources.

[5]The framework has also been embedded within the European Sports Coaching Framework (Lara-Bercial et al., 2017), the International Council for Coaching Excellence standards for higher education sports coaching degrees (Lara-Bercial et al., 2016), and the Chartered Institute for the Management of Sport and Physical Activity (CIMSPA), Professional Standard 'Coaching in High-Performance Sport', and has been adopted by several national governing bodies of sport (e.g., the Football Association, British Triathlon, England Boxing, the British Sailing Team).

Concepts, theories and frameworks were then drawn upon in a more contextual and applied fashion to support the needs of individual coaches and the demands of their coaching role and context. This process necessitated a close cooperation and collaboration between the coach developer and coach. The implication being that learning, and development is not something that can be 'done' to coaches; rather, it is about working alongside coaches to identify and resolve meaningful questions that generate personal and professional growth. Such an approach can more appropriately acknowledge and build on individual's existing resources and those of their embedded context.

Working through this process supported coaches to:

- Explore the relationship between their intentions (goals) and actions (behaviours)
- Explore the reasoning and strategies that underpinned their actions and behaviours
- Explore how their existing beliefs, values, knowledge and perspectives (resources) shaped and influenced their reasoning, reflecting and strategising (Muir, 2018).

Much of the work centred on how coaches used their knowledge and understanding of their athletes, the sport, and learning to:

1. Set the vision, establish what is required to win (target performance), build a curriculum that creates a balanced, coherent, focused and integrated set of experiences that support high performance athletes to maintain momentum and progression towards their desired goals.
2. Shape the culture and environment by nurturing caring, trusting, challenging and supportive relationships with athletes and other key stakeholders to maintain quality relationships and role clarity.
3. Support athletes' learning and development across varying locations (i.e. on or off the training 'pitch'[6]) and events (e.g. training, competing, review meetings, planning discussions, pre-training or competition briefings and post-training or competition debriefs etc.).

It is here where we can see the process and practices of coaches' work with high performance athletes, that we have identified in this chapter.

[6]The expression 'on the pitch' is used to represent the various locations within which athletes train and compete (e.g. pool, court, sea, mat, ring and track etc.), whilst 'off the pitch' is intended to represent all other locations and spaces within which coaches and athletes interact (e.g. meeting rooms, via the telephone, e-mail or other forms of text messaging, travelling to and from venues, in and around the institutional facilities or other public spaces—cafés etc.).

Key Points

Reflecting on the research examining this coaching domain, we suggest that there is much more to explore, understand and explain about coaching high performance athletes. Although reflective of the findings contained in the research reviewed, the themes presented above provide a relatively limited account of coaching high performance athletes imbued with broad ranging principles, metaphors and philosophical maxims. Further research that seeks to undercover what these means in practice is needed. Throughout the chapter we have offered directions for future research. Next we offer four more general reflections and suggestions for researchers:

1. Limited conceptualisation of coaching high performance athletes
   Greater conceptualisation of aspects of coaching under investigation and clarity and consistency in the use of 'high performance' when describing athletes, coaches, and contexts. Much of the research reviewed for this chapter explored aspects of coaching that are relatively under developed conceptually (e.g., vision, philosophy, culture). To further our understanding of coaching high performance athletes, researchers should employ clear conceptual frameworks to interrogate aspects of coaching. Furthermore, the use of terms such as 'elite' and 'high performance' without any additional explanation of context or participants can lead to confusion with regards to the extent to which coaching high performance athletes is truly the focus of the research and therefore limits insights that might be gained. To reduce such confusion, providing a clear description and even criteria for selection of the population participating in the study is critical. In addition, research has often focused on those deemed 'successful' and regularly emphasises winning. Researchers are encouraged to consider whether employing other or multiple criteria in participant selection (e.g., stakeholder perceptions) could provide additional insight into this coaching domain.
2. The 'rosy picture' of coaching high performance athletes
   Greater consideration of the challenges and 'dark sides' of coaching high performance athletes. Although not exclusively, the research reviewed in this chapter paints a relatively 'rosy picture' of high performance sport and this coaching domain. However, coaching is frequently messy, imbued with challenges and setbacks and even potentially negative and damaging practices, however, relatively few are discussed or examined in the research (for exceptions see Cruickshank & Collins, 2015; Purdy & Jones, 2011; Santos et al., 2013; Stirling & Kerr, 2013). Research that continues to explore coaches' and athletes' experiences (the desirable and less desirable) and how they negotiate challenges will provide valuable insight to enhance our understanding and explanations of coaching as well as giving a realistic view of coaching that coaches can relate to.
3. Coaching strategies as continuums and tools
   Greater in-depth examination of coaching strategies as dynamic and varied dependent on athletes, context, coach, and circumstances. Perhaps constrained, to some extent, by conceptualisations such as the motivational climate and

coaching or leadership styles there has been a tendency to present one strategy as superior to another (e.g., task-involving vs. ego-involving; autonomy supportive vs. controlling; playing form activity vs. training form activity; questioning vs. instruction; transformational vs. transactional). However, some of the research reviewed in this chapter challenges these dichotomies, instead suggesting that coaches use a range of strategies when working with high performance athletes. Many of the concepts were not conceptualised as dichotomous and they frequently occur to a lesser or greater extent together. Therefore, although coaches may tend towards and prefer certain strategies over others, we suggest a more accurate representation of how coaches work with athletes is needed, where there is greater recognition of the coaching strategies as continuums which coaches shift along or even as discrete tools employed dependent on the context, situation, individuals and time available.

4. Micro-level analysis of coaching strategies, actions and behaviours

   Greater in-depth and longitudinal examinations of the micro-level practices coaches employ. Much of the research reviewed in this chapter focused on what might be described as meso-level analyses of coaching high performance athletes. Greater in-depth investigations have potential to add to our understanding of the dynamic nature of this coaching domain (e.g., Consterdine et al., 2013; Hall et al., 2016; Purdy & Jones, 2011). For example, Hall et al.'s study of a national rugby team across a season found that the use of playing form versus training form activities varied across training days and the season. They also found that coaching behaviours varied with the different activity forms and between training and competition. Further, research that examines coaches' strategies, actions and behaviours in-depth and over time is needed to develop our understanding of which strategies are used, when, in what circumstances, with whom and why.

Conclusion

In this chapter we sought to provide an overview of the research examining coaching high performance athletes. Recognising the diversity within this coaching domain (i.e., athletes, contexts, and coaches) and in approaches adopted by researchers we attempted to look across disciplinary boundaries to develop themes that represent commonalities in the process and practices within this coaching domain. These themes captured: a clear informed vision for what is possible and detailed plan for implementation; a bringing to life of the coach's philosophy based on values relating to care and consideration for athletes' personal and performance enhancement; facilitated by building and maintaining quality relationships with athletes and among key stakeholders; developing a high performing culture with clear expectations about how things should be done and a desire for improvement; and use of coaching strategies with a prominence of task-involving and autonomy supportive strategies that support athletes' performance progression within challenging sessions which prepare athletes for the demands of competition. In offering an integrative framework we sought to suggest how these commonalities are integrated in the process and practices of coaching. And also, to recognise the relational (it depends) nature of coaching. In doing so, we hope to provide a sense of structure within which coaches and researcher might employ disciplinary-based theory and concepts to understand, reflect, and examine further, the improvisation and realities inherent in day-to-day coaching of, with and for high performance athletes.

References

Abraham, A., & Collins, D. (2011). Effective skill development: How should athletes' skills be developed? In D. Collins, H. Richards, & A. Button (Eds.), *Performance psychology: A guide for the practitioner* (pp. 207–230). London: Churchill Livingstone.

Abraham, A., Collins, D., & Martindale, R. (2006). The coaching schematic: Validation through expert coach consensus. *Journal of Sports Sciences, 24*(6), 549–564. https://doi.org/10.1080/02640410500189173

Abraham, A., Muir, B., & Morgan, G. (2010). *National and international best practice in level 4 coach development*. Leeds: Leeds Metropolitan University & The UK Centre for Coaching Excellence.

Abrahamsen, F. E., & Kristiansen, E. (2015). The dark side of a mastery emphasis: Can mastery involvement create stress and anxiety? *International Journal of Applied Sports Sciences, 27*(2), 76–86. https://doi.org/10.24985/ijass.2015.27.2.76

Abrahamsen, F. E., & Pensgaard, A. M. (2012). Longitudinal changes in motivational climate and performance anxiety among elite handball players. *International Journal of Applied Sport Sciences, 24*, 31–42. https://doi.org/10.24985/ijass.2012.24.1.31

Ames, C. (1992). Achievement goals, motivational climate, and motivational processes. In G. C. Roberts (Ed.), *Advances in motivation in sport and Exercise* (pp. 161–176). Champaign, IL: Human Kinetics.

Barker-Ruchti, N., Rynne, S. R., Lee, J., & Barker, D. M. (2014). Athlete learning in Olympic sport. *Sports Coaching Review, 3*(2), 162–178. https://doi.org/10.1080/21640629.2014.1059136

Bass, B. M. (1985). *Leadership and performance beyond expectations*. New York: Free Press.

Bennie, A., & O'Connor, D. (2010). Coaching philosophies: Perceptions from professional cricket, rugby league and rugby union players and coaches in Australia. *International Journal of Sports Science and Coaching, 5*, 309–320. https://doi.org/10.1260/1747-9541.5.2.309

Blackett, A. D., Evans, A., & Piggott, D. (2017). Why 'the best way of learning to coach the game is playing the game': Conceptualising 'fast-tracked' high-performance coaching pathways. *Sport, Education and Society, 22*(6), 744–758. https://doi.org/10.1080/13573322.2015.1075494

Blackett, A. D., Evans, A., & Piggott, D. (2018). "Active" and "passive" coach pathways: Elite athletes' entry routes into high-performance coaching roles. *International Sport Coaching Journal, 5*, 213–226. https://doi.org/10.1123/iscj.2017-0053

Bowes, I., & Jones, R. L. (2006). Working at the edge of chaos: Understanding coaching as a complex, interpersonal system. *The Sport Psychologist, 20*(2), 235–245. https://doi.org/10.1123/tsp.20.2.235

Callary, B., Werthner, P., & Trudel, P. (2013). Exploring coaching actions based on developed values: A case study of a female hockey coach. *International Journal of Lifelong Education, 32*(2), 209–229. https://doi.org/10.1080/02601370.2012.733974

Carless, D., & Douglas, K. (2011). Stories as personal coaching philosophy. *International Journal of Sports Science and Coaching, 6*(1), 1–12. https://doi.org/10.1260/1747-9541.6.1.1

Collins, J., & Durand-Bush, N. (2014). Strategies used by an elite curling coach to nurture athletes' self-regulation: A single case study. *Journal of Applied Sport Psychology, 26*(2), 211–224. https://doi.org/10.1080/10413200.2013.819823

Collins, J., & Durand-Bush, N. (2016). Coaching strategies to optimize team functioning in high performance curling. *International Sport Coaching Journal, 3*, 240–256. https://doi.org/10.1123/iscj.2016-0073

Consterdine, A., Newton, J., & Piggin, S. (2013). 'Time to take the stage': A contextual study of a high performance coach. *Sports Coaching Review, 2*(2), 124–135. https://doi.org/10.1080/21640629.2014.908626

Cooper, D., & Allen, J. (2018). The coaching process of the expert coach: A coach led approach. *Sport Coaching Review, 7*(2), 142–170. https://doi.org/10.1080/21640629.2017.1361168

Cooper, D., & Allen, J. (2020). "I don't want to give them my brain for the day... and then take it back": An examination of the coach-created motivational climate in adult adventure sports. *International Sport Coaching Journal, 7*(2), 175–188. https://doi.org/10.1123/iscj.2019-0026

Côté, J., & Gilbert, W. D. (2009). An integrative definition of coaching effectiveness and expertise. *International Journal of Sports Science & Coaching, 4*, 307–323. https://doi.org/10.1260/174795409789623892

Côté, J., Salmela, J. H., Trudel, P., Baria, A., & Russell, S. J. (1995). The coaching model: A grounded assessment of expert gymnastic coaches' knowledge. *Journal of Sport & Exercise Psychology, 17*(1), 1-17. https://doi.org/10.1123/jsep.17.1.1

Cronin, C., & Armour, K. M. (2019). *Care in sport coaching: Pedagogical cases*. Boca Raton, FL: Routledge.

Cruickshank, A., & Collins, D. (2012). Culture change in elite sport performance teams: Examining and advancing effectiveness in the new era. *Journal of Applied Sport Psychology, 24*, 338–355. https://doi.org/10.1080/10413200.2011.650819

Cruickshank, A., & Collins, D. (2015). Illuminating and applying "The Dark Side": Insights from elite team leaders. *Journal of Applied Sport Psychology, 27*(3), 249–267. https://doi.org/10.1080/10413200.2014.982771

Cruickshank, A., Collins, D., & Minten, S. (2013). Culture change in a professional sports team: Shaping environmental contexts and regulating power. *International Journal of Sports Science & Coaching, 8*(2), 271–290. https://doi.org/10.1260/1747-9541.8.2.271

Culver, D. M., Gilbert, W., & Sparkes, A. (2012). Qualitative research in sport psychology journals: The next decade 2000-2009 and beyond. *The Sport Psychologist, 26*(2), 261–281. https://doi.org/10.1123/tsp.26.2.261

Cushion, C. J. (2007). Modelling the complexities of the coaching process. *International Journal of Sports Science & Coaching, 2*(4), 395–401. https://doi.org/10.1260/174795407783359650

Cushion, C. J., Armour, K. M., & Jones, R. L. (2003). Coach education and continuing professional development: Experience and learning to coach. *Quest, 55*, 215–230. https://doi.org/10.1080/00336297.2003.10491800

Cushion, C., & Partington, C. (2014). A critical analysis of the conceptualisation of 'coaching philosophy'. *Sport, Education and Society*. https://doi.org/10.1080/13573322.2014.958817

De Backer, M., Boen, F., De Cuyper, B., Høigaard, R., & Vande Broek, G. (2015). A team fares well with a fair coach: Predictors of social loafing in interactive female sport teams. *Scandinavian Journal of Medicine & Science in Sports, 25*(6), 897–908. https://doi.org/10.1111/sms.12303

Din, C., Paskevich, D., Gabriele, T., & Werthner, P. (2015). Olympic medal winning leadership. *International Journal of Sport Science & Coaching, 10*(4), 589–604. https://doi.org/10.1260/1747-9541.10.4.589

Dixon, M., Lee, S., & Ghaye, T. (2012). Coaching for performance: Reflections of Olympic diving coach, Andy Banks. *Reflective Practice, 13*, 355–358. https://doi.org/10.1080/04419057.2002.9674274

Dohsten, J., Barker-Ruchti, N., & Lindgren, E. (2020). Caring as sustainable coaching in elite athletics: Benefits and challenges. *Sports Coaching Review, 9*(1), 48–70. https://doi.org/10.1080/21640629.2018.1558896

Ewing, T. (2019). Rethinking head coach credentials: Playing experience, tertiary qualifications and coaching apprenticeships. *International Sport Coaching Journal, 6*, 244–249. https://doi.org/10.1123/iscj.2018-0092

Felton, L., & Jowett, S. (2013). "What do coaches do" and "how do they relate": Their effects on athletes' psychological needs and functioning. *Scandinavian Journal of Medicine and Sports Sciences, 23*, 130–139. https://doi.org/10.1111/sms.12029

Felton, L., & Jowett, S. (2015). On understanding the role of need thwarting in the association between athlete attachment and well/ill-being. *Scandinavian Journal of Medicine and Sports Sciences, 25*(2), 289–298. https://doi.org/10.1111/sms.12196

Fisher, L. A., Larsen, L. K., Bejar, M. P., & Shigeno, T. C. (2019). A heuristic for the relationship between caring coaching and elite athlete performance. *International Journal of Sports Science & Coaching, 14*(2), 126–137. https://doi.org/10.1177/1747954119827192

Fletcher, D., & Arnold, R. (2011). A qualitative study of performance leadership and management in elite sport. *Journal of Applied Sport Psychology, 23*(2), 223–242. https://doi.org/10.1080/10413200.2011.559184

Fletcher, D., & Streeter, A. (2016). A case study analysis of a high performance environment in elite swimming. *Journal of Change Management, 16*(2), 123–141. https://doi.org/10.1080/14697017.2015.1128470

Gilbert, W. D., Côté, J., & Mallett, C. (2006). Developmental paths and activities of successful sport coaches. *International Journal of Sport Science and Coaching, 1*(1), 69–76. https://doi.org/10.1260/174795406776338526

Gillet, N., Vallerand, R. J., Amoura, S., & Baldes, B. (2010). Influence of coaches' autonomy support on athletes' motivation and sport performance: A test of the hierarchical model of intrinsic and extrinsic motivation. *Psychology of Sport and Exercise, 11*(2), 155–161. https://doi.org/10.1260/174795409789623892

Gomes, A. R., Araújo, V., Resende, R., & Ramalho, V. (2018). Leadership of elite coaches: The relationship among philosophy, practice, and effectiveness criteria. *International Journal of Sports Science & Coaching, 13*(6), 1120–1133. https://doi.org/10.1177/1747954118796362

Gould, D., & Maynard, I. (2009). Psychological preparation for the Olympic Games. *Journal of Sports Sciences, 27*(13), 1393–1408. https://doi.org/10.1080/02640410903081845

Grecic, D., MacNamara, A., & Collins, D. (2013). The epistemological chain in action: Coaching in high level golf. *Journal of Qualitative Research in Sports Studies, 7*(1), 103–126.

Griffo, J. M., Jensen, M., Anthony, C. C., Baghurst, T., & Kulinna, P. H. (2019). A decade of research literature in sport coaching (2005–2015). *International Journal of Sports Science & Coaching, 14*(2), 205–215. https://doi.org/10.1177/1747954118825058

Hall, E. T., Gray, S., & Sproule, J. (2016). The microstructure of coaching practice: Behaviours and activities of an elite rugby union head coach during preparation and competition. *Journal of Sports Sciences, 34*(10), 896–905. https://doi.org/10.1080/02640414.2015.1076571

Hampson, R., & Jowett, S. (2014). Effects of coach leadership and coach–athlete relationship on collective efficacy. *Scandinavian Journal of Medicine & Science in Sports, 24*, 454–460. https://doi.org/10.1111/j.1600-0838.2012.01527.x

Hansen, P. Ø., & Andersen, S. S. (2014). Coaching elite athletes: How coaches stimulate elite athletes' reflection. *Sports Coaching Review, 3*(1), 17–32. https://doi.org/10.1080/21640629.2014.901712

Harvey, S., Cushion, C. J., Cope, E., & Muir, B. (2013). A season long investigation into coaching behaviours as a function of practice state: The case of three collegiate coaches. *Sports Coaching Review, 2*(1), 13–32. https://doi.org/10.1080/21640629.2013.837238

Harwood, C. G., Keegan, R. J., Smith, J. M., & Raine, A. S. (2015). A systematic review of the intrapersonal correlates of motivational climate perceptions in sport and physical activity. *Psychology of Sport & Exercise, 18*, 9–25. https://doi.org/10.1016/j.psychsport.2014.11.005

Hodge, K., Henry, G., & Smith, W. (2014). A case study of excellence in elite sport: Motivational climate in a world champion team. *Sport Psychologist, 28*, 60–74. https://doi.org/10.1123/tsp.2013-0037

International Council for Coaching Excellence (ICCE) and Association of Summer Olympic International Federations (ASOIF). (2012). *International sport coaching framework (Version 1.1)*. Champaign, IL: Human Kinetics.

International Council for Coaching Excellence (ICCE), Association of Summer Olympic International Federations (ASOIF) & Leeds Metropolitan University (LMU). (2013). *International sport coaching framework (Version 1.2)*. Champaign, IL: Human Kinetics.

Jones, J. G., Gittins, M. J., & Hardy, L. (2009). Creating an environment where high performance is inevitable and sustainable: The high performance environment model. *Annual Review of High Performance Coaching and Consulting, 1*, 139–149.

Jones, R. L., Bailey, J., & Thompson, I. (2013). Ambiguity, noticing, and orchestration: Further thoughts on managing the complex coaching context. In P. Potrac, W. Gilbert, & J. Denison (Eds.), *The Routledge handbook of sports coaching* (pp. 271–283). London: Routledge.

Jones, R. L., Potrac, P., Cushion, C., & Ronglan, L. T. (Eds.). (2011). *The sociology of sports coaching*. London: Routledge.

Jones, R. L., & Wallace, M. (2005). Another bad day at the training ground: Coping with ambiguity in the coaching context. *Sport, Education and Society, 10*(1), 119–134. https://doi.org/10.1080/1357332052000308792.

Jowett, S. (2017). Coaching effectiveness: The coach–athlete relationship at its heart. *Current Opinion in Psychology, 16*, 154–158. https://doi.org/10.1016/j.copsyc.2017.05.006

Jowett, S., & Cockerill, I. M. (2003). Olympic medalists' perspective of the athlete-coach relationship. *Psychology of Sport and Exercise, 4*, 313–331. https://doi.org/10.1016/S14690292(02)00011-0

Jowett, S., & Shanmugam, V. (2016). Relational coaching in sport: Its psychological underpinnings and practical effectiveness. In R. Schinke, K. R. McGannon, & B. Smith (Eds.), *Routledge international handbook of sport psychology* (pp. 471–484). London: Routledge.

Junggren, S. E., Elbæk, L., & Stambulova, N. B. (2018). Examining coaching practices and philosophy through the lens of organizational culture in a Danish high-performance swimming environment. *International Journal of Sports Science & Coaching, 13*(6), 1108–1119. https://doi.org/10.1177/1747954118796914

Keegan, R. J., Harwood, C. G., Spray, C. M., & Lavallee, D. (2014). A qualitative investigation of the motivational climate in elite sport. *Psychology of Sport and Exercise, 15*, 97–107. https://doi.org/10.1016/j.psychsport.2013.10.006

Keegan, R. J., Spray, C. M., Harwood, C. G., & Lavallee, D. E. (2014). A qualitative synthesis of research into social motivational influences across the athletic career span. *Qualitative Research in Sport, Exercise and Health, 6*(4), 537–567. https://doi.org/10.1080/2159676X.2013.857710

Kegelaers, J., Wylleman, P., & Oudejans, R. R. (2020). A coach perspective on the use of planned disruptions in high-performance sports. *Sport, Exercise, and Performance Psychology, 9*(1), 29–44. https://doi.org/10.1037/spy0000167

Kristiansen, E., Ivarsson, A., Solstad, B. E., & Roberts, G. C. (2019). Motivational processes affecting the perception of organizational and media stressors among professional football players: A longitudinal mixed methods research study. *Psychology of Sport & Exercise, 43*, 172–182. https://doi.org/10.1016/j.psychsport.2019.02.009

Kristiansen, E., & Roberts, G. C. (2010). Young elite athletes and social support: Coping with competitive and organizational stress in "Olympic" competition. *Scandinavian Journal of Medicine & Science in Sports, 20*(4), 686–695. https://doi.org/10.1111/j.1600-0838.2009.00950.x

Lara-Bercial, S., Jimenez, A., Abraham, A., Bales, J., Colmaire, P., Curado, J., … Rynne, S. (2016). The international sport coaching bachelor degree standards of the International Council for Coaching Excellence. *International Sport Coaching Journal, 3*(3), 344–348. https://doi.org/10.1123/iscj.2016-0085

Lara-Bercial, S., & Mallett, C. J. (2016). The practices and developmental pathways of professional and Olympic serial winning coaches. *International Sport Coaching Journal, 3*, 221–239. https://doi.org/10.1123/iscj.2016-0083

Lara-Bercial, S., North, J., Hämäläinen, K., Oltmanns, K., Minkhorst, J., & Petrovic, L. (2017). *European sport coaching framework*. Champaign, IL: Human Kinetics.

Lombardo, B. (1987). *Coaching in the 21st century: Issues, concerns and solutions*. Springfield, IL: Charles C. Thomas.

Lyle, J. (2002). *Sports coaching concepts: A framework for coaches' behaviour*. London: Routledge.

Lyle, J., & Cushion, C. J. (2017). *Sport coaching concepts: A framework for coaches' practice*. London: Routledge.

Lyons, M., Rynne, S. B., & Mallett, C. J. (2012). Reflection and the art of coaching: Fostering high-performance in Olympic Ski Cross. *Reflective Practice, 13*(3), 359–372. https://doi.org/10.1080/14623943.2012.670629

Magill, S., Nelson, L., Jones, R., & Potrac, P. (2017). Emotions, identity, and power in video-based feedback sessions: Tales from women's professional football. *Sports Coaching Review, 6*(2), 216–232. https://doi.org/10.1080/21640629.2017.1367068

Mallett, C. J. (2010). Becoming a high-performance coach: Pathways and communities. In J. Lyle & C. Cushion (Eds.), *Sports coaching: Professionalisation and practice* (pp. 119–134). Edinburgh: Elsevier.

Mallett, C. J., & Côté, J. (2006). Beyond winning and losing: Guidelines for evaluating high performance coaches. *The Sport Psychologist, 20*(2), 213–221. https://doi.org/10.1123/tsp.20.2.213

Mallett, C. J., & Coulter, T. (2016). The anatomy of a successful Olympic coach: Performer, agent, and author. *International Sport Coaching Journal, 3*, 113–127. https://doi.org/10.1123/iscj.2015-0069

Mallett, C. J., & Lara-Bercial, S. (2016). Serial winning coaches: People, vision, and environment. In M. Raab, P. Wylleman, R. Seiler, A. M. Elbe, & G. Hatzigeorgiadis (Eds.), *Sport and exercise psychology research: theory to practice* (pp. 289–322). Amsterdam: Elsevier. https://doi.org/10.1016/B978-0-12-803634-1.00014-5

Mallett, C. J., Rossi, T., Rynne, S., & Tinning, R. (2016). In pursuit of becoming a senior coach: The learning culture for Australian Football League coaches. *Physical Education and Sport Pedagogy, 21*(1), 24–39. https://doi.org/10.1080/17408989.2015.1072508

Martela, F., & Ryan, R. M. (2016). The benefits of benevolence: Basic psychological needs, beneficence, and the enhancement of well-being. *Journal of Personality, 84*, 750–764. https://doi.org/10.1111/jopy.12215

Mason, J. (2002). *Researching your own practice: The discipline of noticing*. London: Routledge.

Medic, N., Young, B. W., Starkes, J. L., & Weir, P. L. (2012). Relationship between having a coach and master athletes' motivational regulations for sport and achievement goal orientations. *International Journal of Coaching Science, 6*, 65–79.

Mills, J. P., & Boardley, I. (2016). Expert Premier League soccer managers' use of transformational leadership behaviours and attitude towards sport integrity: An intrinsic case study. *International Journal of Sports Science & Coaching, 11*(3), 382–394. https://doi.org/10.1177/1747954116645011

Mills, J. P., & Denison, J. (2013). Coach Foucault: Problematizing endurance running coaches' practices. *Sports Coaching Review, 2*(2), 136–150. https://doi.org/10.1080/21640629.2014.913871

Mouchet, A., & Duffy, P. (2020). Rugby coaches' perceptions of their in-competition role. *Sports Coaching Review, 9*(1), 24–47. https://doi.org/10.1080/21640629.2018.1532650

Muir, B. (2018). *Coach learning and development in the performance domain: An embedded, relational and emergent intervention strategy* PhD thesis. Leeds Beckett University.

Muir, B., Morgan, G., Abraham, A., & Morley, D. (2011). Developmentally appropriate approaches to coaching children. In. I. Stafford (Ed.), *Coaching children in sport*. Routledge: London.

Muir, B., Till, K., Abraham, A., & Morgan, G. (2015). A framework for planning your practice: A coach's perspective. In K. Till & B. Jones (Eds.), *The science of rugby* (pp. 161–172). Malborough: Crowood Press.

Nash, C. S., Sproule, J., & Horton, P. (2011). Excellence in coaching: The art and skill of elite practitioners. *Research Quarterly for Exercise and Sport, 82*(2), 229–238. https://doi.org/10.1080/02701367.2011.10599750

Nicholls, J. G. (1984). Achievement motivation: Conceptions of ability, subjective experience, task choice, and performance. *Psychological Review, 91*(3), 328–346.

North, J. (2009). *The UK Coaching Workforce 2009-2016*. Leeds: The National Coaching Foundation.

North, J. (2017). *Sport coaching research and practice: Ontology, interdisciplinarity and critical realism*. Abingdon, UK: Routledge.

Occhino, J. L., Mallett, C. J., Rynne, S. B., & Carlisle, K. N. (2014). Autonomy-supportive pedagogical approach to sports coaching: Research, challenges and opportunities. *International Journal of Sport Science & Coaching, 9*(2), 401–416. https://doi.org/10.1260/1747-9541.9.2.401

Partington, M., & Cushion, C. (2013). An investigation of the practice activities and coaching behaviors of professional top-level youth soccer coaches practice activities and behaviors of youth soccer coaches. *Scandinavian Journal of Medicine & Science in Sports, 23*, 374–382. https://doi.org/10.1111/j.1600-0838.2011.01383.x

Potrac, P., Jones, R., & Cushion, C. (2007). Understanding power and the coach's role in professional English soccer: A preliminary investigation of coach behaviour. *Soccer & Society, 8*(1), 33–49. https://doi.org/10.1080/14660970600989509

Purdy, L., & Jones, R. (2011). Choppy waters: Elite rowers' perceptions of coaching. *Sociology of Sport Journal, 28*, 329–346. https://doi.org/10.1123/ssj.28.3.329

Richards, P., Collins, D., & Mascarenhas, D. R. (2012). Developing rapid high-pressure team decision-making skills. The integration of slow deliberate reflective learning within the competitive performance environment: A case study of elite netball. *Reflective Practice, 13*(3), 407–424. https://doi.org/10.1080/14623943.2012.670111

Ritchie, D., & Allen, J. (2015). 'Let them get on with it': Coaches' perceptions of their roles and coaching practices during Olympic and Paralympic Games. *International Sport Coaching Journal, 2*, 108–124. https://doi.org/10.1123/iscj.2014-0092

Ritchie, D., Allen, J., & Kirkland, A. (2018). Where science meets practice: Olympic coaches' crafting of the tapering process. *Journal of Sports Sciences, 36*(10), 1145–1154. https://doi.org/10.1080/02640414.2017.1362717

Ronglan, L. T., & Aggerholm, K. (2014). 'Humour helps': Elite sports coaching as a balancing act. *Sports Coaching Review, 3*(1), 33–45. https://doi.org/10.1080/21640629.2014.885776

Ryan, R. M., & Deci, E. L. (2000). Self-determination theory and the facilitation of intrinsic motivation, social development, and wellbeing. *American Psychologist, 55*, 68–78. https://doi.org/10.1037/0003-066X.55.1.68

Rynne, S. B. (2014). "Fast track" and "traditional path" coaches: Affordances, agency and social capital. *Sport Education and Society, 19*(3), 299–313. https://doi.org/10.1080/13573322.2012.670113

Rynne, S. B., & Mallett, C. J. (2012). Understanding the work and learning of high performance coaches. *Physical Education and Sport Pedagogy, 17*(5), 507–523. https://doi.org/10.1080/17408989.2011.621119

Rynne, S. B., Mallett, C. J., & Rabjohns, M. W. (2017). High performance coaching: Demands and development. In R. Thelwell, C. Harwood, & I. Greenless (Eds.), *The psychology of sports coaching* (pp. 114–127). Abingdon, UK: Routledge.

Santos, S., Jones, R. L., & Mesquita, I. (2013). Do coaches orchestrate? The working practices of elite Portuguese coaches. *Research Quarterly for Exercise & Sport, 84*, 263–273. https://doi.org/10.1080/02701367.2013.784722

Schein, E. (2010). *Organizational culture and leadership* (4th ed.). San Francisco: Jossey-Bass.

Schempp, P. G., McCullick, B. A., Grant, M. A., Foo, C., & Wieser, K. (2010). Professional playing experience does not lead to professional coaching experience. *Journal of Coaching Education, 3*(3), 72–82. https://doi.org/10.1123/jce.3.3.72

Simon, S., Collins, L., & Collins, D. (2017). Observational heuristics in a group of high level paddle sports coaches. *International Sport Coaching Journal, 4*, 235–245. https://doi.org/10.1123/iscj.2017-0012

Smith, M. J., Young, D. J., Figgins, S. G., & Arthur, C. A. (2017). Transformational leadership in elite sport: A qualitative analysis of effective leadership behaviors in cricket. *The Sport Psychologist, 31*, 1–15. https://doi.org/10.1123/tsp.2015-0077

Sparkes, A., & Smith, B. (2009). Judging the quality of qualitative inquiry: Criteriology and relativism in action. *Psychology of Sport and Exercise, 10*, 491-497. https://doi.org/10.1016/j.psychsport.2009.02.006

Stirling, A. E., & Kerr, G. A. (2013). The perceived effects of elite athletes' experiences of emotional abuse in the coach–athlete relationship. *International Journal of Sport and Exercise Psychology, 11*(1), 87–100. https://doi.org/10.1080/1612197X.2013.752173

Swann, C., Moran, A., & Piggott, D. (2015). Defining elite athletes: Issues in the study of expert performance in sport psychology. *Psychology of Sport and Exercise, 16*, 3–14. https://doi.org/10.1016/j.psychsport.2014.07.004

Thompson, N. (2000). *Theory and practice in human services*. Buckingham: Open University Press.

Trudel, P., & Gilbert, W. (2006). Coaching and coach education. In D. Kirk, D. Macdonald, & M. O'Sullivan (Eds.), *The handbook of physical education* (pp. 516–539). London: Sage.

United States Olympic Committee Coaching Framework (USOC CF). (2017). The American Development Model. Retrieved from, https://www.teamusa.org/About-the-USOC/Athlete-Development/American-Development-Model

Vallée, C. N., & Bloom, G. A. (2016). Four keys to building a championship culture. *International Sport Coaching Journal, 3*(2), 170–177. https://doi.org/10.1123/iscj.2016-0010

van Puyenbroeck, S., Stouten, J., & Vande Broek, G. (2017). Coaching is teamwork! the role of need-supportive coaching and the motivational climate in stimulating proactivity in volleyball teams. *Scandinavian Journal of Medicine and Science in Sports, 28*, 319–328. https://doi.org/10.1111/sms.12895

Wachsmuth, S., Jowett, S., & Harwood, C. G. (2018a). On understanding the nature of interpersonal conflict between coaches and athlete. *Journal of Sports Sciences, 36*(17), 1955–1962. https://doi.org/10.1080/02640414.2018.1428882

Wachsmuth, S., Jowett, S., & Harwood, C. G. (2018b). Managing conflict in coach-athlete relationships. *Sport, Exercise, and Performance Psychology, 7*(4), 371–391. https://doi.org/10.1037/spy0000129

Waters, A., Phillips, E., Panchuk, D., & Dawson, A. (2019). The coach–scientist relationship in high-performance sport: Biomechanics and sprint coaches. *International Journal of Sports Science & Coaching, 14*(5), 617–628. https://doi.org/10.1177/1747954119859100

Watts, D. W., & Cushion, C. J. (2017). Coaching journeys: Longitudinal experiences from professional football in Great Britain. *Sports Coaching Review, 6*(1), 76–93. https://doi.org/10.1080/21640629.2016.1238135

Yukelson, D., & Rose, R. (2014). The psychology of ongoing excellence: An NCAA coach's perspective on winning consecutive multiple national championships. *Journal of Sport Psychology in Action, 5*(1), 44–58. https://doi.org/10.1080/21520704.2013.866604

Justine Allen is a Senior Lecturer in the Faculty of Health Sciences and Sport at the University of Stirling, Scotland. She is Programme Director for the MSc Sport Performance Coaching and also leads the Post Graduate Diploma Sport Performance Coaching (Paddlesport) in partnership with British Canoeing. Justine's research examines the coaching process and coaching practices, in particular, the 'coach-created' psychosocial environment in sport.

Bob Muir is a Senior Lecturer in Sport Coaching. A senior men's professional basketball coach for over 20 years, Bob is currently the programme director for the MSc Sport Coaching and also leads the Football Association Post Graduate Diploma in Coach Development. His research focuses on sport coaching effectiveness and the development of coaching expertise. Bob has spent the last 10 years working alongside England pathway, national team and Olympic coaches to develop a situated 1to1 coach learning and professional development strategy. He currently works as a coach development consultant with a range of sports organisations and governing bodies in the UK.

Chapter 10
Coaching Life Skills to Young Athletes in Sport Participation Contexts

A. Rui Gomes and Rui Resende

Abstract This chapter is dedicated to analyze sports participation as an alternative to traditional sports for young athletes. Sports participation is directed for individuals interested in benefiting from formal training that stimulates the pleasure and challenges of sports, stimulates learning and developing of life/sports skills, stimulates the benefits of being physically active, and that are not necessary interested in sports for competition purpose. Despite the interest of generalizing sports activity, there are few findings about the relevance of developing sports participation training programs as an alternative of organized sports for youth and recreational sports for adults. In this chapter, we propose the organization of sports participation programs by considering the framework of life skills as a possibility to set the purpose and activities of participation sports. In order to fulfill this goal, we must first present the definition of sports participation, then we will discuss the relation between sports and life skills. Finally, we present a theoretical proposal of life skills applied to sports participation, presenting as framework the example of youth sports. We finish the chapter by reflecting on conditions that can stimulate social recognition of sport programs as a useful proposal to youth athletes.

Keywords Sport leadership · Sport participation · Coaches · Sport coaches · Young athletes · Life skills

Note: The authors wish to express their gratitude to Andy Gillham for his helpful comments on earlier versions of this chapter.

A. R. Gomes (✉)
School of Psychology, University of Minho, Braga, Portugal
e-mail: rgomes@psi.uminho.pt

R. Resende
Life Quality Research Centre, University Institute of Maia, Maia, Portugal
e-mail: rresende@ismai.pt

R. Resende, A. R. Gomes (eds.), *Coaching for Human Development and Performance in Sports*, https://doi.org/10.1007/978-3-030-63912-9_10

Imagine two boys, Arthur and Peter, who started playing volleyball at school at the ages of nine. A couple of years later, they decided to start practicing volleyball in a more organized way and both joined a local club and started playing there. The fact that their parents were able to take them to practice helped the decision to join. After 3 years, Peter quit the team because it was taking up too much of his time. As much as he enjoyed playing, the time consumption was too much for him. Peter never returned to organized sports or other forms of exercise. He started to smoke at 17 and his healthy lifestyle was not the same as before. He experienced increased weight and started to become overweight. Peter later built a family, had a regular job, and never had major health complications. His doctor warned him several times to be more active and careful with his eating habits. One day, Peter suffered a stroke at the age of 53. Fortunately for him, it was not severe enough to cause definitive damage. After receiving medical advice, Peter went to the gym to start rehabilitation with a trainer. It was at that time Peter met his old friend, Arthur. Arthur told Peter that he played volleyball in the second national league until he was 35. After that, Arthur began participating in sports on a regular basis. This included beach volleyball and soccer two times per week besides the cardiovascular training three times per week. Because of all these sports activities, Arthur is in shape and has strong physical health. After meeting his old friend, Peter wondered why he felt so differently about his friend, and Arthur wondered what happened to Peter's physicality and health. Given the opportunity to play sports in a different way, Peter's lifestyle would have most likely been much different. Throughout this chapter, we will defend that sports participation can represent a possibility to prevent negative effects of dropout, sedentary lifestyle, and poor habits of life (as was the case of Peter). Conversely, we will defend that sports participation can reinforce positive effects of sports and contribute to feelings of positive functioning and personal competence (as was the case of Arthur).

Conceptual and Empirical Findings About Sports Participation

Sports participation does not have a clear description. If we consider the International Sport Coaching Framework terminology (ISCF, 2013), sports participation "defines the roles taken on by the coaches according to levels of competence and responsibility and the populations they serve (coaching domains) in participation sport and performance sport" (p. 12). ISCF also consider the role definition from the coach status, meaning fulltime payed, part-time payed, and volunteer involvement.

The definition of ISCF reinforces two distinctive types of sport engagement, one that highlights involvement and enjoyment, and the other that considers the high performance of sports. This spectrum also considers that athletes can change between the several subdivisions set in sports for children, adolescents, and adults considering that sporting pathways are individual, context specific, and non-linear in

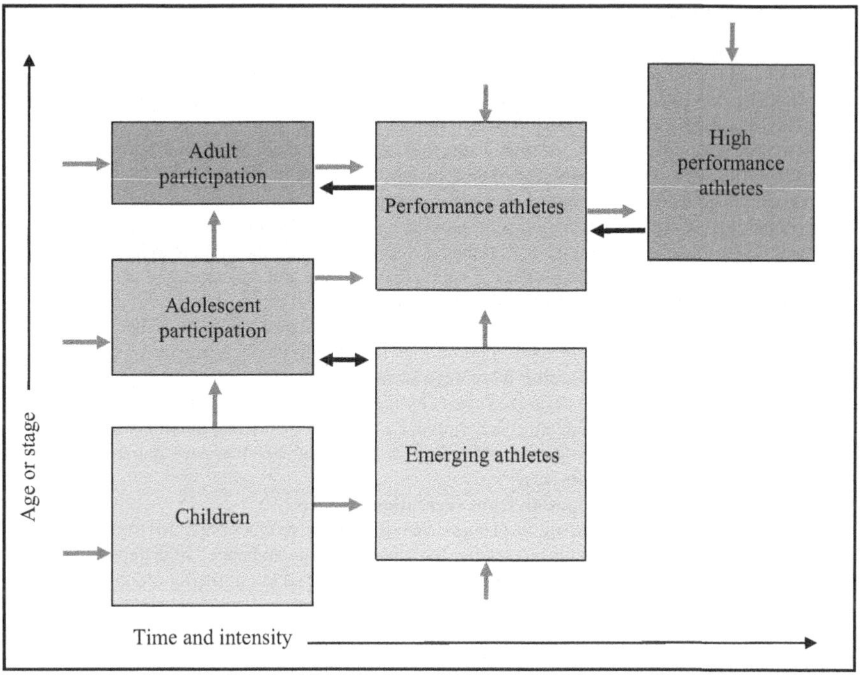

Fig. 10.1 Sports participation spectrum (ISCF, 2013, p. 20)

nature (ISCF, 2013). The performance sport pathway is evident, considering competition and sports achievement as requirements as athletes get older, establishing a bottleneck when they arrive to adult performance sports (Fig. 10.1).

However, what happens to athletes who dropout or change sports engagement when competition is not a focus of interest? What happens to athletes that, despite the interest in organized sports for competition purposes, do not have the opportunity to continue their careers as performance athletes? In our perspective, the alternative for all of these athletes can be sport participation.

Figure 10.2 presents our understanding of sports participation. In the figure, our perspective points to a definition of sports participation. It reinforces the philosophy and goals of sports participation, distinguishes sports participation from organized and recreational sports, and argues what can be the surroundings of sports participation.

Sports participation can lead to very interesting results in society. We may assume that most athletes (from different ages) may be interested in alternatives for performing sports that can be intrinsically motivating, that takes place in a healthy environment and that can be a lifelong project. The assumption is to use sport as an educational tool (Wright, Jacobs, Ressler, & Jung, 2016) that foster positive human development, particularly for youth people (Zuzanek, 2005) not interested in organized sports for competition purposes. Finding alternatives to these traditional forms of organized sports is important due positive benefits of sports and

What is sport participation?

Sport participation is a structured activity, directed by graduate coaches, that offers intrinsically motivated opportunities to individuals interested in benefiting from formal training that stimulates the pleasure and challenges of sports, the learning and developing of life and sports skills, and the benefits of being physically active.

Sports Participation is for everyone who wants to do sports for a variety of reasons, not necessarily related to competition or being better than others.

What are the goals (or philosophy) of sport participation?

The central goal of sport participation is promoting active participation and opportunities to the widest possible audience (Wicker, Hallmann, & Breuer, 2012); the participation should stimulate the pleasure and challenges of sports, the learning and developing of skills related to sports, and the lifetime benefits of being physically active.

The philosophy of sport participation sustains on a "athlete centered perspective" by promoting active participation and equal sport opportunities for all individuals interested in sports.

How different is sport participation from organized sports?

Sport participation is similar to organized sports by including formal and structured sports activities delivered by a graduate coach; however, it differs by the fact that it is not developed for competition purpose being instead directed for all individuals interested in participating in structured programs of sports activity.

How different is sport participation from recreational sports?

Recreational sports are informal sports (Jeanes, Spaaij, Penney, & O'Connor, 2018) with some type of physical activity that is not regular in nature and that can happen in different places and environments. This activity can be more or less organized but normally it does not need a coach as responsible to define and conduct the sport program.

Sport participation is done on a regular basis, typically during a season and it is directed by a coach who leads and takes responsibility for the training process.

What is the age range of sport participation?

The sport participation spectrum can be very wide. However, the onset of sport participation should be the infancy and adolescence period because for some children and teenagers organized sports do not represent an interesting and positive experience.

Who is responsible for the sport participation programs?

The application of sport participation programs should be directed by certificated coaches; however, schools, sports clubs, local recreational clubs, and national agencies of sports represent some of the major promotors of sport participation.

What types of sports are practiced in sport participation programs?

All sports can be included.

Final reflection

Is sport participation about winning? Is it about competing for winning purpose?

Sport participation is about improving and experience positive emotions of sports practice; competition is not forbidden but it does not represent the main purpose of sport participation programs.

Fig. 10.2 Understanding sport participation

exercise. Several studies support the relevance of sports in facilitating human integration (Nanayakkara, 2016) and as a platform of significant learning experiences (Super, Wentink, Verkooijen, & Koelen, 2017). However, Collins (2010) refer that in "England approximately 61% of men and 71% of women over the age of 16 failed to meet the minimum adult recommendation for physical activity (p. 373)". This is a main concern for politics and decision makers. Governments included in EU (EU, 2014; Eurostat, 2018) and outside EU, as Australia (Australian-Government, 2018; Sotiriadou, Quick, & Shilbury, 2006) and Canada (2012) are using sports and psychical activity as useful activities to improve health, well-being, and social cohesion among citizens. As recognized by the United Nations (ONU, 2003), sports can stimulate core principles of human beings. These principles include tolerance, cooperation, respect, discipline, confidence, and effort. Aligning with these principles, sports participation implicates changing the goal from competing for winning purpose (competition centered perspective), to promoting active participation and equal sport opportunities for all individuals interested in sports (athlete centered perspective). Sport participation should be dedicated to developing skills in a variety of sport activities and should promote the lifetime benefits of being physically active. This urges to educate and professionalize coaches to organize sport programs that fit the purposes of sport participation. This is critical because coaches can make the difference between athletes having a positive or negative experience due to their participation in sports (Lefebvre, Evans, Turnnidge, Gainforth, & Côté, 2016). Keeping in mind the main purpose of sports participation (develop the skills of those interested in sports), we will explain what we mean by "skills" (using the concept of "life skills") and we will give particular focus to youth sports because it may represent the outset of sports participation. This does not mean that sports participation is only for children and adolescents; we believe that sports participation may begin at an early age but can continue along human development.

Sports and Life Skills

Sports represent an extraordinary context to learn and develop life skills. In a changing environment, developing personal tools to be able to meet the challenges of everyday life is very significant.

What Are Life Skills?

Jones (Chap. 15), argues that life skills are still not well defined. There are many definitions as there are potential life skills. This is quite interesting because we have already substantial evidence about life skill training programs impact on youth development (Brown & Fry, 2014; Danish, 1996, 1997; Gomes & Marques, 2013; Hardcastle, Tye, Glassey, & Hagger, 2015) without having an agreement of what life skills are. Danish and colleagues understood life skills in a broad perspective: "those skills that enable individuals to succeed in the different environments in which they live, such as school, home and in their neighborhoods" (Danish, Taylor, Hodge, & Heke, 2004, p. 40). Gould and Carson (2008, p. 60) sustains that life skills in sports are "those internal personal assets, characteristics and skills such as goal setting, emotional control, self-esteem, and hard work ethic that can be facilitated or developed in sport and are transferred for use in non-sport settings". World diffusion of life skills mean that they are recognized as important to promote human development. Specifically, for the World Health Organization (2003) life skills are the skills people must have to cope with the demands and challenges of their day-to-day life. These skills increase the possibility of healthy and productive lives. Finally, Jones argues that life skills are acquired through practice to help display competence in socially valuable tasks that predicts similarly useful functions within or across life domains.

In our perspective, life skills encase human potentialities that can be stimulated through systematic training or that are developed "implicitly" from people's everyday experiences, allowing human adaptation to changing events. This definition of life skills sustains in three aspects: (a) a broad understanding of life skills, from intellectual, cognitive, motor, and physical abilities because all of them are reactive to human learning and all of them can have major impact on human adaptation to changing events; (b) life skills can be learned and acquired by exposing the individual to systematic training or by providing the adequate opportunities of learning; although research did not dedicated efforts comparing both sources of life skills learning, there is substantial evidence about the positive impact of intervention programs of life skills (i.e., systematic training) (see Nasheeda, Abdullah, Krauss, & Ahmed, 2018); and (c) the statute of life skills is only achieved when they contribute to human adaptation to changing events. This relation between life skills and adaption to change is important because it provides usefulness to life skills. Thus, we should clarify the concept of adaptation to change. We understand adaptation to change as the efforts assumed by the person when confronted with one or more events (of internal or external nature) that produces a disruption in the habitual pattern of human functioning, and that are assumed in order to restore or stimulate human functioning (Gomes, 2014). The restoration or improvement of human functioning is achieved when the efforts (both at cognitive and behavioral levels) derived from life skills produce desirable effects on dealing with the changing event. However, it is possible that cognitive and behavioral effects do not always produce desirable effects on dealing with the changing event; this means that the individual does not always possess the necessary life skill for that specific event or do not always use proper life skill according the specific constrains of the changing event. In sum, life skills assume meaning when they contribute to human adaptation to change and because we are adapting to change throughout our lives, life skills are useful along the life cycle.

Types of Life skills

Danish et al. (2004) differentiated behavioral (communicating effectively with peers and adults), cognitive (making effective decisions), interpersonal (being assertive), intrapersonal (setting goals), and even physical (e.g., taking the right posture) life skills. This is a very useful life skill categorization, but it may not capture the broad classes and impacts that life skills produce on human functioning.

In our perspective, the determination of life skills should consider the typology and functionality of life skills (see Fig. 10.3). The typology includes intellectual life skills related to abstract thinking (as is the case of solving problems), cognitive life

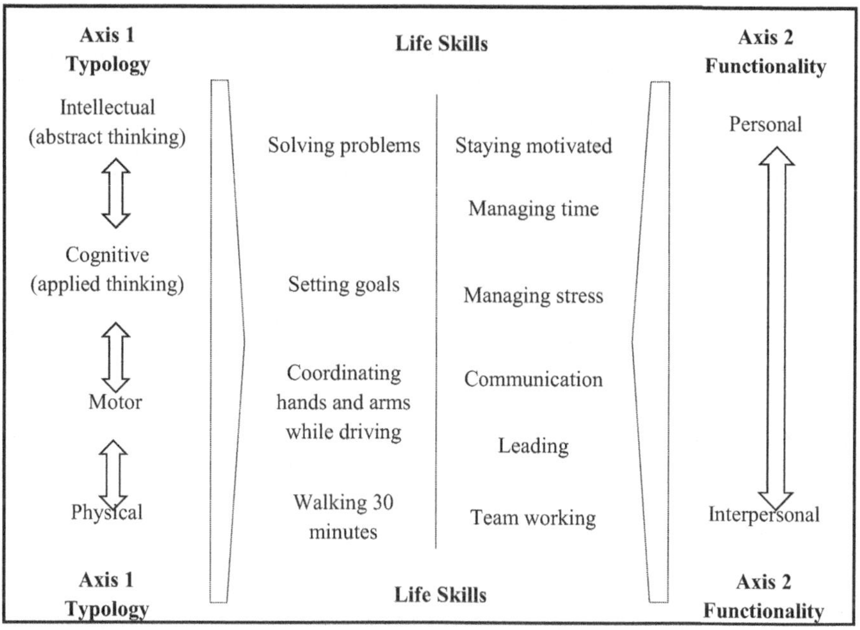

Fig. 10.3 Understanding life skills: typology and functionality

skills related to applied thinking (as is the case of setting goals to stay motivated), motor life skills related to executing simple and complex tasks (as is the case of coordinating hands and arms while driving), and physical life skills related to execute simple and complex tasks (as is the case of walking for 30 min in order to active an healthy condition). The functionality indicates the levels of application and use of the life skill, varying in a continuum of personal and interpersonal life skills. For example, staying motivated, organizing time, and managing stress are typical life skills assumed at a personal level, regardless the possibility of being used in interpersonal relationships (for example, being part of a team in a stressful situation). On the other hand, communication, leading others, and team work are typical life skills assumed at an interpersonal level regardless the possibility of being used as a personal relationship (for example, using positive internal dialogues when executing team tasks). These two types of typology and functionality are useful to determine the areas of life skills, training, and the expected levels of impact produced on human functioning.

Life Skill Acquisition Stages

Life skills can be learned throughout our lives when confronting changing events or they can be trained by using Life Skills Training (LST) programs. In this last case, LST should be implemented in four stages:

1. **Motivation.** Stimulate the participants' interest in the LST and in the training program itself (e.g., what are life skills, what specific life skills are include in the program, what is the typology and functionality of the life skill, what are the applications of the life skill to specific and general life domains of the LST participants, major advantages of participating in the LST program).
2. **Learning.** Transmit information about the life skills of the LST program and internalization of the life skill in the mental and behavioral repertoire of each participant (e.g., what are the components and characteristics of the life skills included in the LST, what information and knowledge is particularly useful in order to assume and become an expert in using the life skill, assuming the relevant tasks implicated in the life skill).
3. **Automatization.** Stimulate the utilization of the life skill in one specific life context of the participants (usually the one where the LST occurs).
4. **Transference.** Stimulate the utilization of the life skill in more than one situation of the same life context of the participants, or in more than one life context of the participant.

Principles of Life Skill Training

Introducing the life skill in cognitive and behavioral repertoire of participants in LST programs is possibly the most challenging factor of the life skills intervention. It is fundamental that stages of life skill acquisition occur, and that transference is successfully achieved. This progress of acquiring the life skills is facilitated when LST programs are implemented by using three principles of life skill training.

(a) **Integral impact of training** (integrality principle). Teaching life skills should spread effects on human functioning on both axis of typology and functionality of skills. This means that acquiring life skills to deal with changing events is stimulated when the LST programs impacts multiple types of human development (intellectual, cognitive, motor, and physical) and distinct levels of human functioning (personal to interpersonal). The integrality principle of training conceives human development as a whole and as a unit, opposing the Cartesian dualism to nondualistic philosophical frameworks (Mehta, 2011). It is evident that some life skills stimulate specific types, and levels, of human functioning. Learning and applying life skills is a multiple experience that evokes and stimulates thinking processes, thoughts and cognitions, emotions, physical and motor reactions, and acting on the changing event.

(b) **Gradual impact of training** (graduality principle). Teaching life skills stimulates them according to the four stages of LST acquisition (e.g., motivation, learning, automatization, and transference). As long as participants progress in the four stages of the LST programs they improve in knowledge and ability, until a point where the skill is part of automatic routines assumed by the participants in multiple life contexts. In this sense, it is fundamental to apply the graduality principle to LST programs by designing activities that fulfill the four stages of training.

(c) **Individual impact of training** (individuality principle). Teaching life skills is improved when it is adapted according to the specific stage of development and skills of participants in LST programs. Adaptation (i.e., individualization) is particularly important when life skills are trained in groups of participants, which is the most frequent option when compared with individual intervention. This implicates that participants in LST programs should have the opportunity to simulate specific activities until a level where they acquire knowledge and ability to assume the life skill. LST programs should be designed in terms of activities and time that allow each participant to successfully proceed in the four stages of life skill acquisition (e.g., motivation, learning, automatization, and transference).

Variables That Influence Life Skill Acquisition

Variables that influence LST programs may be divided among internal and external and both deserve equal attention when designing, implementing, and evaluating the intervention on life skills. Internal variables include demographic characteristics of participants (e.g., age), physical and health status (e.g., motor development), and psychological and emotional abilities and traits (e.g., personality, maturity, openness to new experiences). External variables include situational circumstances where participants are involved (e.g., influence of role models, social support, peer influence, community opportunities for LST), and socioeconomic conditions where participates are included (e.g., financial living conditions). Internal and external variables determine the life skills of participants before the LST intervention, moderate the effectiveness of the LST intervention, and are cumulative with the LST programs in terms of effects produced in the participants.

Efficacy of Life Skill Training

Determination of efficacy of LST is decisive in order to prove the personal and social relevance of stimulating life skills. The efficacy of LST depends on having different indicators suggesting the same pattern of results. Using multiple measures in order to test the LST programs will give a broad and specific vision of effects produced on human functioning. We believe that, at least, four indicators should be considered when testing the efficacy of LST programs:

(a) **Subjective learning acquisition measures.** Indicates the learning and utilization of life skills included in the LST program (ex: training the life skill of motivation should produce positive effects on the perception of motivation of the participants).

(b) **Subjective experiential measures of wellbeing.** Indicates alterations in psychological constructs associated with the LST program (ex: training the life skill of motivation should produce positive effects on the individual's commitment to a given area or task).
(c) **Subjective outcome measures.** Indicates the perceived changes on human functioning by the participants associated with the LST program (ex: training the life skill of motivation should produce positive effects on the perception of achievement of relevant personal goals).
(d) **Objective outcome measures.** Indicates the effective changes on human functioning by the participants associated with the LST program (ex: training the life skill of motivation should produce positive effects on the amount of time dedicated to relevant tasks and on the number of tasks produced by the participant).

Life Skills Acquisition: A Theoretical Proposal

The Life Skills Training Efficacy Model proposes an understanding of major factors that can influence the efficacy of life skills training. Three sets of factors influence the training efficacy: (a) the need for designing LST programs by stages, (b) the need of respecting the principles of life skill training, and (c) the need of considering internal and external variables of participants in the LST programs when designing, implementing, and evaluating the life skills interventions. These factors correspond to three hypotheses about the efficacy of LST programs:

1. The efficacy of LST programs increases if the intervention includes four stages of life skills acquisition (i.e., motivation, learning, automatization, and generalization) compared to programs that do not incorporate these stages.
2. The efficacy of LST programs increases if the intervention respects the principles of life skill training (i.e., integrality, graduality, and individuality) compared to programs that do not incorporate these principles.
3. The efficacy of LST programs is maximized or minimized (i.e., moderate) by internal and external variables of the participants included in intervention program.

Figure 10.4 presents the Life Skills Training Efficacy Model, emphasizing the importance of the variables described above. It is proposed that efficacy measures should be collected before and after intervention (in this last case, at least at the end of intervention and in a follow-up period); the program has higher chances of efficacy if it is implemented in four-stages of intervention and according principles of training, and that internal and external variables of participants influence all of the process of LST. In sum, adaptation to change is increased when individuals use life skills to deal with the constraints of the event (that can have more or less relation with an external situation); this increase of impact on the changing event is maximized when LST programs respects stages, principles, and internal and external variables of life skills.

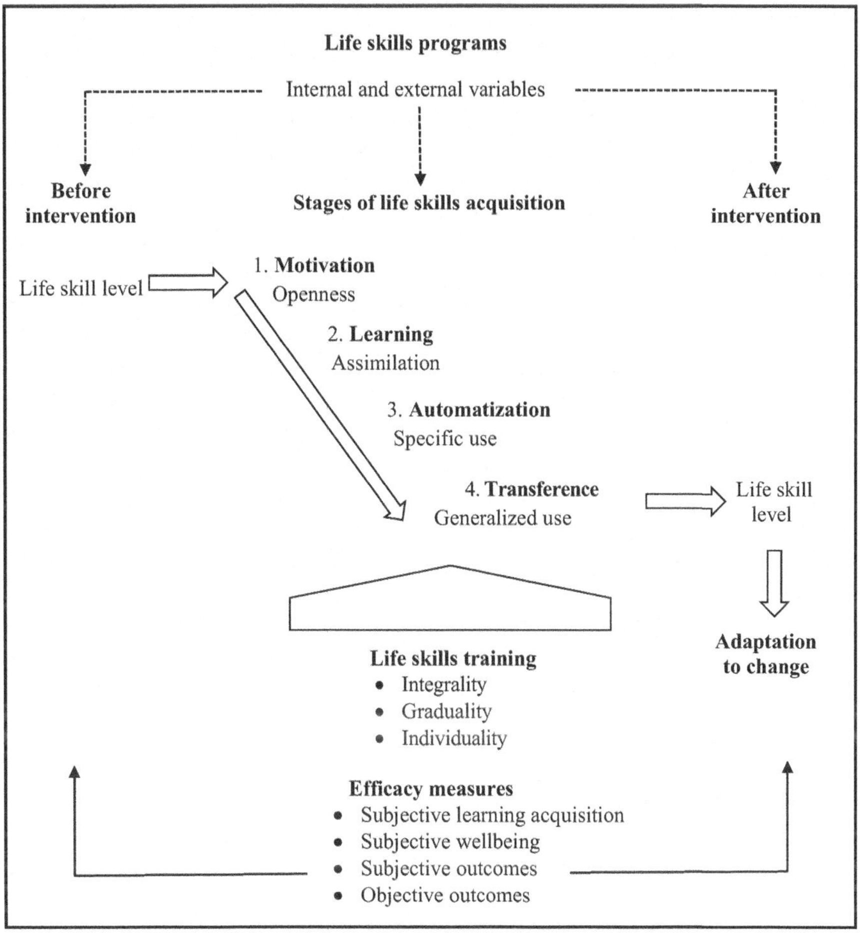

Fig. 10.4 Life skills training efficacy model

Youth Sport Participation: An Opportunity to Life Skills Training

Teaching life skills to young athletes represents a meritorious goal of sports programs. However, some constraints exists when this training occurs in sports organized events for competing purposes. The first, and most obvious, is that coaches may feel pressure to prepare athletes to compete instead of preparing athletes to learn and enjoy sports as a long-life activity. Coaches may have difficulties to organize training plans for all athletes, giving them similar opportunities of learning sports (life) skills. Some evidence suggests that problems related to sport specialization, overtraining, chocking under pressure, and even burnout happens to young athletes (for a review, see DiSanti & Erickson, 2019) which may be interpreted as dysfunctionalities produced by traditional sports. For example, sports specialization of young athletes in order to accelerate sport success is related to several problem, as overuse injuries (Hall, Foss, Hewett, & Myer, 2015), psychological need dissatisfaction (McFadden, Bean, Fortier, & Post, 2016), burnout (Strachan, Côté, & Deakin, 2009), less connection with community (Strachan et al., 2009), and less involvement in organized sports as adults (Russell, 2014).

This indicates that youth sports programs do not necessarily represent a fertile environment to life skills learning. This can be an opportunity to develop youth sports participation programs and an opportunity to relate sports participation to learning life skills. Life skills training may sustain and give purpose to sports participation programs, as an alternative perspective of youth development. By thinking that life skills can be understood in terms of typology and functionality (see Fig. 10.3) and can be trained by stages (see Fig. 10.4), coaches may design sports participation programs in order to develop athletes' life skills by correctly using the principles of training life skills. Coaches are much more prepared to stimulate physical and motor skills than cognitive and intellectual skills, as proposed on the typology axis. This reinforces that sports programs should include other professionals from social and human sciences (as is the case of sport psychologists) besides the coaches, in order to set up training activities that potentiate multiple areas of human development. In the next section, we analyze how coaches can organize sports participation programs, taking into consideration the goal of stimulating life skills.

Coaching for Sport Participation

Sports participation for athletes not interested in traditional sports organized for competitive purpose is a very challenging topic for coaches. The alternative that we suggested in this work is organizing sports participation as a fertile field to teach life skills. In this section, we provide some indications to organize positive activities to athletes included in sport participation, taking as background the Life Skills Training Efficacy Model.

Life Skill Acquisition Stages for Sport Participation

Athletes participating in sports need to be coached as their peers participating in sports for competition purpose, but not by using the same strategies and goals. Because of that, coaches need to rethink their ideas and principles of coaching (philosophy), methodologies and plans of action (practice), and goals (criteria) when designing the training process. This triple relation between philosophy, practice, and criteria (e.g., leadership cycle; see Chap. 4) should consider the stages of life skills training.

Stage 1 of life skills acquisition is challenging for coaches because they have to motivate athletes (and themselves) about the relevance of doing sports for fun, leisure, health, and self-improvement among other related factors. For coaches of traditional sports, the process of training is designed to better prepare athletes for competing. For sports participation coaches, the training process should be organized for other purposes not related to beating other opponents. The alternative implicates that coaches assume a coaching philosophy related to the development of athletes' skills. This would be the main purpose of sports participation coaches: create condition for sports development of athletes in order to stimulate an intrinsic interest of continuing sports along athletes' lives. For sports participation coaches, sports development should be understood in a broad sense, focusing on improvements in social, mental, physical, technical, and tactical abilities that can maximize the chances that sports (and latter exercise) are assumed as a regular routine of athletes. In order to reach this goal, in Stage 1 of skills acquisition, coaches have to motivate athletes for sport participation. This includes discussing motivational topics of what life skills can be learned by athletes (i.e., choice), what level of effort is needed to acquire the skills (i.e., intensity), and what type of obstacles and problems can occur during the learning process (i.e., persistency). This process is well accomplished when athletes develop a personal meaning for sports that is mainly intrinsic and personally challenging, not from competing in order to be ranked by their abilities and success.

Stage 2 of life skills acquisition is dedicated to learning the concepts and behaviors associated with the sports skills that athletes will acquire. For coaches, this a *technical* stage due to their ability to teach the skills and how they should be executed. Thus, *knowing what* and *knowing how* are the two main topics of this stage. For participation athletes, this stage may fulfill major parts of their expectations to do sports because they may be interested in *knowing how to play sports* regardless of their final *comparative expertise of executing* the skill. This process is successful when athletes incorporate their cognitive and behavioral repertoires to the skill, and manifest intensity in the learning process, despite their level of execution can be considered inferior or superior when compared with other athletes.

Stage 3 of life skills acquisition increases the challenge of sports learning by automatizing the skills in the cognitive and behavioral repertoires of athletes. The goal is repeating the skills until a level of expertise is achieved that transmits maximum effort and ability of each athlete. Please note, the goal is not becoming an expert when compared with other athletes, the goal is becoming an expert considering the abilities and efforts made by each athlete in previous executions and actions. For coaches, the challenge is to create the best training conditions that can stimulate the abilities of each athlete. At this stage, the training principle of individualization may become crucial in order to stimulate the strengths and potentialities of each athlete. This process is learned when athletes automatize the skill in their cognitive and behavioral repertoires and manifest persistency when facing obstacles during the learning and execution process.

Stage 4 of life skills acquisition maybe somewhat confusing when compared with traditional sports. In this case, the sports skills automatized in training sessions are stimulated in terms of transference by mainly using the competition setting. For participation sports, competition is not established in the same way. In fact, competition may not occur at all. In this case, coaches may have to find other sports situations and life contexts where athletes can use and apply the sport skills. For example, coordination skills learned in one specific exercise of training may be transferred for other skills implicated in other exercises or, in a broader sense, to life contexts as is the case of driving a bike and then driving a car. When coaches include competition in their coaching plans, they must establish other goals for athletes beyond winning or beating opponents. This is a crucial aspect in order to differentiate participation sports from traditional sports and to prevent the same negative effects that can turn competition into a non-interesting activity for participation athletes (ex: pressure to win, not playing must of the time, adjusting to negative expectations of adults, among others). Thus, for participation athletes, competition may not occur or, if it occurs, it should have other purpose beyond winning. This process is learned when athletes transfer the skill automatized in different exercises or tasks of sports (and life) and manifest the same levels of intensity and persistency in order to execute the learned skill well.

Principles of Life Skill Acquisition for Sport Participation

Organizing life skill training for sports participation implicates using the three principles of life skills training: (a) integral impact of training (integrality principle), gradual impact of training (graduality principle), and individual impact of training (individuality principle).

(a) **Integrality principle.** Training life skills for sports participation should produce multiple impacts on athletes' development, such as, sports skills (technical and tactical), physical skills (motor coordination and physical condition), psychological skills (cognitive and emotional), and social skills (communication and leadership). For sports participation, this principle implicates that coaches think the training process is stimulating skills related to competition by shifting their analysis to think how they can attribute new meanings to sports that motivate athletes not concerned with achieving sports competition success. The alternatives should be integrated in the training plan designed by the coach to participation athletes. For example, the mottos of "developing and improving new abilities" or "executing tasks in different ways" (technical and tactical), "challenging the limits" (physical condition), "thinking positively and experience new sensations" (psychological), and "stimulating the team to their best executions" are starting points that can give a specific purpose to the coaching process of sport participation.

(b) **Graduality principle.** Training life skills for sports participation should recognize the gradual development of athletes' skills, according the four stages of LST (i.e., motivation, leaning, automatization, and transference). Stage 1 of life skills training is particularly important when athletes need to comprehend the advantages of learning the skill, being discussed motivational topics of choice (i.e., why to choose the specific skill), of intensity (i.e., level of effort to dedicate in the learning process), and persistency (i.e., tendency to maintain efforts when facing obstacles and problems during the learning process). Stage 2 of life skills acquisition is particularly important when athletes begin the learning process, analyzing their actual execution by comparing their previous execution. The focus is on the process of executing the skill in order to stimulate the acquisition and the demonstration of the sport skill. Stage 3 introduces performance criteria to skill training by comparing the actual performance of athletes with their previous performance, meaning that acquisition is now related to the *success* on demonstrating the skill. Finally, Stage 4 extends effectiveness criteria by comparing levels of personal performance with other indicators of performance (as for example opponents' performance). For sports participation, this last stage is different by not comparing the performance among athletes in sport participation contexts (the idea is not "beating" or "competing" against others, as it happens in traditional youth sports); the alternative may be testing the skills in different training situations or even in other life contexts (i.e., how good is the athlete in transferring the skills to other situations similar but not equal to the one she/he had acquired the skill).

(c) **Individuality principle.** Training life skills for sports participation should be customized to the specific abilities and expectations of athletes and should include specific training activities for each athlete. The individualization is crucial for coaches of sports participation. Since the beginning, they know that these athletes do not necessarily want to compete against other athletes. They aren't interested in social recognition of sport success. By removing these habitual sources of motivation, coaches may increase the interest of sports by providing athletes equal and individualized opportunities of learning and improving skills. Because coaches are not pressed by competition and by the need of achieving success, they may have the opportunity to give a central role to the ability of each athlete to learn the proposed skills. By learning and executing the skills the best they can, athletes may perceive sports participation as the ideal context to do and enjoy sports.

In sum, sports training should be integral, gradual, and individualized in order to stimulate and develop sports (i.e., life) skills, especially for the case of young athletes of sports participation contexts.

Variables That Influence Life Skill Acquisition for Sport Participation

Internal and external variables of participants in LST programs may influence the efficacy of learning and acquisition of life skills. There is not abundant literature about the influence of these variables on LST efficacy (for a review, see Jones &

Parker, 2014). However, coaches should consider the influence of these variables when designing, implementing, and evaluating the LST provided to athletes. Let's take the example of maturity and complexity, perhaps two major factors that coaches consider when defining training plans for their athletes.

Maturity can be defined as the personal ability to assume a certain skill in a specific moment and context, and that influences readiness for action and final performance. The maturity depends of the emotional predisposition (i.e., levels of self-confidence and motivation) of the individual to learn and assume the skill (psychological maturity), and of the technical predisposition (i.e., levels of competence and knowledge) of the same individual to learn and execute the skill (technical maturity). The principles of life skills training can be used in order to adjust the LST program to the levels of athletes' maturity, as follows:

(a) Integrality of LST should augment as athletes augment their levels of maturity. Coaches may have opportunity to introduce the life skill in one specific context or situation, and only when athletes assume automatization and transference of life skill in the specific situation, coaches should introduce new situations and contexts. For example, teaching basketball player's free throws may first imply to simulate the correct corporal position and associated movements implicated until the shot. Coaches should provide athletes feedback about their execution. Next, coaches may provide feedback about efficacy of execution, and finally, coaches may introduce stress factors (as audience, for example) in order to test the athletes' ability to execute under pressure. By introducing the stress factors only when athletes achieved some maturity on the task (sport life skill), coaches may now use this example to discuss with athletes how they can manage their tension when they are stressed out in other basketball scenarios and even in their lives (psychological life skills).
(b) Graduality of LST should diminish as athletes augment their levels of maturity. Coaches should augment the time and efforts dedicated to each stage of LST when athletes demonstrate lower levels of maturity. Then, augments of athletes' maturity can diminish the time dedicated to each stage of LST.
(c) Individuality of LST should augment in the following situations: (1) when coaches have distinct levels of maturity on their teams, they should provide athletes the necessary adaptations in the LST (this is most applied to collective sports' coaches), (2) when coaches have distinct levels of progression in the LST by the athletes; and (3) when coaches want to stimulate higher levels of expertise in LST of athletes that already learned and acquired the standard levels of execution but they are interested in optimizing their use of the life skill until a point of less interest for the rest of athletes composing the LST.

Complexity refers to specific demands and particularities that characterize the learning and acquisition of the life skill that influences readiness for action and final performance. Complexity can constraint the development and execution of LST programs, and should also consider the levels of maturity of athletes. Once again, the principles of LST can be used in order to adjust the training plan to the complexity of the life skill and also to the athletes' maturity, as follows:

(a) Integrality of LST should decrease as the complexity of the life skill increases, until a point where levels of maturity allows increases of integrality and complexity. Coaches may have advantages in decreasing the integrity of training for complex life skills, and only when athletes assume higher maturity on the life skill is the moment to increase both integrality and complexity.
(b) Graduality of LST should augment as the complexity of the life skill increases, until a point where levels of maturity allows decreases of graduation and increases of complexity. Graduation needs to augment (i.e., giving more time and training activities for the four stages of LST) for complex life skills, and can diminish as long as athletes demonstrates ability to assume the life skill.
(c) Individuality of LST should augment as the complexity of the life skill increases, until a point where levels of maturity allows decreases of individualization and increases of complexity. Individualization is more complex than integrality and graduality, because it has the potential to remain important for longer periods of time despite the maturity of athletes. Normally, we can expect that increases of complexity request higher individualization, until a point where maturity decreases the need of individualization. However, even when athletes assume higher maturity (i.e., become more competent and even experts) they still may have the need for individualization in order to maintain, or ameliorate, their levels of execution. This is quite evident for high performance athletes and, in the case of sports participants, athletes can also expect to assume higher standards of execution on the proposed sports activities.

Figure 10.5 represents the relations between the principles of life skill acquisition and the maturity of athletes and complexity of life skills.

Maturity				Complexity			
****	++++	+	++++	****	+	++++	++++
***	+++	++	++	***	++	+++	+++
**	++	+++	++	**	+++	++	++
*	+	++++	+	*	++++	+	+
Maturity	Integrality	Graduality	Individuality	**Complexity**	Integrality	Graduality	Individuality
	Principles of life skills training				**Principles of life skills training**		

Fig. 10.5 Life skills training principles versus maturity and complexity

Considering the three principles of sports training (integrality, graduality, and individuality), and the relation between skill complexity and maturity, coaches need to establish the effectiveness criteria of their work with athletes.

Efficacy of LST Training for Sport Participation

Coaches of athletes in sport participation contexts need to define the efficacy of their work, as their colleagues of other sport contexts. When it comes to life skills, efficacy measures can be collected from four sources: (a) subjective learning acquisition of life skills (perception of learning the life skills by the participants in the LST program), (b) subjective wellbeing (changes on psychological wellbeing perceived by the participants in the LST program), (c) subjective outcomes (changes on human functioning perceived by the participants in the LST program), and (d) objective outcomes (effective changes on human functioning assumed by the participants in the LST program). Coaches may apply these measures in order to evaluate the efficacy of teaching life skills to athletes. The choice of measures should consider the typology and functionality of life skills. For example, the training of physical or cognitive life skills can implicate selecting distinct measures of subjective learning acquisition; measures of physical activity may be related with perception of strength or endurance of doing training (or life) activities; and measures of cognitive activity may be related with perception of ability to set goals in order to stay motivated in sports (and even in life).

The selection of efficacy measures depend on effectiveness criteria used by coaches to monitor the success of their work with athletes. Coaches for athletes in sports participation should first recognize the need of finding other effectiveness criteria beyond competing and winning competitions in order to fulfill the expectations and needs of athletes. How does one determine the effectiveness criteria for coaches of athletes that are in sport participation? This is a complex question. One possibility is distributing these criteria along the four stages of life skills acquisition.

Stage 1 of motivation intends to stimulate the will of athletes to start the life skills acquisition; effectiveness is achieved when athletes are open (or interested) to learn and acquire the life skill. In this way, effectiveness criteria can be related to athletes' readiness for starting life skills training in terms of choice (i.e., why to choose the specific life skill), of intensity (i.e., level of effort to dedicate in the learning process of the life skill), and of persistency (i.e., tendency to maintain efforts when facing obstacles and problems during the learning process of the skill). Stage 2 of learning intends to stimulate cognitive and behavioral assimilation of the life skills; effectiveness is achieved when athletes understand key aspects of life skills and are able to execute the life skills. In this way, effectiveness criteria can be related to athletes' improvement of life skills execution by comparing their previous use of the life skill (i.e., process of execution). Stage 3 of automatization intends to stimulate the correct use of the life skill in a specific life context (for the sports case, the automation of life skill will be related to sports tasks); effectiveness is achieved when athletes are able to correctly use the life skill in the trained situation. In this way, effectiveness criteria can be related to athletes' effects of using the life skill in the selected situation, comparing their actual performance versus their previous performance. Finally, stage 4 of transference intends to stimulate the correct use of the life skill across distinct life context or across distinct tasks or situations in the same life context (for the sports case, the automation of life skill may occur when athletes use the life skill in other contexts of living or when they use the life skill in other sport tasks); effectiveness is achieved when athletes are able to correctly use the life skill in distinct sport or life situations. In this way, effectiveness criteria can be related to athletes' effects of using the life skill in multiple situations, comparing their actual performances versus previous performances (the use of plural here is intentional). Figure 10.6 summarizes the relation between the efficacy of life skills training and the stages and effectiveness criteria of LST programs.

Efficacy measures	×	Subjective learning acquisition	Subjective wellbeing Subjective outcomes Objective outcomes	Subjective wellbeing Subjective outcomes Objective outcomes
Effectiveness criteria	**Readiness** Choice, intensity, and persistency	**Process** Actual execution versus previous execution	**Specific performance** Actual performance versus previous performance	**Multiple performance** Actual performances versus previous performances
Levels of incorporation of the competence	×	×	×	4 Generalized utilization
	×	×	3 Specific utilization	✓
	×	2 Assimilation	✓	✓
	1 Openness	✓	✓	✓
Stages of life skills acquisition	**Stage 1** Motivation	**Stage 2** Learning	**Stage 3** Automatization	**Stage 4** Transference

Fig. 10.6 Efficacy of life skills training: relation with stages and effectiveness criteria

Stages of life skills acquisition	Athlete discourse
1. Motivation	*I always liked football. However, I was not good enough in my previous club, so I had to leave; but I like to play! I want to play! Winning or not; competing or not, I just want to play!*
2. Learning	*Kicking penalties was always stressful for me... Since I failed a penalty kick in my previous club, I had no more opportunities to score penalties.* *Now I have the opportunity. The coach is training all of us to score penalties.* *It is quite interesting that I also have to assume the role of goalkeeper in order to better understand how goalkeepers think when they have to defend a penalty.*
3. Automatization	*I am improving my ability in penalties. I understand better what I have to do in order to be successful.* *I am now much calmer and concentrate when shooting the penalty.*
4. Transference	*I learned that if I am concentrated in my abilities, I have a better chance of success in football but also in other daily tasks, as for example, doing tests at school.*

Fig. 10.7 Stages of life skills acquisition: example of a football player of sport participation

Considering these four areas of effectiveness criteria (that corresponds to distinct efficacy measures), the question is how can they be applied by sport participation coaches? When we think about athletes in sports for participation purposes, the focus is on intrinsic aspects of training than on extrinsic aspects related to sports success derived from competing with other athletes. Thus, coaches may have to establish effectiveness criteria that fulfills motivation and expectations of sport participation athletes. The main challenge for coaches is how to turn the sports a rewarding experience for athletes not interested on competition for comparative processes, and how to design sports activities that can, indeed, fulfill the four stages of skill acquisition. Figure 10.7 provides an example of an adequate attitude and motivational focus of a sports participation athlete through the four stages of life skill acquisition. As can be seen, the focus is on challenging personal and sport abilities of the athlete, and on providing the athlete the necessary opportunities to improve. This example reinforces the need to clarify the particularities of sports for participation purpose and the implications for coaches. We address this question in the next topic of this chapter.

Philosophy of Sport Participation: Implications for Coaches

Coaching for sport participation should have specific implications on coaches' education and practice. The topic of coach education is addressed in other chapters of this book and is not a central question of our chapter; however, it should be said that curriculum of coach education is much more dedicated to subjects and disciplines related to training youth and adult athletes to compete than on topics of sport participation as an alternative to traditional sport programs. This should deserve the attention of scholars and researchers dedicated to coaching education. Figure 10.8 presents some of the main aspects that characterize sports participation and that should deserve the attention of coaches. By accepting these principles of sports participation, coaches should act accordingly and define plans of training that fulfill the central goal of sports participation: provide unique and positive sport opportunities that significantly contributes to athletes human functioning and developing or, as said before, that increase their ability to deal with changing events in an effective way.

Key Points

Sports participation can be an interesting alternative to traditional sports because not all athletes want play sports for competition purposes, and not all athletes have the right opportunities in traditional sports to develop skills. This is a main concern because there is advantages in having children and teenagers involved in sports in order to develop their skills to stimulate their will to stay active throughout their lives. Stimulating youth to continue sports in order to automatize a healthy life style may also be a profitable social policy due to the costs on the health care systems of treating diseases that results from poor life habits. Sports participation imposes itself; we just need to go to public parks or sports grounds to see so many youth playing sports without adult supervision for hours with high levels of dedication and motivation. This indicates that sports participation represents an opportunity to provide positive and useful activities for a significant number of potential athletes. However, the organization of sports participation should not follow the same logic and rules of traditional sports. Sports participation needs to assume the specific purpose of providing athletes the conditions to develop their skills at their own rhythm. In order to achieve this purpose, some conditions may increase the development of sports participation:

(a) Sport participation has to become an education area for coaches and other professionals involved in this activity, not only at universities, but also along their careers in sport participation. This will increase the interest of coaches, athletes, parents, policy makers, and other individuals about the benefits of sports participation.
(b) Sports participation needs coaches with the right vocational attitude, meaning they should be intrinsically motivated to orientate athletes that do not have competition as their main interest.
(c) Sports participation athletes need to be educated and trained according to the philosophy of this type of sports; sometimes athletes know what they do not like (i.e., competing, social pressure to succeed), but they do not necessarily know that sports participation may be an interesting alternative for them.

1. Every athlete is important and unique. **Implications** o Coaches should treat every athlete equal in terms of their importance for the team and for the sports; it is the individuality of each athlete that matters, not the coaches perspectives of what should be a "good" or "competitive" athlete. o Of course, coaches do not establish equalitarian relations with each athlete (and that was even undesirable) but they need to reinforce the will of each athlete to practice sports the best they can.
2. Every athlete deserves the opportunity to fulfill their expectations and goals. **Implications** o Coaches should understand the desires, needs, and expectations of each athlete. They should not impose their goals for athletes, especially the ones related to competition and sport success. o Of course, coaches may have not the possibility to incorporate all the expectations in training (especially if they work with collective sports), but they should establish specific periods of training where each athlete may feel their expectations are taken into consideration.
3. Every athlete' improvement is a significant improvement. **Implications** o Coaches should recognize the multiple improvements of athletes and should reinforce every progression made by the athletes, regardless of the level of personal or interpersonal expertise achieved by the athletes.
4. Every athlete should be stimulated in multiple life skills. **Implications** o Coaches should provide athletes multiple exercises and activities that do not only develop skills for a specific sport, but they should encourage and include athletes in their training programs for other sports and activities that allow them to develop physical and motor skills and, if intentionally possible, psychological and social life skills.
5. Every athlete needs opportunities to develop. **Implications** o Coaches should evaluate the athlete's abilities and areas of improvement; then, they have to establish plans of training that include opportunities of learning and progress for all the athletes.
6. Every athlete can succeed **Implications** o Coaches should provide specific and utilitarian feedback to each athlete in order to augment the chances of progression; there are multiples forms of feedback (verbal, nonverbal, written, video analysis, etc.) that should be adapted by coaches according to their training plans and the characteristics of athletes.
7. Every athlete can be successful. **Implications** o Coaches should equalize success and the positive attitude of athletes towards sports and to the improvement of their sports/life skills.
8. Every athlete, if competing, needs opportunities to play. **Implications** o Coaches should not design competition the same way as traditional sports; competition can occur from multiple perspectives (ex: comparing previous performance with actual performance) and from multiple indicators beyond winning and losing (executions correctly assumed, efficacy of motor behaviors, fair-play behaviors, tolerance and recovery from errors, team cohesion, communications of behaviors among teammates, etc.).
9. Every athlete should be enthusiastic about a healthy lifestyle after sport participation. **Implications** o Coaches should recognize and stimulate the desire of athletes to maintain sports in their daily routines when they become adults; "sports for life" should be the motto.
10. Every athlete should be trained by coaches that are motivated for sport participation. **Implications** o Coaches should comprehend and accept the differences between participation sports and traditional sports and should act accordingly in an enthusiastic and motivated way.

Fig. 10.8 Philosophy of sport participation: implications for coaches

(d) Sports participation needs adults (parents, managers, policy makers) that comprehend the specificities of this type of sport, and that genuinely support young athletes in their choice for sports participation.

Conclusion

Sports participation has a lot of potential. Not all athletes are interested in traditional sports, some like sports as a non-competitive activity. Sports participation can represent an interesting alternative for this population, but it needs to establish a theoretical and methodological background that can educate interested adults in developing sports participation programs. It is a complex, but fruitful, project to concretize; it just needs the interested adults and the curious athletes. Let this fascinating journey begin!

References

Australian-Government. (2018). *Sport 2030*. Canberra: Australian Government.

Brown, T. C., & Fry, M. D. (2014). Evaluating the pilot of strong girls: A life skills/physical activity program for third and fourth grade girls. *Journal of Applied Sport Psychology, 26*(1), 52–65. https://doi.org/10.1080/10413200.2013.778913

Canada. (2012). *Canadian Sport Policy - 2012*. Retrieved from http://sirc.ca/sites/default/files/content/docs/pdf/csp2012_en_lr.pdf

Collins, M. (2010). From 'sport for good' to 'sport for sport's sake'—not a good move for sports development in England? *International Journal of Sport Policy and Politics, 2*(3), 367–379. https://doi.org/10.1080/19406940.2010.519342

Danish, S. J. (1996). Interventions for enhancing adolescents' life skills. *The Humanistic Psychologist, 24*(3), 365–381.

Danish, S. J. (1997). Going for the goal: A life skills program for adolescents. In G. Albee & T. Gullotta (Eds.), *Primary preventions works* (pp. 291–311). Thousand Oaks, CA: Sage.

Danish, S. J., Taylor, T., Hodge, K., & Heke, I. (2004). Enhancing youth development through sport. *World Leisure Journal, 46*(3), 38–49.

DiSanti, J. S., & Erickson, K. (2019). Youth sport specialization: A multidisciplinary scoping systematic review. *Journal of Sports Sciences, 37*(18), 2094–2105. https://doi.org/10.1080/02640414.2019.1621476

EU. (2014). *White paper on sport*. Retrieved from http://europa.eu/legislation_summaries/education_training_youth/sport/l35010_en.hm

Eurostat. (2018). *Statistics on sport participation*. Retrieved from https://ec.europa.eu/eurostat/statistics-explained/index.php?title=Statistics_on_sport_participation.

Gomes, A. R. (2014). Positive human functioning in stress situations: An interactive proposal. In A. R. Gomes, R. Resende, & A. Albuquerque (Eds.), *Positive human functioning from a multidimensional perspective: Promoting stress adaptation* (Vol. 1, pp. 165–194). New York: Nova.

Gomes, A. R., & Marques, B. (2013). Life skills in educational contexts: Testing the effects of an intervention programme. *Educational Studies, 39*(2), 156–166. https://doi.org/10.1080/03055698.2012.689813

Gould, D., & Carson, S. (2008). Life skills development through sport: Current status and future directions. *International Review of Sport and Exercise Psychology, 1*, 58–78.
Hall, R., Foss, K. B., Hewett, T. E., & Myer, G. D. (2015). Sport specialization's association with an increased risk of developing anterior knee pain in adolescent female athletes. *Journal of Sport Rehabilitation, 24*(1), 31–35.
Hardcastle, S. J., Tye, M., Glassey, R., & Hagger, M. S. (2015). Exploring the perceived effectiveness of a life skills development program for high-performance athletes. *Psychology of Sport and Exercise, 16*, 139–149. https://doi.org/10.1016/j.psychsport.2014.10.005
ISCF. (2013). *International Sport Coaching Framework: Version 1.2*. Leeds Beckett University: Human Kinetics, Champaign, Illinois, United States.
Jeanes, R., Spaaij, R., Penney, D., & O'Connor, J. (2018). Managing informal sport participation: Tensions and opportunities. *International Journal of Sport Policy and Politics, 11*(1), 79–95. https://doi.org/10.1080/19406940.2018.1479285
Jones, M. I., & Parker, J. K. (2014). Life skills programs: What makes them work? In A. R. Gomes, R. Resende, & A. Albuquerque (Eds.), *Positive human functioning from a multidimensional perspective* (Vol. 2, pp. 15–36). New York: Nova.
Lefebvre, J. S., Evans, M. B., Turnnidge, J., Gainforth, H. L., & Côté, J. (2016). Describing and classifying coach development programmes: A synthesis of empirical research and applied practice. *International Journal of Sports Science & Coaching, 11*(6), 887–899. https://doi.org/10.1177/1747954116676116
McFadden, T., Bean, C., Fortier, M., & Post, C. (2016). Investigating the influence of youth hockey specialization on psychological needs (dis)satisfaction, mental health, and mental illness. *Cogent Psychology, 3*(1), 1157975. https://doi.org/10.1080/23311908.2016.1157975
Mehta, N. (2011). Mind-body dualism: A Critique from a health perspective. *Mens Sana Monographs, 9*(1), 202–209.
Nanayakkara, S. (2016). Human integration through Olympism education: A pragmatic engagement of youths in a war-torn society. *Sport, Education and Society, 21*(4), 623–643. https://doi.org/10.1080/13573322.2016.1159956
Nasheeda, A., Abdullah, H. B., Krauss, S. E., & Ahmed, N. B. (2018). A narrative systematic review of life skills education: Effectiveness, research gaps and priorities. *International Journal of Adolescence and Youth, 24*(3), 362–379. https://doi.org/10.1080/02673843.2018.1479278
ONU. (2003). *Sport for development and peace: Towards achieving the millennium development goals. Report from the United Nations Inter-Agency Task Force on Sport for Development and Peace*. Retrieved from http://www.un.org/wcm/webdav/site/sport/shared/sport/pdfs/Reports/2003_interagency_report_ENGLISH.pdf
Russell, W. D. (2014). The relationship between youth sport specialization, reasons for participation, and youth sport participation motivations: A retrospective study. *Journal of Sport Behavior, 37*(3), 286–305.
Sotiriadou, K., Quick, S., & Shilbury, D. (2006). Sport for 'Some': Elite versus mass participation. *International Journal of Sport Management, 7*, 50–66.
Strachan, L., Côté, J., & Deakin, J. (2009). "Specializers" versus "samplers" in youth sport: Comparing experiences and outcomes. *The Sport Psychologist, 23*(1), 77–92.
Super, S., Wentink, C. Q., Verkooijen, K. T., & Koelen, M. A. (2017). How young adults reflect on the role of sport in their socially vulnerable childhood. *Qualitative Research in Sport, Exercise and Health, 11*(1), 20–34. https://doi.org/10.1080/2159676x.2017.1361468
WHO, World Health Organization. (2003). *Skills for health: Skills-based health education including life skills: An important component of a child-friendly/health-promoting school*. Geneva: World Health Organization. Retrieved from http://www.who.int/iris/handle/10665/42818
Wicker, P., Hallmann, K., & Breuer, C. (2012). Micro and macro level determinants of sport participation. *Sport, Business and Management: An International Journal, 2*(1), 51–68. https://doi.org/10.1108/20426781211207665

Wright, P. M., Jacobs, J. M., Ressler, J. D., & Jung, J. (2016). Teaching for transformative educational experience in a sport for development program. *Sport, Education and Society, 21* (4), 531–548. https://doi.org/10.1080/13573322.2016.1142433

Zuzanek, J. (2005). Adolescent time use and well-being from a comparative perspective. *Loisir et Société, 28*(2), 379–423. https://doi.org/10.1080/07053436.2005.10707688

Rui Gomes is an Assistant Professor in the School of Psychology at the University of Minho, Portugal. He received his Ph.D. in Psychology from the University of Minho. He has research interests on human adaptation to stress, leadership and team performance, and training life skills and human performance. He leads the research group "Adaptation, Performance and Human Development", which was created in 2007 (www.ardh.pt). He leads the community and business intervention project "School of Life Skills" (www.e-cv.pt). As a sport psychologist, he consults athletes and their families, coaches, and sport managers.

Rui Resende is an Assistant Professor at University Institute of Maia – ISMAI, Portugal. He does research manly in Sports Pedagogy and Coach Education. He was a Volleyball athlete and coached teams at the high competition level in Portugal and also the junior national coach of the Portuguese national team. Presently is editor director of the Journal of Sport Pedagogy & Research and recently made his graduation as Coach Developer in the ICCE.

Chapter 11
Coaching for Adventures Sports

Vinicius Zeilmann Brasil, Eva Ellmer, Ethan Greenberg, and Vitor Ciampolini

Abstract The increased number of participants in developmental and performance contexts in several adventure sports has led to a demand for coaches to intervene in developing athletic skills and performance. The multifaceted role of the adventure sports coach is a result of a demanding and risky environment and the socio-cultural nature of the practice. Considering that all these variables influence the adventure sports coaching, the purpose of this chapter is to offer insights regarding the coach role and development in bicycle moto-cross (BMX), parkour, and surfing. Thus, the chapter is organized into three sections. The first section presents a conceptualization on adventure sports, adventure sports coaching, and the adventure sports coaching role. The cases of BMX in Australia, parkour in Canada, and surfing in Brazil are presented in the second section to provide an example of the application of concepts presented in the previous section. The third section outlines practical implications related to the development of adventure sports coaches.

Keywords Adventure sports · Adventure sports coaching · Coach development

The purpose of this chapter is to explore how the coaching science agenda has been providing conceptual and empirical support for understanding new trends regarding adventure sports coaching, exploring issues on the coaching role and developments

V. Z. Brasil (✉)
School of Health and Sport Science, Santa Catarina State University, Florianópolis, Brazil

E. Ellmer
School of Human Movement and Nutrition Sciences, University of Queensland, Brisbane, QLD, Australia
e-mail: e.ellmer@uq.edu.au

E. Greenberg
School of Human Kinetics, Faculty of Health Sciences, University of Ottawa, Ottawa, ON, Canada

V. Ciampolini
Sports Center, Federal University of Santa Catarina, Florianópolis, Brazil

R. Resende, A. R. Gomes (eds.), *Coaching for Human Development and Performance in Sports*, https://doi.org/10.1007/978-3-030-63912-9_11

in adventure sports. The chapter begins with a definition of adventure sports and a conceptualization of adventure sports coaching. The remainder of the chapter focuses on coach roles and development in three different scenarios—BMX in Australia, parkour in Canada, and surfing in Brazil. Lastly, this chapter outlines practical implications related to the development of adventure sports coaches.

Conceptual and Empirical Findings

Adventure Sports

Sports such as surfing, skateboarding, snowboarding, and BMX (re-)surfaced in the 1960s and 1970s as a counter-cultural, social movement. Over the past five decades, many action sports have experienced unprecedented growth in participation (Gilchrist & Wheaton, 2016), their increased visibility across public space (Thorpe & Wheaton, 2011) and in academic work (Ellmer, Rynne, & Enright, 2019). Adventure sports have enjoyed impressive rates of growth gaining media coverage through events such as the X Games and the Olympics. The recent inclusion of surfing, skateboarding, sport climbing, and BMX freestyle into the Tokyo 2020 Summer Olympic Games reflects political and cultural changes at the global level (Thorpe & Dumont, 2019) and the growing interest in activities more deeply rooted in adventure and risk (Collins & Brymer, 2018).

Adventure sports is a term that emerge in opposition to traditional sports and the society that foster these sports. On the other hand, adventure sports point to key ideas and developments in modern and post-modern society such as individualism, technology, self-realization, and transcendence (Breivik, 2010). Conceptually, 'adventure sports' embrace a variety of sports or physical activities such as 'alternative', 'extreme', 'gravity', 'lifestyle', and 'action' sports. The term 'adventure' denotes that the activity takes place in a setting that is demanding, challenging, dangerous, or exotic. An adventure is something special and valuable that sticks out from conventional life. In this perspective adventure is a convergence point among a broad range of adventure sport category such as extreme sports, risk sports, alternative sports, action sports, and lifestyle sports where the element of adventure is inherent. In sum, Breivik (2010) considers that the concept 'adventure sports' embraces activities that: (a) have elements of challenge, excitement and (in most sports) risk; (b) take place in demanding natural or artificially constructed environments; (c) are more loosely organized than mainstream sports; (d) represent a freedom from or opposition to the dominant sport culture; and (e) are individualistic pursuits but tend to build groups and subcultures around the activity.

According to Collins and Collins (2012), adventure sports are defined as 'physical activities with a degree of risk that are non-competitive in origin and guided by their own ethics (without specific rules)' (p. 91). Adventure sports require specific technical skills, possess an element of physical challenge and take place within a continually changing dynamic environment (Collins & Collins, 2015). Likewise,

Berry, Lomax, and Hodgson (2015) used the term adventure sport to embrace activities that are typically characterized by: interaction with the environment (e.g., tide, swell, weather condition); challenge by choice/self-determination; an awareness of risk as a critical element demanding attention; independence and autonomy; journeys and; often not overtly competitive and relatively free from arbitrary rules (although may be self-governed by a set of ethics).

The adventure sport perspective assumed in this essay include a variety of other terminologies (e.g., extreme sport, action sport, lifestyle sport) and consider 'adventure' and 'risk' as two intrinsic components that fit in these kinds of sport and physical activities. Collins and Brymer (2018), presenting different categories of nature sports, argued that risk and risk-taking are emphasized in three ways: (1) where the environment is assumed to be dangerous, dynamic, or uncertain; (2) where participants are considered risk-takers or adrenalin seekers; and (3) where participants are presumed to create a personal identity based on fitting in with risk-based counter-cultural characteristics. This standpoint places adventure sports as a concept associated with risk and is increasingly considered in the sports coaching research agenda. Therefore, our purpose is to present how the coaching science agenda has been providing conceptual and empirical support for understanding new trends regarding adventure sports coaching, as well as clarifying issues on the coach role, learning, and development by exploring BMX in Australia, parkour in Canada, and surfing in Brazil.

Adventure Sports Coaching

Face to the institutionalization and commercialization of sports such as snowboarding, skateboarding, windsurfing, and BMX, athletes are increasingly working with coaches, psychologists, agents, managers, and personal trainers to improve their performances (Ojala & Thorpe, 2015). Adventure sports coaching is conceptualized as a distinct sub-discipline of conventional sports coaching and outdoor education practices and has emerged in response to the increased demand for performance development in adventure sports (Collins & Collins, 2012).

Adventure sports coaching is a broad-ranging complex field which utilizes concepts and skills associated with leadership, teaching in the outdoors, and traditional coaching skills (Collins & Collins, 2015). In this line, the book *Adventure Sports Coaching* by Berry et al. (2015) provides a detailed link between coaching science and recent developments in adventure sports coaching and practice. Based on a composition of theory fields (e.g., sport psychology, sport pedagogy, sport biomechanics, sport medicine) associated to a commonly designated mother science (e.g., pedagogy, psychology) (Haag, 1994), coaching science comprises numerous conceptual frameworks and empirical research that has been used to understand and examine coaching, learning, and instructional processes directed by coaches (Gilbert & Trudel, 2004). The development of a conceptual framework over time has helped to fill that vacuum and provides a foundation and reference point for the subsequent emergence of different strands of policy, coach education, academic writing, and research (Lyle, 2018).

Adventure sports coaching is an academic endeavor based on coaching science to establish a consensual language and set of ideas to address perceived shortcomings in the conduct and scope of research and dissemination of these ideas as suggested by Lyle (2018). It aims to analyze and understand a unique set of challenges faced by adventure sports coaches, such as the dynamic natural environment and the requirement to train athletes to levels of high performance outside of traditional structures of competition (Collins & Collins, 2015). Indeed, coaching athletes to achieve high-level performances are not uniquely linked to competition. Performance in adventure sports is dictated by the challenges posed by the environment without necessarily having constructed rules or an opposing athlete (Collins & Collins, 2015).

The Adventure Sports Coach Role The institutionalization and co-option of sports such as snowboarding, BMX, windsurfing, skateboarding, sport climbing, and surfing into the Olympics and other mainstream sporting events highlights new trends in sporting cultures and the role of coaches therein (Ojala & Thorpe, 2015; Thorpe & Dumont, 2019). According to Collins and Collins (2012), the "adventure sport coach's role operates in conjunction with the roles of guides and teachers. The adventure sports coach needs to draw on some skills that are unique and some that are shared. This enables the adventure sports coach to take a role that may, outwardly, appear as guiding, teaching, or coaching. This suggests that a definition of the adventure sports coach role will be complex and broad" (p. 91).

Ojala and Thorpe (2015) suggest that many individuals and groups sought out professionals within their sporting cultures to improve their performance through developing the strength and flexibility necessary for high-demanding performances and to minimize the potential for injury (Thorpe & Dumont, 2019). On the other hand, many athletes pursue less organized careers and thus assume different relationships with coaches (Ojala & Thorpe, 2015). Indeed, given that some individuals practice adventure sports for non-competitive purposes, the coaches' developmental role is underpinned by a personal competence to provide a safe and enjoyable environment (Collins, Collins, & Willmott, 2016).

Moreover, the hybrid role imposed to the adventure sports coach requires a high level of personal competence (i.e., to coach windsurfing in advanced environments requires the coach to actually be able to perform in that advanced environment) as well as a complete grasp of relevant welfare and safety issues inherent to their sport (Collins & Collins, 2015). Thus, the objectives of the session, demands of the environment, and needs of participants demands an adaptive and flexible approach from adventure sports coaches (Cooper & Allen, 2018).

Adventure sports coaches synergize shared skills across outdoor education, leadership, and coaching supported by a clear epistemology (Collins & Collins, 2016). Some of these skills are risk management, risk–benefit exploitation, personal ability, pedagogic expertise, leadership, domain-specific declarative knowledge, and sport-specific experience in order to fulfil their complex and challenging role (Collins & Collins, 2013; Collins, Collins, & Grecic, 2015). With a frequent focus on individualized development (e.g., motor, cognitive, experiential, and psychological), their goal is to enable competent/independent participation in adventure sports, or in adventurous contexts (Collins & Collins, 2012, 2015). In doing so, progress is often managed by the participants themselves rather than levels set by performance (i.e., the goal of greater adventure rather than faster, stronger, further, higher) (Collins & Collins, 2015). In sum, because adventure sports coaching practice comprises a multiplicity of combined roles and a diversity of function, there is a high need to provide an effective management of not only oneself (coach) but also of the performer (athlete) (Collins & Collins, 2013, 2017; Gray & Collins, 2016).

According to Wheaton (2004), the cultural and social aspects of sports such as snowboarding, BMX, windsurfing, parkour, and surfing, often differ from conventional sports in terms of values, socialization processes, and reasons for engagement. Consequently, in-depth knowledge of the particular sporting cultures, their development, and the values held by cultural members offer important implications for coaches in many adventure sports (Ojala & Thorpe, 2015). In fact, it is a consensus that the unique value system of adventure sports (Collins & Collins, 2012) or action sports (Ojala & Thorpe, 2015) should be considered when coaching practices are designed and delivered (Collins et al., 2016). Indeed, these value systems, such as participant control, creativity, cooperativeness, and do-it-yourself ideologies (Wheaton, 2004, 2013), have a significant implication on how athletes perceive cooperation with coaches in their careers and what coaching approaches they prefer (Ojala & Thorpe, 2015).

While recognizing the social and cultural aspects in adventure sports, the perspective presented in this essay is that BMX, parkour, and surfing adhere to the definition of adventure sports due to the inherent risks in these sports. Accordingly, adventure sports coaches must be able to use these risks as learning tools in the development of their athletes, in spite of the potential for harm (Collins & Collins, 2012, 2013). It is up to adventure sports coaches to mediate their athletes' engagement with risk, given that a certain degree of risk can be beneficial in helping adventure sport athletes to learn and develop their skills (Collins & Collins, 2013).

Over the past two decades, adventure sports researchers have increasingly analyzed recreational participants' experiences; however, coaches' experiences have remained largely out of scope (Thorpe & Dumont, 2019). Little is known about the skills adventure sports coaches employ in competitive and non-competitive settings, and how they were developed (Christian, Berry, & Kearney, 2017).

The Adventure Sports Coach in Context

BMX in Australia

BMX Context BMX racing is popular both at an international and national level. Indeed, BMX Australia (BMXA) has been identified as the 'second largest BMX nation behind the United States' (BMXA, 2017a, p. 1), and it produces a number of high quality male and female riders. In 2008, Australia qualified for the Beijing Olympic Games in which BMX debuted. Since then, Australia has been qualified for all Summer Olympic Games and the athletes have presented outstanding results with riders in the finals at each of the Olympics thus fa.. Memberships in BMXA have continued to grow with nearly 20,000 active members registered across the 120 member clubs in Australia (BMXA, 2017b). Since BMX was announced as an inclusion in the program for the 2008 Beijing Olympic Games, BMX Australia has received additional federal and state government funding (as well as commercial partnerships that have arisen due to increased national and international visibility of the sport). At the high-performance level, this funding has supported a national program (High Performance Unit and National Development Academy) and National Training Center programs (through the National Institute Network) that include full-time coaching as well as sport science, sport medicine, sport psychology, and strength and conditioning support (Cycling Australia, 2012).

BMX Coach Adventure sports in Australia still have a somewhat neophyte status in the Australian organized sport landscape. Particularly, the specific cultural background of adventure sports influences how the role of the coach is conceptualized. While adventure sports coaches certainly contribute to the development of the athlete's skills, supporting performance and managing programs and resources, the unique cultural value systems of adventure sports must remain in the foreground of any coach-athlete relationships (Ojala & Thorpe, 2015). There is some overlap between these findings and the observations made within the high-performance context of the sport of BMX in Australia.

While coaches in BMX today contribute to the development of sport specific skills and support performance, many current Australian high performance BMX athletes did not really have a (formally accredited) coach to guide their learning during their early stages participating in the sport (Ellmer, 2019). As the athletes matured and became more experienced riders, many tended to source more experienced individuals (i.e. ex-BMX racers) to facilitate with their problem-solving and their subsequent progression within the sport. These 'coaching' sessions, however, were informal in nature (Ellmer, 2019). The predominantly autonomous and self-organized learning culture of the BMX athletes continued into the high performance sector also. Despite the high performance athletes having access to an accredited coach who contributed to the development of sport specific skills, the coach continued to place the ownership of learning back onto the athletes. It may, therefore, be argued that the coach was trying to make themselves redundant (Ellmer, 2019).

Despite the coach's aim being to teach the athletes to work independently and be accountable for their own learning, the coach-athlete relationship remained personable and athletes had access to the coach's support whenever required. For example, BMX racers in Ellmer's (2019) study had access to one-on-one coaching, even outside of organized training camps. During these sessions, the athletes took control and determined the nature of their training, rather than the coach making these decisions on behalf of the athlete, as commonly seen in more traditional sports. These experiences with the coach contributed to the transformation of the individuals not only in relation to their sport specific knowledge and skills, but also their attitudes, values and beliefs (Ellmer, 2019).

Despite the autonomy of the Australian high performance BMX racers, the coach-athlete relationship was not restricted to the sports context. For example, the coach took interest in the athletes' mental and physical wellbeing and assisted with their programs to ensure they maintained a healthy work-life balance. In addition, the coach organized meals, accommodation and travel during competition season so that athletes only needed to focus on the preparation for and recovery from events (Ellmer, 2019). Indeed, the coach's role within high performance BMX greatly extends beyond the contribution to skill development, program and resource management. The development of relevant attributes and skills should, therefore, be reflected in coach development programs.

Coach Development Coach development and learning programs in sports such as BMX, skateboarding, surfing, and parkour are at varying levels in Australia. BMX is an example in which the coach development and learning is quite advanced in comparison and, therefore, is an example not reflective of all adventure sports in Australia (see Ellmer & Rynne, 2019). Since the sport of BMX has become an Olympic sport, it has vastly professionalized within the country. However, despite BMX being included to the 2008 Olympic program, there was no specific BMX coach education program in place until 2012. Thus, BMX coaches (similar to many in the organized sporting domain) tended to learn largely via informal means (Mallett, Trudel, Lyle, & Rynne, 2009) such as experience as an athlete or practical coach experience (Gilbert & Trudel, 2001; Rynne, Mallett, & Tinning, 2010). Since 2014, the BMX Australia Development Academy offers a three-tier accredited coach development program in line with the National Coaching Accreditation Scheme (NCAS) from the beginner to the elite levels (BMXA, 2017b). The BMXA coach development programs are both interactive and practical, and contain a period of self-directed learning and written assessment tasks. With the combination of formal, non-formal, and informal learning contexts (Nelson, Cushion, & Potrac, 2006), BMXA seems to be offering the coaches a more holistic approach to learning and development.

In order to provide the BMXA coaches with the necessary tools to continue to grow and learn, a Level 2 coaching course was designed, preparing coaches to develop and support higher performing riders. While currently under review, the focus here lies in the coaches developing knowledge in the fields of the psychology of BMX racing, race preparation, recovery, and crisis management while continuing to monitor and assess the athletes' performance (BMXA, 2018). While often working independently, BMXA coaches are encouraged to regularly keep in touch with BMXA Coaching, their State coaching director, and coaching course peers and presenters. This supports the organization of a community of practice (Lave & Wenger, 1991), in an attempt to share their knowledge and experiences while gaining their new accreditation levels. Although the advent of coach education programs in BMX is slow, BMX Australia has come a far way since and continues to review and update their training initiatives to remain at the fore of coach education.

Parkour in Canada

Parkour Context There is a growing interest in parkour across the world, which has led to the development of parkour National Sport Organizations (NSOs) and similar nation-wide associations, such as ParkourUK in the United Kingdom (Parkour UK, 2017), the Australian Parkour Association (APA, n.d.), and the United States Parkour Association (USPK, 2017). While Canada does have NSOs for other adventure sports such as Skiing, Canoe/Kayak, and Snowboarding (Own The Podium, 2015), there is not yet a Canadian parkour NSO. There are, however, a growing number of parkour gyms, clubs, and training facilities across Canada, including but not limited to: Origins Parkour in British Columbia (Origins Parkour, 2014), Breathe Parkour in Alberta (Breathe Parkour, 2017), Play Project in Ontario (Play Project, 2016), and Drummond Parkour in Quebec (Drummond Parkour, 2016). Each of the aforementioned parkour organizations may have their own processes for in-house coach training or apprenticeship programs, but there is no Canadian governing body to oversee them all.

Parkour Coach As parkour is an adventure sport, parkour coaches are in positions to develop values in their athletes that are not traditionally found in other sports (Ojala & Thorpe, 2015). Where parkour athletes often hold common values relating to healthy eating, and choosing to abstain from smoking and drinking, parkour athletes have been noted to value balance, agility, and aesthetics, which might otherwise be considered "feminine" skills, thus suggesting that parkour is less influenced by the white male hegemony that is prevalent in other sports (Gilchrist & Wheaton, 2011). In addition to the physical and skill-based values mentioned above, parkour athletes often hold explicit values or mentalities in the form of two French mottos: *être fort pour être utile* and *être et durer* ('be strong to be useful' and 'to be and to last'). These mottos, which advocate durability and adaptability, originally came from the teachings of George Hébert's Natural Method, which was an inspiration to early parkour practitioners (Brown, 2007).

Greenberg and Culver (2019) interviewed a number of parkour coaches who have described their own personal goals and philosophies, including the values they wish to pass on to their athletes. As the process of coaching is relatively new to the field of parkour, there are many parkour athletes who have become parkour coaches, despite never being coached themselves. Some of these coaches have mentioned that they strive to prevent their athletes from making the mistakes that they themselves made when trying to learn various parkour techniques without the help of a coach (Greenberg & Culver, 2019). Parkour coaches, as well as other adventure sports coaches, have also discussed prioritizing the development of athletes as individuals, including helping the athletes progress to a point in their training when they no longer require a coach (Collins & Collins, 2016; Greenberg & Culver, 2019). However, with the growing popularity of parkour competitions such as the Red Bull Art of Motion (Red Bull, 2017) and the North American Parkour Championships (Sport Parkour League, 2017), there may also come a specific demand for parkour coaches in this competitive context.

Parkour Coach Development There are already a number of organizations across the world that offer parkour coach education programs, such as the American Parkour Instructor Certification Program (American Parkour, 2013), ParkourEDU Coaching Certification (ParkourEDU, 2014), WFPF Parkour Trainer Certification (WFPF, 2017), and the ADAPT Qualification (ADAPT, 2014). All of these programs have offerings in North America, and so North American parkour coaches have the opportunity to participate in multiple parkour coach education programs, if they so desire. Parkour coaches who have participated in these programs have discussed their perceptions of the program contents, with mostly mixed reviews (Greenberg & Culver, 2019). For example, there were disagreements about both the expected difficulty and the experienced difficulty in completing the programs, as well as differences in opinion about what type of content is appropriate to include, such as the history and philosophy of early parkour practitioners (Greenberg & Culver, 2019). These differences in perceptions are not surprising, considering that parkour coach education programs are a very recent addition to the field of parkour, and the participants of those programs are likely to have varying personal histories and levels of parkour coaching experience.

In addition to coach education programs, parkour coaches have also discussed other sources that influenced their learning. One of the most notable sources was the influence of travel on the development of parkour coaches. Where coaches of other sports have reported travelling to learn from coaches in other locations, parkour coaches have described the influence of travel as relating to the destination itself (Greenberg & Culver, 2019). Due to parkour's nature as an adventure sport, parkour athletes and coaches alike rely on dynamic and changing environments to provide new learning opportunities and challenges (Collins & Collins, 2012).

Another influential source of parkour coaches' learning is the fact that many parkour coaches have participated in coach education programs for other sports (Greenberg & Culver, 2019). Greenberg and Culver (2019) have proposed four possible motivations for why parkour coaches engage in coach education specifically for gymnastics: to develop personal parkour skills in gymnastics facilities, to coach in indoor facilities in the absence of available parkour gyms, to develop coaching skills in a different context, and to obtain apparent legitimacy by coaching a regulated sport with a national governing body. In addition to gymnastics programs, Greenberg and Culver (2019) found that parkour coaches have sought out coach education across many other sports, such as personal training, crossfit, breakdancing, and circus training, among others. These findings suggest that cross-training may not only be important to parkour athletes, but that parkour coaches also value the knowledge that they can gain by coaching other sports.

Even though parkour coaches may learn about general coaching principles by coaching other sports, Canadian parkour coaches still do not have a consistent or regulated way to learn to coach parkour. As a result, many parkour coaches, including Canadians, may be forced to learn on the job, and create parkour-specific coaching techniques for themselves. Creating new contributions to the field of coaching is a role often prescribed to innovative coaches who have developed expertise in their respective domains (Trudel, Gilbert, & Rodrigue, 2016), but nevertheless parkour coaches without access to coaching resources may be forced to engage in such innovation, regardless of their experience. However, the complexity and depth of parkour coaches' abilities to innovate may be superficial compared to the innovative coaches described by Trudel et al. (2016), as parkour coaches will typically not have the wealth of experience necessary to significantly impact the fields of parkour coaching, or coaching in general (Greenberg & Culver, 2019).

As the field of parkour coaching is still relatively new, both the prevalence and quality of parkour coaching should continue to grow and become better understood. With the recent development of parkour NSOs worldwide, there should also be an increase in the regulation of parkour coaching, which should accompany a growth in the fields of parkour, adventure sports coaching, and sport coaching as a whole.

Surfing in Brazil

Surfing Context Surfing is a rapidly growing sport in popularity, as well as in the number of participants with over 35 million surfers worldwide (O'Brien & Eddie, 2013) in over 70 countries (ISA, 2017). Also, the International Olympic Committee (IOC, 2017) approved surfing, alongside with a handful of other sports, as a new sport for the Olympic Games Tokyo 2020. Currently, Brazil is seen as a power in surfing with a significant number of participants (Guillén García and Nieri Romero, 2009; Gomes, Souza Neto, Rojo, & Silva, 2017). In addition, Brazilian athletes have kept Brazil among the world powers in this sport such as the USA and Australia, accounting for three world titles in the last 5 years (WSL, 2018). Arguably, these aspects will increase the visibility and excitement surrounding surfing in Brazil, drawing more participants into the sea. As a result, coaches will be required to support the practice and development of surfing practitioners.

Surf Coach In Brazil, surfing has spread in the contexts of sport participation and development. Thus, surfing coaches are mainly working with individuals focused with a leisure activity, tourism, and the development of young athletes. These activities have been offered in specialized schools, clubs, hotels, social projects, and also autonomously by the coach as a kind of "personal trainer in surfing". When coaches supervise surfing as a leisure sport and tourism experience, they meet the 'guide' role (Collins & Collins, 2012). In this perspective, surfing is featured as a sport in which adventure and risk generated by the dynamic nature of the environment provides the practitioner with emotions, sensations, and particular perceptions (Collins & Brymer, 2018).

When coaches focus on developing surfing skills for children, youth, and athletes, it characterizes the typical coaching role (Collins & Collins, 2012). The role of the surf coach in this case is coaching for the development of sport skills so that the practitioner gradually becomes more autonomous and proficient to improve their own practice (Brasil, Ramos, Kuhn, Souza, & Nascimento, 2017; Brasil, Ramos, Souza, Barros, & Nascimento, 2016; Ramos, Brasil, & Goda, 2013). In Brazil, there is a growing number of adults who want to start surfing not only to develop surfing skills, but to learn (about) the surfing culture as a whole. However, the lack of children in surfing training environments has been indicated by many coaches (Brasil et al., 2017) as they often learn by themselves (implicitly) (Lave & Wenger, 1991) when exposed to the beach environment through informal situations of sport participation. Additionally, the informality of the surfing context as well as the learning culture that permeates adventure sports highlights the importance of peer learning and observation in developing skills (e.g., Ellmer & Rynne, 2016; Ojala & Thorpe, 2015) and identity (e.g., Langseth, 2012).

Besides dealing with the surfing practice environment, Brazilian surf coaches usually have to organize several other aspects related to their practice, such as running their own surf school, selling and renting equipment, finding sponsors for their athletes, and setting up surf trips and competitions with their athletes (Brasil, 2015). This multi-task feature of the surf coach role in Brazil reflects the lack of delimitation of the field of work. However, this is also the case for other adventure sports in the country like rafting, canoeing, windsurfing, and kiteboarding (Amaral Junior et al., 2018). Therefore, to be able to work as a surf coach, individuals have found ways that promote the acquisition of knowledge and development of specific skills related to the working practice.

Coach Development Due to the rapid growth in the visibility, interest, and participation in surfing, the need for coach education initiatives and qualified surf coaches is greatly increasing (Correia & Bertram, 2018). In Brazil, the sports coach is a recognized profession and individuals must hold a bachelor's degree in physical education to work with any sport (Brasil, Ramos, Milistetd, Galatti, & Nascimento, 2015). Although surfing is quite an informal sport, there are two complementary "avenues" of formal training for surf coaches nowadays: (a) General Training—Bachelor in Physical Education Courses, organized by public and private universities (Brasil, 1998); and (b) Specific Training—Sports Organizations Programs, provided by specific surfing federations (e.g., Brazilian Institute of Surf—IBRASURF and Santa Catarina State Federation of Specialists in Surf Schools and Stand Up Paddle—FECEESS).

The bachelor's program will prepare professionals capable of working in three areas: health, leisure, and sport performance (all competitive sport activities, from beginner to elite). This program must offer a minimum of 3200 hours over 4 years and include 'Fundamental knowledge' (Human, Social, Biological, Scientific, and Technological Production) and 'Specific knowledge' (Human Movement; Measure and Evaluation; Teaching and Learning). Once coaches graduate from this university-based program, surfing-specific courses offered by sports federations help support the development of further knowledge and competences (Milistetd, Trudel, Mesquita, & do Nascimento, 2014).

While the general training avenue is a broad-based training focused on multiple knowledge areas related to human movement (Brasil, 1998), the specific training avenue is sport-specific and the surfing federations cover several aspects related to the surf coaching practice. These contents are: performance standards of the surf

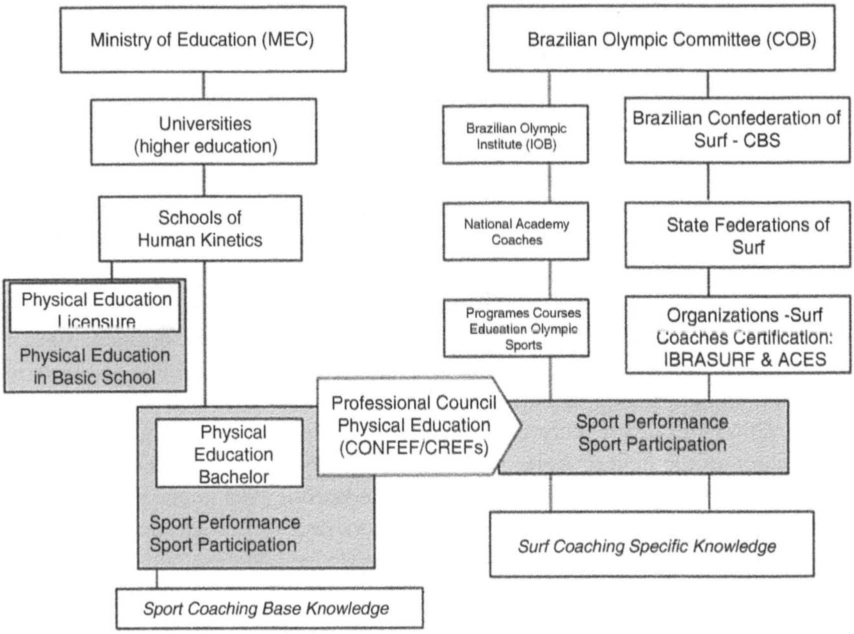

Fig. 11.1 Surf coach education structure in Brazil

coach; surfing-related content (skills, equipment, environment); and safety techniques and pedagogic procedures (Brasil et al., 2015). Nevertheless, it is important to highlight that the specific training avenue does not replace the need for taking the Bachelor of Physical Education course (Fig. 11.1).

The coach education programs offered by the specific training avenue are a fairly recent initiative and have been organized by federations, associations, and private clubs, which are linked to a national level organization that in Brazil corresponds to the Brazilian Olympic Committee (COB) (Milistetd et al., 2016). Although the Brazilian Surfing Confederation (CBS) is part of the list of Olympic sports federations recognized by COB, no training initiatives related to surfing have been provided by COB yet. Thus, IBRASURF have offered courses in Brazil approved by the International Surf Association (ISA). Also, the course offered by FECEESS is an initiative of a group of coaches who together created FECEESS and organized the courses. Both IBRASURF and FECEESS entities are affiliated with CBS. The curriculum structure of these courses has two pillars. The first covers the theoretical knowledge of the laws and professional responsibilities of the surf coach as well as surf-specific content (history, equipment, and technical fundamentals). The second pillar emphasizes the pedagogical procedures for coaching surfing (safety techniques, coaching drills, and risk management). Although coach education programs seem to support the development of surf coaches, other contexts have also contributed as a source of learning.

Based on Nelson et al. (2006) concept for the learning contexts (i.e., formal, non-formal, and informal), Ramos, Brasil, and Goda (2012) found that Brazilian surf coaches valued most informal contexts (e.g., interacting with other coaches, learning by doing and, observation) than formal (e.g., courses that provide certification—university-based programs in Brazil) and non-formal (e.g., training courses offered by organizations—sports federations). Also, Brasil, Ramos, Milistetd, Culver, and Nascimento (2018) analyzed the learning pathways of five Brazilian surf coach developers, in order to understand how they became coach developers. The results showed that becoming a surf coach developer was a result of their experiences as surfers, surf coaches, and surf coach developers, which were strongly influenced by the social relations established with family and other specific groups (e.g., surfers, coaches, and developers). Similarly, Correia and Bertram (2018) identified the ways in which Portuguese surf coaches acquired and developed their coaching knowledge. They concluded that coaches developed most of their knowledge through informal learning (i.e., mainly coaching experience). These results are interesting and seem to be a constant in the surfing context, even with the improvement of training initiatives to support the development of coaches (Correia, 2005; Correia & Bertram, 2018; Correia, Rosado, & Mesquita, 2011).

Adventure Sports Coaching and Coach: Practical Implications

Overall, the concepts (adventure sports, adventure sports coaching, and adventure sports coach role) discussed in this chapter have important implications for researchers and practitioners wishing to better understand this field and to provide some directions to facilitate coaches' development. Indeed, adventure sports coaching and coach conceptualization can be incorporated into a scientific debate on adventure sports coaching research agenda and into the design of initiatives to improve coaches' practice.

Despite being called adventure sports, BMX, parkour, and surfing also adhere to the definition of action and/or lifestyle sport. In comparison to more traditional sports, lifestyle sports promote alternative values, such as individuality, promotion of personal freedom, anti-competitiveness/anti-regulation, and the acceptance of high risks (Wheaton, 2004). Collins and Brymer (2018) suggest that lifestyle sports conceptualizations emphasize the socio-cultural environment where participants are presumed to create a personal identity based on fitting in with risk-based counter-cultural characteristics (Wheaton, 2004). The term action sports embraces sports characterized by individuality and differentiated from competitive sports by the lack of rules and regulations (Collins & Collins, 2016). For the most part participants are assumed to be young, alternative, and searching for hedonistic outcomes associated with risk-taking. Participants are characterized by having a carefree perspective on life while living outside traditional society norms (Collins & Brymer, 2018).

Examples of some values that are commonly held by BMX, parkour, and surfing athletes are the promotion of a healthy lifestyle, including no drinking, no smoking, and healthy eating habits, shared practice, dress codes, and language, while fostering intrinsic motivation through task and mastery orientations (Collins & Brymer, 2018; Gilchrist & Wheaton, 2011).

It might be common to find the promotion of such alternative values in BMX, parkour, and surfing coach education programmes, but not in coach education programmes relating to other sports. In addition to developing sports skills, BMX, parkour, and surfing coaches are in positions to develop values in their athletes that are deeply connected with these sports and also with their lifestyle (Ojala & Thorpe, 2015). This is evident in many coaches, where an individual's personal sports involvement may be intrinsically entangled with their profession. In the case of adventure sports coaches, their involvement in an adventure sports culture are so closely connected and interrelated to many aspects of their lives such as leisure (Filho, 2010), relationships (Greenberg & Culver, 2019), and their enjoyment of outdoor adventure activities and the desire to pass on their knowledge and passion (Lorimer & Holland-Smith, 2012).

As the process of coaching is relatively new to the field of adventure sports (BMX, parkour, and surfing), athletes started to become coaches, despite never being coached themselves. The concepts presented in this chapter may contribute to the debate about how future generations of adventure sports coaches might be educated. In this way, Christian et al. (2017) suggested the integration of longitudinal designs to develop a more coherent understanding of how values and beliefs that underpin coaching are developed. Such approaches would allow us to comment on the extent to which the social-cultural aspects of adventure sports drive the development of an individual's values and beliefs as well as how coach education can contribute to it (Christian et al., 2017; Lorimer & Holland-Smith, 2012).

In addition to coach education programs, BMX, parkour, and surfing coaches have also valued other sources that influenced their learning. Some of the most notable sources are coaching experiences, learn on the sport practice, and the influence of travelling (Brasil, 2019; Correia & Bertram, 2018; Ellmer & Rynne, 2019; Greenberg & Culver, 2019). If in one hand, conventional sports coaches have reported travelling to learn from coaches in other locations (Cushion et al., 2010; Walker, Thomas, & Driska, 2018); on the other hand, BMX, parkour, and surfing coaches have indicated the influence of travelling as relating to the destination itself and to practice their sport in a different setting (Brasil, 2019; Greenberg & Culver, 2019). Additionally, through coaching experience and the sport practice itself, these coaches create specific coaching techniques for their practices (Brasil, 2019; Correia & Bertram, 2018; Greenberg & Culver, 2019).

As BMX, parkour, and surfing coaching are still relatively new, both the prevalence and quality of coaching in these sports should continue to grow and become better understood. With the recent development of these sports worldwide, there should also be an increase in the regulation of BMX, parkour, and surfing coaching, which should accompany a growth in the fields of these sports and adventure sports coaching. Nonetheless, it is important to acknowledge the preliminary characteristics of these adventure sports coaching scenarios and further research is needed to analyze larger samples of coaches. Future researches might carry out cross-cultural comparisons on how adventure sports coaches develop themselves in different countries. Also, studies of adventure sports coach learning pathways in different countries would be worth conducting to see if circumstances are similar across different cultures and settings.

Key Points

1. Due to the hybrid role of the adventure sport coach, and diverse motivations of participants, an effective coach in adventure sport need to be skilled to providing a variety of sport experiences for different learners to help each of them develop in a way that fit with their needs and expectations.
2. Give the cultural issues (values, norms, beliefs, behaviour, etc.) of each adventure sport require of the coach to promote sport experiences implementing teaching approaches that draw on the values and social aspects (interactions, relationships, and power) that are aligned whit the culture of these sports.
3. The research focusing on adventure sport coaches' learning is quite clear. Coaches learn best engaging in sports and coaching experiences. It should prove interesting to see if the influences of coaches' sources of learning will change if adventure sports achieve high levels of institutionalization and performance.
4. Adventure sports (coaching in sports) like BMX, parkour and surfing are at varying levels of professionalization both locally and globally. As such, this presents as an exciting and opportune time for academics, coach learning specialists and program designers collaborate in developing innovative, contemporary, context-specific and evidence-based coach education programs. However, given the varying educational frameworks worldwide, a unified adventure coach education program remains a wishful thought. In doing so, core aspects inherent to the adventure sport culture, ought to be considered. For example, given that adventure sports are often associated with risk (and the subsequent emotion of fear), coach education programs (if not already) should teach prospective coaches skills in relation to creating meaningful learning experiences in both physically and mentally safe environments.

Conclusion

Overall, the aim of this chapter was to present how the coaching science agenda has been providing conceptual and empirical support for understanding new trends regarding adventure sports coaching, as well as clarifying issues on the coach role, learning, and development by exploring BMX in Australia, parkour in Canada, and surfing in Brazil. We expect to offer the reader some insight into how adventure sports coaching and research in sports coaching can be framed into the BMX, parkour, surfing scenarios. We highlight the importance of recognizing adventure sports coaches as individuals who attempt to contribute to develop athletes' performance, continued autonomous participation, and personal development through adventure sport experience. Moreover, intricacies inherent to the nature of adventure sports coaches need to be better understood to provide a continuous improvement on formal, non-formal, and informal learning contexts to contribute the development of coaches.

References

ADAPT. (2014). ADAPT Qualifications. Retrieved from https://adaptqualifications.com/

Amaral Junior, A. J., Vaz, J. M., Correia, P. M., Manfroi, M. N., Figueiredo, J. D., & Marinho, A. (2018). Formação e atuação profissional de instrutores de atividades de aventura na natureza em Florianópolis (SC) [Professional training and work of nature adventure activities instructors from Florianópolis (SC)]. *Licere (Online), 21*(4), 26–59.

American Parkour. (2013). Parkour instructor certification. Retrieved from http://americanparkour.com/academy/parkour-instructor-certification/

APA. (n.d.). Australian parkour association. Retrieved from http://www.parkour.asn.au/index.html

Berry, M., Lomax, J., & Hodgson, C. (2015). *Adventure sports coaching*. Routledge.

BMXA (BMX Australia). (2017a). About BMXA. Retrieved from http://bmxaustralia.com.au/about/about-bmxa/.

BMXA (BMX Australia). (2017b). BMX Australia 2016 annual report. Retrieved from https://issuu.com/bmxa/docs/2016_annual_report_final_.

BMXA (BMX Australia). (2018). Level 2 coach. Retrieved from https://bmxaustralia.com.au/coaches/become-a-coach/level-2-coach/.

Brasil. Lei n°.9696, de 01 de setembro de 1998. Regulamentação da profissão de Educação Física e criação dos respectivos Conselho Federal e Conselhos Regionais de educação física. Diário Oficial da União 02 set 1998; 168:1.

Brasil, V. Z. (2015). *O conhecimento profissional do treinador de surf* [The surfing coaches' professional knowledge]. Master's thesis. Federal University of Santa Catarina, Florianópolis, Brasil.

Brasil, V. Z. (2019). *A construção do conhecimento como um processo de participação social: estudo de caso com uma treinadora de surf* [The knowledge construction through social participation process: Case study with a woman surfing coach]. PhD thesis. Federal University of Santa Catarina, Florianópolis, Brasil.

Brasil, V. Z., Ramos, V., Kuhn, F., Souza, J. R., & Nascimento, J. V. (2017). Os conhecimentos de base para intervenção pedagógica do treinador de surf [The knowledge base for surf coaches' pedagogical instruction]. *Revista Brasileira de Educação Física e Esporte, 31*(4), 807–817.

Brasil, V. Z., Ramos, V., Milistetd, M., Culver, D. M., & Nascimento, J. V. (2018). The learning pathways of Brazilian surf coach developers. *International Journal of Sports Science & Coaching, 13*(3), 349–361.

Brasil, V. Z., Ramos, V., Milistetd, M., Galatti, L. R., & Nascimento, J. V. (2015). A formação profissional para treinadores de surf no Brasil [Professional education for surf coaches in Brazil]. In *Educação física e esporte*: Convergindo para novos caminhos... (p. 357–382). Florianópolis: Editora da UDESC,

Brasil, V. Z., Ramos, V., Souza, J. R., Barros, T. E., & Nascimento, J. V. (2016). As ações pedagógicas para a intervenção do treinador de surf [The pedagogical actions for the surf coach]. *Movimento, 22*(2), 403–416.

Breathe Parkour. (2017). Breathe parkour. Retrieved from http://www.breathepk.com/

Breivik, G. (2010). Trends in adventure sports in a post-modern society. *Sport in Society, 13*(2), 260–273.

Brown, N. (2007). The art of displacement. Parkour as a challenge to social perceptions of body and space. Parkour Generations. Retrieved from http://www.parkourgenerations.com/article/art-displacement

Christian, E., Berry, M., & Kearney, P. (2017). The identity, epistemology and developmental experiences of high-level adventure sports coaches. *Journal of Adventure Education and Outdoor Learning, 17*(4), 353–366.

Collins, L., & Brymer, E. (2018). Understanding nature sports: A participant centered perspective and its implications for the design and facilitating of learning and performance. *Annals of Leisure Research,* 1–16. https://doi.org/10.1080/11745398.2018.1525302

Collins, L., & Collins, D. (2012). Conceptualizing the adventure-sports coach. *Journal of Adventure Education & Outdoor Learning, 12*(1), 81–93.

Collins, L., & Collins, D. (2013). Decision making and risk management in adventure sports coaching. *Quest, 65*(1), 72–82.

Collins, L., & Collins, D. (2015). Conceptualizing the adventure sports coach. In J. Lomax, C. Hodgson, & M. Berry (Eds.), *Adventure sports coaching* (pp. 17–35). London: Routledge.

Collins, L., & Collins, D. (2016). Professional judgment and decision-making in the planning process of high-level adventure sports coaching practice. *Journal of Adventure Education and Outdoor Learning, 16*(3), 256–268.

Collins, L., & Collins, D. (2017). The foci of in-action professional judgment and decision-making in high-level adventure sports coaching practice. *Journal of Adventure Education and Outdoor Learning, 17*(2), 122–132.

Collins, L., Collins, D., & Grecic, D. (2015). The epistemological chain in high-level adventure sports coaches. *Journal of Adventure Education and Outdoor Learning, 15*(3), 224–238.

Collins, D. J., Collins, L., & Willmott, T. (2016). Over egging the pudding? Comments on Ojala and Thorpe. *International Sport Coaching Journal, 3*(1), 90–93.

Cooper, D., & Allen, J. B. (2018). The coaching process of the expert coach: A coach led approach. *Sports Coaching Review, 7*(2), 142–170.

Correia, M. (2005). *Concepções didáticas e metodológicas do ensino do surf* [Didactic and methodologic conceptions in surfing]. Master's thesis. Faculty of Human Kinetics of Lisbon University, Lisbon, Portugal.

Correia, M. C., & Bertram, R. (2018). The surfing coaching: Sources of knowledge acquisition. *International Sport Coaching Journal, 5*(1), 14–23.

Correia, M., Rosado, A., & Mesquita, I. (2011). Concepções didácticas e metodológicas no ensino do surf [Didactic and methodologic conceptions in surfing]. *REDAF: Revista Electrónica de Desporto e Actividade Física, 4*(1), 1–30.

Cushion, C., Nelson, L., Armour, K., Lyle, J., Jones, R., Sandford, R., & O'Callaghan, C. (2010). *Coach learning and development: A review of literature.* Leeds: Sports Coach UK.

Cycling Australia. (2012). 2012 Annual report of the Australian cycling federation Inc. Trading as cycling Australia. Retrieved from https://www.clearinghouseforsport.gov.au/__data/assets/pdf_file/0010/542467/CA_Annual_Report_2012.pdf

Drummond Parkour. (2016). District PK. Retrieved from http://www.drummondparkour.com/

Ellmer, E. (2019). *Learning in action sports: The experiences of high performance BMX racers.* PhD thesis. University of Queensland, Brisbane, Queensland.

Ellmer, E., & Rynne, S. (2016). Learning in action and adventure sports. *Asia-Pacific Journal of Health, Sport and Physical Education, 7*(2), 107–119.

Ellmer, E. M., & Rynne, S. B. (2019). Professionalisation of action sports in Australia. *Sport in Society, 22*(10), 1742–1757.

Ellmer, E., Rynne, S., & Enright, E. (2019). Learning in action sports: A scoping review. *European Physical Education Review.* https://doi.org/10.1177/1356336X19851535.

Federação Catarinense de Especialistas e Escolas de Surf e Stand Up Paddle (FECEESS). (2019). Curso para orientador de surf [Course for surfing coach]. Retrieved from http://www.escolasdesurf.org.br/modules/news/article.php?storyid=441

Filho, S. C. (2010). Rafting guides: Leisure, work and lifestyle. *Annals of Leisure Research, 13* (1–2), 282–297.

Gilbert, W., & Trudel, P. (2001). Learning to coach through experience: Reflection in model youth sport coaches. *Journal of Teaching in Physical Education, 21*, 16–34.

Gilbert, W. D., & Trudel, P. (2004). Analysis of coaching science research published from 1970–2001. *Research Quarterly for Exercise and Sport, 75*(4), 388–399.

Gilchrist, P., & Wheaton, B. (2011). Lifestyle sport, public policy and youth engagement: Examining the emergence of parkour. *International Journal of Sport Policy and Politics, 3*(1), 109–131.

Gilchrist, P., & Wheaton, B. (2016). Lifestyle and adventure sports among youth. In *Routledge handbook of youth sport* (pp. 186–200). Abingdon: Taylor & Francis.

Gomes, L. D., Souza Neto, A., Rojo, J. R., & Silva, M. M. (2017). Nas ondas da ciência: Perfil da produção do conhecimento sobre o surf em periódicos brasileiros [In the waves of science: Profile of knowledge production about surfing in Brazilian journals]. *Licere (Online), 20*(4), 285–311.

Gray, P., & Collins, D. (2016). The adventure sports coach: All show and no substance? *Journal of Adventure Education and Outdoor Learning, 16*(2), 160–171.

Greenberg, E., & Culver, D. M. (2019). How parkour coaches learn to coach: Coaches' sources of learning in an unregulated sport. *Journal of Adventure Education and Outdoor Learning*, 1–15. https://doi.org/10.1080/14729679.2018.1557060

Guillén García, F., & Nieri Romero, D. (2009). Autoestima y competitividad en una selección juvenil peruana de surf [Self-esteem and competitiveness in a Peruvian youth surf team]. *Revista Iberoamericana de Psicología del Ejercicio y el Deporte, 4*(2), 253–270.

Haag, H. R. (1994). State-of-the-art review of sport pedagogy. *Sport Science Review, 3*(1), 1–10.

Instituto Brasileiro de Surf (IBRASURF). (2019). Curso de instrutor de surf e SUP [Course for surfing and SUP instructor]. Retrieved from http://www.fluxexperiences.com.br/cursoinstrutordesurfesup/ocurso/

International Olympic Committee—IOC. (2017). IOC approves five new sports for Olympic Games Tokyo 2020. Retrieved from https://www.olympic.org/news/ioc-approves-five-new-sports-for-olympic-gamestokyo-2020

International Surfing Association (ISA). (2017). Coaching and instructing overview. Retrieved from https://www.isasurf.org/development-programs/coaching-instructing/

Langseth, T. (2012). Liquid ice surfers—the construction of surfer identities in Norway. *Journal of Adventure Education & Outdoor Learning, 12*(1), 3–23.

Lave, J., & Wenger, E. (1991). *Situated learning: Legitimate peripheral participation*. Cambridge: Cambridge University Press.

Lorimer, R., & Holland-Smith, D. (2012). Why coach? A case study of the prominent influences on a top-level UK outdoor adventure coach. *The Sport Psychologist, 26*(4), 571–583.

Lyle, J. (2018). Reflecting on the development of a conceptual framework for sport coaching. *International Sport Coaching Journal, 5*(1), 90–98.

Mallett, C. J., Trudel, P., Lyle, J., & Rynne, S. B. (2009). Formal vs. informal coach education. *International Journal of Sports Science & Coaching, 4*(3), 325–364. https://doi.org/10.1260/174795409789623883

Milistetd, M., Ciampolini, V., Salles, W. D., Ramos, V., Galatti, L. R., & Nascimento, J. V. (2016). Coaches' development in Brazil: Structure of sports organizational programmes. *Sports Coaching Review, 5*(2), 138–152. https://doi.org/10.1080/21640629.2016.1201356

Milistetd, M., Trudel, P., Mesquita, I., & do Nascimento, J. V. (2014). Coaching and coach education in Brazil. *International Sport Coaching Journal, 1*(3), 165–172.

Nelson, L. J., Cushion, C. J., & Potrac, P. (2006). Formal, nonformal and informal coach learning: A holistic conceptualization. *International Journal of Sports Science & Coaching, 1*(3), 247–259.

O'Brien, D., & Eddie, I. (2013, February). Benchmarking global best practice: Innovation and leadership in surf city tourism and industry development. In *Keynote presentation at the Global Surf Cities Conference*.

Ojala, A. L., & Thorpe, H. (2015). The role of the coach in action and adventure sports: Using a problem-based learning approach. *International Sport Coaching Journal, 2*(1), 64–71. https://doi.org/10.1123/iscj.2014-0096

Origins Parkour. (2014). Origins parkour. Retrieved from http://www.originsparkour.com/

Own The Podium. (2015). National sport organizations (NSOs). Retrieved from http://www.ownthepodium.org/Partners/National-Sport-Organizations-(NSOs)

ParkourEDU. (2014). Coaching certification. Retrieved from https://parkouredu.org/seminars/coaching-certification

Parkour UK. (2017). What we do. Retrieved from https://parkour.uk/what-we-do/

Play Project. (2016). Play project. Retrieved from http://www.playproject.ca/

Ramos, V., Brasil, V. Z., & Goda, C. (2012). A aprendizagem profissional na percepção de treinadores de jovens surfistas [Coaches perceptions related to professional learning of young surfers]. *Revista da Educação Física/UEM, Maringá, 23*(3), 431–442.

Ramos, V., Brasil, V. Z., & Goda, C. (2013). O conhecimento pedagógico para o ensino do surf [Pedagogical knowledge for surf teaching]. *Revista da Educação Física/UEM, 24*(3), 381–392.

Red Bull. (2017). Red Bull art of motion. Retrieved from https://www.redbull.com/int-en/events/red-bull-art-of-motion

Rynne, S. B., Mallett, C. J., & Tinning, R. (2010). Workplace learning of high performance sports coaches. *Sport, Education and Society, 15*(3), 315–330. https://doi.org/10.1080/13573322.2010.493312

Sport Parkour League. (2017). North American parkour championship. Retrieved from https://www.sportparkourleague.com/

Thorpe, H., & Dumont, G. (2019). The professionalization of action sports: Mapping trends and future directions. *Sport in Society, 22*(10), 1639–1654.

Thorpe, H., & Wheaton, B. (2011). 'Generation X Games', action sports and the Olympic movement: Understanding the cultural politics of incorporation. *Sociology, 45*(5), 830–847.

Trudel, P., Gilbert, W., & Rodrigue, F. (2016). The journey from competent to innovator: Using appreciative inquiry to enhance high performance coaching. *AI Practitioner, 18*(2), 40–46.

USPK. (2017). The United States parkour association. Retrieved from https://www.uspk.org/

Walker, L. F., Thomas, R., & Driska, A. P. (2018). Informal and nonformal learning for sport coaches: A systematic review. *International Journal of Sports Science & Coaching, 13*(5), 694–707.

WFPF. (2017). World free running parkour federation certifications. Retrieved from https://wfpf.com/certifications/

Wheaton, B. (Ed.). (2004). *Understanding lifestyle sport: Consumption, identity and difference*. Routledge.

Wheaton, B. (2013). *The cultural politics of lifestyle sports*. London: Routledge.

World Surf League (WSL). (2018). Men's championship tour. Retrieved from https://www.worldsurfleague.com/athletes/tour/mct?year=2019

Vinicius Zeilmann Brasil, PhD, is a Researcher and Professor of Sport Coaching in the **Department of Health and Sport Science** at Santa Catarina State University, in Brazil. His research focussed on coaching and coach development in adventure sports (surfing, kitesurfing, and windsurfing).

Eva Ellmer is a PhD candidate and has been teaching in the postgraduate program in Sport Coaching with the School of Human Movement and Nutrition Sciences at The University of Queensland since 2016. Her research focussed on the learning experiences of action sports athletes, specifically within the context of high-performance BMX racing in Australia. Having recently submitted her thesis, Eva now works as a Coach Learning Specialist in a National Sporting Organisation.

Ethan Greenberg has a master degree from the School of Human Kinetics, Faculty of Health Sciences, University of Ottawa, Ottawa, Canada. He is a co-founder of Play Project Inc., an organization in Burlington, Ontario, Canada that is dedicated to teaching parkour, developing coaches, and promoting parkour through community outreach. His research focuses on the learning and development of parkour coaches.

Vitor Ciampolini is a PhD student in the Graduate Program in Physical Education at the Federal University of Santa Catarina, in Brazil. His research focuses on the development of sports coaches and how positive youth development and the teaching of life skills can be integrated in sports.

Chapter 12
Coaching Aging Athletes

Bettina Callary, Bradley W. Young, Diane M. Culver, and Tania Cassidy

Abstract While all athletes are aging, in this chapter we refer to Masters Athletes (MAs) as adults typically over 35 years of age, who are formally registered for sport, and who engage in training to prepare for competitions. While this cohort of athletes is the one of the fastest growing cohorts in sport, research is only beginning to uncover the nuances involved in successfully and effectively coaching them. In this chapter, we first discuss the empirical findings related to coaching MAs from the first and second authors' research endeavours. We then explore challenges for coach development. The practical implications of this research are divulged through the fourth author's personal story of being a MA. Finally, the third author will share her story of being a long-time coach of MAs, including some of the challenges and considerations for coaches who wish to successfully enable these athletes to achieve their respective objectives in sport. We relate the findings to key points that promote coaching in the Masters community, whether professionally or on more of a volunteer basis.

Keywords Masters athletes · Coaching adults · Serious leisure sport · Ageism · Andragogy

B. Callary (✉)
Cape Breton University, Sydney, NS, Canada
e-mail: bettina_callary@cbu.ca

B. W. Young · D. M. Culver
University of Ottawa, Ottawa, ON, Canada
e-mail: byoung@uottawa.ca; dculver@uottawa.ca

T. Cassidy
University of Otago, Dunedin, New Zealand
e-mail: tania.cassidy@otago.ac.nz

R. Resende, A. R. Gomes (eds.), *Coaching for Human Development and Performance in Sports*, https://doi.org/10.1007/978-3-030-63912-9_12

In this chapter, we delve into the topic of coaching aging athletes. We note from the onset that the term 'aging athlete' is somewhat problematic, as all athletes at any point in their athletic pathways are aging. However, with the predominant focus of research being child and youth coached programs, we turn to understanding an oft neglected athletic population of aging adults. Exploring how to coach aging adult athletes is, in our opinion, a unique endeavour as these athletes may be training in their sport, possibly with the same coach, for many years and their training may not necessarily have an upward trend in performance, which in part may be because of their aging bodies. On a psychological level, coaches of these aging athletes need to consider many factors involved in working with mature individuals, and must consider how social aspects of sport play into healthy active aging.

Thus, this chapter aims to explore psychosocial coaching behaviours and characteristics that enable coaches to successfully engage adults in ongoing serious leisure sport activities in ways that cater to their athletes' matured self-concept. Aging athletes are often referred to as Masters Athletes (MAs), meaning that they are typically over 35 years of age (but may be as young as 18 years of age depending on the sport), are formally registered for organized sport activities, and acknowledge that they prepare (train) in order to compete (at any level from recreational competitions through to World Masters Games; Young, 2011). Many of the aging athletes participating at recreational levels can be reluctant to acknowledge that they are "athletes" and that they "train", while those who compete at international levels may "show off" about how much they train. Regardless, MAs all have the expectation that they will participate in a competitive sporting event, the preparation for which engenders a regular routine of physical activity or practice. In this regard, many MAs turn to coaches to provide support and guidance for skill acquisition, performance improvement and motivation to sustain participation.

Empirical and Conceptual Findings About Coaching MAs

MAs are a fast-growing cohort in the Western world with growth paralleling the increasing numbers of aging baby-boomers. Some of these adults are known to have disposable incomes for leisure sport and higher educational levels, and are aware of the broad health benefits of sport participation. MAs participate in a range of events, from multi-sport events open to all abilities, to sport-specific events that often have performance selection criteria. So, while many MAs engaged in recreational events cite fitness, fun, and friendship as key motives for participating, other MAs cite competitive outcomes as key to their engagement in sport, but these motives are not mutually exclusive. Within this scope of aging sport participants, an ever-increasing number are turning to coached sport to provide quality sport experiences. Drs. Callary and Young, two of the authors of this chapter, have been working on a line of research for several years exploring the coached Masters context. The collective findings of our research have led us to understand poignant hallmarks of a quality coached adult (Masters) sport experience as including meaningful competitive and personal strivings, sport mastery, fun, quality relationships, fitness, intellectual stimulation, and feelings of empowerment and validation (e.g., Callary, Rathwell, & Young, 2015; Callary, Rathwell, & Young, 2017; MacLellan, Callary, & Young, 2018; Rathwell, Callary, & Young, 2015). Despite emerging evidence that coaches have a role in affording or shaping such experiences for aging athletes, our research has also indicated that coach development for Masters coaches (i.e., coaches of MAs) is sorely lacking, under-examined, under-considered, and under-resourced.

First, we explored the emerging literature on MAs to orient ourselves and better understand the context in which strategies for coaches and sport programmers might be advanced. This early work was not strictly grounded in coaching research per se, but drew on broader literature in sport psychology, psychosocial studies, and lifelong learning models, including understanding constructivist and adult learning theories (e.g., Jarvis, 2009; Knowles, Holton, & Swanson, 2012). It helped us form a blueprint that would scaffold some of our early inquiries on the topic; including suggestions for tailored programming in the adult sport environment, strategies for coaches to help maximize adults' limited time for sport, to help athletes negotiate issues of age-related performance decline, and approaches to fostering MAs' engagement in sport (Young, Callary, & Niedre, 2014).

We then collected empirical data, exploring what competitive swim MAs said they wanted and preferred from their coaches. They said that they wanted experienced coaches who also had experience as MAs themselves, and who had knowledge through formalized coaching education that they could share. They wanted coaches who fostered accountability to the sport; who displayed integrity in their practices as reflected in the planning, structure, and efficiency of training; and who planned challenging, variable, and flexible practice sessions (Callary, Rathwell, & Young, 2015). They also wanted coaches who understood their personal preferences for feedback delivery; explained the rationale for training activities; and who could cater to different motives, and competitive and personal characteristics. In making sense of our qualitative research, we were struck by the remarkable heterogeneity within groups of coached MAs, with varied abilities, ages, experiences, interests, and expectations.

With this heterogeneity in mind, we wanted to know more about who these athletes were and how they might present themselves to coaches. We knew from the research that MAs have varying motives for being involved in sport and that they are typically a privileged group who have the disposable income, health, ability, and desire to train, compete, and travel for sport (e.g., Dionigi, Baker, & Horton, 2011; Grant, 2001; Tulle, 2007). Although there are relatively more men than women participants, the number of women participants is growing, and Masters sport typically offers gender-inclusive programming. MAs usually do not train with younger athletes in the high-performance stream of sport (e.g., elite teen, young adults, collegiate groups), but can be organized in training groups advertised for Masters. Within these groups, athletes' ages range across decades. For example, it is common to have Masters swimmers in their 30s sharing the same training lane with speedy swimmers in their 60s. Although there is mixing of ages, skills, and experiences, the most regular and/or serious-minded participants assimilate into programs that exhibit structured programming, defined training practices that are associated with a sporting ethos, with a defined hierarchy of roles and identities. Within this context, led by our colleague Scott Rathwell, we conducted a narrative study to determine whether there were distinct profiles of coached MAs (Rathwell et al., 2015). He found that Masters swimmers' could be described according to three profiles: socially driven athletes who want coaches to be involved in and to organize social activities around the sport group; athletes who strove to improve personally and competitively in sport through the use of a coach; and those who enjoyed the shared leadership of Masters sport, liked to have control, and wanted to be part of the team of organizers to satisfy their needs for empowerment and accomplishment.

We next explored what coaches said they are doing with their MAs to cater to their varied personalities, abilities, and goals. Overall, these coaches noted unique approaches when working with MAs including the importance of bi-directional communication, being open to sharing leadership with athletes, understanding MAs' prior and current sport and non-sport experiences, personalizing MAs' goals and knowing their preferences, and utilizing multiple motivational strategies (e.g., Callary, MacLellan, Rathwell, & Young, 2015 in dragon boating; Callary, Rathwell, & Young, 2017 in swimming; MacLellan et al., 2018 in canoe/kayak). What we found was that those coaches who spoke of coaching their MAs with an *andragogical* approach seemed to be the most satisfied that they were matching, or individualizing, to meet their MAs' interests and needs.

Thus, we conceptually framed our understanding of coaching MAs in *andragogy*, which is an adult learning framework (Knowles et al., 2012). Within the Andragogy in Practice Model, there are six adult learning principles that address the individual and situational differences of adult learners, based on the goals and purposes for learning (Knowles et al., 2012). Based on observations of coaches, and both coaches' and athletes' descriptions of their experiences (e.g., MacLellan, Callary, & Young, 2019), our research team has modified Knowles and colleagues' principles to fit the Masters sport context. In particular, we reframed the six principles to characterize effective adult-oriented coaching in sport:

1. The coach enables and allows MAs' self-direction;
2. The coach explains why MAs are working on particular skills or activities;
3. The coach takes into account MAs' prior experiences in and out of sport;
4. The coach makes efforts to include a problem-oriented approach to training;
5. The coach works within the constraints of each adult's readiness to learn; and
6. The coach facilitates an intrinsically motivating environment (Callary et al., 2017; MacLellan et al., 2018, 2019).

Further, adding to Knowles and colleagues' model, we noted that some coaches' ageist assumptions / expectations for their MAs (e.g., how they saw aging and age constraints on sport potential) as well as their focus on learning for competitive goals and purposes (e.g., the degree to which they ascribed to participatory or performance orientations through their actions) will inherently influence the ways in which coaches utilize the six principles. We also concluded that the use of adult-oriented coaching approaches is associated with various positive athlete and coach outcomes.

Overall, these principles allowed coaches to account for the heterogeneity of athletes in their Masters groups, while providing congruency between what MAs say they want (such as individualized feedback) and what coaches say works well when coaching MAs (such as individualizing their communication with each athlete).

While some coaches' and MAs' data were congruent, there were also coaches in Callary et al.'s (2017) study who felt frustrations and ineptitudes in coaching MAs. These experiences often manifest because the coaches tried to use an approach that they claimed worked when coaching youth, or held expectations that their MAs would respond to their coaching like youth did. For example, some coaches made efforts to rearrange practice schedules to ensure adults' attendance at all prescribed training sessions. Although these efforts were well-intentioned and were presented as an accommodation strategy, coaches ended up being frustrated as this expectation proved unrealistic because of adults' other obligations and competing life priorities. Thus, exploring andragogy as a conceptual framework also extended our understanding of why coaches might feel frustrated when they did not ascribe to using the adult-oriented principles.

In an attempt to understand some of the difficulties that coaches faced when coaching MAs, a study was undertaken with the aim of gaining insight into how coaches were learning to coach MAs (Callary, Rathwell, & Young, 2018). What we found was somewhat disheartening. While coaches spoke of learning via several sources, the content was mostly unrelated to psychosocial approaches (e.g., informational, relational, or motivational facets) to coaching adults. That is, there was no formalized coach education, neither large-scale nor bespoke small-scale programming, for understanding how to coach aging athletes. Instead the coaches had compiled information that they had found regarding physiological factors of aging bodies in sport, had learned from experience as a MAs themselves, or in coaching MAs over the years (trial and error), and were minimally learning from other coaches of MAs. Some coaches had a limited understanding of teaching adults. Most had not necessarily considered the psychological and social nuances of Masters sport and thus had not taken steps to develop their knowledge in this domain. They all noted that existing coach education was focused around coaching youth and thus lacked relevance to their Masters context. They also showed a general interest in online resources regarding how to coach MAs (Callary et al., 2018); however, a targeted scope of online psychosocial coaching resources specific to adult athletes' learning yielded sparse findings (Belalcazar & Callary, 2018).

Practical Implications

In this section, the personal stories of Tania and Diane enable readers to see the connections between practice and the research that was presented above. Tania is a long-time MA in field hockey. She provides the reader with an understanding of the types of competitive situations in which she engages in the sport and what might be some of the important implications for coaching within these settings. Diane then provides her story of how she started, and continues, to coach adults in alpine skiing, providing the backdrop for some practical implications of coaching in Masters sport.

Tania's Stories: Introduction

My entrée to becoming a MA did not occur on the sports field, rather it began in a bar. In 2006, and I was having a drink with my sister when a passing patron recognised me and asked; 'you used to be a winger, didn't you? We need a winger'. I could never have anticipated how that chance meeting, and saying 'yes' to that question, would change my life. In the intervening 14 years I have been a regular participant, in a range of capacities, in numerous local, national and international Masters' hockey events. The following discussions focus on three Masters contexts; (1) international Masters multi-sport events, (2) Golden Oldies, (3) representative Masters at a single sport event.

International Masters Multi-sport Event The first World Masters Games (WMG) was held in Toronto, Canada, in 1985, with the aim of meeting the demand for competitive sport among the older population. Since then it has been held every 4 years and has become the biggest multi-sport event on the international calendar. The WMG athletes do not represent their country, although they do have to be a member of their sport's governing body (https://www.imga.ch/en/home/).

In 2009, I took annual leave from work to participate in the WMG held in Sydney, Australia. Its moto was 'Fit, fun and forever young' and had 28,292 competitors, whose average age was 50 years old with the oldest competitor being 101 years old. I was excited to participate because the main sporting venue was the Sydney Olympic Park, which had been the location of the 2000 Sydney Olympic Games. I had also heard that the organisation of the WMG was being modelled on the successful Olympic Games. The managers of the team were also players, and were affectionately known as 'Camp Mum' and 'Camp Leader' after a legendary New Zealand comedy duo. While their titles were humorous, their exceptional organising abilities were legendary, which were arguably informed by the roles they held in their day jobs. While the managers were intent on getting the most competitive team 'on the pitch', they were cognisant that the composition of the team would also be determined by factors such as cost, annual leave entitlement, child care, the desire to have 'low maintenance' team members and players who would socially fit into the team. The 'selection' process needed to be made in conjunction with the decision regarding the age category in which the team would register. At the WMG, hockey teams are required to compete in sex and age categories, e.g., W40, M45, O50 (O = Open, or mixed genders). While the sex categories are non-negotiable, athletes can 'play down' a year category, e.g., you can be 46 years old but play in the O40 category, but athletes cannot 'play up' a category, e.g., you cannot be 46 years old and play in the O50 category.

The members of our informal hockey community do not fit within one age category; instead there is nearly a 40-year age range. Despite the size of the informal group, once all the 'other' factors have been accounted for, we can never get a full squad of 16 who all belong to the same age category. This means that the if older members of the team want to play in competitions like the WMG, they need to agree to 'play down'. So, for the Sydney WMG we agreed our best chance of medalling was to play in the O40 grade, which for me as a 45-year-old meant that I had to 'play down' a grade against younger athletes.

One legacy of the Sydney Olympic Games was that its Olympic Park had been made accessible by public transport, and it was via public transport that many of the thousands of athletes who competed at the WMG arrived. From the center of Sydney, the easiest route was via train, and it took between 40 and 55 min. A change of train was always required and this necessitated walking up and over a bridge to get to the other train tracks. It was here that I met John,[1] a 90+ year old swimmer. He was moving slowly and carrying a largish carry-all bag, from which emanated a clunking sound. One of our team offered to carry his bag up and over the bridge because there was only two minutes between arriving on platform one and departing from platform two. As we walked, he told me that he had to check out from his accommodation that morning and that is why he had to carry his luggage to the pool and that the clunking sound was all the medals he had won at the current swimming meet. Upon alighting from the train, there was still a lengthy walk to the pool so I carried his bag and we talked about his swimming career, which was lengthy. He also talked about why he swam, his family and how at times it was the organisation of the tournaments, rather than the swimming itself, that caused him physical stress. While the public transport was a viable option for many to get from Central Sydney to the Olympic Park, for some of the older participants at the WMG, the logistical and physical requirements of actually getting to the sporting venue were more taxing than the events themselves.

This was the second time I had heard stories about how the organisation of the WMG had physically impacted the athletes. On day one of the tournament all 28,292 participants had to pick up their registration package at the offices at Olympic Park. This had been the process at the 2000 Olympic Games, where the managers from each country had picked up registration packs. However, this approach was not so practical at the WMG. The sheer numbers participating meant that all participants, regardless of age, had to queue, some for up to two hours, to register. Not surprisingly, stories emerged of the discomfort that some of the older MAs had whilst standing in the queue for two hours in the sun. One potential way that organisers could have overcome the discomfort for the athletes, in the team events at least, would have been to allow designated team managers to pick up a team registration pack. That may have gone some way to reduce the size of the queues.

While the queuing did not affect me or my team, we were not immune to what we saw as another organizational blunder on the part of the WMG. Our team had

---

[1]All personal names in this chapter are pseudonyms, except the authors' own names.

registered for the W40 grade along with 16 other teams. The tournament for this grade was not a knock out tournament, nor was it organised along a round robin, neither was it explicitly organised in pools with cross overs at the end of a particular number of games. While it was not clear from the outset what structure was being used, we were pleased to be told that there would be playoffs and that we had qualified for the semi-finals. Upon winning the semi-final, you can imagine our surprise to find that there was no final game and we had finished the tournament in fourth place due to goal difference (https://www.imga.ch/en/data/23). From our perspective, it appeared that whoever had put the draw together in the hockey W40 category did not understand how to organise a tournament draw for 17 teams. This less than satisfactory outcome highlighted a potential weakness of large Masters events, where the organisers, in this case the local sport specific organisers of the hockey tournament at the WMG, whether they are volunteers or paid employees, did not have the appropriate skill set. It appeared from the perspective of my team that the local organizing committee had failed to draw on the expertise in the local Sydney sporting community for assistance. While MAs can be demanding, many of these athletes are also very capable members of the community and, if asked prior to a tournament, are willing to help to make sure Masters events run as smoothly, and are as enjoyable, as possible.

Golden Oldies[2] In 1979, the first Official World Golden Oldies festival took place in Auckland, New Zealand, targeting 35-year old+ rugby players.[3] From that first festival, the Golden Oldies week long festivals are now run biennially in a range of sports, which currently include; rugby, netball, cricket, hockey, golf, and softball. In 2012, the 'Golden Oldies' brand was bought by an events management and travel company, which stated that the 'objective of the company is to keep people who have played sport as keen amateurs—mostly at club level—in the game, despite them getting older'. With this objective in mind the rules of the game in some sports have been modified to 'suit the age groups and reduce the risk of injury and harm'. (https://www.stuff.co.nz/business/industries/74350649/). The motto for the Golden Oldies festivals is 'Fun, Friendship and Fraternity' (https://www.govsl.com/).

I have been participating in the Golden Oldies hockey festivals since 2007 and have attended tournaments in: Rosario, Argentina (2007); Adelaide, Australia (2009); Edinburgh, Scotland (2011); Hawaii, USA 2013; Leipzig, Germany (2015); Cape Town, South Africa (2017); Christchurch, New Zealand (2018); and Vancouver, Canada (2019). My entrée into the Golden Oldies was serendipitous. After competing in the national multi-sport Masters competition in 2006 I was invited by a teammate to play in her local team that competed weekly during the winter season. These weekly games served as 'practice' for the event, as we did not engage in other practices during the week, did not have a coach, and the sideline management of substitutions was organised by either a player who was currently

[2]A South Island (NZ) Golden Oldies women's hockey weekend tournament has been played annually since 1983.

[3]http://www.europeangoldenoldiesrugby.com/festivals/festival-history/

injured, a family member who had come to watch, or it was self-regulated. Some members of the local team had previously attended a Golden Oldies festival and were planning to attend the festival in Rosario in 2007. Half way through the season one of the players had to pull out of the up-coming Rosario Golden Oldies trip and was looking for someone to replace her and recoup the money she had already paid. I was subsequently invited to take her place in the Golden Oldies team because, unbeknown to me at the time, I had been judged by the team to be a 'low maintenance' team member, which meant I was considered to be able to fit in socially with the existing team dynamics, had a sense of humour, was able to pay the required fees on time, was au fait with international travel, and would be open to new experiences. My invitation had nothing to do with my ability to play hockey. The timing to attend the Golden Oldies festival was not great from a work perspective, nonetheless I accepted the invitation because I enjoy travelling and I had not been to Argentina.

While there were similarities between the Masters multi-sport event and the Golden Oldies event, there were also marked differences. The most obvious were that instead of the teams competing in pre-determined 5-year age categories, the composition of the Golden Oldies teams could be anyone over 35 years old. To enable the competition to be fair, teams self-categorised as male, female or mixed, and self-selected the level of competition in which they wanted to play, ranging from 'social' to 'competitive', on a 5-point Likert scale. Further, the scores of each game were not recorded anywhere, there were no league tables and therefore no over-all winner of each grade.[4] Thus, when the games finished, teams did not spend time scouting the upcoming opposition but instead socialized with other teams, enabling the enactment of the Golden Oldies motto, which was furthered by a 'picnic day' to a local tourist destination, playing games on only 3 days, and a final dinner and dance. Despite the motto being clearly evident, the 'competitive' spirit of many participants meant that at times disharmony and the double standards between men's and womens' sport still arose. For example, in 2009 there was uproar in the women's competitive section when a man was found to be surreptitiously playing in goal. Yet when I played in a men's team in Lepzig in 2015 and Christchurch in 2018 no one appeared to disapprove. Instead I got an incredulous comment—'are you a girl?'[5]—from the opposition in Lepzig, and very visible pride from team mates and opposition in Christchurch when the same 'girl' was the leading goal scorer in the section (not that we were keeping count).

Representative Masters at a Single Sport Event Representative Masters hockey, whether at the national or international level, tends to follow the patterns associated with non-Masters representative sport, namely; there are calls for expressions of interest for coaches and managers, trials (aka try-outs) are held for potential players, selections are made, tournaments to attend, and national or international honours for

[4]This is not to say some members of the teams, especially those competing in the competitive grades, did not know how many games they had won throughout the duration of the tournament.

[5]Despite me being in my 50s.

which to play. I have been involved, in various capacities, in representative Masters hockey since 2015 by initially being asked to attend trials for a provincial team.

At the provincial level, the trial and selection process is conducted by the coach and senior players, i.e., the captain and vice-captain, and is primarily about filling in the gaps of a pre-existing team, which was breaking up because a significant number of the players no longer wanted to play 'down an age grade'. The province for which I play is geographically large but small in population, so to field a competitive team it is necessary to select players whose ages cross two 5-year age bands (e.g., O50 and O55). This is not so much of an issue when the older members of the team have just crossed into the older age band but it becomes problematic when they near the top of the age grade because it means a 59-year-old team member can be potentially playing against 49-year old[6] opposition. In the past, when the playing members were in their 40s and this circumstance arose, the younger members of the provincial team were temporarily dropped, until they became 'old enough' to play in the next age grade, and new members are recruited into the older age group.[7] My invitation to trial coincided with this process. Unlike my recruitment to the aforementioned teams, my hockey skills and fitness were assessed at the trial and they did play a part in my subsequent selection.

It appears it does not matter how old you are, when you head off to a tournament playing with a new team, there is a degree of apprehension about how it will go and how you will fit in. I need not have worried because any apprehension quickly evaporated when someone recounted stories of a 1979 national primary (elementary) school representative hockey tournament and we were surprised to find that the majority of our team had played at this tournament, and thus we had been tangentially connected to each other via hockey for 34 years.

At the end of that national tournament, I prepared for the trials for the New Zealand O50s team. I had trained hard and was feeling pretty confident about my fitness level, but because this was my first trial, I was not sure how I compared to the other trialists. In the first part of the trial, I came out on top in all the fitness components so I was beginning to feel more comfortable in the environment. Next was the game play. Within 30 min, I was being carried off the field suffering a dislocated knee and ruptured ACL as a consequence of a dubious challenge from the opposition. Upon returning home and hearing of the diagnosis, I contacted the coach/selector by email to inform her. I never received an acknowledgement of that email, let alone best wishes for a speedy recovery. I remember feeling very cross and wondered what the lack of engagement and empathy by the coach/selector would have meant for an athlete (Master or non-Master) whose identity was closely tied up with becoming a national representative athlete. While I had some investment

[6]The rules state that you can play in a grade that corresponds to the age you will turn that year.

[7]Beyond being an organizational issue, moving into a new competitive age category is often perceived as an advantage by participants, whereas being relatively-older in a category is seen as a competitive disadvantage, a motivational challenge to be navigated (see Medic, Young, & Grove, 2013).

in hockey, it is only one aspect of my identity and there are plenty of other aspects of my life that are reaffirming. So, coaches need to be aware of their possible influence.

During the 18-month recovery period, I became a manager for two hockey teams, my local team that played in a weekly competition and the O50 provincial team. In the process of doing so, I watched plenty of hockey and got a better understanding of positional play and effective practices. Upon returning to play, I surprised myself at how I had become a better hockey player. I was more tactically aware, I was stronger and I enjoyed it more, in part because I knew what it was like not to play. Two years after I was injured, I returned to the national tournament determined to make the national team this time. I was the leading goal scorer for the O50s grade and felt as if I played reasonably well during the tournament. So, I was very pleased when a couple of days before Christmas, I got an email from the coach/selector to say that I had made the squad. I told my family and thanked my physio and then emailed the coach/selector to thank her for the good news. An hour later I got another email from the coach/selector informing me that I had been sent the wrong email, I should have been sent the 'sorry to inform you but you did not make the squad…' email. Once again, I was surprised by the inept email practices of the coach (this was a different coach to the one described above), surely names and messages would have been doubled checked. Again, I was thankful that I had things in my life other than hockey, which meant that I quickly got over the failure to make the squad. But the experience highlighted several things about playing in the Masters context. Specifically, there was a lack of clarity around what criteria was being used in the selection process and lack of rigour in the process of communicating the outcomes of selection to trialist. I also wondered what criteria was being used to discern the competency of the coaches of the Masters teams. Was the same rigour used when selecting a coach for the New Zealand U21 and the New Zealand O50 teams? I am guessing not, especially when the coach of the then O50 team was also a selector and a player.

Finally, in 2019, the trials for the national team were again being held in conjunction with the national Masters hockey tournament. In the intervening 18 months between tournaments, I had become a member of the Hockey New Zealand Masters Advisory Group (MAG). One of the policies the MAG group has instigated in the hiatus between national tournaments was clarity around the selection processes. I decided to put my name forward, and this time trial for the national O55 team (the sands of time wait for no one). In the second game of the tournament, I became aware the selectors were watching the game. The team was playing well and I was making a good contribution, until just before half time when the opposition fullback hit me with a ball at close range. The impact of the ball broke a bone and I was in plaster and a moon boot for 11 weeks. Once again, I had to withdraw from the selection process. A few weeks after the injury, I was invited by Hockey New Zealand to become the Chef de Mission for the biennial Trans-Tasman Masters hockey challenge to be held in Australia. This was the tournament I had been aiming to play in as a player of the New Zealand O55 team, now I was being asked to lead the 14 New Zealand teams (comprising 270 athletes). I decided I would enjoy the challenge, so accepted the invitation. Now my choice for 2020 is complicated; do I trial again in the hope of making the O55 national team to play in the upcoming Masters Hockey World Cup in South Africa or do I continue to develop my leadership skills and express my interest in becoming the Chef de Mission for the World Cup tournament? I cannot do both. Time will tell, but one thing is for sure I will keep being involved in Masters sport for many years to come.

Diane's Story: Becoming a Coach of Masters Athletes

Beginnings I have called this story 'Becoming a coach of MAs' very intentionally, because it has been a long journey, and one that is on-going. My pathway into coaching alpine skiing was quite typical—club, division, provincial, and finally national team ski racer, and after competing on the world stage for about 5 years, I quit racing and moved straight into coaching. Over the next few decades, I coached all levels of athletes, from children to Olympic skiers, but not MAs. During this time, despite doing my coach education training and even training others, I mostly learned in the laboratory of real life, through informal learning situations. These situations included observation, trial and error, interactions with athletes and other coaches, and taking a deep dive into my own learning by leaving coaching for 5 years when I became a ski instructor at a large ski school, which was known for developing the highest level of ski instructor.[8]

During this phase, I continued to train coaches but I focussed mostly on teaching recreational skiers of all levels, and on becoming a serious pedagogue of skiing. Many of my colleagues were astounded that I would leave coaching at the national level, to come to a ski school where I would be teaching beginners and all levels of skiers. But this was my plan—I thought that I would learn about technique from the ground up. Coaching at the national level, I could detect errors and make ski racers go faster, but I did not know everything I wanted to know about what makes an efficient ski turn. Naturally, in this new context, I began working with many adults of Masters age, but 95% of them were not interested in competing. Nonetheless, I got very good at making skiing enjoyable and easier for adults. I also became very familiar with the fears that accompany many adults when they engage in what is perceived as a risky sport. I learned that the affective dimension of learning takes precedence in such situations. You cannot get a fearful learner to listen to and execute motor commands before you deal with the fear.

These, however, were not the only interesting challenges I appraised in teaching adults. I became very good at quickly assessing the psycho-social needs and states of my adult clients. For instance, how do you get a person who is athletic, and thinks

[8]Founded in 1938, the Canadian Ski Instructors' Alliance trains ski instructors across Canada and abroad. While their programs integrate the sport's National Sport Organisation ski coach training as an instructor moves up the instructor pathway, the two organisations are separate. The highest level of ski instructor in Canada is Level 4.

they can use their intuition and athletic prowess to turn, to actually listen to you? Alpine skiing is very counter-intuitive. Most things a person wants to do are actually the opposite of what is required. In general, ski lessons last between an hour to a half day. To achieve good results, an instructor has to quickly adjust to the learner. I also found out that tapping into the previous life and sport experiences of adults allows me to couch my lessons in a language that is easy for the adult to relate to, thereby helping them to learn. Looking back at this part of my career, and thinking about working with adults, I realise there were many things that I did learn about coaching MAs long before I actually tried it out.

First Attempt at Coaching Masters Skiers After coaching youth and high-performance athletes for many years, I returned to coaching children when my children were small. Apart from the enjoyment you get seeing these athletes progress, it is very pleasurable because you do a lot of skiing with them. Such free skiing is an important part of training young skiers. The area where I work (now only holidays and weekends) has a Masters program called 100% Racing, which involves purely 'running gates' (i.e., training in slalom and giant slalom courses). We also run a series of five competitions throughout the season. In the 100% Racing group, coaches do not free ski with the adult skiers.

One day, I was asked at the last minute to replace a coach in the 100% Racing program. Looking back, and knowing what I know now, I can say that I went into this completely unprepared! All morning, I stood there at the bottom of the course, as we do, watching these adults and trying to coach them as I would younger athletes and expecting similar results. I suppose I was quite good at coaching youth and my expectations were that I could change a person's skiing in a morning. At the end, when I was asked if I would consider taking on the program for the season, I said "No thank you!", thinking to myself, "If I am going to stand on the hill and not get to ski, I prefer to do it for children and youth, because at least I get to see almost instantly the fruit of my efforts". I am slightly embarrassed by this admission, which seems somewhat ego-centric, but it is the truth. Coaching MAs requires a major shift in a coach's perspective, and at that point, I was not ready for that shift.

Fifteen Years on Several years after that first experience coaching Masters, I was asked (in advance of the season) if I would join some of my very good colleagues to coach the 100% Racing program. This time, I carefully considered the offer. In weighing it up, I knew that I would need to make some major adjustments in my expectations related to 'a satisfying coaching experience'. I was, at the time, not sure what that would look like for MAs, but my one morning experience told me that it would be very different than a satisfying experience coaching children and youth. In the end, several forces came together to sway me, not the least of which was the opportunity to work with one of my favourite colleagues who had been coaching the group for a few years. I knew that he and I were very much on the same wavelength when it came to ski technique, so I valued the chance to work with him, and see how he coached the MAs.

Over 15 years later, I am still coaching this program. I have found my way into feeling not just 'satisfied enough' but very satisfied with this work. In addition to the knowledge that I carried forward from my early days teaching adults to ski, I have learned many things. I have come to absolutely admire my MAs. Over the 15 years, there are a few MAs that have been consistently there. While I have several serious competitors in the group, there are also those who are really there for the satisfaction of working hard and improving. One MA, Clare, started racing at about 47 years old. She is now 64 and she trains every Saturday and Sunday, no matter the weather. When it is bitterly cold, I am motivated to go out and coach because I know that she (and others) will be there. Through my time coaching Clare, I learned that a small improvement can take, not several days, nor weeks, but several seasons. She continually challenges me to think 'outside of the box' to find solutions to the technical problems that I see in her skiing. I know that I need to work with her physical abilities and find ways to make her go faster. I, along with my coaching partners, have achieved this. But more satisfying is Clare's amazing enthusiasm and smile when she arrives at the bottom of the course and says, "That is so much fun!". One of the great things that we do with our race circuit is that while we produce race results that go to a Masters points list, we calculate special points (called 'beer points') that are based on an individual's improvement in time compared to the fastest time of the day. After each race, we meet in a bar to socialise, get the race and beer points results, and win door prizes (no prizes for winning). This is a wonderful way to recognise self-improvement.

Being a coach of MAs requires that I walk a fine line between friend and coach. I try to respect the limits of my athletes, whether these be physical, psychological, emotional, or social. For example, some of my MAs arrive for training after a hard work week, or after a big social event. I must accept that they have to find the balance in their lives and decide their priorities. In this case, I try to work with them to assess their fatigue and ensure to the best of my ability that they stay safe, within their limits. Occasionally their enthusiasm outweighs their ability. In our set up, we, the coaches, are not responsible for anything in our MAs' lives except their on-hill training, but sometimes we have to recommend that they see a personal trainer to improve their physical abilities. Skiing is a sport that requires a lot of strength, balance, coordination, and agility. Several years ago, we had a very keen new participant join us. He trained with us for a few years, but I was often fearful that he did not have the necessary agility to recover from being out of balance in a slalom course. However, he was so very enthusiastic it was difficult to stop him. One day he fell and broke his wrist badly. This man is a neurosurgeon who could not operate for at least 3 months. I still ponder whether I could have stopped this happening. He, of course, took his own risks, and has since wisely become a volunteer patroller on the mountain. Notably, as a coach of MAs, it is difficult to know when you should step in and remove an adult from an activity that might be dangerous for them. On a regular basis, as coaches, we alter the activity to make it safer. Sometimes this is for the whole group, so we might change the training activity. Most often, though, since the level of competence is quite varied in our groups, we need to find individual solutions. For example, I will change the task for one MA by giving her[9] a drill to do, or getting her to take a different line in the course that would be slower and safer for her but still allow her to focus on some technical aspect on which she needs to work.

One thing that does not change, and I will provide an example to illustrate what I mean, is that I try to stick to my coaching philosophy and coach according to my values. Where I might have to consider slight adaptations to my coaching philosophy when coaching MAs versus youth is in the area of providing each of my MAs the appropriate level of autonomy. It can be difficult to strike the right balance when it comes to pushing your MAs while keeping them safe. Even with MAs, you need to know your athletes, and understand when to push and when to ease up, and when to 'lay down the law', as it were. Understanding MAs' motives for participation is crucial, but even this must be tempered by a realistic evaluation of their capacity to achieve their goals. An example that comes to mind occurred on a day when we were training on a difficult trail under very challenging conditions. The visibility was poor and the snow was very soft. As coaches, we were carefully monitoring the situation for safety but it was frustrating for the skiers as a 'good feeling run' was impossible. Most of the MAs were managing the situation and taking it in stride but one male, who was arguably one of the strongest and most experienced skiers in the group, was not. He was giving up, swearing loudly, and generally complaining. After some time, he stopped near me and asked where we would be training the next day and when I responded the same trail, he said that he thought he might return the following day. I thought a moment about my response, then decided to be frank, believing that this was the best approach to help him move forward. Part of my philosophy is that we create a positive environment and treat others with respect. So, I replied, "That is fine Martin, but not if you are going to continue to swear and be unpleasant". In this instance, I felt as though I was dealing with a young person, but he had in fact been acting like a child. More importantly for coaching, he was making excuses and blaming his results on the conditions rather than adjusting his skiing in order to cope with them. Such conditions are part of the nature of competitive skiing and, as long as he continued to behave in that way, he was not learning how to cope. An on-going challenge is finding a balance between being a coach who partners with my MAs in a collaborative coaching process versus one who uses a more directive approach. There are many occasions when this shift is much subtler than the example of Martin. Sometimes, it is just being very direct and firm about a piece of technical feedback.

If I had to sum up my experience coaching MAs, I would say, rather obviously since I have now been at it for more than 15 years, that it is very rewarding. However, the rewards are quite different than those I get when working with youth. With youth, I get the instant satisfaction of seeing that my coaching know-how works. More long term, I also benefit from seeing my young athletes develop as individuals who carry the lessons they have learned through sport into other areas of their lives. With my MAs, I get a different sort of satisfaction. Yes, I

[9]The use of the feminine in this case refers to either a female or male MA.

see them improve but the learning curve is much flatter than with youth. I have to take joy from the little gains and be very patient. However, these small gains technically come with the added satisfaction of the appreciation demonstrated by the MAs when they become conscious of their improvements. Appreciation of my coaching is definitely demonstrated more by most of the MAs compared to most youth. Finally, and not insignificantly, I am rewarded by my admiration for these MAs. They inspire me with their enthusiasm for my sport. At times, with all my experience as a high-performance skier and coach, I am amazed at their courage and willpower to train in difficult snow conditions and awfully cold weather. Having adjusted my expectations, I have come to love coaching my Masters ski racers. After my work week in the city, I get up every Saturday and Sunday morning at 6 am to be on the mountain at 8 am to set the courses and coach them until noon. With my story, I hope that I will inspire other coaches to consider taking up coaching MAs.

Key Points

Tania's stories generally spoke to her lack of working with coaches at the Masters level. While sport organizations are systematically encouraging and advocating for properly trained coaches at youth sport levels, this is not the case at the Masters level. At the WMG, there may be benefit in teams identifying coaches, which if the organisational structures were supportive, could assist MAs by managing and organizing, facilitating registrations, and helping athletes develop on-site itineraries to negotiate logistics. Having coaches at the Golden Oldies would again require a different skill set. With less competitively-oriented MAs, coaches may need to focus more on creating effective relationships and understanding the interdependence of MAs being on the team for fun and improvement. Finally, in representative Masters single-sport international events, the coaches that Tania had contact with appeared to need training in understanding how to recruit, select, and retain players, dealing with injuries (both physiologically and psychologically), and understanding the anxieties and emotions of high-level competitions as well as the invested interests of MAs and their identities wrapped up in athletic pursuits. It is unclear whether these coaches had any training in coaching MAs, yet Tania's stories also speak to the number of MAs involved in these events, the competitiveness of the MAs, the fun and social aspects of sport, which are all key aspects of sport participation. Tania's stories also spoke about the financial possibilities of working with adults who have money for leisure time sport, and who "pay to play", hoping to get money's worth from their sport experience, in which full immersion and reciprocal loyalty by a coach would help to create quality sport experiences. Thus, coach training for the Masters sport context appears to be important in helping coaches to understand how they contribute effectively to quality sport experiences and environments.

Diane's story is one of a Masters coach with sport-specific experience and training, as well as a passion for coaching and skiing. Her story illustrated how a coach, trained and certified in coaching principles often grounded in pedagogy, refined her craft through experiences over 15 years to adopt a more andragogically-oriented position toward adults. Although Diane did not explicitly call her approach andragogical, her stories embodied many key principles of adult-oriented coaching principles (MacLellan et al., 2019), specifically satisfying MAs' 'need to know', taking efforts to address their 'readiness to train', and employing a 'problem-focused learning orientation'. Her tale also highlighted her adoption of personal attributes related to reciprocal loyalty (Callary, Rathwell, et al., 2015), bidirectional communication skills (Callary et al., 2017; MacLellan et al., 2018), the importance of intellectual stimulation (for both MAs and the coach; Callary, Rathwell, et al., 2015), individualizing approaches and select discretionary skills (e.g., knowing when and how to push your athlete, holding athletes to account for the integrity of practice; Callary, Rathwell, et al., 2015), that proved effective for her in leading Masters skiers. Her story emphasized the importance of coaches' personal interests and rewards in coaching MAs in order to invest in becoming, and remaining, a coach for MAs. She spoke of working with other great coaches, connecting with her athletes, admiring their feats and improvements, and feeling satisfied with their hard work ethic. Also, she spoke of MAs challenging her to become a better and more creative coach, of developing a coaching philosophy specific to MAs, of being realistic and goal oriented. Finally, she noted that adults have competing priorities in life, that she did not spend much time developing adults' life skills or personal development, and that she struggled at times in knowing when to be more collaborative versus when to take a more directive (traditional) coaching approach.

Both Diane and Tania's stories uncover practical aspects that promote Masters sport coaching as a legitimate and professional way of working with adults in sport. However, there exist many challenges in promoting the Masters sport coach as a professional. We note that coaches may not want to undertake coach education or become professional in this context because they do not see the value in it, are not aware of possible psychosocial topics for learning that would be beneficial to their athletes, or cannot financially afford to do it. There may be little demand from some MAs to have an 'official' coach, especially those who do not spend a lot of time training and participate primarily for social reasons. Both Diane and Tania's stories illustrate that MAs note the importance of the coaches being educated and knowledgeable. Further, coaches who use inappropriate approaches in coaching their MAs may in fact detract from quality sport experiences for both the athlete and themselves in terms of lacking the rewarding and beneficial aspects of the coach-athlete relationship in sport, and both may decide to quit. Thus, there is merit in exploring how coaches can act professionally, and effectively promoting the value of adult-coaching principles.

Anecdotally, the lack of professionalism across the Masters system is hindering the growth of quality Masters sport. Yet the issue of professionalizing coaches of MAs is problematic—without organizational or individual push for professional development, there is little incentive. First, on an individual level, some coaches show a lack of professionalism towards coaching MAs (i.e., "MAs aren't trying to get to the Olympics, they just want to have fun and I don't really need to plan for that"). We saw this in Tania's story, in the lack of coaches at events and in coaches' lack of communication during selection processes. While Tania did not give up, some MAs could respond by feeling they do not need coaching and/or do not need to train, they just compete (with potentially unhealthy outcomes such as injury). Second, on an organizational level, there is a lack of interest on the part of sport federations in developing coaches' knowledge specifically for working with adults (i.e., there are no coach education program possibilities for Masters sport and generally the limited sport funding is almost certainly allotted to youth and high performance programming). While Diane's biography gave her a wealth of coaching experience, she still indicated that, when she started coaching MAs she was unsure of what the Masters context would entail and relied on learning about coaching MAs through her experiences with them. Furthermore, most coaches of MAs volunteer or work part time in their role with Masters. Mandatory professional development, which would create a minimum standard for coaching Masters sport, also cuts into the time that these coaches have devoted to sport, and may be overtaxing and not valued. On the other hand, without a minimum standard in understanding how to coach adults, the quality sport experience may be compromised because many coaches do not look, or do not know where to look, to learn how to meet the needs of their athletes. Still, there are numerous Masters coaches who are looking for professional development and have, in our research (Callary et al., 2018), expressed a desire to acquire more knowledge and competencies specific to working with MAs. Thus, our ongoing research aims to better equip coaches, using instructional strategies that provide resources for these coaches without being burdensome.

Conclusion

This chapter highlighted our research initiatives in understanding coaching a group of aging athletes that are oft neglected within both the research and in practice: MAs, a fast-growing cohort of active, competitive, socially-oriented, and passionate group of adults participating in sport. Coaching MAs requires a shift in perspective, knowledge of adult learning, understanding adults' priorities, goals, and challenges in being involved in sport, and a careful negotiation of social, cognitive and emotional aspects to create quality sport experiences. The stories illustrated here also show that coaching MAs requires new sensitivities to the mature identity of adults. This includes a different appreciation for why they are competing and how coach-led learning is framed within their competitive orientation. We also note the importance of coach reflection on how one's role and appreciation for their role changes when leading adults as opposed to youth or younger, high-performance adult cohorts. The stories presented illustrate these challenges and make the case for the importance of developing coaches' professional, interpersonal, and intrapersonal knowledge specific to the Masters context. We are optimistic that as the Masters cohort continues to grow, coaches who are aware of the nuanced nature of MAs will become more common place for the betterment of sport training, events, and competitions.

References

Belalcazar, C., & Callary, B. (2018, March). Facilitating access to online resources for Masters coaches. In *Presentation at the Eastern Canadian Sport and Exercise Psychology Symposium, and Association of Applied Sport Psychology, International regional conference, Montreal, Canada.*

Callary, B., MacLellan, J., Rathwell, S., & Young, B. W. (2015, August). Coaching masters dragon boaters—perspectives from a coach and an athlete. In *Presentation at the International Council for Coaching Excellence, Global Coach Conference, Vierumaki, Finland.*

Callary, B., Rathwell, S., & Young, B. (2015). Masters swimmers experiences with coaches: What they need, what they want, what they get. *Sage Open.* https://doi.org/10.1177/2158244015588960

Callary, B., Rathwell, S., & Young, B. W. (2017). Coaches' report of andragogical approaches with Masters Athletes. *International Sport Coaching Journal., 4*, 177–190. https://doi.org/10.1123/iscj.2016-0102

Callary, B., Rathwell, S., & Young, B. W. (2018). Coach education and learning sources for coaches of Masters Swim Athletes. *International Sport Coaching Journal, 5*(1), 47–59. https://doi.org/10.1123/iscj.2017-0056

Dionigi, R. A., Baker, J., & Horton, S. (2011). Older athletes' perceived benefits of competition. *The International Journal of Sport and Society, 2*(2), 17–28.

Grant, B. C. (2001). "You're never too old": Beliefs about physical activity and playing sport in later life. *Ageing and Society, 21*(6), 777–798.

Jarvis, P. (2009). *Learning to be a person in society*. London: Routledge.

Knowles, M. S., Holton, E. F., III, & Swanson, R. A. (2012). *The adult learner* (7th ed.). New York: Routledge.

MacLellan, J., Callary, B., & Young, B. W. (2018). Same coach, different approach? How Masters and youth athletes perceive learning opportunities in training. *International Journal of Sports Science and Coaching, 13*(2), 167–178. https://doi.org/10.1177/1747954117727202

MacLellan, J., Callary, B., & Young, B. W. (2019). Adult learning principles in master's sport: A coach's perspective. *Canadian Journal for the Study of Adult Education, 31*(1), 31–50.

Medic, N., Young, B. W., & Grove, J. R. (2013). Perceptions of five-year competitive categories: Model of how relative age influences competitiveness in masters sport. *Journal of Sports Sciences & Medicine, 12*(4), 724–729.

Rathwell, S., Callary, B., & Young, B. W. (2015). Exploring the context of coached Masters swim programs: A narrative approach. *International Journal of Aquatic Research and Education, 9*(1), 70–88. https://doi.org/10.1123/ijare.2014-0068

Tulle, E. (2007). Running to run: Embodiment, structure and agency amongst veteran elite runners. *Sociology, 41*(2), 329–346.

Young, B. W. (2011). Psycho-social perspectives on the motivation and commitment of Masters athletes. In N. Holt & M. Talbot (Eds.), *Lifelong engagement in sport and physical activity* (pp. 125–138). London: Routledge and International Council of Sport Science and Physical Education.

Young, B. W., Callary, B., & Niedre, P. (2014). Exploring novel considerations for the coaching of Masters athletes. *International Sport Coaching Journal, 1*(2), 86–93. https://doi.org/10.1123/iscj.2014-0052

Bettina Callary is the Canada Research Chair in Sport Coaching and Adult Learning and an Associate Professor in the Department of Experiential Studies in Community and Sport at Cape Breton University. She researches topics in coach education, learning, and development, coach developers, psychosocial aspects of Masters Athletes and long term development, and qualitative research methods. Dr. Callary is the Editor-in-Chief for the International Sport Coaching Journal. She is also an alpine ski coach and coach developer.

Bradley W. Young is a full professor in the School of Human Kinetics at the University of Ottawa. He publishes on topics relating to the psychosocial aspects of lifelong sport participation, the effective programming of adult sport, and messaging to promote adult sport. His research focuses on how and why older sportspersons commit to sport, barriers to participation, the influence of age-related perceptions, and instructional approaches with older sportspersons.

Diane M. Culver is an Associate Professor in the School of Human Kinetics, University of Ottawa in Canada. Her research interests include coach development and qualitative research. She is currently funded by the Social Sciences and Humanities Research Council of Canada to research parasport coaching, and women in sport organisations. In her teaching, research, and consulting she is particularly interested in social learning theory and building social learning capability in sport. Diane is also an Alpine ski coach who has worked with all levels of skiers from youth to Olympic levels. She now coaches masters skiers and mentors youth coaches.

Tania Cassidy is an Associate Professor in the area of Sport Pedagogy at the University of Otago. She is the first author of a co-authored text entitled *Understanding Sports Coaching: The social, cultural and pedagogical foundations of sports practice* (2004, 2009, 2106; Routledge). Tania is on the Editorial Boards of eight international journals which publish research on, and about, sports coaching. Tania's research interests are informed by both interpretive and critical perspectives and include: the pedagogy of sports coaching and coach education/development; youth development and sports coaching, and; politics and policies of coach development and education. As well as teaching and research in the area of sports coaching Tania is still an active field hockey player, representing her province in national age group tournaments, a competitive lawn bowler as well as an active sport administrator at the local and national level.

Chapter 13
Coaching Athletes with Disabilities

Diane M. Culver, Erin Kraft, Pierre Trudel, Tiago Duarte, and Penny Werthner

Abstract The sport coaching literature on coaching athletes with disabilities is relatively nascent but researchers are becoming increasingly interested in the domain (e.g., Cregan, Bloom, & Reid. Research Quarterly for Exercise and Sport 78 (4):339–350, 2007; Culver & Werthner. Qualitative Research in Sport, Exercise and Health 10(2):167–175, 2017; McMaster & Culver. Qualitative Research in Sport, Exercise and Health 4(2):226–243, 2012; Duarte & Culver. Journal of Applied Sport Psychology 26(4):441–456, 2014). While the majority of the current research has examined the coaching of athletes with physical disabilities, there is a small body of research that looks at coaching athletes with intellectual disabilities. In this chapter, we will describe the context of disability sport coaching and discuss what the current research is telling us. Moreover, we will provide an overview of a selection of international coach education programs for coaches in disability sport and explore the existing landscape of disability sport coaches' learning opportunities (or lack thereof). Examples of the countries reviewed include Canada, United States, United Kingdom, Australia, China, Northern Ireland, New Zealand, Brazil. This section is concluded with a synthesis of the issues present across coach education for disability sport. Finally, we introduce a coach development model and an accompanying vignette to illustrate a pathway for continued learning. This model may enable disability sport coaches to maximize their learning experiences and continue to develop their practices, despite there being a dearth of formal coach education programs. Our hope is that these insights inspire growth in coaches and sport organizations involved in disability sport to better serve this community.

Keywords Intellectual disabilities · Learning opportunity · Coach development model

---

D. M. Culver (✉) · E. Kraft · P. Trudel · T. Duarte
School of Human Kinetics, University of Ottawa, Ottawa, ON, Canada
e-mail: dculver@uottawa.ca; ekraf090@uottawa.ca; ptrudel@uottawa.ca; tduar016@uottawa.ca

P. Werthner
Faculty of Kinesiology, University of Calgary, Calgary, AB, Canada
e-mail: werthner@ucalgary.ca

R. Resende, A. R. Gomes (eds.), *Coaching for Human Development and Performance in Sports*, https://doi.org/10.1007/978-3-030-63912-9_13

Sport for Individuals with disabilities has its roots in the Stoke Mandeville hospital in England where Sir. Ludwig Guttmann promoted sport for rehabilitation purposes (DePauw & Gavron, 2005). The United Nations Convention on Rights for Persons with Disabilities (CRPD) (2006) defines disability as follows: "Persons with Disabilities include those who have long-term physical, mental, intellectual or sensory impairments which in interaction with various barriers may hinder their full and effective participation in society on an equal basis with others" (United Nations [UN], CRPD, 2006, p. 4). Beyond the CRPD, we might ask why is it important to develop and support sport for persons with a disability? According to the World Health Organisation (WHO, 2011), more than one billion people live with a disability; roughly 13% of the world's population. For these people to fully participate in society and be healthy physically and mentally, we would argue they should be provided with sport opportunities similar to those afforded to able-bodied individuals.

Disability sport is a broad term for sport for the disabled, while parasport refers to sport for those athletes, mostly with physical disabilities, who compete in sports that are part of the Paralympics. In terms of numbers of athletes, the Paralympics is now the second largest sporting event in the world, after the Olympics (International Paralympic Committee; IPC, n.d.b), having grown from 400 athletes from 23 countries in Rome in 1960 to 4342 athletes representing 159 National Paralympic Committees in Rio in 2016. The Paralympics are a high-performance competition and athletes need to meet certain performance criteria, while the Special Olympics are open to athletes of any ability over the age of 8 years. To be a Special Olympian, participants must live with an intellectual disability; that is a cognitive delay or a developmental disability. More specifically, the three criteria to be met are: Intellectual functioning level (IQ) below 70–75; important limitations existing in two or more adaptive skill areas assessed in everyday living; and manifestation of the condition before the age of 18. According to the Special Olympics (n.d.a), as many as 200 million people across the globe live with an intellectual disability, and over two and half million of these people compete in Special Olympics programs (Gregg, 2010). Recently, at the World Games in Abu Dhabi, 192 countries participated (Special Olympics, n.d.b).

Coaching disability sport has been identified as a research priority since the 1980s (DePauw & Gavron, 2005). However, the sport coaching literature on coaching athletes with disabilities is relatively recent and researchers have become increasingly interested in this domain (e.g., Cregan, Bloom, & Reid, 2007; Culver & Werthner, 2017; Duarte & Culver, 2014; McMaster, Culver, & Werthner, 2012). While most studies have examined the coaching of athletes with physical disabilities, there are several that look at coaching athletes with intellectual disabilities, which we will also address in this paper. Through our work as researchers and consultants we have explored the perceptions of coaches and athletes, attempting to tease out the skills and knowledge of coaching that are specific to disability sport. Currently, one of the major hurdles facing coaches and sport organizations involved in disability sport is the lack of coach education specific to coaching athletes with a disability. After presenting a brief overview of the context and some of the research, as well as an international scan of the current coach education opportunities (or lack of specific programs) for these coaches, an innovative approach to the training of these coaches is outlined.

Coaching Athletes with Disabilities: The Context and What the Research Tells Us

The two overarching groups of athletes living with a disability are those with physical impairments and those with intellectual disabilities. The opportunities for involvement in sport for those living with a disability range from integration in sport for able-bodied activities (e.g., a swimmer with a disability swims with able-bodied swimmers) to participation in disability specific competitions such as wheelchair sports (e.g., wheelchair basketball, rugby, tennis) or regional Special Olympics programs. There are athletes living with both physical and intellectual disabilities, and some high functioning athletes in this category can compete at the Paralympics in one of a few sports that offer competitions for all categories of disability (e.g., athletics, swimming). The IPC (n.d.c) defines intellectual impairment as follows: "A limitation in intellectual functioning and adaptive behaviour as expressed in conceptual, social and practical adaptive skills, which originates before the age of 18". The other nine IPC categories are: visual, impaired muscle power, impaired passive range of motion, limb deficiency, leg length difference, short stature, hypertonia, ataxia, and athetosis.

Research on coaching disability sport, while still sparse, has increased over the last 15 years. Most of this research has focused on coaching athletes with physical disabilities (e.g., Cregan et al., 2007; McMaster et al., 2012). While some of these studies have been conducted with coaches of elite athletes (e.g., Falcão, Bloom, & Loughead, 2015), others have included those coaching entry and developmental level athletes (e.g., Duarte & Culver, 2014). A handful of studies have examined coaching athletes with intellectual disabilities (e.g., Cybulski, Culver, Kraft, & Forneris, 2016; Kraft, Leblanc, & Culver, 2019; Luiselli et al., 2013). Moreover, in the last decade there have been a number of very informative articles and chapters published about coaching disability sport (e.g., Clark & Woodson-Smith, 2019; Cybulski et al., 2016; Gregg, 2010; MacDonald & Beck, 2014; Martin, 2010). These articles and chapters include specific strategies for coaching athletes living with a variety of different disabilities, both physical and intellectual.

The research on coaching athletes with physical disabilities has examined the overall situation, the pathways and learning opportunities for such coaches, and the views of athletes regarding good coaching. For the latter, there appears to be a paradox in terms of what athletes with a disability wish for in a coach. Despite several researchers recommending that coaches should approach coaching parasport in the same way as able-bodied sport (e.g., Cregan et al., 2007), the situation is in reality more complex. The poem "Same—but Different", constructed from the words of parasport athletes on what they desire in a coach, clearly portrays this paradox (Culver & Werthner, 2017). On one hand, the athletes wish to be treated like any other athlete, but on the other hand, they want a coach who understands their disability and the effects of training on their disability and their life. In regard to the overall situation for coaching disability sport, a notable finding is that until recently as majority of parasport athletes have self-coached; and this is true in both wealthy and developing countries, indicating that there is a shortage of coaches for parasport (Martin, 2010). As well, we have documented a paucity of programmes for para athletes, at least in Canada. One young wheelchair basketball player had to be driven nearly two hours each way to practice (McMaster et al., 2012). In another instance, a wheelchair curler had to travel five or six hours to compete with other wheelchair curling athletes (Duarte, Culver, & Paquette, 2020). Somewhat ironically, our research has uncovered a dearth of opportunities for coaches to work with these athletes due to a lack of participants (e.g., McMaster et al., 2012). It has also been noted that some coaches, particularly those coaching in an able-bodied sport setting like athletics or swimming can find themselves coaching a parasport athlete who turns up looking for a place to train. Such a parasport athlete might rapidly move from grassroots, to developmental, to elite level competitions (Culver, Kraft, & Duarte, 2019). This accelerated pathway of athlete development in parasport presents considerable challenges for the coach.

Studies on coach pathways in parasport portray a picture of mostly able-bodied coaches working with disabled athletes (DePauw & Gavron, 2005; Duarte & Culver, 2014). There are exceptions to this. McMaster et al. (2012) had two of five coach participants who were persons with a disability. Both coached in a wheelchair sport, and both were novice coaches with 3 or less years of coaching, whereas the other three coaches in this study were very experienced, having between 12 and 35 years of coaching experience, much of which was in disability sport. The researchers noted that, given that we know, coaches make use of their own athletic experiences when starting to coach, and it would be important to better understand how being disabled influences a coach's ability to coach disability sport.

The situation in Special Olympics appears to be different, at least in Canada, where more than 21,000 volunteers, including coaches, work in over 5500 programmes across the country. Many of these volunteers are family members of Special Olympics athletes, or high school students doing their ministry of education required volunteer hours. An applied project conducted with Special Olympics Canada documented that other Special Olympics coaches cross over from generic (this is the Special Olympics term referring to sport for athletes not living with a disability) sport and find the experience so rewarding that they never leave. Nonetheless, the challenges for Special Olympics coaches can be considerable, and a strong mentorship program is recommended for those starting out in this context.

In terms of learning opportunities, the next section of this chapter will provide an overview of coach education programmes for coaches of athletes with a disability. Internationally, countries have developed a number of programs to educate and prepare their coaches to coach athletes with a disability. These programs vary greatly between and across countries, from two-hour workshops to 2-year post-secondary programs. The following section will explore a selection of current programs offered globally, along with a discussion of the lack of opportunities available.

Coach Education Programs for Coaching Disability Sport

Canada Since the introduction of The Policy on Sport for Persons with a Disability in 2006 (Canadian Heritage, 2006), numerous policies and initiatives have been put in place across Canada to promote inclusive sport participation. For example, the most recent version of the Canadian Sport Policy (Sport Information Resource Centre, 2012) included a section dedicated to Inclusive opportunities, defined as resources for both equitable and accessible sport. Notwithstanding, programming for coach development to match this progress is lagging behind compared to that for able-bodied / generic sport.

In 2017, the Coaching Association of Canada (CAC) released their first National Coaching Certification Program (NCCP) eLearning module for Coaching Athletes with a Disability (CAC, 2017). A step in the right direction, the module is suggested to take 45 min to complete, acting as an introduction to coaching athletes with a disability. In terms of intellectual disability, the CAC in partnership with Special Olympics Canada offers a Community Sport Coach workshop (1 day) and a Competition Coach workshop (2 days). As with the eLearning module, while these appear to be valuable initiatives there are minimal long-term implications for coach development. Concerningly, these workshops and modules created specifically for coaching athletes with a disability tend to be quite general; often the coach development piece lacks disability specific information. Another example of this general approach is seen in the Long-Term Athlete Development (LTAD) for Athletes with Disabilities, 2nd Edition: No Accidental Champions, developed by Canadian Sport for Life (Higgs et al., 2013). Again, there is a promising compilation of considerations for and influences over LTAD for athletes with a disability. However, in terms of coach education, coaches are directed to their NSOs (National Sport Organization) and DSOs (Disability Sport Organization) without any concrete or applied content for their practice. In sum, such resources provide few practical suggestions for understanding how to effectively coach athletes with a disability.

At the provincial level, PSOs (Provincial Sport Organizations) often facilitate coach education opportunities by sport. For example, the Coaches Association of Ontario (CAO) has a page dedicated to Parasport Coaching Pathways. In many cases however, an exploration of specific sports through their respective websites revealed the only courses actively offered were able-bodied specific. This likely creates a challenge in terms of coach recruitment and retention in disability sport, if there are no educational opportunities for interested coaches to develop their practice.

United States Unlike their Canadian counterparts, the United states does not have a specific national organization to govern their coach education and development although there are a number of organizations offering coach education programs. One example is Disabled Sports USA which aims to provide national leadership and opportunities for persons with a disability, as well as coach development opportunities. They offer sport specific training throughout the calendar year in various states. However, this may cause some challenges for coaches seeking educational opportunities, depending on their location and sport. Additionally, Disabled Sports USA offers online webinars and sport specific manuals for coaches. Webinar content covers topics from "Tips for building successful programs" to "Understanding and Working with People Who Have Traumatic Brain Injury—TBI". Similar to the Canadian programs, these webinars are often quite short, ranging from under 20 min to just over an hour.

Targeting a different population, the American Association of Adapted Sports Programs (AAASP), provides coach education programs for personnel in schools coaching students with physical disabilities. It is a "not-for-profit association dedicated to developing adapted interscholastic sport programs in partnership with national, state, and local educational agencies" (AAASP, n.d., para.1). Although a training tab is available on their website, no current opportunities are provided. However, this organization does provide a number of resources for coaches including: Rules Handbooks, Skills & Drills, and Guides (i.e., terminology, best practices).

In terms of high-performance coach education, the US Paralympic Committee offers a coaches' corner directing coaches to resources for developing athletes with Paralympic-eligible impairments. These resources vary considerably by sport. For example, the Professional Ski Instructors of America (PSIA) offers certification pathways which include adaptive skiing and snowboarding. Others include the adaptive training into their general training, such as the sport of archery. Finally, some sports such as cycling do not offer adaptive specific training, demonstrating the inconsistencies between sports.

United Kingdom The UK is one country that shows a wide range of coach education programs for disability sport from the University level to the recreational level. There are two post-secondary institutions in the UK offering degrees in disability sport coaching. First, the University of Worcester offers a 3-year degree program called the Sports Coaching Science with Disability Sport, BSc. This program includes courses on practice and pedagogy, as well as a professional placement. Similarly, Liverpool John Moores University offers a 2-year foundations degree in the discipline of Disability Sport Coaching and Development and provides courses such as strength and conditioning, and Paralympic sport, along with a placement opportunity.

For those not wishing to pursue their coach education through a degree program, learning opportunities are more challenging to find. UK Coaching is an organization that collaborates with sport organizations to support coach learning (among other activities). In terms of disability sport coaching, their website indicates that they offer two workshops on disability sport coaching which are both accompanied by guides for future coaches. One is titled Inclusive Coaching: Disability, and the other How to Coach Disabled People in Sport. It is important to note there are no currently scheduled versions of these workshops available through their search tool. A second example of an organization in the UK that seems to be geared towards the recreational level is Disability Sports Coach. They offer courses ranging from one to six hours, covering topics from Disability Awareness in Sport to an Adapted Sports Course. Similar to what we see in Canada and the USA, many of these organizations provide one-time educational opportunities that do not necessarily support coaches over the course of their coaching careers.

China In China, there was very little accessible information about their current coach education programs specific to coaching athletes with a disability. A professor at the Beijing Sport University, Dr. Chi Jian produced a document outlining the history of sport for persons with a disability in China and discussed coach education (Jian, n.d.). However, in terms of locating these coach education opportunities, the information is not readily available.

Australia According to Wareham, Burkett, Innes, and Lovell (2018) most Australian coaches of elite athletes with a disability engage primarily in informal and non-formal learning situations for professional development. Nevertheless, there are some Australian organizations offering accreditation and workshops for coaches working with athletes with a disability. These learning opportunities seem to be geared towards both a competitive and recreational level. One example is seen in Sport CONNECT, a partnership between Riding for the Disabled Association Limited and Pony Club Australia. These equestrian organizations offer two courses accredited by the National Coaching Accreditation Scheme (NCAS). In addition to accrediting courses, they provide a number of other basic training opportunities (e.g., Introductory Instructors Certificate).

Disabled Wintersport Australia is another organization offering training clinics. These clinics are geared to specific sports and/or disabilities (e.g., Teach Adaptive Ski or Snowboard to Beginners) and range from 1 to 2 days in length; upon conducting a search of upcoming clinics, no events were currently listed, at the time of writing this paper. As seen with previous countries, long-term development opportunities for coaches do not seem to be available and more concerningly, websites continue to advertise educational opportunities with no concrete dates and times for coaches to participate.

Northern Ireland In Northern Ireland, coach education opportunities seem to generally occur through 1 day workshops and training. One organization that provides training at the recreational level is Disability Sport Northern Ireland. Their workshop is geared to teachers wishing to teach sports to children with intellectual and physical disabilities. Another organization also offering a broad scope of educational opportunities is the CARA Centre in Northern Ireland. According to their website: "CARA coordinates, develops and delivers inclusive training and education workshops across the Sport, Fitness, Adventure and Education sectors. All our workshops are designed to equip participants with the knowledge, competence and skills necessary to include people with disabilities in sport and physical activity and increase quality provision" (CARA, n.d., para.1). These courses range from two to six hours in length and include topics such as Disability Inclusion Training and Autism in Sport. Additionally, CARA was funded by Sport Ireland to create a "CARA Training and Education Framework" to support coach education. A third organization is the Cork Sports Partnership (consisting of a merge between the Cork County Sports Partnership and Cork City Sports Partnership). Their two main training opportunities include the Disability Inclusion Training, taking place over six hours covering both theoretical and practical content, as well as the Disability Awareness in Sport Workshop taking place over two hours. A final example is offered by the Irish Football Association. They provide a four-hour course introducing both practical examples and theoretical concepts for coaching athletes with a disability. But for those looking for more, the association provides a 2-day, 15-h course. In addition to the course, coaches are required to complete 10 h coaching an athlete with a disability. Although promising initiatives, the most recent courses offered (according to their website) were in 2016. Overall, many of Northern Ireland's coach education programs for disability sport are quite general in nature, as is seen in other countries.

New Zealand New Zealand provides several coach development opportunities, with emphasis on their high-performance domain. However, as we have seen previously, high-performance and disability sport are often separated; this is illustrated by the Paralympics New Zealand website. Coaches working with high performance Para-athletes may be invited to participate in a coach development opportunity called the Performance Coach Advance Program. An investigation of the program indicates that it is high-performance focused on able-bodied athletes rather than disability focused. This also seems to be the case for high performance disability sport coaches. Many of their learning opportunities (workshops and programmes) combine Olympic/Paralympic coaches, which might compromise the opportunity for developing disability specific knowledge.

In terms of community Parasport coaching, the New Zealand Paralympic website suggests that coaches contact their NSO for sport specific (e.g., Swimming, Athletics) educational opportunities. For organizations that do not provide these opportunities, the website encourages contacting the Halberg AllSport for their No Exceptions Training. This training offers "a nationwide package of workshops for teachers, teacher aides, coaches, tertiary students and activity providers on adapting sport, physical activity and recreation to ensure they can include physically disabled New Zealanders" (Halberg AllSports, para. 1). The course includes two, one-hour workshops with both practical and theoretical concepts. In addition, their website offers resources which include documents and videos. The videos are one to two minutes in length and cover topics from inclusion to practical games. The documents also provide additional tools including monitor keys.

Brazil Coach development in Brazil has its unique characteristics as the coaching profession is established and regulated by the council of physical education (CREF—Conselho Regional de Educação Física). The Brazilian law requires its coaches to hold a university diploma in physical education in order to work in any type of physical activity (e.g., Milistetd, Penzia, Trudel, & Paquette, 2018). Therefore, Brazilian coaches are formally trained in many areas of sport science. In parasport, a few courses are offered at the university level (e.g., adapted physical activity, adapted sports).

The Brazilian Paralympic Committee (CPB) has created initiatives to stimulate the development of coaches in Brazil. The main hub concerned with coach education is called "Academia Paralímpica Brasileira" (APB) with a mandate to disseminate scientific knowledge on parasport, search for partnerships with educational institutions across the country and around the world, develop and support parasport related researchers, publish and transfer the scientific knowledge through the organization and funding of conferences, congress, books, etc. (CPB, 2018).

The APB organizes a series of events including the "Congresso Paradesportivo Internacional" or the International Parasport Congress that has had six editions since 2010. In 2018, the CPI published the congress annals containing almost 250 abstracts of its oral presentations. Such popularity sparked the creation of regional seminars. The seminars were delivered in six different regions with the goal of facilitating the access of physical educators, occupational therapists, and other people working with athletes with disabilities across the country. Recently, the CPB launched an e-learning module of 40 h entitled "Paralimpic Movement: basic foundations of the sport". According to CPB (2019), the e-learning module had 5000 plus people enrolled in the first week of registration.

While not conclusive, the above provides a global overview of the educational resources available to coaches interested in coaching disability sport. Based on the above, the following section examines the question: What is missing for these coaches?

Issues with Coach Education for Disability Sport

Short-Term and Scarce Coach Development for Coaching Athletes with a Disability As we have seen on an international level, the majority of educational opportunities for coaches take a short-term approach to disability sport coaching education. However, some countries offer full degrees, requiring a several year commitment. In the event a coach does decide to make this multi-year investment in their education, these post-secondary programs still do not seem to provide long-term learning beyond graduation, demonstrating an interesting trend across disability sport coach development. This is not an issue that is exclusive to specific levels of coaching. For example, in the high-performance context, there are many ongoing opportunities for coach development, but often in the able-bodied context. As we saw in New Zealand, coach education is offered in the high-performance context, but not the Paralympic context. Coaches likely have to choose to attend training for high performance sport or disability sport, but not together, demonstrating a gap in learning opportunities. Another barrier is accessing discipline specific training as the opportunities are scarce. For example, in the US, some organizations offer a variety of workshops for a number of sports, but finding one in the right location and in the right sport is not easy thus creating further barriers for disability sport coach education.

Training Generally Broad and Inconsistent Within and Between Countries

Another concern in disability sport coach education is the generalized content of the programming. In many cases there is an emphasis on inclusive sport which is certainly of great importance however this alone will not prepare coaches for the individual needs of their athletes within a specific sport. As well, there are inconsistencies in disability sport coach education across the globe. As mentioned previously, some countries dedicate entire degrees to coach education in disability sport, where in many other countries, coaches may only participate in a one-hour workshop. These inconsistencies pose challenges for coaches in terms of what they need to know to be effective in coaching athletes with a disability.

Research Supporting the Idea that There Is a Lack of Learning Opportunities

Many of the programs discussed above support the findings from recent coach development research, in that disability sport coaches must seek educational opportunities beyond their formal coach education to develop discipline specific knowledge. Considering there are countries where it was quite challenging to find coach education opportunities (e.g., China and Japan) it is not surprising that accessing informal and non-formal training would be sourced to fill this gap. Douglas, Falcão, and Bloom (2018) studied coaches with comparable experiences and noted "The findings revealed that they [coaches] acquired most of their knowledge from a combination of knowledge gained as athletes and informal sources, including trial and error. They also stressed the need for enhanced recruiting of parasport coaches and parasport coach education opportunities that would enhance programs for athletes with physical disabilities, from grassroots to Paralympic levels" (p. 93). Although this article discusses coaches working with athletes with physical disabilities, the lack of educational opportunities seems to be the same for coaches working with athletes with intellectual disabilities: "Coaches primarily learned by doing and by consulting with coaching peers. Information about ideal sources of coaching knowledge demonstrates that coaches would value structured coaching courses, learning from mentors and from administrative support, in addition to learning on their own and from peers" (MacDonald, Beck, Erickson, & Côté, 2016, p. 242). On a final note, Cronin, Angus, Huntley, and Hayton (2018) recently studied coaches who had worked with able-bodied athletes in high-performance sport and transitioned into disability sport. One coach had previously coached basketball at a high level and was confident in his coaching skills, but found it challenging to begin coaching athletes with disabilities. Coach education at the elite level seems to often be categorized into high-performance sport or disability sport, likely causing a barrier for coaches wanting to learn about both contexts.

Becoming a Coach of Athletes with Disabilities

As discussed in the sections above, coaches of athletes with disabilities need knowledge and skills in many different aspects of the coaching process. In many countries, when national governing bodies have developed and implemented coach education programs, to help coaches accomplish their work, they provide certification, which is often needed to coach at a specific level. As a result, the certification process tends to monopolize the discourse on how to prepare coaches to coach. Although essential, these programs will never fully meet the needs of all the coaches because (a) they must be seen as episodic learning experiences—a moment where we are conscious and aware of what we know and don't know (Jarvis, 2006)—that often take place only over a few hours (b) the content comes from or is an adaptation of the programs for coaching able-bodied athletes and is therefore rarely specific to the training of athletes with disabilities, (c) the certifications received correspond only to what coaches knew at a specific moment in the past, and (d) in the research, coaches have mentioned that they learn to coach through different sources of knowledge acquisition (e.g., He, Trudel, & Culver, 2018; MacDonald et al., 2016; Werthner & Trudel, 2009).

In an attempt to provide a global view on how coaches learn to coach, we have recently published an article (Trudel, Gilbert, & Rodrigue, 2016) in which we presented a model (see Fig. 13.1) and also illustrated a typical coach's learning journey by telling the story of a fictional—yet representative—coach coaching able-bodies athletes.

The model contains three components: the coaching contexts, the coach identity evolution, and the learning situations. There is a trend now to recognize the specificities of the different levels of coaching, even for coach education. The three coaching contexts used in the model are the categories suggested by Trudel and Gilbert (2006) as they seem to align relatively easily with those in many countries. The second component, the different learning situations, is separated into three categories: mediated, unmediated, and internal learning situations. This terminology has been used repeatedly in the coaching literature to classify the sources of knowledge acquisition of coaches (e.g., Christensen, 2014; Mesquita, Ribeiro, Santos, & Morgan, 2014; Rynne & Mallett, 2014; Trudel, Culver, & Werthner, 2013). Mediated learning situations are defined as situations 'decided for the learner' (Moon, 2004). In other words, they are situations in which the material presented to

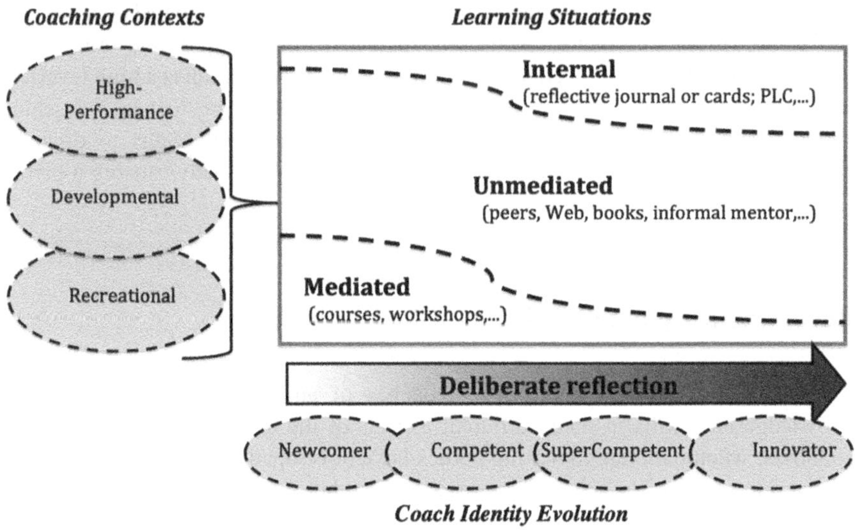

Fig. 13.1 How sport coaches learn to coach. Adapted from "The journey from competent to innovator: Using appreciative inquiry to enhance high performance coaching" by Trudel, P., Gilbert, W., & Rodrigue, F. (2016). *AI Practitioner, 18*(2), 40–46. Permission obtained

the learner is selected and controlled by another entity. Formal coach education programs are the best example of these situations, along with many of the continuous professional development activities. In unmediated learning situations, the learner takes the initiative and is responsible for choosing what/how/when to learn, such as discussing with colleagues or informal mentors, searching on the Web, reading books, etc. In the third type—internal learning situations—the learner is not exposed to new material, but instead reorganizes existing ideas. The expression "cognitive housekeeping" is used to illustrate this type of learning situation. Examples of internal learning situations are scheduling time to reflect, writing in a reflective journal, and even having a personal learning coach (PLC). The third component of the model is labelled "Coach identity evolution". In an early version of the model (Trudel & Gilbert, 2013), the categories were those suggested by Schempp, McCullick, and Mason (2006; beginner, competent, proficient, and expert) to explain the stages to develop expert coaches. Taking into consideration the emergence of new perspectives regarding how coaches learn (e.g., communities of practice, Culver & Trudel, 2008; Stoszkowski & Collins, 2012) and the impact of globalisation and technology (e.g., creativity and innovation, Hoque, 2014; Stack, 2010), the four categories are now: Newcomer, competent, supercompetent, and innovator. A newcomer coach is not a beginner; he/she is a coach entering in a new coaching context. For example, a coach might have many years of coaching experience at the development level but if he/she accepts a position at the high-performance level, he/she will be considered a newcomer. The term competent is often linked with coach education and certification, especially with the growing push to make sport coaching a profession. Therefore a 'competent coach' is a coach who is recognized by an organization as having a minimum of knowledge to coach at a specific level. Nowadays, and especially in sport, it is not enough to be competent; we need to be able to consistently perform at a high level. The 'supercompetent coach' will have the ability to adapt knowledge and skills learned during their training to progressively develop their own coaching style. A coach will reach the category of 'innovator coach' when he/she feels confident enough to challenge the way things are usually done and to take risks in the service of innovation. The dotted lines used in the model stress that the categories that form the three components must be seen as continuums rather than well-defined elements. There are three key aspects of this model that need to be mentioned. First, a coach at the recreational context can move from newcomer to innovator as well as a coach at the high-performance context. Second, the sources of learning for the newcomer and the competent coaches are composed mainly by mediated, and unmediated learning situations. The learning of the supercompetent and innovator coaches depends less on mediated learning situations since they would have completed most of the required certifications. They will still learn by looking for information (unmediated) to address their coaching challenges. Finally, the element that will help coaches to move toward the categories of supercompetent and innovator is their ability to reserve/create moments to deliberately reflect on their coaching practice (internal learning situations). Coaches like most people, often struggle to take the time to step back and reflect, which suggests that there are a lot of competent coaches, a fair number of supercompetent coaches, and very few innovator coaches.

The Coach Learning Model in Action

To illustrate the model, we decided to construct the story of a fictional learning journey of a coach of athletes with disabilities (Rachel). We believe that this story is representative because it is based on ten articles addressing how coaches of athletes with disability learn to coach (Cregan et al., 2007; Douglas et al., 2018; Duarte & Culver, 2014; Duarte, Culver, Trudel, & Milistedt, 2018; Fairhurst, Bloom, & Harvey, 2017; Kraft & Leblanc, 2018; MacDonald et al., 2016; McMaster et al., 2012; Taylor, Werthner, & Culver, 2014; Taylor, Werthner, Culver, & Callary, 2015). If we add the number of coaches interviewed in these studies, we can say that the story is based on the perspectives of 112 coaches.

Rachel's Story I was born in a family where the practice of sports was very strong. Every weekend we left on Friday night for the cottage. During the winter we did cross country skiing, downhill skiing, and skating on the lake; and during the summer it was swimming and sailing. My preference was swimming. I trained intensively when I was at the university for my degree in physical education. I wanted to teach at the secondary level. I won a few medals at national competitions but fell short of making the national team. In my last year at the undergraduate level, I answered an ad asking for an assistant coach for the swimming varsity team. I enjoyed this coaching environment and decided to stay for a couple of years. The main reasons were (a) the head coach was great and I was learning a lot with him, (a) we had a good group of 20 swimmers with a nice balance between men and women, (b) I had the opportunity to register for a master's degree in sport administration, and (c) a new sports complex was opening on campus with a fantastic swimming pool. Because the new building was more accessible for people with disabilities, a few athletes with disabilities knocked at the door to train with us. At this moment, the head coach asked me if I would accept to be in charge of the training of a group of six athletes with disabilities. I said "why not?". In my degree in physical education I had taken a few courses specific to the 'adapted physical activity population' and I had a life experience where I spent time with a person that has a disability. At the cottage we had a very good friend with whom I practiced all sports; Michelle was born with one arm shorter than the other. I have always been impressed by her determination. She always found a way to adapt her environment to be able to follow us. In fact, she was often better than we were. Thus, I thought that it would not be a big deal to coach only six athletes. I was so wrong. Each of them had their own physiological disability, which meant being at a different place in the classification system. Instead of one training plan to prepare and then slightly adapt it to the athletes' needs as I was doing for the able-bodies athletes, it was six completely different training plans. I can say that even if I was a newcomer in coaching athletes with disabilities, I found myself coaching a group of athletes who were evolving in either the recreational, developmental, or high-performance context. To accompany my athletes to competitions I had to be certified by the sport federation even if I had a bachelor in physical education. Unfortunately, coach education programs specific to disability sports are rare and it was suggested to get my certification through the regular able-bodied coach education program in swimming. In reality, what helped me the most was my network. I had kept contact with two of my professors who were experts in sport physiology and sport biomechanics, a friend put me in touch with her father who was a wheelchair athlete trainer and he became my mentor, at competitions I found it very easy to share disability specific knowledge with other coaches, and I frequently searched on the Web for new information. I quickly noticed that my best sources of information were the athletes and their parents. Thus, I needed to establish a good communication system with them and also with some health care specialists, especially doctors and physiotherapists. Progressively, I fine-tuned my coaching approach and after 12 years, I feel a lot more competent; I could say I am supercompetent. This is probably the reason why now I have a group of 15 athletes and one assistant coach that I am mentoring. With the advances in sport training and the new technology, I think we should reflect more about the limits of our program and how to improve things. But to do this effectively, I need to book time, but when? I already work more than 50 h a week. I would need someone to help me to innovate and to keep learning.

Rachel's story highlights that learning to coach in disability sport is a lifelong learning journey and because specific coach education programs for coaches of athletes with disabilities (mediated learning situations) are not fully available, these coaches have to be proactive and deliberately search for, or create their own meaningful learning situations (unmediated). For those experienced coaches who are now certified, acting as mentor, and feel they still need to learn and even innovate; they might look at what is happening in the business world, and secure the support of a personal coach. Recently a few researchers in the sport field have studied the impact of providing a 'personal learning coach' to help experienced coaches reflect on their current coaching practices (Milistetd et al., 2018; Rodrigue, Trudel, & Boyd, 2019).

Key Points

1. It is important for disability sport coaches to be proactive and deliberate in creating/searching for meaningful learning opportunities. As seen above, formalized learning opportunities remain scarce for disability sport coaches across several countries. Thus, a lifelong learning approach serves well for the continuous development of coaching practice.
2. Participation in all three types of learning situations (mediated, unmediated, internal), with specific emphasis on reflection, is significant for disability sport coaches to fine-tune their coaching approaches.
3. Coaches should access several different sources for knowledge/information (coaches, personal coaches, athletes, families, mentors), as each athlete will require a different approach according to their needs.

Conclusion

In conclusion, it is clear that more research is required to better understand how to develop the best learning situations for coaches of athletes with a disability. Formal coach education programmes around the world, while creating a basic and important level of learning for coaches, have several critical limitations. The formal coach education courses are often inconsistent in their availability, rarely have material that is specific to disability sport situations, and are, more often than not, too short in length to allow for rich discussion and reflective practice. As a result, coaches in disability sport turn to unmediated learning situations to continue to learn—talking with other coaches, working and listening to the athletes themselves and their parents, and working with sport science experts in the field. Importantly, unmediated learning situations are most effective when coaches begin to utilize what we call internal learning situations, where they begin to reflect, to perhaps write in a reflective journal, and to reorganize or re-think their coaching practice depending on the athletes they are coaching. An adapted model from Trudel et al. (2016) helps us understand the complexity of learning by illustrating who a coach might be and how they might move from a newcomer coach to an innovator through different learning situations. This complexity is what educators of disability sport coaches must understand in order to allow for on-going learning throughout a coach's career.

References

American Association of Adapted Sports Programs. (n.d.). *About AAASP*. Retrieved from http://adaptedsports.org/about-adaptedsports/overview/

Canadian Heritage. (2006). *Policy on sport for persons with a disability*. Retrieved from www.pch.gc.ca/pgm/sc/pol/spt/tdm-eng.cfm

CARA (n.d.) *Training and education*. Retrieved from https://caracentre.ie/training/

Christensen, M. K. (2014). Exploring biographical learning in elite soccer coaching. *Sport, Education and Society, 19*(2), 204–222.

Clark, B., & Woodson-Smith, A. (2019). Sport for all: Considerations when coaching in disability sport. In R. Thellwell & M. Dicks (Eds.), *Professional advances in sport coaching: Research and practice* (pp. 78–100). Oxon, UK: Routledge.

Coaching Association of Canada (2017). *Coaching athletes with a disability*. Retrieved from https://www.coach.ca/coaching-athletes-with-a-disability%2D%2Ds17345

CPB. (2018). *Regimento interno da academia paralímpica brasileira*. Intern regiment of the Brazilian Paralympic Academy. Retrieved from http://www.cpb.org.br/documents/20181/0/Regimento+da+APB/35fcdca6-44d8-45f5-91f4-946627707141

CPB, (2019). Curso sobre movimento Paralímpico tem cinco mil adesões; Inscrições seguem abertas (Paralympic movement course had five thousand registrations; Subscriptions are still open). Retrieved from http://www.cpb.org.br/web/guest/noticias/-/asset_publisher/lU3LNvrdeyoz/content/curso-sobre-movimento-paralimpico-tem-5-mil-adesoes-inscricoes-seguem-abertas?inheritRedirect=false&redirect=http%3A%2F%2Fwww.cpb.org.br%2Fweb%2Fguest%2Fnoticias%3Fp_p_id%3D101_INSTANCE_lU3LNvrdeyoz%26p_p_lifecycle%3D0%26p_p_state%3Dnormal%26p_p_mode%3Dview%26p_p_col_id%3Dcolumn-3%26p_p_col_count%3D1

Cregan, K., Bloom, G. A., & Reid, G. (2007). Career evolution and knowledge of elite coaches of swimmers with a physical disability. *Research Quarterly for Exercise and Sport, 78*(4), 339–350.

Cronin, C., Angus, R., Huntley, T., & Hayton, J. (2018). 'Sinking and swimming in disability coaching': An autoethnographic account of coaching in a new context. *Qualitative Research in Sport, Exercise and Health, 10*(3), 362–377.

Culver, D., Kraft, E., & Duarte, T. (2019). Social learning in communities and networks as a strategy for on-going coach development. In B. Callary, & B. Gearity (Eds.) *Coach education and development in sport: Instructional strategies*. London: Routledge.

Culver, D., & Trudel, P. (2008). Clarifying the concept of communities of practice in sport. *International Journal of Sports Science & Coaching, 3*(1), 1–10.

Culver, D., & Werthner, P. (2017). Voices: Para athletes speak. *Qualitative Research in Sport, Exercise and Health, 10*(2), 167–175.

Cybulski, S., Culver, D., Kraft, E., & Forneris, T. (2016). Special Olympic coaches: Their views on life skill development and the strategies they use with their athletes. *International Journal of Coaching Science, 10*(2), 3–22.

DePauw, K., & Gavron, S. (2005). *Disability and sport* (2nd ed.). Champaign, IL: Human Kinetics.

Douglas, S., Falcão, W. R., & Bloom, G. A. (2018). Career development and learning pathways of paralympic coaches with a disability. *Adapted Physical Activity Quarterly, 35*(1), 93–110.

Duarte, T., & Culver, D. (2014). Becoming a coach in developmental adaptive sailing: A lifelong learning perspective. *Journal of Applied Sport Psychology, 26*(4), 441–456.

Duarte, T., Culver, D., & Paquette, K. (2020). Mapping Canadian wheelchair curling coaches' development: A landscape metaphor for a systems approach. *International Sport Coaching Journal, 7*(2), 117–128. https://doi.org/10.1123/iscj.2018-0099

Duarte, T., Culver, D., Trudel, P., & Milistedt, M. (2018). Parasport coach development: Evidence from the Canadian context. *LASE Journal of Sport Science, 9*(1), 78–90.

Fairhurst, K. E., Bloom, G. A., & Harvey, W. J. (2017). The learning and mentoring experiences of Paralympic coaches. *Disability and Health Journal, 10*(2), 240–246.

Falcão, W. R., Bloom, G. A., & Loughead, T. M. (2015). Coaches' perceptions of team cohesion in Paralympic sports. *Adapted Physical Activity Quarterly, 32*(3), 206–222.

Gregg, M. (2010). Working with athletes with intellectual disabilities. In S. J. Hanrahan & M. B. Andersen (Eds.), *Routledge handbook of applied sport psychology: A comprehensive guide for students and practitioners* (pp. 441–449). London: Routledge.

Halberg AllSports. (n.d.). *Halberg no exceptions training (NET)*. Retrieved from https://www.halbergallsports.co.nz/no-exceptions-training/halberg-no-exceptions-training-net/

Higgs, C., Bluechardt, M., Balyi, I., Way, R., Jurbala, P., & Legg, D. (2013). *No accidental champions: Long-term athlete development for athletes with disabilities* (2nd ed). Retrieved from http://sportforlife.ca/wp-content/uploads/2016/06/NAC_ENGLISH_SCREEN_rev2013.pdf

He, C., Trudel, P., & Culver, D. (2018). Actual and ideal sources of coaching knowledge of elite Chinese coaches. *International Journal of Sports Science & Coaching, 13*(4), 496–507.

Hoque, F. (2014). *Everything connects: How to transform and lead in the age of creativity, innovation, and sustainability*. New York: McGraw Hill.

IPC. (n.d.-a) *FAQ*. Retrieved from https://www.paralympic.org/frequently-asked-questions

IPC. (n.d.-b). *Paralympics: History of the movement*. Retrieved from https://www.paralympic.org/the-ipc/history-of-the-movement

IPC. (n.d.-c). *Classification introduction*. Retrieved from https://www.paralympic.org/classification

Jarvis, P. (2006). *The theory and practice of teaching* (2nd ed.). New York: Routledge.

Jian, C. (n.d.). *The development of sports for the disabled in China.*. Retrieved from https://sportperformancecentres.org/sites/default/files/7_CHN_Chi_Jian.pdf

Kraft, E., & Leblanc, R. (2018). Instructing children with Autism Spectrum Disorder: Examining swim instructors' knowledge building experiences. *Disability and Health Journal, 11*(3), 451–455.

Kraft, E., Leblanc, R., & Culver, D. (2019). Strategies for teaching children with autism spectrum disorder in recreational aquatics programs. *Journal of Physical Education, Recreation, & Dance, 90*(1), 24–29.

Luiselli, J. K., Duncan, N. G., Keary, P., Nelson, E., Parenteau, R. E., & Woods, K. E. (2013). Behavioral coaching of track athletes with developmental disabilities: Evaluation of sprint performance during training and Special Olympics competition. *Journal of Clinical Sport Psychology, 7*(4), 264–274.

MacDonald, D. J., & Beck, K. (2014). Creating a positive experience for athletes with intellectual disabilities. In D. Hassan, S. Dowling, & R. McConkey (Eds.), *Sport, coaching, and intellectual disability* (pp. 52–68). Oxon, UK: Routledge.

MacDonald, D. J., Beck, K., Erickson, K., & Côté, J. (2016). Understanding sources of knowledge for coaches of athletes with intellectual disabilities. *Journal of Applied Research in Intellectual Disabilities, 29*(3), 242–249.

Martin, J. (2010). Athletes with physical disabilities. In S. J. Hanrahan & M. B. Andersen (Eds.), *Routledge handbook of applied sport psychology: A comprehensive guide for students and practitioners* (pp. 432–440). London: Routledge.

McMaster, S., Culver, D., & Werthner, P. (2012). Coaches of athletes with a physical disability: A look at their learning experiences. *Qualitative Research in Sport, Exercise and Health, 4*(2), 226–243.

Mesquita, I., Ribeiro, J., Santos, S., & Morgan, K. (2014). Coach learning and coach education: Portuguese expert coaches' perspective. *The Sport Psychologist, 28*(2), 124–136.

Milistetd, M., Penzia, L., Trudel, P., & Paquette, K. (2018). Nurturing high-performance sport coaches' learning and development using a narrative-collaborative coaching approach. *LASE Journal of Sport Science, 9*(1), 6–38.

Moon, J. A. (2004). *A handbook of reflective and experiential learning: Theory and practice*. London: Routledge Falmer.

Rodrigue, F., Trudel, P., & Boyd, J. (2019). Learning from practice: The value of a personal learning coach for high-performance coaches. *International Sport Coaching Journal, 6*(3), 285–295. https://doi.org/10.1123/iscj.2018-0078

Rynne, S., & Mallett, C. (2014). Coaches' learning and sustainability in high performance sport. *Reflective Practice, 15*(1), 12–26.

Schempp, P. G., McCullick, B., & Mason, I. (2006). The development of expert coaching. In R. L. Jones (Ed.), *The sports coach as educator: Re-conceptualising sports coaching* (pp. 145–161). London: Routledge.

Special Olympics. (n.d.-a). *Our mission*. Retrieved from https://www.specialolympics.org/about/our-mission

Special Olympics. (n.d.-b). *In the news*. Retrieved from https://www.specialolympics.org/stories/news/abu-dhabi-world-games-sets-special-olympics-record-with-192-participating-nations

Special Olympics Canada. (n.d.). Retrieved from https://www.specialolympics.ca/who-can-be-special-olympics-athlete

Sport Information Resource Centre. (2012). *Canadian sport policy 2012*. Retrieved from http://sirc.ca/sites/default/files/content/docs/pdf/csp2012_en_lr.pdf

Stack, L. (2010). *Super Competent: The six keys to perform at your productive best*. Hoboken, NJ: Wiley.

Stoszkowski, J., & Collins, D. (2012). Communities of practice, social learning and networks: Exploiting the social side of coach development. *Sport, Education and Society, 19*(6), 773–788.

Taylor, S. L., Werthner, P., & Culver, D. (2014). A case study of a parasport coach and a life of learning. *International Sport Coaching Journal, 1*(3), 127–138.

Taylor, S., Werthner, P., Culver, D., & Callary, B. (2015). The importance of reflection for coaches in parasport. *Reflective Practice, 16*(2), 269–284.

Trudel, P., Culver, D., & Werthner, P. (2013). Looking at coach development from the coach-learner's perspective: considerations for coach development administrators. In P. Potrac, W. Gilbert, & J. Denison (Eds.), *Routledge handbook of sports coaching* (pp. 375–387). London: Routledge.

Trudel, P., & Gilbert, W. (2006). Coaching and coach education. In D. Kirk, D. MacDonald, & M. O'Sullivan (Eds.), *Handbook of physical education* (pp. 516–539). Thousand Oaks, CA: Sage.

Trudel, P., & Gilbert, W. (2013). The role of deliberate practice in becoming an expert coach: Part 3—Creating optimal settings. *Olympic Coach Magazine, 24*(2), 15–28.

Trudel, P., Gilbert, W., & Rodrigue, F. (2016). The journey from competent to innovator: Using Appreciative Inquiry to enhance high performance coaching. *AI Practitioner, 18*(2), 40–46.

UN. (2006). *Convention on the rights of persons with disabilities*. New York: United Nations. Retrieved from http://www.un.org/disabilities/documents/convention/convoptprot-e.pdf

Wareham, Y., Burkett, B., Innes, P., & Lovell, G. P. (2018). Coaches of elite athletes with disability: Senior sports administrators' reported factors affecting coaches' recruitment and retention. *Qualitative Research in Sport, Exercise and Health*, 1–18. https://doi.org/10.1080/2159676X.2018.1517388

Werthner, P., & Trudel, P. (2009). Investigating the idiosyncratic learning paths of elite Canadian coaches. *International Journal of Sports Science and Coaching, 4*(3), 433–449.

WHO. (2011). *World report on disability*. Retrieved from https://www.who.int/disabilities/world_report/2011/en/

Diane M. Culver is an Associate Professor in the School of Human Kinetics, University of Ottawa in Canada. Her research interests include coach development and qualitative research. She is currently funded by the Social Sciences and Humanities Research Council of Canada to research parasport coaching, and women in sport organisations. In her teaching, research, and consulting she is particularly interested in social learning theory and building social learning capability in sport. Diane is also an Alpine ski coach who has worked with all levels of skiers from youth to Olympic levels. She now coaches masters' skiers and mentors youth coaches.

Erin Kraft is a doctoral candidate in the School of Human Kinetics at the University of Ottawa. As a former swim coach with over 10 years of experience, Erin primarily coached children with developmental disabilities at the developmental level. She continues working with children with disabilities in the classroom and in the pool as an occasional teacher across Ottawa. Erin's master's in education examined coaches' experiences teaching children with Autism Spectrum Disorders in aquatic programs. Her ongoing doctoral research is focused on Canadian parasport coaches.

Pierre Trudel is an Emeritus Professor in the School of Human Kinetic, University of Ottawa, Canada. His sport research interests focus on the coaching at all levels and the training of high-performance coaches. Pierre has published over 100 articles, and has been a consultant for many sport organizations, developing programmes and supervising coaches. During the last summer Olympic Games in Rio (2016), he conducted a research project for the Canadian Olympic Committee. Trained as a business/life coach, he works with university professors and high-performance coaches in their career development.

Tiago Duarte is a doctoral candidate in the School of Human Kinetics at the University of Ottawa. Since 2004, he has been studying, researching, and working with sport psychology with emphasis on coaches of disability sports. His work has been published in many international outlets such as the "*Journal of Applied Sport Psychology*" and the "*US Olympic Magazine*". Tiago's doctorate studies are funded by the prestigious Joseph-Armand Bombardier scholarship, by the Ontario Graduate Scholarship, and by Sport Canada.

Penny Werthner is a Professor and Dean of the Faculty of Kinesiology, University of Calgary, Penny Werthner's research is in the area of life-long learning from a pedagogical perspective, particularly in the area of high-performance coaches; women and sport; and the use of heart rate variability biofeedback and neurofeedback for optimal performance in high performance sport. She is considered one of Canada's most distinguished consultants in the field of sport psychology. Penny is a former Olympic athlete and has worked with coaches and athletes over the span of 13 summer and winter Olympic Games, from the 1988 winter Olympic Games in Calgary, Canada to the 2018 winter Olympic Games in PyeongChang, Korea. Dr Werthner has written dozens of peer-reviewed papers and book chapters. She currently serves on the editorial board for the *International Sport Coaching Journal* and the *Canadian Journal for Women in Coaching* as well as a reviewer for several journals.

Part III
Challenges of Sports Coaching

Chapter 14
Coaching and Athlete Mental Health

Stewart Vella and Sarah Liddle

Abstract Mental health among athletes has come into sharp focus around the world over recent years. However, the role of the coach in athlete mental health has not been well articulated. This chapter reviews the relationships between sport participation and various indices of mental health, explores the important role of the coach in supporting athlete mental health, and proposes some strategies to increase the likelihood that coaches' have a positive influence on athlete mental health and wellbeing. We outline the potential benefits of an approach to coaching practice and coach education based in self-determination theory for athlete wellbeing. We also discuss the merits of mental health literacy training for coaches. Further, we suggest areas for focus for researchers whereby a meaningful benefit to the field can be made, including strong research designs and methodologies, a focus on non-elite sport, and guidelines for practice. Such advancements will help coaches to engage in evidence- and theory-based practice to the benefit of athlete mental health and wellbeing.

Keywords Wellbeing · Resilience · Motivation · Mental health literacy · Autonomy support

Mental health is an important issue for athletes of all sports, ages, and competitive levels. Numerous positions stand and consensus statements highlight the universal and significant need for attention and action regarding the mental health of sport participants (Henriksen et al., 2019; Moesch et al., 2019; Reardon et al., 2019). The coach may play a particularly important role in the mental health outcomes of sport participation (Ferguson et al., 2019). In this chapter we will outline the relationships between sport participation and various indices of mental health among sport participants, explore the important role of the coach in supporting athlete mental

S. Vella (✉) · S. Liddle
School of Psychology, Faculty of Social Sciences, University of Wollongong, Wollongong, NSW, Australia
e-mail: stvella@uow.edu.au; skl697@uowmail.edu.au

R. Resende, A. R. Gomes (eds.), *Coaching for Human Development and Performance in Sports*, https://doi.org/10.1007/978-3-030-63912-9_14

health, and propose strategies to increase coach competency and intentions to fulfil this role.

Mental health issues are a leading cause of health related burden globally (World Health Organization, 2014), and suicide is the leading cause of death in people aged 15–24 in Australia (Australian Bureau of Statistics, 2017). Although the prevalence of mental illness remains high with approximately 25% of the global population experiencing a mental health problem in their lifetime (Steel et al., 2014; World Health Organization, 2017), help seeking and utilization remains low (World Health Organization, 2014). There is a substantial need to address mental ill-health and promote early intervention for mental health problems around the world.

The importance of athlete mental health has come into sharp focus over the last 2 years. In that time, various sports organisations have published position stands and consensus statements concerning athlete mental health. Such organisations include the International Olympic Committee (Reardon et al., 2019), International Society for Sport Psychology (Henriksen et al., 2019), and the European Federation of Sport Psychology (Moesch et al., 2019). Several reviews have also brought this issue into focus. For example, evidence suggests that athletes experience mental illness at a rate comparable to the non-sporting community (Gulliver, Griffiths, Mackinnon, Batterham, & Stanimirovic, 2015; Rice et al., 2016). Athletes may also experience a range of unique barriers to seeking help (Breslin, Shannon, Haughey, Donnelly, & Leavey, 2017). For these reasons, action on the issue of athlete mental health is both warranted and urgently needed.

Coaches may be in a prime position to act as gate-keepers for athlete mental health. For example, coaches may play a role in identifying possible risk-factors for the development of mental illness, and in facilitating referrals to appropriate mental health resources. Both athletes and their parents have acknowledged that coaches have a role to play in supporting athlete mental health (Brown, Deane, Vella, & Liddle, 2017; Swann et al., 2018). Coaches themselves have also acknowledged support for athlete mental health and wellbeing as part of their role (Ferguson et al., 2019). However, coaches have reported feeling unprepared to take on the role and have requested training in this area (Ferguson et al., 2019; Mazzer & Rickwood, 2015). As such, coaches may currently lack the skill and confidence to act appropriately in the area of athlete mental health (Ferguson et al., 2019; Mazzer & Rickwood, 2015). Therefore, coaches have an important role to play in athlete mental health, but action is needed in order for them to be able to adequately fulfil this role. Specifically, there is a need to develop and implement evidence-based, context-specific mental health training programs for coaches. Those programs should be practical and accessible in order to address the growing concerns around wellbeing and mental illness among sport participants.

Conceptual and Empirical Findings

Conceptualising Mental Health

An understanding of mental health necessitates consideration of both wellbeing and mental illness as distinct components. According to The World Health Organization (2001, p. 1) mental health is not merely the absence of mental illness such as depression, but it is "a state of well-being in which the individual realizes his or her own abilities, can cope with the normal stresses of life, can work productively and fruitfully, and is able to make a contribution to his or her community". This definition of mental health is consistent with Keyes' (2002) model of mental health, in which wellbeing and mental illness are conceptualised as distinct components of mental health. This is in contrast to a conceptualisation of mental illness and wellbeing as sitting on a single spectrum with mental illness at one end of the scale, and wellbeing at the other. According to Keyes (2002) mental illness and wellbeing are two distinct but related continua that contribute to one's overall mental health. This model suggests that, for example, an athlete could simultaneously have high levels of wellbeing while experiencing mental illness, or that they could be free from mental illness but have low levels of wellbeing. If an individual is experiencing low wellbeing and high mental illness, this is termed "languishing". In contrast, if an individual is experiencing high levels of wellbeing and low mental illness, this is called "flourishing". The implication is that an understanding of mental health among athletes necessitates consideration of one's levels of both wellbeing and mental illness as distinct components of mental health.

Individuals who report low levels of wellbeing or high levels of mental illness also report greater levels of impairment and disability (Keyes, 2002, 2005; Keyes & Michalec, 2010). This is important to consider in the context of sport, as an athlete may be free of mental illness but could be experiencing low wellbeing. This could put them at risk of a range of negative outcomes, including impaired performance. The implication for coaches is that they should play a role in simultaneously optimising athlete wellbeing and helping to minimise the harm associated with the onset and development of mental illness.

Sport and Mental Health

At a population level, participation in organised sports has been consistently linked with better mental health. For example, among children and adolescents sport participation is associated with fewer anxiety symptoms, less emotional distress, and fewer mental health problems (Eime, Young, Harvey, Charity, & Payne, 2013b). Among adults, sport participation is associated with lower levels of stress, depression, and emotional distress (Eime, Young, Harvey, Charity, & Payne, 2013a). However, the directionality and causal mechanisms underpinning the association between sport participation and mental health are somewhat unknown. An over reliance on cross-sectional studies limits such assertions. Nonetheless, there are components of the sports environment which may influence the mental health of participants at all levels—for better and worse. Such influences, including the coach, warrant further investigation.

While the prevalence of mental illness among athletes is similar to the general population (Rice et al., 2016), competitive sport may contribute to poor mental health (Bauman, 2016). Athletes may also experience unique risk factors for poor mental health (Donohue, Miller, Crammer, Cross, & Covassin, 2007). For example, stigma may be of a greater concern among athletes when compared to non-athletes (Kaier, Cromer, Johnson, Strunk, & Davis, 2015). A sports culture that typically celebrates masculinity, mental toughness, and disapproval of weakness disclosure (Bauman, 2016) can lead to emotional and psychiatric problems remaining undisclosed (Trojian, 2016). This stigma may perpetuate the under-recognition of mental illness in the sporting population, and therefore risk the delaying of recognition and appropriate treatment for mental illnesses (Bauman, 2016). The role of the coach may therefore include the setting of an appropriate stigma-free climate where athletes feel safe and secure in the disclosure of mental health problems.

Conceptualising mental health as a whole state instead of just the prevention of mental illness may help address the stigma associated with seeking help, and therefore reduce the risk of mental health issues perpetuating and negatively influencing the performance and quality of life of athletes (Uphill, Sly, & Swain, 2016). Athletes and sports participants often have close working relationships with their coaches, and therefore through this relationship coaches may be vital in both the promotion of positive mental health and wellbeing, and the prevention and early intervention of mental illness.

Coaching and Athlete Mental Health

Coaches are an important influence on athlete wellbeing and development across the life-span. Coaches have articulated their own role as inclusive of athlete mental health, including the identification of mental health concerns, facilitating help-seeking, promoting wellbeing, and encouraging ongoing participation in sport (Ferguson et al., 2019; Mazzer & Rickwood, 2015). This is broadly consistent with the definition of coaching effectiveness whereby coaches integrate and apply a broad knowledge base to facilitate positive athlete outcomes which include health and self-worth (Côté & Gilbert, 2009). While mental health outcomes are not explicitly articulated under this definition (see also Côté, Bruner, Erickson, Strachan, & Fraser-Thomas, 2010 for a review)—perhaps owing to the theoretical foundation of positive youth development—mental health outcomes are necessary, desirable, and compatible with current conceptualisations of effective coaching (Vella, Gardner, & Liddle, 2016). This is particularly so with a rapidly increasing focus on athlete mental health (e.g., Reardon et al., 2019). In light of this, it is particularly important to consider the requisite knowledge and most effective coaching strategies to foster optimal mental health and wellbeing in sport.

Despite the increasing prevalence and growing concern regarding mental health problems in sport, it has been shown that sporting organisations are not doing all that they can to promote positive mental health and prevent and intervene with mental health problems. In a recent review of Australian sporting codes by Liddle, Deane, and Vella (2017) it was found that very few sports organisations are addressing mental health at all. Coach education and training guidelines contained no specific mental health content, even among those sports with mental health policies and mental health campaigns. Those coach education guidelines discussed important factors such as "supporting the team", "encouraging a winning mentality", "confidence", "team mentality", "motivation", and "getting involved with family and school", however, the effect these were intended to have on mental health was not explicitly stated or supported with evidence (Liddle et al., 2017). Notably, coach education programs discussed ethical guidelines in regard to physical injury and injury management but contained no mention of the prevention of mental health problems or how to effectively respond to a mental health problem if it were evident. Evidence-based mental health strategies need to be integrated into the ongoing practices of sporting clubs and organisations, and coach education programs could include specific and targeted modules on mental health.

To investigate coaches' perceptions of their role in supporting young athletes' mental health, Ferguson et al. (2019) conducted a series of focus groups. Results indicated that coaches perceived their role as a youth sport coach to be diverse and included the promotion of athlete wellbeing. Consistent with previous research, coaches agreed that their role does include the promotion of mental health (Brown et al., 2017; Mazzer & Rickwood, 2015; Vella, Oades, & Crowe, 2011). For some coaches, this role extended to specific actions to facilitate appropriate help-seeking, however, this view was not shared by all coaches. Despite the variation in the extent to which coaches described their willingness to act regarding athlete mental illness, all coaches articulated some form of role in the identification, referral, and prevention of mental health problems, as well as the facilitation of athlete wellbeing. Similarly, Mazzer and Rickwood (2015) found through a series of interviews that coaches had an understanding of the negative impact of mental health problems, and while they did not feel external pressure to act in this domain, they recognised their potential role to promote mental health and respond to mental health concerns. Furthermore, coaches identified that the relationship they build and maintain with their athletes is a vital mechanism through which they are able to influence athlete mental health and help seeking behaviour. Coaches are also in a position to observe behaviour change which is an important factor in identifying the risk of a mental health problem. In addition to this, coaches acknowledged various ways that they support positive athlete mental health, such as encouraging participation in groups and activities, dealing with bullying, and using behaviour management strategies (Mazzer & Rickwood, 2015). When combined with the increasing recognition of mental health importance in sport (Reardon et al., 2019), the acceptance of athlete mental health as part of a coach's role has implications for coach education, in which there is a lack of focus on mental health and wellbeing (Liddle et al., 2017).

Approaches to Coaching for Mental Health

Autonomy Supportive Coaching

It is widely understood that sport participation and its associated activities has benefits for mental health (Biddle, Mutrie, & Gorely, 2015). Dropout from organised sports is associated with a clinically meaningful increase in risk for mental health problems within 3 years (Vella, Cliff, Magee, & Okely, 2014). One strategy to promote mental health may be to foster good quality athlete motivation, which may in turn increase wellbeing, promote engagement, and prevent burnout and dropout (Langan, Lonsdale, Blake, & Toner, 2015). To do this, coaches may engage in autonomy-supportive coaching (Mageau & Vallerand, 2003). According to self-determination theory (Ryan & Deci, 2000), the quality of athlete motivation can range from more self-determined forms (i.e., autonomous motivation) to less self-determined forms (i.e., controlled motivation), with more self-determined (or autonomous) forms of motivation being associated with more adaptive outcomes. *Autonomous motivation* involves behaving with a sense of volition and choice. In contrast, *controlled motivation* involves behaving under pressure or demand that emanates from something external to the self (Deci & Ryan, 2008). In the sport context, controlled motivation might refer to a sense of obligation to participate in sport in order to receive a desired external outcome (e.g. medals, praise, money).

According to self-determination theory, people will be more self-determined in their motivation when their basic needs for competence, autonomy, and relatedness to others are fulfilled (Ryan & Deci, 2000). Social contexts that facilitate satisfaction of these three basic psychological needs will support people's inherent activity, promote more optimal motivation, and yield the most positive psychological, developmental, and behavioural outcomes (Ryan & Deci, 2000). Conversely, social contexts that neglect these needs can lead to less optimal forms of motivation and can have detrimental effects on wellbeing. Autonomous or self-determined forms of motivation have been associated with greater persistence, more positive affect, enhanced performance, and greater psychological wellbeing (Deci & Ryan, 2008). Considering this, the coach has a responsibility to create a climate and engage in coaching practice that satisfies athletes' basic psychological needs for autonomy, competence, and relatedness.

Autonomy-supportive coaching is an application of self-determination theory to facilitate more adaptive outcomes for athletes (Deci & Ryan, 1985). An autonomy-supportive coach creates an environment that values self-initiation, provides choice, encourages independent problem-solving, and allows athletes to participate in decision-making (Mageau & Vallerand, 2003). Elite swimmers who perceived autonomy support from their coaches were more autonomous in their motivation for swimming, and this predicted greater long-term persistence while amotivation and controlled forms of motivation predicted drop-out (Pelletier, Dion, Slovinec-D'Angelo, & Reid, 2004). It has also been shown that increases in coaches' autonomy-supportive behaviours have been associated with increases in basic psychological need satisfaction, which are in turn associated with increases in athlete wellbeing and decreases in burnout (Balaguer et al., 2012).

Mageau and Vallerand (2003) first conceptualised a model of coaching based on self-determination theory. In this model, coaches' autonomy supportive behaviours, as well as the structure instilled by the coach leads to athletes' perception of autonomy, competence and relatedness. Some of the autonomy-supportive coaching behaviours proposed by Mageau and Vallerand (2003) include: the provision of choice within specific rules and limits; the provision of a rationale for tasks; acknowledgement of other people's feelings and perspectives; the provision of non-controlling competence feedback; the provision of opportunities for initiative; the avoidance of controlling behaviours such as criticisms and tangible rewards; and the prevention of ego-involvement in athletes.

Langan et al. (2015) operationalised an approach to coaching based on self-determination theory with a corresponding coach education program. The authors evaluated the effects of the self-determination theory-based program on athlete motivation and burnout. The authors found that the intervention resulted in a preventative effect on player burnout, particularly with athlete exhaustion, and positive trends for player motivation. Additionally, it was observed that coaches demonstrated an increase in need supportive behaviours. Therefore, coaches can be trained to better meet athletes' psychological needs with positive effects on mental health-related outcomes such as increased motivation and reduced risk of burnout. Vella et al. (2018) subsequently adapted the program developed by Langan et al. (2015) for the purposes of a multi-component mental health intervention for adolescent sport participants. They did so on the basis that higher levels of psychological need satisfaction would lead to greater wellbeing among sport participants and would lead to more self-determined forms of motivation. In turn, self-determined forms of motivation would increase engagement, reduce burnout, and underpin ongoing participation in sport which is associated with greater mental health (Vella et al., 2014). The results of this intervention are not yet known, but it offers a promising way forward in promoting positive mental health and wellbeing for athletes.

Coach Mental Health Literacy

While autonomy-supportive coaching may help to promote athlete wellbeing, coaches also hold concerns about to handling mental health problems among athletes (Ferguson et al., 2019; Mazzer & Rickwood, 2015). Such concerns include self-protection (concern of being "too close" to their athletes), managing privacy (confidentiality) of information between athletes, parents, and other professionals, and inadequate training to support athlete mental health (Ferguson et al., 2019; Mazzer & Rickwood, 2015). Training programs based on the construct of mental health literacy can be utilized to overcome the concerns of coaches. Mental health literacy includes one's knowledge and beliefs about mental health problems which aid their recognition, management, and prevention (Jorm et al., 1997). More specifically, mental health literacy refers to knowledge that is linked to the possibility of action, rather than simply knowledge itself. The components of mental health literacy include: (a) knowledge of prevention strategies, (b) ability to recognize a mental health problem, (c) knowledge of help-seeking options and available treatments, (d) knowledge of effective self-help strategies, and (e) skills and confidence to support others with a mental health problem (Jorm, 2012).

Training programs focused on mental health literacy are commonly available. For example, one such program is Mental Health First Aid (Kelly et al., 2011). The structure and content of the Mental Health First Aid program could equip coaches with the necessary knowledge and skills to alleviate some of the concerns that they have articulated (Ferguson et al., 2019; Mazzer & Rickwood, 2015) and appropriately respond to mental health and mental illness within the sport setting. Offering training in mental health may also address coaches' requests for more training in mental health (Ferguson et al., 2019; Mazzer & Rickwood, 2015). When trialed, mental health training has been shown to increase coaches' confidence and capacity to manage mental health concerns (Pierce, Liaw, Dobell, & Anderson, 2010), and may be the vehicle that equips coaches to be able to assist young people in sport (Bapat, Jorm, & Lawrence, 2009).

Despite recent attention on athlete mental health, specific mental health-related training for coaches has rarely been acknowledged as important, nor has it been systematically provided, at an organisation level. Evidence-based interventions are universally available to enhance mental health and mental health literacy, however very few have been adapted for coaches or sport club settings (Breslin et al., 2017). Increasing coaches' awareness of mental health problems and providing training in mental health literacy can decrease the stigma of mental health problems, and improve the mental health of athletes (Wright, Jorm, Harris, & McGorry, 2007). Despite the demand for context specific programs (Goodheart, 2011), few evidence-based mental health awareness programs are designed for sport-specific populations. Some efforts to meet this need have been trialled in the sport setting with promising results, although mental health literacy training within sport contexts has generally been of low quality (Breslin et al., 2017).

Read the Play is a mental health literacy program that was developed and evaluated in an uncontrolled trial by Bapat et al. (2009) with junior Australian Football and netball sport clubs volunteers. The eight-hour training program ran across three evening sessions over 3 consecutive weeks and was delivered by two experienced mental health clinician trainers. Content of the program was based on the Youth Mental Health First Aid training. The content included helping young people in the early stages of mental health problems as well as those in mental health crises, including suicidal thoughts and behaviours. Bapat et al. (2009) found that mental health literacy scores were high prior to receiving the program, which may have been due to marketing materials or self-selection into the program, and it is likely that those who volunteered to participate already had a greater knowledge (self-selection bias). Despite this, participants in the trial demonstrated significant improvements in knowledge about mental disorders, increased confidence in helping someone with a mental disorder, and more positive attitudes towards people with a mental disorder. Additionally, participants reported greater confidence in helping someone with a mental disorder, particularly depression. Results of this trial demonstrate that mental health training is feasible and potentially effective when delivered in the sport setting. However, the causal effects of the program are not known due to the absence of a control or comparison group—a symptom of much of the research in this area to date (Breslin et al., 2017).

In a region of rural Australia, a mental health initiative called the Coach the Coach project was undertaken. Pierce et al. (2010) delivered Mental Health First Aid training to football coaches in an effort to support early help seeking behaviour of young males within the clubs. Pierce et al. (2010) acknowledge that football clubs are a social hub in rural communities and could be an effective channel to access young people experiencing or at risk of experiencing mental health problems. Mental Health First Aid is an established training initiative that aims to promote response to mental health problems in a similar way to physical health emergencies or 'first aid' (Jorm, Kitchener, O'Kearney, & Dear, 2004). The 12-h program was delivered over 3 weeks to develop the football coaches' knowledge, confidence, and skills in supporting mental health, particularly depressive, anxiety, and psychotic disorders (Kitchener & Jorm, 2002). The program was evaluated in an uncontrolled trial and found improvements in capacity to recognise both depression and schizophrenia, and this capacity was still evident 6 months after training. Coaches also demonstrated improved confidence to help someone experiencing a mental health problem. These results build upon those of Bapat et al. (2009) and suggest that providing mental health training to coaches has the potential to increase their existing skills and knowledge in supporting athletes by providing them with the specific knowledge and words to use to address specific issues if someone is experiencing mental ill health. The results of this study further demonstrate that sports clubs may be appropriate and beneficial avenue for mental health initiatives within the community, and up-skilling coaches may be an advantageous avenue to further support their athletes' wellbeing and performance. Nonetheless, as with the study conducted by Bapat et al. (2009), the absence of a control or comparison group makes it impossible to assign increases in mental health literacy to the training program itself.

In sum, mental health literacy training provides a promising, feasible, and evidence-based way to increase coaches' knowledge and skills to deal with mental ill-health among athletes. It is clear that coaches, and in particular, youth sport coaches, would receive such training well (Ferguson et al., 2019; Mazzer & Rickwood, 2015). However, the quality of the research has generally been poor, with low sample sizes and a lack of control group being major problems for the field (Breslin et al., 2017). Adequately powered controlled trials are needed, as are measures that can give some indication of behaviour change, athlete-level measures of coaching behaviours regarding mental health, and long-term follow-up.

Practical Implications

There has recently been a focus placed on the mental health of athletes. As evidence of this focus, there has been a number of position stands and consensus statements on athlete mental health over the last 2 years, including statements from the International Olympic Committee (Reardon et al., 2019), International Society for Sport Psychology (Henriksen et al., 2019), and the European Federation of Sport Psychology (Moesch et al., 2019). Among these statements, coaches have been identified as the responsible for assisting in the diagnosis and management of mental health problems and creating an environment that supports mental health and resilience (Reardon et al., 2019). Coach education has been identified as key to enabling coaches to fulfil such roles (Henriksen et al., 2019; Moesch et al., 2019; Reardon et al., 2019).

In line with Keyes model of mental health we have put forward two approaches to coach education that could help coaches facilitate athlete mental health and wellbeing. To help coaches improve athlete resilience and wellbeing we propose coach education in line with autonomy supportive coaching and based on self-determination theory (Langan et al., 2015; Mageau & Vallerand, 2003). Such an approach has been a core component of major sport-based mental health initiatives (Vella et al., 2018), and has demonstrated success in improving mental health related outcomes such as burnout (Langan et al., 2015). The topics covered in coach education based on self-determination theory include: building athlete autonomy; appropriate feedback to athletes; ensuring athletes understand your plan; providing athletes with a rationale; building athlete togetherness; providing athletes with choice; developing independent athletes; defining athlete success; building coach-athlete relationships; and, reacting to resentment and negative athlete emotions (Langan et al., 2015; Vella et al., 2018). Systematically implementing coach education based on self-determination theory is one practical way forward to help coaches facilitate athlete wellbeing and create an environment that supports athlete resilience.

To help coaches support the recognition and management of athlete mental health problems, we have recommended mental health literacy training for coaches. The core components of mental health literacy training include: understanding the concept of mental health and various mental health problems; recognising the warning signs of common mental health problems; provision of a framework for assisting those with a mental health problem; knowledge of evidence-based treatments; and knowledge of self-help strategies (Kitchener & Jorm, 2008). This is consistent with the gaps in knowledge identified by coaches themselves at a non-elite level (Ferguson et al., 2019; Mazzer & Rickwood, 2015). In addition, coaches may also benefit from training around setting an appropriate culture whereby stigma is minimised, help seeking and early intervention is encouraged, and mental health is explicitly considered in athlete performance and development plans. While standard training packages are available such as Mental Health First Aid (Kitchener & Jorm, 2008), a sport-specific training program may better serve the needs of coaches by contextualising the content of mental health literacy training to sport.

Despite the increasing focus on athlete mental health (e.g., Reardon et al., 2019), research has systematically lagged the public interest. In a recent systematic review of mental health literacy interventions in sport, Breslin et al. (2017) noted several important limitations in the field. Notably, these include a widespread lack of controlled studies, and systematically underpowered research. If the field is to move forward in an evidence-based manner, adequately powered and adequately controlled trials need to be prioritised. With specific reference to coaching education, robust theory-based education programs should also be a priority (Langan, Blake, & Lonsdale, 2013). We have suggested that self-determination theory and mental health literacy can provide a starting point for research. However, these frameworks should be embedded with holistic, system wide approaches to athlete mental health. Further, alternate approaches to coaching such as an athlete-centred approach may also be beneficial (Kerr & Stirling, 2008). Regardless of theoretical and conceptual approach, high quality research is needed in order to move the field forward.

Key Points

Sport coaches play an important role in athlete mental health and wellbeing. Coach education is also central to efforts to provide the most adaptive environment possible whereby athletes can experience good mental health, wellbeing, resilience, and an environment that facilitates early intervention and help seeking for mental health problems. We have described the potential merits of coach education according to self-determination theory and mental health literacy. However, the coach is only one part of a complex sporting system. For example, the IOC consensus statement on athlete mental health provides multifaceted recommendations for the sport sector, including those relevant to sports organisations, and supporting actors such as physicians, nutritionists and sports scientists (Reardon et al., 2019). As such, in order for the coach to be enabled to promote athlete mental health, they need to work with and with-in sports organisations and systems that are explicitly built to systematically promote athlete mental health and wellbeing.

There has been an emphasis on the mental health of elite athletes with multiple consensus statements (e.g., Henriksen et al., 2019; Moesch et al., 2019; Reardon et al., 2019) and reviews (e.g., Rice et al., 2016) written for this population. However, to this point the mental health of sub-elite populations, including community sport participants, has been neglected. This is an important issue given the popularity of organised sports worldwide (Aubert et al., 2018; Hulteen et al., 2017). Furthermore, there are likely to be considerable differences between the knowledge and skills that are needed by coaches of elite athletes and coaches of various sub-elite athletes including coaches of children and youth (Côté & Gilbert, 2009). An increased research and policy focus on sub-elite contexts will better provide an evidence-base upon which all coaches can found their coaching practice. In the absence of consensus statements and guidelines for non-elite coaches, a large majority of coaches worldwide will not be adequately provided for.

It may be simplistic to assert that one, or a few approaches to coaching are able to make meaningful differences to athlete mental health in the absence of system-wide change. However, at this point, mental health researchers and practitioners working in the sports context largely do so in a theoretical vacuum. The result of this is that researchers and practitioners are unable to systematically account for the various system-wide influences and mechanisms that affect athlete mental health. Knowledge of such influences and mechanisms will enable coaches and coach educators to more fully understand, plan for, and maximise the benefits of the role that they play in athlete mental health.

Finally, guidelines for the promotion of athlete mental health will go a long way to helping coaches clearly understand and enact their role to promote athlete mental health and wellbeing. Concise, clearly articulated, easily understood and easily applied guidelines are necessary to enable coaches to adequately deal with the issue of athlete mental health. At present, many coaches report feeling ill-prepared to deal with issues of athlete mental ill-health (Ferguson et al., 2019; Mazzer & Rickwood, 2015), while parents also feel that coaches of young athletes are ill-prepared for this role (Brown et al., 2017). Visible guidelines to promote athlete mental health would be of enormous benefit for coaches moving forward.

Conclusion

Athlete mental health and wellbeing has become an issue of international importance, particularly with regard to elite athletes. This is evidenced by a proliferation of consensus statements and position stands designed to govern efforts in this area (e.g., Henriksen et al., 2019; Moesch et al., 2019; Reardon et al., 2019). Central to the promotion of athlete mental health and wellbeing are the role of the coach and coach education processes. In line with Keyes' mental health continuum (2002), the role of coach extends to the promotion of athlete wellbeing as well as the promotion of early intervention and help-seeking for mental health problems. As such, we have recommended that coaches consider the merits of coaching practice and coach education based on self-determination theory, as well as mental health literacy. However, coaches should be cognisant that they work within complex sporting organisations and systems that require unified efforts. High quality research to provide a solid evidence base, guidelines for coaches, and a focus on non-elite coaches are necessary to move the field forward in a constructive manner.

References

Aubert, S., Barnes, J. D., Abdeta, C., Nader, P. A., Adeniyi, A. F., Aguilar-Farias, N., . . . Tremblay, M. S. (2018). Global matrix 3.0 physical activity report card grades for children and youth: Results and analysis from 49 countries. *Journal of Physical Activity and Health, 15*(Suppl 2), S251–S273.

Australian Bureau of Statistics. (2017). *Causes of death, Australia, 2016* (No. 3303.0). Canberra, ACT.

Balaguer, I., González, L., Fabra, P., Castillo, I., Mercé, J., & Duda, J. L. (2012). Coaches' interpersonal style, basic psychological needs and the well- and ill-being of young soccer players: A longitudinal analysis. *Journal of Sports Sciences, 30*, 1619–1629.

Bapat, S., Jorm, A. F., & Lawrence, K. (2009). Evaluation of a mental health literacy training program for junior sporting clubs. *Australasian Psychiatry, 17*, 475–479.

Bauman, N. J. (2016). The stigma of mental health in athletes: Are mental toughness and mental health seen as contradictory in elite sport? *British Journal of Sports Medicine, 50*, 135–136.

Biddle, S. J. H., Mutrie, N., & Gorely, T. (2015). *Psychology of physical activity: Determinants, well-being and interventions* (3rd ed.). London: Routledge.

Breslin, G., Shannon, S., Haughey, T., Donnelly, P., & Leavey, G. (2017). A systematic review of interventions to increase awareness of mental health and well-being in athletes, coaches and officials. *Systematic Reviews, 6*, 177–192. https://doi.org/10.1186/s13643-017-0568-6

Brown, M., Deane, F. P., Vella, S. A., & Liddle, S. K. (2017). Parents views of the role of sports coaches as mental health gatekeepers for adolescent males. *International Journal of Mental Health Promotion, 19*, 1–13.

Côté, J., Bruner, M., Erickson, K., Strachan, L., & Fraser-Thomas, J. (2010). Athlete development and coaching. In J. Lyle & C. Cushion (Eds.), *Sport coaching: Professionalism and practice*. Oxford, UK: Elsevier.

Côté, J., & Gilbert, W. (2009). An integrative definition of coaching effectiveness and expertise. *International Journal of Sports Science & Coaching, 4*, 307–323.

Deci, E. L., & Ryan, R. M. (1985). *Intrinsic motivation and self-determination in human behavior*. New York: Plenum Press.

Deci, E. L., & Ryan, R. M. (2008). Facilitating optimal motivation and psychological well-being across life's domains. *Canadian Psychology/Psychologie Canadienne, 49*(1), 14–23.

Donohue, B., Miller, A., Crammer, L., Cross, C., & Covassin, T. (2007). A standardized method of assessing sport specific problems in the relationships of athletes with their coaches, teammates, family, and peers. *Journal of Sport Behavior, 30*(4), 375–397.

Eime, R. M., Young, J. A., Harvey, J. T., Charity, M. J., & Payne, W. R. (2013a). A systematic review of the psychological and social benefits of participation in sport for adults: Informing development of a conceptual model of health through sport. *International Journal of Behavioral Nutrition and Physical Activity, 10*(1), 135.

Eime, R. M., Young, J. A., Harvey, J. T., Charity, M. J., & Payne, W. R. (2013b). A systematic review of the psychological and social benefits of participation in sport for children and adolescents: Informing development of a conceptual model of health through sport. *International Journal of Behavioral Nutrition and Physical Activity, 10*, 98.

Ferguson, H. L., Swann, C., Liddle, S. K., & Vella, S. A. (2019). Investigating youth sports coaches' perceptions of their role in adolescent mental health. *Journal of Applied Sport Psychology, 31*(2), 235–252.

Goodheart, C. D. (2011). Psychology practice: Design for tomorrow. *American Psychologist, 66*, 339–347.

Gulliver, A., Griffiths, K. M., Mackinnon, A., Batterham, P. J., & Stanimirovic, R. (2015). The mental health of Australian elite athletes. *Journal of Science and Medicine in Sport, 18*, 255–261.

Henriksen, K., Schinke, R., Moesch, K., McCann, S., Parham, W. D., Larsen, C. H., & Terry, P. (2019). Consensus statement on improving the mental health of high performance athletes. *International Journal of Sport and Exercise Psychology*. https://doi.org/10.1080/1612197X.2019.1570473

Hulteen, R. M., Smith, J. J., Morgan, P. J., Barnett, L. M., Hallal, P., Colyvas, K., & Lubans, D. R. (2017). Global participation in sport and leisure-time physical activities: A systematic review and meta-analysis. *Preventive Medicine, 95*, 14–25.

Jorm, A. F., Korten, A. E., Jacomb, P. A., Christensen, H., Rodgers, B., & Pollitt, P. (1997). Mental health literacy: A survey of the public's ability to recognise mental disorders and their beliefs about the effectiveness of treatment. *Medical Journal of Australia, 166*, 182–186.

Jorm, A. F. (2012). Mental health literacy: Empowering the community to take action for better mental health. *American Psychologist, 67*, 231–243.

Jorm, A. F., Kitchener, B. A., O'Kearney, R., & Dear, K. B. (2004). Mental health first aid training of the public in a rural area: A cluster randomized trial. *BMC Psychiatry, 4*, 1.

Kaier, E., Cromer, L. D., Johnson, M. D., Strunk, K., & Davis, J. L. (2015). Perceptions of mental illness stigma: Comparisons of athletes to nonathlete peers. *Journal of College Student Development, 56*, 735–739.

Kelly, C. M., Mithen, J. M., Fischer, J. A., Kitchener, B. A., Jorm, A. F., Lowe, A., & Scanlan, C. (2011). Youth mental health first aid: A description of the program and an initial evaluation. *International Journal of Mental Health Systems, 5*, 4.

Kerr, G. A., & Stirling, A. E. (2008). Child protection in sport: Implications of an athlete-centered philosophy. *Quest, 60*, 307–323.

Keyes, C. L. M. (2002). The mental health continuum: From languishing to flourishing in life. *Journal of Health and Social Behavior, 43*, 207–222.

Keyes, C. L. M. (2005). Mental illness and/or mental health? Investigating axioms of the complete state model of health. *Journal of Consulting and Clinical Psychology, 73*, 539–548.

Keyes, C. L. M., & Michalec, B. (2010). Viewing mental health from the complete state paradigm. In T. Scheid & T. Brown (Eds.), *A handbook for the study of mental health: Social contexts, theories, and system* (2nd ed., pp. 125–134). New York: Cambridge University Press.

Kitchener, B. A., & Jorm, A. F. (2002). Mental health first aid training for the public: Evaluation of effects on knowledge, attitudes and helping behavior. *BMC Psychiatry, 2*, 1–6.

Kitchener, B. A., & Jorm, A. (2008). Mental health first aid: An international programme for early intervention. *Early Intervention in Psychiatry, 2*, 55–61.

Langan, E., Blake, C., & Lonsdale, C. (2013). Systematic review of the effectiveness of interpersonal coach education interventions on athlete outcomes. *Psychology of Sport and Exercise, 14*, 37–49.

Langan, E., Lonsdale, C., Blake, C., & Toner, J. (2015). Testing the effects of a self-determination theory-based intervention with youth Gaelic football coaches on athlete motivation and burnout. *Sport Psychologist, 29*(4), 293–301.

Liddle, S. K., Deane, F. P., & Vella, S. A. (2017). Addressing mental health through sport: A review of sporting organizations' websites. *Early Intervention in Psychiatry, 11*, 93–103.

Mageau, G. A., & Vallerand, R. J. (2003). The coach-athlete relationship: A motivational model. *Journal of Sports Sciences, 21*, 883–904.

Mazzer, K. R., & Rickwood, D. J. (2015). Mental health in sport: Coaches' views of their role and efficacy in supporting young people's mental health. *International Journal of Health Promotion and Education, 53*, 102–113.

Moesch, K., Kentta, G., Kleinert, J., Quignon-Fleuret, C., Cecil, S., & Bertollo, M. (2019). FEPSAC position statement: Mental health disorders in elite athletes and models of service provision. *Psychology of Sport & Exercise, 38*, 61–71.

Pelletier, L. G., Dion, S. C., Slovinec-D'Angelo, M., & Reid, R. (2004). Why do you regulate what you eat? Relationships between forms of regulation, eating behaviors, sustained dietary behavior change, and psychological adjustment. *Motivation and Emotion, 28*, 245–277.

Pierce, D., Liaw, S. T., Dobell, J., & Anderson, R. J. (2010). Australian rural football club leaders as mental health advocates: An investigation of the impact of the Coach the Coach project. *International Journal of Mental Health Systems, 4*, 10.

Reardon, C. L., Hainline, B., Miller Aron, A., Baron, D., Baum, A. L., Bindra, A., . . . Engebretsen, L. (2019). Mental health in elite athletes: International Olympic Committee consensus statement (2019). *British Journal of Sports Medicine, 53*, 667–699.

Rice, S. M., Purcell, R., De Silva, S., Mawren, D., McGorry, P. D., & Parker, A. G. (2016). The mental health of elite athletes: A narrative systematic review. *Sports Medicine, 46*, 1333–1353.

Ryan, R. M., & Deci, E. L. (2000). Self-determination theory and the facilitation of intrinsic motivation, social development, and well-being. *American Psychologist, 55*, 68–78.

Steel, Z., Marnane, C., Iranpour, C., Chey, T., Jackson, J. W., Patel, V., & Silove, D. (2014). The global prevalence of common mental disorders: A systematic review and meta-analysis 1980–2013. *International Journal of Epidemiology, 43*, 476–493.

Swann, C., Telenta, J., Draper, G., Liddle, S. K., Fogarty, A., Hurley, D., & Vella, S. A. (2018). Youth sport as a context for supporting mental health: Adolescent male perspectives. *Psychology of Sport and Exercise, 35*, 55–64.

Trojian, T. (2016). Depression is under-recognised in the sport setting: Time for primary care sports medicine to be proactive and screen widely for depression symptoms. *British Journal of Sports Medicine, 50*, 137–139.

Uphill, M., Sly, D., & Swain, J. (2016). From mental health to mental wealth in athletes: Looking back and moving forward. *Frontiers in Psychology, 7*, 935.

Vella, S. A., Cliff, D. P., Magee, C. A., & Okely, A. D. (2014). Associations between sports participation and psychological difficulties during childhood: A two-year follow up. *Journal of Science and Medicine in Sport, 18*, 304–309.

Vella, S. A., Gardner, L. A., & Liddle, S. K. (2016). Coaching, positive youth development, and mental health. In N. L. Holt (Ed.), *Positive youth development through sport* (pp. 205–215). New York: Routledge.

Vella, S. A., Oades, L., & Crowe, T. (2011). The role of the coach in facilitating positive youth development: Moving from theory to practice. *Journal of Applied Sport Psychology, 23*, 33–48.

Vella, S. A., Swann, C., Batterham, M., Boydell, K. M., Eckermann, S., Fogarty, A., . . . Deane, F. P. (2018). Ahead of the game protocol: A multi-component, community sport-based program targeting prevention, promotion and early intervention for mental health among adolescent males. *BMC Public Health, 18*(1):390.

World Health Organization. (2001). *The world health report 2001. Mental health: New understanding. New hope*. Geneva: World Health Organization.

World Health Organization. (2014). Mental health: Strengthening our response. Retrieved from: https://www.who.int/news-room/fact-sheets/detail/mental-health-strengthening-our-response.

World Health Organization. (2017). *Depression and other common mental disorders: Global health estimates*. Geneva: World Health Organization.

Wright, A., Jorm, A. F., Harris, M. G., & McGorry, P. D. (2007). What's in a name? Is accurate recognition and labelling of mental disorders by young people associated with better help-seeking and treatment preferences? *Social Psychiatry and Psychiatric Epidemiology, 42*, 244–250.

Stewart Vella is a Senior Lecturer in the School of Psychology at the University of Wollongong. He has led large scale mental health promotion programs in sport over the last 5 years. His research interests include the design, implementation, translation and dissemination of mental health programs for youth sport participants.

Sarah Liddle is a registered psychologist and Ph.D. (Clinical Psychology) candidate. Her research is focused on the prevention of mental illness through mental health literacy training in adolescent males through sport. Her research interests extend to the role of positive mental health in sport performance, and the role that sport and physical activity can play in both preventing and managing mental health and mental illness.

Chapter 15
Coaching Life Skills in Sports People

Martin I. Jones

Abstract The purpose of this chapter is to explore how to coach life skills through sport. A life skill is a commonly used term with sport psychology literature. However, there is a conceptual ambiguity that surrounds what life skills are and consequently which positive outcomes are labeled as life skills. Rather than listing potential life skills (e.g., communication skills), there is a need to define what life skills are based upon shared characteristics. Thus, the first part of this chapter will focus on what constitutes a life skill to enable coaches to understand what it is that they are aiming to develop. Life skills are defined as skills that are acquired through practice to help an individual to display competence in socially valuable tasks that predicts similarly useful tasks within or across life domains. The consequence(s) of the process of learning a life skill is a change in assumptions about oneself and the world and therefore, requires corresponding changes in behavior and relationships. The next focus of the chapter will be on discussing the salient features of practical life skills coaching. This section will emphasize the environmental features of useful life skills programs by analyzing literature from the broader field of positive youth development. Moreover, this section on features of practical life skills programs will highlight the role of the coach to show how coaches' personal qualities and beliefs are central to the development of life skills. The chapter concludes with a discussion of how to move life skills research and practice forward by providing areas for critical consideration and future research directions.

Keywords Learning Life Skills · Change behaviour · Positive development

The purpose of this chapter is to explore how to coach life skills through sport. Before delving into the extant research, I invite you to engage in a brief thought experiment. Consider two people. Imagine that these imaginary people are two youth sport participants: Jesse and Chris. Both Jesse and Chris play tennis. They both play on the same courts, at the same club in the same town. Both players train

M. I. Jones (✉)
University of Exeter, Exeter, UK

R. Resende, A. R. Gomes (eds.), *Coaching for Human Development and Performance in Sports*, https://doi.org/10.1007/978-3-030-63912-9_15

and compete under the same rules and governance provided by their national governing body. Both athletes have coaches who have received the same coaching qualifications from a relevant national governing body. Both athletes have supportive parents and siblings who endorse psychosocial growth. Imagine now that you have been asked to conduct a "personal development audit" (if such a thing is possible) to try to measure which positive skills, values, and virtues that the two athletes have developed because of their participation in tennis.

On the one hand, you observe that Jesse demonstrated a range of skills that you think are important for young people in your society. For example, Jesse is a great communicator, is organized, and can work well in teams. On the other hand, you observe that Chris does not possess the skills that Jesse has shown you. Chris is selfish, narcissistic, and will do anything to win (for example, cheat). What might "cause" these differences if their youth sports experience appears so similar?

Developmental psychologists have shown that some of the difference between the two athletes might be relatively stable and inherited individual differences (i.e., personality traits). However, inherited dispositions cannot account for all the variability in the behaviors shown by athletes. Instead, many skills, values, and virtues appear to be learned. If we were to extend our audit of personal development to the tennis club, we might observe subtle differences that could help us understand why the two athletes appear to be very different. For example, although the coaches have been trained under the same system, their coaching behaviors and foundational coaching philosophy (i.e., winning vs. personal development) are vastly different. For instance, Jesse's coach creates coaching sessions that promote teamwork, require clear and concise communication, and endorse the value of organization skills. Chris's coach, on the other hand, creates coaching sessions that promote winning at all costs, demonstrating competence by beating opponents and ignoring the needs of others. While it is not my place to say which coaching session is better—they both have value in different ways—it is apparent (I hope) that one session will probably develop a broader range of positive life skills than the other. Moreover, the positive skills that Jesse demonstrates (i.e., communication, organization, teamwork) should be more useful in most (not all) life domains outside of sport (e.g., the workplace) compared with the skills that Chris demonstrates (i.e., winning at all costs and selfishness).

This idea of developing skills for life is a central principle of life skills through sports literature. In the previous example of the two tennis players, it should also be apparent that a crucial element of developing life skills is the role of the coach. Now, that is not to say that the coach is the only way to develop life skills. Young people do not grow up on the tennis court, the football pitch, the swimming pool. They grow up in a complex developmental system that includes (but is not limited to) organized sport. While acknowledging that other social agents and structures in combination with ranges of life experiences, genetic influences, and cultural and historical nuances influence how people develop, the purpose of this chapter is to consider how sports coaches can contribute to the development of life skills in their athletes.

Life Skills and Sports Coaching

In the past two decades, sport and exercise psychologists have examined the procurement of life skills through sport and have generated models to delineate how life skills are developed and possibly transferred to different life domains. Gould and Carson (2008) provided an excellent review of some of this early work and set up several areas for future research. Since then, other researchers have examined life skills (e.g., Pierce, Gould, & Camiré, 2017) and more broadly the positive youth development through sports literature (e.g., Holt, 2016) and despite the excellent suggestions that these research teams made several pervasive limitations exist. One of the main barriers to progress (in my opinion) is the lack of clear guidance about how to coach life skills. While it is not within the scope of this chapter to provide definitive answers, I hope that I present relevant research and points of discussion that stimulates debate and plants the seed of innovation in any readers who wish to develop new or improved methods of coaching life skills through sport.

What Are Life Skills?

Despite a growing body of literature in this area, life skills are still not well defined. A cursory glance at the existing life skills literature reveals that there are nearly as many definitions as there are potential life skills. Life skills researchers have erected an unnecessary obstacle to coaching life skills by listing examples of life skills without identifying a common feature inherent to life skills that makes them thus. In this way, we (as consumers of the research) are exposed to Meno's paradox that a coach cannot search for life skills (or means of coaching) because s (he) does not know what to look for.

Therefore, step one in this chapter is to set out the stall and present a definition of life skills. While this may add to already lengthy list of definitions presently available, I hope that by clarifying what I mean by life skills I can ease into the discussion of how to coach them more easily.

I (Jones & Lavallee, 2009a) have previously defined life skills are ranges of transferable skills needed for daily living, by everybody that helps people thrive. On reflection, I believe that this definition has problems, and I suggest a significant amendment. The first issue regards the misinterpretation and fragility of thriving. In the context of positive youth development, thriving is a developmental concept that signifies a healthy change process linking a young person with an adult status (Lerner, Dowling, & Anderson, 2003). Benson (1993) first used thriving to refer to a set of "vital signs" in adolescence. Along these lines, Benson advocated thriving as an outcome of positive development, rather than a process of growth (Bundick, Yeager, King, & Damon, 2010). In the context of sport, coaches are more likely to use discrete indicators of thriving (e.g., successful performance, talent identification) rather than seeing it as a process. However, that should not detract from the likely reality that young people can be on the longitudinal path of thriving in the absence of visible indicators. Adults may only identify a thriving young person when the young person demonstrates a socially valuable behavior such as volunteering or volitionally engaging in extracurricular activities that the adult sees or about which they are informed. Cognitive and emotional development is not so readily observed, yet emotional and cognitive development is probably equally important in terms of life skill development.

Thriving is also considered a fluid developmental process and is regarded as a positive positioning toward life and a focus on adaptive goals (Benson & Scales, 2009). Benson and Scales (2009, p. 85) stated that "thriving represents the dynamic and bi-directional interplay of a young person intrinsically animated and energized by discovering his or her specialness, and the developmental contexts (people, places) that know, affirm, celebrate, encourage, and guide its expression." Coaches could identify a "thriver" if he or she is on the path to an adult status marked by making culturally valued contributions to self and institutions (Lerner et al., 2003). From the positive youth development perspective, thriving incorporates the absence of problem behaviors (e.g., drug abuse) and pathology (e.g., mental illness) with indicators of healthy growth (e.g., academic achievement: Scales, Benson, Leffert, & Blyth, 2000). If coaches are to use life skills to help people thrive, coaches must know what thriving in sport entails. Brown, Arnold, Reid, and Roberts (2018) suggested that in the context of elite sport thriving involved being optimistic, focused, and in control; having an active awareness of areas for improvement; possessing high-quality motivation; experiencing holistic development; displaying progression upward; and having a sense of belonging. They also suggested that their participants identified various personal (e.g., desire and motivation, goal setting and creating challenge) and contextual (e.g., coach support, training environment) enablers that potentially interact to facilitate thriving in sport. Whether Brown et al. (2018) conceptualization of thriving is practically useful for coaches is yet to be seen. Therefore, researchers could consider how to measure thriving so that they can have a meaningful outcome measure when establishing whether coaching interventions produce desired changes. At this time, there are no standardized measures of thriving.

Next, I would like to draw upon Pierce et al. (2017) review of life skills transfer and specify what life skills transferability might mean in real-world terms. Pierce et al. (2017, p. 194) conceptualized life skill transfer as

> The ongoing process by which an individual further develops or learns and internalizes a personal asset (i.e., psychosocial skill, knowledge, disposition, identity construction, or transformation) in sport and then experiences personal change through the application of the asset in one or more life domains beyond the context where it was originally learned.

The point that life skill transfer is an ongoing process is particularly salient for the coaching of life skills. I do not believe that life skill transmission is dichotomous (transferred vs. not transferred) and therefore coaches should be aware the life skills transfer could be happening both when positive behavior is observed and when it is are not. The nature of the transfer process could be happening within the thoughts and feelings of the individual. Therefore it is not readily observable. The absence of visible behavior should not lead coaches to conclude that skill has not transferred; the process could still be underway. To date, there is no evidence to show how long the process of life skills transfer takes; therefore, coaches must demonstrate patience.

It could be more useful for coaches to think in magnitudes of the transfer rather than transfer vs. no transfer. For example, a coach may want to know how much skill could transfer across life domains or how much a given outcome variable (e.g., life skill in a new life domain) will improve if the athlete learns a particular life skill in the sport. Ideally, researchers could report real-world effects derived from the possession of life skills. For example, it would be useful to know that a 50% increase in (for instance) communication skills in the sport will result in a 20% improvement of communication competency in the workplace. To date, the reliance on retrospective interviews to understand life skills development and transfer has meant that the previous research question remains unanswered. A significant research question for researchers to answer is "to what extent does a life skill from one life domain predicts life skills (or associated outcomes) within and across life domains." For the research to progress, it is crucial for scholars to establish the predictive validity of life skills by moving away from historical qualitative inquiry toward experimental psychology. To help move the field forward, practitioners need to know whether they can predict the acquisition and expression of a single life skill within and across life domains.

Finally, it would likely be useful for practitioners to know whether a given life skill predicts a different outcome (e.g., communication predicting confidence) and whether those outcomes mediate valued behaviors (e.g., job performance). The absence of evidence of predictive validity erects unnecessary obstacles for researchers who need to sell the benefits of life skill programs to athletes and coaches, or for coaches to sell the benefits to sporting directors and policymakers. When considering the time and monetary investment required to coach life skills, practitioners and coaches need to demonstrate value by providing a return on investment. Currently, the evidence base is insufficiently robust for practitioners or coaches to offer anything but an anecdote. Even if the amount of variance in the desired outcome is small, it could still be meaningful and significant to coaches, so should be examined and reported. Therefore, research is needed that reveals how much learning of life skills provided quantifiable benefits across life domains or epochs.

Analysis of Pierce et al. (2017) definition of transfer could lead some coaches to assume that life skills must cross some life skills boundary (i.e., from sport to work). However, another way of conceptualizing transfer is to think longitudinally about the skill in question (i.e., maintenance within a life domain). By within domains I mean that transfer could encompass transmitting given skills over time. The traditional conceptualization of life skills transfer alludes to transmission from one life domain (e.g., sport) to another (e.g., education). For instance, a diligent rugby player will be a diligent student. Transfer of skills might happen within the same domain, specifically from training to competition or from participation in youth to participation in adulthood.

Haskell (2001) alluded to the transfer of learning as the application of prior learning to similar and new situations. These situations could be within the same life domain at different time points. For example, a young athlete may learn about time management as an adolescent and then continue to apply that skill to her sport in adulthood.

Similarly, a young person could determine the value of physical activity by playing youth sport. Physical activity could be a life skill or could be the outcome of one or a set of life skills (e.g., discipline or diligence). Either way, the person in question might then continue to be physically active across the lifespan by playing the same sport he or she performed in youth. In this example, no cross-domain transfer has occurred (i.e., application of the asset in one or more life domain beyond the domain where it was learned initially: Pierce et al., 2017). However, I believe that skill maintenance in the same life domain warrants equal attention.

Moreover, I contend that transfer within domains may serve as an essential moderator of transfer across areas (i.e., more significant across domain transfer in conditions of longer within domain transfer). I welcome researchers to test this hypothesis. In closing, I believe that the maintenance of a life skill is just as valuable as moving skills from one life domain to another.

Further reflection on the Jones and Lavallee (2009a) definition raises additional points of critique. Using simple language such as "everybody" and "every day" to conceptualize a life skill presents a break from the reality of what a life skill is for most people. It is unlikely that people use their life skills every day. Similarly, people are different, and life experiences are unique, so it is doubtful that everyone will require the same skills (based on the novel interactions of individual assets and ecologies in which people live: Lerner et al., 2006). Lerner and colleagues suggested that thriving is a consequence of the potentially infinite number of adaptive developmental regulations that exist in a young person's life. Because of the billions of developmental trajectories that could emerge across the lifespan, it would be brave to suggest that life skills are the primary driving force behind thriving.

Discussing life skills in absolute terms will undoubtedly present unnecessary obstacles to coaches and researchers who wish to conduct life skills research and help young people in the real world. Coaches may better serve the needs of youth by defining life skills in more practical terms. Showing that people do not need life skills but rather acquiring transferable skills improves the probability of securing a desirable outcome could be a better solution to the problem of life skills definition. Simple definitions of life skills may paint a picture that young people cannot thrive in the absence of a rich repertoire of life skills. Thriving is such an elusive construct; it is highly unlikely that life skills alone account for the variance in a person's prosperity to thrive. Instead, life skills will interact with a plethora of other assets, resources, genes, dispositions, and ecological conditions to improve people's chances of thriving.

It is plausible that life skills are culturally valued and subjective (Jones & Parker, 2014). There will be cultural and individual differences in life skills classification.

Therefore, the coaching of specific life skills may engender growth in some people, but not all. Clarifying boundary conditions is crucial. It is not for me to impose these boundary conditions but rather to open debate so that researchers and coaches consider cultural nuances when attempting to intervene in young people's lives. For example, coaching life skills to young people in neo-liberal western societies will be vastly different to coaching life skills to young people from nationalist or socialist societies because of the value assigned to the ranges of life skills within each society (i.e., individualism vs. collectivism).

To refine existing definitions of life skills, I recommend adopting Simonton's (1999) work on talent development. In a similar vein to Simonton's definition of talent, I suggest that life skills could enable an individual to display competence within or across life domains, and life skills require specialized training. I recommend this adaptation to existing definitions because it is useful to clarify that life skills must be learnable (i.e., need training) and are not fixed (or are relatively stable personality traits). It may be that people believe that sport taught a life skill in a young person because of a disposition or an ability and was already present before the young person started playing sport. For example, it may be reasonable to conclude that golf helps to develop conscientiousness. However, an alternative explanation is that people high in conscientiousness are attracted to golf, and the sport experience has done nothing to improve this trait. It is possible that traits like conscientiousness are then considered typical in golf because golfers may value traits like conscientiousness, and coaches identify them as precursors of performance (i.e., talent identification). The result could be that people high in conscientiousness progress through the talent development system while their low conscientiousness counterparts drop out. Ultimately, people may observe that golfers (as a population) are conscientious and draw the conclusion that golf teaches conscientiousness when this is not the case. The same or similar narratives could play out across ranges of sports.

Even though I recommend that life skills be defined based on their learnability, I do not suggest that scholars ignore relatively stable traits completely. It is possible that some of the moderators of life skill development could be innate. For example, an open personality trait may moderate the development of communication skills in the sport. However, openness alone probably cannot help people display competence in communication. Instead, communication skills are refined with specialized training, but openness increases the magnitude of the effect. In here lies the complexity of life skill development. It is improbable that all the available or desired life skills are all learned in the same way as each other. Each life skill will require a different path of development to others. Equally, (and probably more importantly) each person will learn a given skill differently based on a range of individual differences (e.g., personality). Thus, any model of life skill coaching should acknowledge and at least try to reconcile the variability in how life skills are developed based on what the individual brings to the table (see Gould & Carson, 2008).

In closing this section of the definition of life skills, I would like to offer my thoughts on how life skills can be defined. I believe that life skills are acquired through practice to help the owner to display competence in socially valuable tasks that predicts similarly useful functions within or across life domains. The consequence of the process of learning a life skill is a change in assumptions about oneself and the world and therefore requires corresponding changes in behavior (affect and cognition) and relationships (i.e., a transition: Schlossberg, 1981).

Potential Features of Positive Life Skills Coaching

Before delving into this discussion, it is essential to note that any debate about the features of life skills coaching programs is provisional. It is based on the current body of research, which is delimited to a particular range of social and cultural groups. Therefore, some features of practical life skills programs that are culturally nuanced will possibly be omitted.

Lerner (2004) described that "Big Three" features of optimal youth development programs. In the context of sport, coaching is most likely to promote life skills when the coaching environment and the coaching process involve possibilities for sustained adult-youth relationships, youth skill-building activities, and opportunities for youth participation in the leadership of community-based activities. Outside of sport, Catalano, Berglund, Ryan, Lonczak, and Hawkins (1998) found that the majority (about 75%) of effective affirmative youth development programs focus on the "Big Three" features effective affirmative youth development programs. Catalano et al. (1998) classified positive youth development programs as any youth-based program that promoted bonding, resilience, competence, self-determination, spirituality, self-efficacy, clear and positive identity, belief in the future, provided recognition for positive behavior and opportunities for prosocial involvement, and prosocial norms. Catalano and colleagues identified 25 affirmative youth development programs that had robust evaluation designs (experimental or quasi-experimental with viable comparison groups), had an acceptable standard of statistical proof, provided sufficient methodological detail to allow an independent assessment of the study's soundness, and produced evidence of significant effects or behavioral outcomes.

The most effective programs addressed a wide range of positive youth development objectives rather than concentrating on just one area. Similarly, the best programs were rigorously evaluated, made assessments of positive and problem outcomes, had a structured curriculum, lasted for a minimum of 9 months, and had high implementation fidelity. Precious few life skills programs that are delivered by coaches through sport participation are rigorously evaluated, made assessments of positive and problem outcomes, had a structured curriculum, lasted for a minimum of 9 months, and had high implementation fidelity.

The characteristics of effective positive youth development programs identified by Catalano et al. (1998) are similar to those identified by Roth and Brooks-Gunn (2003). They noted that effective programs transcend an exclusive focus on the prevention of risky behaviors to include attempts to instil behaviors that emphasize youth competencies and abilities (e.g., life skills) through increasing exposure to supportive and empowering environments where activities create opportunities for skill-building and horizon-broadening experiences. Also, Roth and Brooks-Gunn (2003) indicated that effective positive youth development programs offer opportunities for youth to nurture their interests and talents, practice new skills, and gain a sense of personal and group recognition.

Finally, the National Research Council and Institute of Medicine (NRCIM, 2002) outlined four primary areas of youth development: physical, intellectual, psychological/emotional, and social. For each developmental domain, several developmental assets are suggested. For example, right eating and physical activity habits are assets that facilitate positive physical development. Knowledge of interpersonal skills, vocational skills, and decision-making skills contribute to positive intellectual development. Mental health, positive self-regard, coping skills, mastery motivation, and conflict resolution skills characterize positive psychological and emotional development. Assets contributing to positive social development include connectedness with parents, peers, and other adults, a sense of social place, and an attachment to society. In addition to the developmental assets, the NRCIM (2002) also outlined eight features of settings that are most likely to foster these developmental assets. These features are physical and psychological safety, appropriate structure, supportive relationships, opportunities to belong, positive social norms, support for efficacy and mattering, opportunities for skill building, and integration of family, school, and community efforts. The NRCIM (2002) also discussed contrast poles for their feature of positive programs. These contrast poles that characterize potential negative youth development program features are relevant in this discussion because they could provide coaches with things to avoid.

Moreover, coaches might recognize strategies and behaviors that they regularly demonstrate, which the coach may have thought were adaptive (e.g., focussing on winning). For example, rather than physical and psychological safety poor (and potentially damaging) programs may comprise dangers, fear, and feeling of insecurity, sexual and physical harassment, and verbal abuse. The opposite of appropriate structure could be a range of conditions including chaos, disorganized, laissez-faire, rigid, over controlled or autocratic.

Unsupportive relationships could be identified as cold, distant, over-controlling, ambiguous support, untrustworthy, focused on winning, inattentive, unresponsive, and rejecting. Exclusion, marginalization and intergroup conflict could be seen as opposite of opportunities for belonging, mainly if the exclusion was based on the excluded individual's gender, ethnicity, sexual orientation, or disabilities, which can sometimes be the case. For example, female youth soccer players may be able to play with male players up to a certain age but are then restricted to female only teams. Recent changes to rules in international athletics also highlight the potential for exclusion and derision of some female athletes because of elevated (compared to norms) levels of the androgenetic hormone testosterone. To date, gender screening of youth sports athletes is rare (if seen at all); however, it is not outside the realms of possibility see some young people being tested and excluded in the future as the professionalization of youth sport takes hold.

Positive social norms are always going to reflect the society in which they are applied, thus in western societies, positive norms are probably things like adhering to rules of behavior, values, and morals, and obligations for service.

In contrast, harmful norms could be laissez-faire practices, antisocial and amoral norms, norms that encourage violence, reckless behavior, consumerism, poor health, practices, and conformity. Lack of support for efficacy and mattering could be manifested in coaching behavior and structure that is non-challenging, over-controlling, disempowering, and disabling and promotes an excessive focus on current relative performance level rather than improvement. Finally, practices that promote bad physical habits and habits of mind; and practices that undermine school and learning are considered features of harmful youth programs. Although some features are extreme and are unlikely to be intentionally set into a life skills program (e.g., harassment and neglect), some aspects of the aforementioned contrast poles may "sneak in" without the coach realizing the effects (e.g., winning over development). Therefore, coaches need to reflect on their coaching practices and structures to consider whether they are inadvertently scuppering attempts to develop life skills by creating conditions that are not conducive to personal growth.

The Role of the Coach

Bailey (2008) stated that whether an athlete reaps the developmental benefits of sports participation depends a great deal on the coach and how the coach transmits his or her behaviors, beliefs, and values and how coach behaviors, beliefs, and value determines the valence of the sports experience for young people. It is, therefore, important to discuss and critically examine how coaches can coach life skills.

Gould and Carson (2008) constructed a broad exploratory model for coaching life skills through sport. In their model, Gould and Carson (2008) emphasized how, under what conditions, and why life skills develop. Gould and Carson (2008) considered the range of assets that young people bring to the sport setting, and they suggested that these prior factors can debilitate or facilitate development (see my earlier discussion of personality). The next section of Gould and Carson's model examined what coaches do (and what they believe) that could encourage life skills development. Gould and Carson (2008) clarify that coaching philosophy and relationship skills (i.e., empathy, rapport building, and communication) are central to the development of life skills. For example, in the hypothetical scenario in the opening paragraphs, it should be clear that the two coaches had different coaching philosophies that underpinned their coaching strategies. It would be fair to assume that Jesse's coach had a philosophy build around tenets of cooperation and personal development, whereas Chris's coach has a philosophy centered on winning and competition. It may be more complicated than a simple dichotomy of one philosophy versus another. In reality, a coach probably holds several beliefs about the value of youth sport and some (if not most) will probably want positive youth development and winning. In this case, the important thing is that the coaches hold philosophies that place a high priority on athletes' personal development over nondevelopmental goals (i.e., personal career development, trophies). Primarily, coaches strive to help athletes become better people if they improve as an athlete as well; that is a bonus. To understand coaching philosophy Gould, Medbery, and Collins (2003) recommended that coaches consider answering these questions: why do I coach, what are my aim and objectives for coaching, what do I get out of coaching, and why did I get into coaching? Coaches can use the answers from these questions to understand their coaching philosophy.

Gould and Carson (2008) proposed that the way (and when) coaches use of direct teaching strategies also influences life skill development. For instance, the absence of clear rules or inconsistent application of rules and boundaries could hinder life skill development. Likewise, limited reinforcement of skills could encumber skill development that, the presence of appropriate feedback and instruction could flourish. Sports participants could derive feedback directly from the coach. In this way, what the coach says and does is paramount. This is not the only that coaches can influence feedback and reinforcement. Coaches can engender social reinforcement of life skills by educating parents and asking them to deliver support young people that are coherent with the lessons that coaches deliver on the pitch, at the pool, in the gym, and the changing rooms. Coaches can also influence the policy of national governing bodies in a bottom-up fashion (as opposed to top-down when governing bodies inform coach behavior). Rather than passively following guidelines, coaches are sometimes in a position to provide feedback to sporting directors, head coaches, and policymakers in national governing bodies that could be disseminated across the relevant communities of knowledge (through coaches continued professional development programs and through coach education).

Turnnidge, Côté, and Hancock (2014) suggested that coaches could develop life skills through sport in two different ways: the implicit approach and the explicit approach. Pierce et al. (2017) noted that there had been growing debate and discussion amongst sport psychology researchers about which approach to life skills transfer is optimal. I add that these approaches are not necessarily mutually exclusive, and I suggest that coaches consider a combination approach rather than exclusively relying on one method over the other. In reality, it is likely that some skills will be developed in the absence of intentional instruction and skills can be developed and reinforced in the presence of deliberate teaching.

Coaches could adopt an explicit method while recognizing that implicit learning could occur in the background. The implicit approach is characterized by the absence of deliberate coaching strategies to develop life skills. Instead, athletes can develop life skills based on the nature of the sport and the athletes' experiences of playing, training, and competing in the sporting environment. Certain sports require skills and values without which athletes will either be unsuccessful or lack enjoyment. To demonstrate this idea, I encourage you to participate in another brief thought experiment and reflect on your answer. Contemplate the reality of sport participation in a developing nation where athletes do not have access to well-trained coaches, league competition, or pervasive national governing bodies. In this case, sports participation is better described as unstructured play rather than training or competition. Consider that the sport young people are playing is cricket. To play cricket, the young people must develop or demonstrate a range of skills including (but not limited to) working together in a team, developing communication skills, managing disappointment (for example getting out), and negotiation (picking teams, applying rules). There is no youth development policy at play and no coach to teach the skills in question. Instead, it is more likely that young people learn skills through trial and error, practice, and peer observation. In this way, continued participation is contingent on developing a set of skills. Failure to acquire necessary life (and sport) skills may result in lowered enjoyment, reduced functioning, and probably dropout from the sport in question (perhaps to other activities that are coherent with an individual's assets, values, and skills).

The explicit approach refers to coaches who intentionally teach life skills and forms the basis of the majority of life skills programs. Intentional life skill teaching does not necessarily mean traditional didactic style teaching. The deliberate instruction can also involve dialectics and the creation of the conditions so that implicit skill development occurs. For example, coaches can condition practice to develop game knowledge and life skill proficiency within representative game activities, akin to a "teaching games for understanding" style model of practice.

The third part of Gould and Carson's explanatory model of life skill development attempts to explain why the sport experience and individual factors may promote life skills development. Gould and Carson (2008) highlighted possible mechanisms that explain the relationship between sport and life skills development. Gould and Carson (2008) proposed two broad sets of explanations: social environment influences and the utility of the life skill strategies themselves. The social environment group mechanisms focus on how sports facilities positive identity formation, development, and consolidation, membership in a positive peer group, developing social capital, and the formation and maintenance of attachments with non-familial adults. By entering different social settings, young people can learn about different social norms, and they can positively enhance their perceived competence, locus of control, self-worth, and autonomy. Without doubt, the positive development of self-worth, locus or control, and perceived autonomy is not automatic and is often confounded and suppressed by many factors (e.g., unsupportive adults and peers, social exclusion, peer conflict). Thus, coaches should appreciate that while young people can learn life skills in the absence of direct teaching and just being in the sports environment can teach skills (i.e., an implicit approach to life skill development) there are sometimes obstacles that can blunt the positive effect of the sports environment.

Thus, one job (among many) for a coach could be to coach life skills by removing these so-called blunting factors. The other general explanation for understanding how life skills development is the utility of life skills (and in my opinion, how aware young people are of the skills they have). According to Gould and Carson (2008), several life skills such as stress management, goal setting, and communication are directly transferable to other settings and used throughout life because this is the most utile.

The final components of Gould and Carson's explanatory life skills model list possible outcomes that coaches, athletes, and parents might label as life skills and role transfer plays in life skills development. According to Gould and Carson (2008), the absence of transfer to another setting occludes observation of whether life skills have developed. In their model, Gould and Carson (2008) stated that transfer is influenced by the perceived value of the transferable skill (by both coach and athlete), awareness of one's skill and similarity of learning and transfer contexts, confidence in the ability to transfer, external support for transfer, and perseverance in the face of failure. Coaching based life skills interventions could, therefore, focus on any one of these areas.

Regarding transferability, the athlete must be aware of the skills that they are learning. Without awareness, the transfer of life skills will be implausible. Danish, Petitpas, and Hale (1993) suggested that one of the main obstructions to life skill acquisition is that young people are aware of the skills they possess. To create the conditions for the transfer of life skills, Gould and Carson's (2008) suggested that young people believe that skills can be of value in other situations. They also require awareness of possessing physical and psychological skills and an understanding and knowledge of how skills are learned. Life skill transfer is also facilitated if young people have the confidence to use skills in different situations and motivation to explore non-sporting roles. Finally, it is plausible that young people will benefit if they seek and finding sources of social support and have the ability to adjust and cope with initial setbacks and failures. Pierce, Kendellen, Camiré, and Gould (2018) also recommended that within the implicit method of life skills development transfer of life skills occurs if the individual deems the skill to be useful in other areas of life. A coach could be well placed to engage with athletes to help them see how skills could be used and by doing so, influence an athlete's perception of the utility of skill across life domains and epochs.

In addition to the Gould and Carson (2008) several other researchers have considered how to teach life skills (e.g., Camiré, Trudel, & Forneris, 2012; Gould, Collins, Lauer, & Chung, 2007). The majority of these researchers have done so by interviewing coaches and asking them to recall what they believe, they did, and how they facilitated growth in their athletes. Aligned with this research, other scholars have asked athletes to reflect on what they thought their coaches did to help them develop life skills (e.g., Jones & Lavallee, 2009b). The result of both approaches to understanding how life skills have been developed is a rich description of the experience. However, what is missing is experimental research that tests the ideas of coaches and athletes. The Gould and Carson (2008) model indicate several areas that could contribute to life skill development. Likewise, similar qualitative research is based on recall of life skills experiences that might not accurately reflect the reality of the sport experience. In the absence of high-quality experimental research, it is impossible to know which areas in Gould and Carson's (2008) model drive the process of life skill development and which areas might be cognitive (i.e., confirmatory) biases on the part of coaches and athletes. To reiterate, I am not saying that the existing qualitative research is redundant, but I do not see the need to adopt the same research design (i.e., retrospective interviews) repeatedly. It is my opinion that this type of research has run its course, and scholars and practitioners are approaching saturation in terms of what this type of research can contribute to knowledge. Other researchers may disagree with me!

The next step is to take the findings from qualitative research and to examine whether independent coaches (i.e., not the coaches' who were interviewed) can adopt specific life skills development strategies. Scholars and practitioners could then consider experimental research designs that compare different coaching conditions to control conditions to see whether athletes believe that they have learned life skills and whether any evidence of life skill transfer can be identified.

The obvious challenge is the longitudinal nature of personal development that cannot be captured through single shot cross-sectional research. The best research designs will be longitudinal that assess life skill development and demonstration over a period (possibly years). The more critical limitation will be the funding available to fund such longitudinal endeavors. Despite these limitations, researchers should strongly consider this type of research (longitudinal and experimental) because publishing the same qualitative papers that ostensibly ask the same question (i.e., what life skills have you learned from sport) have genuinely run their course.

Key Points

- Life skills are latent constructs and as such there is a lack of agreement on how life skills should be operationalised.
- There are also some noteworthy conceptual challenges associated with defining and measuring transferability of skills across life domains.
- Scholars and practitioners need to be considerate of the ranges of outcomes associated with the coaching life skills and also be aware that some outcomes will be moderated by extraneous variables.
- Life skills coaching involves an interaction of personal and environment variables.
- Coaches could play an active role in life skill development however there is a paucity of experimental research to support this claim

Conclusion

In closing, I would like to highlight a range of issues that I believe need reconciling before meaningful progress can be made, and coaches can use research to develop life skills in the sport. Before coaches can coach life skills through the sport, they need to know what life skills are and what they are not. Coaches need objective outcome measures so that they can demonstrate quantifiable benefits to the athlete, the other coaches, and the sports administrators and policymakers. These outcome measures can then be employed to reveal the magnitude of transfer of a life skill from one domain to another or from one time to another. Models of life skill coaching exist, but they are mainly anecdotal and lack sufficient high-quality evidence to support their implementation. These models should be used as a guide but should not be prescriptive. Clearly, future research is required to demonstrate that life skills can be coached and that life skills that are coach can be transferred across life domains or periods. The current literature is not of a high enough quality to conclude that coaching is employed to develop life skills; however, in the absence of high-quality experimental data, there is enough anecdote to suggest that coaching probably does contribute to young sports peoples' life skill development. There is no smoke without fire!

References

Bailey, R. (2008). Youth sport and social inclusion. In N. L. Holt (Ed.), *Positive youth development through sport* (pp. 85–96). Oxford, UK: Routledge.

Benson, P. L. (1993). *The troubled journey: A portrait of 6th-12th grade youth*. Minneapolis, MN: The Search Institute.

Benson, P. L., & Scales, P. C. (2009). The definition and preliminary measurement of thriving in adolescence. *The Journal of Positive Psychology, 4*, 85–104.

Brown, D. J., Arnold, R., Reid, T., & Roberts, G. (2018). A qualitative exploration of thriving in elite sport. *Journal of Applied Sport Psychology, 30*, 129–149.

Bundick, M. J., Yeager, D. S., King, P. E., & Damon, W. (2010). Thriving across the life span. In R. M. Lerner, M. E. Lamb, A. M. Freund, & W. F. Overton (Eds.), *Handbook of life-span development: Cognition, biology and methods* (pp. 882–923). Hoboken, NJ: Wiley.

Camiré, M., Trudel, P., & Forneris, T. (2012). Coaching and transferring life skills: Philosophies and strategies used by model high school coaches. *The Sport Psychologist, 26*, 243–260.

Catalano, R. F., Berglund, M. L., Ryan, J. A. M., Lonczak, H. S., & Hawkins, J. D. (1998). *Positive youth development in the United States: Research findings on evaluations of youth development programs*. Washington, DC: Department of Health and Human Services.

Danish, S. J., Petitpas, A. J., & Hale, B. D. (1993). Life development intervention for athletes: Life skills through sports. *The Counseling Psychologist, 21*, 352–385.

Gould, D., & Carson, S. (2008). Life skills development through sport: Current status and future directions. *International Review of Sport and Exercise Psychology, 1*, 58–78.

Gould, D., Collins, K., Lauer, L., & Chung, Y. (2007). Coaching life skills through football: A study of award winning high school coaches. *Journal of Applied Sport Psychology, 19*, 16–37.

Gould, D., Medbery, R., & Collins, K. (2003). Coaching philosophy-developing winners in football and life. In D. Gould (Ed.), *Coaching academy playbook* (pp. 3–9). Morristown, NJ: The National Football Foundation and College Hall of Fame.

Haskell, R. E. (2001). *Transfer of learning: Cognition, instruction and reasoning*. San Diego, CA: Academic Press.

Holt, N. L. (2016). *Positive youth development through sport* (2nd ed.). London, UK: Routledge.

Jones, M. I., & Lavallee, D. (2009a). Exploring the life skills needs of British adolescent athletes. *Psychology of Sport and Exercise, 10*, 159–167.

Jones, M. I., & Lavallee, D. (2009b). Exploring perceived life skills development and participation in sport. *Qualitative Research in Sport and Exercise, 1*, 36–50.

Jones, M. I., & Parker (2014). Life skills programs: What makes them work? In R. Gomes, R. Resende, & A. Albuquerque (Eds.), *Positive human functioning from a multidimensional perspective* (pp. 15–36). London, UK: Nova.

Lerner, R. M. (2004). *Liberty: Thriving and civic engagement among American youth*. Thousand Oaks, CA: Sage.
Lerner, R. M., Dowling, E. M., & Anderson, P. M. (2003). Positive youth development: Thriving as the basis of personhood and civil society. *Applied Developmental Science, 7*, 172–180.
Lerner, R. M., Lerner, J. V., Almerigi, J., Theokas, C., Phelps, E., Naudeau, S., & Von Eye, A. (2006). Toward a new vision and vocabulary about adolescence: Theoretical and empirical bases of a "positive youth development" perspective. In L. Balter & C. S. Tamis-LeMonda (Eds.), *Child psychology: A handbook of contemporary issues* (pp. 445–469). New York: Taylor & Francis.
National Research Council and Institute of Medicine. (2002). *Community programs to promote youth development: Committee on community-level programs for youth. Board of children, youth, and families, division of behavioral and social sciences and education*. Washington, DC: National Academy Press.
Pierce, S., Gould, D., & Camiré, M. (2017). Definition and model of life skills transfer. *International Review of Sport and Exercise Psychology, 10*, 186–211.
Pierce, S., Kendellen, K., Camiré, M., & Gould, D. (2018). Strategies for coaching for life skills transfer. *Journal of Sport Psychology in Action, 9*, 11–20.
Roth, J. L., & Brooks-Gunn, J. (2003). What exactly is a youth development program? Answers from research and practice. *Applied Developmental Science, 7*, 94–111.
Scales, P. C., Benson, P. L., Leffert, N., & Blyth, D. A. (2000). Contribution of developmental assets to the prediction of thriving among adolescents. *Applied Developmental Science, 4*, 27–46.
Schlossberg, N. K. (1981). A model for analyzing human adaptation to transition. *The Counselling Psychologist, 9*, 2–18.
Simonton, D. K. (1999). Talent and its development: An emergenic and epigenetic model. *Psychological Review, 106*, 435.
Turnnidge, J., Côté, J., & Hancock, D. J. (2014). Positive youth development from sport to life: Explicit or implicit transfer? *Quest, 66*, 203–217.

Martin I. Jones has a PhD in sport and exercise psychology from Loughborough University and has held research and teaching posts in universities in the UK and Canada. Martin is a British Psychological Society Charted Psychologist and a UK Health and Care Professions Council Practitioner Psychologist. Martin conducts research in the areas of positive youth and talent development, mental toughness, and sleep and fatigue management. Martin currently works as a research psychologist in UK defence.

Chapter 16
Coaching Cohesive Teams

Todd M. Loughead, Matthieu M. Boisvert, and Katherine E. Hirsch

Abstract Cohesion has historically been viewed as one of the most important small-group variable (Golembiewski. The small group. Chicago: University of Chicago Press, 1962; Lott & Lott. Psychological Bulletin 64:259–309, 1965). Given its importance for sport, a considerable amount of research has examined this construct over the last six decades. Therefore, the purpose of this chapter is to provide an overview of the area of cohesion in sport. The chapter opens by examining the key definitions and characteristics of cohesion. Next, a conceptual model of cohesion is presented proposing that cohesive teams manifest themselves in four ways. First, team members have perceptions of the team from two perspectives—the closeness of the team and team members' motivation to join and remain on the team. Second, team members have two types of orientations towards the team—task and social cohesion orientations. Based on this conceptualization, research is presented to highlight the findings that cohesion is related to a variety of correlations such as individual cognitions, leadership, sacrifice behavior, and role clarity. In order for coaches to maximize the benefits of having cohesive teams, the chapter concludes with an overview of team building and the role of the coach in facilitating its development.

Keywords Conceptual model · Team · Task · Social cohesion

Given the importance of having cohesive sport teams, it is not surprising that those involved in sport, such as coaches, have been interested in this construct. However, the importance of cohesion dates further back than sport. In fact, the cohesion of groups has been a focal topic in the disciplines of sociology, social psychology, counseling psychology, military psychology, organizational psychology, and educational psychology, dating back to the 1950s (Mudrack, 1989). Historically, authors (Golembiewski, 1962; Lott & Lott, 1965) have suggested that cohesion is

T. M. Loughead (✉) · M. M. Boisvert · K. E. Hirsch
Department of Kinesiology, University of Windsor, Windsor, ON, Canada
e-mail: loughead@uwindsor.ca; boisverm@uwindsor.ca; hirschk@uwindsor.ca

R. Resende, A. R. Gomes (eds.), *Coaching for Human Development and Performance in Sports*, https://doi.org/10.1007/978-3-030-63912-9_16

the most important variable impacting groups. With its perceived prominence, there were several attempts to define what is meant by the term "cohesion". These early definitions were related to "forces" that acted on individuals to remain in the group (e.g., Festinger, 1950; Festinger, Schachter, & Back, 1950) or the "resistance" of a group to disruptive forces (e.g., Gross & Martin, 1952). Unfortunately, these definitions were fraught with issues including practical, conceptual, and measurement perspectives. Consequently, Mudrack (1989) boldly stated that "the history of research into group cohesiveness has been dominated by confusion, inconsistency, and almost inexcusable sloppiness with regard to defining the construct" (p. 45).

Given the issues surrounding these early definitions of cohesion, sport psychology researchers, Carron, Brawley, and Widmeyer (1998) advanced what is considered to this day the most comprehensive and widely used definition of cohesion, which has been used in hundreds of studies. They defined cohesion as "a dynamic process which is reflected in the tendency for a group to stick together and remain united in the pursuit of its instrumental objectives and/or for the satisfaction of member affective needs" (Carron et al., 1998, p. 213).

Carron et al.'s (1998) definition of cohesion highlighted four fundamental characteristics in understanding the nature of cohesion. These characteristics are important for coaches to understand since it will help them understand and subsequently help them enhance the cohesion on their respective teams. The first characteristic is that cohesion is a *multidimensional* construct. In other words, there are many factors that influence a team to remain united. The second characteristic is the *dynamic* nature of cohesion whereby factors which cause a team to unite at one point may not have the same effect at another time. The third characteristic of cohesion is the *instrumental* nature of groups. That is, all groups, including sport teams, form for a specific purpose. The fourth characteristic is that cohesion involves an *affective* component. That is, social relationships may already exist in a group or they may develop over time. Even those groups that are highly task-oriented will develop social cohesion given that team members communicate with each other and have social interactions.

Conceptualization and Measurement of Cohesion

It is important for coaches to understand that there are different types of cohesion. In order to systematically study the construct of cohesion, Carron, Widmeyer, and Brawley (1985) advanced a conceptual model founded on three central assumptions. The first assumption, based on social cognitive theory (Bandura, 1986), stated that cohesion can be measured through individual perceptions. Carron et al. (1985) argued that members of a team have observable properties (e.g., roles, status relationships), are socialized into the team, experience social situations, and developed personal beliefs about the team. The second assumption argued that researchers need to differentiate between the team and the individual (Ver Bergen & Koekebakker, 1959; Zander, 1971). That is, each team member's personal

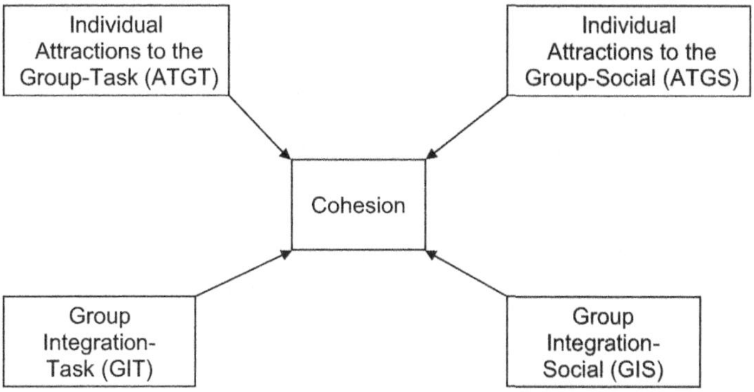

Fig. 16.1 Conceptual model of the four dimensions of cohesion. Adapted from "The Development of an Instrument to assess Cohesion in Sport Teams: The Group Environment Questionnaire", by A. V. Carron, W. N. Widmeyer, and L. R. Brawley, 1985, *Journal of Sport Psychology, 7*, pp. 248

perception regarding cohesion is related to the degree that the team satisfies the needs of the athlete personally and the team as a whole. As a result, two specific categories emerged to classify each of these social cognitions. The first, *individual attractions to the group*, is reflected in the interaction between the motives influencing the athlete to remain in the team (Carron et al., 1985). The second is, *group integration*, and is viewed in the athlete's perceptions regarding the closeness, similarity, and bonding within the team as a whole (Carron et al., 1985). The third assumption argues the need to discriminate between task-oriented and social-oriented perceptions of the team and its members (Loughead & Hardy, 2006). Task-oriented perceptions refers to the motivation toward achieving the team's goals and objectives. Social-oriented perceptions are the motivation toward establishing and maintaining social relationships and activities with fellow group members (Carron et al., 1985).

Based on these three assumptions, Carron et al. (1985) advanced a theoretically driven conceptual model of the specific factors constituting cohesion (see Fig. 16.1). Taken together, the conceptual model consists of four dimensions: *individual attractions to the group-task* (ATGT), *individual attractions to the group-social* (ATGS), *group integration-task* (GIT), and *group integration-social* (GIS). Specifically, ATGT represents individual team member's feelings of personal involvement with the team's goals and objectives. ATGS refers to an individual's feelings about their personal acceptance and social interaction with the team. GIT is the individual team member's feelings towards the similarity, closeness, and bonding around the group's goals and objectives. GIS represents individual team member's perceptions of the similarity, closeness, and bonding around the team as a social unit (Carron et al., 1998).

For those coaches interested in assessing the four types of cohesion, Carron et al. (1985) developed an inventory known as the Group Environment Questionnaire (GEQ). The GEQ is a relatively short inventory for coaches to administer as it contains 18 items that measures each of the four dimensions of cohesion. To date, the

GEQ is the most widely used measure of cohesion (Burke, Davies, & Carron, 2014). Specifically, ATGT is represented by four items and an example item includes "This team gives me enough opportunities to improve my personal performance". ATGS is composed of five items and an example item is "Some of my best friends are on this team". GIT is represented by five items. An example GIT item is "Our team is united in trying to reach its goals for performance". GIS is comprised of four items and an example GIS item is "Members of our team would like to spend time together in the off season". All items are measured on a 9-point Likert scale anchored with the extremes of 1 (strongly disagree) and 9 (strongly agree).

Conceptual Framework for the Study of Cohesion

To help coaches understand the factors that influence and are influenced by cohesion, a review of Carron' (1982) conceptual framework for the study of cohesion (see Fig. 16.2) is useful. This framework is a linear model consisting of inputs, throughputs, and outputs. The inputs represent the antecedents believed to influence cohesion, the throughputs are the different types of cohesion (e.g., ATGT, ATGS, GIT, GIS), and the outputs are the consequences of cohesion. In particular, the antecedents include the following factors: leadership, environmental, personal, and team, which in turn contribute to perceptions of cohesion. The leadership factor is comprised of four types: leader behaviors, leadership style, coach-athlete relationship, and the coach-team relationship. The environmental factor includes factors

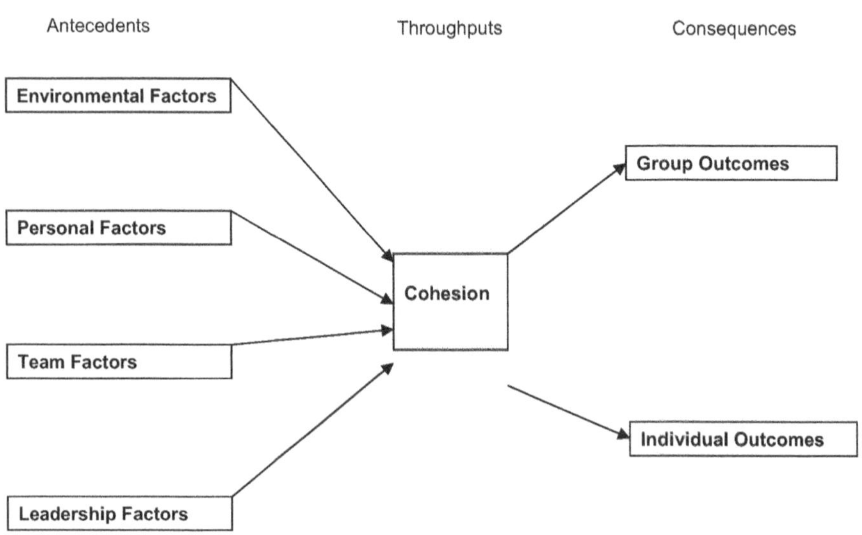

Fig. 16.2 Conceptual framework for the study of cohesion. Adapted from "Cohesiveness in Sport Groups: Interpretations and Considerations", by A. V. Carron, 1982, *Journal of Sport Psychology, 4*, pp. 131

such as the physical proximity of team members, group distinctiveness, and contractual responsibility. While Carron noted that it is difficult to outline a complete list of personal factors, he highlighted that constructs such as athlete ability, attitude, commitment, and satisfaction would impact perceptions of cohesion. Lastly, team factors represent aspects related to the groups' task, desire for group success, group productivity, team ability, team stability, team goals, team roles, and group outcomes. Concerning the throughputs, Carron noted at the time that cohesion was composed of task and social dimensions of cohesion. As noted in the previous section, cohesion has since been conceptualized as being comprised as a four-dimensional construct. As for the consequences that are theorized to be influenced by cohesion, Carron classified them into two general categories (i.e., group and individual outcomes). On the one hand, group outcomes involve team-level aspects such as group productivity, conformity, and role clarity. On the other hand, individual outcomes include facets related to behavioral consequences, individual performance, and personal satisfaction.

Research on Cohesion in Sport Teams

The advancement of the conceptual model of cohesion, the GEQ, and the conceptual framework for the study of cohesion has given rise to a substantial body of research involving the construct of cohesion. In order to give coaches a comprehensive overview of the research conducted in this area, we have organized this section based on the conceptual framework for the study of cohesion. Specifically, it is organized into the antecedents (i.e., environmental, personal, leadership, and team factors) and consequences (group and individual outcomes) of cohesion.

Antecedents

Environmental Factors Literature examining the environment in which athletes and teams function show that the nuances within the sport team environment can result in differences concerning an athlete's perception of cohesion (Eys et al., 2015) and the importance of cohesion as it pertains to performance (Carron, Colman, Wheeler, & Stevens, 2002). To date, most of the research examining environmental factors has examined variables that fall within what is known as the *organizational orientation*. The most common organizational orientation variable examined has been gender, and how it influences cohesion. For instance, interviews with coaches have shown that male and female athletes view cohesion differently on factors such as the importance of cohesion, role differentiation, status, and conflict management (Eys et al., 2015). Additionally, research has shown that female teams differ in their preferences for specific transformational leadership behaviors that, in turn, influence perceptions of cohesion than do male teams (Cronin, Arthur, Hardy, & Callow,

2015). One reason why gender has been examined in relation to cohesion is related to the moderating role that gender plays in the cohesion-performance relationship (Carron et al., 2002; Filho, Dobersek, Gershgoren, Becker, & Tenenbaum, 2014).

In addition to gender, coaches are reminded that there are other environmental factors reported to affect cohesion such as *age*, *maturity of members*, and *team goals*. For instance, research examining positive youth development (PYD) has reported differences in the goals of youth sport compared to adult sport, whereby youth sport encourages the development of cohesion by emphasizing the development of personal and social skills (Bruner, Eys, Wilson, & Côté, 2014). Furthermore, younger athletes perceive cohesion differently, as demonstrated in the development of a youth specific cohesion measure (i.e., Youth Sport Environment Questionnaire; Eys, Loughead, Bray, & Carron, 2009).

Personal Factors Coaches are reminded that individuals' thoughts, feelings, and characteristics impact the functioning of the team and thereby affects a team's level of cohesiveness. For instance, the personal factor of motivational climate has been shown to be related to cohesion (García-Calvo et al., 2014). Specifically, a task-motivational climate (i.e., where effort and skill development are encouraged) have been shown to be positively associated with both task and social cohesion. In contrast, an ego-motivational climate (i.e., where being better than others is encouraged) is negatively associated with task cohesion (García-Calvo et al., 2014; McLaren, Newland, Eys, & Newton, 2017). Further, the personal factor of satisfaction has revealed that the more an athlete feels satisfied the more cohesive they feel with their teammates (Onağ & Tepeci, 2014). These perceptions of satisfaction not only affect a team's cohesiveness by also affect other group constructs such as organizational citizenship behavior (i.e., helping behaviors, sportsmanship, and civic virtue; Aoyagi, Cox, & McGuire, 2008). Lastly, teams who are comprised of individuals with different characteristics (e.g., ethnicity, cultural background) were initially thought to have weaker team cohesion because these individual differences would foster clique formation (Eitzen, 1975). However, these individual differences amongst team members such as ethnic diversity and gender have been positively associated with cohesion (Filho et al., 2014; Shapcott, Carron, Burke, Bradshaw, & Estabrooks, 2006).

Leadership Factors The influence of coaches has been shown to be related to perceptions of cohesion. In an examination of transformational leadership received by their coaches, Cronin et al. (2015) surveyed intercollegiate athletes and found that the transformational leadership behaviors of individual consideration, inspirational motivation, fostering acceptance of group goals, high performance expectations, and appropriate role model were positively related to task cohesion. Similarly, when leadership behaviors are measured using the Leadership Scale for Sports (Chelladurai & Saleh, 1980), coaches who exhibit the leadership behaviors of training and instruction, democratic behavior, social support, and positive feedback have athletes who feel more task and social cohesive (Jowett & Chaundy, 2004).

Coaching research also supports the use of leadership behaviors that reduce physical and psychological distance (i.e., immediacy behaviors) between coaches and athletes as a method of improving task and social cohesion (Turman, 2008). Additionally, coaches play a large role in creating a positive motivational climate through their leadership fairness behaviors which have been shown to be positively correlated with task cohesion (De Backer, Boen, De Cuyper, Høigaard, & Vande Broek, 2015). Moreover, research has indicated that self-perceptions of the coach-athlete relationship is positively related to task and social cohesion, whereas meta-perceptions are related to task cohesion (Jowett & Chaundy, 2004).

Team Factors Coaches should also be cognizant of the type of sport they are coaching. For instance, in coactive sports (e.g., baseball) findings show a stronger cohesion-performance relationship than interactive sports (e.g., football; Carron et al., 2002). Further, a team's interpretation of their collective efficacy has been shown to be positively related to cohesion (Leo-Marcos, Sánchez-Miguel, Sánchez-Oliva, & García-Calvo, 2010). Further, the degree to which task and social behaviors are present within teams is believed to impact team's level of cohesion (Carron, 1982). Therefore, it is not surprising that high levels of communication and prosocial behaviors have been demonstrated to positively impact task cohesion (Al-Yaaribi & Kavussanu, 2017; McLaren & Spink, 2018), while variables such as jealousy, ego-related task climates, and antisocial behaviors have been shown to be negatively related to task and social cohesion (Al-Yaaribi & Kavussanu, 2017; García-Calvo et al., 2014; Kamphoff, Gill, & Huddleston, 2005; McLaren et al., 2017).

Consequences

Group Outcomes An important group outcome for coaches is whether athletes want to return to their teams. Spink, Wilson, and Odnokon (2010) examined eight ice hockey teams and their players to determine which athletes returned to their teams the following season. The analysis revealed that players who returned the following season had significantly stronger perceptions of task cohesion than those players who did not return. In a sample of athletes from soccer, basketball, volleyball, handball, and water polo, Onağ and Tepeci (2014) found that both task and social cohesion predicted intention to return. Therefore, coaches who would prefer to keep their team together for subsequent seasons should aim to enhance social and task cohesion as a means of increasing the likelihood of retaining players.

One of the most examined relationship concerning cohesion is its relation to performance. Carron et al. (2002) performed a comprehensive sport specific meta-analysis on the cohesion-performance relationship. Their meta-analysis included a total of 46 studies representing the response of 9988 athletes from 1044 teams. Overall, the results indicated that there was a moderate to large effect size ($ES = .66$) in the cohesion-performance relationship. Specifically, social cohesion ($ES = .70$) was found to have a stronger effect on performance than task cohesion ($ES = .61$). However, the differences between social and task cohesion were not statistically significant indicating that both types of cohesion are important when it comes to enhancing performance. In addition, the meta-analysis also examined various moderating variables believed to influence the cohesion-performance relationship. In particular, sport type, gender, measures of performance, level of skill, and direction of the cohesion-performance relationship were examined. As for sport type, the results indicated that coactive sports (*ES* = .77) have a slightly larger effect than interdependent sports (*ES* = .66) although the difference was not statistically significant. The results also showed a large cohesion-performance relationship existed for female athletes (*ES* = .95) while a moderate relationship existed for male athletes (*ES* = .56). It should be noted this difference was statistically significant. As for measures of performance, the findings found no difference between self-report measures of performance (*ES* = .58) and actual performance indices (*ES* = .69). In terms of level of competition, there were no significant differences amongst professional (*ES* = .20), club (*ES* = .23), intercollegiate (*ES* = .55), high school (*ES* = .83), and intramural (*ES* = .74) level athletes. Finally, the causal relationship between cohesion and performance displayed no significant difference, suggesting that both social and task cohesion are a cause of (*ES* = .57) and a result of (*ES* = .69) performance. More recently, Filho et al. (2014) conducted a similar meta-analysis on the cohesion-performance relationship on studies published between 2000 and 2010. Similar to Carron et al., there was a moderate cohesion-performance relationship. However, there were some notable differences. First, gender was found to be a moderating variable between the cohesion-performance relationship with mixed gender teams showing the strongest relationship compared to either female or male teams. Second, there was a stronger cohesion-performance relationship for coactive sports (r = .49) than interdependent sports (r = .17). Third, there were differences in level of competition with the strongest cohesion-performance relationship for recreational (r = .43) and college level athletes (r = .40) compared to high school (r = .13) and professional athletes (r = .19). Taken together, the results of these two meta-analyses demonstrate that there is indeed a positive cohesion-performance relationship, however, there are some differences amongst the moderating variables. These differences may suggest that societal dynamics are likely to change over time.

Individual Outcomes Researchers who have addressed performance from an individual athlete perspective have reported that cohesion impacts performance. Bray and Whaley (2001) examined high school basketball players by examining individual athlete performance measures (e.g., individual athlete game statistics) and found that the cohesion dimension of ATGS significantly predicted individual performance. Similar findings have also been reported at the collegiate basketball level (Bird, Foster, & Maruyama, 1980). In addition, athletes who reported having strong task cohesion were more likely to have higher levels of collective and self-efficacy (Leo-Marcos et al., 2010; Leo-Marcos, González-Ponce, Sánchez-Miguel, Ivarsson, & García-Calvo, 2015) and higher perceptions of ATGT and ATGS were predictors for positive coping demands for competition (Wolf, Eys, Sadler, & Kleinert, 2015). In an examination of positive youth development, athletes who reported higher levels cohesion were more likely to have a stronger PYD experience in that task cohesion was positively related to an increase in social skills, goal setting, and initiative, while social cohesion positively impacted social skills, goal setting, and cognitive skills (Bruner et al., 2014). Cohesion is also associated with greater affective commitment (Ha & Ha, 2015), stronger conformity to team norms (Prapavessis & Carron, 1997), and lower levels of social loafing (De Backer et al., 2015).

Team Building in Sport

Given the importance of cohesion, it is not surprising that researchers, mental performance consultants, and coaches alike invest time and effort attempting to enhance cohesion on sport teams. This process can be accomplished through a process called team building. In fact, team building interventions are among the most effective methods of enhancing team functioning (Yukelson, 1997). Some have operationalized team building as "a method of helping the group to a) increase effectiveness, b) satisfy the needs of its members, or c) improve work conditions" (Brawley & Paskevich, 1997, p. 13), whereas others view team building as a way to "promote an increased sense of unity and cohesiveness and enable the team to function together more smoothly and effectively" (Newman, 1984, p. 27). Although there is no agreed upon definition of team building, a consistent feature of team building is improving group effectiveness by enhancing cohesion (Carron, Spink, & Prapavessis, 1997).

Conceptual Model of Team Building in Sport

For those interested in team building, such as coaches, Carron and Spink (1993) advanced a conceptual model highlighting the factors that can be targeted when enhancing cohesion (see Fig. 16.3). The model is linear in nature and consists of inputs, throughputs, and outputs. The inputs consist of individual and team characteristics that need to be taken into consideration prior to the start of the team building intervention and include two categories: team environment and team structure. Team environment refers to the team's distinctiveness (e.g., wearing matching team uniforms) and togetherness (e.g., working out together). According to Carron and Spink (1993), when aspects related to the team's environment and/or the appearance of team members themselves are distinct, team members develop a strong sense of "we", allowing them to distinguish themselves from non-group members (i.e., "they"), which ultimately help to foster stronger perceptions of cohesion. Team structure includes factors such as clarity and acceptance of team roles (e.g., team captain, social organizer), team norms (e.g., team fitness standards), position on team (e.g., mentor), and leadership (e.g., taking teammate opinions into consideration when making decisions). Carron and Spink suggest that as team norms and

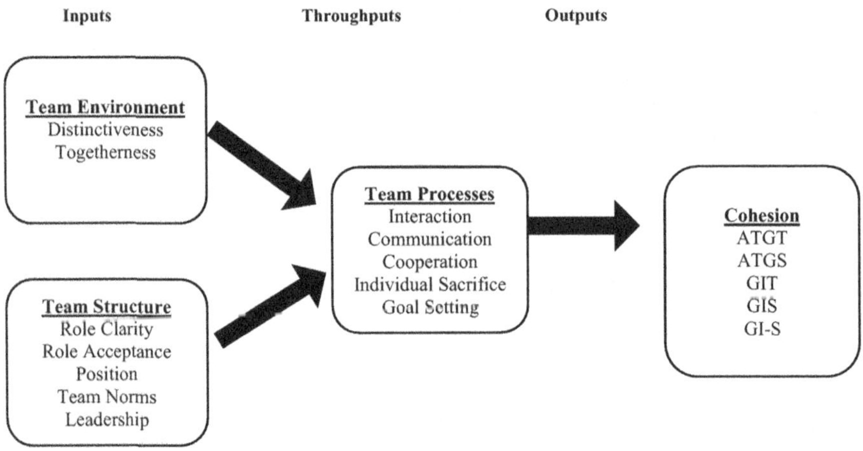

Fig. 16.3 Conceptual model for team building in sports. Adapted from Carron and Spink (1993), Carron et al. (1997)

collective expectations are developed, the team's structure becomes more stable. Additionally, having team members consistently occupy a certain position on the team contributes to the stability of the team structure. These two inputs are presumed to then influence the throughput, operationalized as group processes. Group processes include factors such as team interaction, team communication, cooperation amongst team members, individual athlete sacrifice, and goal setting (team and individual). These throughputs in turn influence the outputs, operationalized as cohesion.

Approaches to Team Building in Sport

A common query for coaches is how to best deliver team building programs to their teams. The literature highlights two primary ways in which team building programs can be delivered: directly (e.g., Yukelson, 1997) or indirectly (Carron et al., 1997). A direct approach involves a mental performance consultant working directly with the team to implement the team building program. For instance, Yukelson (1997) advocates for the use of a four-stage protocol for the implementation of team building program using a direct approach. The first stage involves the mental performance consultant assessing the team's needs by meeting with coaches, athletes, and support staff to learn more about the team's dynamics. During the second stage, the mental performance consultant describes the rationale behind the team building program. The third stage involves team members brainstorming about areas where the team needs improvement. In the final stage, the mental performance consultant implements the team building program.

In contrast, the indirect approach to team building involves a mental performance consultant working with the coaching staff to help them develop and implement the team building program. In order to facilitate the implementation of a team building program using an indirect approach, Carron and Spink (1993) developed a four-stage protocol consisting of an introductory, conceptual, practical, and intervention stage. The introductory stage serves to introduce the team building intervention program to the team and outline the potential benefits. The benefits include greater communication, team stability, trust, acceptance of roles, and conformity to team norms. This stage is particularly important because athletes will exhibit greater motivation and adherence when they understand the rational of the team building intervention program (Spink, 1988). In the conceptual stage, the team building model is introduced (see Fig. 16.3) to facilitate the transition from theoretical to practical. That is, theoretical constructs are simplified and explained that allow athletes to better understand how the team will benefit from the team building program. It is also at this stage that the mental performance consultant identifies the factors that will be targeted for development throughout the intervention. The presentation of the conceptual model during this stage should last approximately 20 min (Carron & Spink, 1993). At the practical stage, coaches and athletes become active agents in developing potential strategies to be used in their team's team building program, based on what they deemed the most important during the conceptual stage. Allowing the coaches and athletes to generate the intervention strategies has be shown to contribute to increased commitment (Loughead & Bloom, 2011). Finally, at the intervention stage, team building protocols developed in the previous three stages are implemented by the coaches.

Research on Team Building in Sport

In the sport literature, team building programs have been implemented in an attempt to enhance a variety of variables, including cohesion. However, the effectiveness of these programs has yielded mixed results in terms of enhancing cohesion. A number of studies have found a positive team building-cohesion relationship (e.g., Rovio, Arvinen-Barrow, Weigand, Eskola, & Lintunen, 2012; Senécal, Loughead, & Bloom, 2008; Stewart, Carreau, & Bruner, 2016), whereas some studies have failed to find any significant changes in perceptions of cohesion (e.g., Bloom & Stevens, 2002; Prapavessis, Carron, & Spink, 1996).

As for studies showing a team building as effective, Rovio et al. (2012) conducted a season-long team building program with a junior Finish ice hockey team. The results indicated that social cohesion significantly increased throughout the season. That is, team members reported an increase in feelings of similarity, closeness, and bonding within the team. However, task cohesion did not significantly increase at post-intervention. The authors mention that this may be due to team members reporting high levels of personal involvement towards team task productivity and goals at the start of the season. Similarly, Stewart et al. (2016) conducted a ropes course team building intervention program, using a mixed methods design, with the purpose of increasing cohesion. Overall, the team building intervention proved to be effective at increasing cohesion and improving the overall team environment. Specifically, task cohesion increased significantly post-intervention, however, social cohesion did not significantly change from pre- to post-intervention. However, focus group interviews conducted with every athlete revealed that cohesion was perceived to have increased throughout the season and that this contributed to their increased performance.

Although the previously mentioned studies reported significant increases in cohesion using mixed method designs, these studies did not contain a control group. As such, it is difficult to determine whether the increases in cohesion were a consequence of the team building program. One study that involved a control group was Senécal et al. (2008) who conducted a season-long team building intervention program with female high school basketball teams examining the effectiveness of team goal setting on cohesion. The results revealed that athletes in the team building condition showed no significant increase in cohesion from the beginning to the end of the season. However, athletes in the control condition showed a significant decrease in cohesion during the season. Therefore, it appears that the team building intervention was helpful in maintaining levels of cohesion throughout the season. Without the use of a control condition, the authors would have simply concluded that the team building intervention was unsuccessful at increasing cohesion.

As for studies showing no change in cohesion, Prapavessis et al. (1996) conducted a team building intervention program with eight soccer teams. Coaches were randomly assigned to a team building, placebo-control, or control condition. Coaches in the team building condition developed strategies related to role clarity and acceptance, leadership, conformity to standards, sacrifices, goals and objectives, and cooperation which were subsequently implemented with their respective teams. Coaches in the placebo-control condition were provided with information covering topics such as nutrition, strength, flexibility, endurance, and tactics. The results revealed that the team building intervention was unsuccessful at increasing perceptions of cohesion compared to a placebo-control or control conditions. Similarly, Bloom and Stevens (2002) implemented a team building mental skills training program with a female NCAA Division I equestrian team. The team building program included topics such as leadership, team norms, communication, how to handle being chosen for competition, and preparing for Nationals. The results demonstrated no significant differences in perceptions of cohesion from pre- to post-intervention.

In order to shed light on the equivocal results of team building research in sport, Martin, Carron, and Burke (2009) conducted a meta-analysis examining not only the effectiveness of team building intervention programs, but also the impact of potential moderating variables. A total of 17 studies were included in the meta-analysis. The results showed that team building had a significant small to moderate positive effect on cohesion, performance, roles (i.e., clarity, acceptance, and satisfaction), self-confidence, and athlete satisfaction. Additionally, team goal setting was found to be the most effective type of team building activity. When examining approaches to team building, both direct and indirect approaches were equally effective, which would tend to indicate that coaches can choose the method they are the most comfortable with. The length of the team building program influences the effectiveness of the intervention. Team building programs lasting less than 2 weeks were found to be ineffective, whereas programs lasting from 2 to 20 weeks, and 20 weeks or longer were both effective. When examining the impact on outcome variables, team building programs had a small positive effect on social cohesion and a large positive effect on performance and enhanced cognitions.

Another type of team building that has received attention is personal disclosure and mutual sharing (PDMS) (e.g., Barker, Evans, Coffee, Slater, & McCarthy, 2014; Dunn & Holt, 2004; Evans, Slater, Turner, & Barker, 2013; Pain & Harwood, 2009; Windsor, Barker, & McCarthy, 2011). According to Crace and Hardy (1997), mutual understanding between team members is the cornerstone of the team building process. Interpersonal problems among teams typically result from individual team members lack of understanding of their teammates' needs, motives, and feelings (Orlick, 1990). Orlick argued that "it is difficult to be responsive to another's needs or feelings when you do not know what they are. It is difficult to respect another's perspective if you do not understand what it is or where it came from" (p. 144). To allow team members to gain a deeper understanding of one another, Yukelson (1997) recommended that mutual sharing activities (e.g., sharing thoughts, feelings, and ideas) be integrated into team building intervention programs.

Among the early studies utilizing a personal disclosure and mutual sharing (PDMS) team building approach, Dunn and Holt (2004) examined the effect of a PDMS program with 27 male intercollegiate ice hockey players delivered during a national championship tournament. The athletes were encouraged to share personal information related to why they play hockey, how and they got started in the sport, and the reasons for their continued participation. The goal of these open discussion was to get athletes emotionally engaged and foster a sense of cohesiveness. Overall, the athletes reported benefiting from the PDMS program. These benefits included an increase in cohesion, confidence, and a greater sense of understanding of themselves and their teammates. Similarly, Pain and Harwood (2009) examined the effectiveness of a team building program utilising a PDMS approach in their study of 18 English university soccer players. The program consisted of four workshops delivered on a weekly basis concentrating on creating open discussions relating to the team's performance environment. Overall, the PDMS team building intervention appeared to be effective at encouraging open discussion regarding team functioning. Specifically, athletes reported an increase in perceptions of team functioning (i.e., cohesion, communication, trust, and confidence in teammates), training quality, self-understanding, player ownership, and team performance. Windsor et al. (2011) sought to examine the effects of a PDMS intervention program on team cohesion and communication among 21 male professional soccer players in the United Kingdom. The PDMS program was administered before a critical match in the latter stages of the team's domestic cup competition. The results revealed that the PDMS program did not statistically increase cohesion or communication. However, the authors argue that these results may have been due to the limited time frame during which the data were collected. In contrast, data from a social validation questionnaire conducted with 14 players after the intervention revealed that the program was beneficial to the team by enhancing closeness, understanding of teammates, and communication.

More recently, Evans et al. (2013) conducted a single-session PDMS team building program with 14 male professional youth soccer academy players. The PDMS targeted the outcomes of social identity, friendships identity content, results identity content, collective efficacy, and team performance. The results revealed an increase in team performance and friendship identity content, whereas social identity, results identity content, and collective efficacy remained stable. In addition, Barker et al. (2014) examined the effects of a dual-session PDMS team building intervention program on multiple group variables, including social identity, social identity content, and collective efficacy. The PDMS program included 15 elite academy cricketers and took place during an 11-day preseason cricket tour. The findings showed that the PDMS program was successful at increasing social identity, social identity content, and collective efficacy.

In sum, it appears that personal disclosure and mutual sharing (PDMS) team building programs can influence various group factors, including trust, understanding (e.g., Dunn & Holt, 2004) communication, cohesion, and collective efficacy (Barker et al., 2014; Pain & Harwood, 2009), which can in turn influence team performance (Evans et al., 2013).

Key Points

Coaches play a valuable role in developing the cohesiveness amongst their athletes. However, the simple existence of athletes on a team does not ensure that positive outcomes will result. Teams must be nurtured, supported, and developed. When coaches facilitate and properly conduct team building, it can have a lasting and positive impact on their teams. As it has been shown in this chapter, having cohesive teams is beneficial in facilitating team effectiveness. Consequently, coaches and sport psychology consultants are reminded that athletes are active participants in the team building process and their involvement in the team building process is vital for establishing cohesive teams. It is also important when conducting team building that both social and task elements be developed to help ensure that all aspects of the team environment are being cultivated. For instance, team building efforts that focus on social elements such as interpersonal relations are likely to influence affective outcomes. While focusing on task related aspects such as team goal-setting are more likely to impact team performance. Therefore, coaches are encouraged to be holistic in the team building activities.

Conclusion

The objective of this chapter was to present an overview of cohesion to help coaches better understand this construct. To achieve this goal, we presented some of the earliest definitions of cohesion and then forwarded the Carron et al. (1998) definition that best describes cohesion in sport. Using the Carron et al. definition, we then describe the multidimensional nature of cohesion. Following this, we discuss how cohesion can be best measured in sport teams using the Group Environment Questionnaire. In order to provide coaches with a comprehensive understanding of how cohesion operates within a sport environment, we describe two conceptual frameworks—one that describes the different dimensions of cohesion (i.e., ATGT, GIT, ATGS, GIS) and the other highlighting the factors that influence these different dimensions cohesion and how these dimensions of cohesion influence certain outcomes. Next, we review some of the literature relating to the variables associated with cohesion (i.e., environmental, personal, leadership, and team) and how cohesion is related to a team's performance. Lastly, we end the chapter with a section on team building by highlighting models and approaches in which coaches can foster more cohesive teams along with the research supporting the building of cohesive teams. It is our hope that the chapter presented will assists coaches, athletes, mental performance consultants, and scholars in developing the highly cohesive teams.

References

Al-Yaaribi, A., & Kavussanu, M. (2017). Teammate prosocial and antisocial behaviors predict task cohesion and burnout: The mediating role of affect. *Journal of Sport & Exercise Psychology, 39*, 199–208.

Aoyagi, M. W., Cox, R. H., & McGuire, R. T. (2008). Organizational citizenship behavior in sport: Relationships with leadership, team cohesion, and athlete satisfaction. *Journal of Applied Sport Psychology, 20*, 25–41.

Bandura, A. (1986). *Social foundations of thought and action: A social cognitive theory*. Englewood Cliffs, NJ: Prentice Hall.

Barker, J. B., Evans, A. L., Coffee, P., Slater, M. J., & McCarthy, P. J. (2014). Consulting on tour: A dual-phase personal-disclosure mutual-sharing intervention and group functioning in elite youth cricket. *The Sport Psychologist, 28*, 186–197.

Bird, A. M., Foster, C. D., & Maruyama, G. (1980). Convergent and incremental effects of cohesion on attributions for self and team. *Journal of Sport Psychology, 2*, 181–194.

Bloom, G. A., & Stevens, D. E. (2002). Case study: A team-building mental skills training program with an intercollegiate equestrian team. *Athletic Insight: The Online Journal of Sport Psychology, 4*, 1–16.

Brawley, L. R., & Paskevich, D. M. (1997). Conducting team building research in context of sport and exercise. *Journal of Applied Sport Psychology, 9*, 11–40.

Bray, C. D., & Whaley, D. E. (2001). Team cohesion, effort, and objective individual performance of high school basketball players. *The Sport Psychologist, 15*, 260–275.

Bruner, M. W., Eys, M. A., Wilson, K. S., & Côté, J. (2014). Group cohesion and positive youth development in team sport athletes. *Sport, Exercise, and Performance Psychology, 3*, 219–227.

Burke, S. M., Davies, K. M., & Carron, A. V. (2014). Group cohesion in sport and exercise settings. In M. R. Beauchamp & M. A. Eys (Eds.), *Group dynamics in exercise and sport psychology: Contemporary themes* (2nd ed., pp. 147–163). New York: Routledge.

Carron, A. V. (1982). Cohesiveness in sport groups: Interpretations and considerations. *Journal of Sport Psychology, 4*, 123–138.

Carron, A. V., Brawley, L. R., & Widmeyer, W. N. (1998). Measurement of cohesion in sport and exercise. In J. L. Duda (Ed.), *Advances in sport and exercise psychology measurement* (pp. 213–226). Morgantown, WV: Fitness Information Technology.

Carron, A. V., Colman, M. M., Wheeler, J., & Stevens, D. (2002). Cohesion and performance in sport: A meta-analysis. *Journal of Sport & Exercise Psychology, 24*, 168–188.

Carron, A. V., & Spink, K. S. (1993). Team building in an exercise setting. *The Sport Psychologist, 7*, 8–18.

Carron, A. V., Spink, K. S., & Prapavessis, H. (1997). Team building and cohesiveness in the sport and exercise setting: Use of indirect interventions. *Journal of Applied Sport Psychology, 9*, 61–72.

Carron, A. V., Widmeyer, W. N., & Brawley, L. R. (1985). The development of an instrument to assess cohesion in sport teams: The Group Environment Questionnaire. *Journal of Sport Psychology, 7*, 244–266.

Chelladurai, P., & Saleh, S. D. (1980). Dimensions of leader behavior in sports: Development of a leadership scale. *Journal of Sport Psychology, 2*, 34–45.

Crace, R. K., & Hardy, C. J. (1997). Individual values and the team building process. *Journal of Applied Sport Psychology, 9*, 41–60.

Cronin, L. D., Arthur, C. A., Hardy, J., & Callow, N. (2015). Transformational leadership and task cohesion in sport: The mediating role of inside sacrifice. *Journal of Sport & Exercise Psychology, 37*, 23–36.

De Backer, M., Boen, F., De Cuyper, B., Høigaard, R., & Vande Broek, G. (2015). A team fares well with a fair coach: Predictors of social loafing in interactive female sport teams. *Scandinavian Journal of Medicine & Science in Sports, 25*, 897–908.

Dunn, J. G., & Holt, N. L. (2004). A qualitative investigation of a personal-disclosure mutual-sharing team building activity. *The Sport Psychologist, 18*, 363–380.

Eitzen, D. S. (1975). Group structure and group performance. In D.M. Landers, D.V, Harris, & R.W. Christina (Eds.), *Psychology of sport and motor behavior* (pp. 262–270). University Park, PA: College of HPER, Pennsylvania State University.

Evans, A. L., Slater, M. J., Turner, M. J., & Barker, J. B. (2013). Using personal-disclosure mutual-sharing to enhance group functioning in a professional soccer academy. *The Sport Psychologist, 27*, 233–243.

Eys, M., Evans, M. B., Martin, L. J., Ohlert, J., Wolf, S. A., Van Bussel, M., & Steins, C. (2015). Cohesion and performance for female and male sport teams. *The Sport Psychologist, 29*, 97–109.

Eys, M., Loughead, T., Bray, S. R., & Carron, A. V. (2009). Development of a cohesion questionnaire for youth: The Youth Sport Environment Questionnaire. *Journal of Sport & Exercise Psychology, 31*, 390–408.

Festinger, L. (1950). Informal social communication. *Psychological Review, 57*, 271–282.

Festinger, L., Schachter, S., & Back, K. (1950). *Social pressure in informal groups*. New York: Harper & Row.

Filho, E., Dobersek, U., Gershgoren, L., Becker, B., & Tenenbaum, G. (2014). The cohesion–performance relationship in sport: A 10-year retrospective meta-analysis. *Sport Sciences for Health, 10*, 165–177.

García-Calvo, T., Leo-Marcos, F., Gonzalez-Ponce, I., Sánchez-Miguel, P. A., Mouratidis, A., & Ntoumanis, N. (2014). Perceived coach-created and peer-created motivational climates and their associations with team cohesion and athlete satisfaction: Evidence from a longitudinal study. *Journal of Sports Sciences, 32*, 1738–1750.

Golembiewski, R. (1962). *The small group*. Chicago: University of Chicago Press.

Gross, N., & Martin, W. E. (1952). On group cohesiveness. *American Journal of Sociology, 52*, 546–554.

Ha, J. P., & Ha, J. (2015). Organizational justice–affective commitment relationship in a team sport setting: The moderating effect of group cohesion. *Journal of Management & Organization, 21*, 107–124.

Jowett, S., & Chaundy, V. (2004). An investigation into the impact of coach leadership and coach-athlete relationship on group cohesion. *Group Dynamics: Theory, Research, and Practice, 8*, 302–311.

Kamphoff, C. S., Gill, D. L., & Huddleston, S. (2005). Jealousy in sport: Exploring jealousy's relationship to cohesion. *Journal of Applied Sport Psychology, 17*, 290–305.

Leo-Marcos, F. M., González-Ponce, I., Sánchez-Miguel, P. A., Ivarsson, A., & García-Calvo, T. (2015). Role ambiguity, role conflict, team conflict, cohesion and collective efficacy in sport teams: A multilevel analysis. *Psychology of Sport and Exercise, 20*, 60–66.

Leo-Marcos, F. M., Sánchez-Miguel, P. A., Sánchez-Oliva, D., & García-Calvo, T. (2010). Interactive effects of team cohesion on perceived efficacy in semi-professional sport. *Journal of Sports Science & Medicine, 9*, 320–325.

Lott, A. J., & Lott, B. E. (1965). Group cohesiveness as interpersonal attraction: A review of relationships with antecedent and consequence variables. *Psychological Bulletin, 64*, 259–309.

Loughead, T. M., & Bloom, G. A. (2011). Team building for coaches: Developing cohesion to build an effective team. In J. Denison, P. Potrac, & W. Gilbert (Eds.), *The Routledge handbook of sports coaching*. New York: Routledge.

Loughead, T. M., & Hardy, J. (2006). Team cohesion: From theory to research to team building. In S. Hanton & S. Mellalieu (Eds.), *Literature reviews in sport psychology* (pp. 257–287). Hauppauge, NY: Nova.

Martin, L. J., Carron, A. V., & Burke, S. M. (2009). Team building interventions in sport: A meta-analysis. *Sport and Exercise Psychology Review, 5*, 3–18.

McLaren, C. D., Newland, A., Eys, M. A., & Newton, M. (2017). Peer-initiated motivational climate and group cohesion in youth sport. *Journal of Applied Sport Psychology, 29*, 88–100.

McLaren, C. D., & Spink, K. S. (2018). Team member communication and perceived cohesion in youth soccer. *Communication & Sport, 6*, 111–125.

Mudrack, P. E. (1989). Defining group cohesiveness: A legacy of confusion? *Small Group Behavior, 20*, 37–49.

Newman, B. (1984). Expediency benefactor how team building saves time and gets the job done. *Training and Development Journal, 38*, 26–30.

Onağ, Z., & Tepeci, M. (2014). Team effectiveness in sport teams: The effects of team cohesion, intra team communication and team norms on team member satisfaction and intent to remain. *Procedia-Social and Behavioral Sciences, 150*, 420–428.

Orlick, T. (1990). *In pursuit of excellence* (2nd ed.). Champaign, IL: Human Kinetics.

Pain, M., & Harwood, C. (2009). Team building through mutual sharing and open discussion of team functioning. *The Sport Psychologist, 23*, 523–542.

Prapavessis, H., & Carron, A. V. (1997). Sacrifice, cohesion, and conformity to norms in sport teams. *Group Dynamics: Theory, Research, and Practice, 1*, 231–240.

Prapavessis, H., Carron, A. V., & Spink, K. S. (1996). Team building in sport groups. *International Journal of Sport Psychology, 27*, 269–285.

Rovio, E., Arvinen-Barrow, M., Weigand, D. A., Eskola, J., & Lintunen, T. (2012). Using team building methods with an ice hockey team: An action research case study. *The Sport Psychologist, 26*, 584–603.

Senécal, J., Loughead, T. M., & Bloom, G. A. (2008). A season-long team building intervention: Examining the effect of team goal setting on cohesion. *Journal of Sport & Exercise Psychology, 30*, 186–199.

Shapcott, K. M., Carron, A. V., Burke, S. M., Bradshaw, M. H., & Estabrooks, P. A. (2006). Member diversity and cohesion and performance in walking groups. *Small Group Research, 37*, 701–720.

Spink, K. S. (1988). Facilitating endurance performance: The effect of cognitive strategies and analgesic suggestions. *The Sport Psychologist, 2*, 97–104.
Spink, K. S., Wilson, K. S., & Odnokon, P. (2010). Examining the relationship between cohesion and return to team in elite athletes. *Psychology of Sport and Exercise, 11*, 6–11.
Stewart, K. L., Carreau, J., & Bruner, M. W. (2016). Team building using a challenge ropes course experience in youth sport. *Revue phénEPS/PHEnex Journal, 7*, 1–15.
Turman, P. D. (2008). Coaches' immediacy behaviors as predictors of athletes' perceptions of satisfaction and team cohesion. *Western Journal of Communication, 72*, 162–179.
Ver Bergen, A., & Koekebakker, J. (1959). Group cohesiveness in laboratory experiments. *Acta Psychologica, 16*, 81–98.
Windsor, P. M., Barker, J., & McCarthy, P. (2011). Doing sport psychology: Personal-disclosure mutual-sharing in professional soccer. *The Sport Psychologist, 25*, 94–114
Wolf, S. A., Eys, M. A., Sadler, P., & Kleinert, J. (2015). Appraisal in a team context: Perceptions of cohesion predict competition importance and prospects for coping. *Journal of Sport & Exercise Psychology, 37*, 489–499.
Yukelson, D. (1997). Principles of effective team building interventions in sport. A direct services approach at Penn State. *Journal of Applied Sport Psychology, 9*, 73–96.
Zander, A. (1971). *Motives and goals in groups*. New York: Academic Press.

Todd Loughead is a Professor and co-director of the Sport Psychology and Physical Activity Research Collaborative at the University of Windsor, Canada. His research uses a group dynamics perspective to investigate coaching and athlete leadership, and how these two sources of leadership impact team functioning. He is also interested in cohesion and how this contributes to an enhanced team environment. He consults with coaches, sport teams, and athletes at various competitive levels.

Matthieu Boisvert is a PhD student studying sport and exercise psychology at the University of Windsor, Canada. He is a member of the Sport Psychology and Physical Activity Research Collaborative. His research is primarily focused on athlete leadership and group dynamics. His doctoral research examines the usefulness of an online athlete leadership development program.

Katherine Hirsch is a PhD student studying sport and exercise psychology at the University of Windsor, Canada. She is a member of the Sport Psychology and Physical Activity Research Collaborative. Her research is largely focused on the role of athlete leaders in promoting positive group dynamics in team sports. Her research examines leader fairness and outcomes of fair treatment and unfair treatment, including cohesion and athlete satisfaction.

Chapter 17
Coaching Girls and Women

Diane M. Culver and Erin Kraft

Abstract In recent years, there have been many advances in sport to support girls and women, however, they are still experiencing instances of discrimination (Adams & Leavitt. International Review for the Sociology of Sport 53(2):152–172, 2018) and in some cases are still considered second rate to men (McGinnis, Chun, & McQuillian. Academy of Marketing Science Review 5:1–24, 2003); all of which are indicative of the continuing, predominant view of sport: the androcentric model. In this chapter, the authors build on LaVoi, Becker, and Maxwell (Women in Sport and Physical Activity Journal 15(4):7–20, 2007) synthesis of literature by discussing additional key papers on coaching girls and women. It is our hope that synthesizing current research findings and the scarcity of literature on this topic may inspire researchers to contribute to this area and sport administrators to take actionable steps to support girls and women in sport. Following the synthesis, the authors provide practical recommendations (e.g., including more women coaches on girls' teams) and future recommendations for research (e.g., coaching non-binary/gender non-conforming/transgender athletes/children). Finally, we provide personal stories from the field and the practical implications of those experiences.

Keywords Coaching girls · Coaching women · Gender · Best practice · Research

Considering sport operates within the context of societal practices (Burton, 2019) and cultural beliefs (LaVoi, Becker, & Maxwell, 2007) coaching and other aspects of sport are impacted by gender expectations. These expectations and assumptions towards gender are so predominant in sport, that we begin not to take notice. In a recent study, one coach developer in training explained that she will often catch herself saying "man-on" when speaking to a group of all female athletes (Kraft, Culver, & Din, 2020). In fact, we see this gendered language across sport on all levels; for example, the titles of tournaments are often called "the" tournament for

D. M. Culver (✉) · E. Kraft
University of Ottawa, Ottawa, ON, Canada
e-mail: dculver@uottawa.ca; ekraf090@uottawa.ca

R. Resende, A. R. Gomes (eds.), *Coaching for Human Development and Performance in Sports*, https://doi.org/10.1007/978-3-030-63912-9_17

men and "the women's" tournament for women (McGinnis, Chun, & McQuillian, 2003). Although we have come a long way in terms of supporting girls in sport, in some cases (take hockey for an example) girls are still considered second rate and experience discrimination (Adams & Leavitt, 2018). These instances of perpetuating inequality and gendering language, driven by the androcentric model of sport also have implications on how we coach girls in sport. The way we treat girls in sport holds significant weight, as girls only have a 10% chance of being physically active as adults if they did not participate in sport before the age of 10 (CAAWS, 2016). In the 2016 CAAWS report *Women in Sport: Fueling a lifetime of participation*, it was suggested that coaches who understand emotional, psychosocial, physical and hormonal changes that girls are experiencing can be instrumental in retaining girls in sports. An important question therefore is: What is current literature suggesting in terms of effectively coaching girls and women to maintain their sport participation despite the current climate?

In 2007, LaVoi and colleagues conducted a content analysis on books with a focus on 'coaching girls'. The authors suggested that many of the books focused on inflated gender differences and stereotypes between female and male athletes. They recommended that:

> Those who produce coaching books and deliver coaching education workshops should rely predominately on coaching science evidence, and strive to use non-gendered, non-stereotypical language. The primary focus should not be on differences between coaching boys and girls. A focus on differences among girls and among boys—or better yet—a focus on the similarities between boys and girls may be more productive—focus should also be on the child (p. 16).

The purpose of the following chapter is to synthesis current literature with a focus on coaching girls, as the most recent content analysis was 12 years ago (LaVoi et al., 2007), and it may be informative to explore the changes that have (or have not) occurred in the literature on coaching girls. The scope of this synthesis is limited as research on this topic is relatively scarce. In addition, we will make recommendations for future research areas and opportunities on this topic. Finally, we share the experiences of several coaches with experience coaching girls and women.

What the Literature Is Telling Us

The next section discusses a selection of coaching publications with a focus on 'coaching girls' (and in some cases women) to explore what the research is telling us. Following this, the authors will make practical and future research recommendations based on the review.

Gilbert (2001) In this article, Gilbert set out to examine girls' (age 8–13) experiences with sport as minimal research explores how physical educators and coaches impact girls' sport participation. Specifically, girls were interviewed to see what positive and negative experiences impacted their involvement in sport. This article is of particular interest as the girls themselves discuss the qualities they preferred in their coaches. Gilbert explains:

> The primary impression gleaned from the girls' opinions about coaching qualities they like and dislike was the clarity of their opinions. They all had opinions about what they thought it took to be a good or bad coach. When discussing their perceptions of good or bad coaches, the girls identified skills the adults had which affected the ways they interacted with their players. If coaches behave in a patient and caring manner, take time with the girls to teach them skills, or get out on the fields or court to play with them, they are seen as good coaches (p. 41).

Additionally, Gilbert appends a list of "Do's and Don't of Coaching" based on the perceptions of the interviewees. Examples of these do's include: be patient, be positive, make sure your criticism is constructive, and remember we are here to have fun. As for don't, examples include: don't expect the impossible, don't show favorites, and don't argue with the officials. With this understanding, coaches may have a stronger sense of what may be effective in their practice when coaching young girls and maintaining their involvement in sport.

de Haan and Knoppers (2019) Although sources are out there, research indicating how coaches gender their practices is scarce. In this article, the authors suggest that coaches are coaching their athletes the way they were coached and replicating similar discourse. Twelve rowing coaches were interviewed to capture their 'regimes of truth' when it came to coaching different genders. Interestingly, many of the coaches were under the impression that they treated everyone the same way and that gender did not matter. However, their descriptions of how they spoke to and thought of their female athletes would suggest that they perceived their female athletes as inferior to their male counterparts and to "the norm". For example, one coach expressed that girls ask too many questions and waste his time. He continued: "The girls need the feedback and they want to be listened to. If girls don't understand they quit" (p. 10). Overall, we can see by this article that some coaches' attitudes towards coaching girls and women is quite problematic. Moreover, there is concern with the assumptions that male athletes are "the norm", perpetuating the stereotype that in sport there is "the" sport (for men) and then, women's sport.

Lumpkin, Favor, and McPherson (2013) Although this article does not specifically look at practices for coaching girls, it addresses some of the barriers experienced by female coaches wishing to get involved in coaching female teams. This is an important topic considering females' exposure to female coaches may encourage them to begin coaching in the future (LaVoi, 2016). In terms of qualifications and education between male and female coaches, there were minimal differences; however, the years of experience varied greatly. Women were appearing as coaches of girls' teams, but the lifespan of their careers was considerably shorter than those of their male counterparts. Although the study did not look into the specific reasons for this, the authors suggested that barriers such as family priorities and a lack of veteran female coach role models may have contributed. As well, time away from family was the main reason both men and women resigned from coaching roles. Another potential barrier is that male coaches were overwhelmingly in the positions to hire coaches for female teams. The authors suggest that there is a need for more women to take on higher positions (such as athletic directors) to set an example for female athletes. For additional barriers -experienced by women in coaching see LaVoi and Dutove (2012).

Bolter and Lucas (2018) In addition to coaching for the purposes of developing physical abilities, coaches are tasked with developing a host of other skills. In this article, the authors look at strategies used for teaching sportspersonship to different genders, which highlights the differences seen when coaching girls and boys. Six male and six female coaches were interviewed to collect their experiences of coaching different genders and to examine how these experiences may differ. In some cases, the coaches expressed that there were no distinct gender differences, but rather the person had to be coached based on their individual needs. In other instances, the coaches used the same standards to coach boys and girls, but different strategies. They explained that the game for girls is different because they are functioning in a society where boys and girls are not treated the same; it was suggested that the games were refereed differently, and that parents responded differently, but they viewed their coaching strategies are similar. In one example, the coaches suggested that: "Girls need immediate intervention during conflict to prevent further conflict, whereas it is possible to take a more hands-off approach with boys and "let them go for a while" before intervening" (p. 624). Taking these experiences into account, the authors concluded:

> It is possible that coaches who detailed similar sportspersonship behaviors among boys and girls more often teach about sportspersonship the same to boys and girls, whereas coaches who perceive gender differences in sportspersonship also coach girls and boys differently when teaching about sportspersonship (p. 625).

Similarly, to what de Haan and Knoppers (2019) discussed, it may be the coach's perception of gender differences and their 'regime of truth' that influences how they go about coaching boys and girls; and this, despite whether or not differences are in fact present.

Culver and Trudel (2000) Anecdotal evidence suggests that many coaches, particularly male coaches, prefer to coach boys/men; backing this up with comments such as 'it is much less complicated'. One aspect critical to all coaching is communication and early research in sport coaching noted differences in the perceptions of coaches and athletes regarding the same message (Horne & Carron, 1985). Laker (1993), who studied messaging in physical education, found that such differences might be greater when the subject of a message was social or affective versus technical and tactical. Culver and Trudel (2000)[1] studied coach-athlete communication in a junior women's national team (Alpine skiing). The coaches of the team were both men about 30 years old and the athletes were young women aged between 17 and 19 years. This qualitative study examined coach-athlete communication from the pre-season through to the end of the season. Using the Fuoss and Troppmann

[1]See also Culver (1999).

(1981) two-way circular model of coach-athlete communication, various scenarios of communication break downs were analyzed with the help of observation and interviews. The participants also commented (pre-season) on their ideas of good communication. Both coaches and athletes agreed that this involved a two-way communication process. However, when the heat was on, that is, when emotions and outcomes were important, this ideal of two-way communication frequently broke down.

In one scenario entitled 'Silence is not golden', the coach did not speak to an athlete after a race because he was facing pressure for results from his organization and the day had not gone well. This was revealed when he was asked about the incident at the end of the season; he had not really thought about the effect of his silence until then. The adolescent female athlete interpreted this silence as the coach being angry with her and she did not approach him for feedback. The consequence of this was that she was very depressed and indeed the rest of her competitive season she did not perform very well.

The following are some comments made by the head coach at the end of season, after the scenarios were presented to him.

> I think that emotionally that they're (the female athletes) more fragile, at least that they show that they're more emotionally fragile. Guys sort of don't really, they don't talk about that stuff and they don't... Don't really show it. You know and the girls need a lot of reassurance and building of self-confidence it seems to me, especially the younger ones who haven't had a lot of success yet.... The other thing with girls, you have to be really careful what you say. They are really sensitive to everything. Or what you don't say, as we've talked about.... You know, silence can be deadly, and be careful, a lot of things, they don't say anything about it, when you've said something, but you know that it comes back to haunt you later, or does well for you later... they remember everything, they never forget anything you say... I think guys are a little less like that. They are a little less sensitive to what you say. You can be a little tough and rougher with them and you don't have really bite your tongue all the time with guys. It's more like water just beads off, it doesn't soak into the material.

When the participants were asked about who (coach or athlete) initiates messages relating to the different components of sport performance, the coaches and athletes generally agreed that for technical and tactical messages the coaches were the initiators. However, when it came to more social or affective issues, the head coach said "If they have a problem they need to tell me. I think they need to initiate and then we can talk". On the flip side, the athletes said that initiating this type of message was very difficult for them. This is understandable given the power differential between athletes and coaches, whereby coaches are in a position of deciding such things as who gets to compete in what competitions. The girls did not want to appear 'weak' by disclosing personal or psychological issues to their coaches. While this situation could certainly occur with coaching boys, given that girls seem to remember everything their coaches say to them, the consequences are much more likely to be long lasting.

Another scenario is particularly interesting and speaks to some of the differences between coaching girls/women versus boys/men. This scenario relates to a radio communication between the assistant coach and one of the athletes, just before she took the start in a race (Culver, 1999). The coach told her to change her line for the race saying 'The course is much straighter down here than we thought (during the course inspection), you can go straighter'. The athlete came down and did not straighten her line and when the coach approached her after the race she said, "The course was much straighter than I thought". To this, the coach said nothing. When I interviewed the skier later that day, I asked her what would make her change her line just before she started. Her response is very revealing. She said, "If the coach had said 'all the girls are overturning—you can go much straighter', I would have straightened my line". This highlights the significance that women put on relationships. The fact that the skier would have changed her line if the coach had referred to how the other girls were skiing rather than just referring 'to the course' indicates the significance that she put on herself relative to the other women athletes.

Culver and Werthner (2012) In a chapter (in French) Culver and Werthner wrote about what to expect in coaching girls versus boys. Drawing on the literature and their experience they made suggestions for coaches. For example, they cite Tannen Deborah (1995) in stating that research (in North America) shows boys are concerned in their group play with establishing their superiority by demonstrating their skills and knowledge, whereas girls are more concerned with interacting with other girls and minimizing their rank vis à vis the others. As a coach instead of putting a hard-working, high performing female athlete in a team on a pedestal in front of her teammates, in order to create better team cohesion it would be better to individually suggest to such an athlete that she help her teammates train harder to improve. Another important difference noted by Culver and Werthner (2012) relates to confidence and self-esteem. While confidence is fragile in most adolescents, it can be particularly fragile in female athletes. Again, according to Tannen, men are more likely to minimize their doubts whereas women will minimize their certainty. There are also differences in how women and men react to criticism. Women tend to take criticism personally and literally, and the reader will remember that, as noted by the head coach in the Culver (1999) study, they do not forget! In general, female athletes tend to be more self-critical than their male counterparts.

What Still Needs to Be Done

In the following section, the authors make practical suggestions for coaching girls based on the articles discussed above, along with recommendations for future research on this topic.

Practical Suggestions

Removing Gender Assumptions and Raising Our Awareness of Gender Bias In the de Haan and Knoppers (2019) and Bolter and Lucas' (2018) articles, there were instances of coaches making assumptions about their players and making decisions based on gender bias. Some coaches felt that they should be coaching their players differently (based on gender) because others in sport treat them differently (i.e., referees and parents). Thus, the coaches were willing to intervene immediately during a conflict with girls but wait before intervening with boys, likely without reflecting on the message this is sending. By relying on other perspectives of sport for make gender-based decisions, the coaches are similarly perpetuating and reinforcing (at times) damaging gender stereotypes. Even more concerning is that some coaches seem to lack an awareness of this gender-based decision making and their uncritical alignment with male 'norms'. They may say that they believe girls and boys (women and men) should be coached the same, as their perception of them is equal; however, in some of the coaches' interviews, it is clear that their actions show something quite different, displaying their internal 'regimes of truth'. In order to break this cycle, the authors recommend that coaches participate in more reflective activities directed at helping coaches to become aware of their gender biases. Additionally, coach education programs and those facilitating coach learning opportunities may consider integrating more reflective activities to heighten this awareness in the hopes of encouraging more intentional coaching practices when it comes to coaching girls.

The Need for More Women Coaching Girls' Teams There is a current lack of women in coaching and leadership positions (see Burton, 2015; Kane & LaVoi, 2018; LaVoi & Dutove, 2012) which has potential implications towards girls' willingness to take on coaching roles in the future. Lumpkin et al. (2013) suggest that it is important for women to coach girls' teams so that girls have female role models. This is also the case for women in coaching; there is a need for more women to take on leadership positions in sports so that female coaches may also have role models, and that there be more women in 'gatekeeper positions' and on hiring committees to recruit and retain more female coaches.

Research Recommendations

Integrating Recommendations into Practice Gilbert (2001) suggested a number of strategies for coaching girls, based on her interviews with girls in sport. Although they are evidence based, there may be some variability in terms of applying these strategies in practice. For example, one of the suggestions is to 'make sure your criticism is constructive'. Although this is a wonderful idea, perhaps a new coach or a coach who has just begun to coach girls may not know exactly what this type of criticism looks or sounds like. Researchers may wish to apply some of these 'do's' and other recommended strategies for working with girls in practice and provide more tangible examples of best practices. Additionally, coaches may wish to apply some of these coaching 'do's' with a boys team context. Many of the strategies would likely transfer well to a boys' team as they do not seem to be gender specific (i.e., be patient, be positive, be respectful). This may also reinforce that many strategies are useful for both girls and boys, and it is the perception of the coach that may be more significant in coaching practice. Since many of these coaching strategies seem to make good sense for all athletes, it might also be worth examining how girls versus boys rank the importance of such characteristics. For example, there is some evidence that a coach's level of playing expertise is one of the most important characteristics for boys. Girls may rank this characteristic of less importance than patience, for instance.

Coaching Non-binary/Gender Non-conforming/Transgender Athletes/Children? In our current society, there has been a recent heightening in our awareness of gender as a spectrum. We have also seen more inclusion in sport, particularly in regard to the LGBTQ+ community. However, there are still a number of obstacles in sport, particularly for transgender athletes as sport is usually categorized by women's and men's teams (Krane, 2016). Moreover, in writing this chapter, we found little literature (e.g., Viel & Demers, 2013) in terms of coaching non-binary, gender non-conforming, and transgender athletes and children. This is not to suggest that athletes that do not conform to the girl/boy binary are in need of being coached differently, but rather, current literature is perpetuating the girl/boy stereotypes by constantly focusing on the differences between the two. Although the purpose of this paper was focused on coaching girls, we suggest that researchers consider exploring the coaching practices of individuals who have coached a variety of persons across the gender spectrum to gain additional insight into the coaching differences and similarities that may or may not exist.

Stories from the Field and Practical Implications

This section recounts the experiences of three women coaches (two Alpine skiing and one rugby) and one male coach (individual winter sport[2]) who have had experience coaching boys and girls. These coaches began their comments with the caveat that their comments are to be taken as generalizations and that there are girls who prefer to be 'coached like a boy' and vis versa.

Alpine skiing is a sport in which the girls and boys train together much of the time until they reach the international level. The following comments are from two coaches: one a millennial and the other a senior. Both of these coaches have worked with girls and boys from age 7 and up. The coaches tell us about their experiences by age group.

U12 and Less As a female coach it takes longer to win the boys over—to get to know them. Girls at this age are reaching out and vying for attention and more confident in their interactions. Boys are more shy.

---

[2]Sport not specified for anonymity.

U14–U16 Boys become more confident. Girls are more in tune emotionally and they internalize a lot more. With girls, a coach has to do a lot more work in terms of following up and checking back in about things in previous conversations—getting a pulse about how they feel about something. The boys are much more in the moment; day by day. If you ask them about something that you talked about with them last week they don't remember. With the boys, you can be more competitive/challenging in terms of communication. For example, a coach might say "You were 2 seconds faster yesterday; what happened today?" Many girls hearing this would lose confidence. But with the boys you can drive them with competition. With the girls you can get more analytical about tactics and technique; you can go deeper into one concept. You can drive the girls by getting them to internalize, and reflect, and really own the process. It is important with the girls to read their emotional state on any given day and adapt to it. With boys it is more constant; although, when something is wrong with a boy it might be harder to know what that is.

Many coaches might have issues with coaching girls because they do not treat them differently. Girls need an emotional connection with their coaches in order to trust them; they need to feel that you are 'in it' together with them. With the girls, the coach-athlete relationship it a team mentality (i.e., collaborative) rather than a teacher mentality (i.e., more top down). With boys you can be more prescriptive.

In order to get respect from boys a coach needs to be firmer. With boys, a coach might ask "Do you want me to be honest with you?" Then if the answer is 'yes' you can be blunter. Boys have their focus for less time. With girls, it might be more like "On a scale from 1–10, to what degree do you think you have achieved what we talked about?"

A coach might be better to use less praise with boys, but they will value it more. Girls might need more praise. Not just the same type of praise as the boys, but words of affirmation. So, for girls a coach might use more of this type of language, "I really like the way you have been working today".

U20 and Above The following are comments from a rugby coach with experience coaching college/university age women and men aged 20–35 years. In short, this coach says: Boys do and girls ask! For her, there is also a difference in how she actually coaches the women versus the men. For example, rugby is a very physical sport, and for teaching plays, it is necessary to physically keep the boys away from each other with cones to prevent them hitting each other too hard. With the girls she sets them up closer to each other to encourage them to 'go at each other', which they would not do if the distance was too great since this would mean the forces would be greater and there would be more chance of injury. The girls are also 'smarter' when it comes to technique and tactics.

Finally, we provide a true story told by a highly successful (e.g., coached a World Championship Gold medal athlete) coach, Peter. This story supports the proposition made above by the head coach in the coach-athlete communication study. The sport that Peter coaches is an individual sport, but one in which the team travels and trains together throughout the year, which entails living in hotels and sharing meals together. When asked about coaching the young women, Peter said,

> You have to be *very* careful what you say! I have learned my lesson the hard way! Sometimes when, at the dining table, one of the girls asks me a question, and I am not sure what to say, I get up and pretend that I have an important phone call to make—this to give me the time to decide how to answer so that I do not do any damage to my relationship with the girl asking the question, and importantly, with the others!

None of the coaches who shared their stories like making these generalizations, but at the same time, they stated firmly that it is really not the same coaching girls and boys. Coaches do need to adapt.

Key Points

1. Coaching girls and women is different! While most aspects of technique and tactics etc., are the same or very similar, the coach-athlete relationship that lays the foundation for effective coaching, while always needing to be individualised, tends to be quite different for coaching girls/women versus boys/men. Coaching girls and women mean that as a coach you are a partner in your athletes' sport endeavours. Therefore, a more collaborative versus a more prescriptive approach often works better with females.
2. Boys/men want to jump into the action—and do! Girls/women may have important questions that need to be answered before the action starts, and when feedback and instructions are given.
3. Girls and women tend to have very long memories when it comes to what you say to them as a coach! Consequence for coaches: Think before you speak! Be aware of what the potential consequences are of your words.

Conclusion

Androcentrism is defined as "the personal pattern of thinking and acting that takes the characteristics of ruling men to be the normative for all humanity" (Johnson, 1992, p. 23). In this framework, 'normal' and 'standard' ways of thinking and acting are based on what works for men. There are many domains beyond sport that have been historically dominated by this worldview (e.g., research in medicine and psychology). In sport, a glance at the media affirms the androcentrism of sport. Outside of major games like the Olympics, the exploits of women athletes receive much less attention that those of men. It is therefore not surprising that the dominant model of coaching in sport is androcentric (Werthner, Culver, & Mercier, 2010); that is, it is based on the coaching of males. This is what makes it difficult for many coaches to coach women. Coaches need to understand that, in general, girls are different than boys. The author Susan Pinker (2008) argued that despite the feminist movement having "created the expectation that all differences between men and women were created by unjust practices. . ." (p. 9) there are indeed important gender differences which require us to thinking much more carefully about we interact with girls and women. Importantly for coaches, Pinker has found that, in general "girls' and women's style of competing looks different" (p. 199) to that of boys and men. In one study of pre-school children, whereas the girls used talking and turn-taking twenty times more than their male counterparts, the boys employed physicality and competition fifty times more than the girls. Both the research presented in this chapter and the stories from the field support these tendencies. Therefore, those who wish to have success in coaching girls and women need to realise that there are some important gender differences that require at least some aspects, notably those related to communication (e.g., establishing trust and providing feedback), that require a different approach than the androcentric model of coaching.

References

Adams, C., & Leavitt, S. (2018). 'It's just girls' hockey': Troubling progress narratives in girls' and women's sport. *International Review for the Sociology of Sport, 53*(2), 152–172.

Burton, L. J. (2015). Underrepresentation of women in sport leadership: A review of research. *Sport Management Review, 18*(2), 155–165.

Burton, L. J. (2019). Under-representation of women in leadership roles in women's sport. In N. Lough & A. Geurin (Eds.), *Routledge handbook of the business of women's sport* (pp. 255–268). London, UK: Routledge.

Bolter, N., & Lucas, S. (2018). Female and male youth sport coaches' perceptions of teaching sportspersonship to female and male athletes. *Sports Science & Coaching, 13*(5), 619–628.

CAAWS. (2016). Retrieved from https://www.caaws.ca/gender-equity-101/facts-and-stats/

Culver, D. (1999). *Coach-athlete communication within a National Alpine Ski Team.* Master's thesis. Ottawa, Canada: University of Ottawa.

Culver, D., & Trudel, P. (2000). Coach-athlete communication within a national alpine ski team. *Journal of Excellence, 3*, 28–54.

Culver, D., & Werthner, P. (2012). À quoi s'attendre lorsqu'on entraîne des filles versus des garçons (What to expect when coaching girls versus boys). In L. Morency & C. Bordeleau (Eds.), *Le manuel de l'entraîneur sportif* (pp. 123–130). Montréal: Québec Amérique.

Deborah, T. (1995). The power of talk: Who gets heard and why. *Harvard Business Review, 73*, 138–148.

de Haan, D., & Knoppers, A. (2019). Gendered discourses in coaching high-performance sport. *International Review for the Sociology of Sport.* https://doi.org/10.1177/1012690219829692

Fuoss, D. E., & Troppmann, R. J. (1981). *Effective coaching: A psychological approach.* New York: Wiley.

Gilbert, E. (2001). Towards a richer understanding of girls' sport experiences. *Women in Sport and Physical Activity Journal, 10*(2), 117–143.

Horne, T., & Carron, A. (1985). Compatibility in coach-athlete relationships. *Journal of Sport Psychology, 7*, 137–149.

Johnson, E. A. (1992). *She who is: The mystery of God in feminist theological discourse.* New York: Crossroad.

Kane, M. J., & LaVoi, N. (2018). An examination of intercollegiate athletic directors' attributions regarding the underrepresentation of female coaches in women's sport. *Women in Sport and Physical Activity Journal, 26*(1), 3–11.

Kraft, E., Culver, D. M., & Din, C. (2020). Exploring a women-only training program for coach developersin. *Women in Sport and Physical Activity Journal, 28*(2), 173–179. https://doi.org/10.1123/wspaj.2019-0047

Krane, V. (2016). Inclusion to exclusion: Sport for LGBT athletes. In R. Schinke, K. R. McGannon, & B. Smith (Eds.), *Routledge international handbook of sport psychology* (pp. 238–247). London: Routledge.

Laker, A. (1993). *Teachers and pupils perceptions of lesson content in physical education (PhD thesis)*. Colorado: University of Northern Colorado.

LaVoi, N. M. (2016). *Women in sports coaching*. New York: Routledge.

LaVoi, N. M., Becker, E., & Maxwell, H. (2007). "Coaching girls": A content analysis of best-selling popular press coaching books. *Women in Sport and Physical Activity Journal, 15*(4), 7–20.

LaVoi, N. M., & Dutove, J. K. (2012). Barriers and supports for female coaches: An ecological model. *Sports Coaching Review, 1*(1), 17–37.

Lumpkin, A., Favor, J., & McPherson, L. (2013). Who is coaching high school girl's sport teams? *Journal of Coaching Education, 6*(2), 27–64.

McGinnis, L., Chun, S., & McQuillian, J. (2003). A review of gendered consumption in sport and leisure. *Academy of Marketing Science Review, 5*, 1–24.

Pinker, S. (2008). *The sexual paradox: Extreme men, gifted women, and the real gender gap*. Toronto: Random House Canada.

Viel, B., & Demers, G. (2013). Coaching gay, lesbian, bisexual, and transgender athletes: Needs, challenges, and fears of top-level coaches. *Canadian Journal for Women in Coaching, 13*(3), 1–4.

Werthner, P., Culver, D., & Mercier, R. (2010). Changing the androcentric world of sport – Is it possible? In *Taking the lead* (pp. 37–55). Edmonton, AB: University of Alberta Press.

Diane M. Culver is an Associate Professor in the School of Human Kinetics, University of Ottawa in Canada. Her research interests include coach development and qualitative research. She is currently funded by the Social Sciences and Humanities Research Council of Canada to research parasport coaching, and women in sport organisations. In her teaching, research, and consulting she is particularly interested in social learning theory and building social learning capability in sport. Diane is also an Alpine ski coach who has worked with all levels of skiers from youth to Olympic levels. She now coaches masters' skiers and mentors youth coaches.

Erin Kraft is a doctoral candidate in the School of Human Kinetics at the University of Ottawa. As a former swim coach with over 10 years of experience, Erin primarily coached children with developmental disabilities at the developmental level. She continues working with children with disabilities in the classroom and in the pool as an occasional teacher across Ottawa. Erin's master's in education examined coaches' experiences teaching children with Autism Spectrum Disorders in aquatic programs. Her ongoing doctoral research is focused on Canadian parasport coaches.

Chapter 18
Coaching Efficacy and the Use of Technology

Hugo Sarmento, Filipe Manuel Clemente, Adam Field, and Pedro Antonio Sánchez Miguel

Abstract The last 20 years has seen an exponential increase in the use of novel technologies in sports science. This chapter aims to assess how these technologies are applied by researches and practitioners in their respective fields. This chapter also provides examples of how science and applied practice is linked and how technology has facilitated this process. Furthermore, coach learning is best understood in terms that recognize the interests and subjectivities of individuals, within a context shaped by the physical, social and educational provisions. Other applications such as positional data and network analysis are revealed in order to enhance the knowledge about current technologies in sport. Indeed, a better understanding of new technologies will ultimately assist in improving athletic performance.

Keywords Performance · Game analysis · Technology · Measurement

Historical Background

At the beginning of the twenty-first century, Lyle (2002) revealed that "a lack of conceptual and theoretical development" in the field of sports coaching has resulted in "a poor research framework and an incomplete appreciation of the role and

H. Sarmento (✉)
Faculty of Sport Sciences and Physical Education, Research Unit for Sport and Physical Activity (CIDAF), University of Coimbra, Coimbra, Portugal

F. M. Clemente
Polytechnic Institute of Viana do Castelo, School of Sport and Leisure, Melgaço, Portugal

A. Field
School of Human and Health Sciences, University of Huddersfield, Huddersfield, UK
e-mail: Adam.Field@hud.ac.uk

P. A. S. Miguel
Behavioral Analysis of Physical Activity and Sports Research Group, Teacher Training College, University of Extremadura, Badajoz, Spain
e-mail: pesanchezm@unex.es

R. Resende, A. R. Gomes (eds.), *Coaching for Human Development and Performance in Sports*, https://doi.org/10.1007/978-3-030-63912-9_18

effectiveness of the coach" (p. 12). In recent years, sports coaching has evolved since the increased research attention afforded to conceptual issues that underpin coaching practice. Furthermore, considerable technological advancements now enable the tracking of athletes during competition and training to monitor load in professional team sports (Akenhead & Nassis, 2016).

The continued developments in technology are assisting coaches in seeking competitive advantages and marginal gains. However, previous innovations in technology and their application to sport were mainly ad hoc rather than systematic initiatives (Adair & Vamplew, 1997).

During the mid twentieth century, technological innovations were easier to integrate and essential in individual sports, such as cycling, track and field and rowing. In the late twentieth century, innovative methods, perspectives and techniques were employed by coaches and sport scientists in swimming and athletics in an attempt to produce performance excellence in international competition with the assistance of more reliable and sophisticated tools (Phillips, 2000).

Sport coaches have a vital role to play in changing social norms through individual and community engagement and empowering or enabling individuals to take part in physical activity and sport (Griffiths & Armour, 2013). Some sporting organizations are relatively opposed towards adopting new technologies and promoting the preservation of sporting 'traditions' (Smith & Stewart, 2010). However technological innovations, especially those related to sports science and improvements in on-field performance, are often viewed positively for most of the practitioners and public (Bastida, Gómez-Carmona, De la Cruz, & Pino, 2018). Nevertheless, research and scientific study into contemporary technologies has grown exponentially in recent years with the majority of professional team and individual sports using Global Positioning Systems (GPS) to monitor the external loads placed on athletes (Hausler, Halaki, & Orr, 2016; Polglaze, Dawson, Hiscock, & Peeling, 2015).

The monetary implications associated with success in team sports has contributed to the rise in a wealth of technological advancements regarding match analysis tools such as, inter alia, semi-automatic multiple-camera video technology (VID), radar-based local positioning system (LPS), as well as the GPS, with the purpose of measuring a players' external load. Furthermore, since the International Football Association Board (IFAB) approved the use electronic tracking systems, GPS devices are commonly worn by players in soccer training and in competitive matches (Page, Marrin, Brogden & Greig, 2016).

Previously, some researches have attempted to reproduce specific competitive situations with non-ecological environments by creating simulations that attempt to replicate actual competition and match-play (Cust, Sweeting, Ball, & Robertson, 2018). However, manual notational analysis or coding in sports has some limitations. Such methods are typically time consuming, subjective in nature, and prone to human error and bias. On the contrary, automating sport movement recognition and its application towards coding has the potential to enhance both the efficiency and accuracy of sport performance analysis.

Furthermore, VID is a methodology used for analysing physical (i.e., number of sprints, accelerations, decelerations) and skill (i.e., number of passes, dribbles shots etc.) variables from footage obtained from high-definition cameras. This system produces the movement of players throughout a match and allows researchers to quantify the actions individual players and teams, formulating statistics, sequences and patterns of play (Bartlett, Button, Robins, Dutt-Mazumder, & Kennedy, 2012).

To assess the validity of the VID, comparisons have been made to other devices such as GPS (Pons et al., 2020) and electronic tracking systems (Hennessy & Jeffreys, 2018). This process is currently in process and will be discussed further in the following sections.

Dellaserra, Gao, and Ransdell (2014) highlighted that over the last 10 years, time-motion analysis systems such as video recordings, hand notation, and computer digitizing have been used to objectively assess the locomotion of athletes for the purpose of improving performance. However, several logistical issues exist, including, validity, time constraints, and a requirement of manual hand-notation techniques. Additionally, the authors discussed another concern relating to the failure of these systems to provide real-time locomotion information (e.g., athlete position, movement displacement, velocity, and accelerations) which are considered vital quantitative data for athletes and teams.

Despite the exponential increase in the development of technology intended to assist coaches and practitioners in the development of sporting performance, there still exists a lack of the literature devoted to this topic. There are also few studies that have appraised a broader set of technologies (Chen & Bassett, 2005; Liebermann & Franks, 2004, 2008). In contrast, some papers have assessed specific technology (Aughey, 2011) and, more recently, there are a significant number of articles devoted to machine learning techniques to improve sports performance (Geurkink et al., 2019; Razali, Mustapha, Yatim, & Ab Aziz, 2017) or prevent injury (Ruddy et al., 2018; Sutter, Orenduff, Fox, Myers, & Garrigues, 2018).

From Science to Practice

It is common for sports to accept the use of new technology to improve performance, especially with the arrival of large-scale manufacturing of consumer products which can be easily accessible for professional sports teams and athletes. Taking into account new conceptual backgrounds, training load is considered as the addition of several factors that emerge from the athlete them self (Seirul-lo Vargas, 2017), which depend on each other and are connected, so that the load in training tasks appears unified and is indivisible (Balagué, Torrents, Pol, & Seirul·lo, 2014).

The use of GPS is currently widespread in sport as it provides pertinent feedback for performance analysis and monitoring personnel (Coutts & Duffield, 2010). This technology is based on a signal concentration system of different brand sensors, designed for the control and monitoring of physical activity in a plethora of sports (Coutts & Duffield, 2010). This equipment permits practioners to measure performance variables such as average heart rate (mean HR), maximum heart rate (peak HR), distance covered per minute (distance/min.), average velocity, maximum velocity, and number of sprints, which provides relevant information to coaches with the view to improving performance.

Taking into account this idea, Mallett, Rynne, and Billett (2016) have assessed high performance coaches to identify those features that constitute effective learning in situ. This research suggests that coach learning is best facilitated through the interests and subjectivities of individuals, within a context shaped by the physical, social and educational provisions. However, within the coaching literature, questions remain about in situ learning, including how coaches' dispositions towards learning engagement develop over time (Griffiths & Armour, 2013), how cultural context influences learning (Barker-Ruchti, Barker, Rynne, & Lee, 2016), and how learning affordances might be shaped over the lifecycle of the organization. It is possible that some of these questions are better answered through further understanding of the technologies used within a given sport.

Currently, the majority of research has focused on testing the effect of the modification of tasks on the physical load (Bujalance-Moreno, Latorre-Román, & García-Pinillos, 2019), although further research into technologies that assess mental, cognitive and/or affective load are warranted (Alarcón, Castillo-Díaz, Madinabeitia, Castillo-Rodríguez, & Cárdenas, 2018).

A question that has emerged from the application of new technologies in sport is the change in relationships and dynamics among technical staff within the team environment. The increase in invention and implementation of technology and, subsequent data outputs available for coaches, requires new skill sets such that data must be collected, analyzed and interpreted effectively. Accordingly, new 'roles' are materializing in professional sport, namely the role of the 'match analyst' or 'performance analyst', that is, the member of technical staff responsible for match and training data.

Depending on the level of football and financial status, teams adopt different solutions in order to integrate this job role into their structure. Teams with substantial resources have specific departments that work full time on performance data analysis. Due to monetary factors, there are clubs/teams that preferer to acquire this service from specific companies that provide professional data analysis. In other cases, and specially in teams with lesser resources, the head coach plays several roles including the analysis of data, among other things.

The organization of technical staff depends highly on the competitive level and type of sport. For example, volleyball and baseball requires a good ability to analyze quantitative data, while in football or rugby, the analyses assume mainly a qualitative character. In this sense, the skills of the scouts need to be, necessarily, different.

Positional Data and Network Analysis as Tools for Coaching Intervention

The contemporary sporting climate requires a large undertaking of data collection by use of technological devices and feedback systems (Gyarmati, Kwak, & Rodriguez, 2014). Among others, tracking methods to determine the positional data of players is widely used in team sports. Such approaches are made possible by the availability of devices that can determine the position of an individual in a given space. One of the most common technological devices used in sports is the GPS system combined with inertial measurements units (IMU) that can accurately determine the position of the players and assess the efficiency of accelerations (Aughey, 2011). Additionally, other methods may accurately track players using video-tracking systems or radio frequency identification (Buchheit et al., 2014). However, GPS usage is more common due to the fact that it provides a feasible (i.e., easy-to-use and portable) approach to monitoring load. Conversely, GPS is limited in that it is unable to be used in indoor spaces. Therefore, sports played indoor, typically use IMU systems or other tracking systems that provide positional-data information.

Despite the fact that GPS and IMU systems being more commonly used in sport, the information provided regarding positional data may allow further analysis that can help coaches to interpret the collective organization or the tactical strategies adopted by team sport athletes (Sarmento et al., 2018).

Collective organization in team sports is one of the main concerns associated with the training process and match analysis. Such collective organization emerges from the match, always depending from the capacity of the players to synchronize individual behaviours in a dynamic system (Duarte, Araújo, Correia, & Davids, 2012). Despite that, the training process aims to regulate guidelines so as to optimize the collective organization in different scenarios, preparing the players for more predictable and/or unpredictable playing scenarios and under dynamic and changing circumstances (McGarry, 2005).

Match analysis has been used to determine the conditions in which specific behaviours emerge to identify areas of improvement and highlight opponents' weaknesses (Sarmento et al., 2014). Among many different approaches, analysis based on positional-data seems to provide useful information that complements the traditional observational methodology (Memmert, Lemmink, & Sampaio, 2017). In fact, positional-data can be particularly applicable considering that it is derived from tracking systems (that are well established in team sports), is automated, valid and reliable (in most cases) and necessary to run the algorithms for coaches to assess outcomes (Clemente, Sequeiros, Correia, Silva, & Martins, 2017). Such approaches make data collection and processing less time consuming, however, there is still question as to whether observational analysis provides an increasingly feasible approach. For instance, many tracking systems are not designed to dispense raw data or run algorithms to provide outcomes. However, in well-established sports sciences departments, the process is easier with the assistance of the multi-disciplinary approach by using human resources from computational sciences or

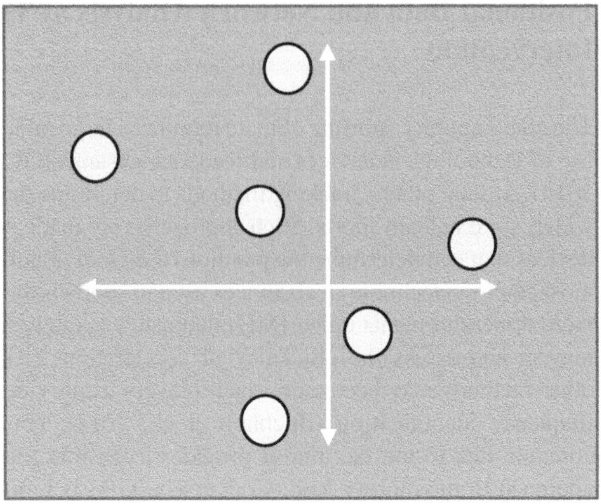

Fig. 18.1 Determining the furthest distances among teammates

physics (as used in elite team sports) to solve the problem. These outcomes do not solve the ultimate goal of the analysis; the possible inference and translation to the practice.

This section will introduce some examples of how this positional data may help coaches to interpret the game and make decisions based on the data. One of the main behaviors that are fundamental to tactical principles in team sports is the exploitation of width during ball possession aiming to spread the opponent's team (i.e., increasing gaps between players) and create spaces in the central region to penetrate (Garganta & Pinto, 1994). Indeed, at the same time, the opposition team are attempting to reduce these gaps so as to protect the center of the pitch (Clemente, Couceiro, Fernando, Mendes, & Figueiredo, 2013). Despite the possibility of being able to observe these patterns, it is difficult to be accurate and precise to determine the distances of players in relation to each other according to observations of the naked human eye.

However, just by using positional data analysis, it is possible to accurately quantify the distances between spaces occupied by players. As outlined in Fig. 18.1, positional data allows us to accurately determine the position of players (white dots) in a given plane. Moreover, it is possible to determine the distance between the two furthest players of the team from (i.e., from goal-to-goal and side-by-side).

By using this approach, the width and length of the team and the length per width ratio can be determined. These simple, but effective concepts, were proposed in some studies (Duarte et al., 2013; Folgado, Lemmink, Frencken, & Sampaio, 2014) to identify the variations of such measures in specific task conditions or game moments. Hypothetically, during ball possession in an indirect playing style the distances between individual players will increase both in width and length. On the other hand, the team in the defensive phase will typically reduce the length and width in an attempt to remain compact. By using the algorithms that allow us to compute

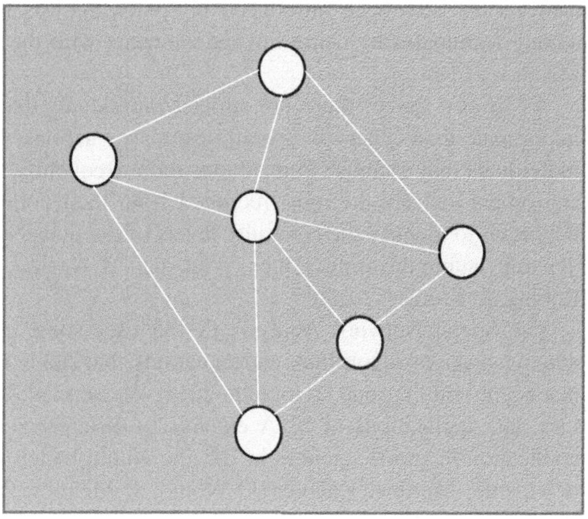

Fig. 18.2 Determining the triangulations among teammates

the width, length and length per width ratio (Clemente et al., 2017) it may be possible to split the game into moments or periods to analyze parameters further. This can be completed with the view to making tactical adjustments (i.e., ensuring compactness when defending and increasing width when attacking) with the objective of ultimately improving performance.

However, these two concepts are not unique in that the positional-data analysis may provide knowledge for coaches to understand the dispersion of the players. The relationships between teammates are composed by triangulations during both attacking and defensive moments. These triangulations should be understood as the lines that link all the dots in the Cartesian plane, with the minimum number of lines possible (Fig. 18.2).

These triangulations also reveal the shape of the team in a specific moment. Starting from this shape, it is possible to quantify the area of the shape or the sub-areas within the shape. This will assist in determining the space "covered" by a team during the match and, in a translation to practice scenarios, eventually to build exercises based on the typical dimensions of the team during specific moments of the match as proposed in previous studies (Caro, Zubillaga, Fradua, & Fernandez-Navarro, 2019; Fradua et al., 2013). Moreover, from a match analysis point-of-view, it is also possible to overlap the shape of both teams and the triangulations aiming to identify the more effective ones as proposed by some authors (Clemente, Couceiro, Martins, Mendes, & Figueiredo, 2013).

The two previous examples reveal the "usability" of the positional data analysis to inspect the collective organization of the teams and how the information can be interpreted by coaches to inform decisions during matches or to adjust exercises or drills in training scenarios. Despite the rate of growth in technology, it is difficult, at present, to establish relationships between these measures and the ball due to the fact that GPS is used to track merely players. Taking this into consideration, the network analysis has also been introduced in sports analysis to establish the connections among teammates by using linkage elements with the ball (Clemente, Martins, & Mendes, 2016).

As in any group, there are athletes/individuals that assume a greater level of importance than others in specific events or actions. Furthermore, there are also individuals that establish connections more frequently, others that act as mediators and others that are the most recruited from their colleagues. In team sports, it is important to identify the centrality levels of the players or to characterize the group dynamic within the group (Duch, Waitzman, & Amaral, 2010; Grund, 2012; Lusher, Robins, & Kremer, 2010).

The Social Network Analysis (SNA) uses some concepts of graph theory to employ a set of algorithms and equations that helps to understand the dynamics that occur within groups (Horvath, 2011; Wasserman & Faust, 1994). The possibilities and applications of SNA extends to different scientific areas, however, the application in sports sciences in specific within-match analysis is somewhat recent (Clemente, Martins, Kalamaras, Wong, & Mendes, 2015b; Lusher et al., 2010; Passos et al., 2011).

Fundamentally, SNA allows the interpretation of three levels of analysis in team sports (Clemente, Martins, et al., 2016): (1) centrality levels of the player(s), (2) interdependency levels between player(s), and (3) characterization of the network and its properties. For each level of analysis, there are many equations and measures that provide different information that can be interpreted.

The procedures involved with using SNA in daily practice are much easier compared with positional data and is a feasible alternative to using notational analysis. This approach involved the observer coding the passing sequences and registering the order of passes and directions in a weighted adjacency matrix. After that, the adjacency matrices of all passing sequences are calculated and imported into an SNA-specific software. Detailed information on how to complete this procedure can be found in specialized books and articles (Clemente, Silva, Martins, Kalamaras, & Mendes, 2016; Clemente, Martins, et al., 2016).

Some studies have characterized the network properties of teams (considering the pass as the linkage between teammates) and possible relationships with performance indicators (Clemente, 2018; Clemente, Martins, Kalamaras, Wong, & Mendes, 2015a; Grund, 2012). Briefly, the results suggest that more homogeneous teams (i.e., the passes and the connections are balanced among teammates) seems to correlate with increased team success and performance during matches (e.g., shots, goals scored etc.) (Clemente, 2018; Clemente et al., 2015a; Grund, 2012). However, how can the coach use such information to inform decisions or interpret the data? It is possible that the coach may use this information to identify possible variations across the periods of match-play or compare between matches (i.e., match-to-match). It may also make sense to compare the properties of teams under various circumstances such as whilst competing against different opponents. Moreover, it can be interesting to identify how specific player(s) may change the overall characteristics of team dynamics.

Few studies have utilized interdependency network measures to analyze how teammates are related and to identify the most dependent (Clemente, Couceiro, Martins, & Mendes, 2014). The particular case of topological overlap measure or scaled connectivity may help coaches to understand the most independent/dependent players and the relationships of the players within the team. Previous research in professional football teams revealed that lateral and central defenders were more connected with teammates and midfielders were the most independent players (Clemente et al., 2014). The results may vary in accordance with the type of analysis, namely if the adjacency matrices are split by critical moments as shots or goals or by moments of counterattacks or indirect attacks.

Also it is possible to determine the most prominent players during passing sequences through the use of network analysis considering that such prominence is understood as the player most recruited (i.e., the most passed to player(s), that recruits (i.e., makes a pass) or the mediator (i.e., has an involvement). There are many centrality measures in SNA, however the most commonly used in match analysis studies are the degree centrality, degree prestige, eigenvector or betweenness centrality (Clemente et al., 2019; Hurst et al., 2016; Praça et al., 2019). Considering the pass as the linkage factor, degree centrality reveals the players that are frequently passed to by teammates are likely to hold stronger relationships with teams. The degree prestige provides information about the players that are more recruited from the teammates, thus if the passes are considered as the link will be the players that more receive passes from the teammates. The eigenvector represents the influence of a player in the passing sequences made by the team. Betweenness centrality can be considered the mediator of the network or in other words, players that are connecting the remaining teammates. The results vary depending on who the adjacency matrices are split, however defenders and midfielders are typically the players with greater degree prestige, centrality or betweenness (Clemente et al., 2019; Clemente & Martins, 2017). However, when counterattacking, the wingers and strikers will have the greater degree prestige and the midfielders and defenders the greater degree centrality (Malta & Travassos, 2014). This emphasizes that depending on the type of analysis, the feedback given to the coach may be different and the inferences drawn from such information should be carefully considered.

Network analysis can help coaches identify the consequences of specific drills or exercises in the centralities, interdependency or global network measures of teams. Moreover, utilizing this information in matches will help establish comparisons and make decisions about which type of player can be more adequate to use in specific circumstances or contexts.

Training Load Monitoring

As previously mentioned, GPS systems are widely implemented in sports science departments of clubs, namely, to monitor the external load of players (Malone, Hughes, Roe, Collins, & Buchheit, 2017). However, one must be aware that the physical demands do not describe the entire contribution of a player or increase the understanding of the impact of the training stimulus on players. The concept of training load has developed in sports science, providing relevant information about how to manage training and match schedules (Williams, Trewartha, Cross, Kemp, & Stokes, 2017). Training load can be further categorized as either internal or external. The external load represents the physical demands imposed on the athlete or player whilst exercising (Halson, 2014). Whereas the internal load is reflective of the biological (e.g., heart rate [HR])) responses of the athlete to a given external load (Halson, 2014). Both are closely related, however, provide different information for coaches (Casamichana, Castellano, Calleja-Gonzalez, San Román, & Castagna, 2013).

Technological devices used to measure and quantify training loads have increased in popularity in sports science departments, mainly to detect fatigue status, optimize player readiness, prevent injury, and ultimately improve performance (Gabbett et al., 2017). The idea behind the systematic collection of training load data is to follow the main principle that "without data you're just another person with an opinion", quoting the famous data scientist W. Edwards Deming.

In fact, the concept of collecting data to understand the effects that training has on players has been around for many years and started before to the invention of technological devices. Well known scales such as the rating of perceived exertion (RPE) (Borg, 1998; Foster et al., 2001) have been used to monitor internal training loads through the perception of effort in athletes. However, employing the use of technology such as HR monitors, accelerometers or GPS are an effective and complimentary addition when used alongside subjective scales (Twist & Highton, 2013).

Monitoring training load is one of the methods that inform training prescriptions which can be broken down into various categories (Gabbett et al., 2017): (1) monitoring external workload; (2) monitoring internal workload; (3) monitoring perceptual well-being; and (4) monitoring readiness.

External load is usually measured by using GPS, accelerometers and IMU and can be organized into the following classifications (Buchheit & Simpson, 2017): (1) level 1, typical distances covered in different speed zones; (2) level 2, events related to changes in velocity, including accelerations, decelerations and changes of direction; and (3) level 3, events derived from the IMU and accelerometers (e.g., player load). The use of external load for coaches should be well applied, namely considering the typical movements performed by players. In fact, some coaches use this information to analyze distances covered during a match, however caution should be exercised when comparing, as disparities in distances between matches may not represent reduced performance per se. In fact, physical within-match demands are dependent on tactical approaches, and subsequent pacing strategies may affect distances rather than the fitness of players (Buchheit & Simpson, 2017). Therefore, it may be considered that levels 1 and 2 of external load analysis may not be suitable for monitoring training status, based on the fact that it does not account for contextual factors and inherent variations in physical performance (Buchheit & Simpson, 2017). On the other hand, the IMU and accelerometer derived measures (e.g., player load and metabolic power) can be collected and used for monitoring fatigue during matches (Buchheit & Simpson, 2017).

External load is a small part of the monitoring "puzzle". In fact, it is really important to understand the biological impact that load has on players. Typically, HR monitors are used to assess the exercise intensity (e.g., using the reserve HR, maximal HR or training HR) or analyze the overall load accumulated during a session (e.g., using the training impulse) (Manzi, Iellamo, Impellizzeri, D'Ottavio, & Castagna, 2009). Moreover, HR variability is commonly used to assess adaptations to training or analyze the recovery status of players prior or following exercise (Rabbani, Baseri, Reisi, Clemente, & Kargarfard, 2018). In the absence of HR monitors, it is also possible to monitor/control effort using RPE. In fact, there is strong evidence that suggests session-RPE is a valid and reliable method to assess internal load and can be utilized either in isolation to monitor training load or combined with other physiological parameters (Haddad, Stylianides, Djaoui, Dellal, & Chamari, 2017). The RPE is also feasible, cost-effective and a practical alternative to monitoring the intensity of sessions (Foster et al., 2001). It can also be used to assess training monotony (the variability of the load within the week) (Foster, 1998), training strain (sum of training loads for all training sessions during a week multiplied by training monotony) (Foster, 1998), acute training load (sum of workloads attained during training sessions across each week), chronic workload (mean of training load of the previous 4 weeks) and the acute: chronic workload ratio (Blanch & Gabbett, 2016).

Currently, sports scientists are able to detect training loads to assist in developing individual training statuses and adapt training prescriptions in order to avoid injury/ fatigue and increase performance (Buchheit, 2019). Therefore, it is highly recommended that practitioners and coaches adapt training loads so as to meet individual needs of the player within team sports.

Key Points

- Over the past few years there has been an exponential increase in the development of specific technology to support coach activity.
- Technologies are assisting practitioners mainly in assessing fatigue, reducing injury and improving the performance of athletes.
- Despite all the advantages that have brought new technologies for coach activity, the large amount of information that some technologies provide can be a barrier for coaches when they do not have the skills to select only the information that really matters.

Conclusion

This chapter has highlighted the evolution of technology over recent years. The use of technology is now commonly used to monitor loads in both team sports and individual athletes. This chapter has revealed the importance of monitoring training load and how this has evolved our understanding of individual training status. The scientific evidences discussed in this chapter suggests that technologies are assisting practitioners in assessing fatigue, reducing injury and improving the performance of athletes.

References

Adair, D., & Vamplew, W. (1997). *Sport in Australian history*. Melbourne: Oxford University Press.

Akenhead, R., & Nassis, G. P. (2016, July). Training Load and Player monitoring in high-level football: Current practice and perceptions. *International Journal of Sports Physiology and Performance, 11*(5), 587–593. https://doi.org/10.1123/ijspp.2015-0331. Epub 2015 Oct 9. PMID: 26456711.

Alarcón, F., Castillo-Díaz, A., Madinabeitia, I., Castillo-Rodríguez, A., & Cárdenas, D. (2018). La carga mental deteriora la precisión del pase en jugadores de fútbol [Mental load impairs pass accuracy in soccer players]. *Revista de Psicología Del Deporte/Journal of Sport Psychology, 27* (2), 155–164.

Aughey, R. J. (2011). Applications of GPS technologies to field sports. *International Journal of Sports Physiology and Performance, 6*(3), 295–310. https://doi.org/10.1123/ijspp.6.3.295

Balagué, N., Torrents, C., Pol, R., & Seirul·lo, F. (2014). Entrenamiento integrado. Principios dinámicos y aplicaciones [Integrated training. Dynamic principles and applications]. *Apunts Educación Física y Deportes,* (116), 60–68. https://doi.org/10.5672/apunts.2014-0983.es. (2014/2).116.06.

Barker-Ruchti, N., Barker, D., Rynne, S. B., & Lee, J. (2016). Learning cultures and cultural learning in high-performance sport: Opportunities for sport pedagogues. *Physical Education and Sport Pedagogy, 21*, 1–9.

Bartlett, R., Button, C., Robins, M., Dutt-Mazumder, A., & Kennedy, G. (2012). Analysing team coordination patterns from player movement trajectories in soccer: Methodological considerations. *International Journal of Performance Analysis in Sport, 12*, 398–424.

Bastida, A., Gómez-Carmona, D., De la Cruz, E., & Pino, J. (2018). Accuracy, intra- and inter-unit reliability, and comparison between GPS and UWB-based position-tracking systems used for time–motion analyses in soccer. *European Journal of Sport Science, 18*(4), 450–457. https://doi.org/10.1080/17461391.2018.1427796

Blanch, P., & Gabbett, T. J. (2016). Has the athlete trained enough to return to play safely? The acute: Chronic workload ratio permits clinicians to quantify a player's risk of subsequent injury. *British Journal of Sports Medicine, 50*(8), 471–475. https://doi.org/10.1136/bjsports-2015-095445

Borg, G. (1998). *Perceived exertion and pain scales*. Champaign, IL: Human Kinetics.

Buchheit, M. (2019). Managing high-speed running load in professional soccer players: The benefit of high-intensity interval training supplementation. *Sport Performance & Science Reports, 53* (1), 1–5.

Buchheit, M., Allen, A., Poon, T. K., Modonutti, M., Gregson, W., & Di Salvo, V. (2014). Integrating different tracking systems in football: Multiple camera semi-automatic system, local position measurement and GPS technologies. *Journal of Sports Sciences, 32*(20), 1844–1857. https://doi.org/10.1080/02640414.2014.942687

Buchheit, M., & Simpson, B. M. (2017). Player-tracking technology: Half-full or half-empty glass? *International Journal of Sports Physiology and Performance, 12*(Suppl 2), S2-35–S2-41. https://doi.org/10.1123/ijspp.2016-0499

Bujalance-Moreno, P., Latorre-Román, P. A., & García-Pinillos, F. (2019). A systematic review on small-sided games in football players: Acute and chronic adaptations. *Journal of Sports Sciences, 37*(8), 921–949. https://doi.org/10.1080/02640414.2018.1535821

Caro, O., Zubillaga, A., Fradua, L., & Fernandez-Navarro, J. (2019). Analysis of playing area dimensions in Spanish professional soccer. *Journal of Strength and Conditioning Research.* https://doi.org/10.1519/JSC.0000000000003226

Casamichana, D., Castellano, J., Calleja-Gonzalez, J., San Román, J., & Castagna, C. (2013). Relationship between indicators of training load in soccer players. *Journal of Strength and Conditioning Research, 27*(2), 369–374. https://doi.org/10.1519/JSC.0b013e3182548af1

Chen, K. Y., & Bassett, D. R., Jr. (2005). The technology of accelerometry-based activity monitors: current and future. *Medicine Science Sports Exercise, 37*(11 Suppl), S490–S500.

Clemente, F. (2018). Performance outcomes and their associations with network measures during FIFA World Cup 2018. *International Journal of Performance Analysis in Sport, 18*(6), 1010–1023. https://doi.org/10.1080/24748668.2018.1545180

Clemente, F., Couceiro, M. S., Fernando, M. L., Mendes, R., & Figueiredo, A. J. (2013). Measuring tactical behaviour using technological metrics: Case study of a football game. *International Journal of Sports Science & Coaching, 8*(4), 723–739.

Clemente, F., Couceiro, M. S., Martins, F. M., & Mendes, R. S. (2014). Using network metrics to investigate football team players' connections: A pilot study. *Motriz, 20*(3), 262–271. https://doi.org/dx.doi.org/10.1590/S1980-65742014000300004

Clemente, F., Couceiro, M. S., Martins, F. M., Mendes, R., & Figueiredo, A. J. (2013). Measuring collective behaviour in football teams: Inspecting the impact of each half of the match on ball possession. *International Journal of Performance Analysis in Sport, 13*(3), 678–689.

Clemente, F., & Martins, F. M. (2017). Who are the prominent players in the UEFA champions league? An approach based on network analysis. *Walailak Journal of Science and Technology, 14*(8), 1–8.

Clemente, F., Martins, F. M., Kalamaras, D., Wong, D. P., & Mendes, R. S. (2015a). General network analysis of national soccer teams in FIFA World Cup 2014. *International Journal of Performance Analysis in Sport, 15*(1), 80–96.

Clemente, F., Martins, F. M., Kalamaras, D., Wong, D. P., & Mendes, R. S. (2015b). Midfielder as the prominent participant in the building attack: A network analysis of national teams in FIFA World Cup 2014. *International Journal of Performance Analysis in Sport, 15*(2), 704–722.

Clemente, F., Martins, F. M., & Mendes, R. S. (2016). *Social network analysis applied to team sports analysis*. The Netherlands: Springer. https://doi.org/10.1007/978-3-319-25855-3

Clemente, F., Sarmento, H., Praça, G. M., Nikolaidis, P. T., Rosemann, T., & Knechtle, B. (2019). Variations of network centralities between playing positions in favorable and unfavorable close and unbalanced scores during the 2018 FIFA World Cup. *Frontiers in Psychology, 10.* https://doi.org/10.3389/fpsyg.2019.01802

Clemente, F., Sequeiros, J. B., Correia, A. F., Silva, F., & Martins, F. M. (2017). *Computational metrics and Its applications on the analysis of soccer: Connecting the dots*. Singapore: Springer.

Clemente, F., Silva, F., Martins, F. M., Kalamaras, D., & Mendes, R. S. (2016). Performance analysis tool for network analysis on team sports: A case study of FIFA Soccer World Cup 2014. *Proceedings of the Institution of Mechanical Engineers, Part P: Journal of Sports Engineering and Technology, 230*(3), 158–170. https://doi.org/10.1177/1754337115597335

Coutts, A. J., & Duffield, R. (2010). Validity and reliability of GPS devices for measuring movement demands of team sports. *Journal of Science and Medicine in Sport, 13*(1), 133–135. https://doi.org/10.1016/j.jsams.2008.09.015

Cust, E. E., Sweeting, A. J., Ball, K., & Robertson, S. (2018). Machine and deep learning for sport-specific movement recognition: A systematic review of model development and performance. *Journal of Sports Sciences, 37*(5), 1–33. https://doi.org/10.1080/02640414.2018.1521769. PMID: 30307362.

Dellaserra, C. L., Gao, Y., & Ransdell, L. (2014). Use of integrated technology in team sports: a review of opportunities, challenges, and future directions for athletes. *Journal of Strength and Conditioning Research, 28*(2), 556–573. https://doi.org/10.1519/JSC.0b013e3182a952fb

Duarte, R., Araújo, D., Correia, V., & Davids, K. (2012). Sports teams as superorganisms: Implications of sociobiological models of behaviour for research and practice in team sports performance analysis. *Sports Medicine, 42*(8), 633–642.

Duarte, R., Araújo, D., Folgado, H., Esteves, P., Marques, P., & Davids, K. (2013). Capturing complex, non-linear team behaviours during competitive football performance. *Journal of Systems Science and Complexity, 26*(1), 62–72.

Duch, J., Waitzman, J. S., & Amaral, L. A. (2010). Quantifying the performance of individual players in a team activity. *PLoS One, 5*(6), e10937.

Folgado, H., Lemmink, K. P., Frencken, W., & Sampaio, J. (2014). Length, width and centroid distance as measures of teams tactical performance in youth football. *European Journal of Sport Science, 14*(Suppl 1), S487–S492. https://doi.org/10.1080/17461391.2012.730060

Foster, C. A. (1998). Monitoring training in athletes with reference to overtraining syndrome. *Medicine and Science in Sports and Exercise, 30*, 1164–1168.

Foster, C., Florhaug, J. A., Franklin, J., Gottschall, L., Hrovatin, L. A., Parker, S., ... Dodge, C. (2001). A new approach to monitoring exercise training. *Journal of Strength and Conditioning Research, 15*(1), 109–115.

Fradua, L., Zubillaga, A., Caro, O., Iván Fernández-García, A., Ruiz-Ruiz, C., & Tenga, A. (2013). Designing small-sided games for training tactical aspects in soccer: Extrapolating pitch sizes from full-size professional matches. *Journal of Sports Sciences, 31*(6), 573–581. https://doi.org/10.1080/02640414.2012.746722

Gabbett, T. J., Nassis, G. P., Oetter, E., Pretorius, J., Johnston, N., Medina, D., ... Ryan, A. (2017). The athlete monitoring cycle: A practical guide to interpreting and applying training monitoring data. *British Journal of Sports Medicine, 51*(20), 1451–1452. https://doi.org/10.1136/bjsports-2016-097298

Garganta, J., & Pinto, J. (1994). O ensino do futebol. In A. Graça & J. Oliveira (Eds.), *O ensino dos jogos desportivos* (pp. 95–136). Faculdade de Ciências do Desporto e de Educação Física da Universidade do Porto: Rainho & Neves Lda.

Geurkink, Y., Vandewiele, G., Lievens, M., de Turck, F., Ongenae, F., Matthys, S. P. J., ... Bourgois, J. G. (2019). Modeling the prediction of the session rating of perceived exertion in soccer: Unraveling the puzzle of predictive indicators. *International Journal of Sports Physiology and Performance*, 1–6. https://doi.org/10.1123/ijspp.2018-0698

Griffiths, M., & Armour, K. (2013). Volunteer sport coaches and their learning dispositions in coach education. *International Journal of Sports Science and Coaching, 8*, 677–688.

Grund, T. U. (2012). Network structure and team performance: The case of English Premier League soccer teams. *Social Networks, 34*(4), 682–690.

Gyarmati, L., Kwak, H., & Rodriguez, P. (2014). Searching for a unique style in soccer. In *2014 KDD Workshop on Large-Scale Sports Analytics* (pp. 5–8). Physics and Society. Retrieved from http://arxiv.org/abs/1409.0308

Haddad, M., Stylianides, G., Djaoui, L., Dellal, A., & Chamari, K. (2017). Session-RPE method for training load monitoring: Validity, ecological usefulness, and influencing factors. *Frontiers in Neuroscience, 11*. https://doi.org/10.3389/fnins.2017.00612

Halson, S. L. (2014). Monitoring training load to understand fatigue in athletes. *Sports Medicine, 44*(2), 139–147. https://doi.org/10.1007/s40279-014-0253-z

Hausler, J., Halaki, M., & Orr, R. (2016). Application of global positioning system and microsensor technology in competitive rugby league match-play: A systematic review and meta-analysis. *Sports Medicine, 46*(4), 559–588. https://doi.org/10.1007/s40279-015-0440-6

Hennessy, L., & Jeffreys, I. (2018). The current use of GPS, its potential, and limitations in soccer. *The Journal of Strength & Conditioning Research, 40*, 83–94. https://doi.org/10.1519/SSC.0000000000000386

Horvath, S. (2011). *Weighted network analysis: Applications in genomics and systems biology*. New York: Springer.

Hurst, M., Loureiro, M., Valongo, B., Laporta, L., Nikolaidis, T. P., & Afonso, J. (2016). Systemic mapping of high-level women's volleyball using social network analysis: the case of serve (K0), side-out (KI), side-out transition (KII) and transition (KIII). *International Journal of Performance Analysis in Sport, 16*(2), 695–710. https://doi.org/10.1080/24748668.2016.11868917

Liebermann, D., & Franks, I. (2004). The use of feedback-based technologies. In M. Hughes & I. Franks (Eds.), *Notational analysis of sport* (2nd ed.). London: Routledge.

Liebermann, D., & Franks, I. (2008). Video feedback and information technologies. In M. Hughes & I. Franks (Eds.), *The essentials of performance analysis. An introduction*. London: Routledge.

Lusher, D., Robins, G., & Kremer, P. (2010). The application of social network analysis to team sports. *Measurement in Physical Education and Exercise Science, 14*(4), 211–224.

Lyle, J. (2002). *Sports coaching concepts: A framework for coaches' behaviour*. London: Routledge.

Mallett, C., Rynne, S., & Billett, S. (2016). Valued learning experiences of early career and experienced high-performance coaches. *Physical Education and Sport Pedagogy, 21*, 89–104.

Malone, S., Hughes, B., Roe, M., Collins, K., & Buchheit, M. (2017). Monitoring player fitness, fatigue status and running performance during an in-season training camp in elite Gaelic football. *Science and Medicine in Football, 1*(3), 229–236. https://doi.org/10.1080/24733938.2017.1361040

Malta, P., & Travassos, B. (2014). Characterization of the defense-attack transition of a soccer team. *Motricidade, 10*(1), 27–37.

Manzi, V., Iellamo, F., Impellizzeri, F., D'Ottavio, S., & Castagna, C. (2009). Relation between Individualized training impulses and performance in distance runners. *Medicine & Science in Sports & Exercise, 41*(11), 2090–2096. https://doi.org/10.1249/MSS.0b013e3181a6a959

McGarry, T. (2005). Soccer as a dynamical system: Some theoretical considerations. In T. Reilly, J. Cabri, & D. Araújo (Eds.), *Science and football V* (pp. 570–579). London: Routledge, Taylor & Francis.

Memmert, D., Lemmink, K. A., & Sampaio, J. (2017). Current approaches to tactical performance analyses in soccer using position data. *Sports Medicine, 47*(1), 1–10. https://doi.org/10.1007/s40279-016-0562-5

Page, R. M., Marrin, K., Brogden, C. M., & Greig, M. (2016, November). The biomechanical and physiological response to repeated soccer-specific simulations interspersed by 48 or 72 hours recovery. *Physical Therapy in Sport, 22*, 81–87. https://doi.org/10.1016/j.ptsp.2016.06.011. Epub 2016 Jul 4. PMID: 27614926.

Passos, P., Davids, K., Araújo, D., Paz, N., Minguéns, J., & Mendes, J. (2011). Networks as a novel tool for studying team ball sports as complex social systems. *Journal of Science and Medicine in Sport, 14*(2), 170–176.

Phillips, M. (2000). *From sidelines to center field: A history of sports coaching in Australia*. Sydney: University of New South Wales Press.

Polglaze, T., Dawson, B., Hiscock, D. J., & Peeling, P. (2015). A comparative analysis of accelerometer and time-motion data in elite men's hockey training and competition. *International Journal of Sports Physiology and Performance, 10*(4), 446–451.

Pons, E., Martín-Garcia, A., Guitart, M., Guerrero, I., Tarragó, J. R., Seirul lo, F., & Cos, F. (2020). Training in team sports: Optimising training at FCB. *Apunts. Educación Física y Deportes, 142*, 55–66. https://doi.org/10.5672/apunts.2014-0983.es.(2020/4).142.07.

Praça, G. M., Lima, B. B., Bredt, S. G., Sousa, R. B., Clemente, F. M., & Andrade, A. G. (2019). Influence of match status on players' prominence and teams' network properties during 2018 FIFA World Cup. *Frontiers in Psychology, 10*. https://doi.org/10.3389/fpsyg.2019.00695

Rabbani, A., Baseri, M. K., Reisi, J., Clemente, F. M., & Kargarfard, M. (2018). Monitoring collegiate soccer players during a congested match schedule: Heart rate variability versus subjective wellness measures. *Physiology & Behavior, 194*, 527–531. https://doi.org/10.1016/j.physbeh.2018.07.001

Razali, N., Mustapha, A., Yatim, F. A., & Ab Aziz, R. (2017). Predicting football matches results using Bayesian networks for English Premier League (EPL). *International Research and Innovation Summit, 226*(1–6). https://doi.org/10.1088/1757-899X/226/1/012099

Ruddy, J. D., Shield, A. J., Maniar, N., Williams, M. D., Duhig, S., Timmins, R. G., . . . Opar, D. A. (2018). Predictive modeling of hamstring strain injuries in elite Australian footballers. *Medicine and Science in Sports and Exercise, 50*(5), 906–914. https://doi.org/10.1249/mss.0000000000001527

Sarmento, H., Clemente, F. M., Araújo, D., Davids, K., McRobert, A., & Figueiredo, A. (2018). What performance analysts need to know about research trends in association football (2012–2016): A systematic review. *Sports Medicine, 48*(4), 799–836. https://doi.org/10.1007/s40279-017-0836-6

Sarmento, H., Marcelino, R., Anguera, M. T., Campaniço, J., Matos, N., & Leitão, J. C. (2014). Match analysis in football: A systematic review. *Journal of Sports Sciences, 32*(20), 1831–1843. https://doi.org/10.1080/02640414.2014.898852

Seirul-lo Vargas, F. (2017). *El entrenamiento en los deportes de equipo [Training in team sports]*. Barcelona: Mastercede, Ed.

Smith, A., & Stewart, B. (2010). The special features of sport: A critical revisit. *Sport Management Review, 13*(1), 1–13.

Sutter, E. G., Orenduff, J., Fox, W. J., Myers, J., & Garrigues, G. E. (2018). Predicting injury in professional baseball pitchers from delivery mechanics: A statistical model using quantitative video analysis. *Orthopedics, 41*(1), 43–53. https://doi.org/10.3928/01477447-20171127-05

Twist, C., & Highton, J. (2013). Monitoring fatigue and recovery in rugby league players. *International Journal of Sports Physiology and Performance, 8*(5), 467–474.

Wasserman, S., & Faust, K. (1994). *Social network analysis: Methods and applications*. New York: Cambridge University Press.

Williams, S., Trewartha, G., Cross, M. J., Kemp, S. P., & Stokes, K. A. (2017). Monitoring what matters: A systematic process for selecting training-load measures. *International Journal of Sports Physiology and Performance, 12*(Suppl 2), S2-101–S2-106. https://doi.org/10.1123/ijspp.2016-0337

Hugo Sarmento is an assistant professor at Faculty of Sport Sciences and Physical Education, University of Coimbra, Portugal. His research covers the areas of athletic performance, training load monitoring, training methodology, performance analysis, and match analysis.

Filipe Manuel Clemente is an assistant professor at Escola Superior Desporto e Lazer, Instituto Politécnico de Viana do Castelo, Portugal. His research interest includes performance analysis, match analysis, motivation in athletes, and physical activity and health in young athletes.

Adam Field is a PhD candidate in the School of Human and Health Sciences at the University of Huddersfield based in the United Kingdom. His research interests include: (1) the effectiveness of recovery modalities following exercise, (2) research and the application of science in team sports, (3) the investigation of ergogenic aids to improve exercise performance, (4) sports nutrition and, (5) recreational team sport activities to improve health and wellbeing.

Pedro Antonio Sánchez Miguel is an assistant professor at Teacher Training College, University of Extremadura, Spain. His research interest include athletic performance, motivation and well-being in athletes, match analysis and physical activity and health in young athletes.

Chapter 19
Coaching Under Stress and Burnout

Peter Olusoga, Göran Kenttä, and Marte Bentzen

Abstract This chapter will explore stress and burnout in the context of sports coaching. First, an effort will be made to provide some conceptual clarity in defining the stress, burnout, and related terms, and in exploring the multiple and often overlapping, theoretical perspectives underpinning coach stress and burnout research. The coach stress literature that has examined stressors, coping methods, and the impacts of coach stress will be critically discussed, and relationships between stress, burnout, and coach well-being/ill-being will also be highlighted. Avenues for future coaching research related to stress, burnout, and well-being will be outlined, and practical implications for coaches, coach educators, and other key stakeholders are also provided. More specifically, existing research reveals a real need to place coach well-being at the forefront of the coaching agenda by coach educators and developers, and this chapter will conclude by suggesting potential strategies for promoting coach well-being in various high-performance and developmental contexts.

Keywords Coaching · Stress · Well-being · Exhaustion · Mindfulness

Stress is and will always be an inevitable part of sport. The ability to manage the vast range of stressors arising from organisational issues, performance-demands, and the

P. Olusoga (✉)
Sheffield Hallam University, Sheffield, UK

Department of Public Health and Sport Sciences, Inland Norway University of Applied Sciences, Elverum, Norway
e-mail: p.olusoaga@shu.ac.uk

G. Kenttä
The Swedish School of Sport & Health Sciences, Stockholm, Sweden
e-mail: goran.kentta@gih.se

M. Bentzen
Norwegian School of Sport Sciences, Oslo, Norway
e-mail: marte.bentzen@nih.no

R. Resende, A. R. Gomes (eds.), *Coaching for Human Development and Performance in Sports*, https://doi.org/10.1007/978-3-030-63912-9_19

personal domain is a significant factor influencing both performance outcomes and subjective well-being for any sports performers. Sport and performance psychology researchers have attempted to shine a light on the ways in which the experience of stress might impact upon these performers, often limited to the athletes under the spotlights. However, this chapter will shift the spotlight to the coach. The consensus view is that given the multiple roles a coach must take on, as well as the technical, physical, organisational, and psychological challenges those roles entail, sports coaches should be regarded as—*performers*—in their own right (Didymus, 2017; Frey, 2007; Gould, Greenleaf, Guinan, & Chung, 2002; Olusoga, Butt, Hays, & Maynard, 2009).

Coaching has been described as an all-consuming, demanding, and oftentimes frustrating profession (Didymus, 2017; Raedeke, 2004), and the impact of stress on sports coaches has become a popular topic of investigation (e.g., Olusoga, Butt, Maynard, & Hays, 2010; Thelwell, Weston, Greenlees, & Hutchings, 2008). Coaches have reported stress leading to anxiety, losing confidence, and withdrawal from sport, in addition to the physical and emotional exhaustion and cynicism often associated with burnout (Frey, 2007; Kelley, 1994; Kelley & Gill, 1993; Olusoga et al., 2010; Olusoga & Kenttä, 2017). In addition, these negative impacts on coaches, have also been linked to a host of potentially detrimental athlete outcomes, including damaged coach-athlete relationships, impacts on the coaching environment, athletes' performance and development, and athlete burnout (Price & Weiss, 2000; Thelwell, Wagstaff, Chapman, & Kenttä, 2017; Thelwell, Wagstaff, Rayner, Chapman, & Barker, 2017).

This chapter will critically examine research exploring coach stress and burnout. The ability to understand and manage stress and burnout is of paramount importance for sports coaches operating in various performance contexts. Thus, we will first make an effort to provide some conceptual clarity in defining the terms and exploring the various, often competing and overlapping, theoretical perspectives underpinning coach stress and burnout. We will discuss the stress process as applied to sport coaches and review the coach stress literature that has examined stressors, coping methods, and the impacts of coach stress on both athletes and coaches themselves. The chapter will also explore the relationships between stress, burnout, and coach well-being/ill-being based on a review of the growing body of coach burnout literature. Avenues for future coaching research will be suggested, and practical implications for coaches, coach educators, and other key stakeholders are provided. More specifically, we emphasize the need for coach well-being to be placed high on the coaching agenda by those responsible for coach education and coach development and suggest potential strategies for promoting coach well-being in various contexts.

The Context of HP Coaching

Before any meaningful or detailed discussion of stress and burnout in high-performance (HP) coaching can take place, it is important to understand key elements of the specific context of HP coaching. Gould et al. (2002) asserted that coaches are performers in their own right and much of the research into coaching stress and burnout has adopted a similar perspective (Didymus, 2017; Frey, 2007; Olusoga et al., 2009). While there is no doubt that coaching can be extremely rewarding, coaching is certainly a challenging and oftentimes frustrating profession (Didymus, 2017; Raedeke, 2004). Within HP contexts in particular, coaches are often compelled to work long and irregular hours, spending substantial amounts of time away from their homes and families (Norris, Didymus, & Kaiseler, 2017). This can lead to isolation and loneliness in the role (Olusoga et al., 2009) and issues with work-home interference (Bentzen, Lemyre, & Kenttä, 2016b), again representing further stressors for coaches.

At the same time, HP coaches are exposed to unrelenting pressure related to performance expectations, alongside the ever-present threat of unemployment and/or funding cuts (Mallett & Lara-Bercial, 2016). In addition, HP coaches might have to endure constant scrutiny from media and fans, amplified by social media, so that their decisions, team selections, and perceived mistakes can be replayed, criticized, and shared around the world even before the competition has ended.

Taken together, the context of HP coaching appears to be one in which coaches experience a combination of extreme, overlapping, and often conflicting demands on their time, energy, and resources (Kenttä, Olusoga, & Bentzen, 2020). Moreover, several negative consequences for coaches' mental health have been reported in the literature and include psychophysiological outcomes such as sleep disturbance, mood changes, emotional responses, and burnout (Bentzen et al., 2016b; McNeill, Durand-Bush, & Lemyre, 2016; Olusoga et al., 2010).

While it is clear that the HP coach has a somewhat challenging role to fulfil, the strict expectation on the coach is to take responsibility for the well-being and performance of their athletes (Olusoga, Maynard, Hays, & Butt, 2012). Unfortunately, this often has the result of relegating coaches' self-care to a secondary concern, if considered at all. Moreover, the hyper-masculine environment of elite sport (i.e., one that is dominated by supposedly desirable characteristics like mental toughness, strength, grit, and resilience), is another context-specific factor that can contribute to coaches' stress and experiences of burnout (Hägglund, Kenttä, Wagstaff, & Thelwell, 2019). Traditionally, this environment is not one in which showing vulnerability or engaging in help-seeking behaviors has been encouraged. As such, coaches have reported masking emotional difficulties to maintain an appearance of being under control and able to cope with stress. The impact of this on coaches' well-being has recently been reported (Kenttä et al., 2020; Olusoga & Kenttä, 2017) and will be discussed throughout this chapter.

Stress in HP Coaching

The generally accepted definition of stress within the sport psychology literature views stress as "an ongoing process that involves individuals transacting with their environments, making appraisals of the situations they find themselves in, and endeavoring to cope with any issues that may arise" (Fletcher, Hanton, & Mellalieu, 2006, p. 329). Put simply, coaching stress is the process by which coaches weigh up the demands that they face, against their perceived ability to cope with those demands. In the past, it has been suggested that failure to consistently define stress has limited our theoretical understanding of stress and its associated key concepts. However, our current understanding that *stressors* are the environmental, organisational or personal demands placed on an individual, *strain* is the psychological, physiological, or behavioral response to those demands, and *coping* represents all attempts to manage either the demands or the responses, has led to a conceptual clarity that advanced this field of research and practice.

Using Lazarus' transactional theory of stress as a theoretical underpinning, a large proportion of the coaching stress literature has focussed on identifying stressors in various coaching contexts (Norris et al., 2017). The rationale for this seemed to be that a more comprehensive understanding of the stressors experienced by coaches would allow sport organisations (and sport psychology practitioners and coaches themselves) to more effectively manage the multifaceted demands of working in sport (Hanton, Fletcher, & Coughlan, 2005). Based largely on research in occupational settings, and on his own applied practice experience, Taylor (1992) suggested that stressors in coaching fall into three broad categories: factors intrinsic to the individual, such as lack of experience or self-doubts (personal stressors), interactions with others both in and outside of the immediate working environment (social stressors), and factors originating "within the team's organisational superstructure," such as long hours, lack of support, and financial concerns (organisational stressors). Stressors falling broadly into Taylor's three categories have been identified in the coach stress literature. For example, concerns related to athletes and athlete performances (e.g., Didymus, 2017; Kroll & Gundersheim, 1982; Rhind, Scott, & Fletcher, 2013; Wang & Ramsey, 1998), pressure to produce results (e.g., Frey, 2007; Olusoga et al., 2009; Pastore, 1991; Thelwell et al., 2008), demands on time (e.g., Frey, 2007), and lack of control (e.g., Robbins, Gilbert, & Clifton, 2015) have all been cited as stressors by coaches operating at various levels.

Knight, Reade, Selzler, and Rodgers (2013) identified further personal and situational factors influencing coaches' perceptions of stress. Unclear expectations, long working hours, lack of agreed criteria for evaluation, higher salaries, and a lack of social support were all related to higher perceptions of stress in coaches working in a broad a range of performance and developmental contexts. In addition, several studies highlighted the self-imposed pressure that coaches create, which acts as a further stressor. For example, Durand-Bush, Collins, and McNeill (2012) reported that women coaches placed high levels of expectation on themselves based on a desire to meet their preferred standards and to create an environment in which their athletes could enjoy themselves and excel. While coaches' concerns regarding their own performances and the pressure they place on themselves to meet expectations have been commonly referred to in the literature (e.g., Chroni, Diakaki, Perkos, Hassandra, & Schoen, 2013; Knights & Ruddock-Hudson, 2016; Olusoga et al., 2009; Thelwell et al., 2008), women coaches perhaps face several unique challenges in the male-dominated culture of elite sport. The relatively small number of women HP coaches (ranging between 8.4 and 20% in Canada, Norway and Sweden; Bentzen et al., 2016b; Kidd, 2013) is itself a potential stressor for this population. Carson, McCormack, and Walsh (2018) explored perceptions of women coaches, and suggested that the coaching role might be incompatible with general well-being and healthy family living. This perception might create an environment in which women coaches' blame themselves for this incompatibility, rather than the coaching context, and feel the need to 'toughen up' to 'fix' the problem (La Voi, 2016). Problematizing the coach, rather than the organisational culture might have the effect of adding to the unique set of stressors already associated with women's HP coaching.

Another under-researched area with regards to coach stress and burnout is the rapidly growing domain of Para sport. A few authors have explored some of the unique challenges of coaching in this performance context. For example, Wareham, Burkett, Innes, and Lovell (2017) highlighted practical (operational and physical), knowledge-based (e.g., concern about lack of disability specific knowledge), psychosocial (e.g., athletes' emotional issues, stigma around disability) and funding-related (e.g., inequity of resources compared to non-disabled sports) issues, unique to coaches in HP disability sport. Yet Paralympic sport has received relatively scant attention in relation to the specific demands placed upon coaches' and their well-being in this environment (Lundqvist, Ståhl, Kenttä, & Thulin, 2018).

A significant proportion of the coaching stress research has been conducted with high-school and collegiate, teacher-coaches, based in North American schools. The often dual-role nature of some of the coaches sampled might well have an impact on their perceptions of stress, while the nature of HP coaching, as described above, might bring with it some particular stressors, not apparent in sub-elite/amateur contexts. A number of researchers also recognized the importance of exploring coaching stress in HP coaching contexts. For example, Thelwell et al. (2008) interviewed eleven British coaches of elite athletes, with performance stressors (performances of the coach and performances of the athlete), and organisational stressors (environmental, leadership, personal, and team issues) being highlighted by coaches. Olusoga et al. (2009) investigated the stressors experienced by 12 world class coaches from a variety of individual and team sports. Ten distinct stressor themes reflecting organisational, competitive, and personal issues emerged from the interviews (*conflict, pressure and expectation, managing the competition environment, athlete concerns, coaching responsibilities to the athlete, consequences of the sport status, competition preparation, organisational management, sacrificing personal time,* and *isolation*). More recently, Didymus (2017) also investigated the stress experiences of international level sports coaches, with a similar personal, organisational, and competition-related stressors being reported. In addition to reporting coaches' perceived stressors, however, Didymus also outlined the situational properties of stressors experienced by these coaches (e.g., ambiguity, imminence, novelty), and the appraisal mechanisms underpinning their perceptions of stress (e.g., challenge, threat, benefit, and harm/loss).

Indeed, exploring stressors in HP sport is only part of the puzzle. There is no question that coach stress research has identified many, multifaceted, overlapping, complex stressors. Yet, overall, this research has suffered from limited indication from the coaches involved as to whether or not these stressors represented significant challenges to their performances or well-being, or whether they merely represented daily hassles associated with the coaching role.

Stress Responses and Burnout in HP Coaching

Fletcher and Scott (2010) proposed four types of stress response: behavioral (e.g., observable actions such as withdrawal), affective (e.g., emotional states like anxiety), cognitive (e.g., negative thinking and maladaptive attributions), and physiological (e.g., increased heart rate). Importantly, distinctions have also been made between more immediate responses to stress and longer-term effects of stress on coaches' well-being and performance (Olusoga et al., 2010). While the majority of the coach stress literature has focused on the deleterious effects of coaching stressors, it is important to note that coaches' stress responses are not always unwelcome. Heightened awareness, increased energy, and motivation have all been reported as desirable consequences of acute stress (Frey, 2007; Olusoga et al., 2010). Nevertheless, acute responses to stress might often have undesirable consequences as well. Indeed, a number of immediate effects on coaches' behaviors (e.g., agitated body language, sharper tone of voice), emotions (e.g., anger, irritability), and cognitions (e.g., lack of focus, worry, poor decision making) have been reported in the coach stress literature, alongside various physiological changes including tension, shaking, and numbness (Frey, 2007; Olusoga et al., 2010).

Olusoga et al. (2010) reported on some of the longer term effects of stress for the coaches themselves. Negative affect (e.g., emotional fatigue, depression), decreased motivation (e.g., reduced enjoyment), relationships with others (e.g., work-home interference), and withdrawal (becoming more introspective) were all discussed by the HP coaches in the study. Moreover, these unwelcome impacts on coaches have also been linked to a host of potentially damaging athlete outcomes (Bentzen, Lemyre, & Kenttä, 2014; Price & Weiss, 2000; Thelwell, Wagstaff, Rayner, et al., 2017). For example, Thelwell and colleagues (2017), suggested that coach-athlete relationships might be damaged as a result of coach stress, and that athletes' performance and development might also suffer, with athlete burnout being one potential end result. In addition, a handful of studies have provided anecdotal reports of excessive alcohol consumption, severe problems of work life interfering with private life, and divorces attributed to the stress of coaching (Bentzen, Lemyre, & Kenttä, 2017; Olusoga et al., 2012; Roberts, Baker, Reeves, Jones, & Cronin, 2018).

The more chronic symptoms of stress, such as emotional and physical exhaustion and withdrawal from sport, are often associated with burnout and have often been observed among HP coaches (Olusoga, Bentzen, & Kenttä, 2019). As such, research exploring the enduring effects of stress on coaches has largely focused on the relationship between stress and burnout (e.g., Caccese & Mayerberg, 1984; Capel, Sisley, & Desertrain, 1987; Tashman, Tenenbaum, & Eklund, 2010; Vealey, Udry, Zimmerman, & Soliday, 1992). Burnout is "an enduring experiential syndrome" (Maslach & Jackson, 1986, p. 1) characterized by emotional and physical exhaustion (feelings of being emotionally depleted by work), depersonalisation (perceived lack of value of the role and a cynical attitude towards, or withdrawal from, personal relationships at work), and reduced personal accomplishment (perceived lack of competence and low self-esteem).

Early research into coaching burnout was largely based on Smith's (1986) Cognitive-Affective Stress Model, with burnout hypothesized to be a result of exposure to chronic stress (e.g., Caccese & Mayerberg, 1984; Capel et al., 1987; Kelley, 1994; Kelley & Gill, 1993; Vealey et al., 1992). Kelley (1994) and Kelley and Gill (1993), for example, found that stress appraisals (e.g., perceived stress, role conflict, and 'coaching issues') were significantly related to all three dimensions of burnout for male and female collegiate coaches. As Raedeke (1997) argued though, exposure to stress is not a sufficient condition for burnout to develop, so there must be other factors at play. Consequently, authors have variously examined the coach burnout using self-determined motivation and workload (e.g., Bentzen et al., 2014, 2016b; Bentzen, Lemyre, & Kenttä, 2016a, 2017), emotional labour (e.g., Lee & Chelladurai, 2016), work-home interference (e.g., Lundkvist, Gustafsson, Davis, & Hassmén, 2016), passion (e.g., Donahue, Forest, Vallerand, Lemyre, Crevier-Braud, & Bergeron, 2012; Moen, Bentzen, & Myhre, 2018), recovery (Altfeld & Kellmann, 2015; Altfeld, Mallett, & Kellmann, 2015), and commitment (e.g., Raedeke, 2004) as their theoretical underpinnings.

Research taking a commitment perspective (e.g., Raedeke, Granzyk, & Warren, 2000) found that coaches displaying characteristics of entrapment (i.e., perceived high costs and low benefits of the role, lack of attractive alternatives to coaching, high investments and social pressure to continue), were more likely to experience burnout than coaches displaying low commitment- or attraction-type commitment profiles. Coakley (1992) argued that the culture within a sport organisation might lead to the development of a singular and sport-related identity. When combined with limited personal autonomy, burnout (conceptualized by Coakley as premature withdrawal from sport) is a likely result. While it is important to recognize that Coakley's assertions regarding burnout were based on interviews with a small sample of adolescent athletes, organisational culture, particularly that related to HP sport, might play a role in coach burnout, especially when considering the organisational demands faced by coaches (Norris et al., 2017). Donahue et al. (2012) explored burnout from a motivational perspective, finding that professional coaches' obsessive passion was associated with their use of ruminative thoughts, which were, in turn, positively associated with emotional exhaustion. Harmonious passion was thought to prevent rumination and, thus, indirectly protect coaches from experiencing emotional exhaustion.

Also from a motivational perspective, a series of studies from Bentzen and colleagues (Bentzen et al., 2014, 2016a, 2016b, 2017), suggested that higher levels of workload and work-home interference were associated with higher levels of exhaustion in high-performance coaches, and that lower levels of self-determined or autonomous motivation explained increasing risk of burnout over time. Lundkvist et al. (2016) explored the relationships between burnout and workaholism (compulsive addiction to work/working beyond what is required), and work-home interference (conflicts arising as a result of sacrificing family time or work due to competing demands) and found both had associations with emotional exhaustion. More recent explanations have therefore focused on work-home interference and lack of recovery as major determinants of burnout (e.g., Bentzen et al., 2016b, 2017; Altfeld et al., 2015; Lundkvist et al., 2016; Lundkvist, Gustafsson, Hjälm, & Hassmén, 2012). Taken together, the existing research certainly seems to suggest that a number of psycho-socio-environmental influences, rather than just the experience of stress, play a role in the development and maintenance of burnout in coaches.

In 2019, Olusoga et al., published a scoping review, providing an up-to-date and critical review of the coaching burnout literature. Altogether, 45 published, peer reviewed studies investigated coaching burnout between 1984 and 2017 (see Table 19.1). While a detailed review of the findings is beyond the scope of this chapter, several key conclusions were drawn. While the overall levels of burnout found in various coaching populations varied across the studies included in the review, a small number of authors have adopted longitudinal designs in order to capture the enduring nature of the burnout syndrome. Although Altfeld et al. (2015) found no significant changes in burnout over the course of a season in their study of 70 full-time coaches from a variety of coaching contexts, Bentzen and colleagues have uncovered some variations in the way that coaches' burnout might fluctuate over time. In one study, 343 HP coaches were evaluated in terms of their perceived goal attainment, workload, perceived autonomy support, need satisfaction, quality of motivation, burnout, and well-being at the beginning and end of a competitive season. Findings indicated that, on average, their well-being had decreased, and their levels of burnout increased during that time period (Bentzen et al., 2016a). Bentzen et al. (2016b) found four different trajectories of perceived emotional exhaustion among 299 HP coaches from multiple sports. Although exhaustion either decreased, or remained consistently low for 70% of the coaches, it increased over the three time points from start to end of season for 15% of the coaches involved, while 10% of the coaches perceived their level of exhaustion to be consistently high across the entire season. In sum, one out of four HP coaches (25%) were found to be high in emotional exhaustion at the end of the season. This is a high number and sends a strong message to the community of HP-coaching—stress, burnout, and mental health need attention.

These conflicting findings might, in part, be explained by the nature of HP coaching where the stressors related to job insecurity and performance expectations (less prominent in other contexts) could become more salient towards the end of a

Table 19.1 Summary of studies included in the scoping review

		N	Sex M/F MIX	Level HP PRO AM COLL HS YS	Country	Methodology QUANT QUAL MIXED	Main findings	Theoretical framework
1	Altfeld, S., & Kellmann, M. (2015). Are German coaches highly exhausted? A study of differences in personal and environmental factors. *International Journal of Sports Science and Coaching*, *10*(4), 637–654	158	MIX F = 9% M = 91%	MIX HP = 46% PRO = 37% Other = 27	Germany	QUANT Survey	Overall stress and overall recovery demonstrated significant effects on exhaustion. Sense of wellbeing and feeling of meaningfulness both significantly related to exhaustion	Stress/Recovery
2	Altfeld, S., Mallett, C. J., & Kellmann, M. (2015). Coaches' burnout, stress, and recovery over a season: A longitudinal study. *International Sport Coaching Journal*, *2*(2), 137–151	70	MIX F = 18% M = 82%	MIX	Germany	QUANT Survey	Burnout levels did not significantly change over the course of a season. Full-time coaches whose values of perceived success decreased over the season showed increased emotional stress and decreased recovery values	Stress/Recovery
3	Bentzen, M., Lemyre, P. N., & Kenttä, G. (2014). The process of burnout among professional sport coaches explored through the lens of Self-	4	MIX F = 50% M = 50%	HP	Norway	QUAL Interview	Heavy workloads, lack of leader support, and work-related conflicts affected motivation. Psychological need thwarting and more controlled motivation	SDT Workload

(continued)

Table 19.1 (continued)

		N	Sex	Level	Country	Methodology	Main findings	Theoretical framework
			M/F MIX	HP PRO AM COLL HS YS		QUANT QUAL MIXED		
	determination theory: A qualitative approach. *Sports Coaching Review*, *3* (2) 101–116						explained increasing risk of burnout over time	
4	Bentzen, M., Lemyre, P. N., & Monna, G. (2016a). Changes in motivation and burnout indices in high-performance coaches over the course of a competitive season. *Journal of Applied Sport Psychology*, *28*(1), 28–48	343	MIX F = 8.7% M = 91.3%	HP	Norway & Sweden	QUANT Survey	Coaches increased in burnout and decreased in wellbeing over the course of a season. SDT process model of change useful for explaining differences in burnout and wellbeing in professional work experiences	SDT Workload
5	Bentzen, M., Lemyre, P. N., & Kenttä, G. (2016b). Development of exhaustion for high performance coaches in association with workload and motivation: A person-centered approach.	299	MIX F = 8.4% M = 91.6%	HP	Norway & Sweden	QUANT Survey	Higher levels of workload and work-home interference were associated with higher exhaustion. Higher levels of recovery, intrinsic and identified regulations associated with lower levels of exhaustion	SDT Workload

	Psychology of Sport and Exercise, *22*, 10–19							
6	Bentzen, M., Lemyre, P. N., & Kenttä, G. (2017). A comparison of high-performance football coaches experiencing high- versus low-burnout symptoms across a season of play: Quality of motivation and recovery matters. *International Sport Coaching Journal*, *4*(2), 133–146	92	MIX F = 6.5% M = 93.5%	MIX HP PRO	Norway	MIXED Survey Interview	Motivational profile, work-home interference, and ability to meet recovery demands were variables that contributed to explain differences in coaches' burnout symptoms	SDT Workload
7	Caccese, T., & Mayerberg, C. (1984). Gender differences in coaches Perceived burnout of college coaches. *Journal of Sport Psychology*, *6*(3), 279–280	231	MIX F = 40.3% M = 59.7%	COLL NCAA/ AIWA Div. I	USA	QUANT Survey	Female coaches reposted significantly higher levels of emotional exhaustion and significantly lower levels of personal accomplishment than male coaches	Stress
8	Capel, S. A., Sisley, B. L., & Desertrain, G. S. (1987). The relationship of role conflict and role ambiguity to burnout in high school basketball coaches. *Journal of Sport Psychology*, *9*, 106–117	235	MIX No Info	HS Dual Role Teacher Coaches	USA	QUANT Survey	Higher role conflict, higher role ambiguity, and lower student enrolment in the school contributed significantly to higher burnout frequency and intensity	Stress Workload

(continued)

Table 19.1 (continued)

		N	Sex M/F MIX	Level HP PRO AM COLL HS YS	Country	Methodology QUANT QUAL MIXED	Main findings	Theoretical framework
9	Dale, J., & Weinberg, R. S. (1989). The relationship between coaches' leadership style and burnout. *The Sport Psychologist*, *3*, 1–13	302	MIX F = 23% M = 77%	HS & COLL NCAA Div. I	USA	QUANT Survey	Coaches displaying consideration style of leadership scored higher on freq. and int. of emotional exhaustion and depersonalisation. Male coaches scored higher in freq. and int. of depersonalisation	Stress Leadership
10	Donahue, E. G., Forest, J., Vallerand, R. J., Lemyre, P. N., Crevier-Braud, L., & Bergeron, E. (2012). Passion for work and emotional exhaustion: The mediating role of rumination and recovery. *Applied Psychology-Health and Well Being*, *4*(3), 341–368	117	MIX F = 11.1% M = 88% (1 = N.S.)	Study1 MIX Study 2 conducted with Nurses	Norway	QUANT Survey	Obsessive passion predicted ruminative thoughts which, in turn predicted emotional exhaustion. Harmonious passion prevented the use of rumination and indirectly protected coaches against emotional exhaustion	Dualistic Model of Passion
11	Drake, D. & Herbert, E. P. (2002). Perceptions of occupational stress and strategies for avoiding burnout: case studies of two female teacher/coaches.	2	F	HS	USA	QUAL Case Study Interview	Stressors included intra-role conflicts, coaching multiple sports, and inter-role conflicts. Coaches described a cyclical pattern of stress over each	Stress

	Physical Educator, *59*(4), 170–184						academic year, and over a career	
12	Gencay, S., & Gencay, O. A. (2011). Burnout among Judo coaches in Turkey. *Journal of Occupational Health*, *53*, 365–370	65	MIX F = 15.4% M = 84.6%	HP	Turkey	QUANT Survey	Burnout levels of coaches ranged from low to moderate. More experienced Judo coaches (over 16 years) had higher levels of emotional exhaustion than less experienced Judo coaches. Coaches who did not feel satisfaction from their sport administrators had significantly higher levels of emotional exhaustion than those who did	Stress
13	Hardin, R., Zakrajsek, R., & Gaston, B. (2015). The relationship between job satisfaction and burnout in fast-pitch softball coaches. *Journal of Contemporary Athletics*, *9*(1), 1–14	326	MIX F = 22% M = 78%	MIX COLL 40.8% (all divisions) HS = 42.6%	USA	QUANT Survey	Softball coaches were moderately burned out. Operating conditions, nature of work, contingent rewards, and promotion influenced coaches' levels of burnout	SDT
14	Hjälm, S., Kenttä, G., Hassménan, P., & Gustafsson, H. (2007). Burnout among elite soccer coaches. *Journal of Sport Behavior*, *30*(4), 415–427	47	M	HP	Sweden	QUANT Survey	71% of coaches in the Women's Premier League experienced moderate to high levels of emotional exhaustion, compared to 23% of coaches in the men's league. Increased leadership demands place coaches in the women's	Stress

(continued)

Table 19.1 (continued)

		N	Sex M/F MIX	Level HP PRO AM COLL HS YS	Country	Methodology QUANT QUAL MIXED	Main findings	Theoretical framework
							league at higher risk of burnout	
15	Hunt, K. R., & Miller, S. R. (1994). Comparison of levels of perceived stress and burnout among college basketball and tennis coaches. *Applied Research in Coaching and Athletics Annual*, *9*, 198–222	915 & 955	N.S.	COLL NCAA Div. I and III)	USA	QUANT Survey	Burnout rates were higher for basketball than tennis and were higher at T2 (1990–91) than T1 (1982–83). For both coaching groups, self-imposed pressure to win was the greatest stressor	Stress
16	Karabatsos, G., Malousaris, G., & Apostolidis, N. (2006). Evaluation and comparison of burnout levels in basketball, volleyball and track and field coaches. *Studies in Physical Culture and Tourism*, *13*(1), 79–83	452	N.S	N.S	Greece	QUANT Survey	Basketball coaches reported higher emotional exhaustion and depersonalisation than coaches from other sports and displayed explicit tendencies for burnout. Team sports coaches experienced "considerable" levels of professional burnout	Stress
17	Kelley, B. C. (1994). A model of stress and burnout in collegiate coaches—	249	MIX F = 47.4% M = 52.6%	COLL NCAA Div. III	USA	QUANT Survey	Male and female coaches higher in coaching issues and lower in hardiness were	Stress

	Effects of gender and time of season. *Research Quarterly for Exercise and Sport*, *65*(1), 48–58						higher in perceived stress. Both male and female coaches' stress appraisal was predictive of all burnout components	
18	Kelley, B. C., Eklund, R. C., & Ritter-Taylor, M. (1999). Stress and burnout among collegiate tennis coaches. *Journal of Sport & Exercise Psychology*, *21*(2), 113–130	265	MIX F = 37.4% M = 62.6%	COLL NCAA Div. I (30.2%) Div. II, III, or NAIA (69.8%)	USA	QUANT Survey	High levels of burnout among the sample A significant multivariate effect was found for gender but not competition level. Women had higher tendency to find coaching stressful than men Women higher on CIS	Stress
19	Kelley, B. C., & Gill, D. L. (1993). An examination of personal situational variables, stress appraisal, and burnout in collegiate teacher coaches. *Research Quarterly for Exercise and Sport*, *64*(1), 94–102	214	MIX F = 53.7% M = 46.3%	COLL NCAA Div. III & NAIA	USA	QUANT Survey	Greater satisfaction with social support, less experience, and gender (females higher), were related to stress appraisal. All stress appraisals were positively related to burnout	Stress
20	Kilo, R. A., & Hassmén, P. (2016). Burnout and turnover intentions in Australian coaches as related to organisation support and perceived control. *International Journal of Sport Science & Coaching*, *11*(2), 151–161	406	MIX F = 28% M = 72%	MIX All levels	Australia	QUANT Survey	Higher perceived organisational support was associated with lower coach burnout scores. Internal locus of control and use of approach coping strategies predicted lower levels of burnout. All three burnout dimensions were strong predictors of	Conservation of Resources (COR)

(continued)

Table 19.1 (continued)

		N	Sex	Level	Country	Methodology	Main findings	Theoretical framework
			M/F MIX	HP PRO AM COLL HS YS		QUANT QUAL MIXED		
							coaches' turnover intentions	
21	Koustelios, A. (2010). Burnout among football coaches in Greece. *Biology of Exercise*, *6*(1), 5–12	132	M	AM	Greece	QUANT Survey	Low overall levels of burn-out. No significant differ-ences between age groups and Emotional Exhaustion was highest among 30–39 year olds	Stress
22	Koustelios, A. D., Kellis, S., & Bagiatis, K. (1997). The role of family variables ion football coaches' burn-out. *Coaching and Sport Sciences Journal*, *2*(3), 41–45	203	M	N.S.	Greece	QUANT Survey	Single coaches experienced a statistically higher level of depersonalisation than married coaches. An inter-action effect found single coaches with no children scored higher on depersonalisation than married coaches with children	Stress
23	Lee, Y. H., & Chelladurai, P. (2016) Affectivity, emo-tional labor, emotional exhaustion, and emotional intelligence in coaching.	430	MIX F = 34.7% M = 65.3%	COLL NCAA Div. I	USA	QUANT Survey	Positive affectivity predicted three forms of emotional labour. Coaches' surface acting and genuine expression significantly	Emotional Labour

	Journal of Applied Sport Psychology, *28*, 170–184						predicted their Emotional Exhaustion. Emotional intelligence moderated the relationship between surface acting and Emotional Exhaustion	
24	Li, L. (2012). The study on effects resulted from job burnout on performance appraisal of professional coaches in China. *Advanced Materials Research*, *345*, 405–410	213	N.S	MIX	China	QUANT Survey	Burnout is the Independent here Low potency and knowledge drain elements of burnout predict task performance (KD being the primary factor)	Stress Workload
25	Lundkvist, E., Gustafsson, H., Hjälm, S., & Hassmén, P. (2012). An interpretative phenomenological analysis of burnout and recovery in elite soccer coaches. *Qualitative Research in Sport, Exercise and Health*, *4*(3), 400–419	8	M (from Hjälm, Penttä, Hassmén, & Gustafsson, 2007)	HP	Sweden	QUAL Interview	Findings describe coach burnout as stemming from a combination of issues related to home and work Two profiles of burnout identified: – Handling performance culture – Overall situation including workload, family, and health	Stress/Recovery Workload
26	Lundkvist, E. Gustafsson, H., Davis, P., & Hassmén. (2016). Workaholism, home-work/work-home interference, and exhaustion among sports coaches. *Journal of Clinical Sport Psychology*, *10*, 222–236	261	MIX 261	MIX 17% PRO Rest HS	Sweden	QUANT Survey	Workaholism associated with Emotional Exhaustion for coaches high on EE. Negative work-home interference has a stronger association with EE than negative home-work interference. Coaches in the	Work-Home Interference

(continued)

Table 19.1 (continued)

		N	Sex M/F MIX	Level HP PRO AM COLL HS YS	Country	Methodology QUANT QUAL MIXED	Main findings	Theoretical framework
							higher percentiles have a higher risk for burnout	
27	Malinauskas, R., Malinauskiene, V., & Dumciene, A. (2010). Burnout and perceived stress among university coaches in Lithuania. *Journal of Occupational Health*, *52*(5), 302–307	203	MIX F = 33% M = 67%	COLL	Lithuania	QUANT Survey	Burnout was more common among university coaches with over 10 years' experience. Higher levels of perceived stress were associated with burnout	Stress
28	McNeill, K., Durand-Bush, N., & Lemyre, P. N. (2016). Understanding coach burnout and underlying emotions: A narrative approach. *Sports Coaching Review*, *6*(2), 1–18	5	MIX, F = 2 M = 3	MIX	Canada	QUAL Interview	Coaches described a variety of emotions including anger, anxiety, apathy, and dejection, which have negative implications on their well-being and coaching practice. Emotions were linked to the three dimensions of burnout	Emotions
29	Nikolaos, A. (2012). An examination of a burnout model in basketball coaches. *Journal of*	170	M	PRO At least 1 season with Nat.	Greece	QUANT Survey	26% variance in perceived stress was accounted for by coaching level, social support, and years in present	Stress

	Physical Education & Sport, *12*(2), 171–179			Division Club			position 23% of variance in burnout level was accounted for by combination of indirect and direct variables, with perceived stress being a major predictor	
30	Olusoga, P., & Kenttä, G. (2017). Desperate to quit: A narrative analysis of burnout and recovery in sports coaching. *The Sport Psychologist*, *31*(3), 237–248	2	M	HP	Sweden	QUAL Interview	Findings highlighted the experiences of burnout including antecedents, experiences of coaching with burnout, withdrawal from sport, and recovery and personal growth. Role-clarity, work-life balance, counselling, and mentoring all important in facilitating recovery	Stress Work Home Interference
31	Omotoya, O. O. (1991). Frequency of burnout among selected soccer coaches in Nigeria. *Asian Journal of Physical Education*, *14* (1), 83–88	40	M	PRO	Nigeria	QUANT Survey	No significant differences between successful and less successful coaches on emotional exhaustion and depersonalisation. Successful coaches (win-loss) scored significantly higher in personal accomplishment than less successful coaches	Stress
32	Pastore, D. L., & Judd, M. R. (1993). Gender differences in burnout among coaches of women's	232	MIX F = 35% M = 65%	COLL	USA	QUANT Survey	A main effect for gender revealed females scored higher on emotional exhaustion then males.	Not explicitly stated Reference to work life balance

(continued)

Table 19.1 (continued)

		N	Sex M/F MIX	Level HP PRO AM COLL HS YS	Country	Methodology QUANT QUAL MIXED	Main findings	Theoretical framework
	athletic teams of 2-year college. *Sociology of Sport Journal*, *10*, 205–212						Female coaches were more burned out on all three burnout subscales than norms. Male coaches were less burned out than norms	
33	Pastore, D. L., & Kuga, D. J. (1993). High school coaches of women's teams: an evaluation of burnout levels. *Physical Educator*, 50 (3), 123–131	167	MIX F = 39% M = 61%	HS	USA	QUANT Survey	Female coaches reported higher levels of emotional exhaustion, depersonalisation, and personal accomplishment than male coaches. The overall degree of burnout was average for males, and average to high for females	Stress
34	Price, M. S., & Weiss, M. R. (2000). Relationships among coach burnout, coach behaviors, and athletes' psychological responses. *The Sport Psychologist*, *14*, 391–409	15 + 193	Coaches (15) MIX F = 5 M = 10	HS	USA	QUANT Survey	Coaches higher in EE were perceived as providing less training and instruction and less social support and making fewer autocratic and democratic decisions Athletes' perceptions of more training and instruction, social support,	Leadership

							positive feedback, more democratic and less autocratic styles were related to more positive (perceived competence, enjoyment) and less negative (anxiety burnout) psychological consequences	
35	Quigley, T. A., Slack, T., & Smith, G. J. (1987). Burnout in secondary school teacher coaches. *Alberta Journal of Educational Research*, *34*, 260–274	75 > 21	N.S.	HS	Canada	MIXED Survey Interview	Coaches had moderate levels of EE, lower personal accomplishment, and moderate depersonalisation compared to norms. More females in were in the upper phases of burnout than males and less experienced coaches appeared more prone to burnout Size of School (smaller = greater burnout), Amount of Admin, Compensation, and recognition and reward all factors influencing burnout	Golembiewski's (1983) Phase Model of Burnout
36	Raedeke, T. D. (2004). Coach commitment and burnout: A 1-year follow-up. *Journal of Applied Sport Psychology*, *16*, 333–349	141	MIX 141 F = 43.3% M = 56.7%	YS Age group swimmers	USA	QUANT Survey	Coaches with characteristics suggesting increased entrapment showed the largest increase in exhaustion. Those with decreased coaching interest had the lowest commitment	Commitment

(continued)

Table 19.1 (continued)

		N	Sex	Level	Country	Methodology	Main findings	Theoretical framework
			M/F MIX	HP PRO AM COLL HS YS		QUANT QUAL MIXED		
37	Raedeke, T. D., Granzyk, T. L., & Warren, A. (2000). Why coaches experience burnout: A commitment perspective. *Journal of Sport & Exercise psychology*, *22*, 85–105	295	MIX F = 43% M = 57%	YS Age group swimmers	USA	QUANT Survey	Three clusters of coaches were identified (Commitment, Entrapment, Less Interested). Cluster differences explained 38% of variance in burnout and commitment scores. Entrapped coaches higher on burnout than other groups	Commitment
38	Richards, K. A. R., Templin, T. J., Levesque-Bristol, C., & Blankenship, B. T. (2014). Understanding differences in role stressors, resilience, and burnout in teacher/coaches and non-coaching teachers. *Journal of Teaching in Physical Education*, *33*(3), 383–402	413	MIX Teacher Coaches M = 21.3% F = 28.8% Non-Teacher Coaches F = 42.1% M = 7.8%	MIX HS YS	USA	QUANT Survey	All participants reported low Role Ambiguity and depersonalisation, moderate levels of role conflict, emotional exhaustion, and high levels of role overload, and personal accomplishment A small interaction effect found—emotional exhaustion lower for teacher coaches in non-core subjects	Role Theory

39	Short, S. E., Short, M. W., & Haugen, C. R. (2015). The Relationship Between Efficacy and Burnout in Coaches. *International Journal of Coaching Science*, *9*(1), 37–49	101	MIX T1 (101) F = 13.9% M = 86.1% T2 (68) F = 16.1% M = 83.9%	HS	USA	QUANT Survey	Coaches had lower coaching efficacy scores and higher burnout scores at post-season compared to pre-season. Correlations between coaching efficacy and burnout were negative at both time points. Low efficacy coaches were more burned out as time passed compared to high efficacy coaches	Coaching Efficacy
40	Sisley, B. L., Capel, S. A., & Desertrain, G. S. (1987). Preventing burnout in teachers and coaches. *Journal of Physical Education, Recreation and Dance*, *58*, 71–75	235	MIX F = 7% M = 93%	HS	USA	QUANT Survey	None of the teacher coaches reported high levels of burnout, emotional exhaustion, depersonalisation, or low personal accomplishment	Stress
41	Stebbings, J., Taylor, I. M., Spray, C. M., & Ntoumanis, N. (2012). Antecedents of perceived coach interpersonal behaviors: the coaching environment and coach psychological well-and ill-being. *Journal of Sport & Exercise Psychology*, *34* (4), 481–502	418	MIX 418 M = 73.2% F = 26.8%	MIX All levels	UK	QUANT Survey	Higher work-life conflict and fewer opportunities for professional development were associated with a distinct maladaptive process of thwarted psychological needs, psychological ill-being, and perceived controlling interpersonal behaviour	SDT

(continued)

Table 19.1 (continued)

		N	Sex	Level	Country	Methodology	Main findings	Theoretical framework
			M/F MIX	HP PRO AM COLL HS YS		QUANT QUAL MIXED		
42	Tashman, L. S., Tenenbaum, G., & Eklund, R. (2010). The effect of perceived stress on the relationship between perfectionism and burnout in coaches. *Anxiety, Stress, & Coping*, *23*(2), 195–212	177	MIX F = 35.5% M = 66.4%	COLL All levels	USA	QUANT Survey	Results indicated an indirect effect of self-evaluative perfectionism on burnout through perceived stress, as well as a significant direct link to burnout, accounting for 56% of its variance. Conscientious perfectionism did not impact burnout either directly or indirectly	Stress Perfectionism
43	Vealey, R. S., Armstrong, L., Comar, W., & Greenleaf, C. A. (1998). Influence of perceived coaching behaviors on burnout and competitive anxiety in female college athletes. *Journal of Applied Sport Psychology*, *10*, 297–318	12 + 149	Coaches MIX F = 11 M = 1	COLL NCAA Div. I = 7 Div. II = 2 Div. III = 3	USA	QUANT Survey	Coach burnout significantly related to perceived coaching styles/behaviour. Coaches higher in emotional exhaustion and depersonalisation were perceived by their athletes to use dispraise and an autocratic coaching style	Stress
44	Vealey, R. S., Udry, E. M., Zimmerman, K., & Soliday, J. (1992). Intra-personal and situational predictors of coaching	848	MIX 848 F = 23.7% M = 75.5% NS = 0.8%	MIX HS & COLL	USA	QUANT Survey	Trait anxiety emerged as the strongest predictor of burnout. Several other cognitive perceptions of the coaching role (perceived	Stress

	burnout. *Journal of Sport & Exercise Psychology, 14*, 40–58						overload of demands, control or autonomy, attainment of meaningful accomplishment, value, professional support, rewards, success, excitement) were also predictive of burnout	
45	Wilson, V. E., & Bird, E. I. (1988). Burning out in coaching – Part two: Results from survey of national coaches. *Sport Science on Research and Technology in Sport, 8*(9)	144	MIX F = 13.2% M = 85.4%	N.S.	Canada	QUANT Survey	Coaching was reported to be stressful (although no indication of how this was measured is provided). Full-time coaches reported higher levels of burnout and 'stress related symptoms' than part-time coaches	Stress

Level: HP, high performance; PRO, professional; AM, amateur; COLL, collegiate; HS, high-school; YS, youth sport
All categories: N.S., not stated

competitive season. Only eight out of the 45 studies identified by Olusoga et al. (2019) used longitudinal designs. Given the enduring and often fluctuating nature of coach burnout, it would be prudent for future research to capture that with more longitudinal approaches.

Gender differences in the experience of stress and burnout have also been documented. Caccese and Mayerberg (1984) for example, found female collegiate coaches to have significantly higher levels of emotional exhaustion and lower perceived personal accomplishments than their male counterparts. Research has also found that female collegiate and high school coaches scored higher on all three burnout dimensions than male coaches (Pastore & Judd, 1993; Pastore & Kuga, 1993). Kelley, Eklund, and Ritter-Taylor (1999) suggested that female collegiate coaches found coaching more stressful than their male coaches with higher scores in the Coaching Issues Survey (CIS: Kelley & Baghurst, 2009). In addition, Hjälm et al. (2007) found that 71% of coaches in the Swedish Women's Premier League (soccer) experienced moderate to high levels of emotional exhaustion, compared to 23% of coaches in the men's league. It should be noted, however, that rather than being attributed the gender of the coach (all coaches were men) these differences were primarily related to the inequality of resources available to the coaches of elite clubs for men (more resources) compared to women.

It does seem plausible that women might face additional challenges in their roles as coaches and experience the impacts of stress more strongly than male coaches. Alternatively, it may be that women are less likely to mask and more likely to accurately report their stress and burnout in the research. It is, however, suggested that female coaches face added mental health challenges that they need to overcome in the context of sport (Carson et al., 2018). For example, it is often reported that female coaches, to a greater extent, experience challenges with work-life balance, a lack of trust from sport organizations, a lack of job security, and fewer opportunities to network than their male colleagues (Norman, 2010a, 2010b).

Beyond Burnout: Mental Health and Well-Being in Coaching

Within the community of elite sports, the darker side of mental health is beginning to receive much more attention and conversations about mental well-being are far more commonplace. Many high profile athletes have openly discussed mental health issues, and coaches are also beginning to open up about their own well-being. One of the most successful football managers of all time, Joesp 'Pep' Guardiola took a year off after four seasons and 14 trophies with FC Barcelona to "recharge his batteries." In a 2019 interview with Sky Sports, Guardiola cited exhaustion, coupled with the pressure and expectation placed on him, as major precipitating factors in his temporary withdrawal from coaching. Marco van Basten famously quit as coach of Dutch club AZ Alkmaar, after experiencing stress-related heart palpitations.

> That made things too difficult for me. It was specifically my problem. I couldn't do it. I kept suffering from stress. I was the one who needed to take the decisions. Everybody's looking at you. 'What, when, who, how and where?' – Marco van Basten (Lawrence, 2015).

Gary Speed, manager of Sheffield United FC and, later, the Welsh national team, tragically took his own life in 2011. Only later was it revealed that Speed had most likely been battling depression for much of his adult life.

Within the academic community too, the shift towards a focus on well-being issues in sport is clearly evidenced by several recent position statements on mental health targeting athletes (Henriksen et al., 2019; Moesch et al., 2018; Schinke, Stambulova, Si, & Moore, 2018; Van Slingerland, Durand-Bush, & Rathwell, 2018). Beyond burnout, however, research on major mental health disorders in the coaching population is still lacking, with a notable absence of studies exploring depression, anxiety disorders, addiction, and sleep disorders in coaching. Although alcohol consumption has been mooted as a coping strategy in a number of coaching stress studies (e.g., Olusoga et al., 2012), and coaches have described experiencing depression associated with burnout (Olusoga &締enttä, 2017), to our knowledge, only one study has attempted to shed some light on issues of depression and alcoholism in sports coaching (Roberts et al., 2018). Coaching is a demanding profession and coaches at the elite level have reported a culture in which showing vulnerability is regarded as a weakness, while suppressing the symptoms of burnout and avoidance of help-seeking is the norm (Olusoga & Kenttä, 2017). It seems obvious that in the high-pressured context of elite sports coaching, seriously addressing mental health issues and mental well-being among coaches is a logical next-step for researchers and practitioners in this field.

Interventions

While research points to coaches being at risk of experiencing burnout, there is a notable absence of intervention studies targeted at stress and burnout in coaches (Olusoga et al., 2019; Raedeke & Kenttä, 2013). However, a small number of studies have been directed towards developing and implementing coach stress and well-being intervention strategies. Olusoga, Maynard, Butt, and Hays (2014) developed a Coaching under Pressure, mental skills training (MST) program for coaches, aimed at developing coaches' coping and stress management skills. As a result of this 6-week, group intervention program coaches relaxation skills improved, their somatic anxiety was perceived as less debilitative, and they used self-blame less often as a coping strategy. Importantly, post-intervention, coaches also indicated that going through the intervention program helped them to pay greater attention to their own mental preparation and well-being.

Mindfulness-based interventions have slowly emerged in sport science and are now at the forefront of intervention research in sport (Schinke et al., 2018). This development is often credited to Gardner and Moore who introduced mindfulness interventions into sports in the early 2000s. Again though, it is athletes' mental health that has predominantly been the focus of such interventions, and those targeting coaches are restricted to two notable studies (Longshore & Sachs, 2015; Lundqvist et al., 2018). Longshore and Sachs (2015) developed Mindfulness Training for Coaches, with the aim of increasing mindfulness and emotional stability, and reducing anxiety. Incorporating elements of Mindfulness Based Stress Reduction (MBSR: Kabat-Zinn, 1982) and Mindful Sport Performance Enhancement (Kaufman, Glass, & Arnkoff, 2009), their program was delivered via a 90-min initial training session and a 6-week home program (20 min/day). Coaches in the treatment group ($n = 12$) reported significantly greater emotional stability and less anxiety after participating in the program, as well as positive impacts in work-life balance, athlete interactions, and coaching performance.

Lundqvist et al. (2018) conducted a mindfulness intervention aimed at preparing Paralympic leaders for managing challenges typically associated with major events. Conducted in a real-world context, this study was an integral part of a larger support program prior to the London 2012 Paralympic Games. An initial session introduced mindfulness (theory and practice) to the intervention group of Swedish Paralympic leaders (six women and four men). This was followed by eight web-based seminars led by a professional trainer (once a week), while a reference group of Norwegian Paralympic leaders ($n = 6$) received no intervention. Three assessments (baseline 5 days before the intervention started, post-intervention, and 6-week follow-up) were conducted. In brief, results suggested that the intervention group displayed greater psychological flexibility, less rumination, and lower perceived stress. Taken together, the findings from these two studies suggest that mindfulness-based interventions might have important implications for coaches' overall well-being.

In addition, McNeill et al. (2016) conducted a study with 250 Canadian developmental and HP coaches with the aim to explore if the capacity to self-regulate could explain their perception of stress. Results revealed that coaches higher in self-regulation capacity perceived lower stress than coaches as compared to their counter parts.

Finally, mindfulness and acceptance-based interventions continue to receive greater attention outside of sport science. A recent systematic review by Rudaz, Twohig, Ong, and Levin (2017) that targeted mental health professionals reported improvements over time in mindfulness, self-compassion, and psychological flexibility. Altogether, MBSR (Kabat-Zinn, 1982), Mindful Self-Compassion (MSC; Neff & Germer, 2013) and Acceptance Commitment Therapy (ACT; Hayes, Strosahl, & Wilson, 2012) tend to reduce stress or burnout. Interestingly, results so far are less supportive for psychological well-being, which prompts the need for further research.

Future Research

While it is clear that stress and burnout research in coaching continues to develop, there are still a number of areas on which future researchers might concentrate in order to advance the field. In their 2019 scoping review, Olusoga and colleagues highlighted the dominant tendency toward cross-sectional and quantitative designs. Perhaps most importantly, we recommend that future researchers endeavor to capture the enduring and dynamic nature of the burnout phenomenon. Although time consuming and challenging to complete, greater use of longitudinal research designs, perhaps extending beyond a single competitive season might illuminate coaches' experiences of the shifting and seasonal situational and environmental factors that contribute to burnout. While longitudinal research is certainly important to advance knowledge in this area, researchers should also ensure that their choice of analysis considers within-person changes over time as potential predictor variables (e.g., Stenling, Ivarsson, Hassmén, & Lindwall, 2017). On a related note, only five studies in Olusoga et al.'s review addressed coach burnout using qualitative methodologies. Qualitative researchers should take up the challenge of bringing the lived experiences of coaches to the fore and shedding further light on coach burnout, withdrawal from sport, and the processes of recovery.

Another important and critical issue is the choice of measurement of coaching burnout. More specifically, we should question whether we are studying coaches who are truly burned out, or coaches who are only displaying some symptoms of one burnout dimension (i.e., by only measuring emotional exhaustion). In summary, future research on coach burnout should carefully consider the most appropriate research design. One obvious challenge with much of the burnout research is the use of self-report measures. However, Baumeister, Vohs, and Funder (2007) suggested that "self-reports may be the most appropriate method, and sometimes are all that is possible" (p. 399). Yet we should also take care to interpret research findings and avoid drawing definitive conclusions based solely on self-report measures. It could also be argued that the ultimate consequence of severe burnout is a temporary (but enduring) or definite withdrawal from sport (Smith, 1986). We should therefore be especially cautious when inferring relationships between personal and situational variables and dimensions of burnout, based on data from coaches who are still active in the profession.

The quality of the interdependent relationship between a coach that is gradually burning out and their athletes is another research topic that has a high relevance in practice. To our knowledge, only two studies (Price & Weiss, 2000; Vealey, Armstrong, Comar, & Greenleaf, 1998) explored athletes' responses to coach burnout symptoms. On a similar note, Thelwell, Wagstaff, Rayner, et al. (2017) explored athletes' responses to coach stress. Based on this limited number of studies, it is suggested that future burnout research should further consider the interplay between coaches and athletes with special attention to mental health and performance of both parties.

Finally, we argue that future research should explore both prevention and clinical treatment of burnout. Based on previously described interventions, there is a growing evidence base supporting the efficacy of Mindfulness-Based Interventions. In particular, MBSR (Kabat-Zinn, 1982) and Mindfulness-Based Cognitive Therapy (MBCT; Segal, Williams, & Teasdale, 2018) have shown effectiveness in improving a range of clinical and non-clinical psychological outcomes (cf., Gu, Strauss, Bond, & Cavanagh, 2015). While there has been a notable rise in the use of Mindfulness-Based Interventions for athlete mental health and stress management (Schinke et al., 2018), performance enhancement (e.g., Röthlin, Birrer, Horvath, & Holtforth, 2016), and indeed in other interpersonal professions such as nursing (e.g., Song & Lindquist, 2015), such programs might also be beneficial for coaches, particularly in terms of them developing recovery and self-care strategies (Lundqvist et al., 2018). Moreover, given the cost of burnout at individual, organizational, and community sport levels, future research should explore the wider impact of coach burnout, within and beyond the work environment.

Practical Implications

Before considering interventions and practical steps to promote coach well-being, it is vital that a distinction is made between the expected and normal fatigue associated with the role, and the maladaptive emotional/physical exhaustion associated with burnout. At the elite level in particular, coaches have reported a culture in which vulnerability and help-seeking are avoided, and suppression of emotional difficulties is considered the norm (Olusoga & Kenttä, 2017). Old stereotypes persist (e.g., "*if you cannot handle it, you should quit*"), but are damaging when attempting to promote sustainable coach careers. The United States Olympic Committee recently published a Quality Coaching Framework (USOC, 2017), including a chapter on coach well-being, in which the importance of designing self-care strategies (monitoring of energy, sleep, physical activity and regular wellness checkups) to foster positive change in professional practice was highlighted. In order to make real progress in this area, however, the practical implications to reduce stress and burnout must be discussed at educational and organizational levels. Specifically, by suggesting that coaches should learn relaxation skills, be more mindful, or engage more with self-care strategies, there is a danger that managing stress and burnout becomes the coach's own responsibility (and, by definition, their fault if something goes wrong). In 'awakening' a coach population to ideas about their own sustainability, this topic of coach well-being needs to be embraced within a broader context including coach education and sport organizations, as well as by individual coaches.

The Micro-politics of Sport Research has shown how coaches can be unprepared for the complex and wide range of work assignments that they are expected to fulfill (Bentzen et al., 2014), and are often overwhelmed by the potential role ambiguity and political complexity they meet in their everyday work life (Potrac & Jones,

2009; Thompson, Potrac, & Jones, 2013). Time in direct contact with athletes is often just a minor part of the coach role, so coach education should prepare coaches for the organizational structures of clubs/teams, policy making, funding, and other organizational elements of the role that have been consistently identified as coach stressors in the research literature. Within sports organizations, younger coaches, newly qualified coaches, and coaches who enter a new expertise level, are especially in need of attention, not only from supportive leaders (Gagné & Deci, 2005), but also in terms of opportunities for adequate education and professional development (Côté & Gilbert, 2009). The use of mentors could be favorable for these coaches when guiding them in relation to new and unexpected challenges at new expertise levels (Erickson, Côté, & Fraser-Thomas, 2007).

Workload, Irregular Work Hours, and Work-Home Interference As a consequence of high workload and inconvenient workhours, work-home interference is a key topic that should be addressed in coach education, and coaches should be afforded the opportunity to reflect on and discuss sustainability of workload. Too often, coaches have not considered this challenge before entering the coach profession, or when establishing a family. Even though coaches could develop strategies to maintain a sustainable workload and to handle work-home interference, the responsibility to avoid this is first and foremost that of the sports organization as an employer. Early research highlighted clear role expectations as important for the prevention of coach burnout (Capel et al., 1987) and an employer has the responsibility of providing clear and realistic expectations for work assignments. Organizations must manage the expectancy of the coach/coaching team in relation to the available resources and constraints, thereby guiding them in prioritizing their energy on the most important work assignments.

Additionally, it is the sport organization's responsibility to put coaches' work-home interference on the agenda. This is not about controlling or interfering with the coaches' private lives; it is about concern and understanding that the coach role involves challenges for their lives beyond coaching. Moreover, high performance directors and leaders should be open about discussing this matter with coaches, regularly help set long-term plans, and foresee and discuss possible obstacles in relation to work-home interference. Sport organizations should be aware of the benefits that might be gained if coaches have a sound and solid private life (Geurts, Rutte, & Peeters, 1999).

Self-Care: Have Fun and Recover To maintain optimal energy levels and high quality motivation in the job, coaches needs to find their jobs interesting, valuable, fun, and rewarding over time (Bentzen et al., 2014, 2016a, 2016b, 2017). Through coach education, coaches need to learn about how to detect and monitor their energy levels based on their own quality of motivation (Bentzen et al., 2016a). A powerful strategy to maintain a healthy motivation is to facilitate coaches' awareness of which work assignments fuel their energy, and which ones drain their energy. While coaches obviously cannot just stop doing the less stimulating tasks, they can make attempts to maintain efforts on work assignments they find enjoyable. As coaches enter the profession with a high intrinsic motivation for the sport, finding it fun, interesting, and valuable are aspects that are of great importance to preserve. Moreover, increasing coaches' self-awareness related to when their own physical and emotional responses to the demands of the role are 'normal' and when they might be symptoms of early burnout might (a) normalize stress and burnout in coaching, and (b) encourage coaches to seek help when they recognize changes in their responses to the demands of the coaching role.

At the organizational level, leaders should raise their own awareness of their coaching staff, and be able to identify coaches who are no longer enjoying their work and are at risk of leaving the organization, and coaches who are enjoying their work, thriving, and will put effort into their jobs. Consequently, it is of importance, both for the coach and the organization, that high performance directors and leaders support coaches in order to find value, interest and enjoyment in their work (Bentzen et al., 2016b). While the quality and type of motivation for coaches is important for coach sustainability, coaches also need to balance their coaching duties with other areas in their life. The importance of recovery for coaches has long been neglected in coach research and practice (Raedeke & Kenttä, 2013), despite the relationships between recovery and burnout being highlighted (Altfeld et al., 2015). Coach education should help coaches learn about efficient recovery strategies that can be employed when traveling and when at home in the training environment, and sport organizations should be responsible for facilitating a healthy work-life balance, and for emphasizing recovery and self-care as integral parts of the coaching role.

Key Points

We began this chapter by stating that stress is and will always be an inevitable part of sport. For sports coaches, attempting to manage ongoing performance, organisational, and personal stressors in an often extremely challenging environment can have a significant impact on their personal well-being. Sleep disturbance, mood changes, emotional responses, and burnout have all been reported in the coach stress literature (e.g., Bentzen et al., 2016b; McNeill et al., 2016; Olusoga et al., 2010), while impacts on coach-athlete relationships, and athletes' performance and development have also been noted (Price & Weiss, 2000; Thelwell, Wagstaff, Chapman, et al., 2017; Thelwell, Wagstaff, Rayner, et al., 2017).

While we feel it is clear that coaches should be considered as performers in their own right (Gould et al., 2002), research points to coaches' self-care often becoming a secondary concern, with the performance and well-being of athletes being of paramount importance (e.g., Olusoga et al., 2012, 2014). In order for sports coaching, especially at the elite level, to be a truly sustainable profession, we argue that coaches must adopt a performer's mindset. Specifically, while the coach has a duty of care (not to mention contractual responsibilities) towards their athletes, they must also develop appropriate stress-management skills, and ensure adequate recovery for themselves. Although further research is required, evidence points to the benefits of mindfulness-based interventions for sports coaches (Longshore & Sachs, 2015; Lundqvist et al., 2018).

More importantly, however, is the need for sports coaches to genuinely challenge the status quo regarding conversations about mental health in sport. However, we recognise that this is not, nor should it be, the responsibility of individual coaches. Elite sport seems to engender a culture that values toughness, strength, resilience, and grit, and one in which showing vulnerability is regarded as a weakness, and is feared and avoided (Olusoga & Benttä, 2017). A significant culture shift is needed. Showing vulnerability, seeking help when needed, and becoming comfortable with conversations about stress and mental health, represent significant steps towards more appropriate methods of ensuring sustained well-being for those working in high-performance environments.

Conclusion

In this chapter, we have made the case for coaching being a demanding profession. Research has highlighted the complex, overlapping, organisational, environmental, and personal stressors that coaches at all levels experience, as well as the consequences of stress, including burnout and challenges to coaches' mental health and well-being. We have discussed several avenues that future burnout researchers might wish to explore, including more longitudinal research to capture the enduring, dynamic nature of the burnout experience, and intervention studies, aimed at reducing the incidence of burnout and promoting well-being for coaching populations. Finally, we argued that practical steps taken to ensure sustainability in the coaching profession should be taken at individual and organizational levels. Although mindfulness-based interventions have shown promise for enhancing coach well-being, it is important that the responsibility for managing coach stress and burnout is not placed on individual coaches, but instead becomes a collaborative effort between coaches, coach educators, sport organizations and stakeholders.

References

Altfeld, S., & Kellmann, M. (2015). Are German coaches highly exhausted? A study of differences in personal and environmental factors. *International Journal of Sports Science and Coaching, 10*(4), 637–654.

Altfeld, S., Mallett, C. J., & Kellmann, M. (2015). Coaches' burnout, stress, and recovery over a season: A longitudinal study. *International Sport Coaching Journal, 2*(2), 137–151.

Baumeister, R. F., Vohs, K. D., & Funder, D. (2007). Psychology as the science of self-reports and finger movements: Whatever happened to actual behaviour? *Perspectives on Psychological Science, 2*(4), 396–403.

Bentzen, M., Lemyre, P. N., & Benttä, G. (2014). The process of burnout among professional sport coaches explored through the lens of self-determination theory: A qualitative approach. *Sports Coaching Review, 3*, 110–116.
Bentzen, M., Lemyre, P. N., & Kenttä, G. (2016a). Changes in motivation and burnout indices in high-performance coaches over the course of a competitive season. *Journal of Applied Sport Psychology, 28*, 28–48.
Bentzen, M., Lemyre, P. N., & Kenttä, G. (2016b). Development of exhaustion for high performance coaches in association with workload and motivation: A person-centered approach. *Psychology of Sport and Exercise, 22*, 10–19.
Bentzen, M., Lemyre, N., & Kenttä, G. (2017). A comparison of high-performance football coaches experiencing high-versus low-burnout symptoms across a season of play: Quality of motivation and recovery matters. *International Sport Coaching Journal, 4*, 133–146.
Caccese, T. M., & Mayerberg, C. K. (1984). Gender differences in perceived burnout of college coaches. *Journal of Sport Psychology, 6*(3), 279–288.
Capel, S. A., Sisley, B. L., & Desertrain, G. S. (1987). The relationship of role-conflict and role ambiguity to burnout in high-school basketball coaches. *Journal of Sport Psychology, 9*(2), 106–117.
Carson, F., McCormack, C., & Walsh, J. (2018). Women in sport coaching: Challenges, stress and well-being. *ACTIVE: Journal of Physical Education, Sport, Health and Recreation, 7*, 63–67.
Chroni, S., Diakaki, E., Perkos, S., Hassandra, M., & Schoen, C. (2013). What stresses coaches in competition and training? An exploratory inquiry. *International Journal of Coaching Science, 7* (1), 25–39.
Coakley, J. (1992). Burnout among adolescent athletes: A personal failure or social problem? *Sociology of Sport Journal, 9*(3), 271–285.
Côté, J., & Gilbert, W. (2009). An integrative definition of coaching effectiveness and expertise. *International Journal of Sports Science & Coaching, 4*(3), 307–323.
Dale, J., & Weinberg, R. S. (1989). The relationship between coaches' leadership style and burnout. *The Sport Psychologist, 3*, 1–13.
Didymus, F. F. (2017). Olympic and international level sports coaches' experiences of stressors, appraisals, and coping. *Qualitative Research in Sport, Exercise and Health, 9*, 214–232.
Donahue, E. G., Forest, J., Vallerand, R. J., Lemyre, P. N., Crevier-Braud, L., & Bergeron, E. (2012). Passion for work and emotional exhaustion: The mediating role of rumination and recovery. *Applied Psychology-Health and Well Being, 4*, 341–368.
Drake, D., & Herbert, E. P. (2002). Perceptions of occupational stress and strategies for avoiding burnout: Case studies of two female teacher/coaches. *Physical Educator, 59*(4), 170–184.
Durand-Bush, N., Collins, J., & McNeill, K. (2012). Women coaches' experiences of stress and self-regulation: A multiple case study. *International Journal of Coaching Science, 6*(2), 21–43.
Erickson, K., Côté, J., & Fraser-Thomas, J. (2007). Sport experiences, milestones, and educational activities associated with high-performance coaches' development. *Sport Psychologist, 21*(3), 302–316.
Fletcher, D., Hanton, S., & Mellalieu, S. D. (2006). An organizational stress review: Conceptual and theoretical issues in competitive sport. In S. Hanton & S. D. Mellalieu (Eds.), *Literature reviews in sport psychology* (pp. 321–374). New York: Nova.
Fletcher, D., & Scott, M. (2010). Psychological stress in sports coaches: A review of concepts, research, and practice. *Journal of Sports Sciences, 28*(2), 127–137.
Frey, M. (2007). College coaches' experiences with stress— "Problem solvers" have problems, too. *The Sport Psychologist, 21*, 38–57.
Gagné, M., & Deci, E. L. (2005). Self-Determination theory and work motivation. *Journal of Organizational Behavior, 26*, 331–362.
Gencay, S., & Gencay, O. A. (2011). Burnout among Judo coaches in Turkey. *Journal of Occupational Health, 53*, 365–370.
Geurts, S., Rutte, C., & Peeters, M. (1999). Antecedents and consequences of work-home interference among medical residents. *Social Science & Medicine, 48*(9), 1135–1148.

Gould, D., Greenleaf, C., Guinan, D., & Chung, Y. (2002). A survey of US Olympic coaches: Variables perceived to have influenced athlete performances and coach effectiveness. *The Sport Psychologist, 16*(3), 229–250.

Gu, J., Strauss, C., Bond, R., & Cavanagh, K. (2015). How do mindfulness-based cognitive therapy and mindfulness-based stress reduction improve mental health and well-being? A systematic review and meta-analysis of mediation studies. *Clinical Psychology Review, 37*, 1–12.

Hägglund, K., Kenttä, G., Wagstaff, C. R. D., & Thelwell, R. C. (2019). Is there an upside of vulnerability in sport? A mindfulness approach applied in the pursuit of psychological strength. *Journal of Sport Psychology in Action*. https://doi.org/10.1080/21520704.2018.1549642

Hanton, S., Fletcher, D., & Coughlan, G. (2005). Stress in elite sport performers: A comparative study of competitive and organizational stressors. *Journal of Sports Sciences, 23*(10), 1129–1141.

Hardin, R., Zakrajsek, R., & Gaston, B. (2015). The relationship between job satisfaction and burnout in fast-pitch softball coaches. *Journal of Contemporary Athletics, 9*(1), 1–14.

Hayes, S. C., Strosahl, K. D., & Wilson, K. G. (2012). *Acceptance and commitment therapy: The process and practice of mindful change* (2nd ed.). New York: Guilford Press.

Henriksen, K., Schinke, R., Moesch, K., McCann, S., Parham, W. D., Larsen, C. H., & Terry, P. (2019). Consensus statement on improving the mental health of high performance athletes. *International Journal of Sport and Exercise Psychology*. https://doi.org/10.1080/1612197X.2019.1570473

Hjälm, S., Kenttä, G., Hassmén, P., & Gustafsson, H. (2007). Burnout among elite soccer coaches. *Journal of Sport Behavior, 30*(4), 415–427.

Hunt, K. R., & Miller, S. R. (1994). Comparison of levels of perceived stress and burnout among college basketball and tennis coaches. *Applied Research in Coaching and Athletics Annual, 9*, 198–222.

Kabat-Zinn, J. (1982). An outpatient program in behavioral medicine for chronic pain patients based on the practice of mindfulness meditation: Theoretical considerations and preliminary results. *General Hospital Psychiatry, 4*, 33–47.

Karabatsos, G., Malousaris, G., & Apostolidis, N. (2006). Evaluation and comparison of burnout levels in basketball, volleyball and track and field coaches. *Studies in Physical Culture and Tourism, 13*(1), 79–83.

Kaufman, K. A., Glass, C. R., & Arnkoff, D. B. (2009). Evaluation of mindful sport performance enhancement (MSPE): A new approach to promote flow in athletes. *Journal of Clinical Sport Psychology, 3*, 334–356.

Kelley, B. C. (1994). A model of stress and burnout in collegiate coaches—Effects of gender and time of season. *Research Quarterly for Exercise and Sport, 65*, 48–58.

Kelley, B. C., & Baghurst, T. (2009). Development of the coaching issues survey (CIS). *The Sport Psychologist, 23*(3), 367–387.

Kelley, B. C., Eklund, R. C., & Ritter-Taylor, M. (1999). Stress and burnout among collegiate tennis coaches. *Journal of Sport & Exercise Psychology, 21*(2), 113–130.

Kelley, B. C., & Gill, D. L. (1993). An examination of personal situational variables, stress appraisal, and burnout in collegiate teacher coaches. *Research Quarterly for Exercise and Sport, 64*, 94–102.

Kenttä, G., Olusoga, P., & Bentzen, M. (2020). Coaches: Health, well-being, and burnout. In D. Hackfort & R. J. Schinke (Eds.), *The Routledge international encyclopedia of sport and exercise psychology* (pp. 154–165). London: Routledge, Taylor & Francis.

Kidd, B. (2013). Where are the female coaches? *Canadian Journal for Women in Coaching, 13*, 1–8.

Kilo, R. A., & Hassmén, P. (2016). Burnout and turnover intentions in Australian coaches as related to organisation support and perceived control. *International Journal of Sport Science & Coaching, 11*(2), 151–161.

Knight, C. J., Reade, I. L., Selzler, A. M., & Rodgers, W. M. (2013). Personal and situational factors influencing coaches' perceptions of stress. *Journal of Sports Sciences, 31*, 1054–1063.

Knights, S., & Ruddock-Hudson, M. (2016). Experiences of occupational stress and social support in Australian Football League senior coaches. *International Journal of Sports Science & Coaching, 11*, 162–171.

Koustelios, A. (2010). Burnout among football coaches in Greece. *Biology of Exercise, 6*(1), 5–12.

Koustelios, A. D., Kellis, S., & Bagiatis, K. (1997). The role of family variables ion football coaches' burnout. *Coaching and Sport Sciences Journal, 2*(3), 41–45.

Kroll, W., & Gundersheim, J. (1982). Stress factors in coaching. *Coaching Science Update, 23*, 47–49.

La Voi, N. M. (2016). Concluding thoughts. Creating change for woman coaches. In N. LaVoi (Ed.), *Women in sports coaching* (pp. 257–260). London: Routledge.

Lawrence (2015). 'Marco van Basten: Why stress prompted manager to leave role.' *BBC Sport*. Retrieved from https://www.bbc.co.uk/sport/football/30854083

Lee, Y. H., & Chelladurai, P. (2016). Affectivity, emotional labor, emotional exhaustion, and emotional intelligence in coaching. *Journal of Applied Sport Psychology, 28*, 170–184.

Li, L. (2012). The study on effects resulted from job burnout on performance appraisal of professional coaches in China. *Advanced Materials Research, 345*, 405–410.

Longshore, K., & Sachs, M. (2015). Mindfulness training for coaches: A mixed-method exploratory study. *Journal of Clinical Sport Psychology, 9*(2), 116–137.

Lundkvist, E., Gustafsson, H., Davis, P., & Hassmén. (2016). Workaholism, home-work/work-home interference, and exhaustion among sports coaches. *Journal of Clinical Sport Psychology, 10*, 222–236.

Lundkvist, E., Gustafsson, H., Hjälm, S., & Hassmén, P. (2012). An interpretative phenomenological analysis of burnout and recovery in elite soccer coaches. *Qualitative Research in Sport, Exercise and Health, 4*, 400–419.

Lundqvist, C., Ståhl, L., Kenttä, G., & Thulin, U. (2018). Evaluation of a mindfulness intervention for Paralympic leaders prior to the 2012 London Paralympic Games. *International Journal of Sport Science & Coaching, 13*, 62–71.

Malinauskas, R., Malinauskiene, V., & Dumciene, A. (2010). Burnout and perceived stress among university coaches in Lithuania. *Journal of Occupational Health, 52*(5), 302–307.

Mallett, C. J., & Lara-Bercial, S. (2016). Serial winning coaches: People, vision and environment. In M. Raab, P. Wylleman, R. Seiler, A-M. Elbe, & A. Hatzigeorgiadis (Eds.), *Sport and exercise psychology research: Theory to practice* (pp. 289–322). Amsterdam: Elsevier.

Maslach, C., & Jackson, S. E. (1986). *MBI: Maslach Burnout Inventory; Manual research edition*. Palo Alto, CA: Consulting Psychologists Press.

McNeill, K., Durand-Bush, N., & Lemyre, P. N. (2016). Understanding coach burnout and underlying emotions: A narrative approach. *Sports Coaching Review, 6*, 1–18.

Moen, F., Bentzen, M., & Myhre, K. (2018). The role of passion and affect in enhancing the understanding of coach burnout. *International Journal of Coaching Science, 12*, 3–34.

Moesch, K., Kenttä, G., Kleinert, J., Quignon-Fleuret, C., Cecil, S., & Bertollo, M. (2018). FEPSAC position statement: Mental health disorders in elite athletes and models of service provision. *Psychology of Sport and Exercise, 38*, 61–71.

Neff, K. D., & Germer, C. K. (2013). A pilot study and randomized controlled trial of the Mindful Self-Compassion Program. *Journal of Clinical Psychology, 69*(1), 28–44.

Nikolaos, A. (2012). An examination of a burnout model in basketball coaches. *Journal of Physical Education & Sport, 12*(2), 171–179.

Norman, L. (2010a). Feeling second best: Elite women coaches' experiences. *Sociology of Sport Journal, 27*(1), 89–104.

Norman, L. (2010b). Bearing the burden of doubt: Female coaches' experiences of gender relations. *Research Quarterly for Exercise and Sport, 81*(4), 506–517.

Norris, L. A., Didymus, F. F., & Kaiseler, M. (2017). Stressors, coping, and well-being among sports coaches: A systematic review. *Psychology of Sport and Exercise, 33*, 93–112.

Olusoga, P., Bentzen, M., & Kenttä, G. (2019). Coach burnout: A scoping review. *International Sport Coaching Journal, 6*, 42–62.

Olusoga, P., Butt, J., Hays, K., & Maynard, I. W. (2009). Stress in elite sports coaching: Identifying stressors. *Journal of Applied Sport Psychology, 21*, 442–459.

Olusoga, P., Butt, J., Maynard, I. W., & Hays, K. (2010). Stress and coping: A study of world class coaches. *Journal of Applied Sport Psychology, 22*, 274–293.

Olusoga, P., & Konttä, G. (2017). Desperate to quit: A narrative analysis of burnout and recovery in sports coaching. *The Sport Psychologist, 31*, 237–248.

Olusoga, P., Maynard, I. W., Butt, J., & Hays, K. (2014). Coaching under Pressure: Mental skills training for sports coaches. *Sport & Exercise Psychology Review, 10*, 31–43.

Olusoga, P., Maynard, I., Hays, K., & Butt, J. (2012). Coaching under pressure: A study of Olympic coaches. *Journal of Sports Sciences, 30*, 229–239.

Omotoya, O. O. (1991). Frequency of burnout among selected soccer coaches in Nigeria. *Asian Journal of Physical Education, 14*(1), 83–88.

Pastore, D. L. (1991). Male and female coaches of women's athletic teams: Reasons for entering and leaving the profession. *Journal of Sport Management, 5*, 128–143.

Pastore, D. L., & Judd, M. R. (1993). Gender differences in burnout among coaches of women's athletic teams at 2-year colleges. *Sociology of Sport Journal, 10*(2), 205–212.

Pastore, D. L., & Kuga, D. J. (1993). High school coaches of women's teams: An evaluation of burnout levels. *Physical Educator, 50*(3), 126.

Potrac, P., & Jones, R. L. (2009). Micropolitical workings in semi-professional Football. *Sociology of Sport Journal, 26*(4), 557–577.

Price, M. S., & Weiss, M. R. (2000). Relationships among coach burnout, coach behaviors, and athletes' psychological responses. *The Sport Psychologist, 14*, 391–409.

Quigley, T. A., Slack, T., & Smith, G. J. (1987). Burnout in secondary school teacher coaches. *Alberta Journal of Educational Research, 34*, 260–274.

Raedeke, T. D. (1997). Is athlete burnout more than just stress? A sport commitment perspective. *Journal of Sport and Exercise Psychology, 19*, 396–417.

Raedeke, T. D. (2004). Coach commitment and burnout: A one-year follow-up. *Journal of Applied Sport Psychology, 16*(4), 333–349.

Raedeke, T. D., Granzyk, T. L., & Warren, A. (2000). Why coaches experience burnout: A commitment perspective. *Journal of Sport & Exercise Psychology, 22*, 85–105.

Raedeke, T. D., & Kenttä, G. (2013). Coach burnout. In P. Potrac, W. Gilbert, & J. Denison (Eds.), *Handbook of sports coaching* (pp. 424–435). New York: Routledge.

Rhind, D. J., Scott, M., & Fletcher, D. (2013). Organizational stress in professional soccer coaches. *International Journal of Sport Psychology, 44*, 1–16.

Richards, K. A. R., Templin, T. J., Levesque-Bristol, C., & Blankenship, B. T. (2014). Understanding differences in role stressors, resilience, and burnout in teacher/coaches and non-coaching teachers. *Journal of Teaching in Physical Education, 33*(3), 383–402.

Robbins, J. E., Gilbert, J. N., & Clifton, A. M. (2015). Coaching stressors in a Division II historically black university. *Journal of Intercollegiate Sport, 8*, 183–205.

Roberts, S. J., Baker, M., Reeves, M. J., Jones, G., & Cronin, C. (2018). Lifting the veil of depression and alcoholism in sport coaching: How do we care for carers? *Qualitative Research in Sport, Exercise and Health, 11*(4), 510–526. https://doi.org/10.1080/2159676X.2018.1556182

Röthlin, P., Birrer, D., Horvath, S., & Holtforth, M. (2016). Psychological skills training and a mindfulness-based intervention to enhance functional athletic performance: Design of a randomized controlled trial using ambulatory assessment. *BMC Psychology, 4*(39), 1–11. https://doi.org/10.1186/s40359-016-0147-y

Rudaz, M., Twohig, M. P., Ong, C. W., & Levin, M. E. (2017). Mindfulness and acceptance-based trainings for fostering self-care and reducing stress in mental health professionals: A systematic review. *Journal of Contextual Behavioral Science, 6*(4), 380–390.

Schinke, R. J., Stambulova, N. B., Si, G., & Moore, Z. (2018). International society of sport psychology position stand: Athletes' mental health, performance, and development. *International Journal of Sport and Exercise Psychology, 16*, 622–639.

Segal, Z. V., Williams, J. M. G., & Teasdale, J. D. (2018). *Mindfulness-based cognitive therapy for depression* (2nd ed.). New York: Guilford.

Short, S. E., Short, M. W., & Haugen, C. R. (2015). The relationship between efficacy and burnout in coaches. *International Journal of Coaching Science, 9*(1), 37–49.

Sisley, B. L., Capel, S. A., & Desertrain, G. S. (1987). Preventing burnout in teachers and coaches. *Journal of Physical Education, Recreation and Dance, 58*, 71–75.

Smith, R. (1986). Toward a cognitive-affective model of athletic burnout. *Journal of Sport Psychology, 8*, 36–50.

Song, Y., & Lindquist, R. (2015). Effects of mindfulness-based stress reduction on depression, anxiety, stress, and mindfulness in Korean nursing students. *Nurse Education Today, 35*(1), 86–90.

Stebbings, J., Taylor, I. M., Spray, C. M., & Ntoumanis, N. (2012). Antecedents of perceived coach interpersonal behaviors: The coaching environment and coach psychological well-and ill-being. *Journal of Sport & Exercise Psychology, 34*(4), 481–502.

Stenling, A., Ivarsson, A., Hassmén, P., & Lindwall, M. (2017). Longitudinal associations between athletes' controlled motivation, ill-being, and perceptions of controlling coach behaviors: A Bayesian latent growth curve approach. *Psychology of Sport and Exercise, 30*, 205–214.

Tashman, L. S., Tenenbaum, G., & Eklund, R. (2010). The effect of perceived stress on the relationship between perfectionism and burnout in coaches. *Anxiety, Stress, & Coping, 23*(2), 195–212.

Taylor, J. (1992). Coaches are people too: An applied model of stress management for sports coaches. *Journal of Applied Sport Psychology, 4*, 27–50.

Thelwell, R. C., Wagstaff, C. R. D., Chapman, M. T., & Kenttä, G. (2017). Examining coaches' perceptions of how their stress influences the coach-athlete relationship. *Journal of Sports Sciences*, (19), 1928–1939.

Thelwell, R. C., Wagstaff, C. R., Rayner, A., Chapman, M., & Barker, J. (2017). Exploring athletes' perceptions of coach stress in elite sport environments. *Journal of Sports Sciences, 35*, 44–55.

Thelwell, R. C., Weston, N. J. V., Greenlees, I. A., & Hutchings, N. V. (2008). Stressors in elite sport: A coach perspective. *Journal of Sports Sciences, 26*, 905–918.

Thompson, A., Potrac, P., & Jones, R. (2013). I found out the hard way: Micro-political workings in professional football. *Sport, Education and Society, 20*(8), 976–994.

United States Olympic Committee. (2017). *USOC quality coaching framework*. Champaign, IL: Human Kinetics.

Van Slingerland, K. J., Durand-Bush, N., & Rathwell, S. (2018). Levels and prevalence of mental health functioning in Canadian university student-athletes. *Canadian Journal of Higher Education/Revue Canadienne D'enseignement Supérieur, 48*, 149–168.

Vealey, R. S., Armstrong, L., Comar, W., & Greenleaf, C. A. (1998). Influence of perceived coaching behaviors on burnout and competitive anxiety in female college athletes. *Journal of Applied Sport Psychology, 10*(2), 297–318.

Vealey, R. S., Udry, E. M., Zimmerman, V., & Soliday, J. (1992). Intrapersonal and situational predictors of coaching burnout. *Journal of Sport & Exercise Psychology, 14*(1), 40–58.

Wang, J., & Ramsey, J. (1998). The relationship of school type, coaching experience, gender and age to new coaches' challenges and barriers at the collegiate level. *Applied Research in Coaching and Athletics, 13*, 1–22.

Wareham, Y., Burkett, B., Innes, P., & Lovell, G. P. (2017). Coaching athletes with disability: Preconceptions and reality. *Sport in Society, 20*, 1185–1202.

Wilson, V. E., & Bird, E. I. (1988). Burning out in coaching—Part two: Results from survey of national coaches. *Sport Science on Research and Technology in Sport, 8*(9).

Peter Olusoga is a Senior Lecturer in Psychology at Sheffield Hallam University in the United Kingdom and currently holds an Associate Professor II position at Inland Norway University of Applied Sciences. His current research focuses on stress, burnout and wellbeing in sports, with a particular interest in high-performance environments and elite coaching. In addition to research, Dr Olusoga is a Chartered Psychologist with the British Psychological Society (BPS) and is an active sport psychology consultant.

Göran Kenttä earned his PhD in psychology at Stockholm University in 2001. The majority of his research has focused on elite sports with a stress–recovery perspective. Göran currently holds a research position in Stockholm at The Swedish School of Sport and Health Sciences, and has been a director of the Coach Education Program at the university; he is also the past president of the Swedish Sport Psychological Association. In addition, Göran currently holds a position at the Swedish Sport Federation as Head of Discipline in sport psychology and an adjunct professor position at Ottawa University.

Marte Bentzen works as an Associate Professor at the Norwegian School of Sport Sciences, lecturing in sport psychology and adapted physical activity. Her research is focused on processes related to enhancement of well-being and prevention of ill-being within occupational psychology in general and among high-performance sport coaches in particular.

Chapter 20
Coaching the Coach: Helping Coaches Improve Their Performance

Andy Gillham and Pete Van Mullem

Abstract Sport coaches work in a distinctive and multifaceted environment (Hall, Gray, & Sproule. Journal of Sports Sciences 34(10):896–905, 2016) influenced by multiple stakeholders on and off the field of play. To find success in these settings coaches must be able to adjust and adapt, often within a short amount of time. Thus, coaches are challenged to grow professionally to remain relevant, knowledgeable, and effective in leading their teams. This ongoing professional development is a difficult endeavor to accomplish without the assistance of a more knowledgeable professional (e.g., coach consultant or coach developer; Lauer, Driska, & Cowburn. Sport psychology professionals as trusted advisors in high performance environments. In Davis (Ed.), The psychology of effective coaching and management (pp. 385–407). New York: Nova, 2016) to facilitate and overcome potential roadblocks in coach development. The purpose of this chapter is to offer insight for those working with a coach to help improve coach performance. Well-established coach development activities such as mentorship, communities of practice (CoP), and learner centered teaching will be discussed in relation to the role of a coach consultant. The role biases play in a coach's ability to self-assess coaching performance along with information from the field of education on maximizing retrieval, assessment of learning, and reflective practice techniques will be shared. Practical suggestions for the coach consultant to assist the coach in reflection of current practice, identification of professional development activities, and evaluation of areas for improvement will be provided.

Keywords Coach developer · Professional development · Coach evaluation · Mentorship · Community of practice

---

A. Gillham (✉)
Sanford Orthopedics and Sports Medicine, Sanford Health, Sioux Falls, SD, USA

P. Van Mullem
Lewis-Clark State College, Lewiston, ID, USA
e-mail: pwvanmullem@lcsc.edu

R. Resende, A. R. Gomes (eds.), *Coaching for Human Development and Performance in Sports*, https://doi.org/10.1007/978-3-030-63912-9_20

The purpose of this chapter is to provide guidance on working with coaches to improve their coaching performance. Nash, Sproule, and Horton (2017) point out that the process through which coaches received feedback on their own coaching is unclear. While information from more large-scale coach education programs will be referenced (e.g., Misener & Danylchuk, 2009), the focus within this chapter will be on the role of trusted others within the network of coaches. This approach is consistent with a suggestion from Lauer, Driska, and Cowburn (2016) that in working with coaches, the sport consultant should strive to become a trusted advisor to the coach they are working with. In addition, the sport consultant should adopt the approach that they do not have all the answers, instead demonstrating the ability to listen and ask insightful questions (Lauer et al., 2016). In an applied example of coach development showcasing the utility of insightful questions, Gillham (2016b) provided suggestions on specific questioning approaches that could be valuable for consultants working with coaches. Two prominent factors regarding providing coach development are (a) who is eligible to provide the service and (b) what areas or topics are included within the coach development activities. In working with different coaches, it is important to remember that each coaching scenario is different and unique based on personal experience, social norms, and contextual influences (Hall, Gray, & Sproule, 2016) which further highlights the need to adopt a perspective of ask questions first and provide suggestions later.

When referring to individuals that provide coach development services, there are a variety of terms available. The most recent version of the International Sport Coaching Framework (ICCE, 2013) uses the term coach developer as does recent research (e.g., Nash et al., 2017). One additional alternative is coach consultant which is often utilized by authors with more of a sport psychology background (e.g., Lauer et al., 2016). Throughout this chapter those two terms, coach developer and coach consultant, are utilized interchangeably when referring to the individual providing coach development services. Finally, the term mentor is also used when referring specifically to mentor-mentee type relationships congruent with the research on mentorship in sport coaching.

Conceptual and Empirical Findings

While coaching science, and more specifically the science of coach development, has progressed tremendously, some principles from education and learning theory have largely been omitted (Nelson & Cushion, 2006). Excellent examinations of elite coaches across sports have provided in-depth studies of individual coaches: (a) analyses of John Wooden (e.g., Gallimore & Tharp, 2004) and Pat Summitt (e.g., Becker & Wrisberg, 2008) in college basketball, (b) Anson Dorrance in college soccer (e.g., Wang & Straub, 2012), (c) J. Robinson the wrestling coach (e.g., Gould, Pierce, Cowburn, & Driska, 2017), and (d) Anatoly Tarasov, ice hockey (Bespomoshchnov & Caron, 2017). Outside of the academic literature, entire books can be found devoted to describing individual coaches and what led them to coach at a high level: (a) Bill Belichick in American football (Halberstam, 2005), (b) Mike Matheny in baseball (Matheny & Jenkins, 2015), and (c) Harry Parker in rowing (Ayer, 2016). Across the series of high profile coach stories, one prominent finding is that while there are similarities, the career paths of the individual coaches are also quite unique. This diversity of experiences and backgrounds should serve as a reminder that becoming a successful coach has more to do with taking advantage of the opportunities presented rather than some set of predetermined variables. Moreover, it shows that coach education or coach development has yet to establish a paradigm that has proven to be singularly effective which leaves space for improvements at both the individual coach level as well as a broader programmatic level.

Large-scale studies of coach development programs do exist (e.g., Callary, Culver, Werthner, & Bales, 2014), yet those studies are relatively rare and coaches have consistently reported mixed feelings about their experiences with formal coach development programs (e.g., Gilbert & Trudel, 1999; Mallett, Trudel, Lyle, & Rynne, 2009). In a study with sport coaches that asked about their ideal and actual sources of professional development information, Erickson, Bruner, MacDonald, and Côté (2008) found that almost 33% of coaches reported receiving information from a national coach certification program as their top source of actual coaching knowledge. Two frequent concerns with formal coach development programs have been that the content of the program has seemed overly formalized (Abraham & Collins, 1998; Nelson & Cushion, 2006) and topics were selected by the organization or coach developers themselves and less by the coaches in attendance (Vella, Crowe, & Oades, 2013). If coaches repeatedly attend workshops, conferences, or seminars (i.e., professional development experiences) and come away feeling it was not valuable or was not applicable to them, it is unlikely the experience will lead to positive coaching behavior changes or a better or more successful experience for the athletes. This situation has created an opportunity to examine alternative solutions to providing coach development.

Descriptions of coaches learning to coach are well-represented in the literature (Cushion, Armour, & Jones, 2003; Mallett et al., 2009; Nelson, Cushion, & Potrac, 2006). Throughout the process of becoming and developing as a coach, a coach will engage in a variety of learning situations. Typically, a coach's experience as an athlete will be their first learning experience. Research on athletic playing experience has demonstrated that this experience is impactful in the coach's development (Carter & Bloom, 2009). In moving from athlete to coach, the coach will engage in formal, non-formal, and informal learning environments. In coaching education, a coach engaged in formal learning would be completing coursework from an institution of higher learning or completing certification requirements under a governing body of sport (Erickson et al., 2008). A non-formal learning environment in sport may include less formalized educational opportunities that may or may not lead to certification or a degree program (i.e., clinics and/or workshops; Nelson et al., 2006). While coaches seek training from formal and non-formal learning environments, when asked, coaches frequently indicate a preference for informal learning opportunities (i.e., discussion with other coaches) away from the structure and guidance of a formal or non-formal setting (Mallett et al., 2009; Van Mullem & Van Mullem,

2014). Within formal, non-formal, and informal learning scenarios the coach may be led by a more knowledgeable professional in a mediated learning environment or be left to learn on his or her own in an unmediated learning environment. An unmediated learning experience challenges coaches to initiate the learning process by selecting what they are learning and how they wish to obtain the knowledge. There are some biases and potential confounds to this approach that will be detailed later in the chapter. In a mediated learning environment, the coach is being directed by another individual (e.g., sport consultant) and being supported in the learning process (Werthner & Trudel, 2006). A mediated learning environment is congruent with two established areas of research in sport coaching where a sport consultant can assist a coach as an identified mentor, or as a member of a community of practice.

Mentorship in Sport Coaching

Research into mentorship in sport coaching seems to lag behind the practical applications of mentorship (Bloom, 2013). Essentially, mentorship for sport coaches is understudied from a research perspective, yet is routinely practiced, even if in a non-formalized manner, by coaches across contexts. Research into mentorship in the workplace (e.g., Allen & Eby, 2010; Beres & Dixon, 2014; Bozeman & Feeney, 2008; Kram, 1988; Ragins & Kram, 2007) is substantially more developed than mentorship research within sport coaching. The literature within a sport context that does exist (e.g., Bloom, Durand-Bush, Schinke, & Salmela, 1998; Chambers, 2015; Gould, Giannini, Krane, & Hodge, 1990; Jones, Harris, & Miles, 2009; McQuade, Davis, & Nash, 2015) has been supportive of both the concept of mentoring and the practical applications. For example, for novice coaches the presence of a specific identified mentor was found to be critical to the novice coach's development (Bloom et al., 1998). Finding support for the concept of mentorship for sport coaches is not difficult within the literature, even considering different countries: (a) Canada (Bloom et al., 1998; Marshall, 2001), (b) Spain (Jimenez, Lorenzo, & Ibanez, 2009), (c) Australia (Layton, 2005), (d) United Kingdom (Cushion, 2006; Nash, 2003), (e) Ireland (Bertz & Purdy, 2011), (f) Germany (Kozel, 1997), and (g) the United States (Gould et al., 1990). Beyond sport coaches, strength and conditioning coaches were unified in their receptivity to mentorship. Their advice for novice coaches was to seek out information and learn from a variety of individuals and within a variety of contexts (Gillham, Doscher, Schofield, Dalrymple, & Bird, 2015). One significant complicating factor within mentorship research across contexts is the lack of a unified model or even a definition of what constitutes a mentorship situation. The Coaching Association of Canada (CAC) has developed some mentorship components to coach development and coach learning as part of their National Coaching Certification Program (NCCP; Bloom, 2013). Much like the remainder of the literature in sport coaching surrounding mentorship, the CAC's program is entirely logical and seems to conform to what coaches already do as part of the culture of coaching (i.e., talking with other coaches, networking at conferences and clinics). However, the CAC's recommendations on mentorship has yet to be formally investigated via academic research.

Bozeman and Feeney's (2008) model of mentorship from a business context contains valuable information for working with sport coaches. While eight characteristics are presented, those eight seem able to be reduced to a critical foursome: (a) information is exchanged between two individuals, wherein one of the individuals typically has more information to share, (b) there is some amount of duration to the collaboration (i.e., a one-off meeting or workshop is purposely excluded), (c) both individuals feel some degree of reciprocity due to participating in the mentoring collaboration, and (d) while some of the social exchanges may occur in the presence of others, a meaningful amount of the interactions are in dyads only (i.e., one-on-one time with the mentor). These are instructive components for a number of reasons. First, the emphasis on information exchange puts fewer restrictions on who can serve as a mentor. The point being that the mentor need only have more information than the mentee on a given topic which allows for a greater number of individuals in a greater number of contexts to serve as mentors. In other words, the mentor need not have achieved some significant milestone or accomplishment in sport coaching or more narrowly to a particular sport in order to have valuable information to share with the mentee. Second, the expectation of an extended time duration (i.e., multiple meetings) showcases that mentorship is not something that simply gets checked off and then left alone. Mentorship should be part of ongoing professional development.

Finally, the point that others can be involved and mentorship sessions can be inclusive of more than only the mentor and mentee has significant ramifications. The group mentoring context would seem to benefit from some of the same aspects of a focus group. When comparing the difference between a one-on-one setting (e.g., an interview) to a focus group where multiple respondents are present, the group setting is ideal when the participants are similar and likely interested in collaboration (Creswell, 2008). Erickson et al. (2008) and Mallet and colleagues (2009) found coaches do actively seek and participate in peer discussions and learning furthering the face validity of conducting some cohort mentoring sessions. While research on mentorship for sport coaches has not greatly increased of late, the research on communities of practice for sport coaches has garnered significant attention over the last decade (e.g., Bertram, Culver, & Gilbert, 2017). It is noteworthy that many of the components described in community of practice studies conform to Bozeman and Feeney's (2008) model of mentorship characteristics.

Communities of Practice in Sport Coaching

A community of practice (CoP) is a term to describe the social learning atmosphere within a group (Wenger, 1998). Establishing communities of practice for coaches has gained recognition as a viable coach development technique (e.g., Bertram et al., 2017; Garner & Hill, 2017). Initially CoP for coaches were recommended as more of an exploratory technique (Gilbert, Gallimore, & Trudel, 2009). However, more recently the concept of CoP has been applied to both strength and conditioning coaches (Murray, Zakrajsek, & Gearity, 2014) and sport coaches (Garner & Hill, 2017). There are two noteworthy consistencies within these CoP studies (e.g., Bertram et al., 2017; Garner & Hill, 2017). First, the coaches included in the CoP directly contributed to the topic areas, format, and schedule of the CoP sessions, which can be seen as a direct improvement for coaches that have critiqued wide-scale coach education programs as not meeting their needs. Second, there was an outside facilitator of the CoP sessions that provided some direction, expertise, and guidance to the execution of the sessions which helps alleviate some problems consistent with unmediated learning situations.

Particularly remarkable in these CoP studies is that the focus was clearly on knowledge dissemination and application for the coaches that participated. Gilbert and Trudel (1999) pointed out the need for coach development activities to be mindful of the distinction between decontextualized knowledge and specific applicable coaching knowledge. Going further, Côté and Gilbert's (2009) definition of coaching effectiveness includes the component of context and provides ample support for its inclusion. The greater focus on context specific problems offered through CoP activities addresses a consistent problem identified within coaching science research (Gould, 2016) and coach education programs have been accused of focusing too much on techniques, tactics, and strategies (Garner & Hill, 2017). More specifically, Gould (2016) has made direct pleas for coaching science researchers, academic faculty members, and the field of sport science as a whole to remember the importance of, and value in, getting the knowledge from academic journals and textbooks into the hands of coaches and administrators that can directly apply that knowledge on a daily basis with the athletes and programs they oversee. This call for more collaboration between researchers and practitioners has been echoed elsewhere (Stoszkowski & Collins, 2016) and one that is worth repeating here. One recommendation that has shown promise for consultants working with coaches is to adopt a learner centered teaching approach.

Learner-Centered Teaching

Learner Centered Teaching (LCT) is described as a shift from giving information to students and becoming a facilitator of student learning, with a focus on how students learn (Blumberg, 2016). In other words, LCT is "... teaching focused on learning—what the students are doing is the central concern of the teacher" (Weimer, 2013, p. 15). The groundwork for LCT is embedded in educational theory (i.e., constructivism, transformative) and aligned around already established leader-centered tactics (i.e., self-directed learning, problem-based learning; Weimer, 2002). To implement a learner-centered approach in teaching, Weimer (2013) outlined key changes teachers can make in practice by establishing the following five dimensions,

(1) the role of the teacher, (2) the balance of power, (3) the function of content, (4) the responsibility for learning, and (5) the purpose and processes of evaluation.

A coach consultant using an LCT approach could implement all five dimensions. For example, a hockey coach has contracted with a coach consultant to help her create more effective practice sessions. To get started, the coach consultant could observe the coach in practice sessions and through feedback and conversation collaborate with the coach to create a learning environment that fits the developmental needs of the coach in that particular scenario (i.e., role of a teacher). Once the learning environment is established, the coach consultant can identify and offer areas where the coach can improve her planning approach, motivation tactics, and communication skills to design and facilitate a more effective practice. Simultaneously, the coach consultant can utilize questions to help the coach select a specific method to improve on each identified area (i.e., balance of power). As she gains new knowledge in the identified areas of improvement, the coach consultant, through continued conversations and questions, would provide the coach with up-to-date information to apply the new knowledge directly into planning and implementing more effective practice sessions (i.e., function of content). In addition, under the LCT approach, the coaching consultant will design short self-assessment activities the coach could implement on a daily basis as she applies the new knowledge to practice (i.e., purpose and processes of evaluation). This also allows the coach consultant to slowly remove themselves from the learning process and assist the coach in becoming a self-directed learner (i.e., responsibility for learning). In short, each dimension requires the coach consultant to become more self-aware and take a deliberate approach explicitly focused on what the student is learning compared to a more traditional approach fixated on what information the teacher is going to share.

To provide guidance for faculty moving to a learner-centered approach, Blumberg (2009) created a framework for assessment of the five dimensions of LCT. Blumberg's framework is considered a leading resource in the assessment of LCT (Paquette & Trudel, 2018) and delineates the five dimensions into 29 specific components to evaluate instructor behaviors using an LCT approach. The framework is centered on rubrics to assist in the assessment of each component (i.e., teaching behaviors) relative to the five dimensions of LCT (Blumberg, 2009). Identification of specific coaching behaviors thought to lead to more effective coaching has long been part of studying coaches (Horn, 2008). For that reason alone, it seems worthwhile to hold coach developers to the same type of expectations. Arguably, all 29 components for evaluating instructor behavior have implications for coach developers when implementing an LCT approach. However, five instructional behaviors that seem particularly relevant to coach developers working with specific coaches are: (a) creation of an environment for learning through organization and use of material, (b) use of content to facilitate future learning, (c) self-directed, lifelong learning skills, (d) demonstration of mastery and ability to learn from mistakes, and (e) determination of course content. In sum, learning through LCT is built on an environment that focuses on what students are learning, how they are learning, and how they can use learning (Tagg, 2003).

While much of the focus on LCT has been in the training of educators (i.e., K-12 teachers, faculty in higher education) on how to more effectively reach the learner (i.e., student), LCT concepts can be applied in the training of coaches both in wide-scale coach development contexts and in smaller more individualized coach development contexts. In a recent study, Paquette and Trudel (2018) examined a coach education program claiming to use an LCT approach. Using Blumberg's (2009) framework for assessing LCT, they identified six components of particular interest to those developing coach education programs and determined that with the aid of a facilitator in the program studied, coaches were encouraged to learn on their own, learn through the development of coaching skills, develop awareness of the learning process, reflect on coaching practice, and be assessed of their progress and how it applies to real-world applications (Paquette & Trudel, 2018). While this is just one example of a coaching education program implementing LCT principles, it does hint at the possibility of an LCT approach being effective in coach development.

The success of LCT rests on the ability and knowledge of the facilitator (i.e., coach developer) to help the student (i.e., coach) link new knowledge with prior knowledge (Blumberg, 2016; Deek, Werthner, Paquette, & Culver, 2013; Paquette & Trudel, 2016; Weimer, 2013) and be able to apply the new knowledge in practice (Blumberg, 2016). Therefore, the coach educator is in prime position to serve as a facilitator, while meeting the needs of the coach in the learning process. In working with coaches of master athletes Callary, Rathwell, and Young (2018) discussed the intricacies of adult learners, "… adults need to know why they are learning something, while understanding that their readiness to learn is heightened by linking their learning to real life experiences and accounting for their prior experience in current learning activities (p. 48)." In working with coaches, the consideration of the adult learner is exacerbated by a coach's unique learning background (Nelson, Cushion, & Potrac, 2013) and the context in which they coach (Callary et al., 2018). Coaches are accustomed to being in positions of expert and legitimate power (Rylander, 2015). Thus, when a coach engages with a coach educator she is likely seeking an LCT-type environment, where the focus is on both helping the coach construct her own knowledge (Paquette & Trudel, 2018) and find the relevance to her current coaching practices within her current coaching context (Blumberg, 2016).

Using Weimer's (2013) five dimensions and Blumberg's (2009) framework for evaluating instructor behavior related to LCT, coaching consultants can implement the LCT approach by creating an environment where the coach identifies as an active participant in the learning process (see Table 20.1). In addition, with the coaching consultant providing constructive feedback during assessment of coach learning the coach would likely be challenged to connect new material with prior experience. Thus, the end goal in working with coaches through the LCT process is to help coaches construct their own learning outcomes (Werthner, Culver, & Trudel, 2012) and become self-directed learners by linking new learning to current practice (Trudel, Culver, & Werthner, 2013). The coaching educator can facilitate this outcome by creating a learning environment where the learner (i.e., coach) assists in the construction of knowledge (Paquette & Trudel, 2016). One area where the value of the coach consultant operating under an LCT approach may be impactful is

Table 20.1 Learner-centered teaching dimensions in coaching education

Five key changes to practice (Weimer, 2013)	The role of the coach educator (CE) (Instructor behaviors)	Component of learner-centered teaching (Blumberg, 2009)	Examples of CE in action
1. Role of the Teacher	Recognize learning styles and provide an individualized learning approach	Creation of an environment for learning through organization and use of material	The CE observes the coach in action and engages with the coach through feedback and conversation to develop a learning environment built on the developmental needs of the coach within their context
2. Balance of Power	Allow the coach to feel in control of the learning environment	Determination of course content	The CE identifies keys areas for coach improvement, but allows the coach to select the approach in how they learn the material
3. Function of Content	Facilitate the linking of new knowledge to current practice	Use of content to facilitate future learning	The CE provides up-to-date content related to the context the coach operates in and then provides resources and feedback to assist the coach in applying the concepts
4. Responsibility for Learning	Assist the coach in becoming a self-directed learner	Self-directed, lifelong learning skills	The CE develops trust with the coach and shifts the focus from certification and degree requirements to lifelong learning activities
5. Purpose and Processes of Evaluation	Offer the coach some strategies for self-assessment of coaching practice	Demonstration of mastery and ability to learn from mistakes	The CE designs short self-assessment activities for the coach and assists the coach in adapting their approach in everyday coaching practice

Note: Adapted from Weimer, M. (2013). *Learner-Centered Teaching: Five Key Changes to Practice (2nd Ed)* and Blumberg, P. (2009). *Developing learner-centered teaching: A practical guide for faculty*

assisting coaches in overcoming the role of biases in identifying areas to target for personal and professional development.

The Role of Biases in Identifying Areas for Development

There is a potential confound when identifying target areas for coach development because allowing coaches to self-select their own areas for development may be problematic. Gilbert and Trudel (2001, 2004, 2005), when examining coach reflective practices, argued that coaches process information through their own view of their role frame. In practice, this means that coaches enter learning situations with their own set of beliefs and their own coaching philosophy (Gilbert & Trudel, 2001, 2005). That coaches come in with their own unique background in and of itself is not noteworthy or surprising. The concern grows though because a coach may not naturally be willing to address topics that seem antagonistic or only tangentially related to what the coach wants to work on or is already part of her own coaching philosophy. Nash et al. (2017) found that novice coaches were more likely to rely on players and peers for coaching feedback which inherently reduces the objectivity of the feedback. Mallett, Rabjohns, and Occhino (2016) pointed out that what coaches are actually doing and what they think they are doing is not always equivalent which highlights the need for improved self-awareness. Additionally, there are a number of known (i.e., they exist outside of sport too) biases that could prevent the coach from identifying areas where coaching performance can most improve. A full accounting of biases is beyond the scope of this chapter, but there are four that are worth highlighting within this context: confirmation bias, actor-observer bias, fundamental attribution error, and self-serving bias.

Confirmation Bias Confirmation bias is about what data is judged as relevant and meaningful (Nickerson, 1998). Put differently, when suffering from a confirmation bias, data that matches (i.e., confirms) what a coach already believes to be true will be actively looked for and noticed more while contrary evidence is ignored or misused (Rajsic, Wilson, & Pratt, 2015). Consider the example of a coach that finds her team consistently loses late in contests. The coach does not do a full accounting of her own actions late in the contest because she believes she is a great in-game manager regarding strategies, player substitutions, and clock management. As a result, the coach may reject the analytics or statistical analysis of percentage chances to win based on certain actions believing those data points are not relevant or meaningful. The coach may miss or not even consider the conditioning level of the players and her role in their conditioning during training sessions. In considering that coach's development plan, if the coach is left to self-select topics for development, that coach may never identify, or even consider, her actions late in contests.

Actor-Observer Bias There is a difference between being an actor (i.e., actively involved) in the game and an observer (i.e., no direct impact on the contest) of the game. This difference also can lead to what is called an actor-observer bias which is when someone emphasizes internal and stable explanations for other people's behaviors but relies primarily on situational factors to explain her own behavior (Nisbett, Caputo, Legant, & Marecek, 1973). In the earlier example when the team lost close contests late in the competition, the coach may ascribe player failures to personality types (i.e., they are a bunch of chokers) while explaining away any of her mistakes to being caught up in the situation. It may be helpful here to understand Weiner's (1972) two-dimensional attribution model. In Weiner's (1972) model, attributions, or the explanation for why something happened, are ascribed via a 2 × 2 framework. The two dimensions are internal/external and stable/unstable. The coach ascribing failure to her players' personality was making an internal-to-the-players and stable (i.e., it is just a part of those players) attribution pattern while adopting an external and unstable (i.e., it was not me, it was the situation) attribution for her own mistakes. This combination highlights the possible confound of allowing a coach to self-select areas for professional development. When a coach suffers from actor-observer bias and blames her failures on external situational characteristics the coach may fail to consider areas of improvement that she has control over. Identifying attribution-based biases are important not just for the sake of identifying them, but because research has shown positive effects of attribution retraining in sport contexts (e.g., Orbach, Singer, & Murphey, 1997; Orbach, Singer, & Price, 1999).

Fundamental Attribution Error Generally, people are more forgiving of someone else's negative behavior when it can be attributed to external characteristics (Weiner, Amirkhan, Folkes, & Verette, 1987). For example, the coach may judge the football defender that allowed the offensive player a shot on goal less harshly because the offensive player is faster and more skilled than the defender. The converse is also true then and this helps explain why coaches get so frustrated when players make what are often called mental mistakes (i.e., mistakes that were under the control of the player). This phenomenon is called the fundamental attribution error and it is characterized by an over-emphasis on internal causes paired with a neglecting of legitimate contextual external factors (Nisbett & Ross, 1980). While this type of attribution error is focused on judging other people's behaviors that does not make it less relevant for coaches' professional development.

There are a number of ways professional development could be ineffective, but near the top of that list is if the activities selected do not actually address a problem in the coach's performance. If the coach consistently judges his players as inadequate that coach is less likely to identify his own coaching weaknesses and thus professional development will be less effective. It is also important to note that athletes and parents make attributions about coaches too. Therefore, coaches that react to player mistakes with aggression, such as via a verbal tirade, are likely to prompt athletes and parents to attribute that aggression as internal to the coach and their judgement would be harsh. It should not be difficult to see how the fundamental attribution error can play a destructive role in any coach's career, beyond the identification of areas for professional development.

Self-Serving Bias The final bias directly pertinent to coaches self-selecting their own areas for professional development is the self-serving bias. A self-serving bias is a form of attribution bias wherein people take credit for successes they experience while blaming others for any failures encountered (Miller & Ross, 1975). There is a substantial history of self-serving bias investigations within sport. In a study where collegiate wrestlers served as participants, De Michele, Gansneder, and Solomon (1998) found the winning wrestlers adopted attribution patterns that were significantly more internal and stable than did the losing wrestlers. Self-serving bias has been seen in racket sports (Mark, Mutrie, Brooks, & Harris, 1984) and volleyball (Gill, Ruder, & Gross, 1982). There are two competing explanations for the occurrence of this bias: (a) it feels good to succeed so people want to take credit for that and (b) people do not intend to fail and thus any failures must be due to some external unforeseen circumstance (Hanrahan & Biddle, 2008). For the purpose of coach development, it does not seem to matter which of the explanations of the bias is adopted. The reality is that coaches accepting undue success or negating their blame obscures what really happened. That obscuring of facts critical to the situation can easily lead to erroneous conclusions and those mistakes will be compounded if the coach adopts a professional development plan based upon faulty data.

In summary, leaving a coach to self-select areas for professional development is fraught with difficulties. Identifying the topics that are most relevant to individual coaches is a fundamental step toward a coach improving her performance. Stodter and Cushion (2016) cautioned that coaches are learning through experience, but that experience is influenced by their existing coaching biography (i.e., a combination of experience, beliefs, and current practice) meaning that how they learn through that continued experience could be limited. This is similar to Gilbert and Trudel's (2001, 2004, 2005) description of a role frame. Fortunately, coach learning occurs through the influence of key collaborators, interactions with athletes, and informal interactions with others that have expertise (Taylor, Werthner, & Culver, 2016). In addition, coach learning can be greatly enhanced when those with expertise (i.e., coach developers) provide guidance in the learning process through mentorship, CoP, or an LCT approach. A coach developer can include anyone that provides guidance, programming, or assessment in the ongoing learning and training of coaches. This coach developer operates, ideally, as an unbiased source of insight, unburdened by many of the complexities associated with mandatory learning environments in coach education. The following section will build upon considering who can be involved in coach development and what can be covered within coach development and move to examining some of the mechanisms of how this process of coach development can be carried out.

Practical Implications

Once the coach development team is put in place to support the coach's development the actual work of improving coach performance can begin. Coaches have often been compared to teachers (Wooden & Jamison, 2005) and this provides an opportunity to examine the education literature for identification of problems and solutions from this highly correlated field. There are two critical principles from education and learning theory that seem underrepresented and underutilized in coach development programs: (a) assessment of learning and (b) the importance of maximizing retrieval. Relatedly, an embrace of desirable difficulties within the learning process seems a worthy endeavor. It will likely take some creativity to build some of these principles into the coach development process, but the available evidence (e.g., Werthner et al., 2012) from current coach development programs suggests a more effective path is possible.

Identifying the Topics for Professional Development Activities

While the opening section of this chapter was focused more on who is, or can be, involved with providing coach development opportunities, an equally important component is what areas of a coach's performance are to be developed. Thus, what professional development activities can the coach consultant identify to assist the coach? The question of who a good coach is seems simple enough. Yet, the answer, of course, depends largely on context. It is for that reason that context was included in Côté and Gilbert's (2009) definition of coaching effectiveness. The other two components of their definition are coach knowledge and athlete outcomes (Côté & Gilbert, 2009). The masterful part of the definition offered in their work is that it is broad enough in scope to allow for a great number of activities to be considered as a means through which coaching effectiveness can be improved. For example, improving a coach's ability to promote a mastery climate would fall within the coach knowledge area and that knowledge could be assessed via any number of athlete outcomes. The connection between mastery climate and positive athlete outcomes (e.g., continued sport participation and enjoyment) is well established in the literature (MacDonald, Côté, Eys, & Deakin, 2011). It is also important to note that outside of the research literature, coach effectiveness is still often measured succinctly by whether or not a coach won enough games (Gillham, Burton, & Gillham, 2013; Horn, 2008). Adopting the position that more wins directly equates to a more effective coach is a position that is unnerving from a research position because the literature is clear that the responsibilities of a coach at nearly any competitive level extend far beyond wins and losses. Yet, in a practical sense competitive outcome is the most visible aspect of any team and thus a coach's performance is often reduced to a simple winning percentage.

Coach Evaluation to Identify Areas for Development

Multiple questionnaires have been published as a means to better operationalize coaching effectiveness and extensive listings of the options can be found elsewhere (e.g., Gillham, Dorsch, Walker, & Taylor, 2018; Horn, 2008). Two instruments in particular stand out due to their conformity with Côté and Gilbert's (2009) definition of coach effectiveness and because the instruments were expressly developed with the intention of utilizing them as coach development tools, as well as the tools having yielded viable psychometrics: The Coaching Behavior Scale for Sports (CBS-S; Côté, Yardley, Hay, Sedgwick, & Baker, 1999) and the Coaching Success Questionnaire-2 (CSQ-2; Gillham et al., 2013). Gillham, Hansen, and Brady (2015) included the perspectives of an athletic director, a coach, and a consultant in discussing how the CSQ-2 was used as part of both formal coach evaluation and follow-up coach development work. An interesting point made was that both the coach and the administrator welcomed the more objective information gained from using the CSQ-2 as a way to guide coaches' professional development needs (Gillham, Hansen, et al., 2015). Supporting Gillham, Hansen et al. (2015) was a roundtable discussion with strength and conditioning coaches (i.e., Gillham et al., 2017) wherein the same sentiment of welcoming a more in-depth evaluation system was highlighted with one coach outright stating "Yes, I would be supportive of a more complete or in-depth evaluation for me and across my profession" (p. 642).

What is striking about this coach evaluation leading to coach development discussion is that it simply does not get utilized often enough in applied settings, or at the least the literature shows a dearth of those types of projects. The Coach Evaluation Questionnaire (CEQ; Rushall & Wiznuk, 1985) was published 35 years ago with the authors' expectation being that the instrument would be used by coaches as a professional development tool. Later, Mallett and Côté (2006) put forward specific recommendations for coach evaluation that included collecting questionnaire data, providing a summary report, and then utilizing that information for specific coach development activities. For any number of reasons, the expectations that started with Rushall and Wiznuk (1985) have rarely come to fruition. Current coaches and administrators (e.g., Gillham et al., 2017; Gillham, Hansen, et al., 2015) have stated being open to the use of more in-depth coach evaluations. There is concern over time and financial resources needing to be devoted to proper coach evaluations and the subsequent coach development activities (Hoffmann, Duguay, Guerrero, Loughead, & Munroe-Chandler, 2017). Additionally, this problem seems indicative of Gould's (2016) concern about the growing gap between the knowledge within the research literature and the application of that knowledge. That gap is unlikely to be narrowed by the coaches on their own as journal articles are not high on the list of sources where coaches get their professional development information (Erickson et al., 2008; Stodter & Cushion, 2017).

Sport psychology consultants also seem to have to some work to do in order to help narrow the gap. In a recent review examining perceptions of sport psychology trained consultants, Fortin-Guichard, Boudreault, Gagnon, and Trottier (2018) found that administrators rarely are even aware of the services that sport psychology consultants can offer. In the same review Fortin-Guichard et al. (2018) found coaches to be largely supportive of sport psychology consultants but that support was obviously dependent upon the coaches being aware of the services offered. Barker and Winter (2014) similarly reported coaches being supportive but also largely unaware of how sport psychology consultants could be best utilized.

If the purpose of coach professional development is to improve coaching performance, then evaluation is a necessary step. The evaluation does not inherently need to be an intimidating experience for anyone involved. There is evidence from sport coaches and administrators (Gillham, Hansen, et al., 2015) and strength and conditioning coaches (Gillham et al., 2017) that evaluation can be used as a means to identify opportunities for professional growth. Those opportunities are what should be focused on within the professional development activities, whoever is delivering those activities. This is consistent with a learner-centered approach to coach development (Trudel et al., 2013) as well as addressing what has been a consistent critique of wide-scale coach development programs (Deek et al., 2013; Misener & Danylchuk, 2009).

Coach Profiles to Identify Areas for Development

Employing performance profiles for athletes has been recommended by multiple authors (e.g., Dale & Wrisberg, 1996; Weston, Greenlees, & Thelwell, 2011) as a way for sport psychology consultants to gain additional information. The same approach can be used by and for coaches too (Burton & Raedeke, 2008; Nicholls, 2017). The premise of a coach profile is to consider a variety of areas important to performance and provide some degree of rating of effectiveness on the coach's ability to successfully implement those important areas. Nicholls (2017) suggested three specific steps to developing a performance profile: (a) generate a list of skills important to success, (b) rank-order those skills as well as operationalizing them with specific examples and identified meanings (i.e., 'leadership' is not sufficient and would need clarification), and (c) provide a self-report rating of effectiveness or current aptitude level for each of the identified skills. The subsequent step, likely involving a coach developer, mentor, or sport consultant is to identify action steps that could be employed to improve each of those identified skills. See Table 20.2 for an example of what this might look like for a basketball coach.

Utilizing this approach of performance profiles is congruent with Côté and Gilbert's (2009) definition of coach effectiveness. A variety of observation-based coaching behavior tools exist (e.g., Coaching Behavior Questionnaire; Williams et al., 2003) with one of the more novel approaches being a state space grid (SSG) methodology. The basic premise of employing a state space grid (Hollenstein, 2007; Lewis, Lamey, & Douglas, 1999) is to capture the dynamics of a social interaction. A key principle of SSGs is that this approach strives for a middle-ground between coach-athlete by treating them as co-actors as opposed to distinct individuals acting entirely independent of one another (Erickson & Côté, 2013). The importance of the coach-athlete relationship, which also highlights the importance of interactions between the two individuals, is well documented in the literature (e.g., Camiré, 2015; Erickson & Côté, 2016; Ferrar et al., 2018; Jowett & Carpenter, 2015; Lorimer & Jowett, 2013). Delving further into examining the holistic interactions between the coach and athlete via SSG can serve a valuable role for creating a coach's performance profile.

Table 20.2 Interscholastic basketball coach performance profile example

Rank order of importance skill/area	Skills/areas important for success	Explanation of why the skill/area is important	Self-reported aptitude level on scale of 1 (room for improvement) to 6 (accomplished)
1	Planning effective practices	Designing productive on-court training sessions that maximize player repetition and development	3
2	Providing quality feedback	Recognizing key moments to provide appropriate and instructional feedback	2
3	Building team cohesion	Being able to consistently provide team building activities	4
4	Player evaluation and squad selection	Keeping an open mind during talent evaluation	5
5	Strategic game management	Knowing when to make tactical decisions to improve the team's chances at success	4

Note: Adapted from Nicholls, A. (2017). *Psychology in Sports Coaching*. 2nd ed

Consider the performance profile included in Table 20.2. A skill such as using space effectively (i.e., not remaining stationary for too long) and the behavior of interacting with most athletes (i.e., not simply favoring the starters) in a single training session can be ranked according to perceived current skill level. A trusted other (e.g., mentor, peer, or sport consultant) could then observe the coach's training session and record interactions congruent with the state space grid methodology wherein further specific examples are provided thus operationalizing the skills to the specific context of the coach. Erickson, Côté, Hollenstein, and Deakin (2011) utilized the SSG and found the more successful team had a coach that exhibited a greater focus on individuals one-at-a-time thereby creating meaningful dyadic interactions. After employing an SSG to detail the specific examples of coach-athlete interactions, a series of action steps could be agreed upon between the consultant and the coach. Associated follow-up activities could include establishing goals for the coach to provide technical feedback to at least 75% of the team members within a training session. There are a variety of resources and examples available for coaches to properly utilize goal setting (e.g., Burton & Raedeke, 2008; Gillham, 2016a; Gillham & Weiler, 2013; Weinberg, 2010). Another option would be to increase coach movement throughout the training space by tracking her movements and identifying a specific percentage increase in movement for a single training session. In conjunction with the definition of coaching effectiveness (Côté & Gilbert, 2009), the example offered here seems likely to fall within the coach knowledge domain. However, success or improvement on the part of the coach, could well be assessed via the second domain of athlete outcomes. While more research needs to be done on

SSGs (Erickson & Côté, 2013) the initial findings show merit for improving coaching performance.

Assessment of Learning

One critique from coaches regarding coach development is that they report not actually learning anything of value (Nelson et al., 2013). A variety of reasons have been offered: (a) topics seem irrelevant to the coaches in attendance (Trudel et al., 2013), (b) perceived lack of knowledge or proper training of the person delivering the coach development activity (Gray, 2011), and (c) a lack of effective assessment procedures which prevent any conclusions about learning from being settled on (Gilbert & Trudel, 1999). Adopting a learner centered approach, as suggested by Paquette and Trudel (2018), may help with the first two critiques. Introducing better assessment procedures though is something under the control of whomever is offering the coach development activity. While there is debate about whether indirect (e.g., attitudes or opinions) or direct (e.g., actual work products or specific knowledge components) is the best method for assessment within education (Luce & Kirnan, 2016), the bigger reality for coach education is that some assessment of the coach development activities should be included. That is true whether the coach development activity is offered through a wide-scale program or through a smaller setting such as CoP or even one-on-one. It is entirely reasonable that after any professional development activity there is some form of assessment of what the coach learned having participated in the activity. This assessment need not be summative in nature and it could simply be used as a gauge toward further progression of learning.

The validity of any selected assessment method must be considered. Gillham et al. (2018) advised that assessments need to be in alignment between the purpose of the assessment, who will be completing the assessment, and if the assessor has the knowledge to accurately rate what is being assessed. For example, a youth sport athlete seems unlikely to be able to accurately rate a coach's ability to prevent athlete injuries. This can be especially problematic as novice coaches may rely too much on player feedback of the coach's performance even when the players are less than 10 years of age (Nash et al., 2017).

Additionally, administrators or parents that do not routinely attend training sessions inherently have less information from which to base their assessments. Within coach development activities, there are two prominent areas for potential misalignment. The first is the difference in value of the assessment by the organization and the students completing the evaluative forms (Huffman, Adamapoulos, Merdock, Cole, & McDermid, 2011; Liu, Bridgeman, & Adler, 2012). This problem is one of learner motivation to accurately report their perception of the learning experience. One recommendation to solve this dilemma is to add a specific statement to the assessment highlighting the value of respondents providing honest and forthright responses (Huffman et al., 2011; Liu et al., 2012). Secondly, there is what could be called a "j" effect often present in interventions. Barker, McCarthy, Jones, and Moran (2011) described this as an initial short-term performance degradation (i.e., when drawing a "j" from left to right the first stroke of the pen will be downward) followed by an increase in performance over the long-term. This is an important consideration when testing coach learning after a professional development activity.

Coaches may arrive at the activity believing they are above average on a particular skill or topic that is included in the coach development workshop or activity. During the course of that activity the students learn more about the topic and subsequently rate their skill or knowledge level on the topic at a lower level (Barker et al., 2011). Without an understanding of this common occurrence, the assessment would show a decrease in coach knowledge which is unlikely to have truly occurred and would be problematic to both the organization that offered the development activity and the coach. Including a more long-term follow-up assessment is one solution to this particular problem. Longitudinal studies are difficult to execute in a research setting, but this is one specific area where reality could far out-pace the research as administrators have the ability, and in some cases responsibility, to maintain year-after-year coaching evaluations.

Maximizing Information Retrieval

Coaches participate in professional development for a variety of reasons, but ultimately the assumption is those activities are completed to improve coaching performance ideally leading to increased competitive successes. This has been seen in training of higher education faculty members with a clear concern that post-workshop ratings by those in attendance (i.e., faculty, coaches) does not inherently mean the attendee will be able to represent adequate change for the benefit of those they serve (i.e., students, athletes; McAlpine, Oviedo, & Emrick, 2008). Given the assumption that any professional development activity is intended to result in improved coaching performance and that the information presented is, at least, theoretically beneficial to the coaching participants, there should also be a concerted effort to present the information in a manner that maximizes coach retention of the materials presented. Indeed, this is a robust assumption across fields as Gaspelin, Ruthruff, and Pashler (2013) expressed a belief that all of society is better when learning occurs more efficiently, particularly in the case where learning was supposed to occur.

Retrieval Including a long-term follow-up assessment after the professional development activity would place a greater emphasis on coaches being able to access the knowledge they were taught during the coach development activity. Accessing this material is typically called retrieval (Hopkins, Lyle, Hieb, & Ralston, 2016). Degradation of the new knowledge is unavoidable (Hopkins et al., 2016) over time, but that has given rise to a plethora of studies on finding ways to limit the decay of learned material and increase the utilization of the new knowledge. One of the most widely accepted learning and memory phenomenon is that of the retrieval practice effect, or the testing effect (Rowland, 2014). In short, this retrieval effect shows that long-term retention is increased via repeated tests (i.e., accessing the necessary stored information to answer a question) more than simply restudying the material at a later date. Moreover, in situations where attentional processes are diverse and quickly change (i.e., coaching), Mulligan and Picklesimer (2016) found significant advantages for the group of participants that used retrieval methods in the distraction condition versus the full attention group. Retrieval methods can be included within the original learning activity which is consistent with pedagogy recommendations (Karpicke, 2017). However, Morehead, Rhodes, and DeLozier (2016) found that educators rarely sufficiently inject retrieval methods into the normal process of learning instead favouring the more traditional formalized end-of-section or end-of-course assessment approaches. Retrieval techniques can also be applied after the initial learning activity and can be self-directed (Ariel & Karpicke, 2018). There is concern though that students across contexts rarely use retrieval methods effectively (Dunlosky & Rawson, 2015) on their own which both provides another opportunity for coach developers to improve the learning of the coaches they work with and yet also adds another task to the to-do list.

Whenever it occurs, the retrieval activities can either be massed or spaced. The massed versus spaced retrieval in education parallels the blocked versus random practice from motor learning. Consider the basketball shooter practicing her shot. In discussing blocked versus random practice for that athlete, the question is whether it is better for her to shoot ten times from the same location (i.e., blocked) before moving on to a different location or if her ten shots should come from ten different locations (i.e., random) on the court. The literature is mounting in support of the random practice condition (Fazeli, Taheri, & Kakhki, 2017). The coach in a professional development activity is likely to continue to retain greater amounts of information by answering questions across the various topics covered in the workshop than to focus specifically on one topic, and then move to the second topic, and so on. Additionally, topics already addressed should reappear later within the workshop and the testing methods should parallel that approach. Going back to previous topics also helps avoid the "one and done" phenomenon where students successfully recall the desired information one time and then consider themselves as having learned the material thereby no longer studying it (Dunlosky & Rawson, 2015). It would not be difficult for an individual coach developer to text message or email some questions to the coaches after a professional development workshop. Those questions could be repeated again after a number of days or weeks and the questions could be revised or adjusted to cover different topics from the workshop.

This body of research has direct implications for anyone providing professional development activities for coaches. If the purpose of the activity is truly to help the coaches improve their own coaching performance, then the coaches must continue to retrieve the information that was taught once they leave the original learning situation. Gilbert and Trudel (1999) described the need for assessments to move beyond simple decontextualized paper-pencil tests. Collins, Abraham, and Collins

(2012) astutely pointed out that any evaluation of the impact of a coach training program must consider that some of the responsibility for the success of the training program lies with the coach. However, that does not absolve the provider of the training program from doing all that they can to maximize coach learning and retention of the material presented. Part of that process may well include teaching, or at least reminding, the coaches in attendance how best to retrieve the information they have been taught during the professional development activity.

Desirable Difficulties An intriguing approach is to introduce desirable difficulties into the learning process. Bjork (1994) coined the term "desirable difficulty" to describe instances where retrieval of learned information is more effortful. The theory is that retrieval that requires more effort strengthens the connections to the material and thus it is a better method for long-term memory than less effortful learning (Maddox & Balota, 2015). Gaspelin et al. (2013) summarized the desirable difficulty research into three general areas: (a) spaced retrieval practice is superior to massed retrieval practice, (b) testing is better than restudying, and (c) mixing topic areas is superior. For example, re-reading of highlighted passages is an example of less effort-demanding recall than would be answering novel questions or attempting to apply the material to a different context. An important consideration with desirable difficulty recall studies is that immediate recall (i.e., during or immediately following) is often superior when the learning was easy or less effortful. However, as Cepeda et al. (2009) found recall is significantly better in subsequent recall situations at a more removed time from the initial learning activity. While the term desirable difficulties are likely novel to many coach educators, the practical applications of the concept should seem logical.

A final point with regards to introducing desirable difficulties is a parallel to the earlier discussion on what topics are beneficial to be included within a coach's professional development activities. When learners control their learning environment there may be an over-reliance on practicing topics and learning strategies that come easy to the participant or already exist within their role frame. This may serve as a partial explanation for why coaches often select attending conferences and workshops or reading books on topics they are already familiar with. While not specific to coaching, or even learning, there is ample research demonstrating people prefer stimuli that are easy to process and a familiarity or prior experience with the stimuli may be enough to prompt positive emotions (Labroo & Kim, 2009; Schwarz, 2004). However, the desirable difficulty literature would surmise those activities may be less than effective at improving long-term coaching performance. Taking that information and applying it directly to a single basketball coach wishing to improve her coaching, it seems more likely that attending a sport psychology conference may yield a higher degree of coaching performance improvement than returning to her fifth consecutive offensive strategy clinic. Coaches may recognize the same behavior in their athletes: A basketball player has a favorite spot to shoot from and only wishes to practice shots from that location. The coach is likely to challenge that player to move around on the court and tackle shots less comfortable to the player. A similar challenge to the coach to address topics outside her comfort zone is offered here.

Reflective Practice Reflective practice is one tool that coaches can use to help with retrieval. Encouraging coaches to utilize reflection as part of their career development is not a novel recommendation as it exists in the literature for both sport coaches (Gilbert & Trudel, 2001; Knowles, Tyler, Gilbourne, & Eubank, 2006; Stodter & Cushion, 2016) and strength and conditioning coaches (Kuklick & Gearity, 2015). The systematic use of reflection can also be a way for coaches feeling isolated to continue their professional development despite their perceived isolation (Nash et al., 2017). Reflective practice is a deliberate process of stepping back and examining one's actions to enhance personal and professional growth (Moon, 2013; Schön, 1987). A coach will likely engage in some type of reflective practice by simply looking back on a recent training session or contest and subsequently make adjustments to improve performance or coaching practice (Knowles et al., 2006). While this is a deliberate action and likely a common approach taken by a coach, what is substantially less clear is if a coach is given any training on how to reflect, why it will help them in their learning pursuits, or what the process actually entails (Lee, Chesterfield, Shaw, & Ghaye, 2009). To assist a coach in more purposeful reflection coaching educators have employed a variety of methods including, but not limited to, (a) reflective journaling (Gilbert & Trudel, 2001; Knowles, Gilbourne, Borrie, & Nevill, 2001), (b) reflective conversation (Gilbert & Côté, 2012), (c) R-cards (Hughes, Lee, & Chesterfield, 2009; Winfield, Williams, & Dixon, 2013), (d) Think Aloud (Whitehead, Cropley, Miles, Quayle, & Knowles, 2016), and (e) a personal leadership narrative (Gearity, 2014).

Reflective journaling is a deliberate action by the coach to step back and examine a recent experience (i.e., practice session, contest) and make note of the experience either manually or electronically (Gilbert & Trudel, 2001). A reflective conversation can occur in-action (i.e., while engaged in the practice of coaching) or on-action (i.e., after a recent practice session). The conversation is with oneself or a more knowledgeable other and often involves identifying the problem, making adjustments through experimentation, evaluating the outcome, and determining if further adjustments need to be made (Gilbert & Côté, 2012). An R-card is an index card with a list of pre-determined areas for improvement or a blank card that provides the coach quick access to make and record observations in-action. The R-card approach functions as an initial reflection in-action, which subsequently allows the coach to revisit the R-card after the practice session and focus on specific areas for improvement when reflecting on-action (Hughes et al., 2009). 'Think Aloud' occurs when a coach verbalizes what she is thinking concurrently during task execution. The verbalized comments can be recorded via audio or documented by another person. Thus, 'Think Aloud' can be a valuable technique for collecting the coach's thought processes, without negatively influencing the experience of the participants (Whitehead et al., 2016). Lastly, a personal leadership narrative flows from the concepts of autoethnography, where the coach examines life experiences, her current role as a coach, and previous learning experiences in an attempt to make sense of how her life history has influenced her development as a coach (Gearity, 2014).

Thus, the assessment of reflective practice is ideally improvement in coach performance (Werthner et al., 2012). However, the impact of reflective practice may be limited unless the coach takes a more critical approach to the reflection process. It is important to note that reflection is a great deal different than rumination. Gilbert (2017) recommends that in addition to reflective practice, coaches engage in more critical reflection. In other words, coaches should make time to focus on why they coach and reflect on their core values compared to reflecting on a specific problem they are trying to solve. Essentially, critical reflection "... provides coaches with a more vivid awareness of their general coaching philosophy, potential areas for targeting future continuous improvement efforts, and a more authentic and humble view of what it takes to succeed as a coach" (Gilbert, 2017, p. 314). For a coach, the power of critical reflection lies in the ability to increase self-awareness regarding the impact of the coach's actions on team and individual performance (Whitehead et al., 2016). The use of reflective practice techniques mimic and support many of the retrieval procedures outlined above. However, absent a critical reflection approach, it seems unlikely that the coach will fully engage in meaningful reflective practice and this negates the tool as a key step toward improving knowledge retrieval.

Key Points

1. Due to the complexity and multifaceted nature of the coaching profession, a coach needs someone to accompany them on their professional development journey.
2. The research on the learning process of a coach is quite clear, coaches learn best when guided by a more knowledgeable other and are able to collaborate in designing their learning experience.
3. When working with coaches it is important to recognize each coach as an individualized learner and the coach development activities need to be customized to reach the learner in the correct context and in a manner in which the material can be applied to current practice.
4. Biases are real and coaches suffer from them which can mask which areas need attention through professional development.
5. The coach consultant serves a vital role in challenging the coach to ensure that learning is actually occurring through assessment of learning, and how to best maximize information retrieval.

Conclusion

As the professionalization of sport coaching continues to intensify (Taylor & Garratt, 2010), it seems the demands placed upon coaches are likely to increase for the foreseeable future. This reality sets up a situation where the coach is unlikely to be able to navigate the options for professional development without seeking help from a network of competent allied professionals, peer coaches, mentors, and administrators. Coach development should be viewed as an on-going process that is well-defined in broad terms and simultaneously ill-defined and nebulous the more specific the context. For some topics (e.g., mentorship) current coaching practices have outpaced the academic research. For other areas (e.g., components of the learning process) the research seems to have outpaced the practices currently utilized by coaches and coach developers alike. Calls for more studies and greater collaboration between academics and practicing coaches are certainly echoed here. But beyond that lies the real world of making those collaborations happen to create meaningful change within the confines of budgets and schedules. The challenge presented here is to move beyond the simple, comfortable, traditional solution and seek out novel approaches to solving problems which may well involve a sport consultant to help bypass biases, a commitment to coach evaluation to identify areas for improvement, and a focus on coach learning to maximize the resources devoted to coach development.

References

Abraham, A., & Collins, D. (1998). Examining and extending research in coach development. *Quest, 50*(1), 59–79.

Allen, D., & Eby, L. T. (2010). *The Blackwell handbook of mentoring: A multiple perspectives approach*. West Sussex, UK: Wiley-Blackwell.

Ariel, R., & Karpicke, J. D. (2018). Improving self-regulated learning with a retrieval practice intervention. *Journal of Experimental Psychology: Applied, 24*(1), 43–56.

Ayer, T. (2016). *The sphinx of the Charles: A year at Harvard with Harry Parker*. Guilford, CT: Lyon Press.

Barker, J., McCarthy, P., Jones, M., & Moran, A. (2011). *Single-case research methods in sport and exercise psychology*. New York: Routledge.

Barker, S., & Winter, S. (2014). The practice of sport psychology: A youth coaches' perspective. *International Journal of Sports Science & Coaching, 9*(2), 379–392.

Becker, A. J., & Wrisberg, C. A. (2008). Effective coaching in action: Observations of legendary collegiate basketball coach Pat Summitt. *The Sport Psychologist, 22*(2), 197–211.

Beres, J. L., & Dixon, J. C. (2014). Exploring mentoring functions within the sport management academy: Perspectives of mentors and protégés. *Sport Management Education Journal, 8*, 14–26.

Bertram, R., Culver, D. M., & Gilbert, W. (2017). A university sport coach community of practice: Using a value creation framework to explore learning and social interactions. *International Journal of Sports Science & Coaching, 12*(3), 287–302.

Bertz, S., & Purdy, L. (2011). Coach education in Ireland: Observations and considerations for high performance. *Journal of Coaching Education, 4*(3), 29–43.

Bespomoshchnov, V. A., & Caron, J. G. (2017). Coaching philosophy and methods of Anatoly Tarasov: 'Father' of Russian ice hockey. *International Sport Coaching Journal, 4*(3), 305–313.

Bjork, R. A. (1994). Memory and metamemory consideration in the training of human beings. In J. Metcalfe & A. Shimamura (Eds.), *Metacognition: Knowing about knowing* (pp. 185–205). Cambridge, MA: MIT Press.

Bloom, G. (2013). Mentoring for sport coaches. In P. Potrac, W. Gilbert, & J. Denison (Eds.), *Routledge handbook of sports coaching* (pp. 476–485). New York: Routledge.

Bloom, G. A., Durand-Bush, N., Schinke, R. J., & Salmela, J. H. (1998). The importance of mentoring in the development of coaches and athletes. *International Journal of Sport Psychology, 29*, 267–281.

Blumberg, P. (2009). *Developing learner-centered teaching: A practical guide for faculty*. San Francisco: Wiley.

Blumberg, P. (2016). Factors that influence faculty adoption of learning-centered approaches. *Innovative Higher Education, 41*(4), 303–315.

Bozeman, B., & Feeney, M. K. (2008). Mentor matching: A "goodness of fit" model. *Administration & Society, 40*(5), 465–482.

Burton, D., & Raedeke, T. D. (2008). *Sport psychology for coaches*. Champaign, IL: Human Kinetics.

Callary, B., Culver, D., Werthner, P., & Bales, J. (2014). An overview of seven national high performance coach education programs. *International Sport Coaching Journal, 1*(3), 152–164.

Callary, B., Rathwell, S., & Young, B. W. (2018). Coach education and learning sources for coaches of masters swimmers. *International Sport Coaching Journal, 5*(1), 47–59.

Camiré, M. (2015). Examining high school teacher-coaches' perspective on relationship building with student-athletes. *International Sport Coaching Journal, 2*(2), 125–136.

Carter, A. D., & Bloom, G. A. (2009). Coaching knowledge and success: Going beyond athletic experiences. *Journal of Sport Behavior, 32*(4), 419–437.

Cepeda, N. J., Coburn, N., Roher, D., Wixted, J. T., Mozer, M. C., & Pashler, H. (2009). Optimizing distributed practice: Theoretical analysis and practical implications. *Experimental Psychology, 56*(4), 236–246.

Chambers, F. (2015). *Mentoring in physical education and sports coaching*. New York: Routledge.

Collins, D., Abraham, A., & Collins, R. (2012). On vampires and wolves—Exposing and exploring reasons for the differential impact of coach education. *International Journal of Sport Psychology, 43*(3), 255–271.

Côté, J., & Gilbert, W. (2009). An integrative definition of coaching effectiveness and expertise. *International Journal of Sports Science & Coaching, 4*(3), 307–323.

Côté, J., Yardley, J., Hay, J., Sedgwick, W., & Baker, J. (1999). An exploratory examination of the Coaching Behaviour Scale for Sport. *Avante, 5*, 82–92.

Creswell, J. W. (2008). *Educational research: Planning, conducting, and evaluating quantitative and qualitative research*. Upper Saddle River, NJ: Pearson, Merrill Prentice Hall.

Cushion, C. J. (2006). Mentoring: Harnessing the power of experience. In R. Jones (Ed.), *The sports coach as educator: Re-conceptualising sports coaching* (pp. 128–144). London: Routledge.

Cushion, C. J., Armour, K. M., & Jones, R. L. (2003). Coach education and continuing professional development: Experience and learning to coach. *Quest, 55*(3), 215–230.

Dale, G. A., & Wrisberg, C. A. (1996). The use of a performance profiling technique in a team setting: Getting the athletes and coach on the "same page". *The Sport Psychologist, 10*(3), 261–277.

Deek, D., Werthner, P., Paquette, K. J., & Culver, D. (2013). Impact of a large-scale coach education program from a lifelong-learning perspective. *Journal of Coaching Education, 6*(1), 23–42.

De Michele, P., Gansneder, B., & Solomon, G. (1998). Success and failure attributions of wrestlers: Further evidence of the self-serving bias. *Journal of Sport Behavior, 21*(3), 242–255.

Dunlosky, J., & Rawson, K. A. (2015). Do students use testing and feedback while learning? A focus on key concept definitions and learning to criterion. *Learning and Instruction, 39*, 32–44.

Erickson, K., Bruner, M. W., MacDonald, D. J., & Côté, J. (2008). Gaining insight into actual and preferred sources of coaching knowledge. *International Journal of Sports Science & Coaching, 3*(4), 527–538.

Erickson, K., & Côté, J. (2013). The state space grid method. In P. Potrac, W. Gilbert, & J. Denison (Eds.), *Routledge handbook of sports coaching* (pp. 108–120). New York: Routledge.

Erickson, K., & Côté, J. (2016). A season-long examination of the intervention tone of coach–athlete interactions and athlete development in youth sport. *Psychology of Sport and Exercise, 22*, 264–272.

Erickson, K., Côté, J., Hollenstein, T., & Deakin, J. (2011). Examining coach–athlete interactions using state space grids: An observational analysis in competitive youth sport. *Psychology of Sport and Exercise, 12*(6), 645–654.

Fazeli, D., Taheri, H., & Kakhki, A. S. (2017). Random versus blocked practice to enhance mental representation in golf putting. *Perceptual and Motor Skills, 124*(3), 674–688.

Ferrar, P., Hosea, L., Henson, M., Dubina, N., Krueger, G., Staff, J., & Gilbert, W. (2018). Building high performing coach-athlete relationships: The USOC's national team coach leadership education program (NTCLEP). *International Sport Coaching Journal, 15*(1), 60–70.

Fortin-Guichard, D., Boudreault, V., Gagnon, S., & Trottier, C. (2018). Experience, effectiveness, and perceptions toward sport psychology consultants: A critical review of peer-reviewed articles. *Journal of Applied Sport Psychology, 30*(1), 3–22.

Gallimore, R., & Tharp, R. (2004). What a coach can teach a teacher, 1975-2004: Reflections and reanalysis of John Wooden's teaching practices. *The Sport Psychologist, 18*(2), 119–137.

Garner, P., & Hill, D. M. (2017). Cultivating a community of practice to enable coach development in alpine ski coaches. *International Sport Coaching Journal, 4*, 63–75.

Gaspelin, N., Ruthruff, E., & Pashler, H. (2013). Divided attention: An undesirable difficulty in memory retention. *Memory and Cognition, 41*, 978–988.

Gearity, B. T. (2014). Autoethnography. In L. Nelson, R. Groom, & P. Potrac (Eds.), *Research methods in sport coaching* (pp. 205–216). New York: Routledge.

Gilbert, W. (2017). *Coaching better every season: A year-round system for athlete development and program success*. Champaign, IL: Human Kinetics.

Gilbert, W., & Côté, J. (2012). A focus on coaches' knowledge. In P. Potrac, W. Gilbert, & J. Denison (Eds.), *Routledge handbook of sports coaching* (pp. 147–159). New York: Routledge.

Gilbert, W., Gallimore, R., & Trudel, P. (2009). A learning community approach to coach development in youth sport. *Journal of Coaching Education, 2*(2), 3–23.

Gilbert, W., & Trudel, P. (1999). An evaluation strategy for coach education programs. *Journal of Sport Behavior, 22*(2), 234.

Gilbert, W. D., & Trudel, P. (2001). Learning to coach through experience: Reflection in model youth sport coaches. *Journal of Teaching in Physical Education, 21*(1), 16–34.

Gilbert, W. D., & Trudel, P. (2004). Role of the coach: How model youth team sport coaches frame their roles. *The Sport Psychologist, 18*, 21–43.

Gilbert, W. D., & Trudel, P. (2005). Learning to coach through experience: Conditions that influence reflection. *Physical Educator, 62*, 32–44.

Gill, D. L., Ruder, M. K., & Gross, J. B. (1982). Open-ended attributions in team competition. *Journal of Sport Psychology, 4*(2), 159–169.

Gillham, A. (2016a). The application of systematic goal setting for strength and conditioning coaches. *NSCA Coach, 3*(2), 4–6.

Gillham, A. (2016b). Using questions to improve coach effectiveness. *NSCA Coach, 3*(4), 6–8.

Gillham, A., Burton, D., & Gillham, E. (2013). Going beyond won-loss record to identify successful coaches: Development and preliminary validation of the Coaching Success Questionnaire-2. *International Journal of Sports Science & Coaching, 8*(1), 115–138.

Gillham, A., Dorsch, T., Walker, B., & Taylor, J. (2018). Coach, parent, and team assessments. In J. Taylor (Ed.), *Assessments for applied sport psychology consulting* (pp. 147–167). Champaign, IL: Human Kinetics.

Gillham, A., Doscher, M., Fitzgerald, C., Bennett, S., Davis, A., & Banwarth, A. (2017). Strength and conditioning roundtable: Strength and conditioning coach evaluation. *International Journal of Sports Science & Coaching, 12*(5), 635–646.

Gillham, A., Doscher, M., Schofield, G., Dalrymple, D., & Bird, S. (2015). Strength and conditioning roundtable: Working with novice coaches. *International Journal of Sports Science & Coaching, 10*(5), 985–1000.

Gillham, A., Hansen, K., & Brady, C. (2015). Coach evaluation from three perspectives: An athletic director, a coach and a consultant. *International Sport Coaching Journal, 2*(2), 192–200.

Gillham, A., & Weiler, D. (2013). Goal setting with a college soccer team: What went right, and less-than-right. *Journal of Sport Psychology in Action, 4*(2), 97–109.

Gould, D. (2016). Conducting impactful coaching science research: The forgotten role of knowledge integration and dissemination. *International Sport Coaching Journal, 3*(2), 197–203.

Gould, D., Giannini, J., Krane, V., & Hodge, K. (1990). Educational needs of elite US national team, Pan American, and Olympic coaches. *Journal of Teaching in Physical Education, 9*(4), 332–344.

Gould, D., Pierce, S., Cowburn, I. H. J., & Driska, A. (2017). How coaching philosophy drives coaching action: A case study of renowned wrestling coach J Robinson. *International Sport Coaching Journal, 4*(1), 13–37.

Gray, D. E. (2011). Journeys towards the professionalisation of coaching: Dilemmas, dialogues and decisions along the global pathway. *Coaching: An International Journal of Theory, Research and Practice, 4*(1), 4–19.

Halberstam, D. (2005). *The education of a coach*. New York: Hyperion.

Hall, E. T., Gray, S., & Sproule, J. (2016). The microstructure of coaching practice: Behaviours and activities of an elite rugby union head coach during preparation and competition. *Journal of Sports Sciences, 34*(10), 896–905.

Hanrahan, S. J., & Biddle, S. J. (2008). Attributions and perceived control. In T. S. Horn (Ed.), *Advances in sport psychology* (3rd ed., pp. 65–97). Champaign, IL: Human Kinetics.

Hoffmann, M. D., Duguay, A. M., Guerrero, M. D., Loughead, T. M., & Munroe-Chandler, K. J. (2017). 360-Degree feedback for sport coaches: A follow-up to O'Boyle (2014). *International Sport Coaching Journal, 4*(3), 335–344.

Hollenstein, T. (2007). State space grids: Analyzing dynamics across development. *International Journal of Behavioral Development, 31*, 384–396.

Hopkins, R. F., Lyle, K. B., Hieb, J. L., & Ralston, P. A. S. (2016). Spaced retrieval practice increases college students' short- and long-term retention of mathematics knowledge. *Education Psychology Review, 28*, 853–873.

Horn, T. S. (2008). Coaching effectiveness in the sport domain. In T. S. Horn (Ed.), *Advances in sport psychology* (3rd ed., pp. 239–268). Champaign, IL: Human Kinetics.

Huffman, L., Adamapoulos, A., Merdock, G., Cole, A., & McDermid, R. (2011). Strategies to motivate students for program assessment. *Educational Assessment, 16*, 90–103.

Hughes, C., Lee, S., & Chesterfield, G. (2009). Innovation in sports coaching: The implementation of reflective cards. *Reflective Practice*, 367–384.

International Council for Coaching Excellence, Association of Summer Olympic International Federations, & Leeds Beckett University. (2013). *International sport coaching framework (version 1.2)*. Champaign, IL: Human Kinetics.

Jimenez, S., Lorenzo, A., & Ibanez, S. (2009). Development of expertise in Spanish elite basketball coaches. *International Journal of Sport Science, 17*, 19–32.

Jones, R. L., Harris, R., & Miles, A. (2009). Mentoring in sports coaching: A review of literature. *Physical Education and Sport Pedagogy, 14*(3), 267–284.

Jowett, S., & Carpenter, P. (2015). The concept of rules in the coach-athlete relationship. *Sports Coaching Review, 4*(1), 1–23.

Karpicke, J. D. (2017). Retrieval-based learning: A decade of progress. In J. Wixted (Ed.), *Cognitive psychology of memory, Volume 2 of learning and memory: A comprehensive reference* (J. H. Byrne, Series Ed., pp. 487–514). Oxford: Academic Press.

Knowles, Z., Gilbourne, D., Borrie, A., & Nevill, A. (2001). Developing the reflective sports coach: A study exploring the processes of reflective practice within a higher education coaching programme. *Reflective Practice, 2*(2), 185–207.

Knowles, Z., Tyler, G., Gilbourne, D., & Eubank, M. (2006). Reflecting on reflection: Exploring the practice of sports coaching graduates. *Reflective Practice, 7*(2), 163–179.

Kozel, J. (1997). Educating coaches for the twenty-first century—a German perspective. *The Sport Educator, 9*(3), 41–44.

Kram, K. E. (1988). *Mentoring at work: Developmental relationships in organizational life*. Lanham, MD: University Press of America.

Kuklick, C. R., & Gearity, B. T. (2015). A review of reflective practice and its application for the football strength and conditioning coach. *Strength & Conditioning Journal, 37*(6), 43–51.

Labroo, A. A., & Kim, S. (2009). The "Instrumentality" heuristic: Why metacognitive difficulty is desirable during goal pursuit. *Psychological Science, 20*(1), 127–134.

Lauer, L., Driska, A., & Cowburn, I. (2016). Sport psychology professionals as trusted advisors in high performance environments. In P. A. Davis (Ed.), *The psychology of effective coaching and management* (pp. 385–407). New York: Nova.

Layton, R. (2005). *Making mentors: A guide to establishing a successful mentoring programme for coaches and officials*. Canberra, ACT: Australian Sports Commission.

Lee, S., Chesterfield, G., Shaw, D. J., & Ghaye, T. (2009). Exploring the potential of reflective learning in sport. *Reflective Practice, 10*(3), 285–293.

Lewis, M. D., Lamey, A. V., & Douglas, L. (1999). A new dynamic system method for the analysis of early socioemotional development. *Developmental Science, 2*, 457–475.

Liu, O. L., Bridgeman, B., & Adler, R. M. (2012). Measuring learning outcomes in higher education: Motivation matters. *Educational Researcher, 41*(9), 352–362.

Lorimer, R., & Jowett, S. (2013). Empathic understanding and accuracy in the coach-athlete relationship. In P. Potrac, W. Gilbert, & J. Denison (Eds.), *Routledge handbook of sports coaching* (pp. 321–332). New York: Routledge.

Luce, C., & Kirnan, J. P. (2016). Using indirect vs. direct measures in the summative assessment of student learning in higher education. *Journal of the Scholarship of Teaching and Learning, 16* (4), 75–91.

MacDonald, D. J., Côté, J., Eys, M., & Deakin, J. (2011). The role of enjoyment and motivational climate in relation to the personal development of team sport athletes. *The Sport Psychologist, 25*(1), 32–46.

Maddox, G. B., & Balota, D. A. (2015). Retrieval practice and spacing effects in young and older adults: An examination of the benefits of desirable difficulty. *Memory and Cognition, 43*, 760–774.

Mallett, C., & Côté, J. (2006). Beyond winning and losing: Guidelines for evaluating high performance coaches. *The Sport Psychologist, 20*, 213–221.

Mallett, C. J., Rabjohns, M., & Occhino, J. L. (2016). Challenging coaching orthodoxy: A self-determination theory perspective. In P. A. Davis (Ed.), *The psychology of effective coaching and management* (pp. 167–181). New York: Nova.

Mallett, C. J., Trudel, P., Lyle, J., & Rynne, S. B. (2009). Formal vs. informal coach education. *International Journal of Sports Science & Coaching, 4*(3), 325–364.

Mark, M. M., Mutrie, M., Brooks, D. R., & Harris, D. V. (1984). Causal attributions of winners and losers in individual competitive sports: Toward a reformulation of the self-serving bias. *Journal of Sport Psychology, 6*(2), 184–196.

Marshall, D. (2001). Mentoring as a development tool for women coaches. *Canadian Journal for Women in Coaching, 2*(2), 1496–1539.

Matheny, M., & Jenkins, J. B. (2015). *The Matheny manifesto: A young manager's old-school views on success in sport and life*. New York: Random House.

McAlpine, L., Oviedo, G. B., & Emrick, A. (2008). Telling the second half of the story: Linking academic development to student experience of learning. *Assessment & Evaluation in Higher Education, 33*(6), 661–673.

McQuade, S., Davis, L., & Nash, C. (2015). Positioning mentoring as a coach development tool: Recommendations for future practice and research. *Quest, 67*(3), 317–329.

Miller, D. T., & Ross, M. (1975). Self-serving biases in the attribution of causality: Fact or fiction? *Psychological Bulletin, 82*(2), 213–225.

Misener, K. E., & Danylchuk, K. E. (2009). Coaches' perceptions of Canada's national coaching certification program (NCCP): Awareness and value. *International Journal of Sports Science & Coaching, 4*(2), 233–243.

Moon, J. A. (2013). *A handbook of reflective and experiential learning: Theory and practice.* New York: Routledge Falmer.

Morehead, K., Rhodes, M. G., & DeLozier, S. (2016). Instructor and student knowledge of study strategies. *Memory, 24*, 257–271.

Mulligan, N. W., & Picklesimer, M. (2016). Attention and the testing effect. *Journal of Experimental Psychology: Learning, Memory, and Cognition, 42*(6), 938–950.

Murray, M. A., Zakrajsek, R. A., & Gearity, B. T. (2014). Developing effective internships in strength and conditioning: A community of practice approach. *Strength and Conditioning Journal, 36*(1), 35–40.

Nash, C. (2003). Development of a mentoring system within coaching practice. *Journal of Hospitality, Leisure, Sport and Tourism Education, 2*(2), 39–47.

Nash, C., Sproule, J., & Horton, P. (2017). Feedback for coaches: Who coaches the coach? *International Journal of Sports Science & Coaching, 12*(1), 92–102.

Nelson, L. J., & Cushion, C. J. (2006). Reflection in coach education: The case of the national governing body coaching certificate. *The Sport Psychologist, 20*, 174–183.

Nelson, L. J., Cushion, C. J., & Potrac, P. (2006). Formal, nonformal and informal coach learning: A holistic conceptualisation. *International Journal of Sports Science & Coaching, 1*(3), 247–259.

Nelson, L., Cushion, C., & Potrac, P. (2013). Enhancing the provision of coach education: The recommendations of UK coaching practitioners. *Physical Education and Sport Pedagogy, 18* (2), 204–218.

Nicholls, A. R. (2017). *Psychology in sports coaching: theory and practice.* New York: Routledge.

Nickerson, R. S. (1998). Confirmation bias: A ubiquitous phenomenon in many guises. *Review of General Psychology, 2*, 175–220.

Nisbett, R. E., Caputo, C., Legant, P., & Marecek, J. (1973). Behavior as seen by the actor and as seen by the observer. *Journal of Personality and Social Psychology, 27*, 154–164.

Nisbett, R. E., & Ross, L. (1980). *Human inference: Strategies and shortcomings of social judgment.* Englewood Cliffs, NJ: Prentice Hall.

Orbach, I., Singer, R. N., & Murphey, M. (1997). Changing attributions with an attribution retraining technique related to basketball dribbling. *The Sport Psychologist, 11*, 294–304.

Orbach, I., Singer, R. N., & Price, S. (1999). An attribution training program and achievement in sport. *The Sport Psychologist, 13*, 69–82.

Paquette, K., & Trudel, P. (2016). Learner-centered teaching: A consideration for revitalizing coach education. In P. A. Davis (Ed.), *The psychology of effective coaching and management* (pp. 53–71). New York: Nova.

Paquette, K., & Trudel, P. (2018). The evolution and learner-centered status of a coach education program. *International Sport Coaching Journal, 5*(1), 24–36.

Ragins, B. R., & Kram, K. E. (2007). *The handbook of mentoring at work: Theory, research, and practice.* Thousand Oaks, CA: Sage.

Rajsic, J., Wilson, D. E., & Pratt, J. (2015). Confirmation bias in visual search. *Journal Experimental Psychology: Human Perception and Performance, 41*(5), 1353–1364.

Rowland, C. A. (2014). The effect of testing versus restudy on retention: A meta-analytic review of the testing effect. *Psychological Bulletin, 140*, 1432–1463.

Rushall, B. S., & Wiznuk, K. (1985). Athletes' assessment of the coach—The Coach Evaluation Questionnaire. *Canadian Journal of Applied Sport Science, 10*(3), 157–161.

Rylander, P. (2015). Coaches' bases of power: Developing some initial knowledge of athletes' compliance with coaches in team sports. *Journal of Applied Sport Psychology, 27*, 110–121.

Schön, D. A. (1987). *Educating the reflective practitioner: Toward a new design for teaching and learning in the professions*. San Francisco: Jossey-Bass.

Schwarz, N. (2004). Metacognitive experiences in consumer judgement and decision making. *Journal of Consumer Psychology, 14*, 332–348.

Stodter, A., & Cushion, C. (2016). Effective coach learning and processes of coaches' knowledge development: What works? In P. A. Davis (Ed.), *The psychology of effective coaching and management* (pp. 35–52). New York: Nova.

Stodter, A., & Cushion, C. (2017). What works in coach learning, how, and for whom? A grounded process of soccer coaches' professional learning. *Qualitative Research in Sport, Exercise and Health, 9*(3), 321–338.

Stoszkowski, J., & Collins, D. (2016). Sources, topics and use of knowledge by coaches. *Journal of Sports Sciences, 34*(9), 794–802.

Tagg, J. (2003). *The learning paradigm college*. Bolton, MA: Anker.

Taylor, W. G., & Garratt, D. (2010). The professionalization of sports coaching: Relations of power, resistance and compliance. *Sport, Education and Society, 15*(1), 121–139.

Taylor, S., Werthner, P., & Culver, D. (2016). Dynamic, evolving, and social: The learning interactions of parasport coaches. In P. A. Davis (Ed.), *The psychology of effective coaching and management* (pp. 91–111). New York: Nova.

Trudel, P., Culver, D., & Werthner, P. (2013). Looking at coach development from the coach-learner's perspective. In P. Potrac, W. Gilbert, & J. Denison (Eds.), *Routledge handbook of sports coaching* (pp. 375–387). New York: Routledge.

Van Mullem, P., & Van Mullem, H. I. (2014). The learning process of a coach: Preferences of coaches in the United States. *Journal of Kinesiology and Wellness, 3*(1), 4–24.

Vella, S. A., Crowe, T. P., & Oades, L. G. (2013). Increasing the effectiveness of formal coach education: Evidence of a parallel process. *International Journal of Sports Science & Coaching, 8*(2), 417–430.

Wang, J., & Straub, W. F. (2012). An investigation into the coaching approach of a successful world class soccer coach: Anson Dorrance. *International Journal of Sports Science & Coaching, 7*(3), 431–447.

Weimer, M. (2002). *Learner-centered teaching: Five key changes to practice*. San Francisco: Wiley.

Weimer, M. (2013). *Learner-centered teaching: Five key changes to practice* (2nd ed.). San Francisco: Wiley.

Weinberg, R. (2010). Making goals effective: A primer for coaches. *Journal of Sport Psychology in Action, 1*(2), 57–65.

Weiner, B. (1972). *Theories of motivation: From mechanism to cognition*. Chicago: Rand McNally.

Weiner, B., Amirkhan, J., Folkes, V. S., & Verette, J. A. (1987). An attributional analysis of excuse giving: Studies of a naïve theory of emotion. *Journal of Personality and Social Psychology, 52* (2), 316–324.

Wenger, E. (1998). *Communities of practice: Learning, meaning, and identity*. Cambridge, UK: Cambridge University Press.

Werthner, P., Culver, D., & Trudel, P. (2012). An examination of a large-scale coach education program from a constructivist perspective. In R. Schinke (Ed.), *Sport psychology insights* (pp. 337–355). Nova.

Werthner, P., & Trudel, P. (2006). A new theoretical perspective for understanding how coaches learn to coach. *The Sport Psychologist, 20*(2), 198–212.

Weston, N. J. V., Greenlees, I. A., & Thelwell, R. C. (2011). Athlete perceptions of the impacts of performance profiling. *International Journal of Sport and Exercise Psychology, 9*(2), 173–188.

Whitehead, A. E., Cropley, B., Miles, T., Quayle, L., & Knowles, Z. (2016). Think aloud: Toward a framework to facilitate reflective practice amongst rugby league coaches. *International Sport Coaching Journal, 3*(3), 269–286.

Williams, J. M., Jerome, G. J., Kenow, L. J., Rogers, T., Sartain, T. A., & Darland, G. (2003). Factor structure of the Coaching Behavior Questionnaire and its relationship to athlete variables. *The Sport Psychologist, 17*, 16–34.
Winfield, J., Williams, J., & Dixon, M. (2013). The use of reflective practice to support mentoring of elite equestrian coaches. *International Journal of Evidence Based Coaching & Mentoring, 11* (1), 162–178.
Wooden, J., & Jamison, S. (2005). *Wooden on leadership*. New York: McGraw-Hill.

Andy Gillham is the lead performance psychology specialist in the Engineering and Applied Sciences department within Sanford Orthopedics and Sport Medicine in Sioux Falls, SD. Previoiusly, he owned his own consulting practice Ludus Consulting LLC (www.ludusconsulting.biz) focusing on performance enhancement for his clients. More specifically, Dr. Gillham works primarily with coaches and athletic administrators on improving systematic coach evaluation and providing targeted coach and program professional development opportunities. His Ph.D. is in Education with a major of sport and exercise psychology from the University of Idaho and has a B.S. in Fitness and a M.S. in Human Performance from University Wisconsin-LaCrosse. He has been a Certified Strength and Conditioning Specialist through the National Strength and Conditioning Association since 2003 and is a Certified Mental Performance Consultant through the Association for Applied Sport Psychology. Dr. Gillham has helped athletes, coaches, administrators and business executives in Canada and the United States improve their performance. Dr. Gillham works across competitive levels ranging from youth through professional levels for both coaches and athletes. In addition to his applied work, he is also an Editorial Board member for *International Journal of Sports Science & Coaching; NSCA-Coach; PHE America,* and an Associate Editor for *International Sport Coaching Journal.*

Pete Van Mullem is an Associate Professor at Lewis-Clark State College (ID) and has over 14 years of professional experience in coaching and athletic administrative positions at the junior high, high school, small college, NCAA Division II and Division I level. He currently serves on the Editorial Board for the International Sport Coaching Journal (ISCJ) and the Editorial Team for PHE America. Dr. Van Mullem recently served as a member of the National Standards for Sport Coaches Revision Task Force (2017-2019).

At LCSC, Dr. Van Mullem is the creator and director of the Annual Dr. Bob Frederick Sport Leadership Lecture Series, held every October on the campus of Lewis-Clark State College. In 6 years the lecture series has welcomed over 100 leaders in the sport industry to share insight and expertise with the LCSC Community. Dr. Van Mullem received his doctorate in Sport Ethics from the University of Idaho and his scholarly interests focus on coach development and ethical sport leadership. He has authored over 40 articles related to coach development.

Chapter 21
Coaching and Effective Leaders: An Overview and Recommended Research Agenda

Marshall Magnusen, Jun Woo Kim, and Matt Robinson

A leader is one who knows the way, goes the way, and shows the way.
– John C. Maxwell

Abstract This chapter is about sports coaching and implications for future research, with specific attention being given to the area of leadership in coaching. Foundational information about leadership is provided. The leadership content is connected to the areas of relational exchanges and culture development. A brief overview of these areas and how they connect to leadership in coaching is an important precursor to the identification of limitations present in the coaching research literature. Without first understanding the basics of leadership and how it impacts essential organizational and team processes such as relationship and cultural building, it is difficult to arrive at recommendations for improving the study of sport coaches as organizational (team) leaders. The chapter also focuses on social effectiveness to introduce readers to an understudied yet essential area of scholarly inquiry that would greatly enhance the leadership effectiveness of coaches. Social effectiveness research is summarized before singling out the concept of political skill as a social effectiveness construct that may hold particular significance to the advancement of leadership and coaching research. The chapter concludes with a brief overview of coaching research and the presentation of an agenda for improving the study of social effectiveness and leadership in the sport sciences.

M. Magnusen (✉)
Department of Educational Leadership, Baylor University, Waco, TX, USA
e-mail: Marshall_Magnusen@baylor.edu

J. W. Kim
School of Global Business, Arcadia University, Glenside, PA, USA
e-mail: kimjw@arcadia.edu

M. Robinson
Department of Exercise Science, Schreiner University, Kerrville, TX, USA
e-mail: MRobinson@schreiner.edu

R. Resende, A. R. Gomes (eds.), *Coaching for Human Development and Performance in Sports*, https://doi.org/10.1007/978-3-030-63912-9_21

Keywords Leadership · Cultural building · Social effectiveness

Coaching is a leadership process that is profoundly relational in nature. Coaches, in their roles as team leaders, craft culture and engage in numerous interpersonal relationships (Laios, Theodorakis, & Gargalianos, 2003). Indeed, achievement in coaching (and life generally) stems in large part from meaningful and successful social exchanges (Ferris, Davidson, & Perrewé, 2005; Magnusen, Kim, & Perrewé, 2014). It is therefore quite surprising that in both the sport coaching and management literatures, scholars have directed minimal attention to better understanding social effectiveness (Magnusen & Perrewé, 2016). That is, exploring why exactly some coaches are better at social exchanges and building personal connections than other coaches. The lack of attention is especially astounding considering the ways in which coaches engage in leader behaviors, such as building relationships with their followers, will notably contribute to the success of their actions (Aditya & House, 2002; Côté, Salmela, Trudel, & Baria, 1995; Knowles, Gilbourne, Borrie, & Nevill, 2001).

Although sport coaching represents a multifaceted social process that is constituted and sustained via mutual, interpersonal relationships (Cushion, 2007), few research efforts have been made to better understand both what leaders do and how they do it. Consider how in a review of social effectiveness in sport management research, Magnusen and Perrewé (2016) reported that only a handful of studies evaluate social effectiveness and that, at best, sport textbooks on leadership and management devote several pages to the topic. Further evidence of the lack of attention to this area is evident in a pair of critical reviews conducted on sport coaching and coaching education. Neither the review by Griffo, Jensen, Anthony, Baghurst, and Kulinna (2019), which included data from 2005 to 2015, nor the review McCullick, Schempp, Mason, Foo, Vickers, and Connolly (2009), which covered coaching data for a period of 13 years after 1995, included social effectiveness. Moreover, in terms of areas of future research, social effectiveness was not recommended as a key area for future scholarship.

Accordingly, in this chapter, the conversation on coaching is steered in the direction of social effectiveness, with special consideration being given to the social effectiveness construct of political skill. Examining relationships and the environments (culture) in which those social exchanges transpire is central to understanding sport organizational behavior. The social dynamic components of dyadic (individual) and team interactions contribute immensely to the success of coaches' actions (Cushion, 2007). Correspondingly, leaders who are social effectively are more likely to be successful than their less socially effective peers (Douglas & Ammeter, 2004; Gentry et al., 2013; Magnusen & Kim, 2016; Robinson, Magnusen, & Kim, 2019). Therefore, studying how coaches lead (instead of just what coaches do when leading) through interpersonal relationships and the formation and maintenance of an organizational culture is an important and underappreciated area of scholarship that can significantly advance the study and practice of coaching.

Figure 21.1 provides a visual outline of this chapter's content. The chapter begins with an overview of fundamental leadership concepts. Leadership content is then

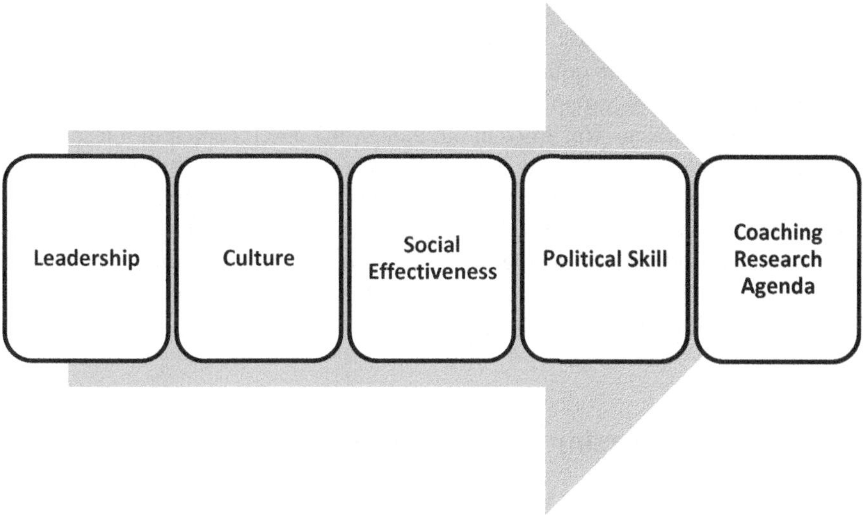

Fig. 21.1 Overview of coaching and leadership chapter content

linked to the areas of culture and relational exchanges. Discussing these areas makes clear the importance of leadership and how leadership impacts crucial organizational and team practices. Next, the chapter focuses on social effectiveness, an area that represents an immensely salient yet understudied area of coaching scholarship. Research on social effectiveness is consolidated before the concept of political skill is identified as a relatively new social effectiveness construct that may hold particular value to the progression of leadership and coaching research.

Leadership at a Glance

The current coaching and sport management literatures are inundated with definitions of leadership. Consequently, the wide array of views concerning leadership can be confusing because there is no single agreed upon definition of leadership. Consider the following observation from Klenke (1994, p. 326):

> Leadership has been defined, constructed and researched from a bewildering number of conceptual perspectives including trait and contingency theories, normative decision theories, leader-follower exchange theories, behavioral and managerial approaches, multiple linkage, transactional, transformational, charismatic and self-leadership. Each of these models has generated its own definitions of leadership, produced a large amount of empirical evidence, yet has failed to serve as the basis for a generally accepted knowledge base.

Bearing that in mind, a relatively straightforward definition of leadership is "the interpersonal influence exercised by a person or persons, through the process of communication, toward the attainment of an organization's goals" (Russell, 2005,

p. 16). Similarly, Yukl and van Fleet (1992) referred to leadership as "a process that includes influencing the task objectives and strategies of a group or organization, influencing people in the organization to implement the strategies and achieve the objectives, influencing group maintenance and identification, and influencing the culture of organizations" (p. 149). In all, though the interpretation of a leader may vary from scholar to scholar and from discipline to discipline, most definitions of a leader (regardless of whether the context of the leader is coaching or corporate) include three important elements. The first element is that leadership is a behavioral process. Next, leadership is interpersonal in nature. Finally, leadership is intended to influence and motivate members toward a set of individual-level, team-level, and/or organizational-level goals (Chelladurai, 2007).

Connecting Leadership and Interpersonal Relationships

Amidst myriad theories considered to explore leadership, a perspective that is often used to understand the interactions that take place between leaders and their followers/subordinates is leader-member exchange (LMX) theory (Dansereau, Graen, & Haga, 1975; Graen & Uhl-Bien, 1995). LMX theory is different from other leadership paradigms in that it positions leadership as a relational exchange between a leader and a subordinate rather than something done to subordinates (Walumbwa, Cropanzano, & Goldman, 2012). Specifically, LMX represents "(a) a system of components and their relationships, (b) involving both members of a dyad, (c) involving interdependent patterns of behavior, (d) sharing mutual outcome instrumentalities, and (e) producing conceptions of environments, cause maps, and values" (Scandura, Graen, & Novak, 1986, p. 580).

Interactions in any work environment—be they a traditional corporate setting or the realm of sports—are going to vary in terms of relationship quality (Graen & Uhl-Bien, 1995; Henderson, Wayne, Shore, Bommer, & Tetrick, 2008). The frequency of interactions between leaders and their subordinates as well as the quality of those exchanges are two variables (among numerous others) unlikely to be constant over time. Accordingly, LMX theory incorporates a basic categorization scheme originating from leaders differing levels of relational quality with their subordinates.

An argument put forth with LMX theory is that leaders categorize subordinates into two groups: an out-group and an in-group (Graen & Uhl-Bien, 1995). In-groups and out-groups emerge over time from the relationships between leaders and their subordinates. Those who are part of the in-group may benefit from greater access to the leader, more input in decisions, and more responsibilities. Individuals who are part of the out-group tend to have diminished roles in team functions, fewer opportunities for growth and development, and less personalized leader interactions that tend to be based on the hierarchical authority of the leader (Graen & Uhl-Bien, 1995; Walumbwa et al., 2012). A member of a sport team who is part of the in-group, for example, may be given more responsibilities and afforded more organizational resources (e.g., extra funding for continuing education) than a staff member who is not part of the leader's in-group.

Additionally, though the traditional focus of LMX research is leader-follower dyads, contemporary scholars have expanded the scope of this research area to include group-level occurrences (Thomas, Martin, Epitropaki, Guillaume, & Lee, 2013). This expansion takes into consideration that a dyadic relationship between a leader and a follower likely transpires within the context of numerous other LMX relationships (Anand, Vidyarthi, & Park, 2015). Specific to sports and coaching, this means that the interactions between the head coach and a particular assistant coach or player do not occur in isolation of other relationships. Coaches manage many relationships in their leadership role, and the extent to which LMX impacts sport team or organization outcomes is likely to stem from both high-quality individual relationships as well as the management of multiple LMX relationships within the same context.

A leader developing varied LMX relationships with different members of a team has been termed the LMX differentiation process (Epitropaki et al., 2016). LMX differentiation is:

> a process by which a leader, through engaging in differing types of exchange patterns with subordinates, forms different quality exchange relationships (ranging from low to high) with them. As such, LMX differentiation refers to a set and outcome of dynamic and interactive exchanges that occur between leaders and members, the nature of which...may differ across dyads within a work group (Henderson, Liden, Glibkowski, & Chaudhry, 2009, p. 519).

The focus of LMX differentiation is on the variances in LMX quality within a particular organization or team. If a team experiences high levels of LMX differentiation, the LMX relationships between the leader and followers will be varied and in- and out-group differences may be more pronounced because of the presence of both highly personalized and depersonalized relational exchanges. Conversely, teams with low levels of LMX differentiation may still experience in-groups and out-groups but overall the relationships between a leader and his or her followers will be relatively steady and uniform. Meaning, team members generally get the same amount of time with their leader, similar quantities of resources, and consistent performance expectations (Herdman, Yang, & Arthur, 2014; Wu, Tsui, & Kinicki, 2010).

Leadership is an essential aspect of coaching that requires these individuals to be involved in numerous, sometimes untidy, dyads (Cushion, Armour, & Jones, 2003; Laios et al., 2003). Coach-player dyads exist. Coach-assistant coach dyads exist. Numerous dyads exist. Each dyad takes place within an environment consisting of numerous relational exchanges between the head coach and his or her athletes and coaching staff members. To be successful and effective leaders, coaches must carefully navigate the complexities of various dyadic exchanges to create team cohesion and a culture that, though likely to consist of in-groups and out-groups, attempts to make each individual feel included and representative of an important component for overall team success (Case, 1998; Turman, 2003).

Organizational Culture at a Glance

Similar to the study of leadership, the prevailing literature on organizational behavior is inundated with research exploring organizational culture. Indeed, academicians and practitioners across the sport and management disciplines have attempted to define the construct, investigate its importance (or lack of), and provide a rundown of common traits present in successful organizational cultures. Though team culture—the culture of a specific team within the broader context of an organization (e.g., athletic department, professional sport organization)—is distinctive from organizational culture in terms of scope, the fundamental elements of team and organizational culture are the same. That is, the focus of culture regardless of whether it is broad (e.g., organizational culture of a college athletic department) or team-specific (e.g., culture of the basketball team within a college athletic department) centers on creating shared values and beliefs that help guide the behaviors of those who are part of the culture.

The focus of this book chapter is coaches and by extension, team culture more so than organizational culture (in a traditional, managerial sense). However, for the sake of simplicity and reader accessibility, the term, *organizational culture*, is used to capture the essence of culture in the context of sport coaching. This should not prove problematic because of the definitional and conceptual similarity of the two concepts as well as the fact that much of the literature on managing culture discusses the concept using organizational culture terminology rather than team culture terminology.

Great interest in the exploration of culture originates in part from its potential to propel an organization to the top of an industry or conversely, stifle its long-term success potential due to the prominence of undesirable behaviors. Culture matters because the type of behaviors and attitudes accepted and perpetuated within any team or organization will significantly impact its success (Sørensen, 2002). Culture, as an organizational behavior phenomenon, is generally thought to represent a set of shared, taken-for-granted inherent conventions (expectations) that a group holds and that controls how it sees, thinks about, and responds to its different environments (Schein, 2010). For instance, a coach might create a culture within his or her sport team that encourages transparency, open communication, and respect between athletes. These aspects of the culture, though not formally written and expressed in an official document, are still adopted as part of the culture of the team.

Similarly, Deshpande and Webster (1989) framed organizational culture as "the pattern of shared values and beliefs that help individuals understand organizational functioning and thus provide them with norms for behavior in the organization" (p. 4). As well, Ogbonna and Harris (2002) described organizational culture as "the collective sum of beliefs, values, meanings and assumptions that are shared by a social group and that help to shape the ways in which they respond to each other and to their external environment" (p. 34). Overall, what should be clear from the provided definitions is that culture has the potential to positively (or negatively) impact team-level and organizational-level processes when the values, beliefs, and behaviors of those within the organization are conducive (deleterious) to success.

Consider the case of the Australian swimming team at the London 2012 Olympics. After a dismal swimming team performance, which saw the Australians take home only a single gold medal and ten swimming medals collectively (the worst swimming performance for the country in two decades), several external reviews were conducted to determine the cause of the lackluster performance. The conclusions from both reports were nearly identical. A lack of leadership and a toxic team culture, inclusive of bullying, drinking, and prescription drug abuse, were key contributors to the team failures (Rose, 2013).

Connecting Culture to Leadership and Relational Exchanges

A relationship exists between leadership and organization success (Klimoski & Koles, 2001). Coaches in a leadership role have innumerable responsibilities within sport organizations, including vision creation and energizing others to take action (Bennis & Goldsmith, 1997), each of which can contribute to organizational productivity. To be successful, leaders must possess the ability to build meaningful relationships with followers and peers; they also must possess interpersonal influence so that they can move groups of people, such as a team, toward a desired future that requires shared values, focused effort, and the establishment of joint purposes (Cushion, 2007; Ferris, Perrewé, & Douglas, 2002). That is how in part championships are won. Coaches must harness, unify, and direct the knowledges, skills, and abilities of a diverse collection of athletic talent toward the accomplishment of shared goals and a team vision.

The notion that leadership is grounded in relationships and influence, which in turn align values and mutual purposes, is where the link to organizational culture is quite evident. Leaders have significant bearing on the creation, transmission, and maintenance of culture because it is the leader who initiates and maintains changes in the sport environment. Schein (1985) even went so far as to remark that creating and managing culture is the only thing of real importance that leaders do on a daily basis. Culture influences the behaviors of followers (Meng & Berger, 2019) and leaders directly influence LMX relationships and the creation of culture; culture correspondingly impacts how LMX relationships are formed, perceived, and maintained (Herrera, Duncan, & Ree, 2013). Thus, the importance of leaders developing relationships with their followers as well as developing and then managing a team's culture (which includes the ways in which relationships are formed and then sustained) cannot be understated.

How Leaders Do What They Do: The Importance of Social Effectiveness

Discussed up to this point have been several important elements of the leadership role of coaches. The concept of leadership has been defined and connected to relationship formation. Leadership also has been connected to creation and maintenance of organizational culture. The introduction and brief discussion of these areas is important to the study of coaching because if sport teams are to be successful, they require a competent and effective leader who can build multiple relationships with diverse groups of people, influence others, build a positive and constructive culture, and then effectively manage the culture (Ferris et al., 2005). Unfortunately, as observed in the introduction section to this chapter, insufficient scholarly attention has been given to the actual social dynamic components that contribute to leaders being able to successfully interact with others and facilitate the develop of a positive and constructive organizational culture. Therefore, in an effort to bridge a gap in the coaching literature, social effectiveness is connected to the leadership role of coaches.

In a broad sense, leader social effectiveness refers to his or her social competencies, such as the ability to social monitor, network, build relationships, adapt to situations and people, inspire trust, and understand the motivations of others (Ferris et al., 2002). Interest in this area stems from social interactions being a fact of life—both in and outside of work—and that certain individuals are noticeable more successful in their social exchanges than others. Consider the hypothetical scenario of two professional sport team coaches.

Prior to coaching, two coaches had successful careers as professional athletes. Each coach, when a player, had roughly the same career statistics and similar levels of career success. Now, each coach is employed by a reputable professional sport team. In this role, each coach is again, not noticeably distinguishable from the other. In sum, if each coach were to interact with the same athletes and peers, their professional backgrounds and sport experiences would not bias the audience for or against them. With variables such as those being equal, certain coaches are still going to be better able to connect with athletes and peers. Indeed, two coaches can engage in the same sorts of behaviors with the exact same audience and be perceived in radically different ways based on the style (the manner) in which they executed their behaviors (Magnusen, Kim, Perrewé, & Ferris, 2014). Thus, when studying coaches, it is important to not just pay attention to their backgrounds and what they do but also consider how they execute their actions.

Education, professional experiences, and intelligence can all contribute to career success but alone these factors may not be sufficient to achieve career success. Consideration needs to be given to individuals' levels of social effectiveness (Ferris, Treadway, et al., 2005; Magnusen, Kim, Perrewe et al., 2014). For example, a 2006 national study on the nonrenewal of interscholastic sport coaches (Miller, Lutz, Shim, Fredenburg, & Miller, 2006) cited poor coach relations with administration and parents as the top reason for coach dismissal or non-renewal of contract. Other reasons for dismissal cited in the study were coach misconduct and having poor player discipline. It stands to reason that a socially effective leader might avoid these pitfalls and that developing political skill and gaining an understanding of the immediate political landscape has become a crucial element of effective leadership and a successful career in coaching.

An effective leader is a relationship manager who participates in socially effective strategies to influence others' impressions of them and generate support necessary to achieve the objectives of the program (Ferris, Davidson, et al., 2005; Potrac & Jones, 2009). Being proficient in social competencies is necessary to orchestrate these interaction-based outcomes (Ferris, Perrewé, Anthony, & Gilmore, 2000). Thus, a combination of the positive connection between leader effectiveness and social effectiveness as found in a business setting and the importance placed on coaches to be effective leaders lend support to expanding research in the area of various social skills and leader effectiveness among sport coaches.

Examining the style through which leaders conducts themselves is an area of scholarship that advances the study of coaching by elucidating what exactly contributes to leader effectiveness. Think about coach-athlete dyads. Coaches engage in social exchanges with athletes who are part of the in-group and the out-group. If coaches are socially effective, they should be more adept at recognizing the existence of such groups, connecting with members of the out-group, improving relationships with out-group members, and creating a culture that recognizes and appreciates the contributions—however small—of each team member (Case, 1998; Magnusen & Kim, 2016). Therefore, the value of social effectiveness research to sport coaches and scholars is that it combines interest in what coaching behaviors are performed with consideration for how those behaviors are performed.

Provided next in this chapter is short overview of the social influence literature. Social effectiveness includes numerous operationalizations, some of which are more useful than others (Magnusen & Perrewé, 2016). An overview of key social effectiveness constructs is provided before singling out political skill as a specific social effectiveness construct that may hold the most practical and research significance to coaching. Once political skill is explained the chapter transitions to a discussion of several research areas that will improve the study of coaching, with particular attention being paid to social effectiveness and how research in this area can enhance understanding of leadership effectiveness and why certain coaches are better at building relationships and culture.

Social Effectiveness Constructs at a Glance

Social effectiveness is an umbrella term that encompasses the wide array of moderately-connected yet conceptually different approaches to understanding social awareness and capability. Indeed, a wide variety of social effectiveness constructs have been offered, including "social intelligence, emotional intelligence, practical intelligence, self-monitoring, social skill, social competence, political skill, ego

Table 21.1 Summary of key social effectiveness constructs

Construct	Definition	Results relevant to leadership, LMX, and culture
Emotional Intelligence (EI)	Salovey and Mayer (1990) viewed it as the ability to recognize, evaluate, and utilize one's own emotions to guide thoughts and behaviors. Goleman (1995) framed it as intelligence applied to the life domain of emotions	Linked to LMX and follower commitment (Minsu, Mayfield, Hinojosa, & Yooshin, 2018). Can contribute to the type of organizational culture that is created. Leader EI can influence follower task performance and citizenship behaviors (Miao, Humphrey, & Qian, 2018). EI also may influence follower perceptions of leader effectiveness in sport organizations (Megheirkouni, 2019)
Political Skill	Ability to understand others in a work environment and then use that understanding (knowledge) to influence them to act in ways that enhance individual and organizational goals. Includes social astuteness, interpersonal influence, networking ability, and apparent sincerity (Ferris, Treadway, et al., 2005)	Enhances relationship quality between leaders and their followers (Brouer, Douglas, Treadway, & Ferris, 2013; Magnusen & Kim, 2016). Improves follower perceptions of leader effectiveness (Douglas & Ammeter, 2004). Specific to sport, politically skilled leaders have increased subordinate levels of job satisfaction and commitment (Robinson et al., 2019)
Self-Monitoring	Includes social perceptiveness. Ability to perceive a social environment and adapt words and deeds accordingly. Being skilled at controlling emotional expressions to craft an effective impression (Snyder, 1974)	Influences how followers perceive a leader, which can impact social exchanges and followers' commitment levels (Türetgen, Unsal, & Dural, 2017). Results in increases in variability of leader behaviors across situations in response to follower (Sosik, Potosky, & Jung, 2002
Social Intelligence	Possessing situational awareness plus the ability to then act appropriately in diverse environments with the aim of achieving desired social goals (Archer, 1980)	Expected to produce stronger relationships with superiors, enhanced relationships with subordinates, and greater career success (Goleman & Boyatzis, 2008). Shown to influence organizational creativity (Rahim, 2014) and how followers perceive the culture of an organization (e.g., just or unjust) (Nazarpoori, 2017)

resiliency, interpersonal intelligence, sociopolitical intelligence, interpersonal acumen, functional flexibility, and social self-efficacy" (Ferris et al., 2002, p. 49). Given the breadth and depth yet lack of synergy found within the study of social effectiveness, this section of the chapter offers an overview of several prevalent approaches to categorizing social effectiveness. Table 21.1 defines and summarizes relevant research for the following approaches to social effectiveness: emotional intelligence (EI), political skill, self-monitoring, and social intelligence.

The Importance of Political Skill

Political skill is a social effectiveness construct that has benefitted from a rise in popularity and application to the context of sport over the past decade (Magnusen & Perrewé, 2016). Of late, the study of political skill in sport has been directed to a variety of research areas. These areas include coach and athletic director effectiveness (Magnusen & Kim, 2016; Robinson et al., 2019), recruiting effectiveness in intercollegiate athletics (Magnusen, Kim, Perrewe, et al., 2014; Treadway et al., 2014), and career success (Ellen, 2016; Kim, Wells, Chan, & Kim, 2016; Magnusen & Kim, 2016).

A widely used definition of political skill is that it represents the ability to effectively understand others at work and to use this level of understanding to then influence others (e.g., peers, subordinates, superiors) to behavior in ways that improve the odds of accomplishing personal and/or organizational goals (Ferris, Treadway, et al., 2005). Political skill is a multi-dimensional construct consisting of four key dimensions: social astuteness, interpersonal influence, networking ability, and apparent sincerity. Although the extent which individuals are naturally politically skilled may vary, the social effectiveness construct is highly trainable. Meaning, any coach can become politically skilled so long as they were willing to train themselves to be more socially competent leaders (Ferris, Treadway, et al., 2005; Magnusen, Kim, Perrewe, et al., 2014; Magnusen & Perrewé, 2016). Figure 21.2 provides a brief overview of each of the four dimensions of political skill.

Though not the only available social effectiveness construct, when compared to the alternatives, political skill appears to be the strongest social competency option to examine in the context of sport (Magnusen & Perrewé, 2016; Perrewe & Ferris,

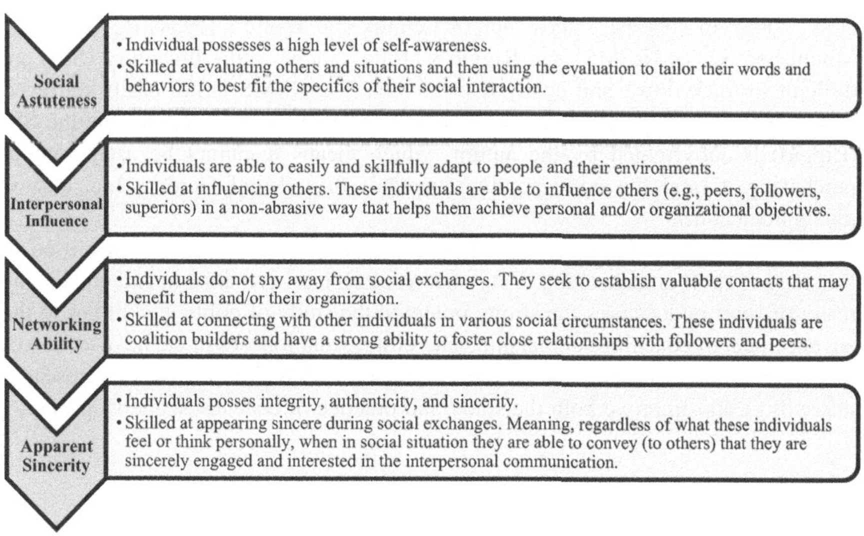

Fig. 21.2 Four dimensions of political skill

2016). In a study by Banister and Meriac (2015), for example, the authors examined the proportion of variance explained by political skill in job satisfaction and turnover intention above and beyond what is explained by other social effectiveness constructs. Political skill was studied alongside social intelligence, emotional intelligence, agreeableness, and conscientious. The results showed that political skill was the strongest predictor of the focal outcomes and also explained a significant proportion of variance that exceeded the other social effectiveness options. A previous study by Semander, Robins, and Ferris (2006) reported similar results. Political skill was compared to self-monitoring, self-efficacy, and EI to determine which social effectiveness construct was the strongest predictor of job performance. The authors reported that political skill was the best predictor.

Additionally, though conceptually overlapping with other social effectiveness constructs, political skill is distinctive in that it explicitly focuses on becoming knowledgeable about people and situations and then leveraging that information with social influence skills to achieve personal and/or professional success (Ferris, Treadway, et al., 2005; Perrewe & Ferris, 2016). Other social effectiveness constructs, such as EI, self-monitoring, and self-regulation, do not account for interpersonal influence. That is a noteworthy distinction considering the ability to sway others is essential for leaders to possess if they are going to build relationships and facilitate a productive organizational culture (Magnusen & Perrewé, 2016).

As well, there are the matters of reliability and validity. Political skill is measured using the 18-item Political Skill Inventory (PSI) and as a construct, political skill has demonstrated strong factorial validity (Ferris et al., 2008; Ferris, Treadway, et al., 2005). Comparable social effectiveness constructs (e.g., EI, self-monitoring) lack valid and psychometrically sound measures. The PSI (Ferris, Treadway, et al., 2005) is also accessible, being available to general audiences through the original research piece as well as the popular press book, *Political Skill at Work* (Ferris, Davidson, et al., 2005). In contrast, scales such as Lennox and Wolfe's (1984) Revised Self-Monitoring Scales (RSMS) and Riggio's (1986) Social Skills Inventory (SSI) are difficult to track down and costly respectively. The RSMS is not easily retrieved absent access to an online database such a Business Source Complete and the SSI (Riggio) is copyrighted by the author, which means it cannot be used without purchasing it (and the corresponding manual) from Mind Garden, Inc. (www.mindgarden.com).

Collectively, social effectiveness constructs have only been minimally used in the study of sport and coaching. Yet, what research has been done in and outside the realm of sport underscores the strong potential the study of political skill has to the advancement of coaching scholarship. Therefore, what follows in the next section of this chapter is the presentation of several avenues of social effectiveness research that will greatly improve both the study and practice of coaches' leadership roles.

Advancing the Study of Coaching: Methodological Recommendations

A chasm exists that divides the worlds of academic research and coaching practice. Academic research in sport is often theoretical and impractical whereas practice-driven scholarship is often atheoretical but much more applied (Stober & Parry, 2005). Even on the academic side there are divides when it comes to theoretical frameworks and agreeing upon definitions of leadership, coaching, and career success and how coaching and leadership should be researched (Griffo et al., 2019; Magnusen & Perrewé, 2016). Though thoroughly evaluating the divide between academic scholarship and coaching practice exceeds the scope of this chapter, recommendations can still be made that will greatly enhance the study and practice of coaching. Accordingly, provided in the following section of this chapter are suggestions for improving coaching research. The recommendations are divided into operational and methodological areas.

Operationalizing Coaching Research

Operationalization is a process of defining a concept that is not measurable (i.e., latent constructs like political skill and coaching satisfaction). The value of more carefully considering operationalization is that the process will help researchers define an ambiguous concept so as to make it clearly distinguishable and measurable via empirical testing. For example, although coaching researchers have developed numerous leadership frameworks (e.g., transformational leadership model, Rowold, 2006; cognitive-mediational model, Smoll & Smith, 1989; servant leadership model, Rieke, Hammermeister, & Chase, 2008), there is a lack of cohesiveness when it comes to definitions of coaching leadership that underpin the processes, knowledge, and behaviors involved in the development of athletes. When a coaching scholar examines the impact of coaching leadership, he or she is then forced to operationalize the concept of coaching leadership before the data collection.

Overall, the absence of critical reviews and analyses of published work on coaching and leadership may limit the potential of researchers to set research agendas and bridge the academic-practitioner divide. As a result, we recommend coaching scholars recognize the need for developing a dialogue with coaching professionals in order to develop theoretical frameworks which inform principle of practices as well as research designs and methods which are testable. Creating standardized and reliable measures will help establish the internal consistency of operationalized sport leadership and coaching concepts. A simplified process of operationalizing the effectiveness of coaching and leadership is offered in Fig. 21.3.

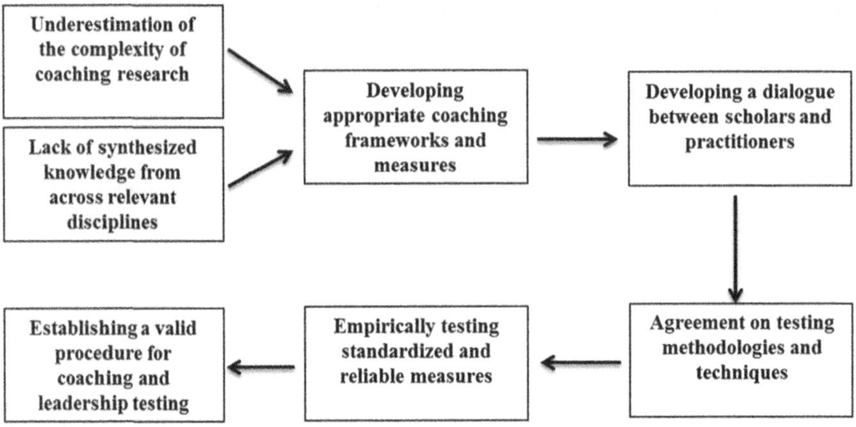

Fig. 21.3 The process of operationalizing coaching and leadership research

Methodological Suggestions

There has been much development in sports coaching research over the past several decades, and the development has been primarily in the usage of methodologies borrowed from other disciplines (e.g., psychology, education, management) that bring to coaching an increased sophistication of data analysis and data presentation. However, the dominance of one research paradigm has led researchers to focus more on hypothesis testing than on the development of new explanatory theories and rich, descriptive detail. Indeed, researchers mainly use a quantitative approach to study coaching, which is similar to what scholars in sport psychology and sport management employ (Chelladurai & Riemer, 1998; Griffo et al., 2019).

The characteristics of a quantitative approach include sampling method (e.g., random vs. non-random sampling), deductive reasoning, sample size (e.g., large vs. small size), and statistical data analysis techniques. Less frequently employed research methods include qualitative and mixed-method efforts (Griffo et al., 2019), which means that much of what is known about coaches is driven by empirical studies rather than observation-based, non-numerical exploratory efforts or the combination both approaches. Future research in the area of coaching would benefit greatly from mixed methodology.

The value of mixed method research to the advancement of coaching and leadership studies is that the findings from one method can be enhanced via the usage of another method. Meaning, qualitative methods can be used to generate new theory and quantitative methods can be used to test the theory or quantitative methods can be used to examine a phenomenon and qualitative methods can then be employed to clarify the results (Rudd & Johnson, 2010). This combination of methods promotes shared responsibility in the pursuit of attaining accountability and credibility with coaching and leadership research quality. Consider the following hypothetical scenario.

Imagine a scenario in which a leadership style failed to improve athlete trust and commitment. The data analysis shows the leadership style did not show a direct significant relationship with the desired outcomes which, depending on the leadership style, might prove puzzling. In response, qualitative follow up could be conducted to better understand the nature of the relationship and why the leader style did not have the anticipated impact on athlete trust and commitment.

Next, consider a scenario that begins with qualitative inquiry. Researchers are interested in understanding the characteristics of an effective coach serving in a leadership role. Even so, they are not quite sure where to begin their study. So, prior to empirical analysis, the researchers examine the nature of effective coaching in order to identify constructs and an appropriate, testable research model. Then, having gathered sufficient qualitative information, the researchers can engage in a quantitative phase and gather empirical information that either confirms or rejects the observational information they gathered. Thus, regardless of whether a study starts qualitative or quantitative, the appropriate combination of these two approaches can be employed to improve how the leadership role of coaches is understood.

Advancing the Study of Coaching: Research Agenda Recommendations

Several specific research agendas are explored in this section. The research agendas build on the previous sections of this chapter by focusing on leader social effectiveness and how the construct of political skill can be applied to sport studies on leadership, LMX, and culture.

Research on Leadership and Political Skill

Few areas of scholarship have received more critical attention than the area of leadership. Of late, there has been a movement in organizations to focus on positive forms of leadership that engage all stakeholders (Van Dierendonck, 2011). This has given way to a rise in interest of servant leadership, a style based on enduring qualities of genuine caring, empathy, and humility and focused on developing quality relationships with subordinates (Robinson, Neubert, & Miller, 2018). Servant leadership is not only focused on meeting follower needs and inspiring follower growth, but also on empowering followers to perform at the highest levels of quality (Stone, Russell, & Patterson, 2004).

Though growing in popularity as an avenue of leadership studies, servant leadership is not a new approach to leadership. Indeed, Greenleaf coined the term, "servant leader," in his book, *The Servant as Leader*, back in 1970. His description of a servant leader, which remains popular to this day, is as follows (Greenleaf, 1977, p. 27):

> The servant leader is servant first... It begins with the natural feeling that one wants to serve, to serve first. Then conscious choice brings one to aspire to lead... The best test, and difficult to administer is this: Do those served grow as persons? Do they, while being served, become healthier, wiser, freer, more autonomous, and more likely themselves to become servants: And what is the effect on the least privileged in society? Will they benefit, or at least not further be harmed?

Given that the practice of leadership has evolved in many sport organizations from leader-focused, controlling relationships to an emphasis on follower-focused relationships and empowering organizational cultures (Burton & Peachey, 2013; Robinson et al., 2018), it is surprising that this area has not benefitted from more scholarly attention. Indeed, the first empirical study on servant leadership with coaches was published by Hammermeister et al. (2008) whereas servant leadership in traditional business contexts has been researched since the 1970s. Though lacking an extensive body of scholarship, what research has been done with servant leadership and coaches elevates support for the idea that servant leaders benefit athletes by improving their task-orientation, intrinsic motivation, athletic success, and levels of satisfaction (Cho & Kim, 2014; Hammermeister et al. 2008; Rieke et al., 2008).

Servant leadership also connects well to social effectiveness research because servant leadership requires leaders to be effective influencers. For instance, servant leadership has been linked to enhancing trust relationships between coaches and athletes (Kim, Kim, & Wells, 2017) as well as positively influencing the ethical culture development within sport organizations (Burton, Welty Peachey, & Wells, 2017). Thus, servant leadership is connected to both leader-follower relationships and culture. Nevertheless, what requires significantly more attention is what factor—or collection of factors—best enable servant leaders to be the greatest possible influencers (Neubert, Hunter, & Tolentino, 2016). Specifically, the social effectiveness construct of political skill needs to be examined in connection to servant leadership.

Servant leadership may influence a variety of outcomes, including athlete commitment, satisfaction, turnover intention, LMX quality, adoption of organizational culture, creativity, and wellbeing. What then needs to be understood is how exactly servant leadership influences those outcomes. That is, investigating the moderating role of political skill on the relationships between servant leadership and any number of the available outcomes that enhance understanding of how coaches can be more effective leaders. For example, scholars could examine the extent to which coach political skill moderates the relationship between servant leadership and athlete commitment and satisfaction levels (see Fig. 21.4). Whether political skill moderates the ability of coaches to facilitate high-quality LMX relationships is another area worth studying. Ultimately, given that servant leadership and political skill are both understudied and important areas of research, the applications of these areas to coaching are only limited by the ability and imagination of the individuals looking to examine these concepts in the context of sport.

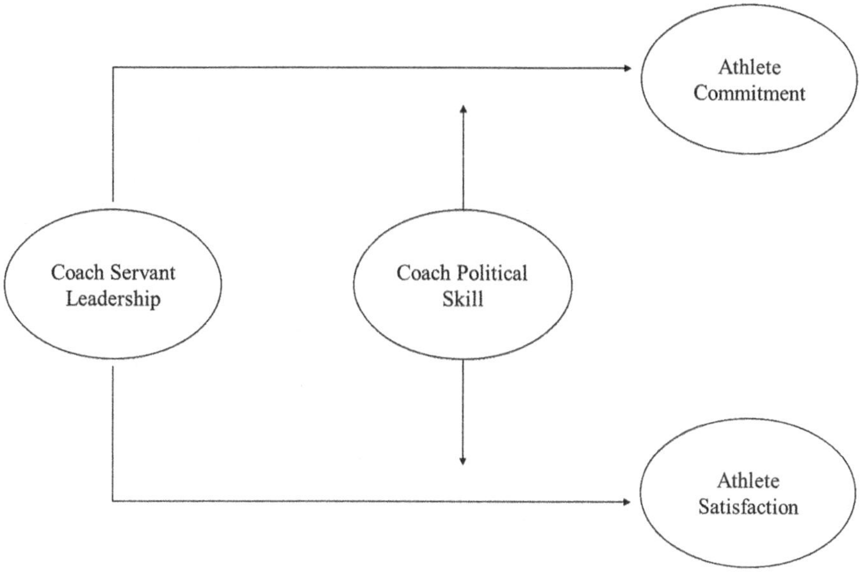

Fig. 21.4 Moderating effect of political skill on the relationship between servant leadership and athlete levels of commitment and satisfaction

Research on LMX and Political Skill

Much has been made in this chapter of the interactive effects of political skill and LMX on leader and work-related outcomes (e.g., team satisfaction with the coach). Moving forward, it would be constructive for sport researchers to explore both LMX and LMX differentiation in the context of sport. Herein we noted that social effectiveness is understudied. Previously, in Griffo et al.'s (2019) critical review of coaching research, the authors noted gender and race are understudied. These gaps in the literature can be simultaneously addressed with research on LMX and coach social effectiveness.

LMX theory (Dansereau et al., 1975) focuses on the relationships between leaders and their followers. Sport is diverse and relationships are unlikely to exist between leaders and followers who are completely similar. Indeed, though gender and racial differences between coaches and their athletes and staffs are not uncommon, such differences and how to overcome them have rarely been considered outside a sociological perspective. It would be of great value to the progression of coaching scholarship to examine the influence of coach (leader) political skill on the quality of LMX relationships when leader-subordinate dyad exists between individuals who are different races or genders. This avenue of exploration should prove especially relevant to female coaches seeking to coach in sports traditionally helmed by male coaches (e.g., American football, soccer, men's basketball). Similar research also can be conducted on LMX differentiation in sport.

LMX differentiation considers the degree of within-group variation that is expected to exist in the workplace due to leaders forming differing quality relationships with different followers. An extension of the previous recommendation would be to expand the study of LMX and political skill to the numerous dyadic exchanges that take place within diverse sport teams. Coaches who are politically skilled should be more aware of the LMX differentiation that takes place within their sphere of leadership influence. They should then be able to use their social effectiveness to perceive relevant social cues, get a sense of how their followers feel, identify influence opportunities, and adapt to their followers and environment to better build relationships, make everyone feel welcome, and foster a positive, productive culture. Thus, it would be worthwhile to investigate the potential interactive effects of leader political skill and follower perceptions of LMX differentiation on LMX quality and perceptions of organizational culture.

Research on Culture and Political Skill

Culture represents the shared set of assumptions and beliefs that guide members' levels of understanding about what is and is not acceptable behavior. Part of the value of culture to the success of teams and organizations is that it represents the underlying framework or explanation for how everyone who is part of the culture should work together (Schein, 2010). Coaches create culture, and consideration for how the culture is both created and maintained must be integrated into the leadership strategies of coaches. Social effectiveness research is important to the advancement of leadership and culture formation because it clarifies how coaches are able to create, adapt, and leverage their culture to produce positive personal and team outcomes. For example, in a study by Meng and Berger (2019), the culture created by a leader had a positive impact on subordinate engagement and trust (in the leader). Leader ability to communicate and embody the culture to his or her subordinates was also shown to enhance engagement and trust.

Given the impact of culture and leadership performance on follower beliefs and behaviors, future research needs to examine the political skill of coaches and how their degree of social effectiveness enhances (diminishes) follower acceptance of the culture and perceptions of leader effectiveness in building and managing the multitude of dyads present within the culture. Studying the mediating effect of culture on the relationship between politically skilled leadership and various sport outcomes (e.g., LMX, satisfaction, commitment, decreased athlete or assistant coach turnover) is one area that is ripe for exploration. Another area worth exploring is how culture impacts athlete health and wellbeing.

In terms of health and wellbeing in the workplace, role stress can contribute to job tension which can then diminish work engagement (Kim, Karatepe, & Chung, 2019). Similarly, in the context of sport, athletes can experience stress in their sport role. This stress can stem from many sources, including ambiguity, role conflict, and poor LMX quality. Such stress heightens job tension—tension that manifests in the individual's athlete role—and tension in what an athlete does can lead to a diminished desire to function in that athletic role. Accordingly, scholars should gather observation data on the predictors and consequences of athlete stress and then consider the direct and mediated effects of coach political skill on follower stress, tension, and engagement in athletic tasks.

Key Points

Researchers need to act on several areas of scholarly inquiry if they are to noticeably advance the study of sport coaches. Better operationalizing the realms of coaching and leadership, for example, needs considerable attention. Knowledge about coaching and leadership from all relevant disciplines (e.g., psychology, management, sport psychology, pedagogy) needs to be organized and synthesized (not just reviewed and rehashed) so that more comprehensive frameworks and measures of coaching can be formulated. From there, conversations about the generated frameworks need to be conducted between researchers and practitioners (e.g., coaches) so that the frameworks can be refined prior to qualitative exploration and empirical examination. Then, mixed methodological approaches over time should lead to the development of more valid and effective ways for coaches to lead their teams in productive and successful manners.

Effective leadership is clearly a practice that sport scholars strive to more comprehensively understand. Given that pro-social forms of leadership in sport and non-sport organizations are on the rise, researcher focus on leadership studies and practice has shifted from traditional authoritarian leadership styles to more positive and less-egoistic forms of leadership aimed at developing subordinates via relationship building and empowerment. This shift in focus has amplified attention being given to sport-based servant leadership, a style of leadership built on foundational principles of other-centeredness and ethical behavior that maintains truly effective and authentic leaders prioritize service to others ahead of personal control and power.

Person-situation and contingency theories of leadership state a leader's effectiveness in influencing others depends in large part on the interaction of a leader's behavior with the characteristics of both leader followers and the environment (context). Though success in the profession of coaching requires the ability to build relationships and influence others, only recently has servant leadership begun to receive consideration as an effective leadership model in the context of sport. Therefore, as proposed in this chapter, servant leadership is deserving of sustained research focus within the domain of sport coaching. Also worth investigating in connection to leadership and coaching are factors, such as the social effectiveness characteristic of political skill, that allow servant leaders to best create successful LMX relationships with their followers, create a positive and productive team culture, and have the greatest possible influence.

Most definitions of leadership are grounded in the assumption that leadership involves a process of intentional influence being exerted over others to provide structure, facilitate activities and relationships, and guide the coordinated efforts of followers. All coaches use influence, be it intentional or unintentional, to achieve desired individual and/or team outcomes. No longer should influence be overlooked with sport coaches. The social influence literature encompasses a broad spectrum of social effectiveness constructs that can be useful in understanding a coach's aptitude at evaluating social situations, self-monitoring, and adjusting to the specific requirements of an environment to modify his/her behaviors and influence the behaviors of others (e.g., subordinates).

Of the available collection of social effectiveness constructs, political skill is a concept that currently has the most potential to advance understanding of why certain coaches are more effective leaders than their peers. Indeed, the available body of evidence on political skill is quite clear. Politically skilled individuals are more likely to achieve greater levels of career success than their less politically skilled counterparts. Research in and outside the arena of sport supports this assertion. Moving forward, researchers interested in what makes for effective coaches need to focus on social effectiveness. These scholars need to incorporate the 18-item PSI (Ferris, Treadway, et al., 2005) into studies on coaching effectiveness, with particular attention being given to the areas of servant leadership, LMX, LMX differentiation, and culture formation and maintenance.

Conclusion

Considering that numerous gaps exist in the literature on the study of coaching, the aim of this chapter was to examine sport coaching and provide suggestions for future research. In focus was the leadership role of coaches and how, in this role, coaches must build and maintain relationships and culture. Several areas impacted by the leadership of a coach were observed and then connected to the important area of social effectiveness. Political skill was then singled out as particularly useful social effectiveness construct to examine in connection to coaching and leadership. Finally, specific recommendations concerning leadership, relational exchanges, culture, and political skill were made to guide and inspire future researchers looking to continue to advance the evolution of how the coaching profession is studied and practiced.

References

Aditya, R. N., & House, R. J. (2002). Interpersonal acumen and leadership across cultures. In R. E. Riggio, S. E. Murphy, & F. J. Pirozzola (Eds.), *Multiple intelligences and leadership* (pp. 215–240). Mahwah, NJ: Lawrence Erlbaum.

Anand, S., Vidyarthi, P. R., & Park, H. S. (2015). LMX differentiation: Understanding relational leadership at individual and group levels. In T. Bauer & B. Erdogan (Eds.), *Oxford handbook of leader-member exchange* (pp. 263–292). New York: Oxford University Press.

Archer, D. (1980). *How to expand your social intelligence quotient*. New York: Evans.

Banister, C. M., & Meriac, J. P. (2015). Political skill and work attitudes: A comparison of multiple social effectiveness constructs. *Journal of Psychology, 149*, 775–795.

Bennis, W., & Goldsmith, J. (1997). *Learning to lead: A workbook on becoming a leader*. Reading, MA: Addison Wesley.

Brouer, R. L., Douglas, C., Treadway, D. C., & Ferris, G. R. (2013). Leader political skill, relationship quality, and leadership effectiveness: A two-study model test and constructive replication. *Journal of Leadership & Organizational Studies, 20*, 185–198.

Burton, L., & Peachey, J. W. (2013). The call for servant leadership in intercollegiate athletics. *Quest, 65*, 354–371.

Burton, L., Welty Peachey, J., & Wells, J. (2017). The role of servant leadership in developing an ethical climate in sport organizations. *Journal of Sport Management, 31*, 229–240.

Case, R. (1998). Leader member exchange theory and sport: Possible applications. *Journal of Sport Behavior, 21*, 387–396.

Chelladurai, P. (2007). Leadership in sports. In G. Tenenbaum & R. C. Eklund (Eds.), *Handbook of sport psychology* (3rd ed., pp. 113–135). Hoboken, NJ: Wiley.

Chelladurai, P., & Riemer, H. A. (1998). Measurement of leadership in sport. In J. M. Williams (Ed.), *Advances in sport and exercise psychology* (pp. 227–253). Morgantown, WV: Fitness Information Technology.

Cho, O., & Kim, S. (2014). *The impact of coaches' servant leadership on athletes' athletic performance*. Paper presented at The American Association of Health, Physical Education, Recreation, and Dance National Convention and Expo.

Côté, J., Salmela, J., Trudel, P., & Baria, A. (1995). The coaching model: A grounded assessment of expert gymnastic coaches' knowledge. *Journal of Sport & Exercise Psychology, 17, 17*(1).

Cushion, C. J. (2007). Modelling the complexity of the coaching process. *International Journal of Sports Science & Coaching, 2*, 395–401.

Cushion, C. J., Armour, K. M., & Jones, R. I. (2003). Coach education and continuing professional development experience and learning to coach. *Quest, 55*, 215–230.

Dansereau, F., Jr., Graen, G., & Haga, W. J. (1975). A vertical dyad linkage approach to leadership within formal organizations—a longitudinal investigation of the role making process. *Organizational Behavior and Human Performance, 13*, 46–78.

Deshpande, R., & Webster, F. E. (1989). Organizational culture and marketing: Defining the research agenda. *Journal of Marketing, 53*, 3–15.

Douglas, C., & Ammeter, A. P. (2004). An examination of leader political skill and its effect on rating of leader effectiveness. *The Leadership Quarterly, 15*, 537 550.

Ellen, B. P., III. (2016). Politics and pigskins: Leader political support and Doug Williams's termination from Grambling State University. *Journal of Applied Sport Management, 8*, 71–92.

Epitropaki, O., Kapoutsis, I., Ellen, B. P., III, Ferris, G. R., Drivas, K., & Ntotsi, A. (2016). Navigating uneven terrain: The roles of political skill and LMX differentiation in prediction of work relationship quality and work outcomes. *Journal of Organizational Behavior, 37*, 1078–1103.

Ferris, G. R., Blickle, G., Schneider, P. G., Kramer, J., Zettler, I., Solga, J., . . . Meurs, J. A. (2008). Political skill construct and criterion-related validation: A two-study investigation. *Journal of Managerial Psychology, 23*, 744–771.

Ferris, G. R., Davidson, S. L., & Perrewé, P. L. (2005). *Political skill at work: Impact on work effectiveness*. Boston, MA: Davies-Black.

Ferris, G. R., Perrewé, P. L., Anthony, W. P., & Gilmore, D. C. (2000). Political skill at work. *Organizational Dynamics, 28*, 25–37.

Ferris, G. R., Perrewé, P. L., & Douglas, C. (2002). Social effectiveness in organizations: Construct validity and research directions. *Journal of Leadership and Organizational Studies, 9*, 49–63.

Ferris, G. R., Treadway, D. C., Kolodinsky, R. W., Hochwarter, W. A., Kacmar, C. J., Douglas, C., & Frink, D. D. (2005). Development and validation of the political skill inventory. *Journal of Management, 31*, 126–152.

Gentry, W. A., Leslie, J. B., Gilmore, D. C., Ellen, B. P., III, Ferris, G. R., & Treadway, D. C. (2013). Personality and political skill as distal and proximal predictors of leadership evaluations. *Career Development International, 18*, 569–588.

Goleman, D. (1995). *Emotional intelligence*. New York: Bantam Books.

Goleman, D., & Boyatzis, R. (2008). Social intelligence and the biology of leadership. *Harvard Business Review, 86*, 74–81.

Graen, G. B., & Uhl-Bien, M. (1995). Relationship-based approach to leadership: Development of leader-member exchange (LMX) theory of leadership of 25 years: Applying a multi-level multi-domain perspective. *Leadership Quarterly, 6*, 219–247.

Greenleaf, R. K. (1977). *Servant leadership: A journey into the nature of legitimate power and greatness*. New York: Paulist Press.

Griffo, J. M., Jensen, M., Anthony, C. C., Baghurst, T., & Kulinna, P. H. (2019). A decade of research literature in sport coaching (2005-2015). *International Journal of Sports Science & Coaching, 14*, 202–215.

Hammermeister, J., Burton, D., Pickering, M., Chase, M., Westre, K., & Baldwin, N. (2008). Servant leadership in sport: A concept whose time has arrived. *International Journal of Servant Leadership, 4*, 185–215.

Henderson, D. J., Liden, R. C., Glibkowski, B. C., & Chaudhry, A. (2009). LMX differentiation: A multilevel review and examination of its antecedents and outcomes. *The Leadership Quarterly, 20*, 517–534.

Henderson, D. J., Wayne, S. J., Shore, L. M., Bommer, W. H., & Tetrick, L. E. (2008). Leader-member exchange, differentiation, and psychological contract fulfilment: A multilevel examination. *Journal of Applied Psychology, 93*, 1208–1219.

Herdman, A. O., Yang, J., & Arthur, J. B. (2014). How does leader-member exchange disparity affect teamwork behaviour and effectiveness in work groups? The moderating role of leader-leader exchange. *Journal of Management, 40*, 1498–1523.

Herrera, R., Duncan, P., & Ree, M. (2013). Aligning organizational culture with leader-member exchange. *Global Business & Organizational Excellence, 32*, 53–65.

Kim, T. T., Karatepe, O. M., & Chung, U. Y. (2019). Got political skill? The direct and moderating impact of political skill on stress, tension and outcomes in restaurants. *International Journal of Contemporary Hospitality Management, 31*, 1367–1389.

Kim, M., Kim, Y., & Wells, J. (2017). Being a servant-leader in sport: Servant leadership as the key to the coach-athlete relationship. *International Journal of Sport Management, 18*, 19–43.

Kim, M., Wells, J. E., Chan, A., & Kim, H. (2016). What are they saying about your head coach? The relationship among political skill, reputation, and effectiveness. *Journal of Applied Sport Management, 8*, 48–67.

Klenke, K. (1994). Information technologies as drivers of emergent organizational forms: A leadership perspective. In R. Baskerville, S. Smithson, O. Ngwenyama, & J. I. DeGross (Eds.), *Transforming organizations with information technology*. Elsevier: North Holland.

Klimoski, R., & Koles, K. (2001). The chief executive officer and top management team interface. In S. Zaccaro & R. Klimoski (Eds.), *The nature of organizational leadership* (pp. 219–269). San Francisco: Jossey-Bass.

Knowles, Z., Gilbourne, D., Borrie, A., & Nevill, A. (2001). Developing the reflective sports coach: A study exploring the processes of reflective practice within a higher education coaching programme. *International and Multidisciplinary Perspectives, 2*, 185–207.

Laios, A., Theodorakis, N., & Gargalianos, D. (2003). Leadership and power: Two important factors for effective coaching. *International Sports Journal, 7*, 150–154.

Lennox, R. D., & Wolfe, R. N. (1984). A revision of the self-monitoring scale. *Journal of Personality and Social Psychology, 46*, 1348–1364.

Magnusen, M., & Kim, J. W. (2016). Thriving in the political sport arena: LMX as a mediator of the political skill – career success relationship. *Journal of Applied Sport Management, 8*, 15–42.

Magnusen, M., Kim, J. W., & Perrewé, P. L. (2014). Gaining a competitive edge when recruiting student-athletes: The role of political skill. *International Journal of Sports Science & Coaching, 9*, 1291–1310.

Magnusen, M., Kim, Y. K., Perrewé, P. L., & Ferris, G. R. (2014). A critical review and synthesis of student-athlete college choice factors: Recruiting effectiveness in NCAA sports. *International Journal of Sports Science & Coaching, 9*, 1264–1286.

Magnusen, M., & Perrewé, P. L. (2016). The role of social effectiveness in leadership: A critical review and lessons for sport management. *Sport Management Education Journal, 10*, 64–77.

McCullick, B., Schempp, P., Mason, I., Foo, C., Vickers, B., & Connolly, G. (2009). A scrutiny of coaching education program scholarship since 1995. *Quest, 61*, 322–335.

Megheirkouni, M. (2019). Responsible leadership as a mediator between emotional intelligence and team outcomes in sport organizations. *International Journal of Sport Management, 20*, 87–107.

Meng, J., & Berger, B. K. (2019). The impact of organizational culture and leadership and performance on PR professionals' job satisfaction: Testing the joint mediating effects of engagement and trust. *Public Relations Review, 45*, 64–75.

Miao, C., Humphrey, R. H., & Qian, S. (2018). A cross-cultural meta-analysis of how leader emotional intelligence influences subordinate task performance and organizational citizenship behavior. *Journal of World Business, 53*, 463–474.

Miller, G. A., Lutz, R., Shim, J., Fredenburg, K., & Miller, J. J. (2006). A national study of nonrenewal in high school coaching. *Journal of Health, Physical Education, Recreation, and Dance, 77*, 40–45.

Minsu, L., Mayfield, C. O., Hinojosa, A. S., & Yooshin, I. (2018). A dyadic approach to examining the emotional intelligence-work outcome relationship: The mediating role of LMX. *Organization Management Journal, 15*, 1–16.

Nazarpoori, A. (2017). A survey of the effect of leader's social intelligence on employee's perception of interpersonal justice: The mediating role of shared leadership. *International Journal of Leadership in Education, 20*, 618–631.

Neubert, M. J., Hunter, E. M., & Tolentino, R. C. (2016). A servant leader and their stakeholders: When does organizational structure enhance a leader's influence? *The Leadership Quarterly, 27* (6), 896–910.

Ogbonna, E., & Harris, L. C. (2002). Managing organisational culture: Insights from the hospitality industry. *Human Resource Management Journal, 12*, 33–53.

Perrewe, P. L., & Ferris, G. R. (2016). The utilization of political skill as leverage in sport management research. *Journal of Applied Sport Management, 8*, 6–14.

Potrac, P., & Jones, R. (2009). Power, conflict, and cooperation: Toward a micropolitics of coaching. *Quest, 61*, 223–236.

Rahim, M. A. (2014). A structural equations model of leaders' social intelligence and creative performance. *Creativity & Innovation Management, 23*, 44–56.

Rieke, M., Hammermeister, J., & Chase, M. (2008). Servant leadership in sport: A new paradigm for effective coach behavior. *International Journal of Sports Science & Coaching, 3*, 227–239.

Riggio, R. E. (1986). Assessment of basic social skills. *Journal of Personality and Social Psychology, 51*, 649–660.

Robinson, G. M., Magnusen, M., & Kim, J. W. (2019). The socially effective leader: Exploring the relationship between athletic director political skill and coach commitment and job satisfaction. *International Journal of Sports Science & Coaching, 14*, 197–204.

Robinson, G. M., Neubert, M. J., & Miller, G. (2018). Servant leadership in sport: A review, synthesis, and applications for sport management classrooms. *Sport Management Education Journal, 12*, 39–56.

Rose, C. (2013). Review details 'toxic' environment on Australian swim team. *Sports Illustrated*. Retrieved from https://www.si.com/more-sports/2013/02/18/australian-swim-team-toxic-environment.

Rowold, J. (2006). Transformational and transactional leadership in martial arts. *Journal of Applied Sport Psychology, 18*, 312–325.
Rudd, A., & Johnson, B. (2010). A call for more mixed methods in sport management research. *Sport Management Review, 13*, 14–24.
Russell, R. V. (2005). *Leadership in recreation*. New York: McGraw-Hill.
Salovey, P., & Mayer, J. D. (1990). Emotional intelligence. *Imagination, Cognition, and Personality, 9*, 185–211.
Scandura, T. A., Graen, G. B., & Novak, M. A. (1986). When managers decide not to decide autocratically: An investigation of leader-member exchange and decision influence. *Journal of Applied Psychology, 71*, 579–584.
Schein, E. A. (1985). *Organizational culture and leadership*. San Francisco: Jossey-Bass.
Schein, E. H. (2010). *Organizational culture and leadership*. San Francisco: Jossey-Bass.
Semander, A., Robins, G., & Ferris, G. R. (2006). Comparing the validity of multiple social effectiveness constructs in the prediction of managerial job performance. *Journal of Organizational Behavior, 27*, 443–461.
Smoll, F. L., & Smith, R. E. (1989). Leadership behaviors in sport: A theoretical model and research paradigm. *Journal of Applied Social Psychology, 9*, 1522–1551.
Snyder, M. (1974). Self-monitoring of expressive behavior. *Journal of Personality and Social Psychology, 30*, 526–537.
Sørensen, J. B. (2002). The strength of corporate culture and reliability of firm performance. *Administrative Science Quarterly, 47*, 70–91.
Sosik, J. J., Potosky, D., & Jung, D. I. (2002). Adaptive self-regulation: Meeting others' expectations of leadership and performance. *Journal of Social Psychology, 142*, 211–232.
Stober, D. R., & Parry, C. (2005). Current challenges and future directions in coaching research. Evidence-based coaching. In M. Cavanagh, A. M. Grant, & T. Kemp (Eds.), *Evidence based coaching: Volume 1 Theory, research and practice from the behavioural sciences* (pp. 13–20). Sydney, NSW: Australian Academic Press.
Stone, A. G., Russell, R. F., & Patterson, K. (2004). Transformational versus servant leadership: A difference in leader focus. *Leadership & Organization Development Journal, 25*, 349–361.
Thomas, G., Martin, R., Epitropaki, O., Guillaume, Y., & Lee, A. (2013). Social cognition in leader–follower relationship: Applying insights from relationship science to understanding relationship-based approaches to leadership. *Journal of Organizational Behavior, 34*, 63–81.
Treadway, D. C., Adams, G., Hanes, T. J., Perrewe, P. L., Magnusen, M. J., & Ferris, G. R. (2014). The roles of recruiter political skill and performance resource leveraging in NCAA football recruitment effectiveness. *Journal of Management, 40*, 1607–1626.
Türetgen, I. Ö., Unsal, P., & Dural, U. (2017). The role of leadership perception as a mediator between managers' self-monitoring and subordinate attitudes. *Journal of Social Psychology, 157*, 295–307.
Turman, P. D. (2003). Coaches and cohesion: The impact of coaching techniques on team cohesion in the small group sport setting. *Journal of Sport Behavior, 26*, 86–104.
Van Dierendonck, D. (2011). Servant leadership: A review and synthesis. *Journal of Management, 37*, 1228–1261.
Walumbwa, F. O., Cropanzano, R., & Goldman, B. M. (2012). How leader-member exchange influences effective work behaviors: Social exchange and internal-external efficacy perspectives. *Personnel Psychology, 64*, 739–770.
Wu, J. B., Tsui, A. S., & Kinicki, A. J. (2010). Consequences of differentiated leadership in groups. *Academy of Management Journal, 53*, 90–106.
Yukl, G., & van Fleet, D. D. (1992). Theory and research on leadership in organisations. In M. D. Dunnette & L. M. Hough (Eds.), *Handbook of industrial and organizational psychology* (pp. 147–197). Palo Alto, CA: Consulting Psychologists Press.

Marshall Magnusen is an Associate Professor of Sport Management at Baylor University. He earned a bachelor's degree in Exercise Physiology and English Literature from Wheaton College (Illinois), a master's degree in Sport Psychology from Texas Christian University (TCU), and a PhD in Sport Management from Florida State University. His current research interests can generally be classified into three areas: (1) social effectiveness in sport, (2) sport leadership, and (3) organizational behavior. To date, his scholarly productivity includes nearly 50 peer-reviewed articles and book chapters and nearly 75 presentations at national and international conferences. He is currently the Editor of the *Journal of Applied Sport Management* and a former Associate Editor of the *Sport Management Education Journal.*

Jun Woo Kim is an Associate Professor of Sport Management at Arcadia University. He earned his PhD in Sport Management from Florida State University. His research interests include sport consumer behavior, leadership, and sports analytics. His recent research involves the application of analytics in sports for testing player performance variables and league policies.

Matt Robinson is Assistant Professor in the Department of Exercise Science and Sport Management at Schreiner University. He completed his PhD in Kinesiology, Exercise Nutrition, and Health Promotion from Baylor University. Prior to becoming a professor, Matt lead a 15-year career in college coaching. His research interests lie in the areas of leadership in sport organizations and social effectiveness among sport coaches and athletic administrators.

Chapter 22
Coaching in Sports: Implications for Researchers and Coaches

Humberto M. Carvalho and Carlos E. Gonçalves

Abstract Sports Coaching research continues to develop, although with a narrow spread of publication, mainly within Sports Psychology, and small impact across Sports Science journals. Nevertheless, Sports Coaching research potentially investigates an array of basic and applied research questions. Hence, there is an opportunity for improvement. Moreover, there is an increased awareness in several scientific areas, including Sports Science, about several problems pertaining to design, transparency, replicability, and trust of research practices. Particularly in Sports Coaching research, these problems include limited or inadequate validation of surrogate outcomes and lack of multidisciplinary designs, lack of longitudinal and replication studies, inappropriate data analysis and reporting, limited reporting of null or trivial results, and insufficient scientific transparency. In this chapter, we initially discuss the trends of publication in Sports Coaching, highlighting research problems as they pertain to their treatment in other disciplines, namely psychology. Lastly, we illustrate an example applied to Sport Coaching research with a repeated measures design and an interdisciplinary approach as a recommendation to promote transparency, replicability, and trust in Sports Coach research.

Keywords Sports coaching · Scholarly publishing · Open science · Reproducibility · Coaching practice

Sports Coaching research continues to develop (Gilbert & Trudel, 2004; Griffo, Jensen, Anthony, Baghurst, & Kulinna, 2019). Nevertheless, the initial argument in this chapter is that Sports Coaching Research still falls mostly within a narrow

H. M. Carvalho (✉)
Federal University of Santa Catarina, Florianópolis, Santa Catarina, Brazil
e-mail: humberto.m.carvalho@ufsc.br

C. E. Gonçalves
University of Coimbra, Estádio Universitário de Coimbra, Coimbra, Portugal
e-mail: carlosgoncalves@fcdef.uc.pt

R. Resende, A. R. Gomes (eds.), *Coaching for Human Development and Performance in Sports*, https://doi.org/10.1007/978-3-030-63912-9_22

spread of publication, mainly within Sports Psychology, and with a small impact across Sports Science journals.

To support our argument, we examined the published Sports Coaching research between 2000 and 2019 in Sports Science journals indexed on Web of Science or Scopus. The records were retrieved limiting the keywords "coach, coaches and coaching" in the titles, abstracts, and keywords in English language manuscripts. The specific syntax for Web of Science or Scopus searches to reproduce our approach is available in a public repository (https://osf.io/vw8yq/). For convenience, we considered journal by main publication theme (Sports Coaching and Pedagogy, Sports Science, Applied Sports Science, Physiology and Nutrition, Biomechanics and Motor Control, Psychology, Social Sciences and Humanities, Sports and Exercise Medicine and Health). After removing duplicate entries, we used mapping analysis to examine on the fly the main trends of Sports Coaching publication. For this step, we used the bibliometrix package (Aria & Cuccurullo, 2017), in R statistical language (R Core Team, 2018). Furthermore, we fitted multilevel ordinal regressions to describe the frequency of Sports Coaching articles published in Sports Sciences journals from 2000 to 2019, adjusting for whether journals were indexed in the Journal of Citations Reports (JCR) in the Sport Sciences section, and for the journal main area of publication. We modeled the data using fully Bayesian methods with the "brms" package (Bürkner, 2017), which calls Stan (Carpenter et al., 2017), in R statistical language (R Core Team, 2018). The data, priors, model specification and computation details, and R codes are available as supplementary material (https://osf.io/vw8yq/).

The frequency of Sports Coaching articles published in Sports Sciences journals increased substantially after about 2009, apparently coincident with the increase of volume of non-JCR indexed publications (Fig. 22.1, upper panel). This indicates a trend of decrease in the proportion of Sports Coaching articles published in the JCR indexed journal, adjusting for journals' main area of publication (Fig. 22.1, lower panel).

Our analysis is consistent with previous analysis of Coaching research (Griffo et al., 2019), as, within Sports Science journals, Psychology appears as the main target area, albeit the trend of increase of Social Sciences and Humanities, and Sports Coaching and Pedagogy areas (Fig. 22.2, upper panel). The latter in particular with the prominence of the *International Journal of Sports Science* and Coaching. Nowadays the proportion of published articles across these three areas appears to be similar (Fig. 22.2, lower panel). The trend of decrease in the proportion of published Sports Coaching articles in Sports Psychology journals became apparent after 2010. Overall, the impact of Sports Coaching research in the field of Sports Sciences is small.

Nevertheless, the inspection of the mapping analysis shows that psychology-related themes remain the main focus and influence of Sports Coaching research. The most frequent words in the abstract (to provide a deeper view of studies), summarized in a word map (Fig. 22.3), are consistently associated with Sports Psychology subjects, and with coach education, given the increase of Sports

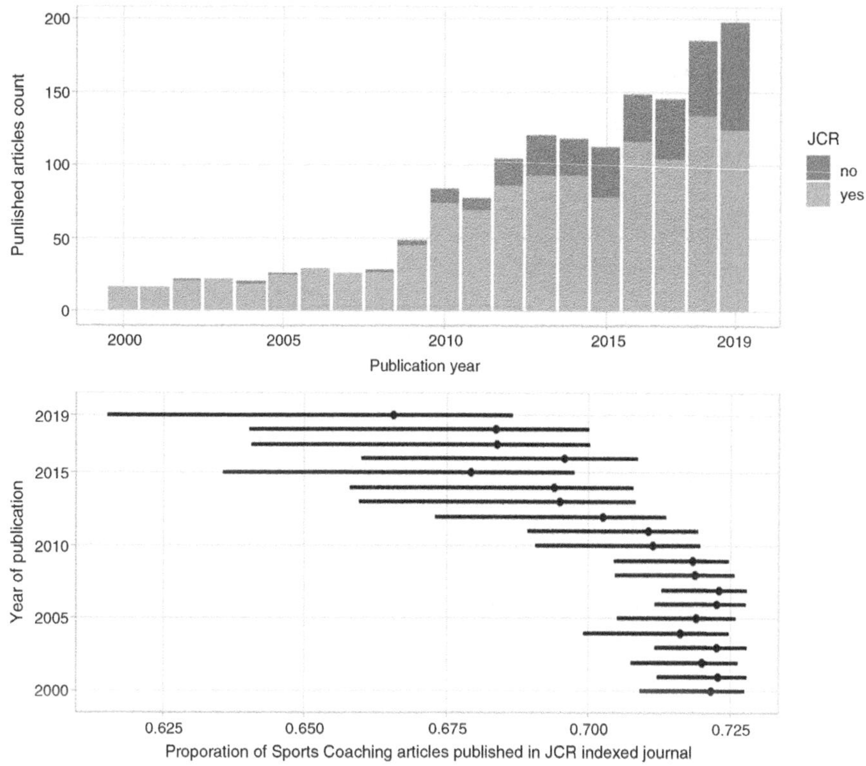

Fig. 22.1 Distribution of Sports Coaching articles across Science journals accounting for JCR from 2000 to 2019 (upper panel) and proportion of articles published adjusting for the area of publication in Sports Science journals (lower panel)

coaching articles in both Sports Coaching and Pedagogy, and Social Sciences and Humanities within Sports Science journals.

Despite the narrow spread of publication, the thematic analysis showed an apparent separation between themes across studies (Fig. 22.4). Considering a thematic map with five clusters with two main labels, it was identified as the main cluster that comprised themes such as coaching and sport (the main two labels), gender, education, expertise, pedagogy, self-determination theory, elite sport or swimming. There was a partial overlap with the second main cluster that identified youth sports and motivation as the main labels, comprised also themes such as self-determination theory, coach-athlete relationship, motivational climate, communication, support, autonomy, team sport, positive youth development or social support. The third cluster was more context-related (coach and soccer as main labels) such as performance, training, youth, or prevention, but there was also psychology associated themes such as leadership or stress. In a more distant quadrant and position, the smaller cluster was labeled as sport and athlete, including themes such as sport psychology, team sports, basketball attitude, burnout, performance analysis,

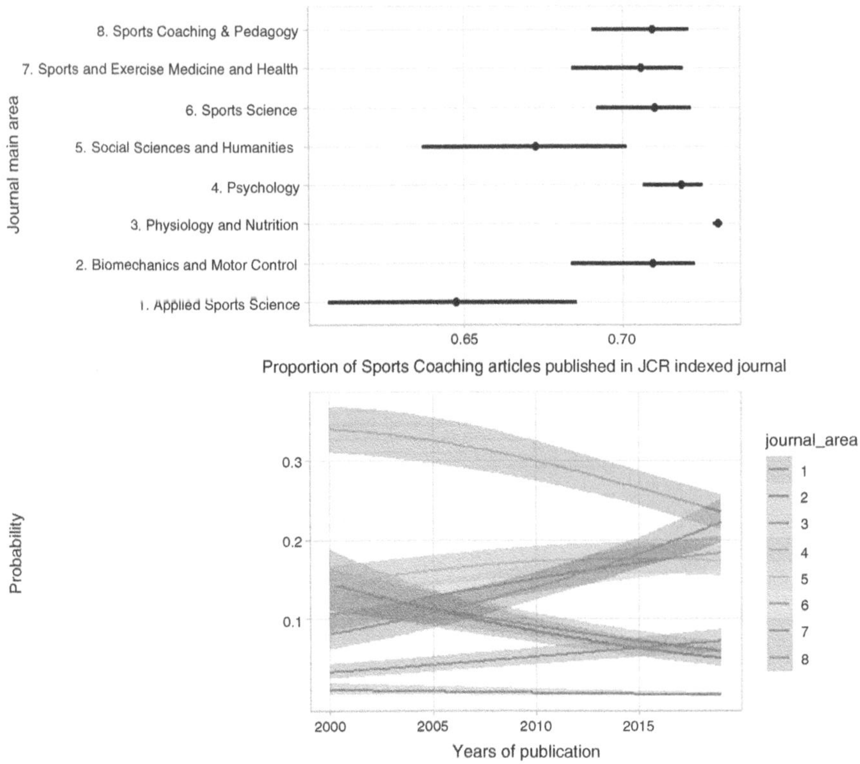

Fig. 22.2 Proportions of articles published in JCR journal by area of publication in Sports Science journals (upper panel), and by year of publication (lower panel)

coaching philosophy, or knowledge. Lastly, the most distant cluster from the three main clusters was identified with coach education and sports coaching as labels. The cluster included themes such as coach development, coach learning, professional development, mentoring, physical education, or qualitative analysis.

Our second argument lies in the increased awareness in several scientific areas (Gelman & Geurts, 2017; Pashler & Wagenmakers, 2012; Simmons, Nelson, & Simonsohn, 2011), including Sports Science (Halperin, Vigotsky, Foster, & Pyne, 2018; Knudson, 2017; Schweizer & Furley, 2016), about several problems of transparency, replicability, and trust of research practices. Note that there is also an intense discussion in medicine and health sciences (Bartell, 2019; Begley & Ioannidis, 2015; Gelman & Geurts, 2017). However, given the influence of Sports Psychology and Social Sciences and Humanities in Sports Coaching research, we can extrapolate that problems in our field may be similar. Particularly in Sports Science, these problems may include limited or inadequate validation of surrogate outcomes and lack of multidisciplinary designs, lack of longitudinal and replication studies, inappropriate data analysis and reporting, limited reporting of null or trivial results, and insufficient scientific transparency.

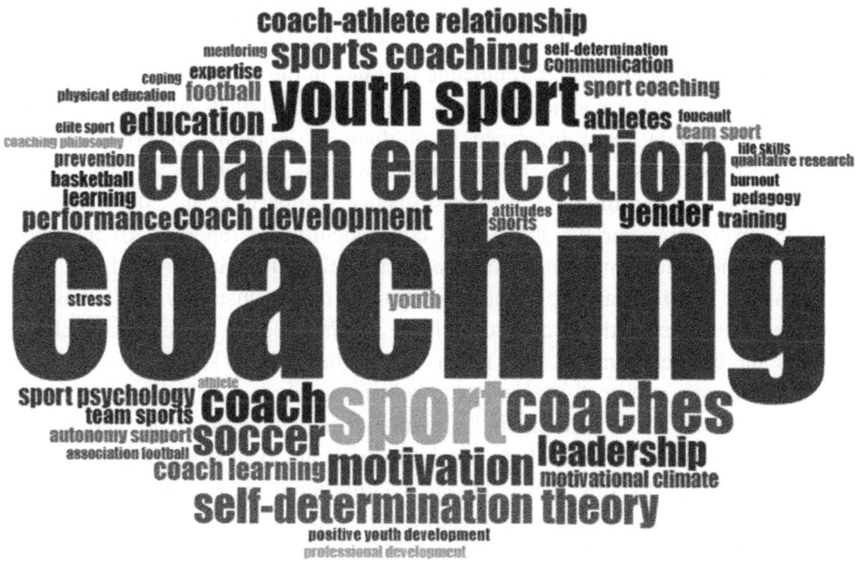

Fig. 22.3 Word map of most common words in the abstracts of Sports Coaching articles from 2000 to 2019

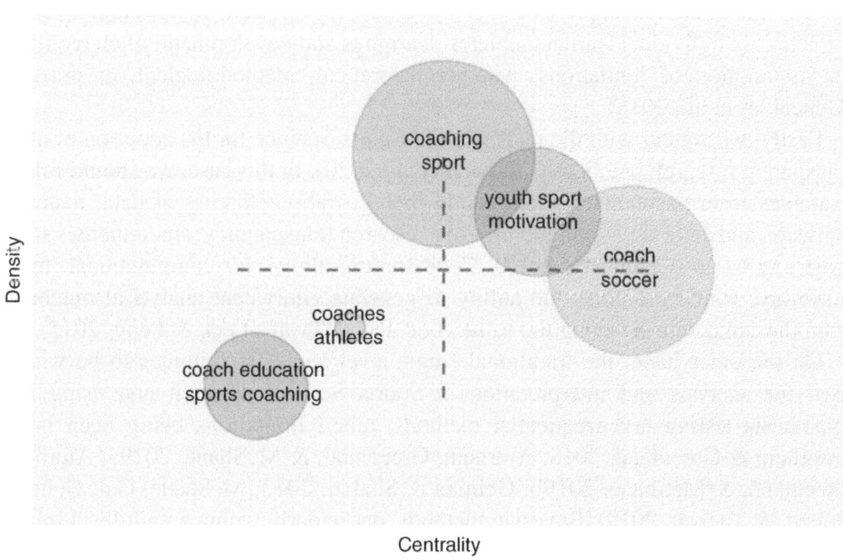

Fig. 22.4 Thematic map clustering the main themes across Sports Coaching articles from 2000 to 2019

The first reason to supports our extrapolations lies in the lack of culture for replication studies in Sports Science, and by extension in Sports Coaching research. The awareness of potentially unreplicable findings in our field has likely risen with the discussion about the validity of a broadly used analytical approach in Sports Science, magnitude-based inference (Batterham & Hopkins, 2006), was noted (Sainani, 2018; Welsh & Knight, 2015). Incorrect statistical analysis and limited sample sizes, as often the case in Sports Science (Halperin et al., 2018; Knudson, 2017; Schweizer & Furley, 2016), and consequently the reporting of inaccurate inferences and inflated magnitude of effects can be common in our field.

Secondly, Sports Coaching research tends to be unidimensional, mostly based on cross-sectional observations, and comprising a narrow scope of behavioral characteristics and applied contexts. Not undervaluing the body of knowledge, sport is a living laboratory where diversity is the rule (Gonçalves, Carvalho, & Catarino, 2018). Coach practice and research deal with an extensive array of applied research questions. Often, the tension between biological and behavioral areas has been evident (Grecic & Collins, 2013; Jacobs, Claringbould, & Knoppers, 2016), and this situation likely limits researchers and coaches to develop a clear understanding of the coaching practice. Given the considerations about Sports Coaching research presented above, there is a clear need for interdisciplinary approaches to explore the interactions between individual learners/athletes exposed and responding to the coach's intervention within the different learning environments. Hence, research designs and analytical approaches need to adjust for different sources and levels of influence on individual learners/athletes' learnings and development, often requiring the assumption of limitations, whether theoretical, methodological, or practical (Gonçalves et al., 2018).

Lastly, we concur with the recent call in Sports Science for the adoption of more transparent research practices (Caldwell et al., 2020). In this case, we should follow examples from psychology where study preregistration, sharing of data, material, software, and code are helping to improve research transparency, albeit there is still a long way to go (Chambers, 2017). Code sharing allows for computational reproducibility, which promotes the ability to generate equivalent analytical outcomes from the same data set using the same code and software (Leek & Peng, 2015).

On the other hand, the traditional single-level analysis continues to be widely used for analysis and interpretation in Sports Science research and using null hypothesis testing and frequentist methods, albeit limitations being been noted (Amrhein & Greenland, 2018; Amrhein, Greenland, & McShane, 2019a; Amrhein, Greenland, & McShane, 2019b; Gelman & Shalizi, 2013; McShane, Gal, Gelman, Robert, & Tackett, 2019). Bayesian methods, particularly within a multilevel framework, offer a very natural alternative, especially for accounting for different sources of inferential uncertainty when making estimations and predictions for a target population (Kennedy & Gelman, 2020; McElreath, 2015). Assuming a Bayesian perspective allow for direct probabilistic interpretations, by combining the available information with the observed data to update the knowledge, expressed as the posterior distribution (Lee & Wagenmakers, 2013). Bayesian estimates are potentially valid for any sample size, given that plausible assumptions are stated (McElreath, 2015). Nevertheless, the process should be transparent and be inspected.

Practical Implications

Lastly, we illustrate an applied to Sport Coaching research with a repeated measures design and an interdisciplinary approach as a recommendation to promote transparency, replicability, and trust in Sports Coach research. Using simulated data based on an ongoing research project, we provide (as supplementary material) an application of analysis and interpretation of the coach intervention (different pedagogical coaching approaches) on athletes' physiological performance and behavioral characteristics across a competitive season period among adolescent players in a team sport (e.g., 11–16 years). Game-centered approaches are advocated to improve decision-making, skill execution, and physical fitness in sports coaching. However, available data is scarce. In this example, the researcher initially should consider the need to adjust for different levels and sources of variation on the outcomes, such as coach-level (e.g., age, previous experience as a coach and/ or with the pedagogical coach approach), player-level (e.g., chronological age, maturity status or accumulated experience) or environmental-level variation (e.g., club competitive level, competitive age group or youth sport program expectations). Measures include anthropometry, maturity status (estimated age at peak height velocity), a composite score of physiological capacity, scores from the motivation for deliberate practice, considering a context of talent development as an example, and a measure of collective-efficacy (collective efficacy questionnaire for sports). We simulated data for 6 teams of 12 players where three coaches used game-centered approaches and the other three used skill-based and coach-oriented approaches. To deal with the different levels and sources of variation we used Bayesian multilevel regressions to consider each measurement (level 1) within each player (level 2) nested by the coaching approach (Level 3). Furthermore, we illustrate individual and contextual variation accounting for the age group (U12, U14, U16), maturity status (early, on-time and later maturers), and the onset of sport-specific deliberate practice (pre-puberty, during puberty and late puberty) as group-level effects. The data generation, model specifications, priors, codes and computation details, and R codes are available as supplementary material, allowing for replication, manipulation of our example, and transparency in the interpretations (https://osf.io/vw8yq/).

Coaches interpret reality and make decisions based on several observable parameters, mediated by their knowledge of the sport, and by their philosophies (Gonçalves et al., 2018). The coach must know how to locate and rank the athlete among his/her peers and must track the personal development trajectory of the athletes he/she coaches. Longitudinal research designs considering multidimensional approaches and available advanced modeling are essential to advance Sports Coaching research. This may contribute to provide meaningful information for coaching education/science exposure in academic settings and to develop research questions and designs applicable to applied coaching practice.

Key Points

Journal articles are the main means of disseminating Sports Coaching research. In our field, there is a growth in the body of knowledge, particularly in the last decade. Nevertheless, the range of topics remains mostly in the area of Sports Psychology and more recently growing in Social Sciences, and Coaching and Pedagogy. Hence, it will be key to increase interdisciplinary research in Sports Coaching research, which given the complexity of coaching practice should be the standard, as noted in general for Sports Sciences research (Burwitz, Moore, & Wilkinson, 1994; Piggott, Muller, Chivers, Papaluca, & Hoyne, 2018).

Moreover, there is a trend of an increase in non-JCR indexed publications, also in the last decade. This may partially reflect the positive trend of emergence of Sports Coaching specific journals (*International Journal of Sports Science and Coaching*, *Sports Coaching Review*, *International Sport Coaching Journal*). On the other hand, it may reflect an increased publication of less rigorous studies that would not be considered in many JCR indexed publications, in particular journals with a broader range of areas published in Sports Science.

Reproducibility and transparency are key issues as scientists across disciplines increasingly recognize the challenges of reproducing published results and the threats that irreproducible results pose to the scientific process (Powers & Hampton, 2019). Hence, this is a key point in our field, where researchers need to be aware that there may be a reproducibility crisis in Sports Coaching research. Scientific claims should not gain credence because of the status or authority of their originator but by the replicability of their supporting evidence (Open Science Collaboration, 2015). Hence, the estimation of reproducibility in Sports Coaching Science is an open area that warrants urgent attention. Furthermore, Sports Coaching researchers need more transparent research practices and reporting, as recently highlighted for Sports Sciences (Caldwell et al., 2020). This will require the incorporation and generalization of practices such as study pre-registration, sharing data and codes, and use of of appropriate statistical analysis. Overall, there is much to do to improve the potential translation of Sports Coaching research to the field.

Conclusion

The chapter focused on the trends of published Sports Coaching Science in reference journals of Sports Sciences. We advocate the need to have a wider range of questions and to incorporate interdisciplinary approaches and longitudinal designs in Sports Coaching research. Like in other scientific areas, Sports Coaching research potentially has problems of design, transparency, replicability, and trust of research practices. There is the need to advance on the examination of the reproducibility of the research in the field, as well as to adopt more transparent research practices that will allow developing trust in Sports Coach research.

References

Amrhein, V., & Greenland, S. (2018). Remove, rather than redefine, statistical significance. *Nature Human Behaviour, 2*(1), 4. https://doi.org/10.1038/s41562-017-0224-0

Amrhein, V., Greenland, S., & McShane, B. (2019a). Scientists rise up against statistical significance. *Nature, 567*(7748), 305–307. https://doi.org/10.1038/d41586-019-00857-9

Amrhein, V., Greenland, S., & McShane, B. B. (2019b). Statistical significance gives bias a free pass. *European Journal of Clinical Investigation, 49*(12), e13176. https://doi.org/10.1111/eci.13176

Aria, M., & Cuccurullo, C. (2017). Bibliometrix: An R-tool for comprehensive science mapping analysis. *Journal of Informetrics, 11*(4), 959–975. https://doi.org/10.1016/j.joi.2017.08.007

Bartell, S. M. (2019). Understanding and mitigating the replication crisis, for environmental epidemiologists. *Current Environmental Health Reports, 6*(1), 8–15. https://doi.org/10.1007/s40572-019-0225-4

Batterham, A. M., & Hopkins, W. G. (2006). Making meaningful inferences about magnitudes. *International Journal of Sports Physiology Performance, 1*(1), 50–57.

Begley, C. G., & Ioannidis, J. P. (2015). Reproducibility in science. *Circulation Research, 116*(1), 116–126. https://doi.org/10.1161/CIRCRESAHA.114.303819

Bürkner, P.-C. (2017). brms: An R package for Bayesian multilevel models using Stan. *Journal of Statistical Software, 80*, 1–28.

Burwitz, L., Moore, P. M., & Wilkinson, D. M. (1994). Future directions for performance-related sports science research: An interdisciplinary approach. *Journal of Sports Science, 12*(1), 93–109. https://doi.org/10.1080/02640419408732159

Caldwell, A. R., Vigotsky, A. D., Tenan, M. S., Radel, R., Mellor, D. T., Kreutzer, A., … Boisgontier, M. P. (2020). Moving sport and exercise science forward: A call for the adoption of more transparent research practices. *Sports Medicine, 50*(3), 449–459. https://doi.org/10.1007/s40279-019-01227-1

Carpenter, B., Gelman, A., Hoffman, M. D., Lee, D., Goodrich, B., Betancourt, M., … Riddell, A. (2017). Stan: A probabilistic programming language. *Journal of Statistical Software, 76*(1), 32. https://doi.org/10.18637/jss.v076.i01

Chambers, C. (2017). *The seven deadly sins of psychology: A manifesto for reforming the culture of scientific practice*. Princeton, NJ: Princeton University Press.

Gelman, A., & Geurts, H. M. (2017). The statistical crisis in science: How is it relevant to clinical neuropsychology? *Clinical Neuropsychology, 31*(6–7), 1000–1014. https://doi.org/10.1080/13854046.2016.1277557

Gelman, A., & Shalizi, C. R. (2013). Philosophy and the practice of Bayesian statistics. *British Journal of Mathematical and Statistical Psychology, 66*(1), 8–38. https://doi.org/10.1111/j.2044-8317.2011.02037.x

Gilbert, W. D., & Trudel, P. (2004). Analysis of coaching science research published from 1970–2001. *Research Quarterly for Exercise & Sport, 75*(4), 388–399. https://doi.org/10.1080/02701367.2004.10609172

Gonçalves, C. E., Carvalho, H. M., & Catarino, L. M. (2018). Body in movement: Better measurements for better coaching. In S. Pill (Ed.), *Perspectives on athlete-centered coaching* (pp. 116–126). Abingdon: Routledge.

Grecic, D., & Collins, D. (2013). The epistemological chain: Practical applications in sports. *Quest, 65*(2), 151–168. https://doi.org/10.1080/00336297.2013.773525

Griffo, J. M., Jensen, M., Anthony, C. C., Baghurst, T., & Kulinna, P. H. (2019). A decade of research literature in sport coaching (2005–2015). *International Journal of Sports Science & Coaching, 14*(2), 205–215. https://doi.org/10.1177/1747954118825058

Halperin, I., Vigotsky, A. D., Foster, C., & Pyne, D. B. (2018). Strengthening the practice of exercise and sport-science research. *International Journal of Sports Physiology and Performance, 13*(2), 127–134. https://doi.org/10.1123/ijspp.2017-0322

Jacobs, F., Claringbould, I., & Knoppers, A. (2016). Becoming a 'good coach'. *Sport, Education and Society, 21*(3), 411–430. https://doi.org/10.1080/13573322.2014.927756

Kennedy, L., & Gelman, A. (2020). Know your population and know your model: Using model based regression and poststratification to generalize findings beyond the observed sample. *ArXiv e-prints, 1906.11323* (1906.11323 [stat.AP]).

Knudson, D. (2017). Confidence crisis of results in biomechanics research. *Sports Biomechanics, 16*(4), 425–433. https://doi.org/10.1080/14763141.2016.1246603

Lee, M. D., & Wagenmakers, E.-J. (2013). *Bayesian cognitive modeling: A practical course*. Cambridge: Cambridge University.

Leek, J. T., & Peng, R. D. (2015). Opinion: Reproducible research can still be wrong: Adopting a prevention approach. *Proceedings of the National Academy of Sciences, 112*(6), 1645. https://doi.org/10.1073/pnas.1421412111

McElreath, R. (2015). *Statistical rethinking: A Bayesian course with examples in R and Stan*. Boca Raton, FL: Chapman & Hall/CRC Press.

McShane, B. B., Gal, D., Gelman, A., Robert, C., & Tackett, J. L. (2019). Abandon statistical significance. *The American Statistician, 73*(suppl 1), 235–245. https://doi.org/10.1080/00031305.2018.1527253

Open Science Collaboration. (2015). Estimating the reproducibility of psychological science. *Science, 349*(6251), aac4716. https://doi.org/10.1126/science.aac4716

Pashler, H., & Wagenmakers, E. J. (2012). Editors' introduction to the special section on replicability in psychological science: A crisis of confidence? *Perspectives on Psychological Science, 7* (6), 528–530. https://doi.org/10.1177/1745691612465253

Piggott, B., Muller, S., Chivers, P., Papaluca, C., & Hoyne, G. (2018). Is sports science answering the call for interdisciplinary research? A systematic review. *European Journal Sport Science, 19* (2), 1–20. https://doi.org/10.1080/17461391.2018.1508506

Powers, S. M., & Hampton, S. E. (2019). Open science, reproducibility, and transparency in ecology. *Ecological Applications, 29*(1), e01822. https://doi.org/10.1002/eap.1822

R Core Team. (2018). *R: A language and environment for statistical computing*. Retrieved from http://www.R-project.org/

Sainani, K. L. (2018). The problem with "Magnitude-Based Inference". *Medicine Science Sports Exercise, 50*(10), 2166–2176. https://doi.org/10.1249/MSS.0000000000001645

Schweizer, G., & Furley, P. (2016). Reproducible research in sport and exercise psychology: The role of sample sizes. *Psychology of Sport and Exercise, 23*, 114–122. https://doi.org/10.1016/j.psychsport.2015.11.005

Simmons, J. P., Nelson, L. D., & Simonsohn, U. (2011). False-positive psychology: Undisclosed flexibility in data collection and analysis allows presenting anything as significant. *Psychology Science, 22*(11), 1359–1366. https://doi.org/10.1177/0956797611417632

Welsh, A. H., & Knight, E. J. (2015). "Magnitude-based inference": A statistical review. *Medicine Science Sports Exercise, 47*(4), 874–884. https://doi.org/10.1249/MSS.0000000000000451

Humberto M. Carvalho is an Assistant Professor at the School of Sports at the Federal University of Santa Catarina in Florianópolis, Santa Catarina, Brazil.

His research focuses on understanding and improving the development of youth athletes. This includes promoting multidisciplinary research in youth sports and the use of advanced statistical analysis. Dr. Carvalho has extensive experience and continues his activity as a basketball coach .

Carlos E. Gonçalves is a Professor Faculty of Sport Sciences and Physical Education of the University of Coimbra in Coimbra, Portugal.

His research interests are focused on the field of youth sport, namely the factors that contribute to the "rocky" path of expertise development in sport. For decades, Dr. Gonçalves has been a basketball coach at an elite level and contributed to the development and delivery of basketball coach education .

The manufacturer's authorised representative in the EU is Springer Nature Customer Service Centre GmbH, Europaplatz 3, 69115 Heidelberg, Germany. If you have any concerns regarding our products, please contact ProductSafety@springernature.com

Printed and bound by CPI Group (UK) Ltd, Croydon, CR0 4YY

30/09/2026

02225296-0017